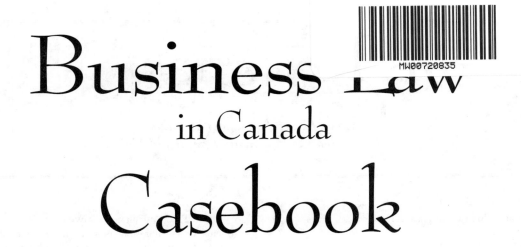

Business Law
in Canada
Casebook

D'ANNE DAVIS

British Columbia Institute of Technology

Prentice Hall Canada Inc.
Scarborough, Ontario

DEDICATION

To Craig, his children Lauren and Ethan,
and to the memory of his parents, Harrell and Marjorie

Canadian Cataloguing in Publication Data

Davis, D'Anne
　　　　Business Law in Canada Casebook

2nd Edition
ISBN 0-13-080597-1

1. Commercial law–Canada–Cases. I. Title.
KE918.5.D3 1999　346.71′07　C98-930285-7
KF888.D3 1999

© 1999, 1995 Prentice-Hall Canada Inc.,
Scarborough, Ontario Division of
Simon & Schuster/A Viacom Company

Prentice-Hall, Inc., Upper Saddle River, New Jersey
Prentice-Hall International (UK) Limited, London
Prentice-Hall of Australia, Pty. Limited, Sydney
Prentice-Hall Hispanoamericana, S.A., Mexico City
Prentice-Hall of India Private Limited, New Delhi
Prentice-Hall of Japan, Inc., Tokyo
Simon & Schuster Southeast Asia Private Limited, Singapore
Editora Prentice-Hall do Brasil, Ltda., Rio de Janeiro

ISBN 0-13-080597-1

Publisher: Patrick Ferrier
Acquisitions Editor: Mike Ryan
Senior Marketing Manager: Ann Byford
Production Editor: Kelly Dickson
Editorial Assistant: Sherry Torchinsky
Copy Editor: Camille Isaacs
Production Coordinator: Jane Schell
Cover Design: Mary Opper
Cover Image: Dan Paul
Page Layout: Heidi Palfrey

1 2 3 4 5 H 03 02 01 00 99

Printed and bound in the USA.

Visit the Prentice Hall Canada Web site! Send us your comments, browse our catalogues, and more at **www.phcanada.com**. Or reach us through e-mail at **phcinfo_phcanada@prenhall.com**.

Every reasonable effort has been made to obtain permissions for all articles and data used in this edition. If errors or omissions have occurred, they will be corrected in future editions provided written notification has been received by the publisher.

TABLE OF CONTENTS

TABLE OF CASES

This table contains two groups: the first is of cases recorded from the decision itself; the second of cases primarily summarized.

    An asterisk (*) following the case indicates it is a decision of the Supreme Court of Canada (S.C.C.) or it was upheld by the S.C.C. or the S.C.C. refused permission to appeal.

LIST OF ABBREVIATIONS

A.C.	Appeal Cases (British)
A.P.R.	Atlantic Provinces Reports
B.C.L.R.	British Columbia Law Reports
C.C.C.	Canadian Criminal Cases
C.C.L.I.	Canadian Cases on the Law of Insurance
C.C.L.T.	Canadian Cases on the Law of Torts
C.E.L.R. (N.S.)	Canadian Environmental Law Reports (New Series)
C.P.R.	Canadian Patent Reporter
D.L.R.	Dominion Law Reports
E.R.	English Reports
F.C.	Canada Law Reports, Federal Court
K.B.	King's Bench (British)
Man. R.	Manitoba Reports
Nfld. and P.E.I.R.	Newfoundland and Prince Edward Island Reports
O.A.C.	Ontario Appeal Cases
O.R.	Ontario Reports
R.P.R.	Real Property Reports
S.C.R.	Supreme Court Reports
Sask. R.	Saskatchewan Reports
W.W.R.	Western Weekly Reports

TABLE OF RELEVANT CASES

This table shows cases in this textbook that correspond to *The Law and Business Administration in Canada, Eighth Edition* by Smyth, Soberman, and Easson.

PREFACE

You can't play the game well if you don't know the rules. Your ability to conduct your business with success is necessarily enhanced by learning about our legal system, the basic principles of tort and contract law, the terms of the contracts between buyer and seller, debtor and creditor, employer and employee, the law of partnerships and corporations, and the law governing administrative tribunals.

Knowledge of these principles and an appreciation for judicial reasoning, which you gain from reading the court decisions, also equips you for your role as lawmaker. Humans, intrinsically complex, often perverse, adjusting to a multiplicity of events, inventions and discoveries, provide us with more than good entertainment—they force us, the ultimate lawmakers, to create new rules to cover the unexpected. We do that not only through our legislators but also through our judges who everyday must decide between opposing views and must justify that decision. The law from both sources, from legislation and court decisions, incorporates the community standard of what is right. When the court, especially the Supreme Court of Canada, is responding to new questions it makes frequent and explicit reference to our collective conscience. Your opinions count, directly and indirectly, and your opinion is a more informed opinion when you have an appreciation of the complexity of issues and how the courts strive to balance legitimate but competing interests.

The study of law should also give you respect for human achievement. Our adoption of rule by law rather than by whim is awesome in itself. Our constant effort to apply and create rules to curb our worst human tendencies and to create a just and good society is worthy of admiration, if not reverence. Besides, our laws may be the best definition we have of who we are as a people.

Because I hold the study of law as both practical and honourable, I have collected cases and stories to make your reading something more pleasurable than the word "assignment" suggests. As in the last edition I have tried to include memorable cases that have the best articulation of existing law, but in this edition you will be exposed to more cases in which the law is being created. Because of recent significant cases involving *Charter* and negligence issues, this edition contains more Supreme Court of Canada decisions in which new law is being made in areas of concern to business students, for example, the liability of commercial hosts and employers.

This casebook was not meant to be read in its entirety. Choose the cases most appropriate to your discipline or interests. For example in the area of negligence, our students in our financial management program should read *Hercules Management Ltd. v. Ernst & Young*, students in human resource management should read *Jacobson v. Nike*, whereas students in tourism should read *Stewart v. Pettie*.

As in the last edition there are three types of entries: extracts from cases, summaries of cases and short snippets (which will begin with the symbol •).

The casebook was written to accompany the fifth edition of *Business Law in Canada* by Richard Yates.

It also complements the eighth edition of *Law and Business Administration in Canada* by Smyth, Soberman and Esson in the table on page xi.

ACKNOWLEDGMENTS

I wish to thank Craig, Lauren, Shaun Cathcart, Ethan, Maria Koroneos, Linda Matsuba and my other friends and colleagues who have been supportive and helpful.

D'ANNE DAVIS

I

THE LEGAL SYSTEM

A. PHILOSOPHICAL BASIS OF THE LAW

- "In the preamble to the Constitution we have the rule of law and the supremacy of God. When we enact law, we must make sure that they do not contravene natural law, which is God's law."[1]

B. CONSTITUTIONAL MATTERS

Questions

When does a case involve a "constitutional issue"?
How does a constitutional issue get before the courts?

1. ALLOCATION OF POWERS

R. v. Hydro-Québec

FILE NO.: 24652.
http://www.droit.umontreal.ca/
SUPREME COURT OF CANADA
SEPTEMBER 18, 1997

La Forest, J. ...

[85] This Court has in recent years been increasingly called upon to consider the interplay between federal and provincial legislative powers as they relate to environmental protection. Whether viewed positively as strategies for maintaining a clean environment, or negatively as measures to combat the evils of pollution, there can be no doubt that these measures relate to a public purpose of superordinate importance, and one in which all levels of government and numerous organs of the international community have become increasingly engaged. ...

[87] This latest case in which this Court is required to define the nature of legislative powers over the environment is of major significance. The narrow issue raised is the extent to and manner in which the federal Parliament may control the amount of and conditions under which Chlorobiphenyls (PCBs) — substances well known to pose great dangers to humans and the environment generally — may enter into the environment.

However, the attack on the federal power to secure this end is not really aimed at the specific provisions respecting PCBs. Rather, it puts into question the constitutional validity of its enabling statutory provisions. What is really at stake is whether Part II ("Toxic Substances") of the Canadian Environmental Protection Act, R.S.C., 1985, c. 16 (4th Supp.), which empowers the federal Ministers of Health and of the Environment to determine what substances are toxic and to prohibit the introduction of such substances into the environment except in accordance with specified terms and conditions, falls within the constitutional power of Parliament.

FACTS

[88] The case arose in this way. The respondent Hydro-Québec allegedly dumped polychlorinated biphenyls (PCBs) into the St. Maurice River in Quebec in early 1990. On June 5, 1990, it

was charged with … two infractions under order, P.C. 1989-296 (hereafter "Interim Order"), which was adopted and enforced pursuant to ss. 34 and 35 of the Canadian Environmental Protection Act: …

On July 23, 1990, the respondent pleaded not guilty to both charges before the Court of Québec.

[89] On March 4, 1991, the respondent Hydro-Québec brought a motion before Judge Michel Babin seeking to have ss. 34 and 35 of the Act as well as s. 6(a) of the Interim Order itself declared *ultra vires* the Parliament of Canada on the ground that they do not fall within the ambit of any federal head of power set out in s. 91 of the Constitution Act, 1867. The Attorney General of Quebec intervened in support of the respondent's position. Judge Babin granted the motion on August 12, 1991 [that these provisions of the legislation were *ultra vires*] ([1991] R.J.Q. 2736), and an appeal to the Quebec Superior Court was dismissed by Trottier J. on August 6, 1992 ([1992] R.J.Q. 2159). A further appeal to the Court of Appeal of Quebec was dismissed on February 14, 1995 [1995] R.J.Q. 398, 67 Q.A.C. 161, 17 C.E.L.R. (N.S.) 34, [1995] Q.J. No. 143 (QL). Leave to appeal to this Court was granted on October 12, 1995: [1995] 4 S.C.R. vii. … [La Forest reviews the judicial history of the case.]

Constitutional Questions

[97] On December 21, 1995, Lamer C.J. framed the following constitutional question: Do s. 6(a) of the Chlorobiphenyls Interim Order, P.C. 1989-296, and the enabling legislative provisions, ss. 34 and 35 of the Canadian Environmental Protection Act, [CEPA] R.S.C., 1985, c. 16 (4th Supp.), fall in whole or in part within the jurisdiction of the Parliament of Canada to make laws for the peace, order and good government of Canada pursuant to s. 91 of the Constitution Act, 1867 or its criminal law jurisdiction under s. 91(27) of the Constitution Act, 1867 or otherwise fall within its jurisdiction?

[98] As can be seen, the constitutional question first raises the constitutionality of s. 6(a) of the Interim Order. … It is clear that the Interim Order will be of no force or effect if the enabling provisions pursuant to which it was adopted are themselves found to be *ultra vires*. … [La Forest reviews the legislative structure of CEPA.]

[108] In this Court, the appellant Attorney General of Canada seeks to support the impugned provisions of the Act on the basis of the national concern doctrine under the peace, order and good government clause of s. 91 or under the criminal law power under s. 91(27) of the Constitution Act, 1867. The respondent Hydro-Québec and the *mis en cause* Attorney General of Quebec dispute this. In broad terms, they say that the provisions are so invasive of provincial powers that they cannot be justified either under the national dimensions doctrine or under the criminal law power. The attack on the validity of the provisions under the latter power is also supported, most explicitly by the intervener the Attorney General for Saskatchewan, on the ground that they are, in essence, of a regulatory and not of a prohibitory character. Finally, I repeat that while the Interim Order precipitated the litigation, there is no doubt that the respondent and *mis en cause* as well as their supporting interveners are after bigger game — the enabling provisions.

[110] … [I]n my view, the impugned provisions are valid legislation under the criminal law power — s. 91(27) of the Constitution Act, 1867. It thus becomes unnecessary to deal with the national concern doctrine, which inevitably raises profound issues respecting the federal structure of our Constitution which do not arise with anything like the same intensity in relation to the criminal law power. …

ANALYSIS

Introduction

[112] In considering how the question of the constitutional validity of a legislative enactment relating to the environment should be approached, this Court in *Oldman River, supra*, made it clear that the environment is not, as such, a subject matter of legislation under the Constitution Act, 1867. As it was put there, "the Constitution Act, 1867 has not assigned the matter of 'environment' sui generis to either the provinces or Parliament" (p. 63). Rather, it is a diffuse subject that cuts across many different areas of constitutional responsibility, some federal, some provincial (pp. 63–64). Thus Parliament or a provincial legislature can, in advancing the scheme or purpose of a statute, enact provisions minimizing or preventing the detrimental impact that statute may have on the environment, prohibit pollution, and the like. In assessing the constitutional validity of a provision relating to the environment, therefore, what must first be done is to look at the catalogue of legislative powers listed in the Constitution Act, 1867 to see if the provision falls within one or more of the powers assigned to the body (whether Parliament or a provincial legislature) that enacted the legislation (ibid. at p. 65). If the provision in essence, in pith and substance, falls within the parameters of any such power, then it is constitutionally valid.

[113] Though pith and substance may be described in different ways, the expressions "dominant purpose" or "true character" used in *R. v. Morgentaler*, [1993] 3 S.C.R. 463, at pp. 481–82, or "the dominant or most important characteristic of the challenged law" used in *Whitbread v. Walley*, [1990] 3 S.C.R. 1273, at p. 1286, and in *Oldman River* … appropriately convey the meaning to be attached to the term. …

THE CRIMINAL LAW POWER

[118] Section 91(27) of the Constitution Act, 1867 confers the exclusive power to legislate in relation to criminal law on Parliament. …

[119] What appears from the analysis in *RJR-MacDonald* is that as early as 1903, the Privy Council, in *Attorney-General for Ontario v. Hamilton Street Railway* Co., [1903] A.C. 524, at pp. 528–29, had made it clear that the power conferred on Parliament by s. 91(27) is "the criminal law in its widest sense" (emphasis added). Consistently with this approach, the Privy Council in *Proprietary Articles Trade Association v. Attorney-General for Canada*, [1931] A.C. 310 (hereafter PATA), at p. 324, defined the criminal law power as including any prohibited act with penal consequences. As it put it, at p. 324: "The criminal quality of an act cannot be discerned … by reference to any standard but one: Is the act prohibited with penal consequences?" This approach has been consistently followed ever since and, as *RJR-MacDonald* relates, it has been applied by the courts in a wide variety of settings. Accordingly, it is entirely within the discretion of Parliament to determine what evil it wishes by penal prohibition to suppress and what threatened interest it thereby wishes to safeguard. …

[120] … This power is, of course, subject to the "fundamental justice" requirements of s. 7 of the Canadian Charter of Rights and Freedoms … but that is not an issue here.

[121] The Charter apart, only one qualification has been attached to Parliament's plenary power over criminal law. The power cannot be employed colourably. Like other legislative powers, it cannot, as Estey J. put it in *Scowby v. Glendinning*, [1986] 2 S.C.R. 226, at p. 237, "permit Parliament, simply by legislating in the proper form, to colourably invade areas of exclusively provincial legislative competence." To determine whether such an attempt is being made, it is, of course, appropriate to enquire into Parliament's purpose in enacting the legislation. As Estey J. noted in *Scowby*, at p. 237, since the *Margarine Reference*, it has been "accepted that some legitimate public purpose must underlie the prohibition." ...

[123] ... But I entertain no doubt that the protection of a clean environment is a public purpose ... sufficient to support a criminal prohibition. It is surely an "interest threatened" which Parliament can legitimately "safeguard," or to put it another way, pollution is an "evil" that Parliament can legitimately seek to suppress. Indeed, as I indicated at the outset of these reasons, it is a public purpose of superordinate importance; it constitutes one of the major challenges of our time. It would be surprising indeed if Parliament could not exercise its plenary power over criminal law to protect this interest and to suppress the evils associated with it by appropriate penal prohibitions. ...

[131] ... [T]he use of the federal criminal law power in no way precludes the provinces from exercising their extensive powers under s. 92 to regulate and control the pollution of the environment either independently or to supplement federal action. The situation is really no different from the situation regarding the protection of health where Parliament has for long exercised extensive control over such matters as food and drugs by prohibitions grounded in the criminal law power. This has not prevented the provinces from extensively regulating and prohibiting many activities relating to health. The two levels of government frequently work together to meet common concerns. The cooperative measures relating to the use of tobacco are fully related in *RJR-MacDonald*. ... It is also the case in many other areas. ...

[133] The respondent, the *mis en cause* and their supporting interveners primarily attack ss. 34 and 35 of the Act as constituting an infringement on provincial regulatory powers conferred by the Constitution. This they do by submitting that the power to regulate a substance is so broad as to encroach upon provincial legislative jurisdiction. ...

[134] I cannot agree with this submission. ... As Gonthier J. observed in *Ontario v. Canadian Pacific* ... this broad wording is unavoidable in environmental protection legislation because of the breadth and complexity of the subject and has to be kept in mind in interpreting the relevant legislation. ...

[135] I turn then to the background and purpose of the provisions under review. Part II [is not too broad; it] does not deal with the protection of the environment generally. It deals simply with the control of toxic substances that may be released into the environment under certain restricted circumstances, and does so through a series of prohibitions to which penal sanctions are attached. ... [The judge reviews the scheme established in Part II.]

[147] This, in my mind, is consistent with the terms of the statute, its purpose, and indeed common sense. It is precisely what one would expect of an environmental statute — a procedure to weed out from the vast number of substances potentially harmful to the environment or human life those only that pose significant risks of that type of harm. Specific targeting of toxic substances based on individual assessment avoids resort to unnecessarily broad prohibitions and their impact on the exercise of provincial powers. ...

[149] I turn now to a more detailed examination of the provisions of the Act impugned in the present case, i.e. ss. 34 and 35. ...

[156] In sum, then, I am of the view that Part II of the Act, properly construed, simply provides a means to assess substances with a view to determining whether the substances are sufficiently toxic to be added to Schedule I of the Act (which contains a list of dangerous substances carried over from pre-existing legislation), and provides by regulations under s. 34 the terms and conditions under which they can be used, with provisions under s. 35 for by-passing the ordinary provisions for testing and regulation under Part II in cases where immediate action is required. ...

[157] Since I have found the empowering provisions, ss. 34 and 35, to be *intra vires*, the only attack that could be brought against any action taken under them would be that such action went beyond the authority granted by those provisions; in the present case, for example, such an attack might consist in the allegation that PCBs did not pose "a significant danger to the environment or to human life or health" justifying the making of the Interim Order. This would seem to me to be a tall order. The fact that PCBs are highly toxic substances should require no demonstration. This has become well known to the general public and is supported by an impressive array of scientific studies at both the national and international levels. ... [A list of such studies follows.]

[159] I should say that the respondent and *mis en cause* do not contest the toxicity of PCBs but simply argue that their control should not fall exclusively within federal competence. ... I have already discussed the issue of concurrency. ...

[160] I conclude, therefore, that the Interim Order is also valid under s. 91(27) of the Constitution Act, 1867.

DISPOSITION

[161] I would allow the appeal with costs, set aside the judgment of the Court of Appeal of Quebec and order that the matter be returned to the Court of summary convictions to be dealt with in accordance with the Act. I would answer the constitutional question as follows:

Q. Do s. 6(a) of the Chlorobiphenyls Interim Order, P.C. 1989-296, and the enabling legislative provisions, ss. 34 and 35 of the Canadian Environmental Protection Act, R.S.C., 1985, c. 16 (4th Supp.), fall in whole or in part within the jurisdiction of the Parliament of Canada to make laws for the peace, order and good government of Canada pursuant to s. 91 of the Constitution Act, 1867 or its criminal law jurisdiction under s. 91(27) of the Constitution Act, 1867 or otherwise fall within its jurisdiction?

A. Yes. They fall wholly within Parliament's power to enact laws under s. 91(27) of the Constitution Act, 1867. It is not necessary to consider the first issue.

Appeal allowed with costs

The decision was a 5-4 split: majority — La Forest, L'Heureux-Dubé, Gonthier, Cory, and McLachlin; Lamer C.J., Sopinka, Iacobucci and Major dissenting.

- *T*he Ontario Environmental Protection Act survived a challenge when the Ontario Court of Appeal found the Act was not *ultra vires* the provincial legislature. *R. v. Canadian Pacific Ltd.* (unreported).[2]

- *T*he legislature of the province of Ontario had not acted beyond the powers conferred on the legislatures of the provinces under section 92(8) of the Constitution Act when it passed legislation creating a "megacity."[3]

- *T*he Alberta Court of Appeal was asked by the lieutenant governor in council of Alberta for an opinion as to the validity and effect of the federal statute creating the Goods and Services Tax, the GST. The questions included the following: was the act *ultra vires* the Parliament of Canada. The court held that the GST Act was not *ultra vires* Parliament. (Reference Bill C-62).[4]

2. CHARTER OF RIGHTS AND FREEDOMS

Questions

If the Charter of Rights and Freedoms was entrenched in the Constitution to curb the power of the government, what is the government? [This is the question Madam Justice McLachlin holds will be prominent in future Charter cases before the Supreme Court of Canada.[5] For example, does the Charter bind the conduct of hospitals, universities and other government bodies like the CBC?

Adbusters Media Foundation v. Canadian Broadcasting Corporation

VANCOUVER REGISTRY NO.C940820
http://www.courts.gov.bc.ca/
BRITISH COLUMBIA SUPREME COURT
NOVEMBER 8, 1995

Holmes, J.: — [1] The Adbusters Media Foundation ("Adbusters") is a non-profit society which provides educational services to the media and promotes environmental awareness and media literacy.

[2] Adbusters believes the media is too commercial and hence they seek to "re-define" it through social marketing of their ideas.

[3] The defendant Canadian Broadcasting Corporation ("CBC") is a federal corporation established under the *Broadcasting Act,* S.C. 1991, c.11 which provides a national television and radio network facility.

[4] Adbusters and Greenpeace International devised, financed and produced a 30-second television advertisement they title *"Autosaurus."* It uses animated dinosaurs to convey a message that the automobile is becoming obsolete and the automotive age coming to an end.

[5] Adbusters wished to have the advertisement shown in the commercial television market.

[6] The CBC carried a commercially sponsored television program called *"Driver's Seat."* The basic format was for journalistic reports on the analytic testing and review of new cars and related products. The program also offered automotive consumer advice and safety messages of interest to car owners or prospective purchasers.

[7] The program was co-produced by an independent producer, Mr. Waldin, and the CBC. The CBC provided facilities and the "hardware" for production, Mr. Waldin's company provided the creative talent and administration. The program contained six minutes of advertising of which the independent producers sold and received the proceeds from two minutes and the CBC sold and retained the proceeds of the other four minutes. The advertising of the independent producer was melded into the show as it was produced. The advertisers were related to the automotive product and service industry.

[8] Adbusters considered the *"Driver's Seat"* viewing audience to be an ideal market to deliver its "anti-auto" message. They contacted the CBC sales office to place *"Autosaurus"* on *"Driver's Seat"* and also submitted the advertisement to the Advertising Standards Branch of the CBC for review.

[9] Adbusters was aware that the CBC had a written Advertising Standard with which they must comply. In particular within those Standards was an Advocacy Advertising policy. The preamble to the policy read:

The purpose of this policy is to permit access to the airwaves for advertisements that advocate a point of view or particular course of action on issues of public interest or concern. It is based on the principle that the democratic rights of Canadians will best be served by policies promoting freedom of speech.

[10] The CBC under the written policy would accept advertisements subject to, *inter alia*:

(d) Advocacy advertisements will not be aired within news programs, programs whose regular mandate is to report on controversial public issues, or programs in which the CBC does not schedule advertising.

[11] Through a translation error from the French to English version the italicised words "... and information ..." were omitted in the English version as it existed and was known to the plaintiff in early 1993. The sub-section should therefore have read:

(d) Advocacy advertisements will not be aired within news *and information* programs. ...

[12] The advertisement as submitted for review as to Advertising Standards was approved for broadcast. February 4, 1993 Adbusters and the CBC contracted in writing for the broadcast of *"Autosaurus"* on the February 27, 1993 and March 6, 1993 showing of *"Driver's Seat"*.

[13] The cost of the advertising was paid in full in advance as required. The CBC broadcast *"Autosaurus"* on the February 27, 1993 date as contracted. On March 2, 1993 the CBC however advised Adbusters the March 6, 1993 *"Driver's Seat"* program was preempted and that it had erred in application of its Advertising Standards and was not willing to permit future broadcast of the advertisement within the *"Driver's Seat"* program.

[14] Alternate scheduling of the advertisement was offered including the time period immediately preceding or following the show. Adbusters refused the offers of alternative broadcast placement and the CBC returned its payment.

[15] Adbusters as a result of the cancellation of its advertisement on *"Driver's Seat,"* and the refusal of the CBC to permit the advertisement future access to that program, brought this action claiming damages for a breach of contract, coupled with claims for relief by way of declarations, damages and injunctive relief for breaches of the Canadian *Charter of Rights and Freedoms ("Charter")*. In particular the plaintiff claims the defendant breached the plaintiff's right to freedom of expression under Section 2(b) and discriminated against the plaintiff in violation of s. 15, of the Charter. ... [The judge finds that CBC did breach its contract with Adbusters when it refused to proceed with the second scheduled showing of the advertisement. He further observes that the contract claim was being used "as a platform to launch a Charter challenge" and finds that there were no apparent damages resulting from the breach and makes no award of damages, not even a nominal sum.]

[26] In the event damages at law must be presumed the award should in the circumstances be the minimal or token amount that the law requires.

CHARTER

[27] 1. Does the *Charter* apply to the CBC?
2. If so, was there a violation of Section 2(b) or Section 15?

[28] The plaintiff contends the CBC is amenable to the Charter specifically because it is a governmental body; alternatively, because the *Charter* in the existing circumstances would apply to all broadcasters.

[29] The Charter provides the individual with protection from the coercive power of the State. Section 32(l) of the Charter provides that it applies:

(a) To the Parliament and government of Canada in respect of all matters within the authority of Parliament. ...

[30] As Mr. Justice Campbell in *Trieger v. Canadian Broadcasting Corp. et al* (1988), 54 D.L.R. (4th) 143 said, the *Charter* "... represents a curb on the power of government, not a fetter on the rights of organizations or individuals independent of government which do not exercise the functions of government."

[31] The CBC does have several of the indicia of a governmental body. The test however is conduct based. It must therefore be found that the conduct in issue of the entity in question is governmental in nature to give rise to Charter application. ...

[34] Although the CBC was created by Parliament, it is an agent of the Crown, and remains ultimately responsible through the Minister to Parliament, this form of "ultimate or extraordinary" control is not determinative of operational, routine or regular control... .

[35] In a trilogy of cases decided by the Supreme Court of Canada as to whether entities such as universities and hospitals were subject to the Charter in respect of mandatory retirement policies, *McKinney, supra; Harrison v. University of British Columbia* (1990), 77 D.L.R. (4th) 55 (SCC); and *Stoffman, supra,* the entities were found to be *not* subject to the *Charter* in respect of the activity in question. The judgments of members of the court differ as to factors to be considered in deciding if the entity is governmental in nature but it would appear fair to conclude that a court should give weight to factors indicative of the entity in question being independent or autonomous of governmental control. ...

[37] It is overall control of programming that lays at the base of the issue here. ...

[38] The *Broadcasting Act* makes clear that the CBC in pursuing its objects and in the exercise of its powers enjoys "... freedom of expression and journalistic, creative and programming independence" [Section 46(5)].

[39] The *Broadcasting Act* provides to both the CBC specifically and to broadcasters generally the protection of this independence through directed interpretation of the statute and strongly indicates the importance placed by Parliament upon the preservation of those freedoms from governmental influence or control. [The judge reviews relevant sections of the *Broadcasting Act* and also shows that the CBC is not subject to control under the *Financial Administration Act*. After citing relevant cases he concludes.]

[46] The Advocacy Advertising policy has not been shown to have either government input, influence, or its formulation interfered with in any way. It is a policy clearly appropriate and incidental to the CBC's carefully protected mandate to exercise power and enjoy freedom of expression and journalistic, creative and programming independence under the *Broadcasting Act*.

[47] The conduct of the CBC in the classification of the

"Autosaurus" advertisement cannot fairly be said to be a decision of government, nor is there evidence that the government influenced, interfered, or participated in any sense in the impugned decision-making process. The advertiser complaints brought to light the embarrassing error or omission that occurred regarding the Advocacy Advertising policy during review of the *"Autosaurus"* advertisement under the Advertising Standards.

[48] I do not find the Charter has application to the CBC as contended either specifically or generally as a broadcaster, viewed in the context of the circumstances and conduct of its dealing with the plaintiff in issue here. I find it unnecessary therefore to deal with the issue of breach of specific Charter sections.

[49] The claims for Charter relief are dismissed. In the circumstances of the finding that the CBC was in breach of its contract, but with no damages being shown; and the failure of the plaintiff on its Charter claims, I find it appropriate that each party bear its separate costs.

[Claim for Charter relief dismissed.]

S. 1 AND S. 2

The *Tobacco Products Control Act*, a federal statute, came into force on January 1, 1989 purportedly to address a national public health problem. The Act, among other things, banned advertisement of tobacco products. Cigarette manufacturers challenged the statute, alleging that the statute was unconstitutional. Judge Chabot of the Quebec Superior Court agreed; he struck it down by holding that it was *ultra vires* the federal government.

The judge held that the effect of the law was to eliminate advertising and that such commercial activities were within the jurisdiction of the provinces—covered by *The Constitution Act* s. 92(13) [property and civil rights] or 92(16) [matters of a local or private nature]. He rejected the argument of the lawyers for the Attorney General that the federal government had the right to create the statute under its residual power to pass laws for the "peace, order, and good government of Canada." Furthermore, the judge held that, even if the purpose of the legislation was to protect the public health, such matters came within the jurisdiction of the provinces. The judge also found the legislation offended against the *Charter of Rights and Freedoms* because it violated s. 2(b), the freedom of expression. Nor could it be saved by s.1, as an infringement that could be justified in a free and democratic society.

Imperial Tobacco Ltd. v. Le Procureur General du Canada
Summarized from The Lawyers Weekly *August 23, 1991 p. 9*

This decision was reversed by the Cour d'appel du Québec, District of Montreal. The Supreme Court of Canada gave the tobacco companies leave to appeal.

In 1995, on the question of the Parliament's authority to pass the statute, the majority of Supreme Court of Canada concluded that the legislation was validly enacted under the criminal law power given to the federal Parliament in the constitution, because its essence was to protect Canadians from the injurious effects of tobacco. The court, however, held that the Act's broad prohibition on advertising violated the Charter rights of the tobacco companies, namely the right of freedom of expression. Five of the nine judges found that the violation of the Charter rights could not be saved by s. 1 of the Charter, that is, the government failed to demonstrate that the Act's ban on advertising was justified. The four dissenting judges felt the Charter infringement on free expression was demonstrably justified. Thus, several sections of the Act were struck down as unconstitutional.[6]

RJR-MacDonald Inc. et al. v. Canada (Attorney General) et al.
http://www.droit.umontreal.ca/
Supreme Court of Canada
September 21, 1995

Note: Subsequent to the court's decision to replace the *Tobacco Products Control Act*, Parliament passed the *Tobacco Act* the preponderance of which was given Royal Assent on April 25, 1997.

- **A** case was summarized as follows: "While there might be an expressive quality to lap dancing which could be protected under s. 2(b), an impugned by-law which prohibited such a performance was saved under s. 1."[7]

- **M**r. Thompson, ticketed for failing to wear his seat belt contrary to the *Motor Vehicle Act*, argued that the provincial seat belt law conflicted with his religious freedom guaranteed by s. 2(a) of the Charter, namely his belief in free will and that he "creates his own reality." He lost.[8]

- **T**he ruling mullahs of Iran have banned Abdelkarim Soroush, a philosopher, from teaching, speaking or writing because he challenged the core concept of the late Ayatullah Khomeinis, namely, that the "holy men have a God-given right to rule." Soroush maintains that religion is interpreted by imperfect humans so one infallible interpretation is not possible, not even that of the Supreme Leader.[9]

- **O**n June 22, 1997 Tung Cheewah, designated to be the "chief executive" of Hong Kong after the handover, announced that laws restricting demonstrations would go into effect on July 1, 1997 the date Hong Kong was to be handed over to China.[10]

s. 3

- **O**n July 1, 1997 the British government handed over to China the control of Hong Kong. The Beijing government disbanded the elected representatives and replaced them with an appointed legislature. During its first meeting, the appointed legislature voted to deport children who entered Hong Kong to join their parents. The new law, which required them to first obtain a certificate of entitlement from the government, was criticized as contrary to the "Basic Law" referred to as the mini-constitution of Hong Kong . "Vanquished former legislators looked on powerless from the public gallery and protesters outside played funeral music."[11]

s. 8 AND s. 24(2)

R. *v.* T.L.

THE DISTRICT COURT OF ONTARIO
FILE NO: YOA 2/89 COBURG, ONTARIO
MAY 9, 1990

Summary of the facts: A Crime Stoppers tip led to the search of a teenager, who was found to have a vial of hash oil and a stolen wallet. He was arrested, read his *Charter* rights and charged with possession of stolen property. He was found guilty by the trial court. The conviction was appealed on the grounds that the police, by acting on a Crime Stoppers tip, had breached his rights under s. 8 of the *Charter* to be free from unreasonable search and seizure.

Kerr, D.C.J.:

… It appears that the trial judge took the view that the police have the right, solely on the basis of an anonymous tip, to conduct a search of the accused. While I am sure that anonymous tips are useful tools in enabling police to initiate criminal investigations, I do not accept the proposition that they are entitled to conduct warrantless searches on members of the public without anything further. Constable Dunn at the time of conducting the search of the accused had nothing but a suspicion based on the anonymous call to his fellow officer. There was no evidence of the caller's identity, reputation or motivation. No subsequent investigation by Constable Dunn was conducted which would provide him with reasonable and probable grounds for suspecting the commission of an offence and under these circumstances he could not, in my view, have obtained a search warrant. If such warrantless searches by the police were condoned by the courts the right sought to be protected by Section 8 of the Charter would be meaningless. I conclude that there was a breach of the accused's Charter Rights under these circumstances.

In fact, on the argument of this appeal it was conceded by the Crown that the police had breached Section 8 in searching the accused, but the Crown submitted that the evidence being "real" evidence ought to be admitted notwithstanding the breach and that I ought not to apply Section 24(2) of the Charter to exclude the evidence obtained on the search. He relies on Collins vs. R. (1987) 33 C.C.C. 3rd, 1 (S.C.C.). However I am of the view that the appellant has met the onus upon him to establish on the balance of probabilities that the admission of this evidence would bring the administration of justice into disrepute when one considers the long term consequences of the regular admission of such evidence on the repute of the administration of justice. If the evidence obtained by Officer Dunn under the circumstances of this particular case were extended into a general policy to admit such evidence it would become readily apparent that the right of a private citizen to be secure from an unreasonable search and seizure would evaporate whenever real evidence was found. It is my view that Section 8 of the Charter has been in place for a sufficiently long period of time so that any competent and conscientious officer should realize that he does not have the right to conduct such a search without something more than a mere suspicion. A malicious or mischievous informant protected by anonymity could well create havoc with the rights and reputation of a well-respected, honest, average citizen. It was to protect the security of such citizens against a search of this type that Section 8 was enacted. Accordingly, the appeal succeeds on that ground...

Note: The evidence obtained after an illegal detention is not always inadmissible. In *R. v. Manolikakis,* the Ontario Court of Appeal followed the directions of the Supreme Court of Canada in *R. v. Collins* (the case cited in *R. v. T.L.* above), and held that, among other things, the reputation of the administration of justice would not be brought into disrepute by allowing evidence of the kilo of cocaine and the handgun. See [1997] O.J. No. 3284 (Q.L.) or Docket: C19123, Ontario Court of Appeal, August 12, 1997.

• *T*he police had acted on the basis of a drug-courier profile, a list of suspicious characteristics of the typical drug runner, and stopped a suspect. Andrew Sokolow, nervous, wearing a black jumpsuit and gold jewelry, paid cash for two round-trip tickets from Honolulu to Miami. He returned within three days without luggage. Stopped for identification, he had none. A dog indicated he was carrying drugs. He was arrested and a search revealed 1,000 grams of cocaine. The issue before the U.S. Supreme Court is whether or not the suspect's right to freedom from unreasonable search and seizure under the Fourth Amendment was violated when he was stopped merely because he fit the drug-courier profile.[12] The U.S. Supreme Court upheld the conviction for possession thereby supporting the character profiling used by the Drug Enforcement Administration.[13]

The reasons for judgment began: "In October 1992 Mr. Brazier suffered the dreaded event of an urban driver: his car was towed to an impoundment lot. He had parked it illegally." Mr. Brazier petitioned for a declaration that the impoundment, allowed under s. 3(a) of the City's by-law, violated his right, stated in s. 8 of the *Charter of Rights and Freedoms*, against unreasonable seizure. After examining the precedents dealing with the meaning of s. 8 of the *Charter* the Judge concluded

Certainly the reliance upon an automobile for a traveller far from home cannot be doubted. Nor can the inconvenience of impoundment be denied. Inconvenience and reliance, however, are not the issue. The question is whether the interest of the driver of an illegally parked vehicle is unreasonably affected by its removal, without search, to a place where it can be immediately retrieved. In my view the answer is no. The intrusion on the interest of the driver in the circumstances is not unreasonable. I conclude the effect of the City's actions are not unreasonable.

I have also been mindful of the purpose of the impoundment. Unlike many of the cases referred to me, the purpose was not to obtain evidence or put in peril the future of the driver or his property. In contrast the purpose of this impoundment is to move a vehicle which is parked on City property in a no parking zone.

I conclude that impoundment, as it occurred in the circumstances of this case, is not a seizure. If I am wrong, I conclude the seizure was not, in the circumstances unreasonable as described in s. 8 of the Charter.

For these reasons the petition is dismissed.

Brazier v. The City of Vancouver
Vancouver Registry No. A953086
www.courts.gov.bc.ca
British Columbia Supreme Court
July 16, 1996

s. 9

Green *v.* Her Majesty the Queen

QUEEN'S BENCH, JUDICIAL CENTRE OF WEYBURN
REGISTRY NO. Q. 129
MAY 16, 1995

Matheson J.:—The appellant has appealed from his conviction, in Provincial Court, on a charge that on March 29, 1994, at Weyburn, he did, having consumed alcohol in such quantity that the concentration thereof in his blood exceeded 80 milligrams of alcohol in 100 mlliliters of blood, operate a motor vehicle, contrary to ss. 253(b) and 255(1) of the Criminal Code, R.S.C. 1985, c. C-46, as am. S.C. 1994, c 44.

It has been alleged, firstly, that the trial judge erred in not ruling that the appellant was arbitrarily detained within the meaning of s. 9 of the *Canadian Charter of Rights and Freedoms*, Part I of the Constitution Act, 1982, being Schedule B of the Canada Act 1982 (U.K.), c. 11 and in not thereby excluding the breathalyzer test results ...

FACTS

A police officer stopped the truck being operated by the appellant at approximately 2:35 a.m. on March 29, 1994. After being asked to do so, the appellant produced both his operator's licence and vehicle registration certificate. The police officer testified that he could smell liquor. The appellant was thereupon asked to go to the police vehicle. A demand for an Alcometer test was read to the appellant. The appellant complied with the demand. A 'fail' reading resulted. [Green was informed about his right to retain counsel, spoke with a lawyer, and consented to undergo a breathalyzer test.]

ARBITRARY DETENTION

Section 9 of the *Charter* states that "Everyone has the right not to be arbitrarily detained or imprisoned."

The Supreme Court of Canada has, in a series of decisions, considered the legality of the random stopping of motorists by police officers: *R. v. Dedman*, [1985] 2 S.C.R. 2; *R. v. Hufsky*, [1988] 1 S.C.R. 621; *R. v. Ladouceur*, [1990] 1 S.C.R. 1257; *R. v. Duncanson*, [1992] 1 S.C.R. 836; and *R. v. Mellenthin*, [1992] 3 S.C.R. 615. [A review of each of those decisions follows]...

The police officer who detained the appellant, Lyle Rodney Green, was alone in a patrol car in the City of Weyburn just prior to the stopping of the appellant's vehicle. ... [In cross-examination the police officer explained the reason for the detention:]

Q. Now can you tell me what time, and I think you may have said this, when you first saw the truck? And I understand it was a truck that Mr. Green was operating that night?

A. It was an enclosed type truck or a suburban type only small, small suburban type.

Q. Okay, Okay. And do you recall when you first saw that vehicle?

A. Well, actually I had see it a few minutes before, and it drove onto the Weyburn Inn lot where I'd been sitting, and then I assumed it had parked there, and then a little later I saw it again. ...

Q. Okay. And I understand — would I be correct the concern would be that if it had been on the Weyburn Inn lot, perhaps the person had been in the Weyburn Inn consuming alcohol, something of that nature?

A. No actually I just checked it to see who it was driving around that time of the night and kind of — and I didn't recognize the vehicle from being around town.

Q. Okay. What would be the significance of it being on the Weyburn Inn lot then? Like if it's parked in the Weyburn Inn lot, so what? I mean that's a place where people would come and stay and spend the night and —

A. Yeah, there was no significance really. I just saw it drive onto the lot. ...

Q. Yeah. And again I'm asking — you were kind enough to send me disclosure, and I notice in the disclosure statement that I got, "I decided I would try and stop the vehicle as I had previously seen it drive onto the Weyburn Inn lot." and I'm just wondering what — why that would be significant?

A. Just the idea that it was kind of hanging around downtown. I just wanted to see who it was basically. ..

It is clear from the foregoing that the detention of the appellant was arbitrary. But was it nevertheless a legally valid detention?

In response to the submission on behalf of the appellant that the detention of the appellant was not legally justified, the trial judge concluded:

The reason for stopping the vehicle, which he gave in evidence on cross-examination ... was that it was a strange vehicle. And although Mr. Fox has argued that it's questionable whether he should have stopped it, the — I relate this as good police work. When you see a strange vehicle in town driving around at two thirty in the morning, one would — the reasonable person would expect that the police officers on duty that evening would make inquiries as to what was about. So I interpret it as good police work. He was simply doing what he is trained to do.

There was no evidence before the trial judge that ascertaining the identity of a 'stranger in town' was within the scope of the police officer's duties or responsibilities, which might have justified the detention pursuant to the decision in *Duncanson.*

The detention of the appellant was arbitrary and, therefore, an infringement of the appellant's right, guaranteed by s. 9 of the *Charter,* not to be arbitrarily detained. It could only be justified if it could be established, pursuant to s. 1 of the *Charter,* that the limitation on the guaranteed right was demonstrably justified in a free and democratic society. Crown counsel, quite properly, did not seriously suggest that the identification of a 'stranger in town' was sufficient justification, in a free and democratic society, to override a guaranteed *Charter* right. ...

As was clearly stated in *Mellenthin,* the random stopping of motorists should not be extended beyond checks for sobriety, licences, ownership, insurance and the mechanical fitness of the motor vehicles. Random stopping must not be permitted to be turned into a means of conducting an unfounded general inquisition.

EXCLUSION OF EVIDENCE

...The evidence obtained from the appellant, Green, after his detention, and which resulted in his conviction, consisted, firstly, of his 'fail' reading following the administration of the Alcometer test, which provided the police officer with reasonable and probable grounds to demand a breathalyzer test and, secondly, the results of the breathalyzer test. It was not 'real' evidence. But for the arbitrary detention, the evidence would not have been available. ... [I]f it should be concluded that the breathalyzer evidence was properly admitted, notwithstanding the *Charter* violation, police officers would be entitled, in the future, to arbitrarily detain motorists, merely to ascertain the identity of strangers, with the knowledge that any evidence of an offence, derived from the arbitrary detention in violation of a guaranteed *Charter* right, would be admissible. The guarantee would thereupon be meaningless. Thus, the breathalyzer evidence should have been excluded. ...

There will be an order setting aside the conviction of the appellant and substituting therefore a verdict of acquittal. If the appellant has paid the fine imposed on him, it shall be repaid to him forthwith.

S. 15 AND S. 24

Haig **v.** Canada

[RE HAIG ET AL. AND THE QUEEN IN RIGHT OF CANADA ET AL.]
86 D.L.R. (4TH) 617
ONTARIO COURT (GENERAL DIVISION)
SEPTEMBER 23, 1991

McDonald J: ... The facts surrounding Mr. Birch's complaint are briefly as follows. The applicant Joshua Birch was a member of the Canadian Armed Forces from February, 1985 to April, 1990. Upon informing his commanding officer that he was a homosexual, Captain Birch was informed that the policy directive regarding homosexuals in the Armed Forces would apply to him and that effective immediately Captain Birch would no longer qualify for promotions, postings, or further military career training.

With no career opportunity left to him, Captain Birch was released from the Armed Forces on medical grounds and seeking some kind of redress he turned to the *Canadian Human Rights Act,* S.C, 1976-77, c. 33, only to find that his situation, namely discrimination based solely on his sexual orientation, was not covered in the Act.

Section 3(1) of the *Canadian Human Rights Act* reads as follows:

3(1) For all purposes of this Act, race, national or ethnic origin, colour, religion, age, sex, marital status, family status, disability and conviction for which a pardon has been granted are prohibited grounds of discrimination.

Clearly the Act does not cover discrimination based on sexual orientation.

The applicant then turns his attention to s. 15(1) of the *Canadian Charter of Rights and Freedoms* which states that every individual is equal before and under the law and has the right to equal protection and equal benefit of the law without discrimination and in particular without discrimination based on race, national or ethnic origin, colour, religion, sex, age or mental or physical disability.

He then looks to s. 24(1) of the *Charter* which states that anyone whose rights or freedoms, as guaranteed by this *Charter,* have been infringed or denied may apply to a court of competent jurisdiction to obtain such remedy as the court considers appropriate and just in the circumstances. ...

The applicant's case is based on the proposition that if lesbians and gays are not in the classes of persons set out in s. 3(1) then they as individuals or groups are not afforded the equal benefit of the law as set out in s. 15(1) of the *Charter.*

Captain Birch, as I understand his application, is not asking this court to decide whether or not he has been the victim of sexual discrimination. He is seeking however the right to put his case before an appropriate tribunal convened under the *Canadian Human Rights Act.*

To put the case in its simplest terms: "Should any Canadian who perceives discrimination on sexual grounds not have some recourse to a legislative tribunal?" If the Charter purports to give him such a right then is s. 3(1) of the *Canadian Human Rights Act* not underinclusive and therefore discriminatory as being contrary to the guarantee of equal benefit of the law set out in s. 15 of the *Charter*?

I have concluded in the affirmative and I am therefore declaring that the absence of sexual orientation from the list of proscribed grounds of discrimination in s. 3 of the *Canadian Human*

Rights Act is discriminatory as being contrary to the guarantee of equal benefit of the law set out in s. 15 of the *Charter*.

So far as I am able I also declare that this decision shall be stayed for a period of six months from the date or until an appeal has been heard within which time period the existing legislation shall remain in full force and effect.

Application allowed in part

Note: This judgment of Justice MacDonald declaring the *Canadian Human Rights Act* (CHRA) discriminatory was appealed by the Attorney General of Canada; Graham Haig and Joshua Birch cross-appealed asking the judgment be varied to include (1) a declaration that homosexuals are entitled to equal benefit and equal protection of the CHRA, and (2) a declaration that homosexuals are entitled to seek and obtain redress against discrimination on the ground of sexual orientation from the Canadian Human Rights Commission. The Court of Appeal of Ontario dismissed the appeal and allowed the cross appeal. Following a recent Supreme Court of Canada case (Schachter v. Canada (1992) 10 C.R.R. (2d) 1), the court, instead of striking down the CHRA as invalid, chose to "read in" so that the order of Justice McDonald was varied by a declaration that the CHRA "be interpreted, applied and administered as though it contained 'sexual orientation' as a prohibited ground of discrimination in s 3. of that Act."

Haig v. Canada   9 O.R. (3d) 495   Court of Appeal for Ontario

---

s. 33

- *I*n1977 the Parti Quebecois government in Quebec enacted a Charter of the French Language which banned English from all signs. In 1989, the Supreme Court of Canada found it contrary to the *Charter of Rights and Freedoms*. Subsequently, the Quebec legislature invoked s. 33, the "notwithstanding clause".[14]

- *I*n December of 1993 amendments to this Charter allowed public signs and posters and commercial advertising to also be in another language provided the French is "markedly predominant."[15]

C. CIVIL LITIGATION

1. THE THEORY OF PRECEDENT

Although the litigants won their case without a lawyer, the judge held that he was bound by precedent and could not award them costs in excess of their disbursements. The Court of Appeal, however, allowed their appeal on this point and held that this ban had developed in the common law and as costs were within the discretion of the courts the court could change the common law.

"This is a case dealing with a judge-made common law rule. … [I]n my opinion, the removal of the distinction between self-represented litigants and lawyer-represented litigants is consonant with the principles underlying the Charter."

Skidmore v. Blackmore
122 D.L.R. (4th) 330
B.C.C.A.
1995

2. THE BURDEN OF PROOF IN A CIVIL ACTION

Q u e s t i o n

Who must prove what to win a civil action?

In his reasons for judgment, Judge Bouck began as follows: " On the afternoon of 7 July 1985 Richard Robert Krusel suffered a tragic accident and became a quadriplegic. He alleges he came down a swimming pool slide head first into the water and struck his head on the bottom of the pool. He says the slide was improperly placed at the side of the pool since it was too close to the shallow end. He also contends the slide lacked adequate warning labels." The plaintiff named seventeen defendants including the owners of the pool, the manufacturers, and distributors of the water slide. After reviewing the evidence of sixty-five witnesses who gave testimony over a thirty-five-day trial, the judge concluded that "the plaintiff did not prove the slide theory on a balance of probabilities. There are any number of reasons as to how the plaintiff suffered this tragic injury. First, he could have been pushed in. Second, while standing near the slide and close to the edge of the pool, he could have lost his balance and started to fall into the pool. Instead of just letting himself collapse into the water on his back or stomach, he may have unthinkingly converted the fall into a dive at the shallow end of the pool. Third, the same manoeuvre could have occurred if, as he argues, he was at the bottom of the slide at one time splashing water up onto the dry slide. Fourth, inadvertently, he could have just dived into the shallow end and struck his head on the bottom of the pool. Etc. ... Over all, the proof offered by the plaintiff does not reach that degree of certainty where I can find he proved negligence on the part of any defendant on a balance of probabilities.

"Evidence on the issue of damages illustrated the enormous loss suffered by the plaintiff as a result of this accident. On the morning of 7 July 1985, a bright future lay ahead of him. He was engaged to be married. He just purchased a new house. His employers spoke glowingly of his work skills. He was upgrading his qualifications as an electrician by taking a course at B.C.I.T. The accident took all of that promising future away from him. A catastrophe is the only word that comes close to his situation.

"But, he is not a person who gives up easily. Since the accident he has acquired computer skills. He is optimistic by nature. He is not a quitter. He lives in a group home with 2 or 3 other people with similar kinds of handicaps. Government and community assistance make his life as comfortable as possible.

"This judgment will undoubtedly cause him great anguish and disappointment. The law is sometimes a blunt instrument. Often, a judge is left with two unpalatable choices. Both are before me in stark contrast. Based upon the evidence, the law compels me to dismiss the action as not proven.

"The action is dismissed as against all defendants."

Krusel v. Firth, et al. → all.
Supreme Court of British Columbia
Vancouver Registry No. C862311
August 23, 1993

3. CLASS ACTIONS

- *A* group of voters applied to the court for certification of their proceeding as a class action against the NDP government in British Columbia. The voters allege that the government lied; it announced an $87 million surplus, called an election, and within a month after the election announced a $200 million deficit.[16]

Those applying to the court to certify their proceeding as a class proceeding were "All those persons who have suffered damages as a result of the cracking of a toilet tank manufactured by the defendant Crane Canada Inc. (the "defendant") at its B.C. Pottery ... except those claims or portions of claims that have been finally and fully settled." The proceeding was instigated by the insurers of the homeowners who suffered water damage as a result of what they alleged were faulty water tanks.

The judge certified the action as a class proceeding on the following common issues:

— "Was the Defendant negligent in the manufacture or distribution of Toilet Tanks manufactured at the Defendant's B.C. Pottery Plant between January 1, 1980 and January 1, 1991?"

— "Whether in the circumstances of this case the appearance of a crack in a Toilet Tank raises prima facie evidence, in and of itself, of the negligent manufacture of a Toilet Tank by the Defendant?"

— "Was the Defendant guilty of conduct in the manufacture or distribution of Toilet Tanks, or in the management of claims arising from cracked Toilet Tanks, which justifies an award of punitive damages? If so, what is the amount of punitive damages to be awarded?"

Chase et al. v. Crane Canada Inc.
Vancouver Registry No. C957341
The Supreme Court of British Columbia In Chambers
July 16, 1996

- *I*n Florida, a lawsuit filed on behalf of thousands of flight attendants against tobacco companies for compensation due to illnesses caused by secondhand smoke was settled out of court. The settlement was hailed as the first time the tobacco companies settled with private individuals.[17]

4. EXAMINATION FOR DISCOVERY

- *I*vana Sharp, was sentenced to 89 days in jail for lying during the examination for discovery. During the cross-examination at trial case she admitted the truth. Sharp, a seller of a restaurant business, was sued for fraudulent misrepresentation, for misrepresenting its financial situation.[18]

Q u e s t i o n

What is the scope of the questions that a judgment creditor can ask the judgment debtor at the examination in aid of execution?

Lauzier *v.* Ranger

[1995] O.J. No. 1943 (Q.L.)
DRS 95-15416 COURT FILE NO. 59847/92
ONTARIO COURT OF JUSTICE (GENERAL DIVISION)
JUNE 23, 1995

Charron J.: — Pierre Ranger is a judgment creditor of Jocelyne Lauzier as a result of several orders for costs made against her in these proceedings. He brings this motion seeking various relief with respect to the judgment debtor examination of Ms. Lauzier. He also seeks a declaration that Ms. Lauzier's assets are not exempt from seizure pursuant to section 8(l) of the Execution Act, R.S.O. 1990, Ch. E.24. Finally, Mr. Ranger seeks an order for the payment of [certain] monies. ...

THE EXAMINATION IN AID OF EXECUTION

A dispute has arisen between the parties as to the scope of the examination in aid of execution to which Ms. Lauzier must be subjected to. Rule 60.18(2) of the Rules of Civil Procedure governs in this respect:

> 60.18(2) A creditor may examine the debtor in relation to,
>
> (a) the reason for nonpayment or nonperformance of the order;
> (b) the debtor's income and property;
> (c) the debts owed to and by the debtor;
> (d) the disposal the debtor has made of any property either before or after the making of the order;
> (e) the debtor's present, past and future means to satisfy the order;

(f) whether the debtor intends to obey the order or has any reason for not doing so; and

(g) any other matter pertinent to the enforcement of the order.

It is evident from the language of the Rule that the scope of the examination is wide. It is equally evident from a reading of the transcripts of two aborted examinations that Ms. Lauzier has been generally uncooperative in providing the requested information. For example, during the course of the examination of May 17, 1995 the first seven pages of transcript are spent in an attempt to confirm Ms. Lauzier's name. She then categorically refuses to provide her social insurance number; her counsel intercedes and points out that the number is noted on the income tax return and Ms. Lauzier then concedes that it is her social insurance number. Next comes an objection to producing a list of her assets on the basis that this information is already available to Mr. Ranger as it is contained in various affidavits filed during the course of these proceedings. She then refuses to disclose where some of the assets mentioned in those affidavits are located. All of these examples are taken from the first 27 pages of a 144 page transcript. A perusal of the balance of the transcript reveals that, although some information was provided to Mr. Ranger, the tone of the examination did not improve appreciably over its course. The continuation of the examination on June 2, 1995 proved to be disastrous. Ms. Lauzier was generally uncooperative and belligerent and at times abusive — often swearing at Mr. Ranger and eventually throwing styrofoam cups at him.

Nevertheless, substantial productions have been made to Mr. Ranger through counsel for Ms. Lauzier and some particular issues were raised with respect to the scope of the examination.

a) Disclosure as to matters preceding the debtor's liability

Counsel for Ms. Lauzier contends that there is no basis in law for going behind the time his client's liability was incurred. Mr. Ranger argues that the very language of the Rule says otherwise. Both parties rely on the same jurisprudence in support of their respective positions.

I agree with Mr. Ranger's position. Subsections (d) and (e) of Rule 60.18 make express reference to the time preceding the order from which liability arises and subsection (g) obliges the debtor to disclose any other matter pertinent to the enforcement of the order without limiting the scope as to time. The case of *The Ontario Bank v. Mitchell* (1881), 32 U.C.C.P. 73 (Ont. C.A.), cited by both parties as authoritative, supports Mr. Ranger's position …

… The chief object is to shew what property the debtor has at the time of the examination which can be made available to the creditor, and it is material in making or in the attempt to make out present property, to shew that at some anterior time, no matter how far back, the debtor where that property is, or what has been done with it.

It is not a sufficient account of property acquired before the judgment debt was incurred to say it all had been disposed of before the debt was incurred. The debtor must shew how, when, and to whom, and for what it was disposed of, as he is able to do it.

If the rule were as the defendants contend it is, the examination would be a farce.

The same rationale applies today and furthermore, the language of the present rule expressly widens the scope of the examination to a period of time prior to the time when liability was incurred. Of course, the information sought must be reasonably relevant to the enforcement of the order. …

b) Joint assets

Ms. Lauzier also refused to answer any questions pertaining to assets she owns jointly with another person. Counsel for Ms. Lauzier refers to a decision of the Ontario Divisional Court in support of his client's position: *Director of Support and Custody Enforcement, for Gardiner v. Jones; Bank of Nova Scotia …* [1991] 5 O.R. (3d) 499. While this case reaffirms the common law position that joint assets are not exigible, in no way does it serve to exclude joint assets from the scope of the examination in aid of execution. Nothing in Rule 60.18 can or should be interpreted to so restrict the examination. …

The scope of the examination in this case therefore extends to joint assets and Ms. Lauzier's objection in this respect is not valid. Any objection which may be raised with respect to assets which may be statutorily exempted from execution is likewise not valid. Even though an asset may not be exigible, it can still form the subject-matter of an examination in aid of execution.

c) Examination of third parties

Mr. Ranger seeks an order permitting him to examine four individuals pertaining to Ms. Lauzier's dealings with her assets since December 14, 1993. He maintains that he needs to examine these parties since he is unable to obtain the relevant information from Ms. Lauzier. Provision for such an examination is found in Rule 60.18(6) . …

Counsel for Ms. Lauzier takes the position that a creditor must exhaust all other means of obtaining the information from the debtor before an order for the examination of a third person can be made. I do not agree. The rule simply requires that any difficulty arise concerning the enforcement of an order. A reading of the transcripts of the aborted examination in this case leads to the inescapable conclusion that much difficulty has already been encountered. The evidence from the sheriff's representatives who indicate they were told by Ms. Lauzier to "take a hike," when they first appeared at her residence to enforce the Writ of Seizure and Sale and the subsequent removal of many assets from the residence prior to execution provide additional evidence that enforcement is very difficult in this case.

However I am concerned by the lack of notice to the named persons. This aspect of the motion is dismissed without prejudice to Mr. Ranger's right to bring a new motion with service on the appropriate persons with material in support clearly indicating the basis upon which it is believed relevant information would likely be in their possession.

EXEMPTED ASSETS UNDER THE EXECUTION ACT

Some exemptions are provided in section 2 of the Act. …

Although general claims to exemptions are made both during the course of the examination and at the hearing of this motion, Ms. Lauzier never specifically set out the exact nature of her claim to exempted property. … I will however give directions for the proper resolution of this issue. …

MS. LAUZIER'S STATE OF HEALTH

A medical report dated June 12, 1995 has been filed from Ms. Lauzier's family physician. He states that his patient's mental condition is frail and he recommends she avoid excessive stress for at least one month. In his opinion his patient is physically and psychologically unfit to attend court proceedings for at least one month. Ms. Lauzier's counsel asked that his client be permitted to provide her information by way of affidavit instead of having to appear personally at an examination. He maintains that his client appears unable to withstand the stress of finding herself in the same room as Mr. Ranger. The transcript of the aborted examinations certainly seem to substantiate counsel's views in this respect. I should point out that the transcripts do not reveal any inappropriate behaviour on the part of Mr. Ranger or of Mr. Max.

In the interest of avoiding the cost of further unproductive sessions before a reporter, I am prepared to accede to this request.

CONCLUSION

Consequently, there will be an order [as per my findings above].

D. Enforcement of Judgments

Questions

What can you do if someone owes you money but won't pay?
Do you have to have judgment against the person before you take such steps?

---

1. Garnishment

- *I*ncome Tax legislation which came into effect on February 25, 1992 allows Revenue Canada to garnishee refunds for outstanding delinquent student loans and unemployment insurance overpayments.[19]

2. Execution

- *I*n a California court Mr. Kroll sued the Soviet Union and *Izvestia* for libel. *Izvestia* had called him a spy, which allegation caused him to lose his business license after 15 years of selling medical supplies from a Moscow office. The plaintiff was awarded $413,000. In his effort to collect the award of damages, the plaintiff's lawyer seized a manual Russian-language typewriter used by an *Izvestia* correspondent in Washington.

  The article quotes the lawyer for the plaintiff as saying "The typewriter is just the start.... We had a writ to seize everything in the apartment that belongs to *Izvestia*.... There are also three desks, three metal filing cabinets, some bookshelves and a big color television set. I'm going back for all that tomorrow with a truck."[20]

Mortil	*v.*	**International Phasor Telecom Ltd.**

23 B.C.L.R. (2D) 354
British Columbia County Court
February 16, 1988

Wong, C.C.J.
Secrets are easier heard than kept: Jewish Proverb

This is an application by the defendant judgment debtor, International Phasor Telecom Ltd., for a declaration that its rights in the Phasor Code 1000 Computer Software and instruction manual for same are not liable under s. 49 of the *Court Order Enforcement Act*, R.S.B.C. 1979, C. 75, to seizure and sale under a writ of execution.

At issue is whether a computer software program incorporating a trade secret is exigible for execution purposes.

On 4th May 1987 the plaintiff judgment creditor, Mortil, obtained default judgment against the defendant, inclusive of interest and costs, in the amount of $6,946.11. On 4th December 1987, pursuant to a writ of seizure and sale, one copy of the defendant's two copies of Phasor Code 1000 Computer Software System and one instruction manual were seized by the sheriff.

The defendant's business is now defunct but it is the registered owner under the federal *Trade Marks Act* of the trade mark "Phasor Code" used in connection with the distribution of Phasor Code 1000 Computer Software products and owns the copyright protecting the form in which the idea for the Phasor Code 1000 Computer Software System is expressed. Basically, Phasor Code is a system of cryptography to encode and decode classified information put into computers.

The defendant distributed its Phasor Code 1000 Computer Software products to purchasers only under licence agreements containing non-disclosure provisions. In addition, copyright notices were affixed on all Phasor Code 1000 Computer Software products. The following elaborate security measures were also in place:

(1)   The defendant limited access to the information relating to the software system to key employees;

(2)   The defendant required the author of the Phasor Code 1000 Computer Software System to sign a confidentiality agreement;

(3)   The defendant established work rules affecting access.

However, in January 1987 the master software copy, from which copies are made for subsequent sale, was stolen and never recovered.

There is a concern by the defendant that if the copy seized by the sheriff is sold, under writ of seizure and sale, the secret nature of the Phasor Code 1000 Computer Software System will be lost.

I think it is established law as outlined by Professor Dunlop in his book, *Creditor-Debtor Law in Canada* (1981), at pp. 152-53, that s. 49 of the *Court Order Enforcement Act* and analogous sections of execution statutes in other provinces have been restrictively interpreted by the court to disallow writs of fi. fa. to reach trademarks, patents or industrial design rights because under common law incorporeal or intangible property was not subject to seizure and sale. Section 52 of the same Act, however, extended the common law somewhat by permitting seizure of specified categories of intangible property—which does not include intellectual property rights.

Counsel for the plaintiff submitted that what was seized by the sheriff was only the physical computer software—clearly tangible property and therefore "goods and chattels"—which are expressly exigible assets under s. 49 of the *Court Order Enforcement Act*. Provided the purchaser of the seized computer software does not infringe the trademark or copyright of the defendant, the purchased software is no different than the purchase of any brandname product. She also submitted that if Phasor Code 1000 System was indeed a trade secret, it was no longer such when the master copy was stolen and never recovered.

There is no reported Canadian judicial decision as to whether a tangible asset with a non-divulged trade secret is exigible to a writ of seizure and sale.

After consideration, I have concluded that this tangible property, like any other corporeal asset, is exigible under s. 49 of the *Court Order Enforcement Act*. However, to safeguard the secret process of the Phasor Code, I direct that its sale be subject to terms. The terms of sale will be a requirement that the purchaser enter into a trust agreement with the defendant concerning non-disclosure and prohibition of unauthorized use of the Phasor Code System, similar to the terms of the licence agreement required by the defendant in its ordinary sale to others.

If counsel cannot agree on the wording of the terms of sale, they may apply for directions.

If the potential purchase is to include the defendant's intellectual property rights, that is a matter not within the concern of this application but a matter for negotiation between the purchaser and the defendant.

As this was a novel point of argument with divided success, there will be no order as to costs.

Order accordingly

---

3. LIMITATION PERIODS

Perron **v.** *R.J.R. Macdonald Inc.*

VANCOUVER REGISTRY: DOCKET: CA016982
http://www.courts.gov.bc.ca/
COURT OF APPEAL FOR BRITISH COLUMBIA
OCTOBER 7, 1996

RYAN J.

BACKGROUND

[1] On June 20, 1988 the appellant, Roger Perron, filed a writ and statement of claim in the Vancouver Registry of the British Columbia Supreme Court seeking damages from R.J.R. Macdonald Inc. for the loss of Mr. Perron's legs due to Buerger's Disease, a disease which is said to have a known connection to cigarette smoking. …

[2] On May 29, 1990 the parties filed a consent order pursuant to Rule 39(29) of the Rules of the Supreme Court of British Columbia that the question whether the plaintiff's action was statute-barred be tried separately from, and in advance of, the other issues in the action. The trial of the issue, at which Mr. Perron testified, took place in February 1993.

THE TRIAL DECISION

[3] On March 22, 1993 Mr. Justice Cooper dismissed Mr. Perron's claim on the basis that the action was statute-barred. In so doing the trial judge found that the tort, if there was one, occurred within the Northwest Territories where Mr. Perron made his home from 1976 to 1983 and where he was told for the first time that he had Buerger's disease and suffered the loss of limbs which gave rise to the action. ...

[5] ... He accepted the opinion of Katherine Peterson, Q.C., a lawyer practising in the Northwest Territories, that the common law may provide for the postponement of the running of the limitation period in the Northwest Territories in certain circumstances (the "discoverability test") as set out by the Supreme Court of Canada in *Central & Eastern Trust Co. v. Rafuse* (1986), 34 B.L.R. 187 (S.C.C.). Applying th[at] case, the trial judge determined, for purposes of s. 3(1)(d) [of the Northwest Territories Limitation of Actions Ordinance], that the limitation period will start to run from the time the plaintiff discovers his injury or ought reasonably to have discovered it. He concluded, however, that Mr. Perron had discovered his injuries and their probable cause by October 1983 and that the "discoverability test" thus would provide Mr. Perron no assistance.

THE GROUNDS OF APPEAL ...

[7] The appellant limited his appeal to one issue: Did the learned trial judge err in law in the manner in which he applied the discoverability test in the *Central Trust v. Rafuse* case?

THE FACTUAL BACKGROUND

[8] To appreciate the appellant's position it is necessary to refer briefly to the findings of fact made by the trial judge.

[9] Mr. Perron is forty-four years of age. He began smoking "Export" (the respondent's product) cigarettes when he was twelve or thirteen years old in Geraldton, Ontario. In 1976 he moved to Yellowknife in the Northwest Territories. He lived there until 1983 when he moved to Vancouver. While living in Yellowknife, Mr. Perron was employed in the construction industry as a truck driver and in various other jobs.

[10] In October 1980 Mr. Perron's right leg was removed in a hospital in Edmonton. He was diagnosed as suffering from Buerger's Disease (Thromboangiitis Obliterans). His doctors warned him that he must stop smoking. In spite of the warning, Mr. Perron continued to smoke.

[11] In October 1982 Mr. Perron's second toe on his left foot was removed due to the effects of Buerger's Disease. In January 1983 his left leg was removed for the same reason.

[12] In October 1983 Mr. Perron stopped smoking.

[13] In November 1983 Mr. Perron consulted a lawyer to assist him to recover long-term disability benefits from a former employer in the Northwest Territories. His claim was settled in May 1984.

[14] Mr. Perron consulted a lawyer sometime in 1987 with respect to pursuing an action against the respondent. Mr. Perron's lawyer told him then that the tobacco companies owed him a duty to warn him about the connection between Buerger's Disease and smoking, but it was not until 1988 that this suit was launched. Mr. Perron said that he did not start an action earlier because no cases had been won against tobacco companies and he did not know that he could sue them. He said the action was launched in 1988 because a jury in the United States, in the case of "*Cippolone v. the Liggett Group*," had found a tobacco company liable for damages for failing to warn smokers about the dangers of smoking.

[15] The trial judge made this crucial finding of fact:

> The plaintiff says that he was unable to stop smoking even after the loss of his second leg in January, 1983 as he was so heavily addicted to smoking and despite the urging of his doctor. It is his opinion that doctors instruct patients to stop smoking as a general precaution for many conditions but the relationship between thromboangiitis obliterans was never explained to him and he did not learn of it until his own research revealed it in the Fall of 1983. The numerous references in the medical records as to the concern of the doctors over the plaintiff's smoking and the consequent future exacerbation of his condition, in conjunction with the warnings of his doctor, leads to a conclusion on a balance of probabilities that the plaintiff was so informed of the relationship but elected to disregard it, and I so find.

[16] In the end the trial judge concluded that Mr. Perron had discovered his injuries and their probable cause by at least October 1983. Applying the discoverability test, the limitation period of two years set out in s. 3(1)(d) of the Northwest Territories Ordinance had expired by the time the suit was launched in June 1988.

DISCUSSION

[17] The parties agree that the law as set out in *Central Trust v. Rafuse* may operate to postpone the running of time in the Northwest Territories Limitation of Actions Ordinance. They disagree as to its application in the case at bar.

[18] In *Central Trust v. Rafuse* ... the respondent law firm provided the trust company with a certificate stating that the mortgage ... formed a first charge on the property. Some years later. ... [i]n a judgment released in 1980 the Supreme Court of Canada held that the mortgage was void *ab initio*. Central Trust sued the firm of solicitors for professional negligence in failing to advise them that the mortgage may offend the provisions of the Companies Act. The question was whether the time to file the lawsuit began to run at the time that the damages were incurred, i.e. when the solicitors provided the certificate; or when the damage was discovered, i.e. when the validity of the mortgage was challenged in the foreclosure action.

[19] Mr. Justice LeDain said this for the court, at 250:

> ... [A] cause of action arises for purposes of a limitation period when the material facts on which it is based have been discovered or ought to have been discovered by the plaintiff by the exercise of reasonable diligence, and that that rule should be followed and applied to the appellant's cause of action in tort against the respondents under the Nova Scotia Statute of Limitations. ... Since the respondents gave the Nova Scotia Trust Company a certificate on January 17, 1969 that the mortgage was a first charge on the Stonehouse property, thereby implying that it was a valid mortgage, the earliest that it can be said that the appellant discovered or should have discovered the respondents' negligence by the exercise of reasonable diligence was in April or May 1977 when the validity of the mortgage was challenged in the action

for foreclosure. Accordingly the appellant's cause of action did not arise before that date and its action for negligence against the respondents is not statute-barred.

[20] The appellant's position is that since no successful action had been taken against a tobacco company, to his knowledge, until the "*Cippolone*" case in 1988, he was unaware before that time that he had a cause of action against the respondent. In the appellant's submission this puts him in the same position as the trust company in the *Central Trust v. Rafuse* case. Mr. Perron submits that it was not until the validity of the trust company's mortgage was challenged in court that the company "discovered" its cause of action. Mr. Perron says that this is analogous to his situation — it was not until the "*Cippolone*" case was decided that he "discovered" that he had a cause of action against the defendant.

[21] In my view the analogy is false. In the … *Rafuse* case the trust company had no reason to believe that the facts were other than they believed them to be. The company assumed that the mortgage document in question was valid. The company's solicitors had provided a certificate which implied just that. The company did not discover that the mortgage might be invalid until it was challenged in the foreclosure action. In Mr. Perron's case all the facts required to launch his negligence suit were known to him by October 1983. He chose not to sue the defendant because he believed that he would not win, not because he did not have the facts to support his lawsuit, but because he thought that without other successes against tobacco companies he would fail. It is not argued that the "*Cippolone*" case changed the Canadian law of negligence (and of course it could not), what Mr. Perron is really saying is that the American case gave him the impetus to proceed.

[22] In my view, the trial judge was not wrong in concluding that Mr. Perron's action was statute-barred.

[23] I would dismiss the appeal.

Note: See p. 104 for other actions thwarted because of delays.

[This decision was unanimous.]

ENDNOTES

1. This is a quotation from Roseanne Skoke, while an MP from Nova Scotia, when speaking against allowing special legal status to homosexuals. For a more detailed account see *Maclean's*, November 28, 1994, p. 31. Reprinted by permission.

2. *The Lawyers Weekly*, July 2, 1993, p. 28.

3. For a review of *East York (Borough) v. Ontario (Attorney General)*, see *The Lawyers Weekly*, August 22, 1997, p. 15.

4. *The Lawyers Weekly*, November 22, 1991, p. 23.

5. For a review of the speech given by Justice McLachlin on the Charter issues faced by the Supreme Court see *The Lawyers Weekly*, June 6, 1997, p. 16.

6. *Maclean's*, October 25, 1993, p. 11. Also see *The New York Times*, September 22, 1995.

7. For a more complete summary of the Court of Appeal's decision in *Ontario Adult Entertainment Bar Assn. v. Metropolitan Toronto (Municipality)* see *The Lawyers Weekly*, October 17, 1997, p. 15.

8. See *R. v. Thompson* 30 C.C.C. (3d) 125 The British Columbia Court of Appeal, September 29, 1986.

9. For a more detailed account see *Time Magazine*, June 23, 1997, p. 38 which reports that the followers of Soroush have a homepage on the Internet. The Council of Foreign Relations in New York has a 56-page study on Soroush's political thought.

10. For a more detailed account see *The International Herald Tribune*, June 23, 1997, p. 5.

11. For a more detailed account see *The Herald Tribune*, July 10, 1997, pp. 1, 4.

12. A more detailed account is given in *Newsweek*, October 10, 1988, p. 79.

13. A more detailed account is given in *Newsweek*, April 17, 1989.

14. *Maclean's*, August 22, 1994, p. 7.

15. For an account of these amendments and the changes to the Civil Code of Quebec see *The Lawyers Weekly*, March 18, 1994.

16. For a more detailed account see *The Globe and Mail*, September 29, 1997, p. A4.

17. For a more detailed account see *The Globe and Mail*, October 11, 1997, p. A12. The article reports that the tobacco industry fought lawsuits successfully for 40 years, but since June has paid about $15 billion to settle suits by state governments trying to recoup the medical costs due to tobacco-related sickness.

18. For a more detailed account of the trial *Morrison v. Sharp*, see *The Lawyers Weekly*, January 7, 1994, p. 2. The award of damages, $278,000 for losses and $20,000 as punitive damages, was appealed. The parties settled at $160,000. For a more detailed account of the settlement and perjury action, see *The Lawyers Weekly*, March 22, 1996, p. 19.

19. Summarized from *The Globe and Mail*, March 10, 1992, p. A8.

20. A more detailed account is given in the *Vancouver Sun*, November 14, 1986.

II

THE LAW OF TORT

A. DISTINCTION BETWEEN CRIMINAL AND CIVIL ACTIONS

Questions

What is the difference between a criminal and a civil action?
Can the same incident attract both types of action?

Note: The facts below illustrate behaviour that did or could lead to both a criminal and a civil action.

- *O*.J. Simpson, U.S. football star and T.V. and movie personality, was charged with the criminal offence of the murder his ex-wife, Nicole Simpson, and her friend Ronald Goldman. In the crimial trial in Los Angeles the prosecutors failed to prove beyond a reasonable doubt that Simpson had committed the murders.[1] In a subsequent civil trial taken by the victims' families, Simpson was found liable for the deaths.

- *A* beer fight at Koo Koo Bananas in Whitby, Ontario resulted in charges of common assault being laid against Eric Lindros, a hockey player with the Philadelphia Flyers. The judge, finding the Crown had failed to prove its case beyond a reasonable doubt, dismissed the charge after a four-day trial.[2]

- *I*n Halifax, Mr. Rent repeatedly rammed his house with his tractor after a matrimonial dispute.[3]

- *S*everal women, sexually abused as children, have taken civil actions against their abusers although appropriate criminal actions were taken.[4]

- *I*n Penticton B.C., a snowplow went off the road and crashed into the living room of Ms. Alaric.[5] In New Westminster, B.C., a truck driven by Gary Crawford "smashed into the livingroom" of Ms. Hetherington.[6]

- *I*n Spokane, Washington a naked Mr. Brown injured a policeman and a Mr. Jones by hitting them with a bowling ball.[7]

- *A* funeral director in Halifax had bodies transferred from the chosen expensive caskets into cheap pressboard boxes before cremation.[8]

B. INTENTIONAL TORTS

Q u e s t i o n s

When will the loss suffered by the plaintiff be shifted to the defendant?
When is the defendant at fault in law?

---

1. ABUSE OF PROCESS

The plaintiff law firm brought an action to recover legal fees of approximately $20,000. The defendant, Mr. Kirsch, filed a statement of defence and a counterclaim in which he alleged that the services rendered were not performed professionally. The plaintiff amended his statement of claim to seek damages for the tort of abuse of process.

Judge Campbell reviewed the material, including the decision of the Registrar before whom the lawyer's bill was taxed (examined), and stated the law: "The authorities indicate that the main elements of the tort of abuse of process are a misuse of the court's process for an ulterior or extraneous purpose other than that for which the process was designed to serve, and some damage flowing therefrom." He then concluded "that the evidence is so overwhelmingly against the defendant, that the only possible inference is that he knew his allegations of unprofessional conduct were false and that he made them to delay judgment and injure the plaintiff's reputation." In holding for the plaintiff, the judge applied the reasoning in *Glazer v. Kirsch* [1986] B.C.W.L.D. 159 in which it was found that the defendant was liable for abuse of process by attempting to forestall judgment and blacken the reputation of a creditor suing him on a promissory note. In that case Kirsch, the defendant, had alleged that the plaintiff creditor had threatened to kill or maim him or his family. The defendant in the case cited was the same Mr. Kirsch! Manson, the plaintiff in this action, was his lawyer who had prepared the unsuccessful defence in the 1986 case.

Norton Stewart et al. v. Kirsch
16 B.C.L.R. (2d) 221
August 19, 1987

- *I*n South Carolina, Ms. Martin sued a Bi-Lo store. She alleged that she suffered back injuries after slipping on a wet floor in the store. A witness claimed that the plaintiff herself poured water on the floor and then sat in it. This fraudulent behaviour resulted in a criminal action against her. It could have also resulted in an action by Bi-Lo against Ms. Martin for the tort of abuse of process.[9]

- *A*ware of the enormous costs and disruptions cased by "loony" lawsuits, The Citizens Against Lawsuit Abuse (CALA) not only publicizes the cost to the public of the abuse of the legal system, but also encourages other methods of resolving disputes.[10]

2. ASSAULT

In 1348 a man irritated by a pubkeeper's refusal to open the pub threw a hatchet at her head. He missed. She sued and won. The case, *I de S et Ux*, established the principle that creating in another apprehension of an imminent hit was wrong. In 1994 Nova Scotia gave us a variation.

Freeman, J.A. (orally): — In the course of a heated argument with his companion Sandra Thibodeau, the appellant produced a double-bitted axe he took from under a bed and, in his version of events, threatened to cut the house down around her because she was blocking a doorway, refusing to let him leave because she said she feared he would drive while impaired by alcohol.

He has appealed his conviction by Judge John Nichols of the Provincial Court on a charge of using a weapon to commit a assault, contrary to s. 267(1)(a) of the Criminal Code... .

An axe produced in the circumstances of an angry domestic dispute can only be considered a weapon and its use for the purpose of threatening or intimidating can be inferred. The appellant's expressed intention to use the axe to damage the house rather than to harm Ms. Thibodeau does not overcome the inference that the axe was used for the purpose of intimidation. The appeal is dismissed.

R. v. Lowe
[1994] N.S.J. No. 36 (Q.L.)
DRS 94-06235
Action C.A. No. 02896
The Nova Scotia Court of Appeal
January 26, 1994

3. BATTERY

- ...when a fist-fight broke out Monday between two surgeons performing an operation in a northern English hospital, a junior doctor stepped in to finish the operation.[11]

- *M*r. Umpierrez, a 26-year old Uruguayan man, bit several passengers aboard a jetliner on its flight from Costa Rica to Rio de Janeiro. The crew members reported that his teeth had been filed down to sharp points.[12]

- *A* customer in Bloomingdale's New York City store was sprayed with perfume by a salesperson. The customer suffered a severe allergic reaction which resulted in her being hospitalized for eleven days. The store settled out of court for $75,000.[13]

- *T*he player responsible for the illegal check from behind which left another amateur hockey player a quadriplegic was found liable. The Supreme Court of Canada refused to hear an appeal.[14] This case, *Unruh v. Webber*, was cited in the appeal of *Zapf v. Muckalt* which began with a familiar refrain: "The plaintiff broke his neck while playing in a Junior A hockey game. He is now a quadriplegic. He and the defendant, a member of the opposing team, were chasing the puck in the plaintiff's end when, as a result of a shoulder check by the defendant the platintiff was propelled head first into the end boards."[15]

Malette **v.** *Shulman*

37 O.A.C. 281
ONTARIO COURT OF APPEAL
MARCH 30, 1990

Summary of the facts: Mrs. Malette, seriously injured in an automobile accident, arrived at the emergency ward unconscious. The doctor gave her a blood transfusion even after it was brought to his attention that she was carrying a card indicating her unwillingness to have such treatment. She sued. The only defendant (of many) found liable at the trial level was the doctor; liable for the tort of battery. The plaintiff was awarded $20,000. The following is an excerpt from the decision of the court hearing his appeal.

Excerpts from the Ontario Court of Appeal:
Robins, J.A.:...

[12] I should perhaps underscore the fact that Dr. Shulman was not found liable for any negligence in his treatment of Mrs. Malette. The judge held that he had acted "promptly, professionally and was well-motivated throughout" and that his management of the case had been "carried out in a confident, careful and conscientious manner" in accordance with the requisite standard of care. His decision to administer blood in the circumstances confronting him was found to be an honest exercise of his professional judgment which did not delay Mrs. Malette's recovery, endanger her life or cause her any bodily harm. Indeed, the judge concluded that the doctor's treatment of Mrs. Malette "may well have been responsible for saving her life."

[13] Liability was imposed in this case on the basis that the doctor tortiously violated his patient's rights over her own body by acting contrary to the Jehovah's Witness card and administering blood transfusions that were not authorized. His honest and even justifiable belief that the treatment was medically essential did not serve to relieve him from liability for the battery resulting from his intentional and unpermitted conduct. ...

[22] On the facts of the present case, Dr. Shulman was clearly faced with an emergency. He had an unconscious, critically-ill patient on his hands who, in his opinion, needed blood transfusions to save her life or preserve her health. If there were no Jehovah's Witness card, he undoubtedly would have been entitled to administer blood transfusions as part of the emergency treatment and could not have been held liable for so doing. In those circumstances he would have had no indication that the transfusions would have been refused had the patient then been able to make her wishes known and, accordingly, no reason to expect that, as a reasonable person, she would not consent to the transfusions.

[23] However, to change the facts, if Mrs. Malette, before passing into unconsciousness, had expressly instructed Dr. Shulman, in terms comparable to those set forth on the card, that her religious convictions as a Jehovah's Witness were such that she was not to be given a blood transfusion under any circumstances and that she fully realized the implications of this position, the doctor would have been confronted with an obviously different situation. Here, the patient, anticipating an emergency in which she might be unable to make decisions about her health care contemporaneous with the emergency, has given explicit instructions that blood transfusions constitute an unacceptable medical intervention and are not to be administered to her. Once the emergency arises, is the doctor nonetheless entitled to administer transfusions on the basis of his honest belief that they are needed to save his patient's life?

[24] The answer, in my opinion, is clearly no. A doctor is not free to disregard a patient's advance instructions any more than he would be free to disregard instructions given at the time of the emergency. The law does not prohibit a patient from withholding consent to emergency medical treatment, nor does the law prohibit a doctor from following his patient's instructions. While the law may disregard the absence of consent in limited emergency circumstances, it otherwise supports the right of competent adults to make decisions concerning their own health care by imposing civil liability on those who perform medical treatment without consent. ...

[26] The distinguishing feature of the present case — and the one that makes this a case of first impression — is, of course, the Jehovah's Witness card on the person of the unconscious patient. What then is the effect of the Jehovah's Witness card?

[27] In the appellant's submission, the card is of no effect and, as a consequence, can play no role in determining the doctor's duty toward his patient in the emergency situation existing in this case. ...

[29]... He argues that it could properly be doubted whether the card constituted a valid statement of Mrs. Malette's wishes in this emergency because it was unknown, for instance, whether she knew the card was still in her purse; whether she was still a Jehovah's Witness or how devout a Jehovah's Witness she was; what information she had about the risks associated with the refusal of blood transfusions when she signed the card; or whether, if she were conscious, she would refuse blood transfusions after the doctor had an opportunity to advise her of the risks associated with the refusal.

[30] With deference to Mr. Royce's exceedingly able argument on behalf of the appellant, I am unable to accept the conclusions advocated by him. I do not agree, as his argument would have it, that the Jehovah's Witness card can be no more than a meaningless piece of paper. I share the trial judge's view that, in the circumstances of this case, the instructions in the Jehovah's Witness card imposed a valid restriction on the emergency treatment that could be provided to Mrs. Malette and precluded blood transfusions. ...

[36]... The doctor is bound in law by the patient's choice even though that choice may be contrary to the mandates of his own conscience and professional judgment. If patient choice were subservient to conscientious medical judgment, the right of the patient to determine her own treatment, and the doctrine of informed consent, would be rendered meaningless. ...

[37] In sum, it is my view that the principal interest asserted by Mrs. Malette in this case — the interest is the freedom to reject, or refuse to consent to, intrusions of her bodily integrity — outweighs the interest of the state in the preservation of life and health and the protection of the integrity of the medical profession. While the right to decline medical treatment is not absolute or unqualified, those state interests are not in themselves sufficiently compelling to justify forcing a patient to submit to nonconsensual invasions of her person. ...

[41] At issue here is the freedom of the patient as an individual to exercise her right to refuse treatment and accept the consequences of her own decision. Competent adults, as I have sought to demonstrate, are generally at liberty to refuse medical treatment even at the risk of death. The right to determine what shall be done with one's body is a fundamental right in our society. The concepts inherent in this right are the bedrock upon which the principles of self-determination and individual autonomy are based. Free individual choice in matters affecting this right should, in my opinion, be accorded very high priority. I view the issues in this case from that perspective. ...

Appeal dismissed.

Note: In a constitutional challenge to the Ontario *Child Welfare Act*, which allows a child to be made a temporary ward of the Children's Aid Society when the parents object to the child receiving a blood transfusion deemed necessary by the medical profession, the SCC upheld the validity of the statute.[16]

- *A*fter the Chicago Bears lost to the San Francisco 49ers 41-0, an unidentified woman among a crowd taunting the Bears coach Mike Ditka alleged that Ditka tossed a wad of gum at her and hit her on the head. "Police officer Richard Galliani said the gum 'was found and booked as evidence. What we have is just a basic assault or battery.'"[17]

- *I*n Bridgeport, Conn. Ms. Diorios hired Mr. Fuller, also known as Tickles the Clown, to throw a pie in the face of a school dean who had disciplined her daughter, "who went AWOL during a class trip to New York," by suspending her from school. At the girl's eighth grade graduation ceremony, Tickles the Clown gave the dean some balloons, a song and a pie in the face. After his arrest, he alleged that Ms. Diorios, wife of a lawyer, offered him $10,000 to keep her identity a secret. Mr. and Ms. Diorios were charged with tampering with a witness and Mr. Diorios was charged with conspiracy to bribe.[18] Apparently, a civil action for battery was not taken.

  A year later it was reported that in criminal court Ms. Diorios was found guilty of breach of peace. She was not found guilty of bribery or tampering with a witness.[19]

- *I*n Hamilton, Ontario Mr. Calligan cut about 30 centimetres of Ms. Staracivic's hair and on another occasion about 20 centimetres of Ms. Brown's ponytail.

- *I*n a scuffle, one man bit off the end of the other's nose.[20]

- *T*he Ohio Court of Appeal held that it was a battery when radio talk-show host Andy Furman blew cigar smoke in the face of his guest, Ahron Leichtman, an anti-smoking activist speaking about the health hazard of passive smoke.[21]

- *A*fter a dispute with a customer, Ms. Carson, a cake decorator in Arkansas, gave the customer a cake. The cake was laced with laxatives; seventeen people were made ill.[22]

- *I*n B.C., Kundan Sangha, who felt the family was disgraced because his 20-year-old daughter moved out of the house, waited for her to leave the building in which she took classes and then deliberately hit her and a male friend with a speeding vehicle.[23]

- *A* cyclist landed on the pavement on the left side of his head and on his shoulders after an attack by motorists with a powerful squirt gun. The pranksters were liable for all the consequent damage caused by their "assault and battery."[24]

DEFENCE OF CONSENT

The court found that a consent form signed by a university student who had submitted to a medical experiment at the University Hospital was not valid in law because the doctors failed to give him a fair and reasonable explanation of the proposed treatment and probable effect or risks so that he could make an informed consent. The doctors did not inform him that they were testing an anaesthetic or that a catheter would be advanced to and through his heart. The student, therefore, succeeded in his action for "trespass to the person." He had suffered a complete cardiac arrest during the treatment and was resuscitated by the manual massage of his heart.

Halushka v. the University of Saskatchewan et al.
53 D.L.R. (2d) 426
Saskatchewan Court of Appeal
May 4, 1965

- *I*n 1996 Evander Holyfield won the World Boxing Association title by an upset victory over the reigning champion Mike Tyson. The rematch in Las Vegas on June 28, 1997 illustrates the limits to the defence of consent often used against plaintiffs injured in contact sports. Holyfield had of course consented to bodily contact, but not to the damage inflicted by Tyson. Tyson bit off a chunk of Holyfield's ear.[25]

4. CONVERSION (TRESPASS TO CHATTELS)

- *I*n London, Ontario, Mr. McMahon testified that he had warned his sister's pet budgie that if it did not quit biting his hand he would bite its head off. The budgie paid no heed and continued to bite; Mr. M "followed through with the threat."[26]

5. DECEIT

Note: The tort of deceit is also known as a "fraudulent misrepresentation" when a deceitful representation is used to induce a person to enter a contract. Therefore, see *Sidhu Estate v Bains* on p. 91.

- *I*nvestors may have lost as much as $6 billion when the price of shares in Bre-X Minerals Ltd. collapsed after an independent study found *no* gold at its Busang gold site. It was revealed that the bags of core samples from that site, which had caused investor excitement, had been salted with bought flakes of gold. The company subsequently hired Forensic Investigative Associates Inc. whose report traces the chronology of the fraud and asserts it has evidence that the exploration manager, Michael de Guzman, and others carried out the salting. De Guzman apparently jumped to his death from a helicopter when the fraud was exposed. Stay tuned. This massive fraud has resulted in a lawsuit by the investors against the company.[27]

- *A*lan Eagleson, the founder of the National Hockey League Players' Association, and its executive director from 1967 to 1991 pleaded guilty to "defrauding Labatt Brewing Co. and three sports organizations." As a result of a plea bargain with both U.S. and Canadian authorities, the Ontario Court of Appeal sentenced Eagleson to 18 months in the Mimico Correctional Institute located not far from where he grew up "for frauds that had the effect of skimming thousands of dollars from hockey players' pensions." In addition, it was alleged that he deceived Bobby Orr by failing to disclose to him that Orr had received an offer from the Boston Bruins that included part ownership of the club.[28]

- *I*nvestors, known as "Names," pledged their money to back insurance policies of Lloyd's of London. Lloyd's suffered losses of about $15 billion (Can.) between 1988 and 1991 because of such disasters as the Exxon Valdez oil spill and Hurricane Hugo. In Canada, 214 Names faced bankruptcy. The Names alleged they were victims of fraud.[29]

- *I*n an effort to win a $100-million contract with the Social Security Administration, Paradyne Corp used phony equipment, an "empty box with blinking lights," to pass as an encryptor and put its name on another manufacturer's gear.[30]

- *H*ertz Corp. entered a guilty plea for defrauding 110,000 customers and insurance companies between January 1, 1978 through mid-1985, by billing them for inflated or fake collision repair costs. Hertz agreed to pay a fine of $6.85 million and to refund $13.7 million to those affected from Jan. 1, 1978 through mid-1985.[31]

- **M**s. Burns, claiming she had both a Ph.D in Medical Sciences and an M.D., when she had neither, worked in the field for thirteen years.[32]

> *Note: Although these last two cases resulted in criminal actions against Hertz and Burns, the persons wronged could have sued in a civil action to recover the losses they suffered because of the deceit.*

6. Defamation

Hill *v.* Church of Scientology of Toronto

File No.: 24216
http://www.droit.umontreal.ca/
Supreme Court of Canada
July 20, 1995

CORY J.—On September 17, 1984, the appellant Morris Manning, accompanied by representatives of the appellant Church of Scientology of Toronto ("Scientology"), held a press conference on the steps of Osgoode Hall in Toronto. Manning, who was wearing his barrister's gown, read from and commented upon allegations contained in a notice of motion by which Scientology intended to commence criminal contempt proceedings against the respondent Casey Hill, a Crown attorney. The notice of motion alleged that Casey Hill had misled a judge of the Supreme Court of Ontario and had breached orders sealing certain documents belonging to Scientology. The remedy sought was the imposition of a fine or the imprisonment of Casey Hill.

[2] At the contempt proceedings, the allegations against Casey Hill were found to be untrue and without foundation. Casey Hill thereupon commenced this action for damages in libel against both Morris Manning and Scientology. On October 3, 1991, following a trial before Carruthers J. and a jury, Morris Manning and Scientology were found jointly liable for general damages in the amount of $300,000 and Scientology alone was found liable for aggravated damages of $500,000 and punitive damages of $800,000. Their appeal from this judgment was dismissed by a unanimous Court of Appeal: …

III. ANALYSIS

[62] Two major issues are raised in this appeal. The first concerns the constitutionality of the common law action for defamation. The second relates to the damages that can properly be assessed in such actions. …

(a) Application of the Charter

[65] The appellants have not challenged the constitutionality of any of the provisions of the *Libel and Slander Act*, R.S.O. 1990, c. L.12. The question, then, is whether the common law of defamation can be subject to Charter scrutiny. The appellants submit that by reason of his position as a government employee, Casey Hill's action for damages constitutes "government action" within the meaning of s. 32 of the Charter. In the alternative, the appellants submit that, pursuant to s. 52 of the Constitution Act, 1982, the common law must be interpreted in light of Charter values. I will address the s. 32 argument first.

(1) Section 32: Government Action

[66] Section 32(1) reads:

32.(1) This Charter applies
(a) to the Parliament and government of Canada in respect of all matters within the authority of Parliament including all matters relating to the Yukon Territory and Northwest Territories; and
(b) to the legislature and government of each province in respect of all matters within the authority of the legislature of each province. …

[79] In my opinion, the appellants have not satisfied the government action requirement described in s. 32. Therefore, the Charter cannot be applied directly to scrutinize the common law of defamation in the circumstances of this case.

[80] Even if there were sufficient government action to bring this case within s. 32, the appellants failed to provide any evidentiary basis upon which to adjudicate their constitutional attack. This Court has stated on a number of occasions that it will not determine alleged Charter violations in the absence of a proper evidentiary record. …

[82] There is no government action involved in this defamation suit. It now must be determined whether a change or modification in the law of defamation is required to make it comply with the underlying values upon which the Charter is founded.

(2) Section 52: Charter Values and the Common Law …

[91] It is clear from [case law] that the common law must be interpreted in a manner which is consistent with Charter principles. This obligation is simply a manifestation of the inherent jurisdiction of the courts to modify or extend the common law in order to comply with prevailing social conditions and values.…

[92] Historically, the common law evolved as a result of the courts making those incremental changes which were necessary in order to make the law comply with current societal values. The Charter represents a restatement of the fundamental values which guide and shape our democratic society and our legal system. It follows that it is appropriate for the courts to make such incremental revisions to the common law as may be necessary to have it comply with the values enunciated in the Charter. …

[95] Private parties owe each other no constitutional duties and cannot found their cause of action upon a Charter right. The party challenging the common law cannot allege that the common law violates a Charter right because, quite simply, Charter rights do not exist in the absence of state action. The most that the private litigant can do is argue that the common law is inconsistent with Charter values. It is very important to draw this distinction between Charter rights and Charter values. Care must be taken not to expand the application of the Charter beyond that established by s. 32(1), either by creating new causes of action, or by subjecting all court orders to Charter scrutiny. Therefore, in the context of civil litigation involving only private parties, the Charter will "apply" to the common law only to the extent that the common law is found to be inconsistent with Charter values.

[96] Courts have traditionally been cautious regarding the extent to which they will amend the common law. Similarly, they must not go further than is necessary when taking Charter values into account. Far-reaching changes to the common law must be left to the legislature. …

[99] With that background, let us first consider the common law of defamation in light of the values underlying the Charter.

(b) The Nature of Actions for Defamation: The Values to Be Balanced

[100] There can be no doubt that in libel cases the twin values of reputation and freedom of expression will clash. As Edgerton J. stated in *Sweeney v. Patterson*, 128 F.2d 457 (D.C. Cir. 1942), at p. 458, cert. denied 317 U.S. 678 (1942), whatever is "added to the field of libel is taken from the field of free debate." The real question, however, is whether the common law strikes an appropriate balance between the two. Let us consider the nature of each of these values.

(i) Freedom of Expression

[101] Much has been written of the great importance of free speech. Without this freedom to express ideas and to criticize the operation of institutions and the conduct of individual members of government agencies, democratic forms of government would wither and die. See, for example, *Reference re Alberta Statutes*, [and others]…. More recently, in *Edmonton Journal*, supra, at p. 1336, it was said:

> It is difficult to imagine a guaranteed right more important to a democratic society than freedom of expression. Indeed a democracy cannot exist without that freedom to express new ideas and to put forward opinions about the functioning of public institutions. The concept of free and uninhibited speech permeates all truly democratic societies and institutions. The vital importance of the concept cannot be over-emphasized.

[102] However, freedom of expression has never been recognized as an absolute right. Duff C.J. emphasized this point in *Reference re Alberta Statutes*, supra, at p. 133:

> The right of public discussion is, of course, subject to legal restrictions; those based upon considerations of decency and public order, and others conceived for the protection of various private and public interests with which, for example, the laws of defamation and sedition are con-

cerned. In a word, freedom of discussion means … "freedom governed by law." [Emphasis added.] …

[103] Similar reasoning has been applied in cases argued under the Charter. Although a Charter right is defined broadly, generally without internal limits, the Charter recognizes, under s. 1, that social values will at times conflict and that some limits must be placed even on fundamental rights. As La Forest J. explained in *United States of America v. Cotroni*, [1989] 1 S.C.R. 1469, at p. 1489, this Court has adopted a flexible approach to measuring the constitutionality of impugned provisions wherein "the underlying values [of the Charter] must be sensitively weighed in a particular context against other values of a free and democratic society …".

[104] In *R. v. Keegstra*, [1990] 3 S.C.R. 697, for example, s. 319(2) of the Criminal Code was found to be justified as a reasonable limit on the appellant's freedom to spread falsehoods relating to the Holocaust and thus to promote hatred against an identifiable group. Dickson C.J. adopted the contextual approach to s. 1 and concluded that, since hate propaganda contributed little to the values which underlie the right enshrined under s. 2(b), namely the quest for truth, the promotion of individual self-development, and participation in the community, a restriction on this type of expression might be easier to justify than would be the case with other kinds of expression. …

[106] Certainly, defamatory statements are very tenuously related to the core values which underlie s. 2(b). They are inimical to the search for truth. False and injurious statements cannot enhance self-development. Nor can it ever be said that they lead to healthy participation in the affairs of the community. Indeed, they are detrimental to the advancement of these values and harmful to the interests of a free and democratic society. This concept was accepted in *Globe and Mail Ltd. v. Boland*, [1960] S.C.R. 203, at pp. 08–9, where it was held that an extension of the qualified privilege to the publication of defamatory statements concerning the fitness for office of a candidate for election would be "harmful to that 'common convenience and welfare of society.'" Reliance was placed upon the text *Gatley on Libel and Slander in a Civil Action: With Precedents of Pleadings* (4th ed. 1953), at p. 254, wherein the author stated the following:

> It would tend to deter sensitive and honourable men from seeking public positions of trust and responsibility, and leave them open to others who have no respect for their reputation. …

(ii) The Reputation of the Individual

[107] The other value to be balanced in a defamation action is the protection of the reputation of the individual. …

[108] Democracy has always recognized and cherished the fundamental importance of an individual. That importance must, in turn, be based upon the good repute of a person. It is that good repute which enhances an individual's sense of worth and value. False allegations can so very quickly and completely destroy a good reputation. A reputation tarnished by libel can seldom regain its former lustre. A democratic society, therefore, has an interest in ensuring that its members can enjoy and protect their good reputation so long as it is merited.

[109] From the earliest times, society has recognized the poten-

tial for tragic damage that can be occasioned by a false statement made about a person. This is evident in the Bible, the Mosaic Code and the Talmud. As the author Carter-Ruck, in *Carter-Ruck on Libel and Slander* (4th ed. 1992), explains at p. 17:

> The earliest evidence in recorded history of any sanction for defamatory statements is in the Mosaic code. In Exodus XXII 28 we find "Thou shalt not revile the gods nor curse the ruler of thy people" and in Exodus XXIII 1 "Thou shalt not raise a false report: put not thine hand with the wicked to be an unrighteous witness." There is also a condemnation of rumourmongers in Leviticus XIX 16 "Thou shalt not go up and down as a talebearer among thy people."

[110] To make false statements which are likely to injure the reputation of another has always been regarded as a serious offence. During the Roman era, the punishment for libel varied from the loss of the right to make a will, to imprisonment, exile for life, or forfeiture of property. In the case of slander, a person could be made liable for payment of damages.

[111] It was decreed by the Teutons in the *Lex Salica* that if a man called another a "wolf" or a "hare," he must pay the sum of three shillings; for a false imputation of unchastity in a woman the penalty was 45 shillings. In the Normal Costumal, if people falsely called another "thief" or "manslayer," they had to pay damages and, holding their nose with their fingers, publicly confess themselves a liar.

[112] With the separation of ecclesiastical and secular courts by the decree of William I following the Norman conquest, the Church assumed spiritual jurisdiction over defamatory language, which was regarded as a sin. The Church "stayed the tongue of the defamer at once *pro custodia morum* of the community, and *pro salute anim\ae* of the delinquent." See V.V. Veeder, "The History and Theory of the Law of Defamation" (1903), 3 Colum. L. Rev. 546, at p.551.

[113] By the 16th century, the common law action for defamation became commonplace. This was in no small measure due to the efforts of the Star Chamber to eradicate duelling, the favoured method of vindication. The Star Chamber even went so far as to punish the sending of challenges. However, when it proscribed this avenue of recourse to injured parties, the Star Chamber was compelled to widen its original jurisdiction over seditious libel to include ordinary defamation.

[114] The modern law of libel is said to have arisen out of the case *De Libellis Famosis* (1605), 5 Co. Rep. 125a, 77 E.R. 250. There, the late Archbishop of Canterbury and the then Bishop of London were alleged to have been "traduced and scandalized" by an anonymous person. As reported by Coke, it was ruled that all libels, even those against private individuals, ought to be sanctioned severely by indictment at common law or in the Star Chamber. The reasoning behind this was that the libel could incite "all those of the same family, kindred, or society to revenge, and so tends per consequens to quarrels and breach of the peace" (p. 251). It was not necessary to show publication to a third person and it made no difference whether the libel was true or whether the plaintiff had a good or bad reputation. Eventually, truth was recognized as a defence in cases involving ordinary defamation.

[115] It was not until the late 17th century that the distinction between libel and slander was drawn by Chief Baron Hale in *King v. Lake* (1679), Hardres 470, 145 E.R. 552, where it was held that words spoken, without more, would not be actionable, with a few exceptions. Once they were reduced to writing, however, malice would be presumed and an action would lie.

[116] The character of the law relating to libel and slander in the 20th century is essentially the product of its historical development up to the 17th century, subject to a few refinements such as the introduction and recognition of the defences of privilege and fair comment. From the foregoing we can see that a central theme through the ages has been that the reputation of the individual is of fundamental importance. As Professor R. E. Brown writes in *The Law of Defamation in Canada* (2nd ed. 1994), at p. 1–4:

> "(N)o system of civil law can fail to take some account of the right to have one's reputation remain untarnished by defamation." Some form of legal or social constraints on defamatory publications "are to be found in all stages of civilization, however imperfect, remote, and proximate to barbarism."

[117] Though the law of defamation no longer serves as a bulwark against the duel and blood feud, the protection of reputation remains of vital importance... .This sentiment was eloquently expressed by Stewart J. in *Rosenblatt v. Baer*, 383 U.S. 75 (1966), who stated at p.92:

> The right of a man to the protection of his own reputation from unjustified invasion and wrongful hurt reflects no more than our basic concept of the essential dignity and worth of every human being — a concept at the root of any decent system of ordered liberty. ...

[120] Although it is not specifically mentioned in the Charter, the good reputation of the individual represents and reflects the innate dignity of the individual, a concept which underlies all the Charter rights. It follows that the protection of the good reputation of an individual is of fundamental importance to our democratic society.

(c) The Proposed Remedy: Adopting the New York Times v. Sullivan "Actual Malice" Rule

[122] In *New York Times v. Sullivan*, supra, the United States Supreme Court ruled that the existing common law of defamation violated the guarantee of free speech under the First Amendment of the Constitution. It held that the citizen's right to criticize government officials is of such tremendous importance in a democratic society that it can only be accommodated through the tolerance of speech which may eventually be determined to contain falsehoods. The solution adopted was to do away with the common law presumptions of falsity and malice and place the onus on the plaintiff to prove that, at the time the defamatory statements were made, the defendant either knew them to be false or was reckless as to whether they were or not. ...

(e) Conclusion: Should the Law of Defamation be Modified by Incorporating the Sullivan Principle?

[137] *The New York Times v. Sullivan* decision has been criticized by judges and academic writers in the United States and elsewhere. It has not been followed in the United Kingdom

or Australia. I can see no reason for adopting it in Canada in an action between private litigants. The law of defamation is essentially aimed at the prohibition of the publication of injurious false statements. It is the means by which the individual may protect his or her reputation which may well be the most distinguishing feature of his or her character, personality and, perhaps, identity. I simply cannot see that the law of defamation is unduly restrictive or inhibiting. Surely it is not requiring too much of individuals that they ascertain the truth of the allegations they publish. The law of defamation provides for the defences of fair comment and of qualified privilege in appropriate cases. Those who publish statements should assume a reasonable level of responsibility... .

[141] In conclusion, in its application to the parties in this action, the common law of defamation complies with the underlying values of the Charter and there is no need to amend or alter it.

(f) Should the Common Law Defence of Qualified Privilege be Expanded to Comply with Charter Values?

[143] Qualified privilege attaches to the occasion upon which the communication is made, and not to the communication itself. As Lord Atkinson explained in *Adam v. Ward*, [1917] A.C. 309 (H.L.), at p. 334:

> ... a privileged occasion is ... an occasion where the person who makes a communication has an interest or a duty, legal, social, or moral, to make it to the person to whom it is made, and the person to whom it is so made has a corresponding interest or duty to receive it. This reciprocity is essential. ...

[144] The legal effect of the defence of qualified privilege is to rebut the inference, which normally arises from the publication of defamatory words, that they were spoken with malice. Where the occasion is shown to be privileged, the bona fides of the defendant is presumed and the defendant is free to publish, with impunity, remarks which may be defamatory and untrue about the plaintiff. However, the privilege is not absolute and can be defeated if the dominant motive for publishing the statement is actual or express malice. See *Horrocks v. Lowe*, [1975] A.C. 135 (H.L.), at p. 149.

[145] Malice is commonly understood, in the popular sense, as spite or ill-will. However, it also includes, as Dickson J. (as he then was) pointed out in dissent in *Cherneskey*, supra, at p. 1099, "any indirect motive or ulterior purpose" that conflicts with the sense of duty or the mutual interest which the occasion created. ...

[147] In other words, the information communicated must be reasonably appropriate in the context of the circumstances existing on the occasion when that information was given.

[149] The principal question to be answered in this appeal is whether the recitation of the contents of the notice of motion by Morris Manning took place on an occasion of qualified privilege. If so, it remains to be determined whether or not that privilege was exceeded and thereby defeated... .

[155] ... It is my conclusion that Morris Manning's conduct far exceeds the legitimate purposes of the occasion. The circumstances of this case called for great restraint in the communication of information concerning the proceedings launched against Casey Hill. As an experienced lawyer, Manning ought to have taken steps to confirm the allegations that were being made. This is particularly true since he should have been aware of the Scientology investigation pertaining to access to the sealed documents. In those circumstances he was duty bound to wait until the investigation was completed before launching such a serious attack on Hill's professional integrity. Manning failed to take either of these reasonable steps. As a result of this failure, the permissible scope of his comments was limited and the qualified privilege which attached to his remarks was defeated.

[156] The press conference was held on the steps of Osgoode Hall in the presence of representatives from several media organizations. This constituted the widest possible dissemination of grievous allegations of professional misconduct that were yet to be tested in a court of law. His comments were made in language that portrayed Hill in the worst possible light. This was neither necessary nor appropriate in the existing circumstances. While it is not necessary to characterize Manning's conduct as amounting to actual malice, it was certainly high-handed and careless. It exceeded any legitimate purpose the press conference may have served. His conduct, therefore, defeated the qualified privilege that attached to the occasion. ...[The issue of damages was reviewed at length and the $1.6 million award was upheld.]

The appeal is dismissed with costs.

- *F*ormer prime minister Brian Mulroney sued the federal government, the RCMP and others for $50 million for defamation for alleging in a letter to the Swiss Government that he had taken kickbacks connected with Air Canada's purchase of 34 Airbus jetliners and two military contracts. The matter was settled out of court at the last minute. Part of the settlement consisted of a full apology to Brian Mulroney by the federal government and payment of his legal bill. The RCMP proceeded with its investigation.[33]

- *M*itch Mitchell, the former drummer with the Jimi Hendrix rock band, sued David Henderson, the biographer of Hendrix, for libel. Mitchell alleged that the writer depicted him as a racist bigot. The British jury found that Mitchell had not been defamed.[34]

- *G*eneral Motors Corp. announced it would sue NBC for defamation for its rigged explosion in a purportedly documentary segment on the safety of GM trucks. On *Dateline*, the debate on the safety of the trucks with gas tanks fitted outside the trucks' interior frame was followed by scenes of GM trucks being hit broadside. One burst into flames. On investigation, GM learned that the explosion had been staged; the network had incendiary devises taped under the truck.[35]

- *O*n the grounds that an action for defamation must be "of and concerning individuals," Justice Montgomery dismissed a claim purporting to represent approximately 25,000 Canadian veterans of World War II. In a class action suit, the airmen alleged in the statement of claim that they had been defamed by the book and the episode "Death by Moonlight" of the T.V. series *The Valour and the Horror*.[36] This decision was upheld by the Ontario Court of Appeal in an unanimous decision.[37]

When the Royal Bank of Canada falsely accused a businesswoman of fraud which, in part, caused her business to fail, it was successfully sued for defamation. On appeal, the damages were increased from $20,000 to $50,000.

Royal Bank of Canada (c.o.b. Chargex) v. Battestella
[1994] O.J.No. 1717 (Q.L.)
DRS 94-14617
Action No. C10097
Ontario Court of Appeal
August 12, 1994

- *C*lint Eastwood successfully sued the tabloid, *National Enquirer* for $800,000 for its reporting on an interview with him which, in fact, never took place. Two quotes from this non-existent interview were subsequently used by an article in *People Magazine* which was asked to rectify its error.[38]

7. FALSE IMPRISONMENT

- *I*n Falls Church, Va, Betsy Nelson was detained outside a sporting goods store and accused of shoplifting. Those that detained her demanded she disrobe. The bulge was caused by advanced pregnancy; a baby boy was born the day after the detention and after she had met with her lawyer. She asked for $100,000 compensatory damages and $500,000 in punitive damages.[39]

When two Brinks security guards, replenishing funds at an automatic teller machine, inadvertently signalled to the alarm company that all was *not* well, that it was a hold-up situation, the alarm company notified the police, who apprehended them and took them to the police station where they were detained until identified. The guard who did not trip the alarm sued for false imprisonment. At trial he was successful, but the B.C. Court of Appeal held that the police had reasonable grounds for taking them to the police station and detaining them until their authority to be at the bank was verified.

Freeman v. West Vancouver (District)
71 B.C.L.R. (2d) 387
October 14, 1992

8. INDUCING BREACH OF CONTRACT

Note: See the summary of *Ernst & Young v. Stuart and Arthur Andersen & Co.* on page xxx under the heading Legality. The action was not only against the employee for breach of contract for leaving Ernst & Young, but also against the firm Andersen & Co. which the plaintiff alleged induced Stuart to breach the contract.

9. INJURIOUS FALSEHOOD (TRADE LIBEL)

- *B*efore Christmas of 1994, persons claiming to belong to the "Animal Rights Militia" stated that they had injected some turkeys with rat poison to avenge the mass murder of turkeys. Safeway Canada and Save-on-Food pulled turkeys from the shelves and allowed customers to return bought turkeys. The food store chains lost about $1 million. Of course more turkeys had to be killed to replace those returned or taken from the shelves.[40]

- *I*n a 314-day trial (reported by J. Miller in *The Lawyers Weekly* July 18, 1997, p. 3 as the longest trial in British history), McDonald's won its lawsuit against environmentalists who accused McDonald's, among other things, of destroying the environment, promoting disease, and contributing to starvation. McDonald's was awarded $136,000; its legal expenses may have exceeded $20 million.[41]

- *P*roctor & Gamble sued James and Linda Newton who wrote and distributed pamphlets claiming that the company's 100-year-old trademark depicting the moon and stars was a satanic symbol. The pamphlets claim the company's customers are supporting the Church of Satan. The defendants are distributors of Amway, a commercial competitor.[42]

10. MALICIOUS PROSECUTION

Susan Nelles was charged with four counts of first degree murder in the deaths of four infants at the Hospital for Sick Children in Toronto. After a lengthy preliminary inquiry to determine if there was sufficient evidence to put the plaintiff on trial, the judge concluded there was not and discharged her on all four counts. Ms. Nelles commenced an action in the Supreme Court of Ontario against the Crown in right of Ontario, the Attorney General for Ontario, and several police officers

The Supreme Court of Ontario dismissed her action for, *inter alia*, malicious prosecution. The Ontario Court of Appeal upheld the judgment and ruled that at common law, an action of malicious prosecution cannot be brought against the Attorney-General for Ontario, or its agents, the Crown Attorneys, for their conduct in initiating and conducting a criminal prosecution. The absolute immunity is justified as it allows the public to trust that the Crown will vigorously bring and conduct criminal prosecutions without fear of lawsuit.

On further appeal, the Supreme Court of Canada dismissed the appeal against the Crown, but allowed the appeal against the Attorney General. That is, the Crown is immune from a suit of malicious prosecution, but the Attorney General is not. The matter was returned to the Supreme Court of Ontario for trial of the claim against the Attorney General.

J. Lamar, reviewing the law, wrote as follows:

2. The Tort of Malicious Prosecution

There are four necessary elements which must be proved for a plaintiff to succeed in an action for malicious prosecution:

a) the proceedings must have been initiated by the defendant;

b) the proceedings must have terminated in favour of the plaintiff;

c) the absence of reasonable and probable cause;

d) malice, or a primary purpose other than that of carrying the law into effect.

(See J.G. Fleming, *The Law of Torts* (5th ed. 1977), at p. 598.)

The first two elements are straightforward and largely speak for themselves. The latter two elements require explicit discussion. Reasonable and probable cause has been defined as "an honest belief in the guilt of the accused based upon a full conviction, founded on reasonable grounds, of the existence of a state of circumstances, which, assuming them to be true, would reasonably lead any ordinarily prudent and cautious man, placed in the position of the accuser, to the conclusion that the person charged was probably guilty of the crime imputed." (*Hicks v. Faulkner* (1878), 8 Q.B.D. 167, at p. 171, Hawkins J.)

This test contains both a subjective and objective element. There must be both actual belief on the part of the prosecutor and that belief must be reasonable in the circumstances. The existence of reasonable and probable cause is a matter for the judge to decide as opposed to the jury.

The required element of malice is for all intents, the equivalent of "improper purpose." It has, according to Fleming, a "wider meaning than spite, ill-will or a spirit of vengeance, and includes any other improper purpose, such as to gain a private collateral advantage" (Fleming, op. cit., at p. 609). To succeed in an action for malicious prosecution against the Attorney General or Crown Attorney, the plaintiff would have to prove both the absence of reasonable and probable cause in commencing the prosecution, and malice in the form of a deliberate and improper use of the office of the Attorney General or Crown Attorney, a use inconsistent with the status of "minister of justice." In my view this burden on the plaintiff amounts to a requirement that the Attorney General or Crown Attorney perpetrated a fraud on the process of criminal justice and in doing so has perverted or abused his office and the process of criminal justice. In fact, in some cases this would seem to amount to criminal conduct. ...

Further, it should be noted that in many, if not all cases of malicious prosecution by an Attorney General or Crown Attorney, there will have been an infringement of an accused's rights as guaranteed by ss. 7 and 11 of the *Canadian Charter of Rights and Freedoms*.

By way of summary then, a plaintiff bringing a claim for malicious prosecution has no easy task. Not only does the plaintiff have the notoriously difficult task of establishing a negative, that is the absence of reasonable and probable cause, but he is held to a very high standard of proof to avoid a non-suit or directed verdict (see Fleming, op. cit., at p. 606, and *Mitchell v. John Heine and Son Ltd.* (1938), 38 S.R. (N.S.W.) 466, at pp. 469-71). Professor Fleming has gone so far as to conclude that there are built-in devices particular to the tort of malicious prosecution to dissuade civil suits (at p. 606):

> The disfavour with which the law has traditionally viewed the action for malicious prosecution is most clearly revealed by the hedging devices with which it has been surrounded in order to deter this kind of litigation and protect private citizens who discharge their public duty of prosecuting those reasonably suspected of crime.

Nelles v. Ontario

60 D.L.R. 4th 609 (O.C.A.)

[1989] 2 S.C.R. 170 (S.C.C.)

11. INTENTIONAL INFLICTION OF NERVOUS SHOCK

> Over several years, a female RCMP officer was harassed by the actions of her male colleagues and their sarcastic and sexist remarks, which led to their desired result — her resignation due to depression and anxiety. The court found the Crown liable for the intentional infliction of nervous shock and also for the negligence of her supervisor who consistently breached the standard of care owed her by not stopping the offensive behaviour and by condoning it by his own improper behaviour.
>
> *Clark v. Canada*
> *[1994] 3 F.C. 323 (T.D.)*
> *Federal Court (T.D.)*
> *April 26, 1994*

12. PRIVACY/MISAPPROPRIATION

Note: In some provinces this tort may be codified; for example, see The Privacy Act, R.S.B.C.

- *T*he in-house researchers at Apple Computer Inc. have code-named projects after notorious people such as George Gershwin or Charles Lindbergh. A project that the researchers hoped would result in a computer sold to billions of people was code-named "Carl Sagan" after the astronomer who popularized astronomy in his series *Cosmos,* in which he often referred to the billions of stars. Sagan filed suit alleging such use of his name was illegal exploitation. Apple agreed to quit using the name. Unfortunately, the researchers changed the code to "BHA" for "Butt-Head Astronomer". Sagan was not pleased; a new suit now contained allegations of defamation.[43]

- *T*iger Woods, the young, gifted U.S. golfer, has sued the Franklin Mint for misappropriation for producing a medal imprinted with an image of his face without permission.[44]

- *T*he estate of the deceased genius pianist, Glenn Gould, sued for misappropriation when the book *Glenn Gould: Some Portraits of the Artist as a Young Man* was published. Justice Lederman of the Ontario Court concluded that the book was not an appropriation of Gould's personality.[45]

> An "unknown trouble" call is the name given to a 911 call that has been disconnected before the caller has spoken. Because of the common-law duty of the police to preserve the peace, prevent crime, and protect life and property, if the police are responding to such an interrupted call, they have the right to interfere with the sanctity of a private dwelling by forcing entry to ascertain if the caller is in distress.
>
> *R. v. Godoy*
> *33 O.R. (3d) 445 (Q.L.) [1997] O.J. No. 1408 No. 23324*
> *Court of Appeal for Ontario*
> *April 9, 1997*

13. TRESPASS

- *M*r. Hetu, angry when his lady friend locked him out of the house because he was drunk, razed the house in a twenty-minute attack with a bulldozer.[46]

C. Negligence

Questions

What must the plaintiff prove in order to win an action for negligence?

If the plaintiff proves that the defendant owed the plaintiff a duty of care, fell below the standard of care owed and caused the plaintiff foreseeable damage, does the defendant have any other arguments that may result in the court dismissing the claim, or forcing the plaintiff to absorb some of his or her loss?

---

1. Duty of Care

Question

Did the defendant owe the plaintiff a duty to be careful?

M'Alister (or Donoghue) *v.* Stevenson

[1932] A.C. 562
House of Lords

By action brought in the Court of Session the appellant, who was a shop assistant, sought to recover damages from the respondent, who was a manufacturer of aerated waters, for injuries she suffered as a result of consuming part of the contents of a bottle of ginger-beer which had been manufactured by the respondent, and which contained the decomposed remains of a snail. The appellant by her condescendence [pleadings] averred [stated as a fact] that the bottle of ginger-beer was purchased for the appellant by a friend in a cafe at Paisley, which was occupied by one Minchella; that the bottle was made of dark opaque glass and that the appellant had no reason to suspect that it contained anything but pure ginger-beer; that the said Minchella poured some of the ginger-beer out into a tumbler, and that the appellant drank some of the contents of the tumbler; that her friend was then proceeding to pour the remainder of the contents of the bottle into the tumbler when a snail, which was in a state of decomposition, floated out of the bottle; that as a result of the nauseating sight of the snail in such circumstances, and in consequence of the impurities in the ginger-beer which she had already consumed, the appellant suffered from shock and severe gastro-enteritis. The appellant further averred that the ginger-beer was manufactured by the respondent to be sold as a drink to the public (including the appellant); that it was bottled by the respondent and labelled by him with a label bearing his name; and that the bottles were thereafter sealed with a metal cap by the respondent. She further averred that it was the duty of the respondent to provide a system of working his business which would not allow snails to get into his ginger-beer bottles, and that it was also his duty

to provide an efficient system of inspection of the bottles before the ginger-beer was filled into them, and that he had failed in both these duties and had so caused the accident.

The respondent objected that these averments were irrelevant and insufficient to support the conclusions of the summons.

Lord Atkin. My Lords, the sole question for determination in this case is legal: Do the averments made by the pursuer [plaintiff] in her pleading, if true, disclose a cause of action? I need not restate the particular facts. The question is whether the manufacturer of an article of drink sold by him to a distributor, in circumstances which prevent the distributor or the ultimate purchaser or consumer from discovering by inspection any defect, is under any legal duty to the ultimate purchaser or consumer to take reasonable care that the article is free from defect likely to cause injury to health. I do not think a more important problem has occupied your Lordships in your judicial capacity. ... The law of both countries [Scotland and England] appears to be that in order to support an action for damages for negligence the complainant has to show that he has been injured by the breach of a duty owed to him in the circumstances by the defendant to take reasonable care to avoid such injury. In the present case we are not concerned with the breach of the duty; if a duty exists, that would be a question of fact which is sufficiently averred and for present purposes must be assumed. We are solely concerned with the question whether, as a matter of law in the circumstances alleged, the defender owed any duty to the pursuer to take care.

At present I content myself with pointing out that in English law there must be, and is, some general conception of relations giving rise to a duty of care, of which the particular cases found in the books are but instances. The liability for negligence, whether you style it such or treat it as in other systems as a species of "culpa," is no doubt based upon a general public sentiment of moral wrongdoing for which the offender must pay. But acts or omissions which any moral code would censure cannot in a practical world be treated so as to give a right to every person injured by them to demand relief. In this way rules of law arise which limit the range of complainants and the extent of their remedy. The rule that you are to love your neighbour becomes in law, you must not injure your neighbour; and the lawyer's question, Who is my neighbour? receives a restricted reply. You must take reasonable care to avoid acts or omissions which you can reasonably foresee would be likely to injure your neighbour. Who, then, in law is my neighbour? The answer seems to be—persons who are so closely and directly affected by my act that I ought reasonably to have them in contemplation as being so affected when I am directing my mind to the acts or omissions which are called in question. This appears to me to be the doctrine of *Heaven v. Pender* (1), as laid down by Lord Esher (then Brett M.R.) when it is limited by the notion of proximity introduced by Lord Esher himself and A.L. Smith L.J. in *Le Lievre v. Gould.* (1) Lord Esher says: "That case established that, under certain circumstances, one man may owe a duty to another, even though there is no contract between them. So A.L. Smith L.J.: "The decision of *Heaven v. Pender* (2) was founded upon the principle, that a duty to take due care did arise when the person or property of one was in such proximity to the person or property of another that, if due care was not taken, damage might be done by the one to the other." I think that this sufficiently states the truth if proximity be not confined to mere physical proximity, but be used, as I think it was intended, to extend to such close and direct relations that the act complained of directly affects a person whom the person alleged to be bound to take care would know would be directly affected by his careless act.

There will no doubt arise cases where it will be difficult to determine whether the contemplated relationship is so close that the duty arises. But in the class of case now before the court I cannot conceive any difficulty to arise. A manufacturer puts up an article of food in a container which he knows will be opened by the actual consumer. There can be no inspection by any purchaser and no reasonable preliminary inspection by the consumer. Negligently, in the course of preparation, he allows the contents to be mixed with poison. It is said that the law of England and Scotland is that the poisoned consumer has no remedy against the negligent manufacturer. If this were the result of the authorities, I should consider the result a grave defect in the law, and so contrary to principle that I should hesitate long before following any decision to that effect which had not the authority of this House. I would point out that, in the assumed state of the authorities, not only would the consumer have no remedy against the manufacturer, he would have none against any one else, for in the circumstances alleged there would be no evidence of negligence against any one

other than the manufacturer; and, except in the case of a consumer who was also a purchaser, no contract and no warranty of fitness, and in the case of the purchase of a specific article under its patent or trade name, which might well be the case in the purchase of some articles of food or drink, no warranty protecting even the purchaser-consumer. There are other instances than of articles of food and drink where goods are sold intended to be used immediately by the consumer, such as many forms of goods sold for cleaning purposes, where the same liability must exist. The doctrine supported by the decision below would not only deny a remedy to the consumer who was injured by consuming bottled beer or chocolates poisoned by the negligence of the manufacturer, but also to the user of what should be a harmless proprietary medicine, an ointment, a soap, a cleaning fluid or cleaning powder. I confine myself to articles of common household use, where every one, including the manufacturer, knows that the articles will be used by other persons than the actual ultimate purchaser—namely, by members of his family and his servants, and in some cases his guests. I do not think so ill of our jurisprudence as to suppose that its principles are so remote from the ordinary needs of civilized society and the ordinary claims it makes upon its members as to deny a legal remedy where there is so obviously a social wrong.

In my opinion several decided cases support the view that in such a case as the present the manufacturer owes a duty to the consumer to be careful. …

It is always a satisfaction to an English lawyer to be able to test his application of fundamental principles of the common law by the development of the same doctrines by the lawyers of the Courts of the United States. In that country I find that the law appears to be well established in the sense in which I have indicated. The mouse had emerged from the ginger-beer bottle in the United States before it appeared in Scotland, but there it brought a liability upon the manufacturer. I must not in this long judgment do more than refer to the illuminating judgment of Cardozo J. in *MacPherson v. Buick Motor Co.* in the New York Court of Appeals (2), in which he states the principles of the law as I should desire to state them, and reviews the authorities in other States than his own.

My Lords, if your Lordships accept the view that this pleading discloses a relevant cause of action you will be affirming the proposition that by Scots and English law alike a manufacturer of products, which he sells in such a form as to show that he intends them to reach the ultimate consumer in the form in which they left him with no reasonable possibility of intermediate examination, and with the knowledge that the absence of reasonable care in the preparation or putting up of the products will result in an injury to the consumer's life or property, owes a duty to the consumer to take that reasonable care.

It is a proposition which I venture to say no one in Scotland or England who was not a lawyer would for one moment doubt. It will be an advantage to make it clear that the law in this matter, as in most others, is in accordance with sound common sense. I think that this appeal should be allowed.

Note: Justice Taylor, a retired judge of the B.C. Court of Appeal, who refers to this case as the "most famous case of all time," "the most celebrated victory in the entire 800-year history of our common law," has written a film script on the case to help students understand it and its significance in the common law world.[47]

The plaintiff, Mr. Schlink, lost his case against Mr. Blackburn, the driver of the car which was involved with an accident with a car driven by Mr. Schlink's wife, Ms. Coleman. Citing the work of Professor Fleming which refers to Lord Atkin's speech in *Donoghue v. Stevenson*, Judge Carrothers of the British Columbia Court of Appeal concluded that

> there is not that proximity which is required in order to impose a duty of care on the appellant in this case. Without the limiting factor of proximity I have some doubt as to whether it can be said that Blackburn ought to have foreseen that a near relative of the subject of his negligence, who was not present at the scene of the accident, on learning of the accident would "panic" and rush headlong down the stairs from his bedroom recklessly and without socks or shoes in a hurried attempt to reach the accident scene and 'not paying particular attention to the stairs' injure his foot on the concrete landing of the outdoor porch stairs.
>
> I have no doubt that the necessary ingredient of proximity is wanting here on the facts. The accident could not be and was not seen by the respondent. Hearing it did not move him to it and it was only after he was told his wife was in an accident — not that she was injured — that the respondent moved to the accident scene. I do not think it can be said on these facts the wrongdoer's act complained of so closely and directly affected the respondent as it must to bring about the essential relationship of proximity before a duty of care can be imposed. …

The appeal was allowed, the action dismissed.

Schlink v. Blackburn
87 B.C.R.L. (2d) 129
British Columbia Court of Appeal
December 16, 1993

Note: For the modern approach for determining a duty of care see *Stewart v. Pettie*, page 36, paragraphs 24 through 32.

2. STANDARD OF CARE

Q u e s t i o n

Was the defendant's behaviour below the standard of care owed?

- *A*t the Kingston General Hospital, a food tube, filled with pureed food, was accidentally attached to an intravenous line and the food passed directly into a patient's veins, blocked an artery bringing blood from his lungs to his heart, and killed the patient by causing cardiac and pulmonary arrest.

- *M*s. Hohman sued the heavy metal group Motley Crüe for its failure to provide earplugs or to warn about the decibel level of the sound at their concert. She alleged her right eardrum was shattered and the left ear damaged by the volume.[48]

- *D*onald Parkes, a 41-year-old man, was brought to the emergency ward of the Cambridge Memorial Hospital unconscious from an overdose of anti-depressant drugs. In an effort to revive him, the nurses hooked up an oxygen line directly from a wall outlet through an endotracheal tube to his lungs. The nurses failed to use a device that would have allowed the patient to exhale as well as to receive the oxygen. Consequently the patient was killed by having his lungs "blown up."

Although a defence was entered, the court found "gross, wanton negligence." The case was interesting to the legal community because of the court's reduction of damages due to the deceased's particular background. He had a history of mental illness which led to two suicide attempts. The court concluded that his life expectancy was lower than that of the average man.[49]

- *T*he driver of a garbage truck in Melville, New York failed to see a sunbathing couple and drove over their faces. The couple suffered tire bruises and jaw injuries. The court found more serious damage was averted probably by their having used a sand pillow which gave way under the weight of the truck. The matter was eventually settled out of court for $150,000.[50]

COMMERCIAL HOSTS

Stewart v. *Pettie*

FILE NO.: 23739
http://www.droit.umontreal.ca/
SUPREME COURT OF CANADA
JANUARY 26, 1995

[1] Major J.:—On December 8, 1985, Gillian Stewart, her husband Keith Stewart, her brother Stuart Pettie, and his wife Shelley Pettie went to the Stage West, a dinner theatre in Edmonton for an evening of dinner and live theatre. Before the evening was finished tragedy had struck. After leaving Stage West at the conclusion of the evening a minor single vehicle accident left Gillian Stewart a quadriplegic. Among others, she sued Mayfield Investments Ltd. (Mayfield), the owner of Stage West claiming contribution for her injuries. This appeal is to decide whether on the facts of this case the principles of commercial host liability, first established by this Court in *Jordan House Ltd. v. Menow*, [1974] S.C.R. 239, apply to impose liability on Mayfield. ... [The trial court, The Aberta Court of Queen's Bench found for the defendant, that is, the commecial host was not liable. The Alberta Court of Appeal allowed the appeal and found the commercial host liable.]

III. ISSUES

[18] ... The main issue is:

1. Did Mayfield Investments Ltd. meet the standard of care required of a vendor of alcohol, or was it negligent in failing to take any steps to ensure that Stuart Pettie did not drive after leaving Stage West?

IV. ANALYSIS

1. Was Mayfield Investments Ltd. negligent in failing to take any steps to ensure that Stuart Pettie did not drive after leaving Stage West?

[20] This Court has not previously considered a case involving the liability of a commercial host where the plaintiff was not the person who became inebriated in the defendant's establishment. In both *Jordan House Ltd. v. Menow*, supra, and *Crocker v. Sundance Northwest Resorts Ltd.*, [1988] 1 S.C.R. 1186, it was the plaintiff who became drunk and as a consequence was unable to look after himself.

[21] There are a number of lower court decisions in which commercial establishments have been found liable to third parties injured by a patron who had become inebriated in their establishment. ...

[22] The present appeal is one in which a third party is claiming against the commercial host. This raises the question of whether the establishment owed any duty of care to that third party. If a duty of care is found to exist, then it is necessary to consider what standard of care was necessary and whether that standard was met.

[23] Another consideration is whether there was a causal connection between the defendant's allegedly negligent conduct and the damage suffered by the plaintiff.

A. Duty of Care

[24] The "modern" approach to determining the existence of a duty of care is that established by the House of Lords in *Anns v. Merton London Borough Council*, [1978] A.C. 728, and adopted by this Court in *City of Kamloops v. Nielsen*, [1984] 2 S.C.R. 2, at pp. 10–11. This test, as established by Wilson J. in Kamloops, paraphrasing Anns is:

(1) is there a sufficiently close relationship between the parties ... so that, in the reasonable contemplation of the authority, carelessness on its part might cause damage to that person? If so,

(2) are there any considerations which ought to negative or limit (a) the scope of the duty and (b) the class of persons to whom it is owed or (c) the damages to which a breach of it may give rise?

[25] This approach has been approved in *Just v. British Columbia*, [1989] 2 S.C.R. 1228, and *Hall v. Hebert*, [1993] 2 S.C.R. 159. The basis of the test is the historic case of *Donoghue v. Stevenson*, [1932] A.C. 562, which established the "neighbour principle": that actors owe a duty of care to those whom

they ought reasonably have in contemplation as being at risk when they act.

[26] In *Jordan House Ltd. v. Menow*, supra, it was established that a duty of care exists between alcohol-serving establishments and their patrons who become intoxicated, with the result that they were unable to look after themselves. The plaintiff, who was a well-known patron of that bar, became intoxicated and began annoying customers. He was ejected from the bar, even though the waiters and employees of the bar knew that, in order to get home, he would have to walk along a busy highway. While doing so, he was struck by a car. Laskin J. (as he then was) said that the bar owed a duty of care to Menow not to place him in a situation where he was at risk of injury. ...

[27] Laskin J. held that the hotel had breached the duty owed to Menow by turning him out of the hotel in circumstances in which they knew that he would have to walk along the highway. The risk to Menow that the hotel's actions created was foreseeable. The hotel was therefore found to be liable for one-third of Menow's injuries.

[28] It is a logical step to move from finding that a duty of care is owed to patrons of the bar to finding that a duty is also owed to third parties who might reasonably be expected to come into contact with the patron, and to whom the patron may pose some risk. ...

[29] In this case, there was a sufficient degree of proximity between Mayfield Investments Ltd. and Gillian Stewart that a duty of care existed between them. The more difficult question is what was the standard of care and whether or not it was breached.

[30] ... The duty of care arises because Gillian Stewart was a member of a class of persons who could be expected to be on the highway. It is this class of persons to whom the duty is owed.

[31] On the second point, the respondents argue that Mayfield Investments Ltd. owed two duties of care to Gillian Stewart: first, not to serve Stuart Pettie past the point of intoxication, and second, having served him past the point of intoxication, to take positive steps to ensure that he did not drive a car. The respondents say that Mayfield breached both duties, and therefore should be liable to Gillian Stewart for her injuries.

[32] I believe this argument confuses the existence of the duty of care with the standard of care required of Mayfield. The question of whether a duty of care exists is a question of the relationship between the parties, not a question of conduct. The question of what conduct is required to satisfy the duty is a question of the appropriate standard of care. The point is made by Fleming in his book The Law of Torts (8th ed. 1992). ...

B.   Standard of Care

[34] Laskin J. said in *Jordan House Ltd. v. Menow*, supra, at p. 247, "The common law assesses liability for negligence on the basis of breach of a duty of care arising from a foreseeable and unreasonable risk of harm to one person created by the act or omission of another." The respondents argued, and the Court of Appeal agreed, that Mayfield was negligent because they (a) served Stuart Pettie past the point of intoxication, and (b) failed to take any steps to prevent harm from coming to himself or a third person once he was intoxicated.

[35] I doubt that any liability can flow from the mere fact that Mayfield may have over-served Pettie. To hold that over-serving Pettie *per se* is negligent is to ignore the fact that injury to a class of persons must be foreseeable as a result of the impugned conduct. I fail to see how the mere fact that an individual is over-imbibing can lead, by itself, to any risk of harm to third parties. ...

[36] ... Without a reasonably foreseeable risk of harm to him or a third party, the fact of over-serving Pettie is an innocuous act. Therefore, liability on the part of Mayfield, if it is to be found, must be in their failure to take any affirmative action to prevent the reasonably foreseeable risk to Gillian Stewart.

[37] Historically, the courts have been reluctant to impose liability for a failure by an individual to take some positive action. This reluctance has been tempered in recent years where the relationship between the parties is such that the imposition of such an obligation has been warranted. In those cases, there has been some "special relationship" between the parties warranting the imposition of a positive duty. *Jordan House Ltd. v. Menow*, supra, was such a case.

[38] A similar positive obligation was found to exist in *Crocker v. Sundance Northwest Resorts Ltd.*, supra. The plaintiff entered a "tubing" competition put on by the defendant ski-hill. Before the race, the plaintiff became drunk in the ski-hill's bar, and by the time he was to race, was visibly intoxicated. The organizers of the race suggested that he not compete, but permitted him to do so nevertheless. As a result, he was thrown from his tube, and rendered a quadriplegic.

[39] ... Canadian courts have been willing to expand the kinds of relationships to which a positive duty to act attaches. Wilson J. reviewed cases where the courts will require a positive action on the part of the defendant, and said at p. 1197:

> The common thread running through these cases is that one is under a duty not to place another person in a position where it is foreseeable that the person could suffer injury... .

[41] It is apparent from Wilson J.'s reasoning that there are two questions to be answered. The first is whether the defendant was required, in the circumstances, to take any positive steps at all. If this is answered in the affirmative, the next question is whether the steps taken by the defendants were sufficient to discharge the burden placed on them.

[42] There is no dispute that neither the appellant nor anyone on its behalf took any steps to ensure that Stuart Pettie did not drive. ... Therefore, if Mayfield is to avoid liability, it will have to be on the basis that, on the facts of this case, Mayfield had no obligation to take any positive steps to ensure that Stuart Pettie did not drive. ...

[49] The existence of this "special relationship" will frequently warrant the imposition of a positive obligation to act, but the *sine qua non* of tortious liability remains the foreseeability of the risk. Where no risk is foreseeable as a result of the circumstances, no action will be required, despite the existence of a special relationship. The respondents argue that Mayfield should have taken positive action, even though Mayfield knew that the driver was with three other people, two of whom were sober, and it was reasonable to infer from all of the circumstances that the group was travelling together.

[50] One of the primary purposes of negligence law is to enforce reasonable standards of conduct so as to prevent the creation of reasonably foreseeable risks. In this way, tort law serves as a disincentive to risk-creating behaviour. To impose liability even where the risk which materialized was not reasonably foreseeable is to lay a portion of the loss at the feet of a party who has, in the circumstances, acted reasonably. Tort law does not require the wisdom of Solomon. All it requires is that people act reasonably in the circumstances. The "reasonable person" of negligence law was described by Laidlaw J.A. in this way in *Arland v. Taylor*, [1955] O.R. 131 (C.A.), at p. 142:

> He is not an extraordinary or unusual creature; he is not superhuman; he is not required to display the highest skill of which anyone is capable; he is not a genius who can perform uncommon feats, nor is he possessed of unusual powers of foresight. He is a person of normal intelligence who makes prudence a guide to his conduct. He does nothing that a prudent man would not do and does not omit to do anything a prudent man would do. He acts in accord with general and approved practice. His conduct is guided by considerations which ordinarily regulate the conduct of human affairs. His conduct is the standard "adopted in the community by persons of ordinary intelligence and prudence."

[51] Obviously, the fact that tragedy has befallen Gillian Stewart cannot, in itself, lead to a finding of liability on the part of Mayfield. The question is whether, before 11:00 p.m. on December 8, 1985, the circumstances were such that a reasonably prudent establishment should have foreseen that Stuart Pettie would drive, and therefore should have taken steps to prevent this.

[52] I agree with the Court of Appeal that Mayfield cannot escape liability simply because Stuart Pettie was apparently not exhibiting any visible signs of intoxication. The waitress kept a running tab, and knew that Pettie had consumed 10 to 14 ounces of alcohol over a five-hour period. On the basis of this knowledge alone, she either knew or should have known that Pettie was becoming intoxicated, and this is so whether or not he was exhibiting visible symptoms.

[53] However, I disagree with the Court of Appeal that the presence of the two sober women at the table cannot act to relieve Mayfield of liability. ... Had Pettie been alone and intoxicated, Mayfield could have discharged its duty as established in *Jordan House Ltd. v. Menow* by calling Pettie's wife or sister to take charge of him. How, then, can Mayfield be liable when Pettie was already in their charge, and they knew how much he had had to drink? While it is technically true that Stuart Pettie was not "put into" the care of his sober wife and sister, this is surely a matter of semantics. He was already in their care, and they knew how much he had to drink. It is not reasonable to suggest in these circumstances that Mayfield had to do more. ...

[58] On the facts of this case I conclude that Mayfield Investments Ltd. did not breach the duty of care they owed to Gillian Stewart. On this basis I would allow the appeal.

C. Causation

[59] An equally compelling reason to allow this appeal flows from the absence of proof of causation.

[60] The plaintiff in a tort action has the burden of proving each of the elements of the claim on the balance of probabilities. This includes proving that the defendant's impugned conduct actually caused the loss complained of.

[61] Here, the appellant claims that the respondents have not proved that the failure of Mayfield to intervene actually caused the injuries to Gillian Stewart. They point to the conversation that took place in the parking lot after the group left Stage West, and argue that, even if Mayfield had intervened in some way, Gillian Stewart and Shelley Pettie addressed the issue of Stuart Pettie's fitness to drive in the parking lot after leaving the Mayfield Inn, and came to an independent determination on this point. ...

[66] ... There is nothing unusual or difficult in this case about proving causation. Nor do the facts lie particularly within the knowledge of the defendant. The person who had the obligation and could have provided some evidence, if such existed, on whether intervention by Mayfield would have made any difference was the injured Gillian Stewart. She testified at the trial, but not on this point. This leaves the inference that had she been asked if Mayfield's had intervened, that is to advise her of facts already known to her that would have made any difference to her decision to have Pettie drive, her answer would have been no.

[67] That answer would accord with the circumstances. The respondent Stewart, in the company of an equally sober sister-in-law, concluded that Pettie was competent to drive. The courts should not interfere in such decisions freely made.

[68] This is ... a case where there is no evidence to indicate that Gillian Stewart and Shelley Pettie would have reached any other conclusion than the one they reached even if Mayfield had intervened.

[69] I would therefore also allow this appeal on the basis that the plaintiffs have failed to discharge the onus placed on them to show that Mayfield's failure to intervene actually caused Gillian Stewart's injuries.

[70] Given the fact that I do not find any liability on the part of Mayfield Investments Ltd., it is unnecessary to address the issues relating to Gillian Stewart's contributory negligence, or whether the fact that Stuart Pettie drove while intoxicated could be said to be, in itself, gross negligence.

Appeal allowed with costs; cross-appeal dismissed.

Jacobsen *v.* Nike Canada Ltd.

VANCOUVER REGISTRY NO. C918359
SUPREME COURT OF BRITISH COLUMBIA
FEBRUARY 22, 1996

I. INTRODUCTION

[1] Levine, J.:—On September 6, 1991, Michael Jacobsen, then 19 years old, worked 16 hours in his job as a warehouseman with Nike Canada Ltd. ("Nike"). During working hours, between 8:30 p.m. and 11:30 p.m., he and his co-workers drank substantial amounts of beer, which were provided by Nike. After work, in the company of one of his co-workers, he visited two clubs and drank more beer. Early the next morning, while driving home to Port Moody from B.C. Place Stadium in Vancouver, where he had worked most of the previous day, he drove off the highway into a ditch, was thrown from his car and suffered injuries that left him a quadriplegic.

[2] Michael Jacobsen seeks damages from Nike on account of his injury. He alleges that Nike owed him a duty of care and that this duty was breached when Nike supplied him with alcohol during working hours and then took no positive steps to prevent him from driving his vehicle, in circumstances where Nike knew or should have known that injury to him could result.

[3] Nike concedes that it owed a duty of care to Mr. Jacobsen. It denies that it breached that duty by failing to take positive steps to prevent him from driving his vehicle because in the circumstances it neither knew nor ought to have known that he was impaired when he left work.

[4] Both liability and the quantum of damages are in issue. I will deal first with liability, including contributory negligence, and secondly with the assessment of damages.

II. LIABILITY

A. Issues

[5] Nike concedes that there existed a sufficient relationship of proximity between it and the plaintiff to give rise to a duty of care. To determine the liability of Nike for the injury suffered by the plaintiff, the following issues must be resolved:

1. What is the standard of care to which Nike is held?
2. Did Nike's conduct meet the standard?
3. If Nike's conduct did not meet the standard, did its breach cause or contribute to the plaintiff's injury?

[After a detailed review of the facts of the day in question, the judge turns to the arguments regarding the appropriate law to apply]

C. Duty of Care

[36] The defendant has conceded that it had a duty of care to the plaintiff.

[37] In *Stewart v. Pettie* (supra, para. 6) at pps. 141–142, Major J. for the court analyzed the basis for the existence of a duty of care of tavern-owners or "commercial hosts" to their patrons. The test for establishing a duty of care, as established in *City of Kamloops v. Nielsen*, [1984] 2 S.C.R. 2; 5 W.W.R. 1, paraphrasing *Anns v. Merton London Borough Council*, [1978] A.C. 728 (H.L.), is whether the plaintiff's relationship with the defendant was of sufficient proximity that it was reasonably foreseeable that the defendant's carelessness could cause injury to the plaintiff and whether there were any considerations which ought to negative or limit (a) the scope of the duty and (b) the class of persons to whom it is owed or (c) the damages to which a breach of it may give rise.

[38] In conceding that it owed a duty to the plaintiff, the defendant acknowledges that its relationship with the plaintiff is such that it is reasonably foreseeable that carelessness could cause his injury and there are no considerations which negative or limit the duty, its applicability to the plaintiff or the damages to which a breach may give rise.

D. Standard of Care

[39] The plaintiff says that the nature of the relationship between him and the defendant is significant in determining the standard of care required of the defendant... .

[41] In this case, the relationship between the plaintiff and the defendant was that of employee and employer. That relationship imposes on an employer, as Duff C.J. said in *Regal Oil & Refining Co.* (supra, para. 8) at p. 312:

> an obligation arising out of the relation of master and servant to take reasonable care to see that the plant and property used in the business in which the servant is employed is safe. That is well settled and well known law. ...

[43] The plaintiff's position is that Nike breached its duty to him to provide a safe workplace by providing a large quantity of alcohol in the workplace and not restricting or monitoring its consumption, when it knew he would be driving home, and then not taking steps to prevent him from driving.

[44] The defendant says that the law does not impose such a high standard of care on it. It says that the mere provision of alcohol to its employees is not negligent because there is no reasonably foreseeable risk of injury to an employee from drinking, even where, as here, the employer knows the employee will be driving home after work. The risk of injury arises, it says, when the employee becomes impaired. It is only then that the employer must act to prevent the employee from driving.

[45] Furthermore, it says that an employer is only required to act when it knows or ought to know that an employee is impaired ...

[46] The defendant's position is based on its analysis of the standard of care imposed on tavern-owners. That standard was

recently analyzed by the Supreme Court of Canada in *Stewart v. Pettie*. ...

[48] I disagree with the defendant that the standard of care applicable to tavern-owners is equally applicable to it as the employer of the plaintiff. The law requires an employer to take reasonable care for the safety of its employees.

[49] Furthermore, I disagree with the defendant's analysis of the standard of care imposed on tavern-owners. In *Stewart v. Pettie*, the court held that a tavern-owner cannot escape liability when a patron shows no visible signs of impairment. [The judge reviews that case.]

[52] Thus, the standard of care as established by *Stewart v. Pettie* requires a tavern-owner to:

1. monitor the consumption of its patrons;
2. make reasonable assumptions, from the amount consumed by a patron, that he or she is likely to be impaired; and
3. take steps to prevent a patron from driving when the tavern-owner knows or ought to know the person is likely impaired and is likely to drive.

E. Did Nike Meet the Standard of Care?

[53] I find that Nike failed to meet the standard of care required of an employer by providing alcohol in the workplace in the circumstances in which it did so on September 6, 1991, not monitoring the plaintiff's consumption and taking no steps to ensure the plaintiff did not drive while impaired.

[54] Nike required the employees to bring their cars to work and knew they would be driving home. In effect, Nike made drinking and driving part of the working conditions that day. It effectively encouraged the crew to drink without limit by making freely available large amounts of beer in an atmosphere which induced thirst and drinking games. The supervisors, Mr. Agostino and Mr. Prasad, drank along with the crew, and made no attempts to restrict or monitor the amount the plaintiff or any of the other crew members drank. ...

[55] Nike's responsibility ... for his safety required that it not introduce into the workplace conditions that it was reasonably foreseeable put him at risk. It is hard to imagine a more obvious risk than introducing drinking and driving into the workplace.

[56] If Nike is correct that the standard it must meet is no higher than that imposed on tavern-owners, it did not meet that standard. ...

[60] ... [I]t failed to meet that standard by failing to monitor the consumption of the plaintiff.

[61] Finally, on the evidence, I find that Nike knew or should have known how much the plaintiff had to drink and based on the amount he consumed, that he was likely impaired. On that basis, it should have taken positive steps to prevent from him driving. By failing to do so, it failed to meet the standard of care required of it.

F. Evidence

[62] I have found that Nike failed to meet the standard of care imposed on it as an employer by providing a large quantity of alcohol in the workplace, not monitoring its consumption and not preventing the plaintiff from driving. None of these facts are in dispute. Thus, strictly speaking, it is not necessary to my decision to further review the evidence. In order to meet the defendant's arguments, however, I find it necessary to do so. [The judge embarks on an exhaustive reivew of the evidence to support two conclusions:

1. That the plaintiff did show visible signs of impairment when he left B.C. Place Stadium on September 6, 1991; and
2. That the defendant knew or ought to have known how much the plaintiff had to drink and that such consumption was likely to cause the plaintiff to be impaired.]

G. Did the Defendant's Breach Cause or Contribute to the Plaintiff's Injury?

[147] Did the plaintiff's consumption of beer at the Unicorn and 86 Street Music Hall break the chain of causation between the defendant's negligence and the plaintiff's injury?

[148] The evidence as to the plaintiff's consumption of alcohol before he left B.C. Place Stadium makes it clear that he was impaired when he left. According to the evidence of Ms. Kirkwood, the consumption of further beers at the Unicorn and 86 Street Music Hall increased his level of impairment. The defendant's negligence, however, clearly caused or contributed to the plaintiff's impairment and the subsequent accident (*Myers v. Peel (County) Board of Education*, [1981] 2 S.C.R. 21; *Doern v. Phillips Estate* (1994), 2 B.C.L.R. (3d) 349 (S.C.)).

[149] Had the defendant taken the steps required of it to determine that the plaintiff was impaired and to prevent him from driving, clearly the accident would not have occurred.

H. Contributory Negligence

[150] The plaintiff has admitted that he contributed to his injuries. He knew about the effects of drinking and driving and testified that on previous occasions when he was driving he restricted his consumption of alcohol or if he drank more than he thought would allow him to drive safely he did not drive. He says that he did not restrict his consumption in this case because he was keeping up with his co-workers and by the time he had to drive home his judgment was impaired by how much he had had to drink.

[151] The plaintiff says that as his employer, however, the defendant bears most of the blame. ...

[154] The plaintiff was under the control and supervision of the defendant while the drinking took place on September 6, 1991. He had no prior expectation that he would be drinking that night. He had no opportunity to make plans in advance for the effects of drinking, such as arranging for a designated driver or alternate transportation or lodging, as he testified he normally did before attending a party where there would be drinking or going to a bar. His employer effectively encouraged drinking by providing the alcohol and drinking with the plaintiff. It took no steps to restrict or monitor the plaintiff's consumption, took no steps to determine if the plaintiff was impaired when he left work and took no steps to prevent him from driving when it knew the plaintiff would drive home.

[155] In arguing its case on liability, the defendant said it was not reasonably foreseeable that the plaintiff would become impaired because in the past, when he had participated in events with his co-workers where alcohol was consumed, he had drunk one or two beers and "then gone home". I rejected

the defendant's argument in that context. While the plaintiff has admitted he should have restricted his consumption because he knew he had to drive home, the significant difference on this occasion is that the plaintiff could not leave B.C. Place Stadium until he was told to do so. He was under the control of the defendant and did what his supervisors and his co-workers were doing: drank while he worked, without restriction as to the amount consumed.

[156] In addition to the control that the defendant exercised over the plaintiff, another significant factor in apportioning negligence in this case is that the preventive measures the defendant could have taken were within its control and would have not imposed any serious burden on it. Although the plaintiff could and should have restricted his own drinking, once he had consumed so much that he was impaired, his judgment was impaired and he had few if any alternatives to driving home. He did not have enough money to take a taxi home, a 40-minute ride away from B.C. Place Stadium. His co-workers had also been drinking and so were not reliable drivers. If public transportation was available (there is no evidence of this), it would have taken him a very long time to get home and he had to be back at work early the next morning.

[157] In the circumstances, I apportion liability 75% to the defendant and 25% to the plaintiff.

III. DAMAGES

A. The Result of the Accident

[158] At the time of the accident, the plaintiff, Michael Jacobsen, was a fit, 170–175 pound, 19-year-old man with an interest in body building and other sports. He wanted to become either a policeman or fireman. As a result of the accident, he is what the medical experts term an "incomplete C4-C5 quadriplegic." More than four years after the accident, he is left with many permanent disabilities. [There follows a thorough fourteen-page review of his abilities, needs and the nature and amount of care required: personal attendant care and homemaker services, vehicle expense, house modification, etc.]

IV. SUMMARY

[254] The defendant, Nike Canada Ltd., is liable to the plaintiff, Michael Jacobsen.

[255] Liability is apportioned 25% to the plaintiff and 75% to the defendant.

[256] Damages are assessed at: ... $2,719,213.48.

[258] Counsel may apply to speak to the matters of a management fee, tax "gross-up" and costs, as well as any matters I may have miscalculated or omitted.

Occupiers of premises — The city

Mortimer et al. *v.* Cameron et al.

111 D.L.R. (4TH) 428
ONTARIO COURT OF APPEAL
FEBRUARY 16, 1994

Robins J.A.:—On the afternoon of July 17, 1987, following an accounting examination, Stephen Mortimer attended a party at the apartment of a classmate, Sandra Hunt. The apartment was on the second floor of a house owned by Stingray Holdings Limited in the City of London. Those present were drinking and relaxing; no one was boisterous or unruly. By all accounts, the mood was convivial but subdued. At some point late in the afternoon, Mortimer engaged John Cameron, another classmate, in friendly conversation while they were standing at the top of a short stairway in the apartment. They had both been drinking beer and Mortimer was "mildly intoxicated". Neither of them was angry or hostile. While they were "joking around" with one another, Mortimer made a motion so as to indicate that he was going to pour beer on Cameron. This led to some good natured horseplay. They began to push each other back and forth and, while doing so, moved down the stairs to the interior landing leading to the front door of the apartment. The door was open at the time. When they reached the interior landing, Mortimer, who was moving backwards, tripped over the raised threshold to the apartment and fell backwards. As he did so, he grabbed Cameron and pulled him towards him. Together, they tumbled onto the exterior landing at the top of the enclosed exterior stairway leading to street level, and came

in contact with the exterior wall. Even though they hit the wall with "minimal" or "little" force, it gave way and the two of them plunged to the ground 10 feet below.

Fortunately, Cameron was unhurt. Mortimer, however, suffered devastating injury. His spinal cord was permanently fractured at the C4-5 or neck level. As a result, Mortimer is a complete quadriplegic without any motor function or sensation below the site of the injury.

Mortimer has brought this action to recover damages against a number of defendants. ... The action came on before the Honourable Mr. Justice McDermid in London. After a trial lasting some 35 days, the learned judge granted judgment against the defendants, the Corporation of the City of London and Stingray Holdings Limited. He held these defendants jointly and severally liable to the plaintiffs for the sum of $4,705,052 in damages (including the Family Law Act claims) and $770,209 in prejudgment interest. Liability was apportioned 80% against the city and 20% against Stingray. The actions and cross-claims against all other parties were dismissed. [Reported 9 M.PL.R. (2d) 185, 32 A.C.W.S. (3d) 928.]

The circumstances relevant to this accident and the claims against the various defendants are fully detailed in the comprehensive and carefully considered reasons of the trial judge.

The matters in issue in this appeal can be dealt with under three general headings: the liability issues; the damage issues; and the cost issues.

THE LIABILITY ISSUES

1. The liability of the City of London

The principles governing the liability of a municipal corporation in tort have been settled in recent years by the Supreme Court of Canada. I need refer only to two of the court's decisions: Kamloops (City) v. *Nielsen* ... and *Rothfield v. Manolakos* ... (See also *Just v. British Columbia*) . ...

In *Kamloops (City) v. Nielsen*, a municipality was held liable to a subsequent owner of a building for the manner in which it enforced its own by-laws. Following the approach taken by the House of Lords in *Anns v. Merton London Borough Council*, [1978] A.C. 728, Wilson J., speaking for the majority, at pp. 662–3, formulated the test for determining whether or not a duty of care is owed by a municipality to a particular claimant in terms of the following two questions:

(1) is there a sufficiently close relationship between the parties (the local authority and the person who has suffered the damage) so that in the reasonable contemplation of the authority, carelessness on its part might cause damage to that person? If so,

(2) are there any considerations which ought to negative or to limit (a) the scope of the duty and (b) the class of persons to whom it is owed or (c) the damages to which a breach of it may give rise?

These questions are to be answered by reference to the governing legislation. A distinction is to be made between statutory powers granted to municipalities and the execution of operational functions carried out pursuant to those powers. The distinction, in short, is this: while a municipality's decision to exercise a statutory power, through, for instance, the passage of a by-law, is discretionary and thus not subject to civil suit, once this power has been exercised, there is a duty at the operational level to use due care in giving effect to it. ...

Applying those principles to the facts of this case, I am of the opinion that the trial judge correctly concluded that the City of London owed a duty to persons in the position of the plaintiff. This was a duty to exercise reasonable care both in inspecting the plans which were submitted for the proposed enclosure of the exterior stairway from which the plaintiff fell and in inspecting the construction authorized by the building permit.

In 1971, the city enacted a by-law designed, as its preamble states, "to safeguard life and limb, health, property and public welfare with respect to the design, construction and alteration of buildings by the provision of appropriate minimum standards." This involved a policy decision to inspect building plans and construction in accordance with the provisions of the by-law. The city's operational activities under a by-law of this nature are subject to the ordinary principles of tort law. Having made a policy decision to inspect building plans and construction, the city owed a duty of care to those it could reasonably foresee might be injured should it negligently perform the inspection duties it had assumed under the by-law.

In this case, the city was found, on ample evidence, to have breached its duty of care in 1972 when the building permit was issued and the structure was built. The application for the building permit was not accompanied by drawings or specifications, as required by the by-law, and the permit was issued with insufficient information as to building code compliance. Moreover, and most importantly, the city negligently failed to detect obvious deficiencies in the construction of the enclosed exterior stairway deficiencies which could readily have been detected had there been a proper inspection of the plans or of the work done pursuant to the plans. In particular, the trial judge found that the condition of the wall through which the plaintiff fell did not conform with good building practice. It was not built in accordance with the standards set by the National Building Code, 1970 or the city's by-law, and could not be justified on the basis of the city's past practice. ...

Furthermore, the fact that the accident did not happen until 15 years after the city's negligence cannot serve to insulate the city from liability. The effluxion of time may have that result in other circumstances and is, as I shall indicate later, an important factor in assessing comparative fault between the tortfeasors in this case, but it does not relieve the city of its duty of care to persons in the plaintiff's position. This duty arose and was breached in 1972. The fact that damage was not occasioned until 1987 does not absolve the city of liability. It was the structure as built that was found to be defective. The original condition, and not any subsequent deterioration or alteration, was the cause of the wall's collapse... .

In short, this tragic accident was within the ambit of the risk created by the city's negligent performance of the inspection duties it had assumed under its by-law. In my opinion, there are no policy considerations here which can properly be invoked to limit or negative the scope of the duty imposed on the city, the damages arising from its breach, or the class of persons to whom the duty is owed.

The city submitted in its factum [written argument] that the present case is distinguishable from the cases cited above in that those cases no municipality was held liable to "incidental third party users who are injured on private property after the issuance of a building permit and an inspection". I cannot accept this submission. If, as the Supreme Court of Canada has indicated , a municipality can be held to owe a duty of care to owners and owner-builders, subsequent owners and tenants, and third party neighbours, to protect their health, safety and property when carrying out its operational duties under a building by-law, there is no reason in principle why entrants in the category of the plaintiff should not be afforded like protection . ...

2. The liability of Stingray

Stingray Holdings Limited concedes that it is an "occupier" of the premises for the purposes of s. 3(l) of the *Occupiers' Liability Act*, R.S.O. 1980, c. 322. As such it owes a duty to take reasonable care to see that persons entering the premises are reasonably safe while on the premises; and it may be required in certain circumstances to take positive action to make the premises reasonably safe. In *Waldick v. Malcolm* (1991), 83 D.L.R. (4th) 114 at p. 128, ... where a slip on some ice gave rise to an action under the *Occupiers' Liability Act*, the Supreme Court of Canada affirmed that the purpose of the legislation is, "to promote, and indeed, to require where circumstances warrant, positive action on the part of occupiers to make their premises reasonably safe."

Stingray contends, however, that the trial judge erred in holding it negligent and in breach of s. 3(l) on the basis that it failed to have a qualified person inspect the exterior stairway to assess its structural integrity. The deficiencies which proximately caused the plaintiff's injury came into existence in 1972 when the enclosure was built. Stingray acquired the property in 1979. In Stingray's submission, it ought not to be held liable for failing to correct defects which were not apparent to it and would not have been apparent on a reasonable examination by it.

In my opinion, there is no basis for interfering with the finding of liability against Stingray. The trial judge correctly held that this company, as owner and occupier of the premises, was under an ongoing duty to inspect the enclosed exterior stairway irrespective of any notification from its tenants of any problem relating thereto. Stingray acknowledges that it bore responsibility for the structural adequacy of the enclosure and placed no reliance on the tenants in this regard. ...

The relevant structural defects were the result of noncompliance with the Building Code and good building practice. This wall was not enclosed on the inside and, unlike defects concealed within an enclosed wall, the defective state of this wall was plainly visible to anyone with knowledge of those requirements. I share the trial judge's view that the owner-occupier of this property ought not to be able to escape liability by relying on an examination conducted by a principal of the company who lacked the knowledge and experience to conduct a meaningful inspection. This cannot be considered a "reasonable inspection."

The dangerous condition created by the lack of structural protection required to guard users of the stairway from accidental falls had been in existence for a very long period of time. During this period the condition of the enclosure had generally deteriorated. This deterioration (the full details of which are set out in the trial judge's reasons), while not directly causative of the plaintiffs injuries, was indicative of a general state of disrepair and should have raised concerns about the structural integrity of the enclosure. The condition was such as to warn a reasonable occupier of the need to retain a knowledgeable person to assess the soundness of the entire structure. This should have been done. Had it been done, the dangerous condition that caused the present accident would have been discovered, the foreseeable risk of harm would have been eliminated, and the accident would not have happened. Stingray would have been duty-bound to remedy the defect by installing an additional stud, thereby narrowing the opening and strengthening the wall. The failure of Stingray to have the structure properly inspected at any time constituted an actionable breach of the duty imposed on it by s. 3(l) of the Occupiers' Liability Act.

Moreover, in addition to the warnings sounded by the deteriorating state of the structure, it appears that Stingray made alterations to the lower part of the structure in 1985 without first obtaining a building permit. Had Stingray applied for and obtained a permit, the city would have inspected the work done pursuant thereto. The evidence is that the inspection would have been of the entire enclosure. The structural unsoundness of the upper landing would then, in all likelihood, have been discovered and ordered corrected. Stingray's failure to comply with the building by-law resulted, the trial judge found, in "the continuance of the hazardous condition of the exterior landing." This provides further reason for holding Stingray in breach of s. 3(l).... .

In my opinion, the comparative blameworthiness of these tortfeasors is such that liability for this accident should be apportioned 60% against Stingray and 40% against the city. ...

Note: With regard to the liability of the young men see the comments of the trial judge below p. 49
Note: The Supreme Court of Canada refused to hear an appeal requested by both defendants.[51]

- *M*r. Faust stopped at a rural canyon construction site to use the outhouse. He fell through a plywood covering into a 12-metre-deep cesspool and, according to the UPI news release, "spent 13 hours fighting off a nasty gopher who fell in with him."[52]

Restaurateurs

- *S*tella Liebeck bought a cup of coffee at the drive-through window at McDonald's. Holding the cup between her knees and attempting to take off the lid to add cream and sugar, she spilled the coffee causing third-degree burns which necessitated her undergoing skin grafts. She sued McDonald's Corp. for negligence, namely, for serving coffee too hot. To meet the preference of its customers, McDonald's purposely brews and serves its coffee at high temperatures. After a seven-day jury trial in the U.S. the court concluded McDonald's was liable; serving coffee at that temperature was below the standard of care owed its customers. For compensatory damages the jury awarded Liebeck $200,000; (less $40,000 as the jury found Liebeck 20% at fault); for punitive damges, $2.7 million.[53]

SOCIAL HOSTS

- *A*lthough David Stringer was warned not to crawl through a window and dive from a roof into a pool, he continued to do so until, on his fourth dive, he broke his neck and was rendered a quadriplegic. He sued the hosts of the party under an Ontario home liability statute and succeeded. An insurer commented that the statute placed a standard of care on hosts that is higher than that expected of a reasonable person.[54]

DRIVERS

Galaske *v.* O'Donnell

[1994] 1 S.C.R. 670
http://www.droit.umontreal.ca/
SUPREME COURT OF CANADA
APRIL 14, 1994

Cory J.—The issue raised on this appeal is whether the general duty of care owed by the driver of a car to his passengers includes a duty to take reasonable steps to ensure that a passenger under 16 years of age wears a seat belt. If it is found that such a duty exists then it must be determined whether that duty is negated by the presence of a parent of the child.

FACTUAL BACKGROUND

On August 17, 1985, Karl Galaske, then eight years of age, together with his father Peter came to visit Erich Stauffer, a friend of the family of many years.

It was decided that Karl and his father would go in Erich Stauffer's new truck to visit his vegetable garden, which was located a mile and a half from Stauffer's residence. The truck was fitted with seat belts for all the occupants of the front seat. Karl sat in the middle between his father and Erich Stauffer.

Mr. Stauffer did not suggest that his passengers put on their seat belts. He omitted doing so because, in his words, he did not wish to take the "fathership" away from his friend Peter Galaske. He readily conceded that if young Karl had been in the vehicle alone with him he would have insisted that he wear the seat belt. It was only the presence of the father which prevented him from requiring that the seat belt be worn. He further agreed that he was aware of the importance of seat belts as a safety factor.

The decision not to insist upon Karl wearing his seat belt had tragic results. The route to the vegetable garden required Stauffer to drive by an intersection that he knew to be dangerous. At that intersection, through no fault of his own, his truck was struck by another vehicle, driven by the defendant O'Donnell. The Galaske father and son were thrown from the vehicle as a result of the impact. Peter Galaske was killed and Karl Galaske received serious injuries rendering him paraplegic.

[The court reviewed the decisions of the trial and appeal courts both of which found Stauffer not negligent.]

ANALYSIS

The issues that arise in this case can, I think, be resolved upon an application of the classic principles of tort law.

Basically, a defendant can only be found liable if it is established, first, that he owed a duty of care to the plaintiff and, second, that he was in breach of that duty and failed to exercise the standard of care of a reasonable person placed in the same circumstances. Let us first consider the concept of duty of care.

THE EXISTENCE OF A DUTY OF CARE, GENERALLY

In *City of Kamploops v. Nielsen*, [1984] 2 S.C.R. 2, at pp. 10–11, Wilson J. paraphrased the two-stage test formulated in *Anns v. Merton London Borough Council*, [1978] A.C. 728, for determining whether a duty of care existed. She did so in these words:

(1) is there a sufficiently close relationship between the parties … so that, in the reasonable contemplation of the authority, carelessness on its part might cause damage to that person? If so,

(2) are there any considerations which ought to negative or limit (a) the scope of the duty and (b) the class of person to whom it is owed or (c) the damages to which a breach of it may give rise?

This approach as been quoted with approval in *Just v. British Columbia*, [1989] 2 S.C.R. 1228 and *Hall v. Hebert*, [1993] 2 S.C.R. 159. This is the basis upon which a determination should be made as to whether there is a sufficiently close relationship between the parties to establish that a prima facie duty of care is owed by one party (the defendant) to another party (the plaintiff). The principle was set out in *Donoghue v. Stevenson*, [1932] A.C. 562, at p. 580, in these classic words:

You must take reasonable care to avoid acts or omissions which you can reasonably foresee would be likely to injure your neighbour. Who, then, in law is my neighbour? The answer seems to be — persons who are so closely and directly affected by my act that I ought reasonably to have them in contemplation as being so affected when I am directing my mind to the acts or omissions which are called in question.

Is there then a sufficiently close relationship between the driver of a motor vehicle and his passengers to establish a prima facie duty of care? I think that there undoubtedly is such a relationship. A driver owes a duty of care to his passengers to take reasonable steps to prevent foreseeable injuries. For example, a driver must comply with the rules of the road; a driver must exercise reasonable caution in the operation of a motor vehicle; a driver must not operate a motor vehicle that is known to be mechanically defective, for example without brakes or headlights or an adequate steering mechanism. The next question to be resolved is this: should that duty of care extend to ensuring that passengers under 16 years of age wear their seat belts?

THE GENERAL DUTY RESTING ON ALL OCCUPANTS OF A CAR TO WEAR SEAT BELTS

It has long been recognized that all occupants of a motor vehicle have a duty to wear their seat belts. ... A failure to do so will result in an assessment of contributory negligence against that person. ...

THE DUTY OWED BY A DRIVER TO ENSURE THAT PASSENGERS UNDER 16 WEAR SEAT BELTS

There is therefore a duty of care owed by an occupant of a car to wear a seat belt. This duty is based upon the sensible recognition of the safety provided by seat belts and the foreseeability of harm resulting from the failure to wear them. What then of children in a car? Children under 16, although they may contest it, do require guidance and direction from parents and older persons. This has always been recognized by society. That guidance and protection must extend to ensuring that those under 16 properly wear their seat belts. To the question of who should assume that duty, the answer must be that there may be two or more people who bear that responsibility. However one of those responsible must always be the driver of the car.

A driver taking children as passengers must accept some responsibility for the safety of those children. The driving of a motor vehicle is neither a God-given nor a constitutional right. It is a licensed activity that is subject to a number of conditions, including the demonstration of a minimum standard of skill and knowledge pertaining to driving. Obligations and responsibilities flow from the right to drive. Those responsibilities must include some regard for the safety of young passengers. ...

In my view, quite apart from any statutory provision, drivers must accept the responsibility of taking all reasonable steps to ensure that passengers under 16 years of age are in fact wearing their seat belts. ...

THE EFFECT OF THE MOTOR VEHICLE ACT

Section 217(6) of the Motor Vehicle Act reads as follows: ...

> A person shall not drive on a highway a motor vehicle in which there is a passenger who has attained age 6 but is under age 16 and who occupies a seating position for which a seat belt assemble is provided unless that passenger is wearing the complete seat belt assembly in a properly adjusted and securely fastened manner.

...[T]he statutory requirement pertaining to seat belts is subsumed in the general law of negligence. However, the statute can, I think, be taken as a public indication that the failure of a driver to ensure that children in the vehicle are wearing seat belts constitutes unreasonable conduct. Further, it may be taken as indicating that such a failure on the part of the driver demonstrates conduct which falls below the standard required by the community and is thus negligent. In this case, the legislation is simply another factor which can be taken into account by the Court in the course of determining whether the failure to ensure children in the car are wearing seat belts constituted negligent behaviour on the part of a driver.

IS THE DRIVER'S DUTY OF CARE NEGATED BY THE PRESENCE OF A PARENT?

The duty of a driver to ensure that young passengers wear their seat belts is well established. It then must be asked whether the presence of a parent in the car negates this duty of care owed by the driver. The trial judge and the Court of Appeal took the position that the presence of the parent in the car removed or terminated the duty of care owed by the driver. In support of that position, the respondent relies on the decisions of this Court in *Arnold v. Teno*, [1978] 2 S.C.R. 287, at p. 311, and of the New Zealand Court of Appeal in *McCallion v. Dodd*, [1966] N.Z.L.R. 710, at p. 721. In my view, these decisions simply indicate that there may be a joint responsibility or duty of care resting upon both a parent and a third party. The presence of a parent in the car may mean that the responsibility is shared but it cannot negate the duty owed by the driver to the passenger under the age of 16. ...

It is true that the conclusion I have reached is one of public policy which imposes a positive duty. That in itself is not novel. ...

STANDARD OF CARE OR THE EXTENT OF THE DUTY OWED BY THE DRIVER

The definition of the standard of care is a mixed question of law and fact. It will usually be for the trial judge to determine, in light of the circumstances of the case, what would constitute reasonable conduct on the part of the legendary reasonable man placed in the same circumstances. In some situations a simple reminder may suffice while in others, for example when a very young child is the passenger, the driver may have to put the seat belt on the child himself. In this case, however, the driver took no steps whatsoever to ensure that the child passenger wore a seat belt. It follows that the trial judge's decision on the issue amounted to a finding that there was no duty at all resting upon the driver. This was an error of law.

The extent of the duty owed by the driver of a vehicle to a child passenger when a parent is present will undoubtedly vary with the circumstances. ... The difference in degree of responsibility will vary widely, depending on the circumstance of each case. That degree of responsibility will have to be determined in this case.

DISPOSITION

In the result, the appeal is allowed. The question of the degree of contributing negligence of Stauffer should be remitted to the trial judge for determination at the same time as the determination is made as to whether there was any negligence on the part of the infant Karl Thomas Galaske or the late Peter Helmut Galaske or both. The appellant should have his costs in this Court and throughout.

Appeal allowed.

Majority: La Forest, L'Heureux-Dube, Gonthier, Cory, and McLachlin; Sopinka and and Major dissenting.

- *I*n a bizarre Ontario case, a plaintiff was successful in an action for damages for nervous shock. A high school boy, Snider, out with his friends, got very drunk. At one point the police told his friends, Alford and Berard to take him home or they'd put him in jail. The friends agreed; Snider got into Alford's car. On the way, Snider wanted out and they let him out and drove off. They returned once when Snider was staggering around but went on without him. A passerby, Stroud, tried to help Snider but Snider walked on and collapsed on the road. Stroud pulled over, walked back to help him and as he did an oncoming car struck and killed Snider. The driver of the car, Nespolon, sued for damages for negligence causing post-traumatic stress disorder. (Nespolon showed 20 of 21 symptoms of post-traumatic stress disorder when only 7 symptoms is sufficient for a diagnosis.) The court found for the plaintiff and found the fault fell equally on friends Alford, Berard and the victim Snider.[55]

OTHER PROFESSIONALS

- *J*udge Geatros of the Court of Queen's Bench in Prince Albert, Saskatchewan held that Constable Hunter, "dogmaster," was not negligent by allowing his police dog, Max, to subdue the plaintiff who was pursued after a break-in. The plaintiff, having tried to escape the police three times, was "taken down" by Max.[56]

Question

If a professional follows the standard practices of that profession, is he or she assured of having performed reasonably and therefore not negligently?

A doctor conducting a neurological examination to test the central nervous system of a patient complaining of loss of balance allowed the patient to walk unaided for several feet as was the practice for this type of examination. The patient fell and sustained injuries. She sued the doctor for negligence. His defence: 'I was acting reasonably; I was following an accepted standard practice for that examination.' The court found as a fact that the doctor was conforming to the standard practice, but held [as a matter of law] that the standard practice was in itself negligent. The plaintiff was therefore successful.

Girard v. Genera Hospital of Port Arthur
Summarized from The Lawyers Weekly August 8, 1997 p. 15
Note: Also see Kripps v. Touch Ross below p. 56.

3. CAUSATION

Question

Did the defendant's act or omission cause the injury suffered?

Hendry *v.* Chiang and Chao

VANCOUVER REGISTRY DOCKET NUMBER: A933987
http://www.courts.gov.bc.ca/
SUPREME COURT OF BRITISH COLUMBIA
NOVEMBER 27, 1996

Background facts: The tenant plaintiff, complained to the landlord defendants, that a ground floor window was loose and could easily be removed — a temptation to an intruder. Subsequently an intruder did break in but not by lifting out the loose window, but by breaking the window. The tenant returning home saw the broken window, entered through it, surveyed the situation and returned to the window to call to a friend when he slipped on the broken glass and cut himself severely. He sued the landlords for negligence.

Although the plaintiff advanced several arguments the main issue fell to the question of causation.

Edwards, J.:—

[9]…The question is whether the defendants' failure to repair the window was the cause of the plaintiffs injury. …

[11] The defendants' position is that, even regarding the facts in a manner most favourable to the plaintiff, the plaintiff has failed to prove causation. They accept that the standard of care is that imposed by s 3(1) of the *Occupiers Liability Act* on the basis of the analysis in *Ellington v. Rodgers*, … namely that the defendants as landlord had the same duty of care toward the plaintiff as tenant as the plaintiff had as occupier towards others coming onto the premises. That duty as set out in s. 3(l) is the duty … to take that care that in all the circumstances of the case is reasonable to see that a person, and his property, on the premises, and property of a person, whether or not that person himself enters on the premises, will be reasonably safe in using the premises.

[12] … Did the loose window make it more likely someone would attempt to break in? Did the loose window make it more likely if someone broke in there would be a greater risk from broken glass than if the window had been secure?

[13] Unless those questions can be answered "yes," it cannot be logically concluded that the defendants' failure to secure the window was a breach of the duty in s. 3(1), in so far as creating a risk of physical harm is concerned. The plaintiff did not notice the loose window until some months after he occupied the suite. If it presented a probing intruder with an easier and therefore more tempting means of entry than breaking a secure window, that was because the window frame could be easily lifted out of the track in which it slid. That is it could be opened without breaking it. This might encourage someone to attempt a break-in which would not involve the sound of breaking glass. Oddly then, the defendants' failure to secure the window made it less likely it would be broken by a thief tempted to effect entry because it was loose. That is it made it less likely if a break-in occurred that it would result in the very risk which was created.

[14] In other words the loose window may have made a break-in more likely but it made the creation of a risk of broken glass less likely than if a secure window had been broken to gain entry.

[15] Section 3(1) refers to the safety of both occupiers and their property. The increased likelihood of a break-in certainly increased the likelihood of harm to property, but it did not necessarily increase the risk of harm to occupiers. There is no evidence the intruder broke in intending to attack the occupiers. It appears theft without the inconvenience of dealing with the occupiers was the motive. That being so, the added likelihood that a break-in might occur as a result of the loose window did not translate directly into an increased risk of physical harm to the occupiers.

[16] I conclude the defendants' failure to secure the window, even if it constituted a breach of the s. 3(l) duty to take reasonable care to make the premises reasonably safe for use by the occupiers and their property, by making it perhaps more likely a break-in might occur, did not in fact increase the physical risk to the occupiers consequent on a break-in. The loose window reduced the likelihood a risk of the kind which actually occurred might be created by a break in. That being so, I conclude the defendants' failure cannot be characterised as the cause of the accident which befell the plaintiff. Failure to secure the window did not make it more likely that accident would occur than would have been the case if the window had been secure.

[17] There is another consideration in this case which points to the same conclusion. [The plaintiff was aware of the broken glass.] Indeed he was careful to avoid it when he entered through the window. He failed to do so when he turned, apparently in an agitated state, to exit. It was that negligent act on the part of the plaintiff which was the cause of the accident. At most, defendants' failure to secure the window provided, indirectly through the intervention of the intruder who broke the window, the opportunity for the plaintiff to act negligently in failing to take appropriate precaution in dealing with the risk created by the broken window, which he was aware of and initially took steps to avoid.

[18] The plaintiff's actions were not the voluntary assumption of a risk created by the defendants. They were simply a failure to maintain a proper lookout for his own safety in circumstances he himself had recognized as dangerous. I conclude the plaintiff has failed to prove on a balance of probabilities that the failure of the defendant to secure the window, whether it be characterized as negligence or a breach of contract or statutory duty, was the cause of the tragic accident which befell the plaintiff. …

[32] In summary, I find the plaintiff has not proved causation and his action fails. …

Arndt v. Smith

FILE No. 24943
http://www.droit.umontreal.ca/
SUPREME COURT OF CANADA
JUNE 26, 1997

Background facts. The plaintiff contracted chicken pox while pregnant; the baby was born disabled. The mother sued the doctor for negligence, namely, failure to warn her of the risks to the fetus from her chicken pox and claimed for the costs of rearing the disabled child. The trial judge held that the plaintiff proved a breach of duty but failed to prove the breach caused her loss. That is, she failed to prove that if she had been told of the risk she would have aborted the pregnancy. The plaintiff appealed. The Court of Appeal directed a new trial on the basis that the trial judge had applied the wrong test for determining causation.

The issue before this court is: What is the proper test to determine whether or not the loss claimed by the plaintiff was caused by the doctor's failure to advise of the risk?

Cory J.:

... [2] The starting point for this question must be *Reibl v. Hughes*, [1980] 2 S.C.R. 880, which set out the basic principles for assessing causation in cases involving allegations of negligence by doctors. Reibl involved an action by a patient against a surgeon for failing to warn him of the risk of paralysis associated with the elective surgery performed by that surgeon. One of the defences raised was that even if the surgeon had disclosed all of the risks of the procedure, the plaintiff would nonetheless have gone ahead with the operation. In other words, the physician disputed whether his negligent failure to disclose had, in fact, caused the plaintiff's loss.

[3] The question presented to the Court was how to determine whether the patient would have actually chosen to decline the surgery if he had been properly informed of the risks. ... In trying to craft the appropriate test, Laskin C.J. for a unanimous Court quoted with approval an article from the New York University Law Review, entitled "Informed Consent — A Proposed Standard for Medical Disclosure" (1973), 48 N.Y.U.L. Rev. 548. The article distinguished between a subjective test, which asks whether the particular patient would have foregone treatment if properly informed, and an objective test, which asks whether the average prudent person in the patient's position would have foregone treatment if informed of all material risks. The authors preferred the objective test, since the subjective standard suffered from what they deemed to be a "gross defect": "[I]t depends on the plaintiff's testimony as to his state of mind, thereby exposing the physician to the patient's hindsight and bitterness." (p. 550) ...

[6] To balance the two problems [of the subjective test which places undue emphasis on the evidence of the plaintiff and the objective test which places too much emphasis on the medical evidence], Laskin C.J. opted for a modified objective test for causation. ... The test enunciated relies on a combination of objective and subjective factors in order to determine whether the failure to disclose actually caused the harm of which the plaintiff complains. It requires that the court consider what the reasonable patient in the circumstances of the plaintiff would have done if faced with the same situation. The trier of fact must take into consideration any "particular concerns" of the patient and any "special considerations affecting the particular patient" in determining whether the patient would have refused treatment if given all the information about the possible risks.

[7] This Court recently had occasion to reconsider the modified objective test in *Hollis v. Dow Corning Corp.* [1995] 4 S.C.R. 634... .

[8] ... [In the Hollis case] ... both the majority and minority judgments explicitly endorsed the continued application of the modified objective test from *Reibl* for negligence actions by a patient against a doctor. The decision in *Hollis* is a very strong and recent affirmation of the *Reibl* test and should not be lightly disregarded... .

[15] *Reibl v. Hughes* is a very significant and leading authority. It marks the rejection of the paternalistic approach to determining how much information should be given to patients. It emphasizes the patient's right to know and ensures that patients will have the benefit of a high standard of disclosure. At the same time, its modified objective test for causation ensures that our medical system will have some protection in the face of liability claims from patients influenced by unreasonable fears and beliefs, while still accommodating all the reasonable individual concerns and circumstances of plaintiffs. The test is flexible enough to enable a court to take into account a wide range of the personal circumstances of the plaintiff, and at the same time to recognize that physicians should not be held responsible when the idiosyncratic beliefs of their patients might have prompted unpredictable and unreasonable treatment decisions.

[16] The *Reibl v. Hughes* test ... strikes a reasonable balance, which cannot be obtained through either a purely objective or a purely subjective approach. A purely subjective test could serve as an incitement for a disappointed patient to bring an action. The plaintiff will invariably state with all the confidence of hindsight and with all the enthusiasm of one contemplating an award of damages that consent would never have been given if the disclosure required by an idiosyncratic belief had been made. This would create an unfairness that cannot be accepted. It would bring inequitable and unnecessary pressure to bear upon the overburdened medical profes-

sion. On the other hand, a purely objective test which would set the standard by a reasonable person without the reasonable fears, concerns and circumstances of the particular plaintiff would unduly favour the medical profession. ...

[17] ... In short, I see no reason to abandon the modified objective test to causation set down in *Reibl v. Hughes*, a test which asks whether a reasonable person in the circumstances of the plaintiff would have consented to the proposed treatment if all the risks had been disclosed.

[18] Turning now to this appeal, it is appropriate to infer from the evidence that a reasonable person in the plaintiff's position would not have decided to terminate her pregnancy in the face of the very small increased risk to the fetus posed by her exposure to the virus which causes chicken pox. Ms. Arndt did make a very general inquiry concerning the risks associated with maternal chicken pox. However, it should not be forgotten that the risk was indeed very small. In the absence of a specific and clearly expressed concern, there was nothing to indicate to the doctor that she had a particular concern in this regard. It follows that there was nothing disclosed by Ms. Arndt's question which could be used by the trier of fact as an indication of a particular fear regarding the possibility of giving birth to a disabled child which should be attributed to the hypothetical reasonable person in the patient's situation. Further,

factors such as the plaintiff's desire for children and her suspicion of the mainstream medical profession can be taken into consideration when determining what a reasonable person in the plaintiff's position would have done if informed of the risks. It is not necessary to assess the relative importance these beliefs would have in the determination of the question of causation. It is sufficient to observe that all these are factors indicating the state of mind of the plaintiff at the time she would have had to make the decision, and therefore may be properly considered by the trier of fact. I agree with the trial judge that the failure to disclose some of the risks to the fetus associated with maternal chicken pox did not affect the plaintiff's decision to continue the pregnancy to term. It follows that the failure to disclose did not cause the financial losses for which the plaintiff is seeking compensation.

[19] I would allow this appeal, set aside the judgment of the Court of Appeal and reinstate the judgment of the trial judge. The defendant should have her costs of the proceedings in this Court and the courts below.

Appeal allowed

Majority: Cory, Lamer, La Forest, L'Heureux-Dubé, Gonthier, McLachlin and Major; Sopinka and Iacobucci dissenting.

---

4. INJURY AND FORESEEABILITY

Question

Was there injury, and was that injury or type of injury foreseeable?

The following are excerpts from the decision of the trial judge.

Mortimer **v.** *Cameron et al.*

[1992] O.J. No. 764 (Q.L.)
ACTION NO. 7458/85
ONTARIO COURT OF JUSTICE (GENERAL DIVISION)
APRIL 13, 1992

McDermid J.: —

1. THE ACTION:

After writing an intermediate accounting examination on the morning of July 17, 1987, Stephen Mortimer made the fateful decision to go to a party at the apartment of a classmate, Sandra Hunt. The apartment she shared with Marijo Kale was on the second floor of a home owned by Stingray Investments Limited.

People there were drinking and relaxing. The mood was convivial but subdued. No one was boisterous or unruly. After a time, Mortimer engaged another classmate, John Cameron, in some friendly conversation and horseplay in the hall of the apart-

ment. From the hall, they travelled down the interior stairs, pushing each other back and forth until they reached the interior landing. Both had been drinking but neither was angry nor hostile.

Mortimer, who was moving backwards, tripped over the raised threshold to the apartment. He fell back and pulled Cameron toward him. Together, they tumbled onto an exterior landing, through its exterior wall and plunged to the ground about 10 feet below.

Cameron picked himself up, but Mortimer could not move. As a result of the fall, he sustained a permanent spinal cord injury at the C4-5 level that rendered him a complete quadriplegic without any motor function or sensation below the site of the injury.

This tragic event has spawned complex issues of liability and damages.

Mortimer sues Cameron on the basis of assault, battery, trespass to the person and negligence. He claims that Cameron applied force to him without due care and attention for his safety and caused him to trip and fall through the exterior wall of the stairway.

[In an exhaustive review of the facts, the arguments and the law, the judge, in a 209-page decision, found the City and the owners of the building at fault. (See p. 41 above for the appeal decision.) With regard to the fault of the young men, the judgment was as follows:]

7.   THE ISSUE OF CAMERON'S NEGLIGENCE:

Stairs in residential buildings are potentially dangerous. They connect two different levels, usually about 8 or more feet apart. Stair treads provide a relatively small surface area upon which to place one's foot. Unless one uses a handrail, one has to balance all one's weight first on one foot and then on the other when ascending or descending stairs. If one is not careful, one is liable to fall and sustain injury, which is sometimes serious. Therefore, generally, one ought not to engage in horseplay on a stairway because, in an already potentially dangerous situation, there is an increased risk of harm from falling.

In these potentially dangerous circumstances, Cameron was under a correspondingly high duty to act so as not to cause harm to Mortimer. With respect to the issue of Mortimer's contributory negligence, Mortimer was under a similar duty to act so as not to cause harm to himself. Mortimer and Cameron travelled down the stairway in a controlled manner. The force used by each against the other was measured and not excessive. Each had hold of the other. They managed to traverse the stairs without falling or losing their balance and reached the interior landing safely. At that point, the risk of harm from falling on the interior stairs had expired.

After they had traversed the interior stairs, the action that then set in motion the immediately ensuing chain of circumstances that resulted in Mortimer's injury was the push Cameron gave Mortimer that caused him to trip over the threshold. When he had entered the apartment, Cameron had noticed he had to step over the threshold and he was aware it was 3 or 4 inches high. When Cameron pushed Mortimer, he created the risk that Mortimer might trip over the threshold and fall through the open doorway onto the exterior landing or against the exterior wall of that landing and injure himself. A reasonable and prudent person would not have pushed Mortimer on the interior landing as Cameron did. Therefore, Cameron was in breach of his duty of care to Mortimer when he pushed him.

In Fridman, *The Law of Torts in Canada* (1989), Vol. 1 at pp. 320 to 329, the learned author deals with the issues of "causal connection" and "causation and remoteness." He observes that a plaintiff must establish a causal connection between his or her loss and the negligence of the defendant. He also notes that the "confused situation" in this area of the law in Canada "is a reflection of the uncertainty that prevails in England as a result of various contradictory decisions in the last thirty years." In reviewing some of those decisions, he refers first to the "directness approach" to causation, as set forth in *Re Polemis*, (1921) 2 K.B. 560 (C.A.), which in effect held that a defendant is liable for the direct consequences of his or her negligence,

whether or not those consequences are foreseeable. He states this rule was subject to two exceptions: the "thin skull" situation, and a foreseeable intervening act, perhaps by a third party, an animal or a natural event such as a storm, that occurred in the form and manner that was foreseeable.

At p. 327, he states " ... the directness approach to causation, as stipulated in *Re Polemis*, was rejected" in *The Wagon Mound (No. 1)*, (1961) A.C. 388, which held that a

> ... defendant would only be liable for foreseeable consequences. Anything which could not be foreseen by the reasonable man in advance of his acts or omissions as being the probable outcome would be too remote and could not be attributed to his negligence.

The law in this area was further qualified by *The Wagon Mound (No. 2)*, (1967) 1 A.C. 617, which held that, " ... as long as what happened was within the realm of what was reasonably foreseeable, the defendant did not have to foresee the precise manner in which it came about." ...

Mortimer's injury was caused from hitting the ground. He would not have hit the ground if P1 [the plywood panel] had held or if a vertical 2x4 stud had been inserted properly under the window between SO and S1. Even though Quaile [expert witness] said he would have expected someone to be hurt if P1 had remained in place, I am not prepared to infer from all the evidence that Mortimer would have been seriously injured from striking P1 if it had not given way. ...

Even though there was a failure on Cameron's part to exercise the care that the circumstances demanded, his failure of care was not the proximate cause of Mortimer's injury. The damage ensuing to Mortimer was too remote a consequence of Cameron's breach of his duty to render him liable for its occurrence. ...

...[I]t was not reasonably foreseeable when Cameron pushed Mortimer on the interior landing that P1 would give way and permit Mortimer to fall from the landing to the ground below. It was not reasonably foreseeable when Cameron pushed Mortimer that Mortimer would be rendered a quadriplegic or even that he would be seriously injured. The probability of the sequence of actual events occurring was extremely remote, though obviously possible. In other words, what actually happened was not within the realm of what was reasonably foreseeable. ...

Accordingly, no liability should attach to Cameron's acts or omissions and the claim against him should be dismissed.

8.   THE ISSUE OF MORTIMER'S NEGLIGENCE:

... [In summary], [e]ven though Mortimer initiated the horseplay and was modestly intoxicated, his legal position is not substantially different from that of Cameron, who had also been drinking and whose level of intoxication, according to Dr. LeBlanc, was probably close to Mortimer's. The same reasoning applies in the case of Mortimer as in Cameron's case. If exactly the same sequence of events had occurred, including Mortimer's initiation of the horseplay and his level of intoxication, but P1 had not given way, Mortimer would not be a quadriplegic today, nor would he have been seriously injured. Given the raised threshold and the fact he was going backwards, Mortimer probably would have tripped over it and lost his balance whether he had been sober or intoxicated to the degree he was. Neither his action in initiating the horseplay nor his level of intoxication was the proximate cause of his injury, nor, as in Cameron's case, was what happened to him within the realm of what was reasonably foreseeable. If P1 had held, he and Cameron probably would have picked themselves up from the exterior landing and returned to the party. Accordingly, no liability should attach to Mortimer's acts or omissions.

[With regard to issue of the liability of Cameron and Mortimer at the *appellate level*:]

COURT OF APPEAL 111 D.L.R. (4TH) 428 AT PP. 440 AND 441

There is no basis for disturbing this conclusion. ... Here, neither Cameron's negligence nor Mortimer's contributory negligence en-

tailed an unreasonable or foreseeable likelihood of the risk or hazard that actually befell Mortimer. It was reasonable for them to assume that what purported and appeared to be a properly constructed wall was in fact a properly constructed wall. In regulating their conduct and having regard for their own safety, they were entitled to rely on the wall providing them reasonable protection. The risk to which they exposed themselves was the risk of being injured by falling down the stairs or onto the exterior landing or by hitting the exterior wall. The risk that materialized was of a different nature. ... The accident that in fact occurred was, in sum, beyond the reasonable contemplation of these parties; it was not within the scope of the risk created by their horseplay, no matter how imprudent that conduct may be considered.

- *T*he court of Appeal found the Mental Health Centre was not negligent in its treatment of Stephen Czupor, a paranoid schizophrenic, who stabbed his sister Anna in the back with a hunting knife rendering her partially paralyzed. The court assumed the centre owed a duty of care to the sister, but found that it had not breached its duty to her as the staff neither knew nor ought to have known that Stephen would commit a violent act remotely similar to that attack.[57]

- *A*fter the judge found that the accused was guilty of the criminal charges against him, the accused jumped from the window of the courtroom to his death. The widow sued the lawyer representing her husband for negligence in his duties as the legal representative. At the trial the plaintiff's action was dismissed. The court held that the accused's jumping out the window was not foreseeable. *McPeake v. Cannon*[58]

- *A*fter the funeral service in Dublin, the cars proceeded from the church to the cemetery. The hearse was separated from other cars by a passing train. The driver of the hearse left the hearse running and ran into a store to buy some cigarettes. The hearse was stolen, so the body did not arrive at the cemetery as expected. The wife of the deceased sued the funeral home for negligence.[59]

D. NEGLIGENT MISSTATEMENT

1. FINANCIAL ADVISORS

Haig v. *Bamford*

72 D.L.R. (3D) 68
SUPREME COURT OF CANADA
APRIL 1, 1976

Dickson J.: This appeal concerns the liability of an accountant to parties other than his employer for negligent statements. The Court is asked to decide whether there was in the relationship of the parties to the appeal such kind or degree of proximity as to give rise to a duty of care owed by the respondents to the appellant. The damages involved are not large but the question raised is of importance to the accounting profession and to the investing public. ...

[Haig, the plaintiff, relied on financial statements prepared

by the defendants and invested $20,000 in a company needing an infusion of equity capital. The statements were improperly prepared and Haig lost the invested money plus $2,500 he later advanced to the company. He sued the accountants to recover his losses.]

I come then to the question whether Haig, who received the defective financial statements, and relied on them to his loss, has a right of recovery from the accountants. Mr. Justice MacPherson at trial allowed recovery [32 D.L.R. (3d) 66, [1972]

6 W.R.R. 557]. He held that the accountants knew or ought to have known that the statements would be used by a potential investor in the Company; although Haig was not, in the Judge's words, "in the picture" when the statement was prepared, he must be included in the category of persons who could be foreseen by the accountants as relying on the statement and therefore the accountants owed a duty to Haig. The Judge applied a test of foreseeability.

The majority in the Court of Appeal for Saskatchewan … came to a different conclusion. …

The outcome of this appeal rests, it would seem, on whether, to create a duty of care, it is sufficient that the accountants knew that the information was intended to be disseminated among a specific group or class, as Mr. Justice MacPherson and Mr. Justice Woods would have it, or whether the accountants also needed to be apprised of the plaintiff's identity, as Mr. Justice Hall and Mr. Justice Maguire would have it. …

THE ENGLISH AUTHORITIES

I do not think one can do better than begin with Lord Denning's dissent in *Candler v. Crane Christmas & Co.*, [1951] 1 All E.R. 426 (C.A.), which later found favour in *Hedley Byrne & Co., Ltd. v. Heller & Partners, Ltd.*, [1963] 2 All E.R. 575 (H.L.). After identifying accountants as among those under a duty to use care, Lord Denning, in answer to the question "To whom do these professional people owe this duty?" said, at p. 434:

> They owe the duty, of course, to their employer or client, and also, I think, to any third person to whom they themselves show the accounts, or to whom they know their employer is going to show the accounts so as to induce him to invest money or take some other action on them. I do not think, however, the duty can be extended still further so as to include strangers of whom they have heard nothing and to whom their employer without their knowledge may choose to show their accounts.

and

> The test of proximity in these cases is: Did the accountants know that the accounts were required for submission to the plaintiff and use by him?

One can find some support in these words for the position taken by the majority in the Saskatchewan Court of Appeal but their effect is tempered by what appears later in the judgment. …

In the case at bar, the accounts were prepared for the guidance of a "specific class of persons," potential investors, in a "specific class of transactions," the investment of $20,000 of equity capital. The number of potential investors would, of necessity, be limited because the Company, as a private company, was prohibited by s. 3 (1) (o) (iii) of the *Companies Act* of Saskatchewan, R.S.S. 1965, c. 131, from extending any invitation to the public to subscribe for shares or debentures of the Company. …

In the present case the accountants knew that the financial statements were being prepared for the very purpose of influencing, in addition to the bank and Sedco, a limited number of potential investors. The names of the potential investors were not material to the accountants. What was important was the nature of the transaction or transactions for which the statements were intended, for that is what delineated the limits of potential liability. The speech of Lord Morris of BorthyGest in *Hedley Byrne* included this observation. …

[The judge then reviews the American and Canadian authorities.]

In summary, Haig placed justifiable reliance upon a financial statement which the accountants stated presented fairly the financial position of the Company as at March 31, 1965. The accountants prepared such statements for reward in the course of their professional duties. The statements were for benefit and guidance in a business transaction, the nature of which was known to the accountants. The accountants were aware that the Company intended to supply the statements to members of a very limited class. Haig was a member of the class. It is true the accountants did not know his name but, as I have indicated earlier, I do not think that is of importance. I can see no good reason for distinguishing between the case in which a defendant accountant delivers information directly to the plaintiff at the request of his employer (*Candler's* case and *Glanzer's* case), and the case in which the information is handed to the employer who, to the knowledge of the accountant, passes it to members of a limited class (whose identity is unknown to the accountant) in furtherance of a transaction the nature of which is known to the accountant. I would accordingly hold that the accountants owed Haig a duty to use reasonable care in the preparation of the accounts.

I am of the view, however, that Haig cannot recover from the accountants the sum of $2,500 which he advanced to the Company in December, 1965, because by that time he was fully cognizant of the true state of affairs. It cannot be said that the sum was advanced in reliance upon false statements. Haig had the choice of advancing additional money in the hope of saving his original investment. He chose to make a further advance, but the choice was his and not one for which the accountants are liable.

I would allow the appeal, set aside the judgment of the Court of Appeal for Saskatchewan and reinstate the judgment of MacPherson, J., subject only to disallowance of the claim of $2,500, the whole with costs in this Court and in the Courts below. …

Appeal allowed in part.

Hercules Managements Ltd. et al. *v.* Ernst & Young et al.

FILE NO.: 24882
http://www.droit.umontreal.ca/
SUPREME COURT OF CANADA
MAY 22, 1997

[1] LA FOREST J.—This appeal arises by way of motion for summary judgment. It concerns the issue of whether and when accountants who perform an audit of a corporation's financial statements owe a duty of care in tort to shareholders of the corporation who claim to have suffered losses in reliance on the audited statements. It also raises the question of whether certain types of claims against auditors may properly be brought by shareholders as individuals or whether they must be brought by the corporation in the form of a derivative action.

FACTS

[2] Northguard Acceptance Ltd. ("NGA") and Northguard Holdings Ltd. ("NGH") carried on business lending and investing money on the security of real property mortgages. The appellant Guardian Finance of Canada Ltd. ("Guardian") was the sole shareholder of NGH and it held non-voting class B shares in NGA. The appellants Hercules Managements Ltd. ("Hercules") and Max Freed were also shareholders in NGA. At all relevant times, ownership in the corporations was separated from management. The respondent Ernst & Young (formerly known as Clarkson Gordon) is a firm of chartered accountants that was originally hired by NGA and NGH in 1971 to perform annual audits of their financial statements and to provide audit reports to the companies' shareholders. The partner in charge of the audits for the years 1980 and 1981 is the respondent William Alexander Cox. Mr. Cox held personal investments in some of the syndicated mortgages administered by NGA and NGH.

[3] In 1984, both NGA and NGH went into receivership. The appellants, as well as [other] shareholders or investors in NGA ... brought an action against the respondents in 1988 alleging that the audit reports for the years 1980, 1981 and 1982 were negligently prepared and that in reliance on these reports, they suffered various financial losses. More specifically, the appellant Hercules sought damages for advances totalling $600,000 which it made to NGA in January and February of 1983, and the appellant Freed sought damages for monies he added to an investment account in NGH in 1982. All the plaintiffs claimed damages in tort for the losses they suffered in the value of their existing shareholdings. In addition to their tort claims, the plaintiffs also alleged that a contract existed between themselves and the respondents in which the respondents explicitly undertook, as of 1978, to protect the shareholders' individual interests in the audits as distinct from the interests of the corporations themselves. ...

ISSUES

[14] The issues in this case [with regard to the action for negligent misstatement] may be stated as follows:

(1) Do the respondents owe the appellants a duty of care with respect to

(a) the investment losses they incurred allegedly as a result of reliance on the 1980–82 audit reports; and

(b) the losses in the value of their existing shareholdings they incurred allegedly as a result of reliance on the 1980–82 audit reports? ...

ANALYSIS ...

Issue 1: Whether the Respondents owe the Appellants a Duty of Care

(i) Introduction

[19] It is now well established in Canadian law that the existence of a duty of care in tort is to be determined through an application of the two-part test first enunciated by Lord Wilberforce in *Anns v. Merton London Borough Council*, [1978] A.C. 728 (H.L.), at pp. 751–52:

First one has to ask whether, as between the alleged wrongdoer and the person who has suffered damage there is a sufficient relationship of proximity or neighbourhood such that, in the reasonable contemplation of the former, carelessness on his part may be likely to cause damage to the latter — in which case a prima facie duty of care arises. Secondly, if the first question is answered affirmatively, it is necessary to consider whether there are any considerations which ought to negative, or to reduce or limit the scope of the duty or the class of person to whom it is owed or the damages to which a breach of it may give rise. ...

While the House of Lords rejected the Anns test ... the basic approach that test embodies has repeatedly been accepted and endorsed by this Court. ...

(ii) The Prima Facie Duty of Care

[22] The first branch of the Anns/Kamloops test demands an inquiry into whether there is a sufficiently close relationship between the plaintiff and the defendant that in the reasonable contemplation of the latter, carelessness on its part may cause damage to the former. The existence of such a relationship — which has come to be known as a relationship of "neighbourhood" or "proximity" — distinguishes those circumstances in which the defendant owes a prima facie duty of care to the plaintiff from those where no such duty exists. In the context of a negligent misrepresentation action, then, deciding whether or not a prima facie duty of care exists necessitates an investigation into whether the defendant-representor and the plaintiff-representee can be said to be in a relationship of proximity or neighbourhood. ...

[24] ... The label "proximity", as it was used by Lord Wilberforce in *Anns*, supra, was clearly intended to connote that the

circumstances of the relationship inhering between the plaintiff and the defendant are of such a nature that the defendant may be said to be under an obligation to be mindful of the plaintiff's legitimate interests in conducting his or her affairs. Indeed, this idea lies at the very heart of the concept of a "duty of care," as articulated most memorably by Lord Atkin in *Donoghue v. Stevenson*, [1932] A.C. 562, at pp. 580–81. In cases of negligent misrepresentation, the relationship between the plaintiff and the defendant arises through reliance by the plaintiff on the defendant's words... . To my mind, proximity can be seen to inhere between a defendant-representor and a plaintiff-representee when two criteria relating to reliance may be said to exist on the facts: (a) the defendant ought reasonably to foresee that the plaintiff will rely on his or her representation; and (b) reliance by the plaintiff would, in the particular circumstances of the case, be reasonable... .

[Whereas in other cases when the judges have couched their analysis of duty of care in different terms, such as asking if the defendant had knowledge of the person or the class of person who relied on the statements, they were really motivated by underlying policy concerns.]

[30] ...In other words, criteria that in other cases have been used to define the legal test for the duty of care can now be recognized for what they really are — policy-based means by which to curtail liability — and they can appropriately be considered under the policy branch of the *Anns/Kamloops* test. To understand exactly how this may be done and how these criteria are pertinent to the case at bar, it will first be useful to set out the prevailing policy concerns in some detail.

(iii) Policy Considerations

[31] As Cardozo C.J. explained in *Ultramares Corp. v. Touche*, 174 N.E. 441 (N.Y.C.A. 1931), at p. 444, the fundamental policy consideration that must be addressed in negligent misrepresentation actions centres around the possibility that the defendant might be exposed to "liability in an indeterminate amount for an indeterminate time to an indeterminate class." This potential problem can be seen quite vividly within the framework of the *Anns/Kamloops* test. ...

[32] The general area of auditors' liability is a case in point. In modern commercial society, the fact that audit reports will be relied on by many different people (e.g., shareholders, creditors, potential takeover bidders, investors, etc.) for a wide variety of purposes will almost always be reasonably foreseeable to auditors themselves. Similarly, the very nature of audited financial statements — produced, as they are, by professionals whose reputations (and, thereby, whose livelihoods) are at stake — will very often mean that any of those people would act wholly reasonably in placing their reliance on such statements in conducting their affairs. ...[The judge reviews the work of several authors writing on the topic.]

[36] As I have thus far attempted to demonstrate, the possible repercussions of exposing auditors to indeterminate liability are significant. In applying the two-stage *Anns/Kamloops* test to negligent misrepresentation actions against auditors, therefore, policy considerations reflecting those repercussions should be taken into account. ... In the general run of auditors' cases, concerns over indeterminate liability will serve to negate a prima facie duty of care. But while such concerns may exist in most such cases, there may be particular situations where they do not. ... This needs to be explained.

[40] [For example, t]his Court's decision in *Haig*, supra, can be seen to rest on precisely the same basis. There, the defendant accountants were retained by a Saskatchewan businessman, one Scholler, to prepare audited financial statements of Mr. Scholler's corporation. At the time they were engaged, the accountants were informed by Mr. Scholler that the audited statements would be used for the purpose of attracting a $20,000 investment in the corporation from a limited number of potential investors. The audit was conducted negligently and the plaintiff investor, who was found to have relied on the audited statements in making his investment, suffered a loss. While Dickson J. was clearly cognizant of the potential problem of indeterminacy arising in the context of auditors' liability (at p. 476), he nevertheless found that the defendants owed the plaintiff a duty of care. In my view, his conclusion was eminently sound given that the defendants were informed by Mr. Scholler of the class of persons who would rely on the report and the report was used by the plaintiff for the specific purpose for which it was prepared... . On the facts of *Haig*, then, the auditors were properly found to owe a duty of care because concerns over indeterminate liability did not arise. I would note that this view of the rationale behind *Haig*, supra, is shared by Professor Feldthusen. ...

[41] The foregoing analysis should render the following points clear. A *prima facie* duty of care will arise on the part of a defendant in a negligent misrepresentation action when it can be said (a) that the defendant ought reasonably to have foreseen that the plaintiff would rely on his representation and (b) that reliance by the plaintiff, in the circumstances, would be reasonable. Even though, in the context of auditors' liability cases, such a duty will often (even if not always) be found to exist, the problem of indeterminate liability will frequently result in the duty being negated by the kinds of policy considerations already discussed. Where, however, indeterminate liability can be shown not to be a concern on the facts of a particular case, a duty of care will be found to exist. Having set out the law governing the appellants' claims, I now propose to apply it to the facts of the appeal.

(iv) Application to the Facts

[42] In my view, there can be no question that a prima facie duty of care was owed to the appellants by the respondents on the facts of this case. As regards the criterion of reasonable foreseeability, the possibility that the appellants would rely on the audited financial statements in conducting their affairs and that they may suffer harm if the reports were negligently prepared must have been reasonably foreseeable to the respondents. This is confirmed simply by the fact that shareholders generally will often choose to rely on audited financial statements for a wide variety of purposes. It is further confirmed by the fact that under ss. 149(1) and 163(1) of the *Manitoba Corporations Act*, it is patently clear that audited financial statements are to be placed before the shareholders at the annual general meeting. ... In my view, it would be untenable to argue in the face of these provisions that some form of reliance by shareholders on the audited reports would be unforeseeable.

[43] Similarly, I would find that reliance on the audited statements by the appellant shareholders would, on the facts of this case, be reasonable. ...

[44] Having found a prima facie duty to exist, then, the second

branch of the *Anns/Kamloops* test remains to be considered. It should be clear from my comments above that were auditors such as the respondents held to owe a duty of care to plaintiffs in all cases where the first branch of the *Anns/Kamloops* test was satisfied, the problem of indeterminate liability would normally arise. It should be equally clear, however, that in certain cases, this problem does not arise because the scope of potential liability can adequately be circumscribed on the facts. An investigation of whether or not indeterminate liability is truly a concern in the present case is, therefore, required. ... With respect to the present case, then, the central question is whether or not the appellants can be said to have used the 1980–82 audit reports for the specific purpose for which they were prepared. The answer to this question will determine whether or not policy considerations surrounding indeterminate liability ought to negate the prima facie duty of care owed by the respondents.

[48] What, then, is the purpose for which the respondents' audit statements were prepared? ...

[49] To my mind, the standard purpose of providing audit reports to the shareholders of a corporation should be regarded no differently under the analogous provisions of the Manitoba Corporations Act. Thus, the directors of a corporation are required to place the auditors' report before the shareholders at the annual meeting in order to permit the shareholders, as a body, to make decisions as to the manner in which they want the corporation to be managed, to assess the performance of the directors and officers, and to decide whether or not they wish to retain the existing management or to have them replaced. On this basis, it may be said that the respondent auditors' purpose in preparing the reports at issue in this case was, precisely, to assist the collectivity of shareholders of the audited companies in their task of overseeing management.

[50] The appellants, however, submit that, in addition to this statutorily mandated purpose, the respondents further agreed to perform their audits for the purpose of providing the appellants with information on the basis of which they could make personal investment decisions. ... I have read the relevant portions of the record on this question and I am unable to accept the appellants' submission. ...

To my mind, ... despite the appellants' submissions, the respondents did not, in fact, prepare the audit reports in order to assist the appellants in making personal investment decisions or, indeed, for any purpose other than the standard statutory one. This finding accords with that of Helper J.A. in the Court of Appeal, and nothing in the record before this Court suggests the contrary. [The judge reviews the claims of the appellants: first, for investment losses due to their reliance on the financial statements.]

[52] ... In light of the dissonance between the purpose for which the reports were actually prepared and the purpose for which the appellants assert they were used, then, the claims of Hercules and Mr. Freed with respect to their investment losses are not such that the concerns over indeterminate liability discussed above are obviated; viz., if a duty of care were owed with respect to these investment transactions, there would seem to be no logical reason to preclude a duty of care from arising in circumstances where the statements were used for any other purpose of which the auditors were equally unaware when they prepared and submitted their report. On this basis, therefore, I

would find that the prima facie duty that arises respecting this claim is negated by policy considerations and, therefore, that no duty of care is owed by the respondents in this regard.

[53] With respect to the claim concerning the loss in value of their existing shareholdings[:] [It] suffers from the same difficulties as those regarding the injection of fresh capital by Hercules and Mr. Freed. Whether the reports were relied upon in assessing the prospect of further investments or in evaluating existing investments, the fact remains that the purpose to which the respondents' reports were put, on this claim, concerned individual or personal investment decisions. Given that the reports were not prepared for that purpose, I find for the same reasons as those earlier set out that policy considerations regarding indeterminate liability inhere here and, consequently, that no duty of care is owed in respect of this claim.

[55] As regards ... the appellants' claim concerning the losses they suffered in the diminution in value of their equity, the analysis becomes somewhat more intricate. The essence of the appellants' submission here is that the shareholders would have supervised management differently had they known of the (alleged) inaccuracies in the 1980–82 reports, and that this difference in management would have averted the demise of the audited corporations and the consequent losses in existing equity suffered by the shareholders. At first glance, it might appear that the appellants' claim implicates a use of the audit reports which is commensurate with the purpose for which the reports were prepared, i.e., overseeing or supervising management. ...

[56] ... On the appellants' argument, however, the purpose to which the 1980-82 reports were ostensibly put was not that of allowing the shareholders as a class to take decisions in respect of the overall running of the corporation, but rather to allow them, as individuals, to monitor management so as to oversee and protect their own personal investments. Indeed, the nature of the appellants' claims (i.e. personal tort claims) requires that they assert reliance on the auditors' reports qua individual shareholders if they are to recover any personal damages. In so far as it must concern the interests of each individual shareholder, then, the appellants' claim in this regard can really be no different from the other "investment purposes" discussed above, in respect of which the respondents owe no duty of care.

[57] This argument is no different as regards the specific case of the appellant Guardian, which is the sole shareholder of NGH. The respondents' purpose in providing the audited reports in respect of NGH was, we must assume, to allow Guardian to oversee management for the better administration of the corporation itself. If Guardian in fact chose to rely on the reports for the ultimate purpose of monitoring its own investment it must, for the policy reasons earlier set out, be found to have done so at its own peril in the same manner as shareholders in NGA. Indeed, to treat Guardian any differently simply because it was a sole shareholder would do violence to the fundamental principle of corporate personality. I would find in respect of both Guardian and the other appellants, therefore, that the prima facie duty of care owed to them by the respondents is negated by policy considerations in that the claims are not such as to bring them within the "exceptional" cases discussed above.

Appeal dismissed.

Question

Does an auditor avoid liability by following the Generally Accepted Accounting Principles?

Kripps v. Touche Ross & Co. et al.

COURT OF APPEAL FOR BRITISH COLUMBIA
REGISTRY: VANCOUVER DOCKET: CA019919
http://www.courts.gov.bc.ca/
APRIL 25, 1997

I. [1] Finch J.:—This appeal is from the judgment of Mr. Justice Lowry, pronounced 30 January 1995 in the Supreme Court of British Columbia, which dismissed the plaintiffs' action for economic loss simpliciter for negligent misrepresentation or non-disclosure by the defendant auditors. ...

II. FACTS

[2] The plaintiffs are investors who purchased debentures after the issue of a prospectus by Victoria Mortgage Corporation Ltd. ("VMCL") on 24 September 1984.

[3] VMCL was at all material times owned by Oakside Corporation Limited, a private holding company of Hermann Bessert. The company's primary business was providing loans secured by mortgages on real property. The mortgages held by VMCL were its principal asset, and interest from those mortgages was its main source of income. MCL borrowed money by selling fixed-term debentures which were offered to the public on a continuous basis. The borrowed money was then loaned against mortgage security in real estate. Subject only to the company's bank debt, the debentures constituted a first priority charge on its assets. VMCL's success depended upon making a profit by maintaining the spread between the interest rate it paid to debenture holders and the interest rate it earned on its mortgage loans.

[4] VMCL's policy, as expressed in the notes to its financial statements, was to "capitalize" accrued interest on mortgages in default, if the company's management believed those amounts to be adequately secured. So, where mortgage payments were in arrears, the unpaid interest was added to the principal value of the mortgage. At the same time the uncollected interest was included in VMCL's statement of income. The learned trial judge found that the company policy with respect to capitalizing unpaid interest was consistent with Generally Accepted Accounting Principles (GAAP) applicable during the relevant period. The amount of unpaid interest capitalized in the financial statements was disclosed in publicly-available accounts filed quarterly with the Superintendent of Brokers.

[5] VMCL recognized the risk that some unpaid interest might never be recovered. This was accounted for in VMCL's financial statements by a provision for investment loss. One of the issues in this case is whether the loss provision in the audited 1983 financial statements was adequate. ...

[10] The plaintiffs claim that in making their decisions to pur-

chase debentures between December 1984 and March 1985 they relied, in part, on Touche's auditor's report of the 1983 financial statements, which was included with those financial statements in the prospectus issued in September 1984.

[They claim damages for the losses they suffered on the grounds that the financials were negligently prepared.]

[29] At trial, the plaintiffs contended that the defendant's report was a negligent misrepresentation because three elements of VMCL's financial position ought to have been disclosed in the financial statements and were not, namely: (1) an adequate loss provision; (2) the default of a substantial part of VMCL's mortgage loan portfolio; and (3) transactions with a related company.

[The trial judge held for the defendants, that is, that the auditors were not negligent.]

III. ISSUES

[33] In this Court, the plaintiffs submit that the trial judge erred in failing to find that the defendant made a negligent misrepresentation as a result of the non-disclosure of the $4.9 million worth of mortgage loans in default and in finding that the plaintiffs had not relied on the audited financial statements. ...

IV. ANALYSIS

[35] The required elements for a successful claim for negligent misrepresentation are: (1) a duty of care based on a "special relationship" between the parties; (2) a misrepresentation; (3) negligence by the representor in making the misrepresentation; (4) reasonable reliance by the representee on the misrepresentation; and (5) damages to the representee caused by the reliance: see *Queen v. Cognos Inc.* ...[See p. 58 of this casebook.]

[36] I will consider each of these elements in turn.

(1) The duty of care

[37] The trial judge concluded that the defendant owed a duty of care to the plaintiffs. ...

[38] This conclusion is within the principles enunciated in such cases as *Hedley, Byrne & Co. Ltd. v. Heller & Partners Ltd.,* [1964] A.C. 465, [1963] 2 All E.R. 575 (H.L.); *Haig v. Bamford,* [1977] 1 S.C.R. 466; *Queen v. Cognos*, supra; *Edgeworth Construction Ltd. v. N.D. Lea & Associates Ltd.,* [1993] 3 S.C.R.

206; and *Rangen Inc. v. Deloitte & Touche* (1994), 95 B.C.L.R. (2d) 182 (C.A.)... . [The judge agreed with the trial judge that none of the arguments of the defendants negated the defendant's duty of care.]

(2) and (3)   A negligently made misrepresentation
[53] The issue here is whether the defendant's conduct was in breach of the standard of care. ...

a.   *Was the failure to disclose the amount of arrears a breach of the standard of care?*
[The judge reiterates in detail the complaints of the plaintiffs and the relevant facts found by the trial judge].
[57] The plaintiffs say that whether GAAP was correctly applied does not conclusively determine the issue of whether the defendant met its standard of care. ...
[59] The defendant ... takes the position that it did not make a bald statement that the financial statements presented fairly the financial position of VMCL, but rather that the financial statements presented fairly the financial position in accordance with GAAP. ...
[63] In my view, the critical issue is the effect of the auditor's report. The learned trial judge concluded that the failure to disclose the amount of arrears was an omission of a piece of material information, but that the capitalization of unpaid interest was the universal practice at the time and was in accordance with GAAP. He therefore concluded that since the capitalization of arrears was in accordance with GAAP, the defendant could not refuse to sign the standard form of auditor's report, regardless of whether the practice was misleading . ...
[64] It is my view that the aim of an auditor's report is to allow auditors to provide their professional opinion which may be relied upon as a guide to business planning and investment. GAAP may be their guide to forming this opinion, but auditors are retained to form an opinion on the fairness of the financial statements, not merely on their conformity to GAAP.

[The judge found support for his view in the Handbook of the CICA (Canadian Institute of Chartered Accountants). In his review of the cases submitted by both the plaintiffs and defendant he stated:]
[69] The present judicial attitude towards standards set by professions is set out by Sopinka J. for a majority of the Supreme Court of Canada in *ter Neuzen v. Korn* (1995), 11 B.C.L.R. (3d) 201 at para. 51:

> I conclude from the foregoing that, as a general rule, where a procedure involves difficult or uncertain questions of medical treatment or complex, scientific or highly technical matters that are beyond the ordinary experience and understanding of a judge or jury, it will not be open to find a standard medical practice negligent. On the other hand, as an exception to the general rule, if a standard practice fails to adopt obvious and reasonable precautions which are readily apparent to the ordinary finder of fact, then it is no excuse for a practitioner to claim that he or she was merely conforming to such a negligent common practice. ...

[73] In my view, therefore, while professional standards would normally be a persuasive guide as to what constitutes reasonable care, those standards cannot be taken to supplant or to replace the degree of care called for by law. A professional body cannot bind the rest of the community by the standard it sets for its members. Otherwise, all professions could immunize their members from claims of negligence. A partial immunization would be the result of giving effect to the qualification in unqualified auditor's reports that the financial statements present fairly the financial position in accordance with GAAP. ...
[77] ...Touche had actual knowledge that a simple application of GAAP would omit material information and lead to financial statements that could not be said to have fairly presented the financial position of VMCL. Given this actual knowledge, Touche fell below the required standard of care when it made its auditor's report... .

b.   *Was the acceptance of the deficient loss provision a breach of the standard of care?*
[85] From these submissions [from the plaintiff and defendant] it would appear that there are two or three different tests for materiality. The first test is whether a representation might possibly affect a decision; the second is whether a representation is capable of affecting a decision; and the third is whether a representation would probably affect a decision. I think that the first two tests are the same, and that the real distinction is between a representation that might possibly affect a decision and one that would probably affect a decision.
[86] Even if the higher test of probability is the one properly to be applied, it seems to me that understatement of the loss provision by approximately $275,000 is material. It may be that the trial judge understated the test of materiality, but even if he had applied the correct test he ought to have concluded that the loss provision was a material misrepresentation because it would likely have had a significant effect on the plaintiffs' decision.

(4)   Reliance
[After a review of the arguments and precedents cited on this point of law, he concludes]
[104] Applying the principles derived from the cases referred to above, in my respectful view, the learned trial judge misdirected himself on the law in holding that to succeed the plaintiffs had to prove that the misrepresentation alleged to be relied upon was "fundamental" to their decision, and in holding that affirmative evidence from the plaintiffs was required before actual reliance could be found. In my respectful view, the misrepresentation with respect to the understated loss provision was material, and, because of its effect on retained earnings, borrowing capacity, and interest coverage, was such as would tend to induce the plaintiffs to act in reliance upon it.
[105] Moreover, the non-disclosure of $4.9 million worth of mortgages in arrears and the misrepresentation with respect to the non-performing loans note were decidedly material and misleading. They were misrepresentations in financial statements which the defendant said fairly represented the financial picture of VMCL. They were statements which clearly would tend to induce an investor to purchase VMCL debentures. It was therefore incumbent upon the defendant to rebut the inference that the plaintiffs relied on these misrepresentations, and in my view it failed to do so.

(5)   Damages
[106] The fifth element required in a negligent misrepresentation claim is that the reliance result in damages is not at issue on this appeal.

V. CONCLUSION

[107] I conclude that the plaintiffs have made out a successful claim for negligent misrepresentation. The defendant owed the plaintiffs a duty of care, a material misrepresentation was negligently made, and the plaintiffs relied upon this misrepresentation to their detriment.

[108] I would allow the plaintiffs' appeal.

Concuring: Rowles; Dissenting: Ryan

Dissenting reasons for judgment included the following:

[123] In the case at bar my colleague has found that the generally accepted accounting principles were themselves inadequate. In my respectful view that finding does not assist the appellants. The respondents were asked to determine the prevailing principles (GAAP) and state whether the financial statements met them. They did that. They are not accused of negligently determining the proper generally accepted accounting principles, they are accused of failing to state that the prevailing principles were inadequate. In my view they were under no obligation to offer such an opinion.

---

2. EMPLOYERS

Queen *v.* Cognos

SUPREME COURT OF CANADA
99 D.L.R. (4TH) 626
JANUARY 21, 1993

Background facts: Mr. Queen, a chartered accountant, was interviewed for a position as manager, financial standards, for the development of accounting software. He was not told in the interview that the funding for the project was not guaranteed nor that it was subject to budgetary approval by senior management. He left a secure position to join Cognos, Inc. A few months after he signed the employment contract he was told there would be reassignments because of cuts in research and development. Within two years he had received an effective termination notice; the employment contract had allowed for the termination of his employment at any time.

Mr. Queen sued the employer for negligent misstatement. He won at the trial level, but the decision was reversed by the Ontario Court of Appeal. Below are excerpts from the decision of the Supreme Court.

Per Iacobucci J.: — This appeal involves the application of the tort of negligent misrepresentation to a pre-employment representation made by an employer to a prospective employee in the course of a hiring interview. Specifically, the court is being asked to determine in what circumstances a representation made during a hiring interview becomes, in law, a "negligent misrepresentation". A subsidiary question deals with the effect of a subsequent employment agreement signed by the plaintiff, and its provisions allowing termination "without cause" and reassignment, on a claim for damages for negligent misrepresentation. ...

This appeal involves an action in tort to recover damages caused by alleged negligent misrepresentation made in the course of a hiring interview by an employer (the respondent), through its representative, to a prospective employee (the appellant) with respect to the employer and the nature and existence of the employment opportunity. Though a relatively recent feature of the common law, the tort of negligent misrepresentation relied on by the appellant and first recognized by the House of Lords in *Hedley Byrne, supra,* [*Hedley Byrne & Co. Ltd. v. Heller & Partners Ltd.* [1964] A.C. 465] is now an established principle of Canadian tort law. This court has confirmed on many occasions, sometimes tacitly, that an action in tort may lie, in appropriate circumstances, for damages caused by a misrepresentation made in a negligent manner: . ...

While the doctrine of *Hedley Byrne* is well established in Canada, the exact breadth of its applicability is, like any common law principle, subject to debate and to continuous development. At the time this appeal was heard, there had only been a handful of cases where the tort of negligent misrepresentation was used in a pre-employment context such as the one involved here: ... Without question, the present factual situation is a novel one for this court.

Some have suggested that it is inappropriate to extend the application of *Hedley Byrne, supra,* to representations made by an employer to a prospective employee in the course of an interview because it places a heavy burden on employers. As will be apparent for my reasons herein, I disagree in principle with this view. ...

[T]his appeal may be disposed of simply by considering whether or not the required elements under the *Hedley Byrne* doctrine are established in the facts of this case. In my view, they are.

The required elements for a successful *Hedley Byrne* claim have been stated in many authorities, sometimes in varying forms. The decisions of this court cited above suggest five general requirements:

(1) there must be a duty of care based on a "special relationship" between the representor and the representee;
(2) the representation in question must be untrue, inaccurate, or misleading;

(3) the representor must have acted negligently in making said misrepresentation;

(4) the representee must have relied, in a reasonable manner, on said negligent misrepresentation; and

(5) the reliance must have been detrimental to the representee in the sense that damages resulted.

In the case at bar, the trial judge found that all elements were present and allowed the appellant's claim. …

[After a lengthy review of the decisions of the lower courts, the relevant case law and the facts, the justice concluded.] In my view, the appellant has established all the required elements to succeed in his action. The respondent and its representative, Mr. Johnston, owed a duty of care to the appellant during the course of the hiring interview to exercise such reasonable care as the circumstances required to ensure that the representations made were accurate and not misleading. This duty of care is distinct from, and additional to, the duty of common honesty existing between negotiating parties. The trial judge found, as a fact, that

misrepresentations — both express and implied — were made to the appellant and that he relied upon them, reasonably I might add, to his eventual detriment. In all the circumstances of this case, I agree with the trial judge that these misrepresentations were made by Mr. Johnston in a negligent manner. While a subsequent contract may, in appropriate cases, affect a *Hedley Byrne* claim relying on pre-contractual representations, the employment agreement signed by the appellant is irrelevant to this action. In particular, cls.13 and 14 of the contract [regarding reassignment and termination] are not valid disclaimers of responsibility for the representations made during the interview.

For the foregoing reasons, I would allow the appeal, set aside the judgment of the Ontario Court of Appeal, and restore the judgment of White J., finding the respondent liable and granting the appellant damages in the amount of $67,224. The appellant should have his costs here and in the courts below.

Appeal allowed

3. SUPPLIERS

Mr. and Mrs. Wright purchased a house outside London, Ontario only after having been assured by the telephone company that the house would be within the exchange of London, so that calls to friends and family in London would not be subject to long distance charges. The serviceman who came to install the telephone told them that the house was not within the 666 exchange. The Wrights sued the telephone company for negligent misstatement and claimed damages in an amount equal to their telephone charges for calls within the 666 exchange. The judge who first heard the case in Small Claims Court, relying on *Hedley Byrne v. Heller*, held for the plaintiffs. The Wrights returned with another bill and the judge again held for the plaintiffs on the ground that it was a breach of contract and that the damages were continuing. He urged the telephone company to resolve the difficulty. Its failure to do so would lead to the Wrights' return to court.

Wright v. Bell Canada
Summarized from The Lawyers Weekly
July 3, 1987 p.11

E. VOLUNTARY ASSUMPTION OF RISK / CONTRIBUTORY NEGLIGENCE

Poirier et al. **v.** *Murphy et al.*

36 C.C.L.T. 160
BRITISH COLUMBIA SUPREME COURT
FEBRUARY 17, 1986

MacKinnon J.: — On June 24, 1982 the plaintiff Peter Albert Poirier (Poirier) and the defendant John Anthony Murphy (Murphy), each 18 years of age, agreed to perform and in fact did carry out a "stunt" which resulted in Poirier being injured by the car driven by Murphy. With Poirier and Murphy, as

passengers, were three girls and two boys, all around 17 years of age. They had been driving around with no particular destination and were looking for something to do. A conversation took place between Poirier and Murphy about doing a "stunt." The passengers were unaware of what this meant.

However, they did hear Murphy asking Poirier to do it and Poirier refusing twice and then agreeing. The stunt was done in an underground parking lot of the Lougheed Mall in Coquitlam where Poirier would stand underneath a water sprinkler pipe and Murphy, as the driver of the car, from a position about 100 feet away, would drive towards Poirier and at the last moment Poirier would jump up, grab the pipe, do a chin-up, and swerve his hips and legs to one side, and thereby allow the car to pass under him. The expected clearance between Poirier's body and the car would be approximately 4 to 6 inches. It was intended to be thrilling to the participants and anybody watching. It was certainly a dangerous act. In the past, and on the occasion of the accident, the signal indicating that Poirier was ready for the stunt to commence was a slight nod by Poirier. It was to be seen only by Murphy. On observing the signal (the slight nod by Poirier) Murphy would drive the car toward Poirier and expect him to escape any impact. ...

[After reviewing the testimony of the witnesses, the Judge continued:] Thus, on the first run, it would appear the stunt performance went as planned with one exception. It almost failed. Even though Poirier signalled to Murphy his readiness for the commencement he was not able to completely escape contact with the car. His foot or part of his body was hit by the car. That impact did not release his grip on the pipes so as to cause a fall but it was of a sufficient force to be perceived by two of the passengers.

On the second run there are different stories as to what occurred. I do not accept Murphy's evidence that on the second run he backed up and performed the second stunt in the same way as the first. Other witnesses testified that he made a U-turn, headed at Poirier with his back facing Murphy. I have concluded that, after completing his first run, Murphy turned the car around in some manner and immediately commenced his run from the opposite direction. At this time Poirier was still hanging from the pipe. I find Poirier did not signal his readiness for Murphy to start the second run. Notwithstanding Mark Anderson's cry to stop, Murphy proceeded ahead in the belief that Poirier would pull himself up and avoid the impact. [He did not. He was struck and suffered serious brain injury.]

The issues

1. Does the maxim of *volenti non fit injuria* apply to the circumstances of this case?
2. If not, was there contributory negligence?
3. Damages.

Volenti non fit injuria

The defendant submits the plaintiff knew, or ought to have known, the real risk involved in carrying out the stunt and that, when he agreed to do it, he impliedly exempted the defendant from liability. The defendant says that Poirier consented to assume the risk without compensation, and he absolved Murphy from the duty to take care.

Cartwright J., in delivering the majority judgment of the Supreme Court of Canada in *Stein v. Lehnert*, [1963] S.C.R. 38, 40 W.W.R. 616, 36 D.L.R. (2d) 159 said, at p. 620 [W.W.R.]:

"The decision of this court in *Seymour v. Maloney; Car and Gen. Insur. Corpn. (Third Party)* [1956] SCR 322,...establishes that where a driver of a motor vehicle

invokes the maxim *volenti non fit injuria* as a defence to an action for damages for injuries caused by his negligence to a passenger, the burden lies upon the defendant of proving that the plaintiff, expressly or by necessary implication, agreed to exempt the defendant from liability for any damage suffered by the plaintiff occasioned by that negligence, and that, as stated in *Salmond on Torts*, 13th ed., p.44:

'The true question in every case is: did the plaintiff give a real consent to the assumption of the risk without compensation; did the consent really absolve the defendant from the duty to take care?' "

In *Lackner v. Neath* (1966), 57 W.W.R. 496, 58 D.L.R. (2d) 662 (Sask. C.A.) Culliton C.J.S., quoted the excerpt from *Stein v. Lehnert*, supra, and then stated at p. 489 [W.W.R.]:

Clearly, then, to admit the defence of *volenti non fit injuria* there must be established, either by direct evidence or by inference, that the plaintiff: (a) Voluntarily assumed the physical risk; and (b) Agreed to give up his right for negligence, or, to put it more briefly, that the plaintiff accepted both the physical and legal risk. ...

In *Deskau v. Dziama; Brooks v. Dziama*, [1973] 3 O.R. 101, 36 D.L.R. (3d) 36, the plaintiff agreed to assume the risk of riding with the defendant driver whom he knew was driving the car over hills at high speeds so that the car would fly from the crest of the hill with all four wheels off the ground. Keith J. found the nature of the risk voluntarily assumed by the plaintiff was unlimited. He said at p. 106 [O.R.]:

I respectfully agree with the following statement from Fleming, *Law of Torts*, 4th ed. (1971), pp. 243-4:

'Formerly it mattered nothing whether a plaintiff was defeated on the ground of voluntary assumption of risk or contributory negligence. Now, however, the distinction has become critical, since the relevant legislation does not purport to extend apportionment to voluntary assumption of risk. All the more reason therefore for the courts to have taken an ever more restrictive view of the defence (*volenti no fit injuria*) in order to avoid the distasteful consequence of having to deny the plaintiff all recovery instead of merely reducing his award. In the result, the defence is nowadays but rarely invoked with success.' ...

The defendant submits, and I agree, that had Poirier been injured in the first run the authorities would support the application of the doctrine of *volens*, and his claim would be dismissed. ...

He did not give such approval on the second run. Unlike the first stunt, Poirier was not ready for the second. He did not expect Murphy from that direction. After the first run he may have remained swinging from the water pipes so as to stay out of the way as Murphy was to (but did not) return to the starting position for the second stunt. Had Murphy done so, Poirier could have indicated or withheld his signal to commence the second stunt.

Accordingly, I have concluded that Poirier had not assumed the physical risk of the second stunt and the defence of *volens* does not succeed.

Contributory negligence

Murphy was negligent. As the driver of a motor vehicle, he owed a duty to drive it in a manner different than he did in the underground parking lot where the accident occurred. He was negligent in doing the stunt. He was negligent in failing to hear the noise in the first stunt (Poirier's foot), in failing to pay heed to the passenger's cry to stop, and in failing to recognize that Poirier was not ready for the second stunt. His negligence caused or contributed to the damages suffered by Poirier.

Poirier contributed to his own fate. He failed to take reasonable care for himself. He clearly was negligent in agreeing to the stunt. Though he may not have agreed to the second stunt being done in the manner it was, he placed himself in a hazardous position and failed to remove himself from the risk.

In my view Poirier and Murphy were equally negligent in the first run, and both were negligent in the second. In the second run I attach more blame to Murphy. I apportion the liability two-thirds on the shoulders of Murphy and one-third on Poirier. ...

The plaintiff is entitled to two-thirds of the damages together with court order interest.

Action allowed.

- *A*lthough the defendants were found negligent for failing to have a reasonable system for keeping the premises free from ice, the plaintiff was found 25% contributorily negligent for wearing high-heeled dress shoes instead of "safe footgear for winter conditions."[60]

F. VICARIOUS LIABILITY

- *B*ecause a caretaker's duties did include controlling the conduct of tenants in the rooming house, the owner of the house, as employer of the caretaker, was found vicariously liable for the actions of the caretaker who chose to solve one disturbance by taking a three-foot board "described as a portion of a handrail with the word 'truth' marked on it" and striking a tenant in the face with it.[61]

- *T*he legislature of Manitoba introduced a bill that would create a presumption that parents are liable for the wrongdoing of their children. The parents must then rebut the presumption with evidence of reasonable supervision or be responsible for paying for repairs up to $5000.[62]

When the driver of a white Alfa Romeo 164s saw another driver of an Alfa Romeo 164s the race was on. Unfortunately, a person was severely injured when one of the drivers, Cormier, lost control of the car. Cormier admitted liability and as he was driving with consent of the owner, the owner was also liable. At trial, the driver of the white Alfa, Pieter van der Griend was also found at fault by reason of his participation in the race.

The sole issue on appeal was whether the employer of van der Griend, Carter Motor Cars Ltd., was vicariously liable as van der Griend was not authorized to have the car at the time of the accident. He knew that the use of the Alfa 164s was restricted to actual demonstrations and it was not to be used as a loan car.

The court examined the wording of s. 79(1) of the Motor Vehicle Act, R.S.B.C. 1979, c. 288 as amended:

> ... Every person driving or operating the motor vehicle who acquired possession of it with the consent, express or implied, of the owner of the motor vehicle, shall be deemed to be the agent or servant of that owner and employed as such, and shall be deemed to be driving and operating the motor vehicle in the course of his employment.

The court held the employee had possession of an automobile by virtue of the fact that keys and dealer plates were made available to him as was the key to the place where they were kept.

> Carter ... enabled the Employee to acquire possession of the white Alfa on 23 May 1993 and whether the use to which he put it thereafter was one of which Carter would approve is immaterial if, in his driving or operation of the vehicle, he was at fault.

> The employer was thus vicariously liable.
>
> ***Morrison v. Cormier Vegetation Control Ltd.***
> *Docket: CA021749 Registry: Vancouver*
> *http://www.courts.gov.bc.ca/*
> *Court of Appeal for British Columbia*
> *December 17, 1996*

G. RES IPSA LOQUITUR

Fontaine v. **British Columbia (Official Administrator)**

FILE No.: 25381
http://www.droit.umontreal.ca/doc/csc-scc/
SUPREME COURT OF CANADA
MARCH 19, 1998

MAJOR J.:—[1] This appeal provides another opportunity to consider the so-called maxim of res ipsa loquitur. What is it? When does it arise? And what effect does its application have? This appeal centres on these questions. At the conclusion of the hearing, the appeal was dismissed with reasons to follow. These are the reasons.

I. FACTS

[2] The appellant claimed damages under the Family Compensation Act, R.S.B.C. 1979, c. 120, as amended, with respect to the death of her husband, Edwin Andrew Fontaine.

[3] On November 9, 1990, Edwin Andrew Fontaine ("Fontaine") and Larry John Loewen ("Loewen") left Surrey, B.C. for a weekend hunting trip. They were expected back on November 12, 1990, and were reported missing later that day. Their bodies were found on January 24, 1991 in Loewen's badly damaged truck ("the vehicle"), which was lying in the Nicolum Creek bed adjacent to Highway 3 (approximately seven kilometres east of Hope, B.C.). There were no witnesses to the accident, and no one knows precisely when or how the accident happened.

[4] The weather was bad on the weekend the men went missing. Between 10 p.m. on November 8 and 10 p.m. on November 10, 1990, the area in and around the Hope weather station received approximately 328 mm. of rain. Three highways lead out of Hope. Highway 1 was cut off by a major landslide, Highway 3 was closed owing to the washout of a large culvert from under the highway, and two bridges on Highway 5 were closed because of heavy river flooding and potential damage to the bridges' understructures.

[5] Police investigators concluded that, at the time of the accident, the vehicle had been travelling westbound on Highway 3 and left the roadway at a point approximately 10 metres east of the entrance to a rest area. The vehicle then tumbled down a rock-covered embankment into the swollen flood waters of Nicolum Creek and was swept downstream. The vehicle left the road with sufficient momentum to break a path through some small alder trees. Loewen was found, with his seatbelt in place, in the driver's seat.

[6] A police constable testified that, at the presumed time of the accident, Nicolum Creek was in flood condition with the water within two-thirds of a metre of the edge of Highway 3 at the likely site of the accident. The wind was gusting to "extremely high velocities" and a rainstorm was raging.

[7] The constable also testified that there is a swale in the highway at the point where the vehicle is believed to have left the road. With heavy rains, between 12.5 and 38 mm. of rain may collect in the swale. In the constable's opinion, if the driver continued to drive straight at this point, loss of control would be unlikely. However, if the driver were to suddenly turn the vehicle's wheels in an attempt to avoid the pool of water or engage in any other sudden driving manoeuvres, the vehicle might hydroplane, particularly if the vehicle had worn tires. The police report indicated that the two front tires of the vehicle showed "excessive" wear, with only 4 and 5 mm. of tread on the tires. The constable further testified that the sidewall of the right front tire was cut and the rim was damaged, consistent with the tire hitting a rock or other solid object on the road surface. He considered it difficult to say whether or not a flat tire might have caused the vehicle to go out of control and

leave the roadway. He further agreed that the driver might have swerved to avoid hitting an animal on the road surface. [8] The trial judge found that negligence had not been proven and dismissed the case. A majority of the Court of Appeal dismissed the appeal.

[The judge then reviews the lower courts decisions.]

III. ISSUES

[16] 1. When does res ipsa loquitur apply?
2. What is the effect of invoking res ipsa loquitur?

IV. ANALYSIS

A. When does res ipsa loquitur apply?

[17] Res ipsa loquitur, or "the thing speaks for itself", has been referred to in negligence cases for more than a century. In Scott v. London and St. Katherine Docks Co. (1865), 3 H. & C. 596, 159 E.R. 665, at p. 596 and p. 665, respectively, Erle C.J. defined what has since become known as res ipsa loquitur in the following terms:

> There must be reasonable evidence of negligence. But where the thing is shewn to be under the management of the defendant or his servants, and the accident is such as in the ordinary course of things does not happen if those who have the management use proper care, it affords reasonable evidence, in the absence of explanation by the defendants, that the accident arose from want of care.

[18] These factual elements have since been recast (see Clerk and Lindsell on Torts (13th ed. 1969), at para. 967 at p. 968, quoted with approval in Jackson v. Millar, [1976] 1 S.C.R. 225, at p. 235, and Hellenius v. Lees, [1972] S.C.R. 165, at p. 172):

> The doctrine applies (1) when the thing that inflicted the damage was under the sole management and control of the defendant, or of someone for whom he is responsible or whom he has a right to control; (2) the occurrence is such that it would not have happened without negligence. If these two conditions are satisfied it follows, on a balance of probability, that the defendant, or the person for whom he is responsible, must have been negligent. There is, however, a further negative condition; (3) there must be no evidence as to why or how the occurrence took place. If there is, then appeal to res ipsa loquitur is inappropriate, for the question of the defendant's negligence must be determined on that evidence. . . .

B. Effect of the application of res ipsa loquitur

[The judge reviews the historical use of the rule in court and concludes:]

[26] Whatever value res ipsa loquitur may have once provided is gone. Various attempts to apply the so-called doctrine have been more confusing than helpful. Its use has been restricted to cases where the facts permitted an inference of negligence and there was no other reasonable explanation for the accident. Given its limited use it is somewhat meaningless to refer to that use as a doctrine of law.

[27] It would appear that the law would be better served if the maxim was treated as expired and no longer used as a separate component in negligence actions. After all, it was nothing more than an attempt to deal with circumstantial evidence. That evidence is more sensibly dealt with by the trier of fact, who should weigh the circumstantial evidence with the direct evidence, if any, to determine whether the plaintiff has established on a balance of probabilities a prima facie case of negligence against the defendant. Once the plaintiff has done so, the defendant must present evidence negating that of the plaintiff or necessarily the plaintiff will succeed.

C. Application to this case

[28] In this appeal, the trial judge had to consider whether there was direct evidence from which the cause of the accident could be determined, or, failing that, whether there was circumstantial evidence from which it could be inferred that the accident was caused by negligence attributable to Loewen.

[29] The trial judge found that the only potential evidence of negligence on Loewen's part concerned the fact that the vehicle left the roadway and was travelling with sufficient momentum to break a path through some small trees. She concluded that, when taken together with other evidence concerning the road and weather conditions, this was no more than neutral evidence and did not point to any negligence on Loewen's part. That conclusion was not unreasonable in light of the evidence, which at most established that the vehicle was moving in a forward direction at the time of the accident, with no indication that it was travelling at an excessive rate of speed.

[30] There was some evidence about "excessive wear" on the front tires of the vehicle. In commenting upon this evidence, Gibbs J.A. for the majority of the Court of Appeal stated at p. 379:

> The fact was stated thus in an accident investigation report: "The front tires showed excessive wear with only 4 mm. LF and 5 mm. RF tread depth". The author of the report was not called as a witness. The evidence does not disclose whether the witness who was asked about the effect of "excessive" wear had himself measured the tires as well as observing the wear. There was no evidence of where on the tires the measurement was taken or of whether the wear was uniform over the tires. Perhaps most importantly, there was no evidence of what the tread depth of an unworn tire of that make and style would be, whatever the make and style was. So there was no standard against which to measure the 4 and 5 mm., and no way for the court to attach an objective meaning to the observer's subjective description of "excessive" wear.

In light of these deficiencies in the evidence, I agree with Gibbs J.A. that the trial judge did not err when she apparently treated this evidence as of negligible value.

[31] There are a number of reasons why the circumstantial evidence in this case does not discharge the plaintiff's onus. Many of the circumstances of the accident, including the date, time and precise location, are not known. Although this case has proceeded on the basis that the accident likely occurred during the weekend of November 9, 1990, that is only an assumption. There are minimal if any evidentiary foundations from which any inference of negligence could be drawn.

[32] As well, there was evidence before the trial judge that a severe wind and rainstorm was raging at the presumed time of the accident. While it is true that such weather conditions impose a higher standard of care on drivers to take increased precautions, human experience confirms that severe weather conditions are more likely to produce situations where accidents occur and vehicles leave the roadway regardless of the degree of care taken. In these circumstances, it should not be concluded that the accident would ordinarily not have occurred in the absence of negligence.

[33] If an inference of negligence might be drawn in these circumstances, it would be modest. The trial judge found that the defence had succeeded in producing alternative explanations of how the accident may have occurred without negligence on Loewen's part. Most of the explanations offered by the defendants were grounded in the evidence and were adequate to neutralize whatever inference the circumstantial evidence could permit to be drawn. The trial judge's finding was not unreasonable and should not be interfered with on appeal.

[34] The finding of facts and the drawing of evidentiary conclusions from those facts is the province of the trial judge, and an appellate court must not interfere with a trial judge's conclusions on matters of fact unless there is palpable or overriding error: see Toneguzzo-Norvell (Guardian Ad Litem of) v. Burnaby Hospital, [1994] 1 S.C.R. 114, at p. 121 per McLachlin J. There is no indication that the trial judge committed a palpable or overriding error here.

[35] The appellant submitted that an inference of negligence should be drawn whenever a vehicle leaves the roadway in a single-vehicle accident. This bald proposition ignores the fact that whether an inference of negligence can be drawn is highly dependent upon the circumstances of each case: see Gauthier & Co. v. The King, supra, at p. 150. The position advanced by the appellant would virtually subject the defendant to strict liability in cases such as the present one.

V. DISPOSITION

[36] The trial judge did not err in concluding based on either the direct or circumstantial evidence or both that the plaintiff failed to establish on a balance of probabilities that the accident occurred as a result of negligence attributable to Loewen. The appeal is therefore dismissed with costs.

Appeal dismissed with costs.

The Cohen family had suffered stomach cramps and nausea for a few days before the son noticed white maggots crawling inside the top part of a bottle of Heinz ketchup. The family sued the seller, but also sued H.J. Heinz Co. and argued *res ipsa loquitur*.

The judge did not think that the principle would apply "or even if it did, whether this principle would assist the plaintiffs to any extent, in view of the evidence tendered by Heinz of careful preparation and proper handling of the product, which evidence I have accepted." Heinz submitted evidence showing that a vacuum is created in the bottle before the ketchup is inserted, that the ketchup is inserted at a minimum temperature of 190 degrees Fahrenheit, and that the fruit fly would have had to enter the bottle after it left the manufacturer to have maggots discovered on the date given.

Cohen et al. v. H. J. Heinz Company of Canada Limited and
Valdi Discount Foods
Summarized from The Lawyers Weekly
October 17, 1986 p. 7.

H. STRICT LIABILITY

Question

Should we ever make the defendant pay when he is not at fault?

[As summarized in the law report:]

By joint agreement, the first municipality brought putrescible organic matter on to the lands of the second municipality in order to dispose of the matter by way of land-fill. Subsequently, as this organic matter decomposed, it generated methane gas which escaped into adjoining lands on which private homes had been constructed and on one occasion caused a fire in a garage which led to the residents being required to park their cars on the street. Still later, however, an official of the municipality which owned the land assured the resident who had suffered fire that the problem had been solved and that garages could again be used. Plaintiffs, having heard this information from its original recipient, began to use their garage again. However, methane gas continued to escape from the land-fill site and filled plaintiffs' garage so that on one occasion when the male plaintiff turned on the ignition of plaintiffs' car an explosion destroyed the garage, damaged the car and injured the male plaintiff.

In an action against both municipalities, *held*, both were strictly liable for the escape of the dangerous substance. A land-fill project as a means of disposing of garbage is a non-natural user [sic] of land in a heavily populated residential district. While the first municipality had statutory authority to pass by-laws for acquiring land for the purposes of dumping and disposing of garbage under s.214b (enacted 1956, c.53, s.23) of the *Municipality of Metropolitan Toronto Act*, 1953 (Ont.), c.73 (now R.S.O. 1970, c.295), the project was not carried out pursuant to that statutory authority.

Furthermore, the continuing generation and escape of gas, with injurious consequences reasonably to be anticipated, constituted a nuisance. It would, however, be impractical and unrealistic to require the second municipality to abate the nuisance by removing the garbage fill. Plaintiffs should be awarded damages for the interference with the beneficial use of their land.

Finally, defendants were liable in negligence for the damage in burying the garbage as they did when they knew or ought to have known that its decomposition would result in the production of gas, in failing to take steps to prevent the escape of the gas, in failing to warn the adjoining owners of the risk and, in the case of the second defendant, negligently misrepresenting that the problem had been solved.

Fletcher v. Rylands (1866), L.R. 1 Ex. 265; affd L.R. 3 H.L. 330; *Hedley Byrne & Co., Ltd. v. Heller & Partners Ltd.*, [1964] A.C. 465, apld; ...

Reprinted with permission of Canada Law Book Inc., 240 Edward Street, Aurora, Ontario, L4G 3S9.

Gertsen et al. v. Municipality of Metropolitan Toronto et al.
41 D.L.R. (3D) 646
Ontario High Court
August 21, 1973

ENDNOTES

1. For a more detailed account see the *Vancouver Sun*, September 18, 1996, p. A10.

2. *The Globe and Mail*, February 9, 1993, p. A12.

3. *The Lawyers Weekly*, February 12, 1988, p. 8.

4. For more particulars, see *The Lawyers Weekly*, September 15, 1990, p. 8.

5. A more detailed account is given in the *Vancouver Sun*, January 1987.

6. For a more detailed account of the resulting negligence action see *The Lawyers Weekly*, July 1, 1994, p. 27.

7. A more detailed account is given in the *Vancouver Sun*, March 23, 1982.

8. A more detailed account is given in the *National*, April, 1986.

9. For a more detailed account see *The Lawyers Weekly*, January 19, 1996, p. 11.

10. For a more detailed account see *The Lawyers Weekly*, October 31, 1997, p. 1.

11. A more detailed account is given in the *Vancouver Sun*, December 1, 1987.

12. A more detailed account is given in the *Vancouver Sun*, October 24, 1989.

13. *The Lawyers Weekly*, January 19, 1990, p. 23.

14. For a more detailed account see *Maclean's*, September 19, 1994, p. 21 or the appeal decision *Unruh v. Webber* (1994) 88 B.C.L.R. (2d) 353.

15. See *Zapf v. Muckalt* Vancouver Registry: Docket: CA020937, December 3, 1996 for the unanimous decision of the B.C. Court of Appeal; dismissing the appeal of the defendant found liable by the trial court.

16. See *The Lawyers Weekly*, February 17, 1995, p. 1 for a report of *B.(R.) v. Children's Aid Society of Metropolitan Toronto*, a 160-page decision.

17. A more detailed account is given in the *Vancouver Sun*, January, 1984.

18. *The Lawyers Weekly*, October 12, 1984, p. 2.

19. A more detailed account is given in the *Vancouver Sun*, April 15, 1985.

20. For a more detailed account see the *Vancouver Sun*, January 13, 1993, p. A3.

21. For a more detailed account see *The Lawyers Weekly*, June 24, 1994, p. 7.

22. A more detailed account is given *The Globe and Mail*, August 11, 1992, p. A2.

23. For a more detailed account see *The Province*, September 9, 1994, p. A22.

24. See *Vinthers v. Dumont*, British Columbia Supreme Court, http://www.courts.gov.bc.ca/.

25. For an account of the match, the bite, and subsequent events, see *Newsweek*, July 14, 1997, p. 58.

26. *National*, July, 1988.

27. For a more detailed report see *The Globe and Mail*, October 8, 1997, p. 1. Its article ends with a referral to the Bre-X web site for the executive summary of the FIA report: www.bre-x.com. For the estimate of $6 billion and the status of investor actions see *The Lawyers Weekly*, October 10, 1997.

28. For a more detailed account see *The Globe and Mail*, January 17, 1998, p. A8. Subsequently Eagleson, faced with the possibility of expulsion, resigned from Canada's Hockey Hall of Fame. See *The Globe and Mail*, March 26, 1998, p. A15.

29. For a more detailed account see the *Vancouver Sun*, October 5, 1994, p. D1, in which it was also reported that British investors won a lawsuit against Lloyd agencies on the basis of negligence and the award of damages, perhaps as much as $1 billion Canadian, may be the largest award in British history.

30. *Datamation*, 1983.

31. A more detailed account is given in *Newsweek*.

32. A more detailed account is given in *The Lawyers Weekly*, December 17, 1993, p. 14.

33. For a detailed account see the *Vancouver Sun*, January 6, 1997, p. 1. It was reported in *The Globe and Mail*, October 8, 1997, p. 1 that the amount that was settled by binding arbitration was $2,006,508 plus interest.

34. *The Globe and Mail*, November 5, 1992, p. A13.

35. *The Globe and Mail*, February 9, 1993, pp. B1, 7.

36. For a more detailed account see *The Globe and Mail*, January 6, 1994, pp. 1, 2.

37. *Maclean's*, June 26, 1995, p. 19.

38. For a more detailed account, see *Newsweek*, April 29, 1996, p. 4.

39. *Ontario Lawyers Weekly*, September 6, 1985.

40. *Maclean's*, January 9, 1995, p. 63.

41. For more details see *The Lawyers Weekly*, July 11, 1997, p. 5 and July 18, 1997, p. 3.

42. For a more detailed account see *The Lawyers Weekly*.

43. For a more detailed account see *The Vancouver Sun*, April 13, 1994, p. 1.

44. For a more detailed account see *The Lawyers Weekly*, June 27, 1997, p. 24.

45. For a summary of *Gould Estate v. Stoddart Publishing Co. Ltd.* see *The Lawyers Weekly*, October 25, 1996, pp. 24, 30.

46. A more detailed account is given in the *Vancouver Sun*, July 5, 1993, p. 1.

47. For the story that would warm the heart of a lawyer see the *Vancouver Sun*, November 1, 1996, p. A12.

48. *The Lawyers Weekly*, March 8, 1990.

49. *Ontario Lawyers Weekly*.

50. A more detailed account is given in the *Vancouver Sun*.

51. See *The Lawyers Weekly*, September 16, 1994, p. 4.

52. A more detailed account is given in the *Vancouver Sun*, January 1985.

53. For a more detailed account see *The Globe and Mail*, September 2, 1994, pp. B1, B15.

54. For a more detailed account see the *Vancouver Sun*, February 2, 1994, A6.

55. For the full story see the article on *Nespolon v. Alford* in *The Lawyers Weekly*, July 7, 1995, p. 12.

56. See *Arnault v. The Board of Police Commissioners of the City of Prince Albert et al.*, Case No. Q.B. No. 356, September 25, 1995.

57. If you have the heart for a very tragic tale see *Molnar v. Her Majesty the Queen in Right of the Province of British Columbia*, Vancouver Registry CA015514, June 24, 1993.

58. See *The Lawyers Weekly*, April 21, 1981, p. 20.

59. See *The Lawyers Weekly*, May 4, 1990.

60. See *Britt v. Zagio Holdings Ltd.*, Ontario Court of Justice (General Division) [1996] O.J. No. 1014 (Q.L.) DRS 96-08791 File No. 12941/92 February 23, 1996.

61. See *Fagnan v. Monaghan*, Court of Queen's Bench of Manitoba, Suit No.: CI 93-01-70599, September 15, 1995.

62. For a more detailed account see *The Lawyers Weekly*, June 28, 1996, p. 3.

III

THE LAW OF CONTRACT

A. Freedom of Contract

Question

What kind of deals are we allowed to make?

- *J*apan's Mitsui Real Estate Ltd. learned through its agent that the asking price for the Exxon Building in New York was $375 million. The agent advised Mitsui that Exxon would probably take less. Mitsui instructed its agent to offer $610 million. The agent tried to dissuade it. Lawyers acting for Exxon did not want to accept it; $375 million would be sufficient. Eventually the $610 million offer was formally made and accepted. Why did Mitsui pay $235 million over the asking price? To break the record in the *Guinness Book of World Records* of the top price ever paid for a single building.[1]

- *T*he rock group Guns N' Roses insists that reporters and photographers sign a contract which provides that the interviewer must "acknowledge that [the band] shall own all right, title and interest, including, without limitation, the copyright, in and to the interview and all transcriptions or summaries thereof ..." and that the interviewer be considered an employee. Furthermore, the interview had to be submitted to the band for its written approval which could be withheld for any reason. The contract stipulates that any party in breach of the agreement will pay them $100,000 as damages.[2]

- *W*orldCom Inc.'s bid of $29.4 billion (U.S.) to takeover MCI Communications Corp. was referred to as "stunning".[3] Apparently it wasn't sufficient. The deal was struck at $37 billion — "the most expensive takeover in corporate history." The merger helps create a global network for providing a wide range of services including the provision of local and long distance service and access to the Internet.[4]

B. Formation of Contracts

Question

A contract is often defined as an agreement the law will enforce, but that is not too helpful. What elements in particular must be present before the law will enforce an agreement?

---

1. GENERAL DUTY OF GOOD FAITH

In 1967, Gateway Realty Ltd. (Gateway), the owner of a shopping centre, rented space to Zellers, a retail chain. The lease gave Zellers the right to assign or sublet. The store was successful with annual sales over $14 million by the late 1980s. Mr. Hurst, the owner of a rival shopping centre, Bridgewater Mall, persuaded Zellers to leave those premises and to open a store in the new mall. Zellers did and assigned the remainder of its lease in the shopping centre to another of Mr. Hurst's companies, Arton Holdings and LaHave Developments (Arton). When Gateway Realty learned that its lessee had assigned its premises to its competitor it met with Hurst; Arton signed an agreement to use its best efforts to lease the space to suitable tenants. Gateway received inquiries about the space, but despite notices to Arton from Gateway, Arton did not follow up on any leads. Gateway took possession and eventually leased the space to K-mart.

Gateway took an action against Arton for a declaration that Zeller's assignment to Arton was invalid because Zellers had breached its duty of good faith by assigning the remainder of the lease to Gateway's main competitor; or a declaration that Gateway was entitled to terminate the lease with Arton because it had breached its duty of good faith to find a suitable replacement tenant. Arton defended by relying on the lease, which gave an unrestricted right to assign and by claiming that, in Canada, there was no duty of good faith in the performance of contracts. Justice Kelly of the N.S.S.C. found that "the law requires that parties to a contract exercise their rights under the agreement honestly fairly and in good faith." The duty is breached if a party acts contrary to community standards of honesty, reasonableness or fairness.

On the evidence of Arton's actions, the judge concluded there was a breach of its duty of good faith and that the breach was serious enough to allow Gateway the right to terminate the lease. As an alternative reason for his decision, the Judge found that Gateway's agreement with Arton was an amendment to the Zellers lease, and that agreement was breached in such a way to justify Gateway's termination of the lease. He issued the declaration that the leasehold interest of Arton was terminated.

Gateway Realty Ltd. v. Arton Holding Ltd.
N.S.S.C.
Summarized from The Lawyers Weekly
October 4, 1991 p. 1

Note: This decision was upheld by the Nova Scotia Court of Appeal. The court found that Gateway was justified in breaking the lease when its competitor failed to find a replacement, but the court did not comment on the trial judge's finding about a general duty of good faith.[5]

Smilestone, the defendant, decided to retire from his business of selling homeowner mortgages. Dudka, the plaintiff, contracted to buy the business. The contract provided that Dudka would not become the owner of the company until the remaining mortgages, 11 in all, were sold by Dudka; each of the sales would require the approval of the defendant Smilestone. Smilestone approved nine but within weeks of the anticipated transfer, he refused to approve the sale of the last two mortgages. Smilestone refused to transfer the business on the grounds that Dudka breached the agreement by not selling the last two mortgages. The plaintiff maintained that Smilestone refused to approve the mortgages for a personal reason, to secure a position for his son who was appointed as the operating manager. The following are excerpts from Justice Kelly.

When one party to a contract has a discretionary power which might prevent the other party from completing performance, that discretion must be exercised in good faith. The party with the discretionary power must not be in a position to frustrate the contract for "bad faith" reasons. ...

[He reviews the case law] The common core of all of these examples is that if one party had explicitly reserved in the contract the "right" to exercise its discretion, even when such phrases as "its sole discretion" are used, the courts have held that this does not mean absolute discretion, but that the discretion must be exercised reasonably, honestly, and in good faith, and further that the assessment of such discretionary power should be an objective one.

A party breaches its obligation to act in good faith if, without reasonable justification, the party acts in relation to the contract in a manner which substantially nullifies the bargained for benefits or defeats legitimate expectations of the other party. The imposition of a doctrine of good faith was recommended by the Ontario Law Reform Commission (Report on Amendment of the Law of Contract (1987), p. 166). Since *Gateway v. Arton, supra,* courts in Australia and New Zealand have separately affirmed the doctrine in their jurisdictions. …

[Smilestone] could not void the contract merely by saying he was not going to approve, or that he was going to withdraw his approval, of the two mortgages and then complain that Mr. Dudka had not performed his obligations under the contract to fully sell the mortgage portfolio. …

I conclude from an objective inquiry into the state of mind of Mr. Smilestone that he acted in bad faith … and that the contract should have been completed.

He held Smilestone in breach of contract and seems to have added in the alternative that Dudka had substantially performed his contractual obligations; his failure to assign the mortgages was not a substantial breach ending the contract. He awarded Dudka $25,000 for the loss of the goodwill he would have obtained if the contract would have been honoured by Smilestone.

Dudka v. Smilestone
[1994] N.S.J. No. 187 (Q.L.)
Action S.H. No. 79893
Nova Scotia Supreme Court
April 22, 1994

---

2. OFFER AND ACCEPTANCE

Question

Are all the essential terms of the bargain included and unambiguous?

SALE OF LAND—Certainty of Terms - Mortgage-Back—The plaintiff sought an order of specific performance of an agreement of purchase and sale of property. The financing was to be payable by: "a morgage (sic) of thirty-two thousand dollars to be paid at ten and one half percent interest for a two year morgage (sic) ammortise (sic) over twenty years Plus a two year additional morgage (sic) option (same) Payment to start on January forth (sic) 1984." Cooper L.J.S.C. held that this memorandum was so unclear as to essential terms to be included in the mortgage as to render the agreement unenforceable at law. It did not say how the interest was to be calculated, how and when the mortgage payments were to be made, whether monthly, quarterly, or otherwise. See *Arnold Nemetz Engineering Ltd. v. Tobien,* (1971) 4 W.W.R. 373 (B.C.C.A.). Here, the absence of essential terms as to the manner of calculating interest and payment of the proposed mortgage rendered the agreement uncertain whether the parties were ad idem on all essential terms in order to make the agreement binding and enforceable in law.

> ### Cooper v. Hawes
> *Rossland Registry N. SC 59-1984,*
> *January 6, 1986*
> *Reprinted with permission from* The Advocate *(published by the Vancouver Bar Association), Volume*
> *44, (1986), Part 6, page 922*

- *I*n Louisiana, Ms. Linda Blow sued Jimmy Swaggart, televangelist, in small claims court for the return of her payment of $500. She claims she sent the $500 to the Swaggart Ministries because Mr. Swaggart, in an appearance in December of 1985, said the unsaved could be saved by sending money to the Swaggart Ministries and she wanted her family to change its ways and be saved. After a year had passed and her family had not changed its ways she asked for a refund of the $500.

Question

What test does the court apply to determine if there has been an offer and acceptance?

Campbell v. Sooter Studios Ltd.

MANITOBA QUEEN'S BENCH
AUGUST 22, 1989
UNREPORTED

Summary of the facts: The lease between the plaintiff lessor and the defendant lessee expired on June 30, 1987. After that date, the lessor sent over a draft of a new lease which provided for a significant increase in the rent and for a three-year term commencing July 1, 1987 and ending June 30, 1990. The president of Sooter Studios, the lessee, not satisfied with the document, altered the term of the lease to make it a one-year lease ending June 30, 1988, and changed the rent. He then signed it and sent it back to the lessor with no letter or conversation indicating that the terms were changed. The lessor signed it without noticing the alterations, sent it back to the lessee for affixation of the corporate seal. The lessee did affix the seal and returned the lease to the lessor.

The lessor then noticed the changes and argued that there was no new lease; that the lessee should give up possession or pay double rent as an overholding tenant. The lessee maintained there was a lease and it remained in possession until June 30, 1988.

The lessor sued for double rent, for the cost of certain repairs, and for a share of realty taxes.

Jewers, J. ... Counsel for the plaintiffs submitted that there was no concluded contract of lease between the parties...that the plaintiffs were never aware of the alterations made to the draft lease by the defendant, and that there was, therefore, never a true meeting of minds between the parties.

In *Chitty on Contracts* 25th Ed. p. 25 it is stated:

The normal test for determining whether the parties have reached agreement is to ask whether an offer has been made by one party and accepted by the other. In answering this question, the courts apply an objective test: if the parties have to all outward appearances agreed in the same terms upon the same subject-matter neither can generally deny that he intended to agree. Hence an unexpressed qualification or reservation on the part of one party to an apparent agreement will not normally prevent the formation of a contract. The theory, popular

in England in the nineteenth century, that there can be no contract without a meeting of the minds of the parties, has been largely discredited as it would tend to produce commercially inconvenient results.

The question then is: objectively considered, was there an accepted offer? In my opinion, there was. The original offer was, of course, the draft lease prepared and sent by the plaintiffs to the defendant; this offer was not accepted; the defendant made a counter offer by altering some of the essential terms of the lease, signing the document and then resubmitting it to the plaintiffs for their consideration; the plaintiffs then (objectively at least) accepted the counter offer by executing the lease and returning it to the defendant so that the defendant's seal could be affixed; the contract was finally concluded when the defendant affixed the seal and sent the lease back to the plaintiffs. The defendant had no way of knowing and did not know that the plaintiffs had not noticed the alterations and had not assented to them. The plaintiffs had not agreed to the alterations, but, to all outward appearances, they had. They had signed the document after it had been altered by the defendant and had returned it to the defendant without comment or dissent, except to ask that the defendant's corporate seal be affixed. Subjectively, there was no true meeting of minds, but objectively there was and that is the test. ...

I therefore hold that the defendant did enter into a valid and binding lease of the premises expiring on June 30th, 1988: that the defendant was not an overholding tenant; and that the plaintiffs are not entitled to charge double rent.

[The judge awarded the plaintiffs an amount for a share of the taxes and the cost of repairs to a plate glass window.]

The plaintiffs have been partially successful, but the greater victor has been the defendant. ...

When Alan Eagleson was acting as the executive director of the National Hockey League Players' Association his company Rae-Con represented Michael Gillis. In 1984, Gillis, playing with the Boston Bruins, fractured his right ankle. Eagleson was instrumental in obtaining a settlement between Gillis and the insurer Lloyd's of London. Eagleson, through Rae-Con, sent Gillis a bill for $41,250 U.S. Gillis paid it but he thought the work was done by Eagleson as director of the NHLPA; Eagleson maintained he acted as the lawyer for Gillis and that was the agreed on fee. Justice O'Brien of the Ontario Court (General Division) found there was no fee arrangement between Eagleson and Gillis and ordered the return of the money.

Gillis v. Eagleson
Ontario Court (G.D.)
Summarized from The Lawyers Weekly
January 10, 1997 p. 2

A Toronto film-maker Brigitte Berman, made a documentary about the life of the musician Artie Shaw with the approval of Shaw himself. He wrote a memo "To Whom it May Concern" to indicate that the film was being done "with my cooperation and under my authorization." He also wrote to Ms. Berman indicating which of his music could be used in the film and on what conditions.

Berman worked on the film from the spring of 1982 to the fall of 1984. She raised all the necessary funding — $255,000.

In March, 1997 Berman's "labour of love" won an Academy Award for Best Feature Documentary for 1986.

Subsequently, Shaw had some telephone conversations with Berman who later received a letter from Shaw's lawyer which included the following: "This letter confirms that Artie Shaw has a 35% profit participation in the motion picture." The matter went to court.

The following are excerpts from the judgment:

"It is not disputed that Berman at no time acknowledged any obligation to share profits with Shaw, who admits that the figure of 35% was what he unilaterally considered reasonable. Up to the time that letter was written, Shaw's claim to share in the profit from the film was based on the contention that he would have included such a provision in the agreement if he had anticipated that the film would be exploited commercially, or if he had believed that Berman had even considered such a possibility. Since he did not allege a promise by Berman to not exploit the film commercially, the inevitable conclusion from his testimony is that the reason the film would not be commercially exploited was that it had no commercial value. That the film has earned approximately $145,000 during a nine-year period while its production costs, excluding Berman's salary, are approximately $255,000 may speak mountains about the prescience of both parties. The transmission of this financial information by Berman to Shaw might have nipped this lawsuit in the bud. It is clear that the predominant purpose of this film was a celebration of Shaw's life, which was, by any standard, remarkable. ...

The oral communications between the parties after August 15, 1984, [the letter regarding the music] and the letter from Shaw's counsel on November 15, 1987, purporting to "confirm" that

Shaw had a 35% profit participation in the film cannot, by any canon of construction, be deemed to constitute an agreement of any sort. In fact, Shaw has not even attempted to persuade the court that such an agreement exists. ...

... The action is dismissed. with costs ...

Shaw v. Berman
[1997] O.J. No. 829 (Q.L.)
Court File No. 45222/90
Ontario Court of Justice (General Division)
March 3, 1997

COUNTER OFFER

Question

What is the effect on the offer if the offeree makes a counter offer?

Hyde v. Wrench

1840 49 E.R. 132

The Defendant being desirous of disposing of an estate, offered, by his agent to sell it to the Plaintiff for £1200, which the Plaintiff, by his agent, declined: and on the 6th of June the Defendant wrote to his agent as follows:—"I have to notice the refusal of your friend to give me £1200 for my farm; I will only make one more offer, which I shall not alter from; that is, £1000 lodged in the bank until Michaelmas, when the title shall be made clear of expenses, land tax, &c. I expect a reply by return, as I have another application." This letter was forwarded to the Plaintiff's agent, who immediately called on the Defendant; and, previously to accepting the offer, offered to give the Defendant £950 for the purchase of the farm, but the Defendant wished to have a few days to consider.

On the 11th of June the Defendant wrote to the Plaintiff's agent as follows:—"I have written to my tenant for an answer to certain enquiries, and, the instant I receive his reply, will communicate with you, and endeavour to conclude the prospective purchase of my farm; I assure you I am not treating with any other person about said purchase."

The Defendant afterwards promised he would give an answer about accepting the £950 for the purchase on the 26th of June; and on the 27th he wrote to the Plaintiff's agent, stating he was sorry he could not feel disposed to accept his offer for his farm at Luddenham at present.

This letter being received on the 29th of June, the Plaintiff's agent on that day wrote to the Defendant as follows:—"I beg to acknowledge the receipt of your letter of the 27th instant, informing me that you are not disposed to accept the sum of £950 for your farm at [336] Luddenham. This being the case, I at once agree to the terms on which you offered the farm, viz., £1000 through your tenant Mr. Kent, by your letter of the 6th instant. I shall be obliged by your instructing your solicitor to communicate with me without delay, as to the title, for the reason which I mentioned to you."

[The defendant vendor alleged there was no contract. The plaintiff said there was a contract and] charged that the Defendant's offer for sale had not been withdrawn previous to its acceptance. ...

Mr. Kindersley and Mr. Keene, in support [of the defendant vendor] . ... To constitute a valid agreement there must be a simple acceptance of the terms proposed. *Holland v. Eyre* (2 Sim. & St. 194). The Plaintiff, instead of accepting the alleged proposal for sale for £1000 on the 6th of June rejected it, and made a counter proposal; this put an end to the Defendant's offer, and left the proposal of the Plaintiff alone under discussion; that has never been accepted, and the Plaintiff could not, without the concurrence of the Defendant, revive the Defendant's original proposal.

Mr. Pemberton and Mr. Freeling, *contra*. So long as the offer of the Defendant subsisted, it was competent to the Plaintiff to accept it; the bill charges that the Defendant's offer had not been withdrawn previous to its acceptance by the Plaintiff; there, therefore, exists a valid subsisting contract. *Kenney v. Lee* (3 Mer. 454), *Johnson v. King* (2 Bing. 270), were cited. ...

[337] The Master of the Rolls [Lord Langdale]... I think there exists no valid binding contract between the parties for the purchase of the property. The Defendant offered to sell it for £1000, and if that had been at once unconditionally accepted, there would undoubtedly have been a perfect binding contract; instead of that, the Plaintiff made an offer of his own, to purchase the property for £950, and he thereby rejected the offer previously made by the Defendant. I think that it was not afterwards competent for him to revive the proposal of the Defendant, by tendering an acceptance of it; and that, therefore, there exists no obligation of any sort between the parties. ...

REVOCATION OF OFFER

Q u e s t i o n

When is the revocation of an offer effective?

Mlodinska et al. *v.* Malicki et al.

60 O.R. (2D) 180
ONT. HIGH COURT OF JUSTICE, DIVISIONAL COURT
JANUARY 26, 1988

Hughes J. (orally):—The order in appeal was made by the Honourable Mr. Justice O'Brien in the course of a case involving a will. It discloses an interesting confrontation having occurred in court in the absence of the learned judge in which the validity of a withdrawal of an offer to settle is in question, and I cannot improve of his concise account in describing what happened.

He says:

The settlement now in issue occurred following a discussion between counsel. While there is no complete agreement on the facts occurring in court, there is so little difference in the position of counsel I propose to deal with the matter now rather than direct a trial of an issue on that point. I am reluctant to do anything which would increase the expense to the parties.

It appears there had been offers of settlement made by both sides. The defence made one offer on April 2, 1987, which had not formally been withdrawn. There had been a counter-offer from the plaintiff for a larger amount. A further offer had been made by the defence increasing their prior offer but containing a provision that the offer terminated one hour before the trial commenced.

During an intermission of trial counsel for the defendants obtained further instructions from his client. Pursuant to those instructions, he wrote a formal notice indicating any offer of settlement had been withdrawn and formally withdrawing the offer of April 2, 1987.

He walked into the court-room indicating with thumb and forefinger the gesture of a zero, said words to the effect "Now, it's zero," took a few steps to counsel table, where plaintiffs' counsel was sitting, and handed to him the handwritten notice. As he did so, plaintiffs' counsel handed him a typewritten notice purporting to accept the offer April 2, 1987.

The position of counsel for the defence is, while there may have been a very short period of time between his action and that of plaintiff's counsel, there was a time differential, and counsel's position is "first in time, first in right" and the defendants' settlement offer was withdrawn prior to acceptance.

The position of counsel for the plaintiffs is that there has been ongoing settlement discussions, the gesture and statement made by defence counsel as he walked into the court-room was not unequivocal and the exchange of his acceptance and withdrawal was virtually simultaneous.

Plaintiff's counsel also urges it is unseemly to encourage "races" of this type between counsel during the course of a trial.

[I]n my view (and I am advised that my brother Austin will develop the point), [there was] an undisputed priority in time, however slight of the presentation of the withdrawal by counsel for the appellants before the handing over of the acceptance by counsel for the respondent.

Nonetheless, the learned judge came to the conclusion that because of the apparent unseemliness of this cut and thrust delivery of papers not, albeit, in his presence, and what Carruthers J. had to say about the policy of the rules being to prevent gamesmanship, that a settlement had been concluded, and he made an order to that effect … I am more concerned with an aspect other than seemliness involved in this matter, and that is the real purpose, I would have thought, of the rules, in respect of reaching a just result which, I believe, is to be found in rule 1.04(1).

It seems to me that, in addition to the question of who served first, there is an overriding concern of the court to effect that result, and that to impose a settlement upon a party who, when confronted with a counter-offer or a request to consider a higher offer, concluded that not only the existing one should be withdrawn, but none other substituted in its place. To hold on such tenuous grounds that a settlement had been made would, I think, be unfair to the defendants in the case and the appellants here, and produce an unjust result.

In response to the concern of O'Brien J. that he should be given some direction, I am of the opinion that his order should be set aside and that he should continue with the trial.

Austin J. (orally):—It was apparent that, by virtue of the matters set out in the reasons of my brothers, the learned trial judge was in a very difficult position. In his reasons he said:

It seems to me the purported acceptance and withdrawal were virtually simultaneous. I accept submissions of plaintiffs' counsel it is unseemly for courts to encourage the type of race which might result in gamesmanship in the exchange of paper during the course of trial.

I conclude, therefore, the settlement offer was accepted by the plaintiffs and this litigation is ended.

No one disputes the desirability of settlement. In reaching the result he did, however, the trial judge must have concluded either that the acceptance was given first, or that the exchange was for all intents and purposes simultaneous. In my view, neither conclusion is supported by the evidence.

Counsel for the plaintiffs conceded that counsel for the defendants, "put his piece of paper down on my book prior to me handing mine to him." Leaving aside completely the gesture and oral statement of counsel for the defendants, the uncontradicted evidence is that the defendants delivered their notice of withdrawal before the plaintiffs delivered their notice of acceptance.

The time lapse between the two events may have been very short. Counsel for the plaintiffs described it as a split second. Whatever the length of the period, the withdrawal was first and the acceptance second. In those circumstances it does not seem to me that any offer remained available for the plaintiffs to accept.

It appears that what led to the exchange was the request of counsel for the plaintiffs to counsel for the defendants that he ask his clients to consider increasing their offer. Counsel for the defendants acted on that request. Counsel for the plaintiffs knew, or should have known, that inherent in that exercise was a risk, some risk, that the outstanding offer would be withdrawn. If he was not prepared to run that risk he should not have initiated the exercise. As it was, the risk was realized.

As the evidence stands, it appears that in spite of having initiated the exercise, instead of waiting for the answer, he served or attempted to serve a notice of acceptance. In my view, there was nothing left to accept.

I would allow the appeal and set aside the order of O'Brien J., dated April 24, 1987.

Appeal allowed.

Note: An appeal to the Ontario Court of Appeal was abandoned; the parties settled out of court.

---

3. CONSIDERATION

Degoesbriand **v.** *Radford*

SASKATCHEWAN COURT OF APPEAL
SEPTEMBER 16, 1986
UNREPORTED

Gerwing, J.A. (Orally)

The appellant appeals from a judgment dismissing her claim against the respondent, a shareholder in the company by which she was formerly employed, for a declaration that she was entitled to 5% of the shares owned by him in that company, on the alternate basis of either contract or constructive trust. ...

The appellant had worked for two companies, in which the respondent was interested, between 1979 and 1982. She testified that the respondent had promised to give to her 5% of his shares in the business when he either sold out or retired. Although the respondent denied this the learned trial judge accepted that such promises were made. He said:

> I conclude after considering the testimony of the witnesses, and particularly the evidence of Mr. Wall and Mr. Thomson, that the defendant did indeed state to the plaintiff he would give her five per cent of the shares of the business he was then involved in at some time in the future. I am not satisfied, however, this statement occurred as often as the plaintiff claims and I cannot [accept] her evidence it was made within one week of her becoming employed by the defendant.

The learned trial judge also found that the appellant had worked in excess of reasonable overtime, but then quoted from her examination for discovery [in which she admitted she would have worked just as hard even if she had not been promised the five percent of the company.]

The learned trial judge concludes that the promise was made after the relationship of employer-employee was already in existence, and also that the promise was not made to induce the appellant to work extra overtime. He concludes that there was no action by the appellant in reliance on, or in consideration for this promise. He also found as a fact that the appellant did not intend any promise he made to create a legal obligation.

> This conclusion, however, falls short of holding a legally enforceable contract existed between the parties. The defendant on no occasion stated his promise was contingent on the plaintiff's continuing to work more than reasonable overtime nor did the plaintiff perform these duties as a result of the promise being made. It was only after their cordial relationship cooled, did the plaintiff claim the defendant was legally obliged to give her the shares in return for the hours of extra overtime she provided. The defendant may owe some moral obligation to the plaintiff, however, I am not satisfied the obligation arises from a contract between them.

On the facts as found by the learned trial judge, we are of the view that he was correct to dismiss the contractual claim. He found a bare promise by the respondent to the appellant, with no consideration requested or received by him from the appellant. The suggestion that in some way he made this conditional on performance of extra overtime by the appellant, and that performance of this overtime was a method of accepting this offer, was found by the learned trial judge to be only in the mind of the appellant, arising at a later time after the relationship had terminated.

Further, her services as an employee were already the subject of an employment contract which required her to work a reasonable amount of overtime. There was no evidence she did anything that she was not already contractually obliged to do, or that she was not prepared to do in any event, to do her job properly, in reliance on the promise of the respondent. There was nothing to provide consideration or raise the doctrine of estoppel, and the bare promise remained just that and was unenforceable as a contract. In light of the lack of consideration, it is not necessary to comment on the question of lack of congruence between the offer and acceptance or the question of intention to create a contract.

… In the result, the appeal is dismissed with costs. …

After having worked for the defendant company for about 20 years, the employee, Watson, was asked to sign an agreement which, in effect, reduced her rights. It provided that her employment could be terminated without cause on notice or in lieu of notice, payment of the minimum required under the Employment Standards Act plus one week's salary for every two years of completed service. Five years later, in 1993, she was dismissed without cause and offered 20 weeks' pay in lieu of notice. The employee took an action claiming she was entitled to reasonable notice under the common law and that the signed agreement was of no effect because there had been no consideration flowing to her in exchange for her giving up her common law right. The trial judge held that the consideration given was her "continued employment."

The appeal court held, in a 2-1 split, that continued employment, without something more, is not good consideration. The following are excerpts from the reasons of Chief Justice McEachern, speaking for the majority:

"Consideration

[15] Cases about consideration are no longer common although the recent decision of this court in *Canada West Tree Fruits Ltd. v. T.G. Bright & Co.* (1990), 48 B.C.L.R. (2d) 91 (C.A.) demonstrates that it is still very much a part of our law. The plaintiff in her factum, quoting Fridman, *The Law of Contract*, 3rd ed. (Toronto: Carswell, 1994) pp. 81–2, has provided a useful reminder of what consideration is:

> A contract consists of an exchange of promises, acts, or acts and promises, as a result of which each side receives something from the other. The attempt was made by Lord Mansfield in the eighteenth century to allow valid contracts to be based upon moral obligation, or to be entirely gratuitous. But in the nineteenth century it was held that there had to be some material advantage passing to or promised by one party before a promise given in exchange could be regarded as a contract. There is no doubt that this doctrine is now firmly established in Canadian law as well as English. If there is no consideration there is no contract; and if there is no contract, there is nothing upon or from which to found or create liability. …

[28] There are difficulties with finding that continued employment alone constituted consideration in this case. The plaintiff was already employed and remained employed throughout the relevant period. Unless it can be said that the defendant forbeared discharging her, nothing of value flowed from the defendant to the plaintiff. …

[30] In this case, the provision in issue relates directly to the company's ability to terminate the employee's employment without cause. It cannot be seriously contended that continuation of the plaintiff's existing employment, without more, was consideration for her agreement that she could be discharged without cause with less notice or pay in lieu thereof than she was already entitled to receive.

[31] It follows, in my view, that consideration for the plaintiff's employment contracts cannot be found just in the normal continuation of her existing employment.

Consideration by forbearing to dismiss the plaintiff

[32] … In order to demonstrate forbearance in the context of employment contracts, in my view, an employer must show that it intended to dismiss its employee if he or she refused to sign an employment contract. …

[35] In my judgment, no effective forbearance was proven in the case at bar. ...

[37] The only evidence of anything approaching forbearance on the part of the defendant in this case is its subjective assertion, unexpressed until there was litigation, that the agreement was "required as a condition of continued employment." The plaintiff was not given any specific indication that she would be dismissed if she did not sign. While she and others assumed she might be dismissed if she did not sign, they were merely speculating; indeed, her subjective assumptions would seem to be irrelevant as the consideration must flow from the defendant. In this case, the defendant's officers do not even say now that they would have dismissed the plaintiff if she had declined to sign. It is conjecture what the defendant would have done if the plaintiff had, for example, merely placed the agreement in her file and forgot about it. ...

[42] With respect, it is too easy for the employer to say nothing at the time, and then expect the court to find that this employee would have been dismissed had she not signed the agreement. In *Hollis v. Dow Corning Corp. et al.*, ... Sopinka J. warned of the dangers of accepting self-serving reconstructions of what parties say they would have done at an earlier time, and this is especially so when what they later say is essential to success at trial.

[43] Second, the defendant's position must be that the forbearance consisted in not dismissing the plaintiff prior to her signing and returning the agreement. On the evidence, however, the defendant clearly had no intention of dismissing the plaintiff before that time. On that basis, as the plaintiff signed the agreement, there was no reason at any time for the defendant to discharge the plaintiff, or to forbear doing so.

[44] Counsel argues, however, on the authority of *Alliance*, that the defendant had the right all along to give notice of termination, and that not having done so constituted forbearance which provided consideration for the agreements the plaintiff signed.

[45] With respect, I cannot accept that submission. In my view, it would be excessive and impermissible sophistry to conclude that the defendant furnished consideration to the plaintiff whom it had offered a contract of employment, by refraining from discharging her.

[46] I must accordingly conclude that there was no consideration for the 1987 and 1989 agreements.

Damages

[48] ... Having regard to the authorities and the factors I have mentioned, I would fix the reasonable [notice] period in this case at 18 months. I agree with Mr. Wiebach that the plaintiff's damages should be calculated on the basis of average earnings over the last two years of her employment.

[49] If the parties cannot agree on what the plaintiff should also receive for benefits, they may submit detailed memoranda.

Appeal allowed.

Watson v. Moore Corp.
Vancouver Registry CA019382
http://www.courts.gov. bc.ca/
Court of Appeal for British Columbia
March 14, 1996

Note: As of mid-August, 1997 this case had not been appealed.

- *A* woman in Kansas was charged with "criminal solicitation to commit murder." In exchange for the killing of her common-law husband she offered to give the killers his baseball card collection. She gave them ten cards as a down payment.[6]

• *A*n amendment was proposed to the *NWT Maintenance Act*, which would have allowed court-ordered support payments to be paid in caribou, seal or other take from hunting and fishing to reflect the fact that these "traditional currencies" are more in keeping with an economy not based on cash.[7]

PROMISSORY ESTOPPEL

Central London Property Trust Limited *v.* High Trees House Limited

[1947] 1 K.B. 130

Denning J.

By a lease under seal made on September 24, 1937, the plaintiffs, Central London Property Trust Ld., granted to the defendants, High Trees House Ld., a subsidiary of the plaintiff company, a tenancy of a block of flats for the term of ninety-nine years from September 29, 1937, at a ground rent of £2,500 a year. The block of flats was a new one and had not been fully occupied at the beginning of the war owing to the absence of people from London. With war conditions prevailing, it was apparent to those responsible that the rent reserved under the lease could not be paid out of the profits of the flats and, accordingly, discussion took place between the directors of the two companies concerned, which were closely associated, and an arrangement was made between them which was put into writings. On January 3, 1940, the plaintiffs wrote to the defendants in these terms, "we confirm the arrangement made between us by which the ground rent should be reduced as from the commencement of the lease to £1,250 per annum," and on April 2, 1940, a confirmatory resolution to the same effect was passed by the plaintiff company. On March 20, 1941, a receiver was appointed by the debenture holders of the plaintiffs and on his death on February 28, 1944, his place was taken by his partner. The defendants paid the reduced rent from 1941 down to the beginning of 1945 by which time all the flats in the block were fully let, and continued to pay it thereafter. In September, 1945, the then receiver of the plaintiff company looked into the matter of the lease and ascertained that the rent actually reserved by it was £2,500. On September 21, 1945, he wrote to the defendants saying that rent must be paid at the full rate and claiming that arrears amounting to £7,916 were due. Subsequently, he instituted the present friendly proceedings to test the legal position in regard to the rate at which rent was payable. In the action the plaintiffs sought to recover £625, being the amount represented by the difference between rent at the rate of £2,500 and £1,250 per annum for the quarters ending September 29, and December 25, 1945. … [Accepting that the lessors promised to forgive half the rent during the war years, the court considers whether] they had waived their rights in respect of any rent, in excess of that at the rate of 1,250£, which had accrued up to September 24, 1945. …

There has been a series of decisions over the last fifty years which, although they are said to be cases of estoppel are not really such. In each case the court held the promise to be binding on the party making it, even though under the old common law it might be difficult to find any consideration for it. The courts have not gone so far as to give a cause of action in damages for the breach of such a promise, but they have refused to allow the party making it to act inconsistently with it. It is in that sense, and that sense only, that such a promise gives rise to an estoppel. The decisions are a natural result of the fusion of law and equity: for the cases of *Hughes v. Metropolitan Ry. Co.* (6) *Birmingham and District Land Co. v. London & Northwestern Ry. Co.* (7) and *Salisbury (Marquess) v. Gilmore* (8), afford a sufficient basis for saying that a party would not be allowed in equity to go back on such a promise. In my opinion, the time has now come for the validity of such a promise to be recognized. The logical consequence, no doubt is that a promise to accept a smaller sum in discharge of a larger sum, if acted upon, is binding notwithstanding the absence of consideration: and if the fusion of law and equity leads to this result, so much the better. That aspect was not considered in *Foakes v. Beer* (1). At this time of day however, when law and equity have been joined together for over seventy years, principles must be reconsidered in the light of their combined effect. It is to be noticed that in the Sixth Interim Report of the Law Revision Committee, pars. 35, 40, it is recommended that such a promise as that to which I have referred, should be enforceable in law even though no consideration for it has been given by the promisee. I seems to me that, to the extent I have mentioned, that result has now been achieved by the decisions of the courts.

I am satisfied that a promise such as that to which I have referred is binding and the only question remaining for my consideration is the scope of the promise in the present case. …

I prefer to apply the principle that a promise intended to be binding, intended to be acted on and in fact acted on, is binding so far as its terms properly apply. Here it was binding as covering the period down to the early part of 1945, and as from that time full rent is payable.

Judgment for plaintiffs.

Note: Judgment is for full rent from early 1945 but not for the rent forgiven during the war years.

In a dispute about the amount of the bill and the time for payment, the court found as a fact that the intention of the parties was that the debtor would pay interest on unpaid accounts and that amounts would be due and owing upon receipt of periodic invoices. However, because the creditor drafted and accepted from the debtor a promissory note for $30,934.65 "together with interest at the rate of Nil (0)% per annum," he could not later demand interest. "The plaintiff accepted a note at nil interest. Having done so, it cannot now claim interest."

Chandler Moore v. Jacques
[1997] N.S.J. No. 330 (Q.L.)
S.H. No. 124840
Nova Scotia Supreme Court
July 18, 1997

4. CAPACITY

Re Collins

SUPREME COURT OF BRITISH COLUMBIA
VANCOUVER REGISTRY # A913069
OCTOBER 21, 1991

Holmes, J. The Petitioner Andrea Collins ("Ms. Collins") is the mother of the Petitioner [S.] Collins, an infant aged 15. S and his sister [J] Collins, 19 years of age, are parties to a contract dated December 11, 1989 with Ms. Collins the subject matter of which involves the infants interest in a residential property in Vancouver which is owned by a trust created irrevocably by their father Philip Collins. The contract was unenforceable from inception as both S and J (collectively hereafter referred to as "the children") were minors at that date. A letter of August 9, 1991 purportedly affirming the contract and stated to be pursuant to Section 16.2 (1) (b) of the *Infants Act* was signed by J the day after she reached the age of majority. As S remains an infant the contract is unenforceable against him and the purpose of the Petition is to make the contract enforceable by obtaining an Order under Section 16.4 (1) (b) of the *Infants Act* granting to S: "capacity to enter into a contract. ...specified in the order."

Counsel for Philip Collins and the Public Trustee both are opposed to the Court granting the Order. ...

THE FACTS:

Ms. Collins married Philip Collins in England in September 1975, they separated in 1979, and were divorced in August 1980. ...As a consequence of her divorce from Philip Collins the Petitioner received a lump sum settlement of £100,000 and spousal support of £8,000 per annum. ...Ms. Collins wished to move to Vancouver. ... The cost of houses the Petitioner considered suitable were beyond her means and she was " ... also concerned about the lack of financial security afforded her by the terms of the previous Orders." Discussions ensued with Philip Collins regarding his possible contribution towards the purchase of a residential property. The Petitioner located a suitable house and Philip Collins paid the $750,000 purchase price and created an irrevocable trust

"Collins Children's Trust" to hold title with the Canada Trust Company as Trustee. The purpose of the Trust was to provide a home for J, S and Ms. Collins until S (the youngest child) reached age 20 at which time S and J would receive the property absolutely as tenants in common. Ms. Collins signed a License Agreement requiring her to pay property taxes and cost of maintenance repairs.

... Ms. Collins and the children moved into the house in September 1987 and Ms. Collins remains unhappy about what she considers was a misunderstanding as to the ownership interest she felt was promised in the house. ... The unhappiness and insecurity of Ms. Collins in respect of the property became known to J and S. I am uncertain precisely how that occurred but assume she told them and the three of them discussed the matter. ... [After visiting both a psychologist who assessed the children's' state of mind and a lawyer, the children signed the contract.]

The contract of December 11, 1989 provides that the children transfer their beneficial interest in the Collins Children's Trust to Ms. Collins when their interest vests. In return Ms. Collins agrees to provide financial support for their reasonable maintenance, care, education and benefit until they are age 25. ... Ms. Collins also agrees to create a trust in favour of the children which will see the property, or its remainder, returned to them if she should remarry or die. Ms. Collins is Trustee under the Agreement with extremely wide and unfettered powers, including a power:

3.01 (b) "until the Material DATE (her death or remarriage)...in her absolute discretion, encroach upon the capital of the Trust Property and pay or transfer any amount or amounts of the capital...to or for the benefit of Andrea Collins...as the Trustee, in her absolute discretion, shall determine.

(c) Notwithstanding the generality of clause 3.01 (b), the Trustee may encroach upon the Trust Property to such an extent that the Trust Property is completely distributed and used up.

THE LAW

The relevant provision of the *Infants Act* is Section 16.4(1)(b) and (2):

The court may, on an application on behalf of an infant, make an order granting to the infant…capacity to enter into a contract…(but the Court must be) satisfied that it is for the benefit of the infant and that having regard to the circumstances of the infant, he is not in need of the protection offered by law to infants in matters relating to contracts.

It is obvious that the court's power is discretionary, but to grant the infant capacity to contract it is mandatory that:

(a) the contract be for his benefit, and
(b) considering the infant's circumstances does not need the protection accorded by the law to infants relating to contracts.

Counsel advised that they knew of no case law concerning this section which would be of assistance. Counsel also agree that the phrase "…for the benefit of the infant…" is to be given the same meaning at law as "…in the best interests of the infant…". Counsel for the Public Trustee argues there is a presumption in law that an infant is under the influence of a parent or guardian. I agree there is such a presumption however I concur with Petitioner's counsel that is a rebuttable presumption, and the opinion and evidence of Dr. Elterman [the psychologist] and Mr. Martin [the lawyer] supports the view there was no undue influence or pressure by Ms. Collins and both children fully understood the agreement and wished to enter into it.

I accept S is an intelligent young man who does understand the legal implication of his intended contract. He is not under direct compulsion, duress, or undue influence in respect of his agreement to sign. It is my view however that it was Ms. Collins who set a chain of events in motion by in some manner making it known to S and J how unhappy and insecure she felt because Philip Collins had not given her an ownership interest in the property. The inference has to be that in some manner the children received what she was promised and entitled to. I have no concern as to whether she is right in a moral context, I do have concern that the remedy for her insecurity has involved the children.

I view the contract of December 11, 1989 as a thinly disguised attempt to vary the trust set up by Philip Collins. … In my view the Court's discretionary power should not be exercised on a pretext of being for the benefit of the infants when in essence it is to have Ms. Collins achieve financial security.

The consequence of the agreement of December 11, 1989 is essentially that S would be giving up to Ms. Collins an interest in property which will vest in him within 5 years that has a present market value in excess of $700,000. Ms. Collins would have the ability to encroach upon that property for her exclusive benefit so there might be no reversion to him at all … In my view it is in the circumstances here insulting to suggest that this contract is of any financial benefit to S.

It is suggested that the emotional well being of S is best served by Ms. Collins being happy and secure, and that he genuinely wishes that to be so. I am sure that is true, as it would be in any family relationship. I cannot justify S giving away his interest in the trust to purchase that feeling of security for Ms. Collins. I see no benefit to S in the contract in question. I am of the opinion it is not in his best interest.

The decision to give up as substantial an asset as his interest in this trust is one to be reserved until he reaches the age of majority. Should he feel then, as he does now, he is free to make that gift. If his view, or the circumstances, change in the next five years he is not bound to an improvident contract.

The Petition is dismissed with costs. …

---

5. LEGALITY

Question

In what ways is a contract or a provision of a contract illegal?

A. *IF THE PURPOSE OF THE CONTRACT IS TO DEFRAUD*

Cerilli **v.** Klodt

(1984) 48 O.R. (2D) 260
ONTARIO HIGH COURT
OCTOBER 17, 1984

Southey J. (orally): — This is an action for specific performance of an agreement for the sale by the defendants to the plaintiff of a house property at 242 Ester St. in Sudbury, owned by the defendants as joint tenants.…

On [the] evidence, I find as a fact that the plaintiff Cerilli was party to a scheme with the male defendant Robert Klodt whereby a false price of $45,200 would be stated in the agreement of purchase and sale and other formal documents relating to the transaction so that the female defendant Sheila Klodt would be deceived into thinking that Mr. Cerilli was paying only $45,200. The balance of $4,800 was to be paid by the plaintiff directly to the male defendant without the knowledge of Mrs. Klodt, in the hope that Mr. Klodt could thereby avoid her obtaining any portion of that $4,800.

This scheme, in my judgment, was clearly fraudulent, and the result in law is that the agreement between the plaintiff and Robert Klodt is void and unenforceable in the courts. I think it is necessary to refer only to the passage from the decision of the Court of Appeal in England in *Alexander v. Rayson*, [1936] 1 K.B. 169, which was quoted and applied by the Supreme Court of Canada in *Zimmermann v. Letkeman*, [1978] 1 S.C.R. 1097 at p. 1101, 79 D.L.R. (3d) 508 at p. 519, [1977] 6 W.W.R. 741. Mr. Justice Martland, delivering the judgment of the court, quoted from the decision of Lord Justice Romer in the *Alexander v. Rayson* case as follows:

> It is settled law that an agreement to do an act that is illegal or immoral or contrary to public policy, or to do any act for a consideration that is illegal, immoral or contrary to public policy, is unlawful and therefore void. But it often happens that an agreement which in itself is not unlawful is made with the intention of one or both parties to make use of the subject matter for an unlawful purpose, that is to say a purpose that is illegal, immoral or contrary to public policy. The most common instance of this is an agreement for the sale or letting of an object, where the agreement is unobjectionable on the face of it, but where

the intention of both or one of the parties is that the object shall be used by the purchaser or hirer for an unlawful purpose. In such a case any party to the agreement who had the unlawful intention is precluded from suing upon it. *Ex turpi causa non oritur actio.** The action does not lie because the Court will not lend its help to such a plaintiff. Many instances of this are to be found in the books. ...

...[W]hen the fact that Mr. Cerilli had agreed to pay a total of $50,000 became known, Mrs. Klodt, through her solicitor, Mr. Rivard, confirmed that she was prepared to sell her one-half interest in the matrimonial home to Mr. Cerilli on a basis of a purchase price of $50,000. ...

It is clear from the authorities to which Mr. Humphrey referred, however, that the court is under an obligation to refuse to give effect to an illegal agreement whenever the illegality comes to the attention of the court, even though the parties do not raise it. See the judgment of Mr. Justice Krever in *Menard et al. v. Genereux et al.* (1982), 39 O.R. (2d) 55 at p. 64, 138 D.L.R. (3d) 273 at p. 283, where he quotes from a decision of the Court of Appeal of Saskatchewan in *Williams v. Fleetwood Holdings Ltd. et al.* (1973), 41 D.L.R. (3d) 636 at p. 640 [quoting from *Alexander v. Rayson, supra,* at p. 190]:

> The moment that the attention of the Court is drawn to the illegality attending the execution of the lease, it is bound to take notice of it, whether such illegality be pleaded or not. ...

Action dismissed.

*This clause means that from a base matter no action can arise.

Note: This case was affirmed by the Ontario Court of Appeal 55 O.R. (2d) 399n.

B.   *IF THE PERSON WAS ENGAGED IN AN ILLEGAL ACTIVITY*

Boyd **v.** *Newton*

NEW WESTMINSTER REGISTRY NO. C900402
SUPREME COURT OF BRITISH COLUMBIA
NOVEMBER, 1991

Selbie, J. (In Chambers) This action is for negligence in the operation of a motor-vehicle or, in the alternative, damages for assault and battery. I.C.B.C. applies under Rule 18A that the action be dismissed against it on the basis that the claim is barred by the application of the defense *ex turpi causa non oritur actio* [out of an illegal consideration no action can arise].

This action is about a drug "rip-off." The plaintiff, Boyd, was trafficking in marijuana at a local billiards arcade in Coquitlam. As usual, while waiting for buyers he was playing the video games. He had been there for about five hours. As well as selling the drug he was performing another function for other traffickers—"I just sit there and play video games all day and so people that deal dope up there used to put their drugs on top of the video games. So I got paid a gram for watching drugs." About nine o'clock a stranger approached him about buying some "grass." Boyd told him he had a gram

he could have and the price was settled at $10. The driver of the buyer's car was to pay. Boyd gave over the gram of marijuana and both proceeded outside to a car driven by the defendant Newton. The buyer entered the passenger's seat and Boyd approached the open driver's door to get his $10. He stood in the gap between the door and the car frame waiting for his money. Newton suddenly pushed Boyd away and tried to drive off. Boyd, for the purpose of detaining Newton and getting his money, grabbed Newton by his coat and then grabbed the door frame to keep his balance as the car was driven away. He suffered injuries as he was dragged down the street. In effect, in fighting over the closing of an illegal transaction, he was injured. ... This is not a situation, for instance, where, after a deal was closed, the car in leaving negligently ran over the trafficker's foot. There it could be argued that the injury had no causal connection with the drug deal and the maxim would, arguably, not apply. Here the injuries were directly caused by the action of Boyd in trying to detain Newton in order to complete the transaction.

"No Court will lend its aid to a man who founds his action upon an immoral or an illegal act"—Lord Mansfield in *Holman v. Johnson* (1775) 1 Cowp 342 as quoted by Gibbs JA in *Hall v. Hebert* B.C.C.A., (unreported), Vancouver Registry #CA010498, February 1, 1991. The principle is founded upon public policy.

Gibbs JA in *Hall v. Hebert* (supra), in discussing the maxim, said at p. 12 of the judgment:

> … the principle underlying *ex turpi causa* is not limited to circumstances where the injuries were sustained during the course of a joint criminal enterprise. The compass of the defence is much broader. It will be available wherever the conduct of the plaintiff giving rise to the claim is so tainted with criminality or culpable immorality that as a matter of public policy the court will not assist him to recover. The joint criminal enterprise ground is merely

an example, and perhaps the most common example, of public policy at work.

In the instant case the injuries *were* "sustained during the course of a joint criminal enterprise" and not "after" as is argued. This then is one of those common examples spoken of by his Lordship which give rise to the maxim as a defense.

Speaking of the doctrine of *ex turpi causa* Taylor J. (as he then was) in *Mack v. Enns* (1981) 30 B.C.L.R. 337 at 344 said:

> The purpose of the rule to-day must be to defend the integrity of the legal system, and the repute in which the court ought to be held by law-abiding members of the community. It is properly applied in those circumstances in which it would be manifestly unacceptable to fair-minded, or right-thinking, people that a court should lend assistance to a plaintiff who has defied the law.

It is proper to apply it here. The application of the Third Party, the Insurance Corporation of British Columbia, is allowed and the action is dismissed as against it.

- Mr. Andres sued his brother for breach of contract for failing to oversee the reconstruction of his house damaged by fire and to perform the necessary carpentry work in a workmanlike manner. The contract provided that in exchange for this work Andres would provide him with room and board and $10 per hour. Unfortunately for his case, Andres knew this arrangement would facilitate the brother's ability to keep receiving workers' compensation payments and to avoid paying income tax.[8]

C. IF THE CONTRACT IS CONTRARY TO STATUTE

- "Dynamite Donny Lalonde," later featured as "Golden Boy," was able to have an agreement declared unenforceable because it was not in writing, signed by the parties and approved as being "fair and reasonable" by the Boxing Commission contrary to the provisions of the *Boxing and Wrestling Commission Act*, R.S.M. The alleged contract allowed the defendant to take 50% of the net proceeds from ten fights which he was to promote and produce and 30% of the "total purse" earned by Lalonde even if he did nothing. The wisdom of the legislators is apparent.[9]

D. IF THE CONTRACT OR A PROVISION IS IN RESTRAINT OF TRADE

A partner who left the firm of Ernst & Young and went to work for Arthur Andersen & Co. was sued for being in breach of provisions in the partnership agreement. His new firm was sued for inducing the breach. The case rested on the issue of whether or not the provisions were legal.

In an appeal on an issue of damages, the judge reviewed the facts and findings of the trial and appeal court on the question of liability:

"[1] Ernst and Andersen are both national accounting mega-firms with offices throughout Canada with hundreds of partners.

[2] In 1991, Mr. Stuart was a partner of Ernst, having joined that firm 14 years earlier as a student. He headed the insolvency department of Ernst's Vancouver office and was, in that role, very highly regarded by those in the world of business, banking and law who bring or refer insolvency work to those accountants qualified to perform it.

[3] In May 1991, Mr. Stuart advised Ernst of his intention to leave the firm as soon as possible and start up an insolvency department in the Vancouver office of Andersen. He did so in breach of the terms of the partnership agreement which required a partner to give one year's notice of inten-

tion to retire and included restrictive covenants which imposed severe limits on a retiring partner's right to practise.

[4] In June 1991, Ernst commenced this action alleging breach of contract against Mr. Stuart and, against Andersen, of having induced that breach. ... The action came to trial in 1993 before E.R.A. Edwards J. who, in reasons reported at (1993), 79 B.C.L.R. (2d) 70, dismissed the action against both defendants on the ground that the provisions of the agreement relied on by Ernst were unreasonable and thus unenforceable. He also allowed Mr. Stuart's counterclaim in the sum of $60,148.00 for monies owed to him under the partnership agreement.

[5] On appeal by Ernst, the trial judgment was upheld with respect to the restrictive covenants [unenforceable] but the provision requiring one year's notice was found to be enforceable. In giving judgment for the court ... Southin J.A. said ...:

> [10] I do not agree, however, that cl. 2.8 [notice clause] was vitiated as being part of a scheme in restraint of trade. In my view a notice clause of this kind is a legitimate and proper clause. Therefore, it follows that Mr. Stuart, when he gave less than 12 months notice, was in breach of that term and damages must be assessed against him for that breach.

> [11] Insofar as the respondent, Arthur Andersen & Co., is concerned, the learned trial judge found that it had induced Mr. Stuart to go with it and I see no error in that finding. In my view what was done here was a wrongful interference with contractual relations, the notice clause being known to Arthur Andersen & Co. and they knowing that it was being broken. On that footing I would also allow the appeal as against Arthur Andersen & Co and remit the matter to the court below for an assessment of damages on inducing a breach of that clause only."

The court did allow the appeal on the quantum of damages with these words:
"I would allow the appeal to the extent of varying the award of compensatory damages by fixing the award against Mr. Stuart at $175,000 and against Andersen at $75,000. I would dismiss the appeal in respect of punitive damages."

Ernst & Young v. Stuart and Arthur Andersen & Co.
Vancouver Registry: CAO21297
http://www.courts.gov.bc.ca/
Court of Appeal for British Columbia
March 4, 1997

Note: For a concise statement of the law on restraint of trade see the Ben Johnson case on p. 234 below.

6. THE WRITING REQUIREMENT

THE STATUTE OF FRAUDS

Hoffer *v.* Verdone

[1994] O.J. No. 1967 (Q.L.)
ACTION NO. 2458/89
ONTARIO COURT OF JUSTICE — GENERAL DIVISION
AUGUST 12, 1994

[1] Salhany J.:— Over two centuries ago Mr. Justice Wilmot decried that "Had the Statute of Frauds been always carried into execution according to the letter, it would have done ten times more mischief than it has done good, by protecting, rather than preventing fraud:" *Simon v. Motivos* (1766) 97 E.R. 1170. In this action the plaintiff claims that the defendant John Verdone promised to convey to her a condominium unit in exchange for marketing services rendered on behalf of the de-

fendants. The defendant denies that there was any such agreement. But he also says that if he did agree to do so, that agreement is barred by the Statute of Frauds because it was an oral agreement with respect to an interest in land. At issue in this action is whether the invocation of the Statute of Frauds by the defendant will protect or prevent fraud. ...

FINDINGS

[11] The first issue that has to be determined is whether there was an agreement between the plaintiff and John Verdone that the plaintiff be given unit 37 of the Treetops Project in exchange for marketing services rendered by her to the project. As I have already said, it was conceded by the defence that the plaintiff and Mr. Verdone contemplated moving into two units side by side at Crabtree Keys Project. I am satisfied that Mr. Verdone led the plaintiff to believe that she would get one of the units in exchange for her marketing services and that they discussed how this could be done in view of the fact that the condominiums were legally owned by VHL Construction Ltd. and that Angelo Verdone was a one-half owner of the company. It would seem natural to me that he, planning to marry the plaintiff, or at least giving her the impression that he intended to do so, would lead her to believe that they would set up living arrangements side by side and that he would find a way to ensure that she would have a unit in exchange for her marketing services. The defendant conceded that they discussed putting a door between the units so that they could go back and forth. Moreover, I am also satisfied that after the Crabtree Keys project was abandoned and the Treetops initiated, John Verdone continued to make the same promises to the plaintiff with respect to unit 13 and later unit 37. ...

DECISION

[13] Mr. Thomson, [counsel for the defendants] relying on the Statue of Frauds, argued that if there was any agreement, it was unenforceable. ...

[14] The agreement between the plaintiff and Mr. Verdone was, understandably, not reduced to writing because of their relationship and because of the difficulties that Mr. Verdone would have to eventually face in transferring title from the corporate defendant to the plaintiff. There is no memorandum relied upon by the plaintiff that would satisfy the requirements of the Statute of Frauds.

[15] The plaintiff relied upon the doctrine of part perfor-

mance. The theory of part performance is that it tends to show that the contract really was made and is thus within the spirit of the Statute: See Waddams, *The Law of Contract*, 2nd ed. at p. 173. However, the law is clear that the acts relied upon as part performance must tend to corroborate proof of the agreement. To corroborate proof of the agreement, Canadian authorities have insisted that the acts of performance must not merely show, on balance, that there is an underlying contract between the parties but that "the acts are unequivocally or necessarily referable to some dealing with the land in question:" *Dealman v. Guaranty Trust Co. of Canada* [1954], 3 D.L.R. 785 (S.C.C.).

[16] [The judge reviews the facts submitted by the plaintiff.]
   I am not satisfied that any of these acts relied upon by the plaintiff were necessarily referable to a contract between her and John Verdone. Moreover, the marketing services which she performed on behalf of VHL Construction Ltd. were for the purpose of selling condominiums for which she received $1,000 per unit upon occupancy and later in July, 1987, an agreed monthly fee of $5,000. They were not necessarily referable to their agreement. Thus in my view; the Statute of Frauds bars the plaintiff from recovery on her agreement with the plaintiff.

[17] On the eve of trial, the plaintiff abandoned her claim for specific performance because unit 37 had been already sold and sought damages alternatively for failure to perform the agreement. Counsel for the plaintiff indicated that this damage claim was for the work which she had performed on behalf of the defendants on a *quantum meruit* basis. Mr. Thomson's position was that if the enforcement of the contract was statute barred, there could be no alternative recovery of damages. He also said that a *quantum meruit* should not be entertained because it was not specifically pleaded. Although, the statement of claim did not specifically claim recovery on a *quantum meruit* basis, the general claim for damages did alert the defendant to the fact that this was an issue to be pursued. I am not convinced that the defendant has been prejudiced by this claim.

[18] I am satisfied that the plaintiff is entitled to recover on a *quantum meruit* basis for all of her preparatory work to make the project a successful one and for obtaining a number of reservation agreements. Indeed, Mr. Verdone admitted that it was one of their more successful projects. The work which she performed for the defendants was set out in her letter of November 27, 1987 which was marked as exhibit 1 in this action. I assess the value of her work and services on a *quantum meruit* basis at $25,000.00. ...

C. CHALLENGES TO CONTRACTS

Question

In what instances will the court allow a party to an agreement to avoid his or her obligations?

1. MISTAKE

Marvco Color Research Ltd. *v.* Harris et al.

141 D.L.R. (3D) 577
SUPREME COURT OF CANADA
DECEMBER 6, 1982

Summary of the facts: Mr. and Mrs. Harris were induced by Johnston, a man living with their daughter, to sign a mortgage in favour of Marvco Color Research Ltd. Johnston led them to believe that the document was an unimportant amendment to an existing mortgage when it was, in reality, a second substantial mortgage. Although Mr. and Mrs. Harris did not sign at the same time, neither read the document nor questioned it. When the payments were in arrears, the mortgagee took this action for foreclosure. The sole defence was *non est factum*.

The trial court and the Ontario Court of Appeal held that the plea was effective, that their carelessness did not defeat the defence. The courts were following a precedent set by the S.C.C. in *Prudential Trust Co. Ltd. v. Cugnet et al.* (1956) 5 D.L.R. (2d), *(Prudential Trust)*. This appeal to the Supreme Court of Canada forced a re-examination of the legal principle set out in *Prudential Trust* in light of an English case, *Saunders v. Anglia Building Society* [1971] A.C. 1004 which held that carelessness would defeat the plea of *non est factum*.

Estey J.:—The decision of the House of Lords in *Saunders* has been considered by a number of Canadian courts. In *Commercial Credit Corp. Ltd. v. Carroll Bros. Ltd.* (1971), 20 D.L.R. (3d) 504n (Man. C.A.), the question of whether the principles laid down in *Saunders* are good law in Canada was left open by the court. In a number of more recent decisions, however, the reasoning of the House of Lords has been directly applied. ...

In my view, with all due respect to those who have expressed views to the contrary, the dissenting view of Cartwright J. (as he then was) in *Prudential, supra*, correctly enunciated the principles of the law of *non est factum*. In the result the defendants-respondents are barred by reason of their carelessness from pleading that their minds did not follow their hands when executing the mortgage so as to be able to plead that the mortgage is not binding upon them. The rationale of the rule is simple and clear. As between an innocent party (the appellant) [the mortgagee] and the respondents, the law must take into account the fact that the appellant was completely innocent of any negligence, carelessness or wrongdoing, whereas the respondents by their careless conduct have made it possible for the wrongdoers to inflict a loss. As between the appellant and the respondents, simple justice requires that the party, who by the application of reasonable care was in a position to avoid a loss to any of the parties, should bear any loss that results when the only alternative available to the courts would be to place the loss upon the innocent appellant. In the final analysis, therefore, the question raised cannot be put more aptly than in the words of Cartwright J. in *Prudential, supra*, at p. 5 D.L.R., p. 929 S.C.R.: "...which of two innocent parties is to suffer for the fraud of a third." The two parties are innocent in the sense that they were not guilty of wrongdoing as against any other person, but as between the two innocent parties there remains a distinction significant in the law, namely, that

the respondents, by their carelessness, have exposed the innocent appellant to risk of loss, and even though no duty in law was owed by the respondents to the appellant to safeguard the appellant from such loss, nonetheless the law must take this discarded opportunity into account.

In my view, this is so for the compelling reason that in this case, and no doubt generally in similar cases, the respondents' carelessness is but another description of a state of mind into which the respondents have fallen because of their determination to assist themselves and/or a third party for whom the transaction has been entered into in the first place. Here the respondents apparently sought to attain some advantage indirectly for their daughter by assisting Johnston in his commercial venture. In the *Saunders* case, *supra*, the aunt set out to apply her property for the benefit of her nephew. In both cases the carelessness took the form of a failure to determine the nature of the document the respective defendants were executing. Whether the carelessness stemmed from an enthusiasm for their immediate purpose or from a confidence in the intended beneficiary to save them harmless matters not. This may explain the origin of the careless state of mind but is not a factor limiting the operation of the principle of *non est factum* and its application. The defendants, in executing the security without the simple precaution of ascertaining its nature in fact and in law, have nonetheless taken an intended and deliberate step in signing the document and have caused it to be legally binding upon themselves. In the words of *Foster v. Mackinnon* this negligence, even though it may have sprung from good intentions, precludes the defendants in this circumstance from disowning the document, that is to say, from pleading that their minds did not follow their respective hands when signing the document and hence that no document in law was executed by them.

This principle of law is based not only upon the principle of placing the loss on the person guilty of carelessness, but also upon a recognition of the need for certainty and security in commerce. This has been recognized since the earliest days of the plea of *non est factum*. In *Waberly v. Cockerel* (1542), 1 Dyer 51a, 73 E.R. 112, for example it was said that:

> ...although the truth be, that the plaintiff is paid his money, still it is better to suffer a mischief to one man than an inconvenience to many, which would subvert a law; for if matter in writing may be so easily defeated, and avoided by such surmise and naked breath, a matter in writing would be of no greater authority than a matter of fact...

More recently in *Muskham Finance Ltd. v. Howard, supra*, at p. 912, Donovan L.F. stated:

> Much confusion and uncertainty would result in the field of contract and elsewhere if a man were permitted to try to disown his signature simply by asserting that he did not understand that which he had signed.

The appellant, as it was entitled to do, accepted the mortgage as valid, and adjusted its affairs accordingly. ...

I wish only to add that the application of the principle that carelessness will disentitle a party to the document of the right to disown the document in law must depend upon the circumstances of each case. This has been said throughout the judgments written on the principle of *non est factum* from the earliest times. The magnitude and extent of the carelessness, the circumstances which may have contributed to such carelessness, and all other circumstances must be taken into account in each case before a court may determine whether estoppel shall arise in the defendant so as to prevent the raising of this defence. The policy considerations inherent in the plea of *non est factum* were well stated by Lord Wilberforce in his judgment in *Saunders, supra*, at pp. 1023-4:

> ...the law...has two conflicting objectives: relief to a signer whose consent is genuinely lacking...protection to innocent third parties who have acted upon an apparently regular and properly executed document. Because each of these factors may involve questions of degree or shading any rule of law must represent a compromise and must allow to the court some flexibility in application.

...

[Appeal allowed; the plaintiff lender wins.]

- *M*r. Copperfield bid on a Batmobile; his bid of $189,500 won. He learned that that car was not the actual car used in the film *Batman*, but one of five cars used to promote the film. He sued the seller, Mr. Eisenberg who "has returned the favor."[10]

Two "Oakland Raiders" baseball caps, one "Pro 1" pair of boxer shorts, one Star Wars figurine were among the items stolen from Zellers by two teenagers. The boys were arrested. The mother of one of the boys subsequently received a letter from the lawyer for Zellers which included the following:

> ...I act for Zellers to recover their damages in civil court. The civil recovery process is <u>SEPARATE AND DISTINCT</u> from any criminal action and the two must not be confused.
>
> It is alleged that [J.R.B.], a young person for whose supervision my client holds you legally responsible, took unlawful possession of merchandise from Zellers ... to the value of $59.95.
>
> In order to eliminate additional expense to you, Zellers is willing to settle THE CIVIL <u>CASE ONLY</u> out of court, providing you pay the following amount by August 25, 1995:
>
> Restitution for cost of incident including damages and costs: $225.00.
>
> Should you elect to ignore this demand, refuse or fail to pay the amount of the proposed out of Court settlement, Zellers will take the case before a Civil Court and claim damages, ...

The mother paid the $225.00.

The mother sued for the return of the money on the basis that Zellers was never entitled to claim or get any money from her. The following are excepts from the judgment.

"There is no general rule that parents are liable for the torts of their children by virtue of their status as parents per se. See *Taylor v. King* [1993] 8 W.W.R. 92. The parents would only be liable if they, themselves, were in some way negligent or had engaged in tortious conduct in relation to the activities of their children. There is no suggestion in this case that the plaintiff was negligent or had committed any tort in her personal capacity. ...

"In my opinion, the defendant's claim was not merely a doubtful claim — it was an invalid claim.

"However, the matter is not quite so simple as that because the plaintiff has actually voluntarily paid the money over to Zellers. There was thus an executed compromise and so, ordinarily, the plaintiff would not be entitled to the return of the money. It would be regarded in law as equivalent to an "executed gift" - to borrow the phrase from Chitty . ...To establish a claim for the return of the money, the plaintiff would have to rely on other grounds.

"The ground advanced by counsel for the plaintiff is under the rubric of unjust enrichment: that the money was paid over by reason of a mistake in fact or law or both. ...

"The plaintiff honestly believed that the claim was a serious one and that if she did not pay it the defendant would sue her. ...

"I accept this evidence. After all, the plaintiff had received a letter from a lawyer who should know something about the law and who was making an apparently serious threat of legal action if the claim was not paid. And she paid. She would not have done so if she had not believed that there was something to it.

"In this belief, the plaintiff was mistaken. Whatever legal opinion or opinions Zellers might have had regarding their claims generally, I cannot believe that they seriously thought that this claim could succeed or that they seriously intended to pursue it to court if it was not paid. ...

"The plaintiff subsequently took legal advice, learned of her mistake and now wants her money back.

"The old rule that monies paid under a mistake of fact could be recovered and monies paid under a mistake of law could not, has now been abandoned in this country. Proof of a mistake of fact or law is enough. See *Air Canada v. British Columbia* [1989] 59 D.L.R. (4th) 161. See also *McShane v. Manitoba* (1993) 86 Man. R. (2d) 212.

"The plaintiff was certainly misled by the tone and content of the lawyer's letter. In my opinion, in the particular circumstances of this case, the plaintiff is entitled to a refund on the ground of monies paid under a mistake.

"The appeal is allowed and the plaintiff's claim is allowed with interest and costs. Although the claim is a small one, and was dealt with in the small claims procedure, it appeared to have been treated as a sort of "test" case which will have a bearing on Zellers entire recovery programme. Senior counsel were engaged and I received well-researched arguments on both sides. In the circumstances, I will allow the plaintiff her costs to be assessed as if this were a Class 2 action."

Bond v. Arkin and Zellers Inc.
Suit #CI 96-06-00055
Court of Queen's Bench of Manitoba
July 15, 1996

INTERPRETATION

Implied terms

A contract between a community college and a video game supplier provided that the supplier would supply and maintain tabletop video games and would guarantee a minimum payment to the college of $16,000 a year. The games were installed for the start of the school year. Almost immediately there were problems with vandalism: "machines were overturned, glass was broken, cords and plugs were removed or destroyed, sound equipment was damaged and cash boxes were broken into." The president of the supplier discussed the problem with the operations manager on different occasions and stated that, because the college was not providing security, no money was being earned and no commission could be paid. The supplier agreed to continue on the basis of a 50/50 split of income generated. However, at the end of the term of the contract the college sued the supplier for the full amount owing under the terms of the original contract.

The supplier submitted that the original contract was properly terminated by them because of the college's breach of an essential, though implied term, namely, to provide security for the machines. The court found, on the evidence of several witnesses, that the vandalism was "abnormal, excessive [and] continuous" and that the failure of the college to provide security was a breach of an implied term of the contract entitling the supplier to treat the agreement as at an end. It further held that it was common sense for the college who stood to gain from the games to provide security to prevent the damage. Therefore, the supplier could terminate the contract and need not make the guaranteed payment.

Algonquin College of Applied Arts and Technology v. Regent Vending and Amusement Limited
Summarized from The Lawyers Weekly
May 3, 1991, p. 2

The defendant purchasers bargained for two properties. The seller erroneously forwarded to them three certificates of title instead of two. The defendants paid for the three and the three properties were transferred into their names. When the seller realized its mistake it asked the defendants to transfer back the third property. They refused. In the ensuing case the court found that the defendant purchasers realized the seller had made an error and that they had seized on that error to obtain a benefit they knew or ought to have known they were not entitled to have.

The court ordered them to transfer the title back to the plaintiff.

Farm Credit Corp. v. Mihilewicz
Saskatchewan Queen's Bench
Summarized from The Lawyers Weekly
February 23, 1996 p. 29

2. MISREPRESENTATION

INNOCENT

Mr. Chorkawy co-signed a promissory note for $57,200 with his friend Welch. When Welch went bankrupt the bank looked to Chorkawy for payment. He refused to pay on the basis of misrepresentations made to him in response to his inquiries. The court summarized his position as follows:

> It is Chorkawy's position that the execution of the promissory note was procured by the bank's misrepresentation of Welch's other financial obligations to Chorkawy, and, accordingly, ought to be entitled to rescission.

Despite the bank's denial, the court accepted Chorkawy's testimony that he had been assured by representatives of the bank that Welch had no other indebtedness and that the loan was secure when, in fact, Welch had other debts—a term loan of $46,500, a mortgage of $85,000 and arrears with Revenue Canada of $33,000.

The bank then argued the parol evidence rule: that evidence of an innocent misrepresentation was inadmissible because it contradicted the terms of a written guarantee.

Justice Mykle concluded:

> On the strength of [the] authorities, it is clear that such evidence is admissible. I find that, on Chorkawy's testimony, which I accept, there was a misrepresentation to him by the bank, which misrepresentation directly induced him to sign the promissory note.
>
> In these circumstances, the note cannot bind Chorkawy, and accordingly the bank's claim is dismissed.

Royal Bank of Canada v. Chorkawy
[1994] M.J. No. 561 (Q.L.)
DRS 95-03563
File No. 93.01.70245
Manitoba Court of Queen's Bench
October 20, 1994

• *T*he National Consumer Council and the Plain English Campaign, which promote the use of clear, straightforward English, gave the 1986 "Golden Bull booby prize for gobbledegook" to a firm which used the following in their share prospectus: "[the signers] agree that without prejudice in any other rights to which you may be entitled, you will not be entitled to exercise any remedy of rescission for innocent misrepresentation at any time after acceptance of your application."

FRAUDULENT

B.C. Hydro, the defendant, had decided to contract out the construction of transmission lines in a rugged area of British Columbia. B.C. Hydro advertised for tenders. The trial court found as a fact that the defendant had deliberately omitted information from the tender documents about the condition of the right-of-way. The judge stated that the deliberate omission of words of warning amounted to "a form of tender by ambush." In his opinion, the defendant had a duty to make full disclosure of all information relevant to the project, to give the bidders information that accurately reflected the nature of the work to be done so they could prepare a proper bid. He held that the defendant had fraudulently induced the plaintiff to enter the contract and awarded the plaintiff $2.6 million, "the total loss suffered by the plaintiff as a result of being fraudulently induced to enter into this contract."[11]

B.C. Hydro appealed. After examining the contractual terms relevant to the case, the majority on the B.C. Court of Appeal concluded that the contract meant that the clearing was to have been completed and thus the words constituted a negligent, but not a fraudulent, misrepresentation that induced the plaintiff to enter into a contract at a price less than it would have if it had known the true facts. It reduced the award to $1,087,730 for negligence and remitted the breach of contract issue and the consequent damages back to the trial court.

With regard to the claim of fraudulent misrepresentation, the court agreed that fundamental principles still apply, namely, the plaintiff must prove the defendant's intention to deceive. It concluded that the evidence in the case did not show that any of the twelve members of the committee which prepared the tender documents did so with such an intention.

Judge Southin, although dissenting on the finding of negligent misrepresentation, agreed that the plaintiff failed to prove fraudulent misrepresentation. "[I]n my opinion, in the whole of his judgment, the learned judge never came to grips with the issue of who was fraudulent. To say, as the learned judge does, that the defendant did this or that is to ascribe to the defendant a soul which it does not possess. ... I am persuaded that no one had a guilty mind." [At page 189][12]

B.C. Hydro appealed to the Supreme Court of Canada, which dismissed its appeal. All the judges agreed that B.C. Hydro had breached the contract and the majority held that the plaintiff, Checo, could also sue in tort for negligent misrepresentation even though the representations were also stated expressly in the contract. It sent the matter back to the trial court for the assessment of damages and stated that the law should move to reduce the significance of suing in tort rather than in contract. [In tort, the wronged is to be compensated for all the reasonably foreseeable loss that was caused by the tort; in contract the wronged is entitled to damages that would put him in the position he would have been in if there had been no breach.][13]

BG Checo International Ltd. v. B.C. Hydro and Power Authority
Summarized from The Lawyers Weekly
February 12, 1993, p.1

Note: This case will be remembered less for its finding of negligent rather than fraudulent misrepresentation than for the proposition that a person can bring an action in contract and tort, even if the duty in tort is also an express term of the contract, subject only to the limitations set out in the contract.

Ms. Pitt purchased a ticket from a Toronto agent for a three-hour flight on the Concorde jet, in response to a newspaper advertisement which urged the reader to "see the curvature of the earth from 60,000 feet," "circle the arctic," "fly to vicinity of the North Pole," and travel at "Mach 2—twice the speed of sound (1,360 m.p.h.)." Ms. Pitt did not see the curvature of the earth, the flight did not circle the arctic or fly within the vicinity of the North Pole; it went to Goose Bay.

The judge concluded that the misrepresentations were made with reckless disregard for their accuracy and that the defendant was liable for breach of contract. The plaintiff was awarded punitive damages as well as compensatory damages.

Pitt v. Executive Travel (London) Ltd.
Ontario Provincial Court
Summarized from The Lawyers Weekly
January 12, 1990, p. 4

BY SILENCE

Questions

Can silence be a misrepresentation?
If so, what has to be proved and by whom?

Sidhu Estate v. Bains, Bristow, Third Party

VICTORIA REGISTRY V02469
http://www.courts.gov.bc.ca/
COURT OF APPEAL FOR BRITISH COLUMBIA
JUNE 7, 1996

Background facts: Mr. Bhandar was induced to invest $134,000 in a company by the fraudulent misrepresentations of a Mr. Bristow who told Bhandar that he, Bristow, had invested $600,000 and that Bhandar's good friend Bains had invested $380,000 in cash when in fact neither had invested anything. Mr. Bains permitted Bristow to mislead Bahndar to induce him to invest in the project. Some time later, when Bristow asked Bhandar if he knew of any other investors, Bhandar said his sister might be interested. In the presence of Mr. Bains, Bhandar called his sister, Ms. Sidhu, and innocently relayed the misinformation to her. She invested $80,000.

When Bhandar learned the truth he sued successfully on the basis of fraudulent misrepresentation. The appeal by Bains was dismissed.

The sister, Ms. Sidhu died about three years after she invested in the company and four years before the action on behalf of her estate began. The action by her estate failed at trial on the basis that she had not relied on the misrepresentations; she invested because her brother had invested.

This case is an appeal from that decision.

1 Finch J: . ...

[3] The plaintiffs allege that Ms. Sidhu was induced to invest the sum of $80,000 in IPC in reliance upon representations made to her in a telephone conversation on 18 June 1987 by Mr. Bhandar, who believed the representations to be true, but which, to the knowledge of Mr. Bains, were false. Mr. Bains was present with Mr. Bhandar at the time the latter spoke with his sister by telephone. The plaintiffs allege that in standing silent, and in failing to correct the false information he knew Mr. Bhandar was conveying to Ms. Sidhu, Mr. Bains committed a fraudulent non-disclosure of material facts. The plaintiffs say Mr. Bains is liable for damages in deceit because Ms. Sidhu relied upon the representations, which she would not have done had Mr. Bains disclosed the truth.

[The judge reviewed the conflicting evidence as to what was said to Ms. Sidhu on the telephone, the findings of the trial judge and of the judge in the earlier action of Bhandar v. Bains.]

[28] I am therefore satisfied the only reasonable inference to be drawn in the circumstances was that Mr. Bains had the necessary fraudulent intention [and it was a material misrepresentation that induced Ms. Sidhu to invest.] ...

[30] As to the trial judge's conclusion that a misrepresentation could be made by silence, I respectfully agree. As a general rule, mere silence cannot found a cause of action, but active concealment can: See *Peek v. Gurney* (1873), L.R. 6 (H.L.) 377 at 403; and *Leeson v. Darlow*, [1926] 4 D.L.R. 415 (Ont. C.A.). Mr. Bains's duty to disclose the truth did not arise from a fiduciary relationship to Ms. Sidhu, or from a relationship calling for the utmost good faith on his part. The duty to correct the false information conveyed by Mr. Bhandar to Ms. Sidhu arose on Mr. Bains's part because by remaining silent Mr. Bains tacitly confirmed the false information as true.

[31] The circumstances required for silence to be actionable misrepresentation are articulated in *Spencer Bower & Turner, The Law of Actionable Misrepresentation*, 3d ed. (London: Butterworths, 1974) at 101:

A misrepresentation may be made by silence, when either the representee, or a third person in his presence, or to his knowledge, states something false, which indicates to the representor that the representee either is being, or will be, misled, unless the necessary correction be made. Silence, under such circumstances, is either a tacit adoption by the party of another's misrepresentation as his own, or a tacit confirmation of another's error as truth.

[32] And see also Halsbury's Laws of England, 4th ed., Vol. 31 at 639–40; *Hardman v. Booth* (1863), 1 H. & C. 803, 158 E.R. 1107; and *Howse v. Quinnel Motors Ltd.* (1949), [1952] 2 D.L.R. 425 (B.C.C.A.). ...

[33] The fact that Mr. Bains was present at the time of the communication by Mr. Bhandar to his sister and the fact that Mr. Bains had the opportunity to correct the information that he knew to be false are essential to my conclusion that silence could, in law, constitute a misrepresentation. In the particular circumstances of this case, and on the findings of the learned trial judge, Mr. Bains's silence can only be seen as confirmation of the misinformation which Mr. Bhandar passed on to Ms. Sidhu.

[34] That brings one to the issues most actively addressed in this appeal, namely, whether the learned trial judge erred in finding that the plaintiffs had failed to prove reliance by Ms. Sidhu on the false representations; and whether liability for fraudulent mis-

representation can be found where there are, or may have been, additional representations or factors which induced the representee to act. The learned trial judge appears to have considered the issues of reliance and contributory inducement together. ...

[35] Given his acceptance of Mr. Bhandar's testimony as to what was said, I interpret ... the trial judge's reasons to mean that both Mr. Bhandar's and Mr. Bains's investment in IPC were factors which induced Ms. Sidhu to follow suit. However, the learned trial judge appears to have held the view that the plaintiffs could only succeed by proving that those representations were the sole inducements upon which Ms. Sidhu relied. In so directing himself, in my respectful view, the learned trial judge erred in law. Fleming in *The Law of Torts*, 7th ed. (Sydney: Law Book, 1987), says at 604:

Besides being intended to rely on the misrepresentation, the plaintiff must have actually done so. ... At the same time, a defendant cannot excuse himself by proving that his misrepresentation was not the sole inducing cause, because it might have been precisely what tipped the scales, as in the case of the plaintiff who had taken up debentures, partly by reason of a falsehood contained in the prospectus, partly in the mistaken belief that they created a charge on the company's property. Nor is it a defence that the plaintiff was negligent or foolish in relying on the misrepresentation or had an opportunity for verifying it. (footnotes omitted)

...

[36] It is therefore sufficient in my view to found liability in deceit if the fraudulent representation is a material inducement upon which the representee relied, even if that representation is only one of several factors contributing to her decision.

[37] I am also of the view that the learned trial judge erred in concluding that the plaintiffs had failed to discharge the onus of proving Ms. Sidhu's reliance on the fraudulent misrepresentation. There are two lines of authority on the nature of this onus. ...

[42] I think the preferred view of the law in Canada is that once intention, materiality and causation of loss are proven, the burden of proving non-reliance shifts to the defendant. The antecedent elements are not in question in this case. The burden of proving that Ms. Sidhu did not rely on the statements therefore shifts to the defendant, as it did in *Parallels Restaurant*. Taking the trial judge's reasons as a whole, I am of the view that he did not find that the defendant had proven conclusively that Ms. Sidhu did not rely at all on the statements. He found only that she probably relied on other information as well. As I have observed, this is not enough.

[43] However, even if the other view of the law regarding the burden of proof is the correct one [i.e. that the plaintiff must prove all the elements], the plaintiffs should still succeed. ... The only reasonable inference in all the circumstances is that Ms. Sidhu did rely on the representations made to her by Mr. Bhandar and uncorrected by Mr. Bains and that Mr. Bains has failed to rebut this inference by proving that she did not so rely.

[44] In my respectful view all of the elements of a successful claim in deceit have been proven or are reasonably to be inferred from the proven facts. I would allow the appeal.

[Appeal allowed. The decision was unanimous]

Note: See also the tort of Deceit page 21.

3. UNDUE INFLUENCE

Tannock **v.** *Bromley*

10 B.C.L.R. 62
SUPREME COURT OF BRITISH COLUMBIA
JANUARY 24, 1979

Bouck J.:—

SYNOPSIS OF CLAIM AND DEFENCE

Between approximately July 1974 and January 1977 the plaintiff received treatment from the defendant through the medium of hypnosis. He now says that while he was under her influence he conveyed real estate to her, bought her a car and gave her many other items such as coins, a stereo set, etc. In this action he asks for return of the real property and judgment for the money value of the additional articles transferred to her.

There is not much of a contest over the fact the conveyances occurred and the chattels were given, but the defendant alleges all of this happened by way of gift from the plaintiff to her and so none of the property need be restored. ...

ISSUE

Must the defendant return to the plaintiff the property or its value?

LAW

Where the parties to a contract do not stand upon an equal footing the law has frequently intervened to set aside the contract on the grounds of undue influence by one towards the other. This principle has been applied with particular emphasis in circumstances where there is a fiduciary relationship between the parties. Such a bond has been held to exist between solicitor and client, principal and agent, doctor and patient, priest and penitent, etc.

The main theory of the law is that, when a person who because of his state of mind is incapable of exercising his free will and is induced by another to do an act which may be to his detriment, the other shall not be allowed to derive any benefit from his improper conduct. Conveyances or transfers by the victim are not set aside because of folly or want of prudence but to protect the weak from being forced, tricked or misled into parting with their property.

Once the relationship between the parties is established so that it is clear one has maintained dominion over the other, then a presumption of law arises where a gift is made by the servient to the dominant party. The onus of proof then shifts to the dominant party to uphold the validity of the gift. This presumption is to the effect that the dominant party used undue influence over the servient party and consequently the transaction should be set aside unless the dominant party can show the conveyance or gift was a spontaneous act of the donor performed under circumstances which enabled the donor to exercise an independent will.

The authorities on this branch of the law are not altogether consistent and so the textbook discussions of the cases tend to vary from author to author. Nonetheless, in broad outline the principles I have recited seem to be generally accepted: see for example the following texts and cases cited therein: ...

On the facts there is no question the defendant controlled the plaintiff in much the same way a solicitor may dominate his client or a doctor his patient. Her position was that of a fiduciary in relation to the plaintiff. Indeed, the influence she held is more profound than in the examples of other situations I have mentioned because of the nature of hypnotism and its method of manipulating the mind through suggestion. The plaintiff was incapable of resisting the defendant's influence and became her obedient servant. She either abused her position of trust or took advantage of the inequality which existed between them. As hypnotist and subject a presumption therefore arose that everything given by the plaintiff to her ought to be set aside unless she could prove the plaintiff's acts were spontaneous and done by him through the exercise of his independent will.

I could not find any solid evidence to support the defendant's cause by way of rebutting the presumption. The conveyances and gifts were voluntary in the sense there was no consideration moving from the defendant to the plaintiff. Furthermore the plaintiff did not receive independent advice so that one could say he was acting outside the influence of the defendant. Because of this the transfers must be set aside. ...

JUDGMENT

By way of summary the plaintiff will recover judgment against the defendant in the following terms:

   (a) An order directing the defendant to sign a conveyance of her interest in the Wellington Street farm and in default of her so doing the district registrar of Nanaimo may sign on her behalf;
   (b) An order directing that an account be taken as between the plaintiff and the defendant with respect to the moneys received by the defendant on the sale of the Amsterdam house;
   (c) An order directing that the plaintiff has a charge against the car in question proportionate to his contribution and that the car be sold;
   (d) An order directing the defendant to deliver up the stereo to the plaintiff:
   (e) An order that there be an accounting between the plaintiff and the defendant with respect to any loss suffered by the plaintiff as a consequence of the sale of the car, and the value of the rent the defendant must pay to the plaintiff for her use of the car and the stereo;
   (f) Costs to follow the event;
   (g) Liberty to apply.

Action allowed in main.

- *A*n accountant prepared financial statements for a family business and saw the business was in difficulty. The accountant refused to release the statements to an investor intending to buy the company unless the investor signed an agreement to guarantee payment of his accounting fees. The court held the guarantee was obtained by undue influence and the investor was relieved of his obligation.[14]

4. DURESS

> As reported in *The Advocate:* Mr. and Mrs. B, aged 78 and 72, signed a contract to transfer certain real property to their son Jim. The contract had been prepared by a solicitor. When Jim brought an action for a declaration that he was the beneficial owner of this property Mr. B testified that he and Mrs. B had only signed because Jim had threatened to blow his brother Bill's head off if a family money dispute was not settled. The parents heard this threat through a third brother. Mr. B said that he and his wife, who was very ill at the time and died not long afterwards, were terrified Jim would act on his threat and were prepared to do almost anything to prevent it. Their lawyer had been consulted on how to settle a tangle of money disputes among the members of the family, and he advised that this agreement seemed to be the only way to obtain peace.
>
> Held: the agreement was void for Jim's duress or, alternatively, should be set aside for unconscionability. It was enough if the threat of harm was a reason for executing the document, albeit that the signer might well have done the same if the threat had not been made: *Barton v. Armstrong*, [1976] A.C. 104 (P.C.). A threat of harm to a third party, if acted on by the signer, was duress: *Saxon v. Saxon*, [1976] 4 W.W.R. 300 (B.C. Co. Ct.). Although Mr. and Mrs. B had independent legal advice and chose to sign the agreement, they did so because they feared that Jim would harm Bill unless they signed the agreement. This was a coercion of their will so as to vitiate their consent. Unconscionability was found because through the duress and their lack of understanding of the transaction the parents were in a weak position compared with Jim, and because the agreement was unfairly one-sided.
>
> ### *BYLE v. BYLE et al.*
> *Vancouver S.C. Registry No. C854743 Legg, J.*
> *August 5, 1988*[15]

- *A* bank applied for summary judgment against a guarantor who pled duress and *non est factum*. The guarantor alleged that she signed the document unaware that it was a guarantee secured by a mortgage on her home because her husband threatened, among other things, "to open up your belly and drink your blood." The judge concluded a summary judgment was inappropriate.[16] *TD Bank v. Nabmiache*

5. UNCONSCIONABILITY

Turner Estate *v.* *Bonli Estate*

77 SASK. R. 49
SASK. COURT OF QUEEN'S BENCH
JUNE 2, 1989

[1] Sirois, J.: The plaintiff sues for specific performance of an option to purchase farmland entered into between the purchaser Gordon Turner and the vendor Oli Bonli on the 2nd day of May A.D. 1975. One of the difficulties encountered herein is that both of the main actors are now deceased and their personal representatives stand in their place. ... The defendant resists the claim mainly on the basis that the alleged option agreement should be set aside as the entire transaction was unconscionable in that the purchase price of the land and the method of payment of purchase price by installments are gravely inequitable and constitute equitable fraud on the part of the plaintiff. The evidence must be carefully scrutinized. The sole issue is the validity of the option to purchase.

[2] At the time the lease agreements and option to purchase were entered into, Gordon Turner was 47 years of age and Oli Bonli was 88 years of age. Gordon Turner likely typed out the agreement at his residence on the previous night leaving the land description to be filled out later at his office where he had a municipal map to consult. It was executed bright and early around 7 o'clock in the morning. Oli Bonli who lived at the hotel walked over to Turner's office. Alan Pederson who worked at his brother's service station across the road was hailed to come over and sign as a witness. In five minutes or less the deed was done. This is the text of the agreement entered into:

May 2, 1975

TO WHOM IT MAY CONCERN:

I Oli Bonli do hereby rent all of my land to Gordon A. Turner for the period of five years starting as of today May 2nd 1975. At the end of this time being May 2nd 1980 he may purchase this land for the sum of one hundred thousand dollars, this sum to be paid in twenty equal payments of five thousand dollars each year. This payment to cover principal and interest and there will be no further charges made to him.

If I should decease before the rental agreement is fulfilled, he may purchase the land from my estate under the same terms. The rentor may seed up to four hundred and fifty acres per year and must farm the land in a husbandly manner.

I will receive one third of the crop each year and will pay the taxes on all of this land.

The rentor will haul all my grain to the graneries (sic) and elevator for me at no cost to me, and I in return will let him use any of my machinery that he desires for farming any land at no cost to him.

The rentor will be allowed to store grain in any of my granaries (sic) that I am not using in that crop year at no cost to him.

The legal description of the said land is as follows:. ...

I have clear titles to the above land in the Toronto Dominion Bank.

'Alan Pederson'	*'Oli Bonli'*
WITNESS	Oli Bonli

'G.A. Turner'
Gordon A. Turner"

[3] Gordon Turner was in the fuel business all his life. He drove fuel trucks for Texaco, B.A. Oil and finally Gulf. He was also involved in farming. In 1966-67 he purchased one-half section of land; in 1972 he purchased a further three quarter sections. There was further trading along the way so that by 1975 he owned five quarters of land, besides the Bonli land—the subject of the action. But he had his eyes on this land too. He was very involved in the community. He served on the Town Council for nine years, mayor for two terms and the Elks representative for eight years. In the wintertime he curled for a pastime. From all accounts, he was a mover and doer. He was well-liked and respected in the community. He was married with three children—all boys, with whom he got along well. He enjoyed people and his work. For the last six months of his life his nerves were bad and he suffered from arthritis. He took anti-depressants but finally succumbed, a victim of suicide on the 30th of September 1975.

[4] Oli Bonli appears to have been an entertaining person, always nice, friendly, with a twinkle in his eye. But as a bachelor he kept to himself quite often. He lived on the farm until the winter of 1973-74. He spent his summers on the farm and his winters at the hotel in Kyle. ...

In 1974 and 1975 age was catching up to Oli Bonli. He had good days and bad days when he was very confused. Finally, unable to care for himself properly at the hotel in Kyle, the Social Services Department intervened and he was taken to a nursing home in Langham in the month of November of 1976. In 1980, Oli Bonli was examined by psychiatrists to ascertain the state of his mental condition. In March of 1982 he was declared to be a mentally disturbed person, incapable of managing his affairs through mental infirmity arising from age and the Montreal Trust Company of Canada was appointed Committee of his estate under the *Mentally Disordered Persons Act*, R.S.S. 1978, c. M-4, ss. 5 and 42. He died on the 18th day of February, A.D. 1985 at the age of 98. ...

[13] The leading Canadian case appears to be *Waters v. Donnelly* (1884), 9 O.R. 391, where Fergus, J., held at 409:

> The law which I think applicable to a case of this sort appears to be clearly and briefly stated in a case mentioned by the Chancellor. *Slater v. Nolan* Ir. R. 11 Eq. 386, by the Master of the Rolls, and the decision was afterwards affirmed in appeal. The learned Judge said:—'If two persons, no matter whether a confidential relation exists between them or not, stand in such a relation to each other that one can take undue advantage of the other whether by reason of distress, or recklessness, or wildness, or want of care, and when the facts show that one party has taken undue advantage of the other by reason of the circumstances I have mentioned, a transaction resting upon such unconscionable dealing will not be allowed to stand; and there are several cases to show, even where no confidential relation exists, that where the parties are not on equal terms, the party who gets a benefit cannot hold it without proving that everything has been right, and fair and reasonable on his part.' This decision does not, I think, lay down any new law but rather appears to state concisely what the law was and is. ...

[15] In *Black v. Wilcox*, (1976) 70 D.L.R. (3d) 192; 12 O.R. (2d) 759, at pp. 195-196, Evans, J.A., said:

> In order to set aside the transaction between the parties, the Court must find that the inadequacy of the consideration is so gross or that the relative positions of the parties is so out of balance in the sense that there is a gross inequality of bargaining power or that the age or disability of one of the controlling parties places him at such a decided disadvantage that equity must intervene to protect the party of whom undue advantage has been taken. In considering whether a Court should intervene,

it is necessary to look at all the circumstances surrounding the transaction but it is not necessary to find any intentional fraud. The question is whether the transaction reveals a situation existing between the parties which was heavily balanced in favour of the defendant and of which he knowingly took advantage.

[16] If the bargain is fair the fact that the parties were not equally vigilant of their interest is immaterial. Likewise, if one was not preyed upon by the other, an improvident or even grossly inadequate consideration is no ground upon which to set aside a contract freely entered into. It is the consideration of inequality and improvidence which alone may involve this jurisdiction. Then the onus is placed upon the party seeking to uphold the contract to show that his conduct throughout was scrupulously considerate of the other's interests. This is an accurate statement of the law vide: *Mundinger v. Mundinger*, [1969] 1 O.R. 606; 3 D.L.R.(3d) 338, affd. 14 D.L.R. (3d) 256n...*Knupp v. Bell et al.* (1966), 58 D.L.R.(2d) 466, affd. 67 D.L.R.(2d) 256; di Castri, *The Law of Vendor and Purchaser* (2d Ed.), at pp. 205, 206, 207. ...

[17] In the case at bar the 47 year old Turner and the 88 year old Oli Bonli were certainly not par or of equal bargaining power. Turner drew the agreement himself. ...When questioned by Tony Sander [long time friend, neighbour and helper] about the rumours that his land had been rented to Gordon Turner early in May 1975, Oli Bonli denied that he had either rented or sold any land. On the contrary he declared that he had bought land from Gordon Turner and that Sander would have more work to do for him that spring than he had ever done in the past. Now Oli Bonli was not a liar; he was a nice old man and trickery was not part of his arsenal. I have serious doubts that he really knew all that was contained in Exhibit P-1 or D-2.

[18] Let us look at the agreement itself between this 47 year old active businessman and this failing 88 year old gentleman. The evidence is that he was failing with good days and bad days. One year down the road he could not adequately take care of himself and was taken to a nursing home. This document drawn up by Gordon Turner provides for a five year lease at the end of which, he or his estate could exercise the option

to buy. At that time the rentor, Oli Bonli, would be 93 years of age. Then, on the option being exercised over a 20 year period, Oli Bonli would be 113 years of age by the time it was all paid out. The price was $100,000.00 at a time when the land was worth $167,000.00, or was one third more than the purchase price, and at a time when the price of land was ascending rapidly. Furthermore, the agreement makes no provision for interest on the unpaid portion of the purchase price; the five thousand per year would comprise both principal and interest. Gordon Turner knew very well what land prices were doing at this time; this man was world wise and knew what he was after. The agreement moreover provides that the lessee can use any of the rentor's machinery to farm any land free of charge. And again, the lessee reserves the right to use any of the rentor's granaries to store his grain that the rentor was not using at any relevant time.

[19] Can one honestly conceive a more one-sided or improvident agreement than this? To ask the question is to beg the answer. It was all one-sided in favour of Gordon Turner at the expense of Bonli.

[20] Here, there was no independent legal advice given to Oli Bonli; given the respective ages and state of health of both parties there was inequality of bargaining power; the consideration was grossly inadequate and the terms of purchase were very unfair in the light of all circumstances. The transaction resting upon such unconscionable dealing cannot stand. The plaintiff has failed to discharge the onus that rests upon her to show that everything has been fair, right and reasonable on her part. Equity must intervene to protect the defendant's estate when undue advantage was taken of the deceased. The transaction is set aside and specific performance is refused. In effect, the action is dismissed with costs to the defendant. The caveat against the lands is ordered discharged; that is instrument No. 75-MJ-06745 registered on the 2nd day of June A.D. 1975, dated the 30th day of May A.D. 1975. The lands in question are: N half 29-20-14-W3rd; E half 30-20-14-W3rd; half of NE 31-20-114-W3rd; NW quarter 32-20-14-W3rd. Parties have leave to reapply before me if any differences develop with respect to rentals since 1980.

Action dismissed.

D. PRIVITY AND ASSIGNMENT OF CONTRACTS

Two employees of Kuehne & Nagel International Ltd. caused extensive damage ($33,955.41 worth) to a transformer owned by London Drugs Ltd. They dropped it attempting to lift it with two fork lifts, contrary to the method advised. The storage contract included an exclusion clause limiting liability of Kuehne & Nagel on any one package to $40. London Drugs Ltd. sued the defendant in bailment, contract and tort (negligence); it sued the employees personally for the tort of negligence.

At trial the employees were found liable for the full amount of the damage while the liability of their employer company was limited to $40.

The B.C. Court of Appeal found it unreasonable to hold the employees responsible for the full amount of the loss when their employer's liability was limited to $40. The court reduced the employees' liability to $40. Justice Southin dissented with "regret" because the result is "in a moral sense, unjust," but, she concluded, "it is for judges to state the law and for the legislature to reform it."

London Drugs Ltd. v. Kuehne & Nagel International Ltd. et al.
70 D.L.R. (4th) 51
British Columbia Court of Appeal
March 30, 1990

On appeal, the Supreme Court of Canada focused on the issues of whether or not the employees owed a duty of care to their employer's customers and whether or not the liability clause contained in the contract between the employer company and the customer could afford any protection to the employees.

The court held that the employees did owe a duty of care to the employer's customer, but found the employees beneficiaries of the exemption clause in the contract between the employer and customer. Thus, the court added an exemption to the privity of contract rule: when a service contract between an employer and its customer contains a clause limiting liability, that clause, if it expressly or impliedly covers the employees, should protect the employees charged with performing the contract. The customer should not be able to circumvent the terms of the contract by suing the employees directly in tort.

London Drugs Ltd. v. Kuehne & Nagel International Ltd. et al
S.C.C.
Summarized from The Lawyers Weekly
November 13, 1992, p. 1

• *A* contract by which William Millard borrowed $250,000 from a venture-capital firm, Marriner & Co., allowed the lender to convert the note into 20 percent of the company's stock. The contract was sold to Mr. Martin-Musumeci, who, as the assignee of the contract, claimed the 20 percent of the company, ComputerLand. Millard resisted by claiming he had an oral agreement with Marriner that it could not transfer the right to convert the note. The matter went to court.

The court held that Millard must give 20 percent of his stock to Martin-Musumeci plus punitive damages of $125 million. Twenty percent of ComputerLand, at that time, was estimated to be worth $50 million to $400 million. To appeal, Millard would have to post a cash bond equal to $1\frac{1}{2}$ times the award.[17]

EQUITABLE ASSIGNMENT

Q u e s t i o n

What are the consequences of ignoring a valid assignment?

Bitz, Szemenyei, Ferguson & MacKenzie v. *Cami Automotive Inc.*

34 O.R. (3D) 566 (Q.L.)
[1997] O.J. No. 2463
No. 22747/96
ONTARIO COURT (GENERAL DIVISION)
MAY 30, 1997

Background: This case was very complicated. The court had to determine whether or not the assignment was a matter of contract law, tort law, whether it needed to satisfy the *Conveyancing and Law of Property Act*, and whether it was invalid by the *Wages Act*. In the end it was held to be a valid assignment.

Cavarzan J.:—The plaintiff law firm successfully represented one James Mastronardi, an employee of the defendant corporation, in a grievance arbitration. The arbitrator found that James Mastronardi (hereinafter referred to as J.M.) had been wrongfully dismissed and that he was entitled to be compensated for his losses. Prior to the conclusion of negotiations to settle the amount of the compensation, J.M. executed an "irrevocable direction" to the defendant to pay from the settlement proceeds the sum of $15,120.91 to the plaintiff and the balance to himself.

Although the defendant had intended to comply with the terms of the irrevocable direction, the entire proceeds of the settlement were paid out to J.M. ...

The plaintiff now seeks summary judgment for the amount specified in the direction. Counsel advised me that the facts are not in dispute. They submitted, and I agree, that the only genuine issues are questions of law which should be determined by the court pursuant to rule 20.04(4) of the Rules of Civil Procedure. ...

THE ISSUES

In addition to the grounds alleged in the amended statement of claim, Mr. Mackenzie argued that the "irrevocable direction" amounted to an equitable assignment which was binding upon the defendant and enforceable. ...

WAS THERE AN EQUITABLE ASSIGNMENT?

The following statements from *Halsbury* ... support the position of the plaintiff in this case:

An engagement or direction to pay a sum of money out of a specified debt or fund constitutes an equitable assignment, though not of the whole debt or fund; but it is necessary to specify the debt or fund.

...

Although the precise amount of the award had yet to be calculated, the defendant became a debtor as of the date of the award. ... (*Halsbury*, supra, at para. 37):

Consideration is not required to support the equitable assignment of an existing legal chose in action, provided that the assignor has done everything required to be done by him to make the assignment complete in equity.

...

I conclude ... The irrevocable direction was a binding equitable assignment. ...

Finally, I note that the parties before the court in this dispute are the innocent victims of what appears to be fraudulent behaviour by J.M. He retained the full amount of the arbitration award knowing that one week earlier he had executed an assignment of a major portion of that award. The defendant is by this judgment required to pay twice.

CONCLUSION

The plaintiff is entitled to summary judgment against the defendant . ...

E. Termination of Contracts

1. Performance

Question

Is everybody happy?

- *P*avel Bure's hockey jersey, one of a limited edition bearing a crest marking the National Hockey League's 75th anniversary, was sold for $4,250. The sheet music for Bryan Adams' song "Everything I Do, I Do for You" was sold for $4,100. (The proceeds of both sales benefited fifteen organizations, including Canuck Place, North America's first free-standing hospice for children.)[18]

- *M*r. Mateo of New York City bought fifty $100 gift certificates from Toys 'R' Us and offered one certificate for each gun turned in to the police station. Over a few days 375 weapons had been turned in "almost 40 times as many as the precinct has collected in the past year under the department's amnesty program which pays up to $75 a gun." Donations from others allowed the programme to continue.[19]

- *T*he Ontario housing ministry ordered a landlord to rebate $2,308.80 to his tenant. The tenant received that amount in change that filled two blue recycling boxes. The tenant said he may use the change to pay his rent.[20]

2. AGREEMENT

Q u e s t i o n

Have the parties contracted to call off the deal?

- *A*MR Corp., the parent company of American Airlines, would invest $246 million in Canadian Airlines if Canadian Airlines and its parent compnay PWA Corp. can withdraw from the Gemini computer system, which PWA co-owns with Air Canada. Canadian Airlines requested the federal Competition Tribunal to hear its submission, but Air Canada challenged the tribunal's right to hear the matter. The Federal Court of Appeal ruled that the Tribunal did have the authority to hear the appeal.[21]

  The Supreme Court refused to hear Air Canada's appeal from this decision.[22]

  The Competition Tribunal ruled that PWA Corp. can withdraw from the Gemini computer system, and ordered the dissolution of Gemini Group Automated Distribution Systems Inc. if the partners cannot negotiate a settlement by December 8, 1993. The Tribunal held that PWA would likely fail without AMR's investment and that would lessen airline competion in Canada.[23]

  Air Canada, with Covia, a third owner of Gemini, appealed the ruling of the Competition Tribunal. Before the case was heard, Air Canada abruptly halted its legal fight against PWA.[24]

3. FRUSTRATION

Q u e s t i o n

Has some unforeseen event beyond the control of either party happened after the contract was formed that makes it impossible or meaningless to perform?

Impala Construction Ltd. **v.** *Wade*

115 A.P.R. 437
NEWFOUNDLAND DISTRICT COURT
FEBRUARY 10, 1983

Riche, D.C.J. [orally]: In this case the plaintiff, Impala Construction Ltd., … entered into a contract with the defendant for the performance of certain works consisting of bulldozing a road in the Clarke's Beach area of Newfoundland for a price of $2,000.00 [plus transportation and seeks damages for work done] . …

What then was the legal position of the parties? There was a contract but it was only partly performed. It was only partly completed because it could not be finished, not because of any action of the parties but because of some outside force. The contract became frustrated because of extreme weather conditions. It wasn't until nearly two years afterwards in the summer of 1981 that the work was actually completed. Even if the defendant had requested the plaintiff to complete the contract in 1981, I do not think the plaintiff would be obliged after such a long delay to go back and complete the contract for the price as stipulated. … It should be remembered that the contract consisted of only 3-4 days work.

So what we have is a frustrated contract in November, 1979, which cannot be performed and which has been partly performed. In the circumstances I find from the evidence … that there was at least 50 percent of the work completed and probably something more. The evidence varied the amount from 50 percent to 75 percent. I, therefore, find as a matter of fact that 60 percent of the work was completed. I value the contract at $2,500.00 including transportation; $1,500.00 is the value of the work completed, being 60 percent of the $2,500.00 contract.

In relation to frustration in contracts, I refer to *Canadian Building Contracts*, Goldsmith, (2nd Ed.). It has a fairly concise explanation of frustration, at p. 53 & 54:

> Frustration in the legal sense does not refer to the feeling frequently experienced by both owners and contractors in support of the performance of the work, but occurs when some supervening event for which neither

party is responsible and which was not within the contemplation of the parties renders performance impossible. It is always open to parties to provide in their contract what was to happen in such an event, and many contracts contain what is known as a *force majeure* clause. In the absence of any such provision, however, on the happening of such an event the contract will be frustrated, and the parties are released from further performance. The accrued rights and liabilities at the date of frustration remain unaffected, but future or continuing obligations are discharged.

Frustration also occurs if the performance is rendered impossible by an act of God. In this particular case because of the extreme wet weather in the fall of 1979 and 1980 which anyone who has lived in this province knows. [sic] It was an unbelievable year with regards to the amount of rain we had that summer. I hold this contract impossible of performance as the parties contemplated.

By the common law in a contract which is frustrated, by an act of God, neither party would be entitled to recover. However, under the *Frustrated Contracts Act,* R.S.N. 1970, c. 144, s. 4(3). It states: [if]

> Before the parties were discharged any of them has by reason of anything done by any other party in connection with performance of the contract, obtain a valuable benefit other than a payment of money, the court, if it considers it just to do so having regard to all the circumstances, may allow the other party to recover from the party benefited the whole or any part of the value of the benefit.

On the basis of this legislation and the law relating to frustrated contracts, I find that the contract here had become frustrated. I find the defendant has benefited from the work done under the contract to the value of $1,500.00 and with respect to the contract I allow the sum of $1,500.00 to the plaintiff in respect of that work.

Judgment for the plaintiff in part.

- *Potential* causes of contractual frustration:

    — frozen waste from an airliner. A large chunk of frozen waste from an airliner smashed through the roof of a home in Seattle.[25]

    — a c-130 Hercules cargo plane crashing. Only the chimney was left of Mr. Barnhart's home when such a plane crashed. Mr. Barnhart escaped serious injury.[26]

4. BREACH OF CONTRACT

- "The millennium bug," (also known as Y2K) the name given to the computer software that records the date with only two digits instead of four, causes the computer to record the year 2000 as "00" if it can deal with it at all. *Produce Palace International v. Tec-America Corp. and All American Cash Register, Inc.* may be the first lawsuit resulting from this glitch — the computer system with this type of bug causes the company's cash register to crash whenever a customer uses a credit card with a expiration date in the year 2000.[27]

- *I*n 1994, the New York Rangers won the Stanley Cup under coach Mike Keenan. When the Rangers were a day late with a playoff bonus (of $840,000), he maintained that the Rangers had breached their contract and declared himself a free agent. Within days he signed a five-year $7 million contract with the St. Louis Blues. The Rangers sued him for breach of contract with the argument that their late payment of the bonus did not constitute a material breach.

    Negotiations led to Keenan being free to coach and manage the St. Louis Blues but the NHL commissioner suspended him for 60 days, fined him $138,000 and ordered him to return most of a $691,000 earlier signing bonus.[28]

- *J*ohn Fogerty, former member of the successful band Creedence Clearwater Revival, did not record for almost ten years partly because of a bitter and protracted legal battle. He is reported as saying "I haven't been paid properly in 17 years." When he did record, the title and lyrics of one song referred to these contract disputes: "Zanz Kan't Danz." "Zanz can't dance/But he'll steal your money/Watch him or he'll rob you blind."[29]

• Main Line Pictures, an independent film company, sued actress Kim Basinger for breach of contract for failing to star in a film after promising to do so. The company had sold distribution rights for about $10 million when it advertised the film with Basinger's name. The jury ordered her to pay $8.92 million in damages and ruled that she could also be responsible for punitive damages.[30]

The judge of the Ontario Court (General Division) found the following as facts: The plaintiff, Ontex Resources Ltd. (Ontex) owned eighteen leasehold mining claims. Mr. Chilian, the president of Metalore Resources Ltd. (Metalore) approached the plaintiff about a possible joint venture, with the result that the companies entered into a contract in 1981. The agreement provided that Metalore would take possession of the property, and that if it would spend $1 million, set out a detailed drilling program, and agree to spend a further $5 million, Ontex would either transfer the property to Metalore in return for a 30% net royalty interest, or give Metalore 60% interest in the property and enter into a joint venture agreement. The contract further provided that Metalore would provide Ontex with information on demand and would provide it with a report by July 1 of each year.

Metalore did provide Ontex with a report in 1982, but it did not disclose a previous and positive report that indicated a potential for a successful gold mine in the areas for exploration. Although Metalore was aware of the industry practice to make full disclosure of all information it possessed about the property, Chilian reported to Ontex that the results were disappointing. Chilian did, however, offer to increase Metalore's interest in the property. Metalore further misled the plaintiff about its drilling plans intentionally concealing its optimistic plans.

In 1983, in response to Chilian's offer, the companies entered into an agreement in which Ontex agreed to assign to Metalore 100% of its interest in the property for $40,000 and a 10% net royalty interest.

In 1984 Chilian received an extraordinarily positive report on one drill hole, but those results were not given to Ontex. Chilian secretly purchased stock in both companies; Metalore began staking and acquiring claims. By July 1, 1985 it had acquired 232 claims.

In January of 1986, Ontex demanded reports for 1983, 1984, and 1985 pursuant to the terms of the 1981 agreement. Chilian replied that the 1981 agreement had been replaced by the 1983 agreement but did promise to deliver information. The information provided was confusing, incomplete and inaccurate. Ten days after the information was delivered, Metalore announced its discovery. By then it had acquired another 227 claims.

Ontex sued Metalore and Chilian for breach of contract, fraud, misuse of confidential information, breach of fiduciary duty and claimed ownership of the mining claims.

The trial judge stated the law on the breach of contract as follows:

Breach of Contract

Stephan M. Waddams, *The Law of Contracts*, 2nd ed. (Aurora, Ont.: Canada Law Book, 1984), at pp. 440-442:

A variety of expressions has been used to define the sort of term that, if broken by one party, will excuse the other. "Dependent covenant," covenant which goes to the whole of the consideration," "condition," "condition precedent," "breach going to the root of the contract," "concurrent condition," breach that "terminates" or "frustrates the object" of the contract," "nonseverable breach," "repudiation," "renunciation," "breach of an entire contract," are among the expressions used. Behind them all, it is suggested, lies a single notion—that of substantial failure of performance. Diplock, L.J., said in *Hongkong Fir Shipping Co. Ltd. v. Kawasaki Kisen Kaisha Ltd.*:

"...in what event will a party be relieved of his undertaking to do that which he has agreed to do but has not yet done?..."

The test whether an event has this effect or not has been stated in a number of metaphors all of which I think amount to the same thing; does the occurrence of the event deprive the party who has further undertakings still to perform of substantially the whole benefit which it was the intention of the parties as expressed in the contract that he should obtain as the consideration for performing those undertakings?"

After his examination of the evidence the trial judge concluded that Metalore had breached the 1981 agreement and that "[t]he 1983 agreement rests for its validity on proper disclosure having been made under the 1981 agreement. Given Metalore's intentional failure to make proper disclosure, the 1983 agreement cannot stand."

Ontex Resources Ltd. v. Metalore Resources Ltd.
75 O.R. (2d) 513
Ontario Court (General Division)
December 18, 1990

On appeal, the Ontario Court of Appeal held that, on the facts, the defendant's breach of the 1981 agreement did not entitle Ontex to terminate the agreement. The court did hold that the "deliberate non-disclosure of information" was a "material misrepresentation which induced [Ontex] to enter the 1983 agreement" and that, therefore, Ontex was entitled to rescission of the 1983 agreement. It therefore held that the 1981 agreement, as per its terms, would be "treated as being renewed as of July 1, 1991."

Ontex Resources Ltd. v. Metalore Resources Ltd.
103 D.L.R. (4th) 158
Ontario Court of Appeal
June 4, 1993

- *A* summary of the facts would rob you of the gross details of an outrageous "cruise" with Captain Higginbotham whom the court appropriately found had "fundamentally breached the contract." The plaintiff paid over $20,000 for a luxury 28-day cruise between the mainland and Vancouver Island. To appreciate the reasons for the complete refund of the amount paid, plus special and general damages go to http://www.courts.gov.bc.ca for the story of *Litner and Litner v. Delta Charter Inc. et al.* decided by the Supreme Court of British Columbia on April 16, 1997.

- *T*he plaintiff claimed the Prime Minister and the Progressive Conservative Party were liable for breach of contract. The plaintiff claimed that the defendants failed to honour their election promises to improve postal service and not to enter into a free trade agreement with the U.S. The action was dismissed.[31]
  Ruffolo v. Mulroney

In *Lalonde v. Coleman*, the court held that the boxer was not bound by the agreement not only on the grounds that the agreement was illegal (see p. 83) but also on the grounds that Coleman's breach of the agreement entitled Lalonde to terminate the contract. Judge Scott wrote: "In this case, in my opinion, in light of the magnitude of the defendant's inability to perform, we are dealing with such a fundamental breach as to entitle the plaintiff to treat the contract as being at an end. ... What occurred was a total nonperformance or benefit to the plaintiff. What resulted was something totally different from that which the parties must have contemplated and in my opinion, the plaintiff was quite entitled to walk away from the agreement. ..."

Lalonde v. Coleman
67 Man. R. (2d) 187 at p. 195

ANTICIPATORY BREACH

Q u e s t i o n

What is an "anticipatory breach" and what are the choices of the person faced with such a breach?

Homer et al. **v.** *Toronto Dominion Bank*

(1990) 83 SASK. R. 300
SASKATCHEWAN COURT OF APPEAL
MAY 28, 1990

Sherstobitoff, J.A.: This appeal is from a judgment which awarded damages and interest exceeding $135,000.00 for breach of a lease. The issue was whether the tenant improperly terminated the lease or whether it was entitled to do so by reason of the doctrine of anticipatory breach or repudiation.

In 1978, the appellant bank occupied premises in a shopping centre under the terms of a written offer to lease, signed by the appellant and accepted by the owner of the premises. The offer defined the area to be occupied, fixed the rental to be paid, and fixed the term at ten years, renewable for two ten year periods. The offer was stated, upon acceptance, to be a binding contract and required the tenant to execute the "Landlord's standard form of lease" before occupying the premises, "provided that the lease document shall be in a form mutually satisfactory to both parties." Such a lease was never signed.

In 1980, the respondent became owner of the premises. Over the next four years, the parties negotiated with a view to agreement to the terms of a formal lease, but without success. On October 14, 1984, the respondent, by its solicitors, sent the following letter to the appellant:

> Further to your letter of September 27, 1984, please be advised that I have failed to convince my client that we grant to your client any of the proposed changes contained in your letter of March 22, 1984. My client is most emphatic that they are not prepared to discuss the matter further and have instructed me to advise you that the Lease is either to be executed in the form negotiated between our two respective offices or the Toronto-Dominion Bank is to vacate the premises.

> Although I realize you are having difficulty in receiving instructions from your client, I must insist that the matter be resolved on or before the 31st day of October, 1984 failing which I will seek further instructions from my client.

The appellant, by letter of its solicitors dated November 14, 1984, stated that it was terminating the lease as of May 14, 1985, and would vacate the premises on or before that date, which it did.

The respondent sued for damages, alleging the existence of a binding ten year lease. The appellant admitted the existence of such a lease, but relied on the respondent's letter as either an offer to terminate, which it accepted, or a repudiation, which it accepted, in either case terminating the lease. The

evidence indicated that the respondent was bluffing when it sent the letter, and had no wish to terminate. However, the respondent also admitted that the appellant had no way of knowing that it was bluffing and that even after the bluff was called, the respondent did not make its position clear to the appellant. The trial judge found a binding ten year lease and ... assessed and awarded damages.

The appeal must be allowed.

The appellant admitted the existence of a binding lease, although that was open to doubt. Because of the admission, it will be assumed, for the purpose of this judgment that there was a binding lease.

The judge, in his decision, overlooked entirely the applicable principles of contract law. The issue was not one of the right to terminate under the terms of the existing lease. Rather, the issue was whether there was an anticipatory breach or repudiation of the existing lease by the respondent, followed by an election by the appellant to accept the repudiation, thereby terminating the contract.

Anticipatory breach occurs when a party by express language or conduct, or by implication from his actions, repudiates his contractual obligations. There must be conduct which evidences an intention not to be bound by the terms of the contract and absence of justification for such conduct. The innocent party may then elect either to preserve the contract and seek to enforce its terms, or to accept the repudiation and terminate the contract. In the latter case, the innocent party is freed from his future obligations under the contract, but may pursue such remedies as would have been available to him if the breach had taken place when performance was due.

The case most close to the point emanating from this jurisdiction is *Canadian Doughnut Co. Ltd. v. Canada Eggs Products Ltd.*, [1954] 2 D.L.R. 77 (Sask. C.A.), affd. [1955] S.C.R. 398. Other judgments of this court dealing with anticipatory breach include *Cowie v. McDonald*, [1917] 2 W.W.R. 356; *Smith v. Crawford*, [1918] 2 W.W.R. 298; and *Sunnyside Nursing Home v. Builders Contract Management Ltd.*, 75 Sask. R. 1; [1989] 3 W.W.R. 721 (S.C.A.). A useful text book analysis of the principles involved is found in Fridman on, *The Law of Contract*, (2nd Ed., pp. 558-571).

The letter of October 15, 1984 demanded that the appellant either sign a new lease or vacate the premises, at the same time foreclosing any further discussion of the matter. Even against the background of four years of fruitless negotiation toward a formal lease, the letter amounted to a clear and un-equivocal statement of intention not to be bound by the terms of the existing lease which had three more years to run. No other conclusion is possible because neither of the alternatives given in the letter contemplated continuation of the existing lease. The appellant's letter of reply took no issue with the respondent: it accepted the second of the two alternatives given, that is, to vacate the premises. It was an election to accept the repudiation and to terminate the contract.

The respondent argued that the appellant's letter, which did not agree to give up possession until six months later, May 14, 1985,

was not an acceptance of the demands in the respondent's letter, which required a reply by October 31, 1984. That did not change the character of the appellant's letter as an acceptance of the respondents' repudiation. While the respondent may have been entitled to require the appellant to vacate immediately upon receipt of the appellant's letter, it chose not to do so. …

The appeal is allowed with costs. … The judgment below is set aside and the action stands dismissed with costs.

Appeal allowed.

F. Remedies

1. Laches

> "I say that equity will not leap across an eight-year gulf of acquiescence in what, as a matter of contract, is a clear breach thereof. The right here has been slept on too long; it smacks of a stale claim, and the court will not enforce it."
>
> *Logan v. Williams (Logan)*
> *41 B.C.L.R. (2d) 34*
> *B.C.C.A. at p. 39*
>
> Judge Anderson, quoting from the reasons for judgment of Judge Drake of the lower court which held that a husband's action, commenced in December of 1987 to set aside a separation agreement breached by his wife in December of 1979, was barred by laches. The Court of Appeal agreed with the lower court's decision.

- *A*lna de Bodisco began an action seeking $2 million from the fashion designer Oscar de la Renta based on an agreement to give her half his wealth. De la Renta admitted signing a letter making the promise. The promise was made on June 22, 1956; the lawsuit was filed April 1979. The court held that the suit was barred by the *Statute of Limitations*.

- *A* cyst removed from a Ms. Argue contained a four-faceted diamond one-third of a centimetre across, which apparently was dropped into her by a careless doctor or nurse during the Caesarean birth of her daughter 52 years previously.

2. Exemption Clauses

Questions

A party to a contract has the right to ask the court for a remedy if the other party is in breach. That is the essence of contract law. How does the court help a person if a clause in the contract states that he agrees not to seek a remedy if the other party is in breach?

Do these exemption clauses illustrate the freedom of contract or are they contrary to the essence of contract law?

AN EXEMPTION CLAUSE FAILS TO BE EFFECTIVE:

a. *when there was no reasonable notice of the term.*

The skier was seriously injured while skiing and sued the ski company for negligence for failing to warn of a dangerous drop off. The issue in the case was whether the plaintiff's action was barred by the exclusion clause which the defendant alleged was part of the contract. Although the ticket given to the skier gave notice of an exclusion of liability clause on the back and although it was on stiff cardboard with a string attached so it could be worn around the skier's neck and although red and yellow cards were posted immediately in front of the ticket wickets and although there was another notice at the base of the mountain, the judge found as a fact that the skier, "a stranger to the country and to the mountain" had no actual notice of any term excluding liability. The judge acknowledged that the defendant, as the occupier of the land, could exempt itself from liability, merely by taking reasonable steps to bring an express notice of the exclusion clause to the attention of the skier, but concluded as follows:

"The notices are garish, and are reasonably legible and clear in their wording. But the evidence as to their location in relation to the ticket wickets, as to their number and as to the other circumstances existing on that day, is vague. I cannot conclude that the plaintiff should have seen any of them. There is nothing about the tickets themselves which would necessarily draw to the attention of a reasonably alert person without prior knowledge that they contain writing other than the advertising and definition of the period for which they are issued.

"For these reasons, I hold that the defendant is not entitled to enforce the exclusionary terms against the plaintiff."

Greeven v. Blackcomb Skiing Enterprises Ltd.
Vancouver Registry No. C927644
Supreme Court of British Columbia
September 19, 1994[32]

---

b. *when on its true construction (interpretation) the clause does not cover the incident.*

The defendant courier company promised delivery within four hours of request. The plaintiff bank called the courier company at 12:08 requesting delivery of municipal tax payments due that day. The driver arrived for the envelopes about 1:30, but they were not ready until 2:00. Three of six deliveries were made by 4 p.m. but at that time the driver was erroneously told by the dispatcher that it was too late to deliver the rest of the cheques. The driver delivered them the following morning. Two of the municipalities did not accept late payment without penalty and assessed fines of $54,089 and $39,407.

After the court concluded that the defendant courier was in breach of contract, the defendant argued, *inter alia*, that the regulations to the *Motor Carrier Act* limited its liability for "any loss or damage" to "$2.00 per pound unless a higher value declared."

In a unanimous decision, the B.C. Court of Appeal upheld the trial judge's interpretation that the regulations only applied to loss or damage to the goods themselves and did not apply to damages arising from delay. The court concluded that the courier must pay the $93,000 penalties which were reasonably foreseeable damages.

Bank of Montreal v. Overland Freight Lines Ltd. *(unreported)*
Summarized from The Lawyers Weekly
April 21, 1989, p. 2; June 1, 1990, p. 19

c.   *When there was a fundamental breach and on the true construction of the contract it wasn't meant to cover such a breach.*

Aurora TV and Radio *v.* *Gelco Express*

65 MAN. R. (24) 145
MANITOBA'S QUEEN'S BENCH
MAY 10, 1990

OVERVIEW

Oliphant, J.: The plaintiff owns and operates an audio and video sales and service outlet at Brandon, Manitoba.

The defendant is a national courier company.

The plaintiff's action is for the recovery from the defendant of the value of a videocassette recorder. The defendant contracted to transport the videocassette recorder for the plaintiff. The videocassette recorder was either lost by or stolen from the defendant.

The defendant does not deny liability. It says its liability is limited by virtue of the contract between it and the plaintiff.

THE ISSUES

There are two issues to be resolved:

(1) Is there a clause in the contract between the plaintiff and the defendant which limits the liability of the defendant for the loss of the videocassette recorder?
(2) If so, is the defendant entitled to rely upon the clause?

[After reviewing the facts and the case law, the judge concluded as follows.]

CONCLUSIONS

On the question of notice of the limitation clause, I agree with and adopt the principles set forth in *Firchuk, supra*. The court must carefully scrutinize any clause in a contract which purports to limit the liability of a party, especially where a limitation clause appears in a standard form contract and purports to limit the liability of the drawer of the contract. Before a party can rely upon a clause which purports to limit his liability, reasonable notice of that clause must be given to the other party to the contract. Also the loss must come within the four corners of the limitation clause.

Here, on the face of the bill of lading, there is a reference to the limitation of the carrier's liability. However, the clause which purports to limit that liability appears on the reverse side of the bill of lading in very small print, buried amongst other words under a heading which is not indicative of a limitation clause.

Notice cannot be said to be reasonable, in my view, if the clause is neither legible nor capable of comprehension.

The clause utilized in the case before me was printed in such a manner that it is difficult, if not impossible, to read without the aid of magnification.

The limitation clause becomes incomprehensible in its attempt to cover almost every possibility in terms of limiting the carrier's liability. The wording of the clause is neither plain nor unambiguous. It is unclear. It is, quite simply, legal gobbledygook.

Even if one accepts the proposition that the requirement of notice is met if the nondrawing party to the contract is given the opportunity to read it, the notice cannot, in my opinion, be said to be reasonable if the clause is unintelligible because of its complexity.

I am not persuaded that any notice of the limitation clause was given to the plaintiff here. If notice were given, then I find that such notice in all the circumstances, was not reasonable.

Accordingly, the defendant is not able to rely upon the clause limiting its liability.

Even if it could be said that reasonable notice of the limitation clause had been given, I would still allow the plaintiff's claim.

The essence of the contract here was that the defendant was to carry certain goods being shipped by the plaintiff from Brandon to Calgary and to deliver the goods to an address in Calgary.

In a contract for carriage, the unexplained disappearance of the goods which are the subject of the contract is in my opinion a fundamental breach of the contract.

Where the goods which are the subject of the contract inexplicably disappear, the possibility of theft is real. As stated by Cory, J. A., in *Punch, supra*, a carrier is liable for loss where theft is a possibility unless there is a clause which clearly exempts the carrier from loss occasioned by theft.

I agree that whether an exclusionary or exception clause is applicable where there is a fundamental breach is to be determined according to the true construction of the contract.

Looking at the contract as a whole and bearing in mind the factual circumstances here, I am not able to say that it is fair and reasonable to attribute to the parties the intention that the limitation clause should survive notwithstanding a fundamental breach by the party in whose favour it was drawn. That is the test applied by Grange, J. A., in *Cathcart, supra*. Is my view it is the correct test.

Cathcart, supra, is also authority for the proposition that in a contract for the delivery of goods, the failure to deliver, though not deliberate, is a fundamental breach. I agree with the correctness of that proposition as well.

I disagree with the reasons for judgment given by Rowbotham, J., in *Lotepro Engineering and Construction Ltd., supra*. He took the view that a failure to deliver does not constitute a breach of the fundamental term of a contract for delivery, rather, it is negligent performance of a contract. I respectfully disagree.

Here, we have a contract for the carriage and delivery of goods. The goods were not delivered and there is no explanation for the disappearance of same. The defendant is liable for the fundamental breach of the contract and because of the lack of clarity in the limitation clause, it cannot, in my opinion, rely upon that clause to escape the consequences of the loss of the goods.

For the reasons stated, then, there will be judgment for the plaintiff in the sum of $699.95.

The plaintiff is entitled to its costs in the court below in the sum of $88.99. I award the plaintiff costs here in the sum of $250.00.

Additionally, the plaintiff is entitled to interest as is provided for under Part XIV of the *Court of Queen's Bench Act*, S.M. 1988-89, c. 4; C.C.S. M., c. C-280.

Judgment for plaintiff.

3. EQUITABLE REMEDIES

An insurance company terminated an insurance contract on the basis that it was obtained by a fraudulent misrepresentation. The person who made the fraudulent misrepresentation sued for the return of the premiums paid. After reviewing the facts, the arguments of the parties and the law, the court held in favour of the defendant insurer. The judge cited *Brophy v. North American Life Assurance Co.* (1902), 32 S.C.R. 261 for "perhaps the strongest language against the return of the premiums in any case" and quoted Taschereau J.:

> An interference, in the name of equity, to alleviate the offender's punishment by ordering the return of the premiums into his guilty hands would seem to me an inconsistency. The insured is not in a position to ask the assistance of the court, nor to invoke rules of equity the sole effect of which would be then to benefit the sole culprit. He has received no consideration from the company for the moneys he has paid, it is true, but he owes his loss to his own turpitude, and the court should have no pity upon him and no mercy for him, under any circumstances. I would apply to him the rule that he who has committed iniquity cannot claim equity.

Justice Pitt concludes: "… I believe that the authorities support the position of the insurer, and I also believe that it is the more principled and rational position."

Moscarelli v. Aetna Life Insurance Company of Canada
24 O.R. (3d) 383 (Q.L.)
[1995] O.J. No. 1709
Court File No. 12250/91U
Ontario Court (General Division)
June 14, 1995

Note: see p. 210 for more of the reasons for judgment.

Question

When is the equitable remedy of specific performance available?

Note: See *Semelhago v. Paramadevan* for the answer of the Supreme Court of Canada on p. 219.

4. DAMAGES

LIQUIDATED DAMAGES

Questions

Can the parties to a contract agree in the contract on the amount of damages to be paid in the event of a breach? Is such an agreement binding?

Lee **v.** *Skalbania*

SUPREME COURT OF BRITISH COLUMBIA
VANCOUVER REGISTRY NO. C872510
DECEMBER 21, 1987

Summary of the facts: Lee and Skalbania entered into a contract for the sale of Lee's property at a price of $975,000, the completion date to be March 31, 1987 and the balance of the cash payment to be paid that day. The vendor Lee was to carry a second mortgage of $200,000. The contract also provided that Skalbania pay a deposit of $50,000 which, at the option of the vendor, would be "absolutely forfeited to the owner as liquidated damages" in the event of his breach. He did breach. He failed to tender the cash payment on the completion date, which was extended to April 1, 1987. Lee refused to grant a further extension of time, cancelled the agreement, and sold the property to another for the same price, but for cash. Lee now claims the $50,000 deposit held in trust.

Gow J.:—... The primary issue is whether the deposit of $50,000 was liquidated damages or a penalty.

The position of the defendant is aptly set out in the affidavits of Skalbania.

In his affidavit filed October 2, 1987 he says:

2) That on February 5, 1987 I signed an interim agreement offering to purchase 2487 Point Grey Road, Vancouver, British Columbia ... and at no time was it ever discussed with the plaintiff as to whether the $50,000.00 was or would be a pre-estimate of damages. In fact, the $50,000.00 was not paid until the plaintiff signed the interim agreement on the 10th day of February, 1987. The $50,000.00 was and is not 'non-refundable'.

3) That the present value of a $200,000.00 mortgage at 9% for two years as at April 1, 1987 is approximately $168,336.00. As a result, the plaintiff by virtue of her sale on April 1, 1987 to new purchasers Mr. Koon Yip Lee and Sau Yung Lee has saved the sum of $31,664.00 with the result the plaintiff has suffered no damages but, in fact, made a profit. Now produced and shown to me and marked exhibit 'A' to this my Affidavit is a true copy of a letter dated October 26, 1987 from Fred Whittaker, Chartered Accountant, setting out the present value of a $200,000.00 mortgage as aforementioned.

In his affidavit filed November 4, 1987 he says:

3) That it is unfair that the plaintiff, who has suffered no damages whatsoever, but in reality has made a profit of $31,000.00 by virtue of the fact that the purchase and sale by myself did not take place, to retain the deposit of $50,000.00. It is unconscionable for her to retain the deposit and at no time would I have ever signed or agreed to a deposit of the same had I understood that in the event the Vendor sold the property for the same price and on much more favorable terms to another purchaser, I would lose the $50,000.00 deposit.

Filed on behalf of the plaintiff on October 26, 1987 was an affidavit by one Banu Foroutan, a real estate sales person of Vancouver, who stated "that the usual practice in the real estate business is to obtain a minimum deposit on the sale of residential property of between 5% and 10% of the total purchase price". ...

On the facts I find:

(1) That the plaintiff was ready, willing and able to complete.
(2) That the defendant was unable to complete when the time for performance came, namely, April 1, 1987.
(3) Time remained the essence of the contract.

I hold that the failure of the defendant to perform timeously was a breach of contract on his part which relieved the plaintiff of her obligations to perform under the contract but the contract survived for the purpose of enabling the plaintiff to pursue her remedies thereunder.

I find that she elected the remedy of cancellation of the contract and the forfeiture to her of the deposit as liquidated damages. That is, however, a finding in fact of what the plaintiff did. The question remains is she entitled to that remedy? The answer is "yes" if the $50,000 was a genuine pre-estimate of damages: the answer is "no" if it was a penalty. But even if the answer is a "penalty" the plaintiff will be deprived of the $50,000 only if it were unconscionable for her to retain that sum. *Dimensional Investments Ltd. v. R.*, [1968] S.C.R. 93.

In *Elsley v. J.G. Collins Insurance Agencies Ltd.*, (1978) 2 S.C.R. 916, Dickson J. (as he then was) said at p. 937:

It is now evident that the power to strike down a penalty clause is a blatant interference with freedom of contract and is designed for the sole purpose of providing relief against oppression for the party having to pay the stipulated sum. It has no place where there is no oppression. ...

Of course, if an agreed sum is a valid liquidated damages clause, the plaintiff is entitled at law to recover this sum regardless of the actual loss sustained.

The facts in *Hughes v. Lukuvka* (1970)–75 (BCCA) bear a striking similarity to the facts in this case.

The headnote reads:

Appellant had agreed to buy property for $59,500 and time was expressed to be of the essence; he paid a deposit of $5,000. The contract provided that upon failure by the purchaser to pay the balance of the cash payment and to execute formal documents within the time stipulated the owner could cancel the agreement and retain the deposit as liquidated damages. The purchaser failed to complete as stipulated and the vendor elected to cancel the agreement and claimed the deposit, which claim was upheld by Ruttan, J. The substantial question on the appeal was whether the deposit should be regarded as a penalty and its retention by the vendor relieved against as unconscionable.

It was held per curiam, that the appeal must be dismissed; there was no onus on the respondent to prove that the amount of the deposit was arrived at as a result of a genuine pre-estimate by the parties of the actual damage; the fact that it was described as liquidated damages in the contract freely entered into by the parties afforded evidence that it was a genuine pre-estimate of damages especially where, as here, the amount could not be said to be out of all proportion to the damage; while the use of the words 'liquidated damages' was not conclusive, it should not be disregarded without good reason.

The judgment of the Court was given by McFarlane J.A. who concluded his reasons by citing a dictum of Lord Parmoor in *Dunlop Pneumatic Tyre Co. v. New Garage & Motor Co., 1915 A.C.* 79 PC 101:

No abstract can be laid down without reference to the special facts of the particular case, but when competent parties by free contract are purporting to agree a sum as liquidated damages, there is no reason for refusing a wide limit of discretion. To justify interference there must be an extravagant disproportion between the agreed sum and *the amount of any damage capable of pre-estimate.*

The emphasis added is mine because McFarlane J.A. went on to say:

Applying these principles to the facts, I am of the opinion that the deposit of $5,000 should not be regarded as a penalty and that its retention by the respondent is not unconscionable.

In that case, the amount of the deposit was approximately 1/12 of the purchase price. In the instant case, the amount of deposit is approximately between 1/19 and 1/20.

Applying the principles discussed to the facts of this case, I find that the sum of $50,000 is not a penalty, but a more than reasonable pre-estimate of damage and, therefore, is liquidated damages. Even if I were in error in making that finding, and the sum was a penalty I would find that it was not unconscionable for the plaintiff to "retain" it.

Does it make any difference that the plaintiff was fortunate enough to re-sell for the same price?

Again, the decision in *Hughes v. Lukuvka*, supra, is most helpful. There, in the original contract, the price was $59,500, payable $38,500 in cash and the balance by assumption of an existing mortgage for approximately $21,000 with interest. The completion date was June 30, 1969. Before June 20, 1969, the purchaser informed the vendor that he would not have funds by the completion date and requested an extension of time. The request was refused and on July 22, 1969 the vendor gave the purchaser written notice of her election to exercise her contractual right to cancel the agreement and claim the deposit. On July 25th, she accepted an offer from other purchasers to buy the property for $59,500.

The reason is plain. The test of reasonableness is at the date of the making of the contract and not at the date of the breach or any subsequent date. The reason for that reason is also plain, namely, that at the time when the agreement about liquidated damages is made, each party takes a risk, the vendor that the damages he may in fact suffer from failure on the part of the purchaser to complete will be very much greater, and the purchaser, that the vendor may not suffer any damage at all, or if he does suffer damage that damage is much less in amount than the amount stipulated as liquidated damages.

Nor does it matter that the plaintiff as vendor was to take a mortgage back of $200,000. First of all, that was an advantage to the defendant and a disadvantage to the plaintiff because she could not put that part of the price into her pocket. Secondly, even with respect to the cash balance of $775,000, the $50,000 was only 1/15. ...

I dismiss the counterclaim and application of the defendant.

Judgment for plaintiff.

When the purchaser missed the deadline for tendering the $500,000 for the property, the deadline was extended provided the purchaser pay, in addition to the $10,000 already given as a deposit, $150,000, all to be "treated as a deposit." The failure of the purchasers to meet the second deadline resulted in a struggle for the $160,000. In the words of the court:

"Can the defendants retain the $160,000 as a deposit? Neither law nor equity mandates such an unjust result. ... Such damage is measured by the injury suffered by the vendor but does not include any punitive element. ...[There are no] special circumstances that would warrant a finding that the sum that was 31.25% of the total purchase price could qualify as a true deposit."

Porto v. DiDomizio
[1996] .J. No. 22 (Q.L.)
DRS 96-03898
Court File no. 92-CQ-25469
Ontario Court of Justice (General Division)
January 9, 1996

QUANTUM OF DAMAGES

Question

How does the court approach the problem of determining the amount of damages to be paid by the party found to be in breach of contract?

Parta Industries Ltd. *v.* Canadian Pacific Ltd. et al.

48 D.L.R. (3D) 463
BRITISH COLUMBIA SUPREME COURT
JULY 4, 1974

Summary of the facts from the law report, reprinted with permission of Canada Law Book Inc., 240 Edward Street, Aurora, Ontario L4G 3S9.

The defendant carriers agreed to ship from Montreal to British Columbia certain goods imported from Belgium, described as construction material. The bill of lading was marked "RUSH." The goods consisted of equipment essential to the plaintiff's plan to bring into operation a manufacturing plant. Owing to the derailment of three railway cars the goods were damaged, and as a result, the plaintiff had to reorder the goods from Belgium, and the opening of its plant was delayed for 105 days. [The plaintiffs sued] for damages caused by the delay. ...

Craig, J.:—The plaintiff commenced an action against the defendants (hereinafter referred to as "the defendants") claiming

(a) Special and general damages for breach of contract entered into between the Plaintiff and the Defendants on the l2th day of September 1969, by which contract the Defendants, common carriers, contracted to deliver goods for and to the Plaintiff, and did fail to do so in accordance with the terms, express and implied, of the said contract. Which failure caused financial loss to the Plaintiff.

(b) In the alternative, damages against the Defendants for negligence in the performance of the aforementioned contract, which negligence caused financial loss to the Plaintiff.

The defendants have denied the plaintiff's claim, generally, and have counterclaimed for the sum of $1,548.59 which, they allege, is the net amount owing to them after making financial adjustments between the parties relating to this incident....

Mr. Moran contends that the failure of the defendant to deliver the equipment in usable condition on or before September 19th, or within a reasonable time of this date, was a breach of the contract to "rush" delivery and that the plaintiff suffered damages totaling $129,705. He filed a schedule as ex. "4" which representatives of the plaintiff had prepared, showing how damages were calculated and what items were included. He submitted that these items of damages and the amounts claimed for these items are such damages:

(1) "...as may fairly and reasonable be considered as...arising naturally...", or at least,

(2) "...as may reasonable be supposed to have been in contemplation of both parties, at the time they made the contract, as the probable result of the breach of it".

citing *Hadley v. Baxendale* (1854), 9 Ex. 341, 156 E.R. 145, and the well-known judgment of Asquith, L.J., in *Victoria Laundry (Windsor) Ltd. v. Newman Industries Ltd.; Coulson & Co. Ltd. (Third Parties)*, [1949] 2 K.B. 528, [1949] 1 All E.R. 997. ...

In the *Victoria Laundry (Windsor) Ltd. v. Newman Industries Ltd.* case, *supra*, Asquith, L.J., listed six propositions applicable to damages for breach of contract. His judgment has been referred to on numerous occasions. These propositions are as follows [at pp. 539-40]:

(1) It is well settled that the governing purpose of damages is to put the party whose rights have been violated in the same position, so far as money can do so, as if his rights had been observed: (*Sally Wertheim v. Chicoutimi Pulp Company*, [1911] A.C. 301). This purpose, if relentlessly pursued, would provide him with a complete indemnity for all loss *de facto* resulting from a particular breach, however improbable, however unpredictable. This, in contract at least, is recognized as too harsh a rule. Hence,

(2) In cases of breach of contract the aggrieved party is only entitled to recover such part of the loss actually resulting as was at the time of the contract reasonably foreseeable as liable to result from the breach.

(3) What was at that time reasonably so foreseeable depends on the knowledge then possessed by the parties or, at all events, by the party who later commits the breach.

(4) For this purpose, knowledge "possessed" is of two kinds; one imputed, the other actual. Everyone, as a reasonable person, is taken to know the "ordinary course of things" and consequently what loss is liable to result from a breach of contract in that ordinary course. This is the subject matter of the "first rule" in *Hadley v. Baxendale*. But to this knowledge, which a contract-breaker is assumed to possess whether he actually possesses it or not, there may have to be added in a particular case knowledge which he actually possesses, of special circumstances outside the "ordinary course of things," of such a kind that a breach in those special circumstances would be liable to cause more loss. Such a case attracts the operation of the "second rule" so as to make additional loss also recoverable.

(5) In order to make the contract-breaker liable under either rule it is not necessary that he should actually have asked himself what loss is liable to result from a breach. As has often been pointed out, parties at the time of contracting contemplate not the breach of the contract, but its performance. It suffices that, if he had considered the question, he would as a reasonable man have concluded that the loss in question was liable to result (see certain observations of Lord du Parcq in the recent case of *A/B Karlshamms Oljefabriker v. Monarch Steamship Company Limited*, [1949] A.C. 196).

(6) Nor, finally, to make a particular loss recoverable, need it be proved that upon a given state of knowledge the defendant could, as a reasonable man, foresee that a breach must necessarily result in that loss. It is enough if he could foresee it was likely so to result. It is indeed enough, to borrow from the language of Lord du Parcq in the same case, at page 158, if the loss (or some factor without which it would not have occurred) is a "serious possibility" or a "real danger." For short, we have used the word "liable" to result. Possibly the colloquialism "on the cards" indicates the shade of meaning with some approach to accuracy.

In his judgment, also, Asquith, L.J., said that the case of *British Columbia Saw-Mill Co. v. Nettleship* (1868), L.R. 3 C.P.

499, annexed a rider to the principle laid in *Hadley v. Baxendale* to the effect

…that where knowledge of special circumstances is relied on as enhancing the damage recoverable that knowledge must have been brought home to the defendant at the time of the contract and in such circumstances that the defendant impliedly undertook to bear any special loss referable to a breach in those special circumstances. The knowledge which was lacking in that case on the part of the defendant was knowledge that the particular box of machinery negligently lost by the defendants was one without which the rest of the machinery could not be put together and would therefore be useless.

Having regard to the evidence in this case and the circumstances generally, I find that the only knowledge possessed by the defendant was that he was to "RUSH" delivery of 77 packages of "construction material." There is nothing in the contract to indicate the nature of the material, nor the use to which it was to be put. Certainly, there is nothing to indicate that it was to be used in a large manufacturing plant and that the plant could not operate without the equipment. In other words, the defendant did not have knowledge of the special circumstances of the situation which would bring into operation the second branch of the rule in *Hadley v. Baxendale*. That being so, what damages, if any, in this case should be considered as "…such as may fairly and reasonably be considered as…arising naturally i.e. according to the natural course of things from the breach of contract…"? In my opinion, the defendant could have reasonably foreseen on the facts which were known to it in this case that a delay in delivery, or a failure to deliver was liable to result in:

(a) a delay in actual construction;
(b) extra labour costs;
(c) interest;
(d) depreciation of equipment;
(e) additional overhead expenses;
(f) cost of repairing and replacing equipment.

While I think that the defendant could have reasonably foreseen a delay in construction, I do not think that the defendant could have reasonably foreseen a delay of 105 days. …

Questions

Is a contractor liable in damages to a subsequent purchaser if the building is defective? Can one recover for an economic loss when there is no injury to persons or damage to property?

Winnipeg Condominium Corporation No. 36 *v.* Bird Construction Co.

FILE NO.: 23624
http://www.droit.umontreal.ca/
SUPREME COURT OF CANADA
JANUARY 26, 1995

[On appeal from the Court of Appeal for Manitoba.]

[1] LA FOREST J. — May a general contractor responsible for the construction of a building be held tortiously liable for negligence to a subsequent purchaser of the building, who is not in contractual privity with the contractor, for the cost of repairing defects in the building arising out of negligence in its construction? That is the issue that was posed by a motion for summary judgment and a motion to strike out a claim as disclosing no reasonable cause of action argued before Galanchuk J. of the Manitoba Court of Queen's Bench . ... Galanchuk J. dismissed the motions, but the Court of Appeal of Manitoba allowed an appeal from this decision and struck out the claim against the contractor on the grounds that the damages sought were for economic loss, which were not recoverable in the circumstances, and hence that the claim did not disclose a reasonable cause of action.

[2] For reasons that will appear, I do not, with respect, share the views of the Court of Appeal; I agree with Galanchuk J. that the action should proceed to trial. ...

FACTS

[3] On April 19, 1972, a Winnipeg land developer, Tuxedo Properties Co. Ltd. ("Tuxedo"), entered into a contract ("the General Contract") with a general contractor, Bird Construction Co. Ltd. ("Bird"), for the construction of a 15-storey, 94-unit apartment building. In the General Contract, Bird undertook to construct the building in accordance with plans and specifications prepared by the architectural firm of Smith Carter Partners ("Smith Carter"), with whom Tuxedo also had a contract. On June 5, 1972, Bird entered into a subcontract with a masonry subcontractor, Kornovski & Keller Masonry Ltd. ("Kornovski & Keller"), under which the latter undertook to perform the masonry portion of the work specified under the General Contract. The work called for by the General Contract commenced in April, 1972 and the building was substantially completed by December, 1974.

[4] The building was initially built and used as an apartment block, but was converted into a condominium in October, 1978, when Winnipeg Condominium Corporation No. 36 ("the Condominium Corporation") became the registered owner of the land and building. ...

[5] In 1982, the Board of Directors of the Condominium Corporation became concerned about the state of the exterior cladding of the building (consisting of 4-inch thick slabs of stone), which had been installed by the subcontractor, Kornovski & Keller. The directors observed that some of the mortar had broken away and that cracks were developing in the stone work. As a result of these concerns, the Condominium Corporation retained a firm of structural engineers and the original architects, Smith Carter, to inspect the building. The engineers and Smith

Carter recommended some minor remedial work but offered the opinion that the stonework on the building was structurally sound. The remedial work, costing $8,100, was undertaken at the Condominium Corporation's expense in 1982.

[6] On May 8, 1989, a storey-high section of the cladding, approximately twenty feet in length, fell from the ninth storey level of the building to the ground below. The Condominium Corporation retained engineering consultants who conducted further inspections. Following these inspections, the Condominium Corporation had the entire cladding removed and replaced at a cost in excess of $1.5 million. ...

ANALYSIS

[12] This case gives this Court the opportunity once again to address the question of recoverability in tort for economic loss. ...

[13] Traditionally, the courts have characterized the costs incurred by a plaintiff in repairing a defective chattel or building as "economic loss" on the grounds that costs of those repairs do not arise from injury to persons or damage to property apart from the defective chattel or building itself; see *Rivtow Marine Ltd. v. Washington Iron Works*, [1974] S.C.R. 1189, at p. 1207. For my part, I would find it more congenial to deal directly with the policy considerations underlying that classification. ... However I am content to deal with the issues in the terms in which the arguments were formulated. Adopting this traditional characterization as a convenient starting point for my analysis, I observe that the losses claimed by the Condominium Corporation in the present case fall quite clearly under the category of economic loss. In their statement of claim, the Condominium Corporation claim damages in excess of $1.5 million from the respondent Bird, the subcontractor Kornovski & Keller and the architects Smith Carter, representing the cost of repairing the building subsequent to the collapse of the exterior cladding on May 8, 1989. The Condominium Corporation is not claiming that anyone was injured by the collapsing exterior cladding or that the collapsing cladding damaged any of its other property. Rather, its claim is simply for the cost of repairing the allegedly defective masonry and putting the exterior of the building back into safe working condition. ...

[16] Proceeding on the assumption, then, that the losses claimed in this case are purely economic, the sole issue before this Court is whether the losses claimed by the Condominium Corporation are the type of economic losses that should be recoverable in tort. In coming to its conclusion that the losses claimed by the Condominium Corporation are not recoverable in tort, the Manitoba Court of Appeal, we saw, followed the reasoning of the House of Lords in *D & F Estates*. In that

case, the House of Lords found that the cost of repairing a defect in a building is not recoverable in negligence by a successor in title against the original contractor in the absence of a contractual relationship or a special relationship of reliance. I should say that the Court of Appeal might well have come to the same conclusion on the basis of the majority opinion in *Rivtow*, supra, an issue I will take up later. Here I shall dispose of the arguments relating to *D & F Estates*. ...

[18] [In that case], [t]he House of Lords dismissed the ... [claim by tenants for the cost of repair when plaster fell from the ceiling and a wall] on two principal grounds. First, they decided that any duty owed by a contractor to a home owner with respect to the quality of construction in a building must arise in contract, and not in tort. They based this conclusion upon a concern that allowing recoverability for the cost of repairing defects in buildings would have the effect of creating a non-contractual warranty of fitness; see *D & F Estates*, at p. 1007.

[19] Second, they decided that a contractor can only be held liable in tort to subsequent purchasers of a building when the contractor's negligence causes physical injury to the purchasers, damage to their other property, or where a special relationship of reliance has developed between the contractor and the purchasers along the lines suggested in *Hedley Byrne & Co. v. Heller & Partners Ltd.*, [1964] A.C. 465. See *D & F Estates*, at p. 1014.

[20] There was no contract between the plaintiff and the defendants in *D & F Estates*, and the Law Lords found no special relationship of reliance on the facts of the case. Accordingly, they reasoned that the cost of repairing defective plaster fell under the category of "pure economic loss." Since the negligence in that case did not result in damage to persons or property, they concluded that the plaintiff could not claim that expense against the contractor. ...

[21] Huband J.A. found the reasoning in *D & F Estates* to be compelling and of strong persuasive authority and, on that basis, came to the conclusion that the cost of repair of the defects in the building were not recoverable in tort by the Condominium Corporation against Bird. With respect, I come to a different conclusion. In my view, where a contractor (or any other person) is negligent in planning or constructing a building, and where that building is found to contain defects resulting from that negligence which pose a real and substantial danger to the occupants of the building, the reasonable cost of repairing the defects and putting the building back into a non-dangerous state are recoverable in tort by the occupants. The underlying rationale for this conclusion is that a person who participates in the construction of a large and permanent structure which, if negligently constructed, has the capacity to cause serious damage to other persons and property in the community, should be held to a reasonable standard of care.

[22] My conclusion that the type of economic loss claimed by the Condominium Corporation is recoverable in tort is therefore based in large part upon what seem to me to be compelling policy considerations. I shall elaborate in more detail upon these later in my reasons. However, before doing so, I think it important to clarify why the *D & F Estates* case should not, in my view, be seen as having strong persuasive authority in Canadian tort law as that law is currently developing. [The judge critiques *D & F Estates*.] ...

[34] I conclude, therefore, that the *D&F Estates* decision is not of strong persuasive authority in the Canadian context. Accordingly, the question arising in this appeal must be resolved with reference to the test developed in *Anns* and *Kamloops*. I will

now proceed, applying this test, to discuss whether the costs of repair claimed by the Condominium Corporation are the type of economic loss that should be recoverable in tort. [The first test:]

Was There a Sufficiently Close Relationship Between the Parties so that, in the Reasonable Contemplation of Bird, Carelessness on its Part Might Cause Damage to a Subsequent Purchaser of the Building such as the Condominium Corporation?

[35] ... Buildings are permanent structures that are commonly inhabited by many different persons over their useful life. By constructing the building negligently, contractors (or any other person responsible for the design and construction of a building) create a foreseeable danger that will threaten not only the original owner, but every inhabitant during the useful life of the building. As noted by the Supreme Court of South Carolina, in *Terlinde v. Neely*, 271 S.E. 2d 768 (1980), at p. 770:

> The key inquiry is foreseeability, not privity. In our mobile society, it is clearly foreseeable that more than the original purchaser will seek to enjoy the fruits of the builder's efforts. The plaintiffs, being a member of the class for which the home was constructed, are entitled to a duty of care in construction commensurate with industry standards. [...] By placing this product into the stream of commerce, the builder owes a duty of care to those who will use his product, so as to render him accountable for negligent workmanship.

[36] In my view, the reasonable likelihood that a defect in a building will cause injury to its inhabitants is also sufficient to ground a contractor's duty in tort to subsequent purchasers of the building for the cost of repairing the defect if that defect is discovered prior to any injury and if it poses a real and substantial danger to the inhabitants of the building. ...

[37] Apart from the logical force of holding contractors liable for the cost of repair of dangerous defects, there is also a strong underlying policy justification for imposing liability in these cases. Under the law as developed in *D&F Estates* and *Murphy*, the plaintiff who moves quickly and responsibly to fix a defect before it causes injury to persons or damage to property must do so at his or her own expense. By contrast, the plaintiff who, either intentionally or through neglect, allows a defect to develop into an accident may benefit at law from the costly and potentially tragic consequences. In my view, this legal doctrine is difficult to justify because it serves to encourage, rather than discourage, reckless and hazardous behaviour. Maintaining a bar against recoverability for the cost of repair of dangerous defects provides no incentive for plaintiffs to mitigate potential losses and tends to encourage economically inefficient behaviour. The Fourth District Court of Appeal for Florida in *Drexel Properties, Inc. v. Bay Colony Club Condominium, Inc.*, 406 So.2d 515 (1981), at p. 519, explained the problem in the following manner:

> Why should a buyer have to wait for a personal tragedy to occur in order to recover damages to remedy or repair defects? In the final analysis, the cost to the developer for a resulting tragedy could be far greater than the cost of remedying the condition.

...

[38] This conclusion is borne out by the facts of the present case, which fall squarely within the category of what I would define as a "real and substantial danger." ... The piece of cladding that

fell from the building was a storey high, was made of 4"-thick Tyndall stone, and dropped nine storeys. Had this cladding landed on a person or on other property, it would unquestionably have caused serious injury or damage. Indeed, it was only by chance that the cladding fell in the middle of the night and caused no harm. In this light, I believe that the Condominium Corporation behaved responsibly, and as a reasonable home owner should, in having the building inspected and repaired immediately. Bird should not be insulated from liability simply because the current owner of the building acted quickly to alleviate the danger that Bird itself may well have helped to create. ...

[42] ... I note that the present case is distinguishable on a policy level cases where the workmanship is merely shoddy or substandard but not dangerously defective. ... Accordingly, it is sufficient for present purposes to say that, if Bird is found negligent at trial, the Condominium Corporation would be entitled on this reasoning to recover the reasonable cost of putting the building into a non-dangerous state, but not the cost of any repairs that would serve merely to improve the quality, and not the safety, of the building.

[43] I conclude that the law in Canada has now progressed to the point where it can be said that contractors (as well as subcontractors, architects and engineers) who take part in the design and construction of a building will owe a duty in tort to subsequent purchasers of the building if it can be shown that it was foreseeable that a failure to take reasonable care in constructing the building would create defects that pose a substantial danger to the health and safety of the occupants. Where negligence is established and such defects manifest themselves before any damage to persons or property occurs, they should, in my view, be liable for the reasonable cost of repairing the defects and putting the building back into a non-dangerous state.

[The second step in the *Anns* case is]

Are There Any Considerations that Ought to Negate (a) the Scope of the Duty and (b) the Class of Persons to Whom it is Owed or (c) the Damages to which a Breach of it May Give Rise?

[44] There are two primary and interrelated concerns raised by the recognition of a contractor's duty in tort to subsequent purchasers of buildings for the cost of repairing dangerous defects. The first is that warranties respecting quality of construction are primarily contractual in nature and cannot be easily defined or limited in tort. ...

[45] The second concern is that the recognition of such a duty interferes with the doctrine of caveat emptor. ...

[46] In my view, these concerns are both merely versions of the more general and traditional concern that allowing recovery for economic loss in tort will subject a defendant to what Cardozo C.J. in *Ultramares Corp. v. Touche*, 174 N.E. 441 (N.Y.C.A. 1931), at p. 444, called "liability in an indeterminate amount for an indeterminate time to an indeterminate class." In light of the fact that most buildings have a relatively long useful life, the concern is that a contractor will be subject potentially to an indeterminate amount of liability to an indeterminate number of successive owners over an indeterminate time period. The doctrines of privity of contract and caveat emptor provide courts with a useful mechanism for limiting liability in tort. But the problem, as I will now attempt to demonstrate, is that it is difficult to justify the employment of these doctrines in the tort context in any principled manner apart from their utility as mechanisms for limiting liability.

[The judge rejects each of these concerns and concludes:]

CONCLUSION

[54] I conclude, then, that no adequate policy considerations exist to negate a contractor's duty in tort to subsequent purchasers of a building to take reasonable care in constructing the building, and to ensure that the building does not contain defects that pose foreseeable and substantial danger to the health and safety of the occupants. In my view, the Manitoba Court of Appeal erred in deciding that Bird could not, in principle, be held liable in tort to the Condominium Corporation for the reasonable cost of repairing the defects and putting the building back into a non-dangerous state. These costs are recoverable economic loss under the law of tort in Canada. ...

[56] I would allow the appeal, reverse the decision of the Court of Appeal and make the following orders: that the losses alleged in the statement of claim, to the extent that they may be found to constitute pure economic loss flowing from the negligence of the respondent, be recoverable from the respondent, and that the order of the learned motions judge, that the within action proceed to trial against the respondent Bird Construction Co. Ltd. with respect to the remaining issues raised in the statement of claim, be reinstated. The appellant is entitled to its costs throughout.

Appeal allowed.

Question

Can you recover for lost computer time and lost data if the power system is knocked out?

The case begins:

"[1] Esson, C.J.S.C.:— The parties have stated a case for the opinion of the court under Rule 33. The outline of the facts which follows is a somewhat condensed version of the agreed facts as set out in the stated case.

[2] The plaintiff is a federally incorporated life insurance company which has its head office in

Vancouver. The defendant carries on a trucking business using a truck owned by him. He has no other employees. On May 20, 1993, in the course of his business he was delivering a load of gravel to a construction site across the alley from the rear of the plaintiff's head office building. He knew nothing of the plaintiff or its business. While backing into the site, the truck came into contact with a wooden pole, situate on municipal property, owned by B.C. Hydro. The pole supports distribution wires and carries step-down conductors.

[3] The pole suffered only a minor scar which, from the attached photograph, seems no more serious than scars caused by linemen's spikes. But the impact, although minor, was sufficient to cause a "whiplash" effect which knocked some of the conductors off their insulators at the top of the pole and caused some of the wires to fall, resulting in a power outage which deprived the plaintiff and about 1,500 other customers of B.C. Hydro of power supply. The disruption lasted for about 90 minutes.

[4] The defendant admitted liability to B.C. Hydro for the costs of $202.50 incurred in restoring the power connection. ..."

The questions put before the court were these:...

    (a) Does the loss of computer data constitute property damage?
    (b) If the answer to question (a) is yes, are the plaintiff's losses, measured as expenses thrown away, loss of profit, or otherwise, too remote?
    (c) If the answer to question (a) is no, is the defendant liable to the plaintiff to make good the plaintiff's pure economic loss, measured as expenses thrown away, loss of profit, or otherwise?

In the case he answers question (a) in the negative.

But for the purposes of distinguishing between pure economic loss and damage to property in the law of damages, I consider that it would simply be productive of confusion to treat the loss of the data as anything other than economic loss. In this case, the loss was purely economic. Some employees had to stand by until the computers were operational. Others had to spend some time checking them and "re-inputting" data. All, essentially, a matter of increasing the cost of doing business.

After an examination of the case law he concludes that the Supreme Court of Canada has held that there can be recovery for pure economic loss but that there is no majority judgment establishing what those circumstances are. He answers question (c) in the negative as well. He does not see it governed by any precedent and also finds that allowing recovery would not be wise policy.

... [A]ll of the judgments accepted that the exceptions of the general rule [that pure economic loss is not recoverable] should avoid exposing defendants to, in the famous phrase of Cardozo, J. in *Ultramares Corp. v. Touche*, 174 N.E. 441 (1931) at p. 444, "liability in an indeterminate amount for an indeterminate time to an indeterminate class." The facts of this case offer a classic example of the potential for imposing liability in an indeterminate amount to an indeterminate class. We know that some 1,500 other customers of B.C. Hydro were affected. Depending on the area served by the pole, the number no doubt could have been far larger.

The conclusion:

I would answer questions (a) and (c) in the negative. Question (b) need not be answered.

Seaboard Life Insurance Co. v. Babich et al.
[1995] B.C.J. No. 1868 (Q.L.)
DRS 95-18301
Vancouver Registry No. C933879
British Columbia Supreme Court
(In Chambers)

- *T*he United States Supreme Court struck down a damage award as being grossly excessive. In a five to four split the court held that a US $2 million damage award to a doctor who sued because his BMW had been painted in places to conceal damage from acid rain was in violation of the due process rights of the car manufacturer.[33]

A woman injured in two automobile accidents had worked full time in a bakery co-owned with her husband, and approximately 40 hours a week at home. She appealed from the trial judge's award of damages which she argued were "inadequate." The Saskatchewan Court of Appeal held that she was entitled to an award of damages that would compensate her not only for loss of earning capacity, pain and suffering and loss of amenities, but also for the impairment of her housekeeping capacity. The court would take into account the cost of employing someone to provide the services she had performed, including the value of management.

Dean v. Fobel; MacDonald v. Fobel
Saskatchewan Court of Appeal
83 D.L.R. (4th) 385
August 27, 1991

The Supreme Court of Canada refused leave to appeal in March of 1992.[34]

Note: This "landmark" decision has now been followed in numerous cases. Watch for further cases on and discussion of compensation for lost "housekeeping capacity."

- *P*ennzoil successfully sued Texaco for interfering with its planned merger with Getty Oil and was awarded $10.53 billion by a jury, the largest award in U.S. history. Texaco subsequently filed for bankruptcy. Later the companies reached a settlement by which Texaco would agree to pay to Pennzoil the sum of $3 billion in cash.[35]

DIFFICULTIES IN ASSESSING QUANTUM OF DAMAGES

When Judge Taylor of the B.C. Supreme Court had to assess damages to be awarded to an 88-year-old plaintiff seriously injured when struck by a car, he found the principles for assessing damages "sadly inadequate to the task." The life expectancy tables were not especially helpful to determine the loss to a man of that age who had been active and robust before the accident. Furthermore, the judge did not feel that the practice of awarding a lump sum was appropriate. Nevertheless, following established procedures, he awarded the plaintiff $50,000 non-pecuniary damages.

Olesik v. Mackin et al.
Summarized from The Lawyers Weekly
March 27, 1986 p. 18

- *A* dispensing error by a pharmacist in Vancouver resulted in a fatal dose of an anti-psychotic drug being given to a 94-year-old woman.

- *I*n Louisiana, a coroner deliberately dropped a dead baby to examine the results of a fall on her head. The information would help him as an expert witness in an infant mortality case.

PUNITIVE DAMAGES

The National Bank of Canada was sued because of its role in diverting funds from a public company to a rogue and his companies. The Ontario Court of Appeal found that the bank had conspired to deplete the company's assets and awarded the plaintiff $4.8 million dollars in punitive damages, in addition to the $7 million awarded for compensatory damages. The judges reviewed the law with regard to punitive damages as follows:

"In the words of Schroeder J.A. in *Denison v. Fawcet*, 1958 O.R. 312 at pp. 319-20, 12 D.L.R. (2d) 537 at p. 542 (C.A.), exemplary or aggravated damages may be awarded:

[i]f, in addition to committing the wrongful act, the defendant's conduct is "highhanded, malicious, conduct showing a contempt of the plaintiff's rights, or disregarding every principle which actuates the conduct of a gentleman"…

In *Robitaille v. Vancouver Hockey Club Ltd.* (1981), 124 D.L.R. (3d) 228 at p. 251, [1981] 3 W.W.R. 481, 30 B.C.L.R. 286 (C.A.), it was pointed out that aggravated damages may be awarded on the basis of circumstances which accompany or are associated with the tortious conduct.

A further principle for consideration comes from *Cassell & Co. Ltd. v. Broome*, [1972] All E.R. 801 (H.L.) at pp. 830-31. In an exhaustive analysis of exemplary, punitive or aggravated damages, Lord Hailsham observed, citing Lord Devlin in *Rookes v. Barnard*, [1964] 1 All E.R. 367 (H.L.), that '[e]xemplary damages can properly be awarded whenever it is necessary to teach a wrongdoer that tort does not pay'."

Claiborne Industries Ltd. v. National Bank of Canada
(1989) 59 D.L.R. (4th) 533
June 27, 1989

Note: See also *The Lawyers Weekly* (July 14, 1989 p. 1) which quotes the winning counsel as saying "it was by far the largest punitive award in the history of this country."

- *I*n 1984, The U.S. Supreme Court reinstated a $10 million punitive damages award won by the estate of Karen Silkwood. In Oklahoma a jury had awarded her children $500,000 in actual damages and $10 million in punitive damages. The U.S. Circuit Court of Appeals had overturned the punitive damage award on the basis that the federal government's exclusive regulation of radiation hazards precluded any punitive damage award based on state law.[36]

  In 1986 it was reported that the estate settled for $1.38 million.[37]

8. CONTEMPT OF COURT

Question

Equitable remedies are one type of orders of the court. What can be done if a person ignores an order of the court?

Canadian Imperial Bank of Commerce *v.* Sayani

No. C941062 Vancouver Registry
http://www.courts.gov.bc.ca/
The Supreme Court of British Columbia
June 7, 1996

[1] Hall, J: This is a contempt proceeding brought by the plaintiff against the defendant. The proceeding has its immediate origin in an order made by the Honourable Mr. Justice Vickers on September 27, 1995. The operative part of his order reads as follows:

> THIS COURT ORDERS that the defendant Zarina Sayani appear before this Court at a time and date to be appointed to show cause why she should not be held in contempt of this Honourable Court.

That order was entered on October 20, 1995.

[2] This matter came on for hearing on October 27, was continued on November 9 and ultimately concluded on February 14, 1996. There was extensive written material placed before the Court and the defendant, Mrs. Sayani, gave oral testimony.

[3] In the early 1980s, there were dealings between the plaintiff bank and the husband and brother-in-law of the defendant, Mrs. Sayani. Monies had been borrowed from the bank and in the 1980s the bank was owed hundreds of thousands by the husband and brother-in-law. There were attempts to collect by the bank and I believe a tentative settlement was reached but this did not endure. Attempts at realization were not successful and by 1994, the plaintiff bank was seeking to obtain a judgment against the defendant for about $635,000 based on a guarantee she had executed in March of 1982. I presume the bank felt there was then some likelihood of success in getting some funds from the defendant because as a result of her entering into a venture to manage the Georgian Court Hotel in the late 1980s, she was in receipt from time to time of substantial funds and it was anticipated that further funds would be coming from that venture. ... [Her guarantee was to cover the indebtedness of the Sayani brothers against whom judgment was taken for $518,064.33. Their appeal was dismissed. Leave to appeal to the Supreme Court of Canada was refused.]

[6] Arising out of the Georgian Court Hotel management joint venture, in February of 1993, the defendant received through her private company something in the order of $1.7 million Canadian. This money was initially in the HongKong Bank in Vancouver but was immediately moved to a Swiss bank by the mechanism of two bank drafts. Thereafter, it was moved from one Swiss bank to another because the latter bank was one that Mrs. Sayani's family had dealt with during a time when she lived in Africa. I should observe here that I see nothing sinister or indeed particularly unusual about her placing funds in a Swiss bank account. That was a perfectly lawful thing to do so far as the evidence discloses. The name of the bank where the funds were ultimately lodged was the Habib Bank AG, Zurich, hereinafter called the Habib Bank. The funds remained in that bank from the spring of 1993 until the spring

of 1995, drawing interest at a comparatively modest rate.

[7] Mrs. Sayani testified that in March of 1995, as a result of certain diagnostic tests done by her physician, she discovered that she might have a cancerous lesion on one of her kidneys. She says that this greatly alarmed her and caused her to fear for the future economic well-being of her daughters. She says that there is a custom in her culture whereby if a family member dies, then a sibling may well take over responsibility for the well-being of the children of the deceased sibling. Mrs. Sayani says that these concerns led to her decision in the third week of March of 1995 to transfer the funds in the Habib Bank to the direction of her brother. ...

[8] On March 28, 1995, Habib Bank formally notified Mrs. Sayani by a letter sent to her West Vancouver residence that it had paid out the full amount of her accounts which stood at U.S. $1,408,623.04 to the order of her brother, Mr. Shiraz P. Chatur. ... The bank made efforts in the summer of 1995 to execute on its judgment against Mrs. Sayani. There were applications before my colleagues Paris J. and Thackray J. On July 27, 1995, Thackray J. ordered the defendant to deposit the sum of $750,000 in trust not later than August 8, 1995. This apparently was reckoned to be approximately the figure of the judgment of $668,000 odd dollars plus costs and interest that was owing to the bank. Nothing happened. Thereafter, Vickers J. made the order referred to supra.

[9] [Sayani appealed the judgment against her, but was still required to post security in the amount of $750,000],

[10] As Blackburn J. observed in Skipworth's case (1873), 9 L.R. Q.B. 230, the phrase, contempt of court, can often mislead persons who are not lawyers to misapprehend its meaning. It is sometimes thought that a proceeding for contempt amounts to some process taken for the purpose of vindicating the personal dignity of judges or protecting them from personal insults as individuals. His Lordship observes that in essence contempt of court is a procedure to ensure that the course of justice is not sullied or interfered with. In Skipworth's case, there is a reference to a case in the time of Lord Cottenham, Lechmere Charlton's case, (1837) 40 E.R. 661, where Charlton, a barrister and M.P. had attempted to obstruct the course of justice in the Court of Chancery by what were said to be threatening letters he sent concerning proceedings he was involved in before a Master in Chancery. Mr. Charlton was ultimately committed to the Fleet prison by Lord Cottenham for contempt. In Charlton's case, there is reference to case law in the time of Lord Hardwicke in the century before, where attempted bribery of a judicial officer occurred and was dealt with under the contempt power. It is an ancient power given to superior courts to ensure that the course of justice is not obstructed. It probably has its origins in a species

of the Royal Prerogative. ...

[13] In the case at bar, ... [a]ccording to Mrs. Sayani and her brother [now resident in Uganda] the funds that were originally in the Habib Bank have now been placed in some type of unspecified investment in India. Her brother asserts that he has unnamed partners in his business in an undisclosed location and says that essentially for business reasons, he is not prepared to disclose the whereabouts of the funds or the nature of what is being done with them. It is said that the funds are tied up for a term of years at a favourable rate of return and that it would have harmful economic consequences to the brother and the partners if their location and employment were disclosed. Mrs. Sayani professed no ability to get any further information from her brother. Mrs. Sayani said she was hopeful that some further funds to be generated from the Georgian Court Hotel management joint venture would soon accrue to her and that these could be utilized to pay off her obligations under the judgment held by the plaintiff bank. However, apparently, there exists controversy concerning the ownership of any anticipated dividend coming from the joint venture and so there is a strong element of uncertainty as to when, if ever, that source of funds will yield anything.

[14] Chief Justice Lemuel Shaw once observed that the proper object of jurisprudence is for a court to take a set of facts, proven or admitted, and to declare what rights or obligations flow therefrom. Judges do that everyday. That is the chief aim and purpose of the judicial branch and without that, civil society could scarcely go on. Concomitant with that, if adjudications of courts could be ignored and set at naught by citizens, then society would cease to be orderly.

[15] I think I could properly observe that the evidence of Mrs. Sayani and the evidence emanating by way of affidavit from her brother ... may well be described as fantastic. Having listened carefully to her evidence and having considered all of the material placed before me, I simply say that I do not find her narrative believable. The funds are said to have mysteriously vanished into an unnamed venture in the Indian continent. Her brother professes to be unable to make any disclosure about it. Interestingly, he does assert in his affidavit sworn September 25, 1995 that if the plaintiff bank should seek to move in India to obtain access to the funds (assuming it could ever find where they are), the "slightest hint of any commencement of legal actions by CIBC to collect these funds prematurely could tie up the total investment in litigation quagmire of the Indian Court system for several years." The whole narrative seems improbable in the highest degree . In my view, any "quagmire" that may exist here is one created by brother and sister to keep the plaintiff from getting access to any funds to satisfy its judgment.

[16] Commencing in the year 1994, ... Mrs. Sayani could not have failed to appreciate that she stood increasingly in peril of having a judgment rendered against her for a substantial dollar amount. ... [W]hen she arranged for the movement of the funds, the likely hour of reckoning was near at hand. I have no doubt that her actions were a calculated effort to prevent the plaintiff from being able in future to realize on the fruits of its likely judgment. Apropos of the comments of Chief Justice Shaw

adverted to above, it would be an exceedingly idle enterprise for courts to proceed to adjudicate questions of property rights between citizens if actions as transparently artificial as those disclosed here could be used to frustrate the normal course of justice.

[17] Counsel for the defendant points out correctly that mere failure to pay money is not generally a contempt of court. In connection with that argument, reference was made to a judgment of our Court of Appeal, in *The Royal Bank of Canada v. McLennan* (1918), 25 B.C.R. 183. However, Huddart J. (as she then was), noted in *Manolescu v. Manolescu* (1991), 31 R.F.L. (3d) 421 at p. 433:

> Wilful breach of a court order will always be a contempt of court. A deliberate refusal to pay money pursuant to a court order when one has the ability to pay will constitute a civil contempt of the court. It is also a private injury or wrong to the person who is the beneficiary of the order.

That case concerned a husband who had consistently refused to obey court orders concerning arrears and support. Counsel for the defendant suggested that case was distinguishable but I believe it to be a correct statement of legal principle. The learned judge in that case found that the conduct was a deliberate contempt going beyond a mere failure to pay money. I believe likewise that this case involves much more than a simple failure to satisfy a judgment debt by paying money to a judgment creditor. As I perceive the circumstances, the activity of the defendant undertaken in the month of March 1995 was intentional activity designed to put beyond the reach of any creditor the money she then held on deposit in the Swiss bank. By simply transferring the asset to her brother, she erected an impenetrable and opaque wall between the funds and the plaintiff here. The purpose was to render nugatory any judgment that might be rendered against her, the likelihood of which judgment was becoming extremely imminent. This was conduct calculated and designed to interfere with the due administration of justice in this country and I have no hesitation in characterizing it as contempt. The suggestions concerning her wish to preserve the economic positions of family members is to me a feeble attempt to justify the unjustifiable. Her real purpose was to make sure these funds were put beyond the reach of any power of execution. People are entitled to order their affairs to protect themselves from personal liability for debt and to enhance their economic interests but transparent ruses of the sort disclosed here are to be discouraged. Having considered all of the evidence here, I am fully convinced that the activities undertaken by Mrs. Sayani in Spring, 1995 to put her assets beyond ken and reach of a potential creditor were a calculated course of activity designed to frustrate the course of justice. Her continuing refusal to take steps to satisfy the judgment are merely confirmatory evidence of what was her original intent and purpose. I find her actions to amount to a contempt of court. I leave it in the hands of counsel to decide when they wish to again bring on the case before me so that the question of penalty can be addressed.

See p. 210 for the consequences imposed for failing to obey an injunction.

- *F*aye Leung, the person who arranged the sale of former B.C. premier Vander Zalm's Fantasy Garden theme park, was sued by former business associates who alleged that she had fraudulently induced them to participate in a real estate investment. The court ordered Leung to produce a list of her assets. She not only failed to provide the list, but also violated a court order by attempting to remove "a major asset" from the province. Her conduct was held to be in contempt of court.

    At the hearing in which the Supreme Court Judge was attempting to determine the appropriate remedy, the lawyer for the former associates referred to her as a "whirling dervish of deceit" and in response to the judge's suggestion that she do community service, the lawyer answered "not to be unkind or flippant, but I have some concerns about loosing this woman upon the world."[38]

    In his judgment released February 17, 1992, the judge described her as "obstructive, uncooperative, and dishonest," but suspended her sentence with a two-year probation. He stated that he had considered a sentence of imprisonment with a recommendation for electronic monitoring, "but concluded she is likely to become too much of a nuisance to the corrections authorities."

    Her former associates won their case against her.[39]

- *L*yndon LaRoche, a controversial political figure in the U.S. frequently cited for contempt of court, ran for the U.S. presidency and was quoted as saying "It's a terrible inconvenience running a presidential campaign from prison."[40]

Criminal Contempt

- *A* witness, J. N., who refused to answer questions at a murder trial was sentenced to three years in prison for contempt of court. In his reasons for imposing such a severe sentence the judge said "… individuals like [J.N.] … must know, and all citizens must know, that if they are lawfully required to attend at a court and testify, they must testify. Otherwise, the whole fabric of our system will be torn apart, and this court is not prepared to allow that to happen. We must be stern in guarding all the requirements of the administration of justice." The sentenced was appealed. On appeal the sentence was reduced to the time served which was nine months.[41]

- *W*hen the bailiff told the 18-year-old (who had been arrested for driving without a licence) that he could not go into the courtroom wearing shorts, the accused walked in naked. Found in contempt of court, the judge gave him the Florida maximum — 179 days in jail.[42]

- *A*n inmate, protesting his transfer to a different jail, plugged the toilet in the cell directly above the courtroom so that the overflowing water would fall on the judge below. It was reported that the judge, to continue on with his cases, merely ordered a bailiff to hold an umbrella over his head. The inmate was charged with contempt of court, but the judge, after receiving an apology from the inmate, imposed no sentence.[43]

Endnotes

1. For a more detailed and, therefore, a more astonishing account, see *Harper's Magazine*, August 1995, p. 23 which printed and excerpt from "A Sprocket in Satan's Bulldozer: Confessions of an Investment Banker" issue number 6 of *Might*.

2. *The Lawyers Weekly*, May 24, 1991, p. 2.

3. See *The Globe and Mail*, October 2, 1997, p. B1 and *Time*, October 27, 1997, p. 36.

4. *The Globe and Mail*, November 11, 1997, p. B1.

5. *The Lawyers Weekly*, May 15, 1992, p. 13.

6. *The Lawyers Weekly*, October 2, 1992, p. 17.

7. Summarized from *The Globe and Mail*, April 23, p. 1.

8. For a more detailed account see *The Lawyers Weekly*, July 1, 1994, p. 30 for its summary of *Andres v. Andres* heard by Judge Stach of the Ontario Court General Division.

9. See *Lalonde v. Coleman*, 67 Man. R. (2d) 187 Manitoba Court of Queen's Bench, July 3, 1990.

10. For a more detailed account see *Newsweek*, April 22, 1996, p. 79.

11. Summarized from *The Lawyers Weekly*, July 1, 1988, p. 6.

12. BG Checo International Ltd. v. B.C. Hydro and Power Authority, 44 B.C.L.R. (2d) 145 B.C.C.A. March 21, 1990.

13. *The Lawyers Weekly*, February 12, 1993, pp. 1, 21, http://www.droit.umontreal.ca/.

14. Summarized from *The Lawyers Weekly*, October 23, 1992, p. 24.

15. Reprinted with permission from *The Advocate* (published by the Vancouver Bar Association), Volume 46, (1988), Part 6, p. 986.

16. Summarized from *The Lawyers Weekly*, September 27, 1991, p. 24.

17. A more detailed account is given in *Newsweek*, March 25, 1985, p. 72.

18. A more detailed account is given in the *Vancouver Sun*, November 19, 1992, p. B7.

19. Summarized from *The Globe and Mail*, December 29, 1993, p. A9.

20. A more detailed account is given in the *Vancouver Sun*, December 15, 1993, p. A16.

21. Summarized from *Maclean's*, November 22, 1993, p. 37.

22. A more detailed account is given in the *Vancouver Sun*, October 15, 1993, p. D1.

23. Summarized from *The Globe and Mail*, November 25, 1993, p. B2.

24. For a more detailed account see the *Vancouver Sun*, January 27, 1994.

25. Summarized from *The Globe and Mail*, November 17, 1992, p. A9.

26. A more detailed account is given in the *Vancouver Sun*, October 8, 1992, p. A10.

27. For a more detailed account see *Infoworld Canada*, September, 1997, p. 9. For an account of the potential catastrophic consequences of the bug for the federal government see *The Globe and Mail*, October 8, 1997, p. 1. An article in *The New York Times* in September reports one group estimates the cost of fixing the problem may top $1 trillion.

28. For a more detailed account see *Maclean's*, August 1, 1994, August 8, 1994, p. 11.

29. His latest album released in 1997 is called "Blue Moon Swamp." For a more detailed account see *Time Magazine*, June 23, 1997.

30. A more detailed account is given in the *Vancouver Sun*, March 25, 1993, p. A18.

31. *The Lawyers Weekly*, July 29, 1988, p. 2.

32. For a case in which the court found there *was* reasonable notice see a discussion of *Schuster v. Blackcomb Skiing Enterprises Ltd.* in the *Vancouver Sun*, November, 1994 or in *The Lawyers Weekly*, December 16, 1994, p. 35.

33. For a more detailed account see *The Lawyers Weekly*, June 7, 1996, p. 15.

34. *The Lawyers Weekly*, September 18, 1992, p. 3.

35. More detailed accounts of this case can be found in *The New York Times*. See, for example, December 20, 1987, p. 1.

36. Summarized from *The Globe and Mail*, January 12, 1984, p. 8.

37. *The Globe and Mail*, August 23, 1986.

38. A more detailed account is given in the *Vancouver Sun*, January 29, 1992, p. 1.

39. A more detailed account is given in the *Vancouver Sun*, February 18, 1992, p. 1.

40. A more detailed account is given in the *Vancouver Sun*, October 29, 1992, p. A14.

41. See *The Lawyers Weekly*, August 19, 1994, p. 27 for an extract from *R. v. Deas*. The case was also reported and summarized in *The Lawyers Weekly*, July 15, 1994, p. 27. The accused was found guilty for the murder even without the testimony of J.N. For the ruling of the court of appeal see *The Lawyers Weekly*, March 17, 1995, p. 5 and March 24, 1995, p. 15.

42. See *The Lawyers Weekly*, August 26, 1994, p. 21 which ends the article with a quotation from the judge: "He said he was sorry, but I told him that wouldn't cut it."

43. *The Lawyers Weekly*, June 6, 1986.

IV

COMMERCIAL TRANSACTIONS

A. SALE OF GOODS ACT

Questions

What types of contracts are covered by the Sale of Goods Act?
What contractual terms are implied by the statute?
What additional remedies does the statute give the unpaid seller?

---

1. SCOPE OF THE STATUTE

Mr. Gee and Mr. and Mrs. Pan, customers of White Spot restaurant, claimed they suffered botulism poisoning from food eaten at the restaruant. They sued the restaurant for breach of the implied term of the contract that the food was fit for purpose. The defendant argued that the contract was one for services and not goods and was not properly covered by the *Sale of Goods Act*. The first question the plaintiffs put before the court was whether or not the *Sale of Goods Act* applied to the purchase of a meal from a restaurant.

The B.C. Supreme Court had no binding precedent before it. The Justice reviewed cases from Canada, the United Kingdom and the United States and concluded that "an item on the menu offered for a fixed price is an offering of a finished product and is primarily an offering of the sale of goods and not primarily an offering of a sale of services." In answer to the second question as to what must the plaintiff prove to establish the liability of the defendant restaurant, the court answered that to establish an impled condition of resonable fitness three requirments must be met:

"First, the goods in question must be of a kind in which the seller normally deals in the course of his business. ...

The second requirement is that the proposed use of the food is made known to the seller so as to show the plaintiff's reliance on the seller's skill and judgment...

The third requirement is that the contract is not for sale of a specified article under its patent or other trade name."

Applying the law as stated to the facts of the case, the court held for the plaintiffs. The defendants were liable under s. 18(a) of the *Sale of Goods Act* (the fit for purpose provision).

Furthermore, the facts supported a claim under s. 18(b), namely, the defendants were liable for breach of the implied condition that the goods were of merchantable quality.

The judge commented that fourteen other actions were pending against White Spot on similar allegations.

Gee v. White Spot, Pan et al v. White Spot
32 D.L.R. (4th) 238
British Columbia Supreme Court
October 27, 1986

---

2. IMPLIED TERMS

A. RE: TITLE

• *T*he owner of a mobile home left it with a business outfit to lease it on his behalf. The owner's signature was forged on documents transferring title to another. "Title" of the mobile home passed through approximately eight different purchasers before it was returned to its rightful owner. Relying in part on the implied condition of good title in s. 13 of the *Ontario Sale of Goods Act*, the judge found a series of sellers in breach of contract.[1]

B. FIT FOR PURPOSE/MERCHANTABLE

Sigurdson et al. v. *Hilcrest Service Ltd., Acklands Ltd., Third Party*

73 D.L.R. (3D) 132
SASKATCHEWAN QUEEN'S BENCH
DECEMBER 21, 1976

Estey, J.:—This action arises out of a single vehicle accident in which the plaintiffs allege that they did suffer personal injuries. The said vehicle was owned by the plaintiff Mr. K.E. Sigurdson. The plaintiffs allege that the cause of the accident was a faulty brake hose installed on the vehicle in the defendant's garage. The defendant joined Acklands Limited as a third party as Acklands supplied the defendant with the two hydraulic brake hoses which the defendant through its employees installed on the said vehicle.

The plaintiff Karl Edward Sigurdson stated that he was on June 16, 1973, operating a 1963 Ford vehicle owned by him and had as passengers his wife Hannelore and his children Christopher and Michael. At approximately 4:30 p.m. on June 16, 1973, Mr. Sigurdson was approaching the intersection of Avenue H and 20th St. in the City of Saskatoon intending to make a right-hand turn onto 20th St. when he was confronted with a red stop-light at the said intersection. Mr. Sigurdson stated that pedestrians were crossing the intersection in front of his vehicle and when he applied the brakes they failed to operate. He immediately swung his vehicle to the right hitting a power pole. Mr. Sigurdson stated that at the time of the accident his speed was 15 to 20 m.p.h. and that the brakes of the vehicle had up until the time of the accident been operating in a proper manner. The vehicle as a result of the accident was damaged beyond repair. A few days prior to May 1, 1973, Mr. Sigurdson took his vehicle to the defendant's service station for certain repairs as the defendants had previously serviced his vehicle.

Exhibit P.10 dated May 1, 1973, is the invoice which Mr. Sigurdson received from the defendant covering the repairs and labour performed on his vehicle immediately prior to the said date. This exhibit shows that two brake hoses were on this occasion installed by the defendant on Mr. Sigurdson's vehicle. Mr. Sigurdson as a result of the accident had three teeth removed and now has a partial denture. His son the plaintiff Michael received minor scratches while the plaintiffs Christopher and Mrs. Hannelore Sigurdson received injuries to which I will later refer. Mr. Sigurdson stated that after receiving his vehicle from the defendant's garage on or about May 1, 1973, the brakes on the said vehicle did until the time of the accident operate in a proper manner and that from May 1, 1973, to the date of the accident he had travelled approximately 1,300 miles. Mr. Sigurdson takes the view that the cause of the brake failure was due to a faulty brake hose. Counsel agreed that the brake hose removed from Mr. Sigurdson's vehicle is ex. P.11 and that exs. P.12, 13, 14 and 15 which are portions of a brake hose were cut off P.11 for purpose of examination.

Professor C.M. Sargent, from the faculty of mechanical engineering at the University of Saskatchewan in Saskatoon, examined the said brake hose by means of cutting off portions and found therein at least two particles which were composed of what he described as a "glassy material". His opinion was that due to the operation of the motor vehicle these particles tended to work towards the outside of the brake hose permitting the brake fluid to escape. His evidence was that in order for a garage operator to discover the presence of these "glassy particles" the hose would have to be cut and thereby destroyed. ...

[After reviewing the reports of injuries suffered by the plaintiffs, the judge turned to the evidence of the defendant.]

Evidence on behalf of the defendant was given by Mr. A.P. Halseth who in May, 1973, was an officer of the defendant company and worked in the company's service station. Mr. Halseth admitted that just prior to May 1, 1973, Mr. Sigurdson's vehicle was in the defendant's service station and that the two new brake hoses were installed on the said vehicle. The said brake hoses were obtained by the defendant from the third party Acklands Limited which company had been a supplier to the defendant since 1958. Mr. Halseth stated that the defendant company relied on the third party to supply proper brake hoses. Exhibit D.3 is an invoice from the third party referring to two brake hoses. Mr. Halseth stated that after the accident he inspected the plaintiff's vehicle to determine the cause of brake failure. He filled the master brake cylinder with brake fluid but found there was no build-up of pressure and on examining one of the brake hoses which had been installed by the defendant he found that brake fluid was dripping from the brake hose in the location immediately adjacent to the male end of the hose. The witness stated that he has had considerable experience with brake hoses but does not know of a method of testing a brake hose for leaks prior to installation. Mr. Halseth stated that after installing new brake hoses he puts the fluid under pressure and inspects for leaks. The witness denied that any member of the defendant's staff did anything in the installation of the brake hose which contributed to the rupture of the hose.

The plaintiffs in their statement of claim allege that the cause of their injuries was the failure on the part of the defendant's employee or employees to properly service and repair the vehicle and failure to test and examine the repairs to the vehicle. The plaintiffs also allege the use of defective materials by the defendant in effecting the repairs. The statement of defence pleads the provisions of the *Contributory Negligence Act*, R.S.S. 1965, c.91, and in the alternative that if liability is found the responsibility for such injuries and damages rests with Acklands Limited as its supplier of automotive parts. The third party's statement of defence admits that the said party is engaged in the wholesale automotive parts business and did on or about May 1, 1973, sell and deliver to the defendant's place of business two brake hoses priced at $6.60. The third party also alleges that the hydraulic brake hoses were supplied to it by a firm know[n] as Echlin Limited and that if there was negligence in the "supply and manufacture of the said brake hose, it was the negligence of Echlin Limited the supplier and manufacturer". It should be pointed out that at the time of the trial of the action the manufacturer of the said brake hoses was not a party to the action.

I will first deal with the actions of Mrs. Sigurdson and her son Christopher. My understanding of the law is that in order for these parties to succeed against the defendant they must establish negligence on the part of the defendant in the repair of the vehicle. I am satisfied from the evidence that one of the brake hoses installed by the defendant was defective in that it contained at least two foreign objects as determined by Professor Sargent and that due to the operation of the vehicle these objects moved causing a rupture in the hose which permitted brake fluid to escape. I am further of the view that the cause of the accident was brake failure caused by the escape of the brake fluid. If there be negligence on the part of the defendant it must be carelessness on the part of its employee or employees in the installation of the brake hose or in the installation of the brake hose which the defendant's employees knew or should have known was defective. From the evidence I am unable to find that there was any negligence in the installation of the brake hose. The evidence further established to my satisfaction that no inspection by an employee of the defendant of the brake hose prior to installation would have determined the defects other than that of cutting the hose as was done by Professor Sargent. Indeed the professor stated that he knew of no test which could be made in the garage which would determine the presence of foreign objects in the hose other than by the destruction of the hose. The question of the necessity for an inspection of the brake hose by the defendant is dealt with in *Charlesworth on Negligence*, 5th ed. (1971), para. 654, pp.405-6, when the author writes:

> A retailer is under no duty to examine goods for defects before resale, in the absence of circumstances suggesting that they might be defective, when he obtains them from a manufacturer of repute. ...

Placing the defendant in a position of a retailer I take the view that there were no circumstances in the present case which would suggest to an employee of the defendant that the brake hose was or might be defective when it was delivered to the defendant's place of business by the third party. Indeed there was, prior to installation of the brake hose, no test or examination which could be conducted by the defendant which would locate the foreign object short of destruction of the brake hose. Moreover, the operation of the vehicle from May 1st to June 16th suggests in itself that the actual installation of the brake hose was proper. There is therefore in my opinion no negligence on the part of the defendant in either the installation of the break hose or in the failure to inspect such hose prior to installation. As I have held that there is no negligence on the part of the defendant, I dismiss the actions of the plaintiffs Mrs. Sigurdson and her son Christopher.

The liability of the defendant towards the plaintiff Mr. Sigurdson involves other considerations. While I have already held that the defendant's employees were not guilty of negligence the defendant, in so far as the plaintiff Mr. Sigurdson is concerned, is faced with the provisions of the *Sale of Goods Act*, R.S.S. 1965, c. 388, s. 16, which reads:

16. Subject to the provisions of this Act and of any Act in that behalf there is no implied warranty or condition as to the quality of fitness for any particular purpose of goods supplied under a contract of sale except as follows:

1. Where the buyer expressly or by implication makes known to the seller the particular purpose for which the goods are required so as to show that the buyer relies on the seller's skill or judgment and the goods are of a description that it is in the course of the seller's business to supply, whether he be the manufacturer or not, there is an implied condition that the goods shall be reasonably fit for that purpose;

2. Where goods are bought by description from a seller who deals in goods of that description, whether he is the manufacturer or not, there is an implied condition that the goods shall be of merchantable quality:

   Provided that if the buyer has examined the goods there shall be no implied condition with regard to defects which such examination ought to have revealed;

3. An implied warranty or condition as to quality or fitness for a particular purpose may be annexed by usage of trade;

Waddams in his text *Products Liability* (1974) suggests that even in the absence of negligence a repairer may be liable to the plaintiff Mr. Sigurdson for breach of the implied warranty as set out in said s. 16 when the author writes at pp. 18-9:

> However, insofar as the defect complained of is caused by defective materials supplied by the installer or repairer, there may be liability even in the absence of negligence for breach of an implied warranty that the materials used are reasonably fit.

The said author points out at p.76 of his text:

> …liability for breach of the implied warranties is strict liability in the sense that it is no defence for the seller to show that he exercised reasonable care or that the defect in the goods was undiscoverable.

I am of the view on the facts of the present case that there was by virtue of the *Sale of Goods Act*, an implied warranty or condition that the brake hose would be "reasonably fit" for the purpose for which it was intended. I find that the said brake hose was not "reasonably fit" in that it contained foreign bodies which eventually caused a rupture and brake failure which failure was the cause of the accident.

The defendant's plea of contributory negligence appears to be based on Mr. Sigurdson's failure to keep a proper look-out. The plaintiff was in the situation described by Hodgins, J.A., in *Harding v. Edwards et al.*, [1929] 4 D.L.R. 598 at pp. 599-600, 64 O.L.R. 98 at p.102 [affd 1931] 2 D.L.R. 521, [1931] S.C.R. 167], when he wrote:

> …hence I cannot convince myself that he was sufficiently recovered from the shock of the emergency to be judged by standards involving deliberation and opportunity for conscious decision, or by what is called by Lord Sumner "nice judgment, prompt decision:" *SS. "Singleton Abbey" v. SS. "Paludina"*, [1927] A.C. 16, at p. 26.

The plaintiff when confronted with pedestrians in front of him and a failure of his foot-brakes was faced with an emergency and he chose to turn to his right. There was no time for a "conscious decision" to the effect that he should try the hand-brake for by turning right he would hit a power pole. I do not think that contributory negligence attaches to the plaintiff on the facts of this case.

The question now arises as to the damages to which the plaintiff Mr. Sigurdson is entitled. Counsel for the parties agreed to special damages in the amount of $2,079.56. I therefore award to the plaintiff Mr. Sigurdson special damages in the amount of $2,079.56. I award the said plaintiff general damages in the amount of $2,000. The plaintiff Mr. Karl Sigurdson shall be entitled to his tax [sic] costs in this matter, such costs to be taxed in accordance with column 4 of the Queen's Bench tariff of costs. …

The third party did not take an active part at the hearing. The reason being no doubt that it admitted selling two brake hoses to the defendant. My view is that the defendant may successfully recover from its supplier the third party for a breach of warranty, *i.e.*, that the brake hose was defective or not reasonably fit for the purpose for which it was intended. This point is dealt with by Waddams at p. 189 when the author writes:

> Although it is doubtful that one held liable for breach of warranty has a claim for contribution against the manufacturer of the defective goods as a joint tortfeasor, he may have a remedy against his own supplier (whether manufacturer or other distributor) for breach of implied warranty.

I therefore award judgment in favour of the defendant against the third party in the amount of the judgment recovered by the plaintiff against the defendant, together with the taxed costs paid by the defendant to the plaintiff.

Judgment for the plaintiff

A woman, shopping at Safeway, bought a 7-Up which she began to drink while the cashier packed her other groceries. The can contained a small dry cell battery which had made the fluid toxic. The woman suffered a severe burning of the lining of her mouth, throat and stomach. She sued Safeway for breach of contract, namely, breach of the implied term that the goods were fit for purpose. In the alternative, she sued the manufacturer and bottler and distributors of 7-Up for negligence.

Estrin v. Canada Safeway Ltd., 7-Up Vancouver Ltd., and Gray Beverage Co. Ltd.[2]

Note: Robert Gardner, the lawyer for the plaintiff, confirmed that this matter was settled out of court.

- **W**hen Sharon McClelland of Newmarket, Ontario, took her first free-fall jump from an airplane, the parachute malfunctioned. Miraculously, she fell in a marshy area, landed flat on her back and was able to walk away. When she stood up she apologized to her skydiving instructor.[3]

- **A** California vintner had to recall its 1986 vintage and reseal more than 700,000 bottles of wine. The corks had been covered with a substance that had acted like glue.[4]

- **O**ne lawyer of the new Union of Consumers was quoted as saying "We drank champagne that day;" another, "It was a real holiday. It was a historic day in our country." The cause of the celebration? Ivan Sumkin won a lawsuit against the government store which sold him a defective microwave oven. It may appear to us as commonplace but his victory was hailed as a milestone in post-communist Russia.[5]

EXEMPTION CLAUSES IN CONTRACTS FOR THE SALE OF GOODS

"... TO THE MAXIMUM EXTENT PERMITTED BY APPLICABLE LAW, MICROSOFT DISCLAIMS ALL OTHER WARRANTIES, EITHER EXPRESS OR IMPLIED, INCLUDING BUT NOT LIMITED TO IMPLIED WARRANTIES OF MERCHANTABILITY AND FITNESS FOR A PARTICULAR PURPOSE, WITH RESPECT TO THE SOFTWARE, THE ACCOMPANYING PRODUCT MANUAL(S) AND WRITTEN MATERIALS, AND ANY ACCOMPANYING HARDWARE..."
From the license agreement accompanying the computer program EXCEL.

3. UNPAID SELLER'S RIGHTS

The defendant supplied a company with canola meal in installments as per the contract between them. After some of the meal had been delivered, the purchasing company made an assignment in bankruptcy. The bankrupt company owed $236,858 to the supplier. The trustee in bankruptcy pressed the supplier to continue to supply the meal. When it refused to do so, the trustee petitioned the court, which held that the purchasing company's breach was not sufficient to give rise to the right of the supplier to repudiate. The supplier appealed.

The B.C. Court of Appeal, allowed the appeal. The supplier could retain the canola meal. Pursuant to the *Sale of Goods Act* the unpaid seller had a right to withhold delivery of the goods. Furthermore, the Act provided that a seller could retain the goods if the buyer became insolvent and that a seller had these rights even if he had made part delivery of the goods.

Coopers & Lybrand Ltd. v. Canbra Foods Ltd.[6]

B. OTHER CONSUMER PROTECTION LEGISLATION

- **L**abels on Batman products warn the buyer that the "Armor does not provide actual protection and cape does not enable wearer to fly."[7]

COMPETITION ACT R.S.C.

- **T**he court awarded $102.5 million to the major-league baseball players' union to be paid by the 26 club owners who had conspired to fix the market for free agents.[8]

- **N**intendo did not admit to any wrongdoing, but agreed to send $25 million worth of $5 discount coupons to registered users of Nintendo games who purchased games between June 1, 1988 and December 31, 1990; $1.75 million to the states of New York and Maryland where most of the legal work was done; and $3 million to other states. The company paid these sums to settle charges that it pressured dealers who wanted to sell below the suggested retail price by threatening to slow or reduce delivery of the games.[9]

- *R*oyal LePage Real Estate Services Ltd., when charged with attempting to fix prices contrary to the *Competition Act*, argued that the sections of the statute under which they were charged infringed ss. 2 and 7 of the *Charter of Rights and Freedoms* because the provisions were too broad and vague. The Alberta Court of Queen's Bench held that the provisions were not unconstitutionally vague.[10]

- *J*anet Reno v. Bill Gates. United States of America v. Microsoft. The U.S. Justice Department claims Microsoft has violated antitrust laws by incorporating the Explorer software in Windows 95 instead of competing with other software that has the same functions, for example, Netscape Communicator.[11]

FOOD AND DRUG ACT R.S.C.

- *J*im Pattison Industries Ltd. was fined $5,000 for violations of the *Food and Drug Act* R.S.C. The bakeries operated by Overwaitea Foods claimed the baguette bread had "no preservatives or fat." In fact, it had the same amount of fat as regular bread.[12]

- *B*eech-Nut Nutrition Corp. (owned by Nesfood Inc. a subsidiary of Nestle S.A. of Switzerland) pled guilty to 215 counts of intentionally shipping millions of jars of bogus apple juice for babies. The juice was sold as pure apple juice, but, in fact, was mixed with other juices, beet sugar, corn syrup and other ingredients. The U.S. District Judge imposed a $2-million U.S. fine,, the largest ever paid under the U.S. *Food, Drug and Cosmetic Act*.[13]

BUSINESS PRACTICES ACT/TRADE PRACTICE ACT

Schryvers and Schryvers *v.* *Richport Ford Sales Limited et al.*

BRITISH COLUMBIA SUPREME COURT
VANCOUVER REGISTRY No. C917060
MAY 18, 1993

Tysoe, J.: —On May 15, 1991 Mr. and Mrs. Schryvers acquired two vehicles from Richport Ford Sales Limited ("Richport Ford") through its salesperson, Mr. Stehr. They had intended to purchase the two vehicles in cash but the transactions were ultimately structured as leases with options to purchase. The aggregate amount payable by the Schryvers under the leases is greater than the sale prices of the vehicles plus a financing charge. ...

Did the lease transactions involve a deceptive or unconscionable act or practice in contravention of the Act? [*Trade Practice Act* R.S.B.C. 1979, c 406]

Section 22 of the Act authorizes the Court to grant relief in a case where a consumer has entered a consumer transaction involving a deceptive or unconscionable act or practice by the supplier of the goods. Section 3(1) of the Act states that a deceptive act or practice includes any representation or conduct that has the capability, tendency or effect of deceiving or misleading a person. Subsection (3) of s. 3 lists instances of deceptive acts or practices, including a representation that is such that a person could reasonably conclude that a price benefit or advantage exists when it does not (clause j) and the failure to state a material fact in making a representation which makes it deceptive or misleading (clause r).

Section 4 of the Act deals with unconscionable acts or practices. There is no statement as to what constitutes an unconscionable act or practice. Subsection (2) states that a court shall consider all of the surrounding circumstances and it lists five types of circumstances that should be considered (e.g., undue pressure). Mr. Schryvers was an experienced businessman who has been involved in the purchase of over 100 vehicles in the past [from Richport]. Although the Schryvers may have been getting tired by the end of the dealings, they were not forced to continue. It may be argued that it was unconscionable for the Schryvers to be persuaded to enter into leases when they were too tired to realize that they were leases. However, I believe that Mr. Schryvers did appreciate that he was entering into leases and that he had second thoughts at a later time. In any event, it is clear that the Schryvers appreciated that they were entering into some kind of financing arrangement and I do not think that it would be unconscionable for the Schryvers to have entered into a financing arrangement by way of a lease with an option to purchase rather than a more conventional financing arrangement.

There is more merit in the claim that there was a deceptive act. In *Rushak v. Henneken* (1991), 84 D.L.R. (4th) 87 the B.C. Court of Appeal commented on the wide scope of the Act at p. 95: ....

It is my view that Richport Ford committed deceptive acts with respect to the lease transactions in at least two respects. In view of the fact that Mr. and Mrs. Schryvers had indicated their intention to purchase the vehicle with cash, it was incumbent on Mr. Stehr to have properly explained the financial differences between a lease and a cash purchase. Mr. Stehr failed to state a material fact when he did not advise the Schryvers that the cost of acquiring the vehicles by way of the lease/options was greater than the cost of purchasing the vehicles in cash (after taking into account the savings on the taxes under the lease and the saving of interest by leaving their money in the bank). I believe that Mr. Stehr intentionally left the impression that there was a price advantage by acquiring the vehicles through lease/options when such an advantage did not exist. Even if the "guaranteed" price or the availability of the three options at the end of the terms of the leases represents a significant benefit, the Schryvers should have still been properly advised on the financial comparison so that they could decide whether they were prepared to pay the extra amount for this benefit.

The second deceptive act relates to the position of Richport Ford that the sale prices of the vehicles is no longer relevant when it has been decided that the transaction is to be structured as a lease/option. In the words of counsel for the Schryvers which were adopted by Mr. Stehr, it is like comparing apples to oranges because the transactions are so different. Whether this position is right or wrong, Richport Ford had an obligation to disclose its position to the Schryvers so they would be aware that the two types of transactions could not be compared. I have no doubt that, to the knowledge of Mr. Stehr, the Schryvers believed that the plan was equivalent to a method of financing the purchase of the vehicles in a manner that was advantageous to an outright purchase. Mr. Stehr had a duty to point out to the Schryvers that the two methods of acquisition were not comparable and that the negotiated sale prices would not be utilized for the purposes of applying the lease rate factors to determine the amounts payable under the leases. …

[After lengthy discussion and calculation of damages the court concluded] The total of the general damages in respect of both vehicles is $4,948.31 + $6,630.16 = $11,578.47.

The Schryvers also seek punitive damages in the amount of $10,000. Counsel for the Schryvers relied on the following passage from *Novak v. Zephyr Ford Truck Centre Ltd.* (unreported, B.C.C.A., November 24, 1988, No. CA008534) at p. 7:

> Secondly, I wish to add that while the power of the court to award punitive damages should always be exercised with extreme caution and care, I note in this case that the

learned trial judge found not only that there had been a deceptive trade practice, he also specifically found that upon this matter being questioned the defendant then adopted a series of stalling tactics which led to a heated confrontation and other unpleasantness. In those circumstances it seems to me that the learned trial judge had ample reason to make an award of punitive damages if he thought as he did, and we ought not to interfere.

Counsel for the Schryvers pointed to the fact that Mr. Schryvers complained about the leases well within the 15-day period during which Ford Credit would have allowed Richport Ford to cancel the assignment of the leases.

If the deceptive act committed by Richport Ford was restricted to a failure to properly explain the financial differences between a lease and a cash purchase, I may not be inclined to award punitive damages. However, I have also found that Richport Ford intentionally committed a deceptive act by structuring the leases without regard to the sale prices that were listed on the vehicles. Richport Ford received from the Schryvers and Ford Credit the following amounts (net of taxes) in comparison to the agreed sale prices (as adjusted to reflect the extended warranty, the undercoating and the freight and inspection charges):

	Amount Received	Sale Price
Explorer	$28,244	$26,080
Escort	$19,258	$15,220

Little wonder Richport Ford had a contest for the salesperson who could persuade the most customers to acquire their vehicles by way of a lease transaction. I consider the actions of Richport Ford to be sufficiently flagrant and high handed to warrant an award of punitive damages.

There must be a disincentive to suppliers in respect of intentionally deceptive trade practices. If no punitive damages are awarded for intentional violations of the legislation, suppliers will continue to conduct their businesses in a manner that involves deceptive trade prices because they will have nothing to lose. In this case I believe that the appropriate amount of punitive damages is the extra profit Richport Ford endeavoured to make as a result of its deceptive acts. I therefore award punitive damages against Richport Ford in the amount of $6,000.

Conclusion
I grant judgment against Richport Ford in the amount of $17,578.47 plus costs. …

The plaintiff purchased a truck which the dealer had said had not sustained damage over $2,000. In fact, the truck's original owner had rolled the truck and the repairs to the bent frame had cost $34,000. After learning the story, the plaintiff complained several times to the seller who refused to deal with the matter. The buyer returned the truck, sued for rescission of the contract, return of the purchase price of the truck and punitive damages.

The court found for the plaintiff.

Novak et al. v. Zephyr Ford Truck Centre Ltd.[14]

- *S*omeone sanded off the original grade stamps on millions of board feet of lumber and replaced the stamp with a higher-quality label. The lumber was sold by a B.C. supplier throughout the Seattle area. Some apartments had to be dismantled to find and replace or reinforce the inferior wood.[15]

- *T*he Texas Attorney General began an investigation of televangelist, Robert Tilton, who professed to be the "Prophet of God," for deceptive trade practices. Tilton urged viewers to send him prayers they wanted answered with their donations. It is estimated that Tilton received about $80 million a year, but a report by ABC (American Broadcasting Corporation) suggests that the money was taken from the envelopes but not the letters. Its reporters found the envelopes had been opened, the donation apparently taken and the letters left unread.[16]

- *T*he revelation that Milli Vanilli, a "singing" group, had not actually sung the songs on its best-selling album resulted in more than the rescinding of its Best New Artists Grammy. In California, Sheila Stalder, mother of 14-year-old David, who felt "hurt, cheated" after learning that the group merely lip-synched the songs, began a class action suit asking for restitution to any California consumer who bought its album of performances. The pleadings alleged that "the entire Milli Vanilli success story is a fake foisted upon unsuspecting consumers by the defendants in the action who bilked untold numbers of consumers, many of them children, out of tens of millions of dollars."[17]

- *L*uciano Pavarotti, renowned tenor, agreed to refund money paid by the BBC for broadcast rights to a concert in Modena, Italy when it was learned he had lip-synched his performance.[18]

- *T*he Attorney General in Texas challenged a Volvo ad in which the car withstands the crush of a huge truck. It was learned that the car in the ad had been reinforced with steel or wood. Volvo agreed to run a newspaper ad correcting the false ad, to make no unproved claims and to pay the state $316,250 for the costs incurred investigating the matter.[19]

- "Dear PowerBar consumer,

  Consumer and Corporate Affairs Canada (CCA) is threatening to pull PowerBars from the marketplace.
  After having approved our PowerBar label in April of 1991, the CCA now believes that we are misleading you, the Canadian consumer, with the word "Power" on our label. In their opinion, the term Power is an inherently misleading term that:
  > connotes a time/energy relationship, and is fundamentally different from the term 'energy'. Foods cannot provide power; they can provide the energy component thereof. Therefore the word Power is misleading to Canadian consumers and must be deleted from your product.
  What are your feelings about this department's ruling?
  Please write to: Minister of Consumer and Corporate Affairs ..."[20]

- *L*aidlaw Inc., a company based in Burlington, Ontario, agreed to pay $3 million to settle a consumer protection action commenced in California. The customers alleged that they were sent forms with removable stickers which said the forms should be signed for insurance purposes or as pledges not to dispose of hazardous waste in the companies' garbage bins. In fact, the forms were used by Laidlaw as long-term contracts. Customers who complained were told that they would have to continue with the company or pay a six-month service charge to cancel the contract.[21]

C. Priority of Creditors

Questions

In contracts for loans the debtor promises to repay the creditor,
but if the creditor wants more than just the promise what else can he take as security?
What can this secured creditor do if the debtor doesn't pay?
How does the procedure work?

---

1. Secured Transactions

- *I*n 1985, the entertainer Michael Jackson paid about $45 million for songs written by the Beatles. These and others, including songs by Little Richard, are estimated to be worth as much as $200 million and provide him with a valuable asset to use when borrowing money.[22]

Personal Property Security Act

Question

If the debtor is in default and the creditor seizes the asset, under what circumstances,
in any, can the debtor be reinstated under the contract?

Glenn v. General Motors Acceptance Corporation of Canada

ONTARIO COURT OF JUSTICE (GENERAL DIVISION)
FILE NO. 5274/92
JULY 7, 1992

MacLeod, J.

This is an application brought by Robert Glenn against Canadian Motors Acceptance Corporation of Canada Limited for the return of the applicant's 1990 Mercedes-Benz 500 SL automobile, and for compensations and damages, pre-judgment interest and costs.

On or about the 4th of June, 1992, the respondent, or its agents, repossessed the automobile which was the subject of a conditional sales contract between the applicant and the respondent. On June the 8th and 9th of 1992, Mr. Glenn tendered, or attempted to tender, upon the respondent the sum actually in arrears, pursuant to the conditional sales contract, plus a sum equal to the respondent's reasonable expenses of repossession, pursuant to section 66, subsection 2 of the *Personal Property Security Act*. To date, the respondent has refused to reinstate the security agreement and to return the vehicle to Mr. Glenn.

The issue for the court to determine, on this application, is the interpretation of section 66, subsection 2 of the *Personal Property Security Act*. In particular, that section states as follows:

Where the collateral is consumer goods, at any time before the secured party, under section 63, has disposed of the collateral or contracted for such disposition, or before the secured party under subsection 65(6) shall be deemed to have irrevocably elected to accept the collateral, the debtor may reinstate the security agreement by paying,

(a) the sum actually in arrears, exclusively of the operation of any other default which entitles the secured party to dispose of the collateral; and

(b) a sum equal to the reasonable expenses referred to in clause 63(1)(a) incurred by the secured party.

The section provides, in section (3), that this remedy may only be exercised once during the term of the security agreement, unless leave of the court is obtained.

The issue to be determined by me is whether or not Mr. Glenn can reinstate the security agreement by paying the arrears and the expenses due to the respondent, which is his position on the application. The respondent's position is that they are opposing the reinstatement of the security agreement in relation to the second part of clause 66(2)(a), which is:

…by curing any other default which entitles the secured party to dispose of the collateral…

Counsel for General Motors Acceptance Corporation refers, specifically, to two paragraphs of the terms of the conditional sales contract between Mr. Glenn and G.M.A.C. In the additional terms and conditions of the contract, which is page 2, paragraph 2, in relation to the section, "Default and Repossession" states, in part, that:

…should the Seller [G.M.A.C.] deem itself insecure the unpaid balance of the Total Time price and all other amounts owing under this contract shall immediately become due and payable and the Seller take possession of the vehicle where it may be found, so long as repossession is done peacefully.

The second aspect of the contract referred to by counsel is paragraph 7, which states that:

You … [shall] not … permit to continue any charge, lien or encumbrance of any kind upon the vehicle, and shall not use it illegally or for hire.

The respondent's position on the application is that Mr. Glenn has caused the respondent to deem … [itself] insecure and, secondly, that he has operated, or allowed the vehicle to be operated, illegally.

The cross-examination of Mr. Glenn satisfies me that, in fact, he allowed the motor vehicle licence plates, and registration of the vehicle, to expire in June of 1991. It is clear, from his evidence given on that examination, that he has allowed the vehicle to be operated on the roads and highways in Canada and the United States without it being legally licensed. In my view,

that clearly is an illegal operation of the vehicle, entitling the respondent to repossess the vehicle and prevent reinstatement of the security agreement.

Secondly, the respondent alleges that Mr. Glenn … [has caused G.M.A.C. to feel] insecure. I accept Mr. Glenn's counsel's submission that G.M.A.C. cannot, capriciously, or of its own volition, decide whenever it likes that a creditor is deemed insecure; but having had the full benefit of argument, and the examination of the parties in this case, I am satisfied that the respondent has made its case that Mr. Glenn is, in fact, [causing G.M.A.C. to feel] insecure. There is no reasonable prospect that he will maintain the currency of the contract. There is also a risk to the creditor of removal of the vehicle from the province of Ontario and a history, at least on one occasion, of refusing to advise the respondent of the actual location of the vehicle.

The cross-examination of Mr. Glenn indicates that there are extensive executions registered against him, totalling several hundred thousand dollars, and that he has no present means of income from his corporation, which was his principal business operation, being a numbered company operating "Bandito Video." He refused, on his cross-examination, to disclose his other sources of income.

The *Personal Property Security Act* has a clear legislative policy in favour of reinstatement of security agreements for consumer goods, such as a vehicle, if all of the expenses and amounts owing, "except for an acceleration clause," are paid by the debtor. This is a policy that has been implemented in subsection 2 of section 66 of the Act. Clearly, however, the creditor is not without remedy in a situation where they have established, to the satisfaction of the court, that the deemed insecurity provisions of the contract have, in fact, been met on a reasonableness basis. The creditor also has a remedy for illegal operation of this vehicle.

I find that the respondent, on the facts of this case, is entitled to refuse to reinstate the security agreement. Counsel have advised me there is no law on this section of the *Personal Property Security Act*. The legal argument was novel. I am dismissing Mr. Glenn's application for return of the vehicle, and I am making no award as to costs.

- *M*r. Martins bought a $47,000 Canon laser photocopier. He gave the seller a $25,000 cheque as a down payment. The cheque was returned NSF (not sufficient funds) three weeks after the buyer had taken possession of the copier.

    When the seller repossessed the machine, a piece of paper containing three $50 Canadian bills was discovered. In all, $24,240 in $20, $50, and $100 counterfeit bills had been made using the machine. Despite the arguments of the accused which included his allegation that he was merely testing the colour of the reproduction, he was found guilty and sentenced.[23]

    R. v. Martins Ontario District Court

Questions

Who takes the asset given as security if the secured creditor fails to register his interest or registers it improperly?
At what time do the rights of the Trustee in Bankruptcy take effect?

Plante Estate **v.** *John Deere Finance Ltd.*

[1996] O.J. No. 865 (Q.L.)
28 O.R. (3D) 314
Court File No. C12480
Court of Appeal for Ontario
March 13, 1996

Houlden, J.A.:—By s. 20(1)(b) of the *Personal Property Security Act*, R.S.O. 1990, c. P.10 (the "P.P.S.A."), an unperfected security interest in collateral is not effective against a trustee in bankruptcy. By s. 20(2)(b), the rights of a trustee in bankruptcy in respect of the collateral are to be determined as of the date from which the trustee's representative status takes effect. Where a receiving order in bankruptcy has been made against a debtor, does the trustee's representative status take effect as of the date of the filing of the petition in bankruptcy or as of the date of the making of the receiving order? Brockenshire J., in the court below, in a decision reported in (1992), 13 C.B.R. (3d) 40, held that the representative status takes effect as of the date of the receiving order. With respect, I disagree.

THE FACTS

On March 15, 1990, Julien H. Plante purchased a 41-foot Mainship cabin cruiser from Beacon Bay Marina McKay Yacht Agency for $300,000. At the time of the purchase, Plante executed a consumer purchase security agreement. On the same day, the agreement was assigned by Beacon Bay Marina to John Deere Finance Limited ("John Deere"), the respondent in the appeal.

On April 2, 1990, John Deere registered a financing statement under the P.P.S.A. The debtor was described in the financing statement as Julien H. Plante. The name of the bankrupt on his Quebec birth certificate was Joseph Julien Herv Plante. It appears that the debtor used a variety of names, including Julien Herv Plante, Harvey Joseph Plante, Joseph Julien Plante, and Herv Julien Plante. If a search had been made in the P.P.S.A. registration system under the name Joseph J. Plante, it would not have disclosed the financing statement of John Deere under the April 2, 1990 registration.

On September 4, 1990, a petition in bankruptcy was filed against Plante. The petition was disputed. On January 8, 1991, an interim receiving order was made in which the appellant was appointed interim receiver and directed to take immediate possession of all property of the debtor save for certain real property. On January 9, 1991, the interim receiver took possession of the cabin cruiser.

On January 25, 1991, John Deere filed a new registration in respect of the same collateral. In this registration, the name of the debtor was shown as Joseph J. Plante.

On January 29, 1991, after hearing oral evidence, McGarry J., sitting as Bankruptcy Judge, made a receiving order against the debtor. The appellant, Price Waterhouse Limited, was appointed trustee of the bankrupt estate. The trustee in bankruptcy brought a motion in the bankruptcy court for an order that the interest of John Deere was subordinate to the interest of the trustee in the collateral. The motion was dismissed by

Brockenshire J. with costs.

[The judge reviewed the trial court's decision which rested on his examination of the old and new bankruptcy statutes and the old and new personal security statutes.] …

THE RELEVANT LAW FOR THIS APPEAL

… The relevant portions of s. 20 (of the *Personal Property Security Act*) for the purposes of this appeal are the following:

20(1) Except as provided in subsection (3), until perfected, a security interest,

(a) in collateral is subordinate to the interest of,

(i) a person who has a perfected security interest in the same collateral or who has a lien given under any other Act or by a rule of law or who has a priority under any other Act, or. … .

(b) in collateral is not effective against a person who represents the creditors of the debtor, including an assignee for the benefit of creditors and a trustee in bankruptcy; . … .

(2) The rights of a person,

(a) who has a statutory lien referred to in subclause (1)(a)(i) arise,

(i) in the case of the bankruptcy of the debtor, at the effective date of the bankruptcy, or . …

(b) under clause (1)(b) in respect of the collateral are to be determined as of the date from which the person's representative status takes effect.

… Brockenshire J.[appears to have] arrived at the conclusion that the relevant date was the date of the receiving order for two reasons: (a) the use of the words "effective date of bankruptcy" in s. 20(2)(a)(i) as contrasted with "as of the date from which the person's representative status takes effect" in s. 20(2)(b); and (b) the change from "status has effect" in former s. 22(2) to "status takes effect" in s. 20(2)(b) of the present P.P.S.A.

…[The judge reviews this position and concludes.]

By virtue of s. 71(1) of the *Bankruptcy Act*, when a receiving order is made against a debtor, bankruptcy begins for all purposes at the date of the filing of the petition: *R. v. Minden*, … [1935] 4 D.L.R. 309 (C.A.). The bankruptcy of a debtor is deemed to have relation back to and to commence at the time of the presentation of the petition on which the receiving order is made: *Re Clayton's Women's Wear Ltd.*, … [1933] 2 D.L.R.

767 (C.A.). If Brockenshire J. is right in his interpretation of s. 20(2)(b), then s. 20(2)(b) would, in effect, be amending s. 71(1) of the Bankruptcy Act. By interpreting "the date from which the person's representative status takes effect" as being the date of the filing of the petition, this difficulty is avoided.

...

CONCLUSION

For these reasons, in the case of a receiving order, I am of the opinion that "the date from which the person's representative status takes effect" in s. 20(2)(b) of the P.P.S.A. is the date of the filing of the petition. I would, therefore, allow the appeal, set aside the order below and, in its place, make a declaration that the interest of the respondent John Deere in the cabin cruiser is not effective against the appellant, the trustee in bankruptcy. The appellant will be entitled to its costs here and below.

Appeal allowed.

---

2. GUARANTEES

Q u e s t i o n s

Under what circumstances would a guarantor be relieved of his or her obligation? Under what circumstances would a guarantor be obligated to honour his promise even after the principal debtor and lender changed the terms?

Manulife Bank of Canada *v.* Conlin

FILE NO.: 24499
http://www.droit.umontreal.ca/.
SUPREME COURT OF CANADA
OCTOBER 31, 1996.

Background facts: In 1987 Manulife Bank of Canada lent $275,000 to Dina Conlin. The term of the contract was three years and the interest rate was 11.5% per annum. It was guaranteed by her husband John and a company, Conlin Engineering and Planning Limited. The contract contained a clause that the guarantors would be bound as principal debtors. Furthermore, the contract provided that the guarantors would be bound even if the bank and the principal debtor changed the terms of the agreement. The couple separated in 1989. In 1990 before the contract was to mature Dina and the bank changed the terms: the agreement was renewed for a further three-year term and the rate of interest was to be 13% per annum. In 1992 Dina defaulted on the mortgage. The case reached the Supreme Court of Canada which split 4 to 3 on the issue of whether or not the guarantors were released from their promise to pay when the principal debtor and the bank agreed to extend the term of the mortgage and increase the interest rate without giving notice to the guarantors.

[1] CORY J. — I have read with great interest the clear and concise reasons of Justice Iacobucci [dissenting].... However, I must differ with his conclusion that by the terms of the guarantee, the respondent waived the equitable right of a guarantor to be released upon renewal of the mortgage loan with a different term and interest rates to which the guarantor did not consent.

THE POSITION OF A GUARANTOR AS DEFINED BY EQUITY AND THE COMMON LAW

[2] It has long been clear that a guarantor will be released from liability on the guarantee in circumstances where the creditor and the principal debtor agree to a material alteration of the terms of the contract of debt without the consent of the guar-antor. The principle was enunciated by Cotton L.J. in *Holme v. Brunskill* (1878), 3 Q.B.D. 495 (C.A.), at pp. 505-6, in this way:

> The true rule in my opinion is, that if there is any agreement between the principals with reference to the contract guaranteed, the surety ought to be consulted, and ... if it is not self-evident that the alteration is unsubstantial, or one which cannot be prejudicial to the surety, the Court ... will hold that in such a case the surety himself must be the sole judge whether or not he will consent to remain liable notwithstanding the alteration, and that if he has not so consented he will be discharged.

This rule has been adopted in a number of Canadian cases. ...

[3] The basis for the rule is that any material alteration of the principal contract will result in a change of the terms upon which the surety was to become liable, which will, in turn, result in a change in the surety's risk. The rationale was set out in *The Law of Guarantee* (2nd ed. 1996) by Professor K.P. McGuinness in this way, at p. 534:

> The foundation of the rule in equity is certainly consistent with traditional thinking, but it is a fair question whether it is necessary to invoke the aid of equity at all in order to conclude that in a case where the principal contract is varied materially without the surety's consent, the surety is not liable for any subsequent default. Essentially, a specific or discrete guarantee (as opposed to an all accounts guarantee) is an undertaking by the surety against the risks arising from a particular contract with the principal. If that contract is varied so as to change the nature or extent of the risks arising under it, then the effect of the variation is not so much to cancel the liability of the surety as to remove the creditor from the scope of the protection that the guarantee affords. When so viewed, the foundation of the surety's defence appears in law rather than equity: it is not that the surety is no longer liable for the original contract as it is that the original contract for which the surety assumed liability has ceased to apply. In varying the principal contract without the consent of the surety, the creditor embarks upon a frolic of his own, and if misfortune occurs it occurs at the sole risk of the creditor. A law based approach to the defence is in certain respects attractive, because it moves the surety's right of defence in the case of material variation from the discretionary and therefore relatively unsettled realm of equity into the more absolute and certain realm of law. In any event, it is clear quite certainly in equity and quite probably in law as well, that the material variation of the principal contract without the surety's consent (unless subsequently ratified by the surety) will result in the discharge of the surety from liability under the guarantee. ...

> To require a surety to maintain a guarantee ... [when the terms are changed] would be to allow the creditor and the principal to impose a guarantee upon the surety in respect of a new transaction. Such a power in the hands of the principal and creditor would amount to a radical departure from the principles of consensus and voluntary assumption of duty that form the basis of the law of contract.

THE RIGHT OF A GUARANTOR TO CONTRACT OUT OF THE PROTECTION PROVIDED BY THE COMMON LAW

[4] Generally, it is open to parties to make their own arrangements. It follows that a surety can contract out of the protection provided to a guarantor by the common law or equity. See for example *Bauer v. Bank of Montreal*, [1980] 2 S.C.R. 102, at p. 107. The Ontario Court of Appeal, correctly in my view, added that any contracting out of the equitable principle must be clear. See *First City Capital Ltd. v. Hall* (1993), 11 O.R. (3d) 792 (C.A.), at p.796.

[5] ... It is a question of interpretation whether such changes are authorized or contemplated.

[6] The issue as to whether a surety remains liable will be de-

termined by interpreting the contract between the parties and determining the intention of the parties as demonstrated by the words of the contract and the events and circumstances surrounding the transaction as a whole.

PRINCIPLES OF INTERPRETATION

[7] In many if not most cases of guarantees ... the document is drawn by the lending institution on a standard form. The borrower and the guarantor have little or no part in the negotiation of the agreement. They have no choice but to comply with its terms if the loan is to be granted. Often the guarantors are family members with limited commercial experience. As a matter of accommodation for a family member or friend they sign the guarantee. Many guarantors are unsophisticated and vulnerable. Yet the guarantee extended as a favour may result in a financial tragedy for the guarantor. If the submissions of the bank are accepted, it will mean in effect that a guarantor, without the benefit of notice or any further consideration, will be bound indefinitely to further mortgages signed by the mortgagor at varying rates of interest and terms. ...

[8] In my view, it is eminently fair that if there is any ambiguity in the terms used in the guarantee, the words of the documents should be construed against the party which drew it, by applying the *contra proferentem* rule. This is a sensible and satisfactory way of approaching the situation since the lending institutions that normally draft these agreements can readily amend their documents to ensure that they are free from ambiguity. The principle is supported by academic writers.

[9] G.H.L. Fridman, in his text *The Law of Contract in Canada* (3rd ed. 1994), at pp. 470-71, puts the position in this way:

> The *contra proferentem* rule is of great importance, especially where the clause being construed creates an exemption, exclusion or limitation of liability. ... Where the contract is ambiguous, the application of the *contra proferentem* rule ensures that the meaning least favourable to the author of the document prevails.

...

[14] I would note in passing that the guarantor in this case comes within the class of accommodation sureties.

[15] It follows that if there is a doubt or ambiguity as to the construction or meaning of the clauses binding the guarantor in this case, they must be strictly interpreted and resolved in favour of the guarantor. Further, as a result of the favoured position of guarantors, the clauses binding them must be strictly construed.

[16] Finally, when the guarantee clause is interpreted, it must be considered in the context of the entire transaction. This flows logically from the bank's position that the renewal agreement was an integral part of the original contract of guarantee. ... It follows that fairness demands that the entire transaction be considered and this must include the terms and arrangements for the renewal agreement.

APPLICATION OF THE PRINCIPLES OF INTERPRETATION TO THE GUARANTEE AND RENEWAL AGREEMENT PRESENTED IN THIS CASE

[After reviewing the terms of the original guarantee, the judge continued.]

THE EFFECT OF THE "PRINCIPAL DEBTOR OBLIGATION" SET OUT IN CLAUSE 34

[19] In *Canadian Imperial Bank of Commerce v. Patel* (1990), 72 O.R. (2d) 109 (H.C.), at p.119, it was held that a principal debtor clause converts a guarantor into a full-fledged principal debtor. I agree with this conclusion. If the guarantor is to be treated as a principal debtor and not as a guarantor, then the failure of the bank to notify the respondent of the renewal agreement and the new terms of the contract must release him from his obligations since he is not a party to the renewal. This conclusion does not require recourse to equitable rules regarding material variation of contracts of surety. It is simply apparent from the contract that a principal debtor must have notice of material changes and consent to them. Of course, a guarantor who, by virtue of a principal debtor clause, has a right to notice of material changes, may, by the terms of the contract, waive these rights. However, in the absence of a clear waiver of these rights, such a guarantor must be given notice of the material changes and, if he is to be bound, consent to them.

[20] The appellant contended that the words in clause 34 which provide "the said guarantors ... covenant, promise and agree as principal debtors and not as sureties" indicate that the respondent is bound as a principal debtor yet without any of the usual rights and benefits of a principal debtor such as notice with regard to renewal, and the opportunity to negotiate and consent to its terms. To take this position seems to me to be unfair and unreasonable. ...

[22] Even if it were thought that the principal debtor clause does not convert the guarantor into a principal debtor, the equitable or common law rules relieving the surety from liability where the contract has been materially altered by the creditor and the principal debtor without notice to the surety would apply, in the absence of an express agreement to the contrary. The question is whether in this case, either as principal debtor or as surety, the guarantor has expressly contracted out of the normal protections accorded to him. This question must be determined as a matter of interpretation of the clauses of the agreement, through consideration of the transaction as a whole, and the application of the appropriate rules of construction. ... [After doing so the judge concludes.]

[32] It follows I find that the words used ... [in the original contract] are sufficiently clear to conclude that the guarantor did not waive his equitable and common law rights either as a principal debtor or as a guarantor. The renewal agreement which was entered into without notice to, or the agreement of, the guarantor materially altered the provisions of the original loan agreement. The guarantor was thereby relieved of his obligation.

[33] If the wording of the two clauses should be found to be ambiguous, the *contra proferentem* rule must be applied against the bank. The wording of clause 34 binding the guarantor to variations in the event of an extension of the mortgage should not be applied to bind the guarantor to a renewal without notice since there is ambiguity as to whether clause 34 applies to renewals at all. In these circumstances as well, the guarantor should be relieved of liability.

DISPOSITION

[34] I would dismiss the appeal with costs.

...

Majority: La Forest, Sopinka, Cory and Major; L'Heureux-Dubé, Gonthier and Iacobucci dissenting.

Note: This case gives a very clear statement of the law with regard to a guarantor's liability when there is no clause purporting to extend that liability even when the lender and principle debtor change the terms. But this case is about a contract that contains such a clause and note well that four of the seven judges found *on the facts of this case* the bank had not made it clear to the guarantor that his liability was to survive changes in the terms. The banks are now aware of the cost of being unclear and, most probably, have rewritten their standard form documents. Therefore, read the contract with great care; if you do not want your liability as a guarantor (or as a principal debtor if such a clause is included) to extend past the first term of the contract, delete unwanted provisions.

---

3. BUILDERS' LIENS

Dominion Bridge (of United Dominion Industries Limited) placed two construction liens against the property of Skydome (the Stadium Corp.). The liens totalled more than $46 million. Skydome wanted the liens removed and, pursuant to the provisions of the *Construction Lien Act* of Ontario, asked the court for orders to "vacate" the liens upon its posting security. Dominion Bridge brought a cross-motion for an order under the statute to require Skydome to post security not only for the full amount of the liens but an additional 25% as security for costs which it anticipated to be approximately $6 million. The Master concluded that to remove the liens, Skydome should pay into court the full amount of the liens plus an amount of $50,000 for costs for each lien.

Dominion Bridge appealed; Skydome moved to "quash" the appeals.

The wording of the statute regarding the vacating of a lien is as follows:

s. 44 (1) Upon the motion of any person, without notice to any other person, the court shall make an order vacating,

(a) ...the registration of a claim for lien ... or,

(b) ...the claim for lien,

where the person bringing the motion pays into court, or posts security in an amount equal to, the total of,

(c) the full amount claimed as owing in the claim for lien; and

(d) the lesser of $50,000 or 25 per cent of the amount described in clause (c), as security for cost.

(2) Upon the motion of any person, the court may make an order vacating the registration of a claim for lien, and any certificate of action in respect of that lien, upon the payment into court or the posting of security of an amount that the court determines to be reasonable in the circumstances to satisfy the lien.

s. 71   (3) No appeal lies from,

(b) an interlocutory order made by the court.

The judge quashed the appeals. The court held that the order relating to costs was interlocutory and furthermore, that s. 44(2) could not override the mandatory provisions of s. 44 (1). With regard to costs, Skydome would only have to post $50,000 for each lien, considerably less than 25% of the liens.

United Dominion Industries Ltd. v. Ellis-Don Limited et al.
Ontario Court of Justice (General Division)
File numbers 405/92 and 406/92
January 12, 1993

---

4. Bankruptcy

In The Matter of the Bankruptcy of Margaret Rose Antosh

Action 29493
Court of Queen's Bench of Alberta, Judicial District of Edmonton
July 4, 1991

Wachowich, J.:

I. FACTS

This matter concerns an application by a bankrupt for discharge. ...

The facts leading up to the assignment into bankruptcy, on October 20, 1989, are rather straightforward and are not in dispute. In order to attend university during the period 1982 until 1988 to pursue a Bachelor of Social Work degree, Ms. Antosh was obliged to enter into student loan arrangements with both Canada Student Loans and The Saskatchewan Student Aid Fund. The amount remaining unpaid, as stated in the trustee's report to the Court, is $20,518.07.

Ms. Antosh is currently working as a Child Protection Worker in Moose Jaw, Saskatchewan having moved to Saskatchewan from Alberta sometime in the late spring or early summer of 1990. She supports herself and her 14-year-old son on her modest income. She receives no child support for her son. Ms. Antosh's net monthly income is approximately is $1,632.00. Both the Canada Student Loans and The Saskatchewan Student Aid Fund object to the discharge.

II. ISSUE

Should the Bankrupt, Margaret Antosh, be granted an absolute discharge?

The matter before this Court falls under the Bankruptcy Act, ss. 172 and 173. Consideration of these sections lead to the initial discussion of whether any of the facts referred to in s. 173 have been proven. There is evidence that the assets of the bankrupt are "not of a value equal to fifty cents in the dollar on the amount of her unsecured liabilities." The question is, has she satisfied the Court that this "has arisen from circumstances for which she cannot justly be held responsible"?

Counsel for the bankrupt submits that while there is some common-law support for the notion that student loans are to be treated differently than the claims of other creditors, there is no legislative sanction supporting this. He urges the Court to adopt the reasoning in *Re Cunningham* (1987) 1 W.W.R. 31 (B.C.S.C.). In that case at p. 38, the court decided that in the absence of specific legislative direction to put student loans on a different standing, "it is questionable, that a court should take this task upon itself."

Further, counsel for the Bankrupt urges the adoption of the test in *Re Gill* (1988) 69 C.B.R. (N.S.) 132 (B.C.S.C.) wherein Errico, LJSC held at page 35 that:

For a bankrupt to be justly held responsible for the assets being less than fifty cents in the dollar, there must be some element of culpability or blameworthiness, some recklessness or blind disregard by the bankrupt for his own financial well being.

Counsel for the Bankrupt submits that there is no evidence to show that this test has been met. In the alternative, he emphasizes the honesty, full cooperation and exemplary conduct of the Bankrupt, all held by the Court of Appeal in *Links and Robinson et al* 1970 16 C.B.R. (N.S.) 180 (Alberta C.A.) to be factors to be considered in an application for a discharge by a Bankrupt.

Counsel for the Objecting Creditors, on the other hand, refers to the oft quoted case of *Re Provost* (1974) 19 C.B.R. *(N.S.)* 95 (Sask Q.B.) which suggests that on a bankruptcy, the claims of student loans creditors must be considered very seriously. Bayda, J. at p. 102 states:

… a loan ranks on a moral level as high as a debt for necessaries or alimony, a liability under a maintenance or affiliation order, and a debt arising out of fraud or dishonesty—in short, those classes of debts and liabilities in respect of which an order of discharge does not (by the operation of s. 148(l) of the Act) release the bankrupt. It strikes me as being grossly unfair for a person to be able to go to a financial institution and say "I have no assets but take a chance on me anyway and lend me some money for my education; when I have my new professional status (my new 'asset') I will pay you back out of earnings" and then on getting his education says to his creditor, with impunity, "I am not making as much money as I expected and I am not able to comfortably pay you now, so, I am asking you to forego the debt and if you do not, I will make an assignment in bankruptcy and cancel it out." Judicial approbation of such an attitude could result in a serious undermining of the current system of student loans.

The philosophical underpinnings of Bayda, J.'s words are compelling. Student loans have been made available to persons who would, but for the loan program, be unable to pursue post-secondary education. These loans enable individuals to obtain educational training which, unlike most goods or disposable assets, will remain with the individuals for life. The education which student loans enable an individual to gain should be viewed as a long-term investment which will benefit the recipient throughout his or her working career. Bayda J.'s judgment does not preclude the discharge where the creditor is the student loans program. Rather, he categorizes the obligations undertaken in taking a student loan as being on a high moral level.

This approach is as relevant today as it was in 1974. … It is the approach that should be adopted by this Court in the matter before it.

While the efforts of the Bankrupt in pursuing a university education concurrent with heavy family responsibilities are very laudable, this is not the test for granting a discharge of a bankrupt. Rather, the question that must be answered under s. 173(l)(a) is whether she is in her current situation due to "circumstances for which she cannot justly be held responsible."

The pursuit of a university education is a deliberate choice. Equally, the decision to enter child welfare work with its concomitant demands (including the requirement that a child protection worker provides her own transportation) are circumstances and decisions for which the bankrupt can and should be held accountable.

Ms. Antosh made the decision to relocate from Lac La Biche to Regina in consideration of her personal circumstances and where she could best meet her responsibilities as head of her household, mother of a teenage son, and daughter with aging parents. These circumstances, while important responsibilities, cannot be considered to be the type of circumstances for which she cannot justly be held responsible.

Having concluded that the facts in s. 173(l)(a) have been proven and do not fall within the exception mentioned therein, the next question to be addressed is what action the Court should take under s. 172(2). The Court should be cognizant of the rights of the Bankrupt as outlined in *Industrial Acceptance Corporation et al. v. A. Lalonde et al.* (1952) 32 C.B.R. 191 at 199 to be "rehabilitated as a citizen unfettered by past debts" in the appropriate circumstances.

Ms. Antosh is now a trained child protection worker with good prospects for continuing long term employment in her field. She has now resettled in Saskatchewan and has obtained full-time employment. While her income is modest, it is not negligible. In accordance with *Re Norman* (1987) 65 C.B.R. *(N.S.)* 103 (Nfld T.D.) at p. 106, in making a conditional discharge under s. 172 (2) the Court should be satisfied that the bankrupt has sufficient earnings to properly maintain herself. This Court should find that Ms. Antosh does have the sufficient earnings. What she needs, however, as stated by Halvorson, J. in *Re Lind* (1990) 84 Sask. R. 112 (Q.B.) at p. 113 is "a repayment schedule she can afford."

In light of the above circumstances, a conditional discharge in accordance with s. 172(2)(c) is in order. This conditional discharge should take the form of the following order:

1. If the bankrupt consents to judgment, there will be judgment in favour of the trustee for $5,000 with which the trustee shall pay the student loans.

2. The judgment will not be enforced so long as the bankrupt pays to the trustee the sum of $75 per month commencing-September 1, 1991 and continuing until the amount of judgment is paid in full.

3. The judgment shall bear no interest:

4. As a condition of her discharge, the bankrupt must satisfy the judgment in favour of the trustee.

There will be no costs on the present application.

Dr. Bialik made an application for an absolute discharge from bankruptcy. His debts were substantial. He owed the United States $200,000 for student loans plus interest. He also owed the Royal Bank from whom he borrowed without disclosing his U.S. debt. His application was opposed by both the United States of America and the Royal Bank.

The Ontario judge hearing his application reviewed the causes of the Bialek's financial difficulties:

"...[H]e conceded that the trips to Nepal did interfere with maximizing his earnings. He made it clear in the hearing that he was satisfied that giving priority to his volunteer work in Nepal was entirely appropriate for one in his position, indeed he was quite eloquent on the subject of the poverty in that country.

"His earnings and expense statements bear out his sense of priorities. The expenses show that in the first half of 1993, while bankrupt, he made a gift of over $9,000 to the Nepal Foundation. This is an organization of his creation whose purpose is to fund his travels to Nepal. He then spent April and May 1993 in Nepal, earning no income. His monthly phone expenses of $578 include many calls to Nepal. I admire Dr. Bialek's devotion to improving the lot of the people of Nepal. However, I cannot permit him to force his creditors to bear the brunt of this devotion. For present purposes, I do not recognize his Nepal-related expenses as justifiable.

"Apart from Nepal, there are questionable expenses: his computer, leased for $391 monthly, is not used to earn income; over $700 a month is allocated to Travel, Vacation and Wilderness . ... At over $11,000 a month, his expenses are perhaps twice what a responsible person in his position and station in life would require. They are either artificially inflated to eat up his income or they reflect a wholly inappropriate approach to his finances. Oddly, but perhaps a further expression of financial irresponsibility, he has made no provision for income taxes in this statements.

...

"Counsel for the bankrupt asks for an absolute discharge. He says that it was the bankrupt's devotion to Nepal that caused these troubles, the cause is praiseworthy and is an extenuating circumstance. I do not agree. ... It is not open to an insolvent debtor to divert the funds available to pay his creditors in favour of a charitable enterprise, however worthy, and then come for an absolute discharge. The creditors have the right to pick their own uses for the money owed to them.

After reviewing the relevant law the judge granted a conditional discharge upon the bankrupt's making payments to the trustee in bankruptcy of $2,000 a month for 45 months."

In the Matter of the Bankruptcy of Barry Benjamin Bialek
Court File 31-262202
Ontario Court of Justice (General Division) In Bankruptcy
April 11, 1994

- *O*range County, California, a symbol of wealth and conservative politics, declared bankruptcy after the it lost more than $1.5 billion in high risk investments.[24]

- *T*he Finnish Communist Party filed for bankruptcy. Some of its $19.06 million U.S. debt was incurred by "share investments gone bad."[25]

- *M*.C. Hammer, award-winning rapper, filed for bankruptcy in the U.S. with assets of $1 million and debt of $10 million. At one time, *Forbes* magazine estimated his gross earnings at more than $33 million.[26]

- *A*fter the court decision finding Kim Basinger liable for $8.1 million for breach of contract [see p. 101 above], the actress declared bankruptcy, but the bankruptcy judge rejected her plan for paying her debts as being too vague.[27] It was reported that Ms. Basinger changed her bankruptcy petition, a change that necessitates her selling many of her assets.[28]

Q u e s t i o n

Can the debtor transfer his assets to protect them from the creditors?

After reviewing the evidence, the court found that the transfer by the debtor of farm lands to his wife thirteen months before the debtor declared bankruptcy was an improper transfer and thus void against the claim of the trustee in bankruptcy. The Saskatchewan Queen's Bench found the transfer contrary to the provisions of the *Bankruptcy and Insolvency Act, The Fraudulent Preferences Act* and *The Statute of Elizabeth.*

Goertz (Trustee of) v. Goertz[29]

Q u e s t i o n

Can the debtor prefer one creditor?

Medler-McKay Holdings Ltd. (Trustee of) *v.* *Teac Canada Ltd.*

[1994] O.J. No. 618 (Q.L.)
ACTION No. 35039606
ONTARIO COURT OF JUSTICE—GENERAL DIVISION

[1] Browne J.:— In this action the plaintiff seeks a declaration that a payment made to Teac Canada Ltd. by Medler-McKay Holdings Ltd. in the amount of $108,589.80 is fraudulent and void as against the Trustee as a preference pursuant to the provisions of s. 95 of the *Bankruptcy and Insolvency Act* and he seeks a judgment against the defendant in the amount of $108,589.80.

[2] Section 95 provides that every payment made by an insolvent person in favour of any creditor with a view to giving that creditor a preference over the other creditors shall, if the payment is within three months of bankruptcy, be deemed fraudulent and void as against the Trustee in the bankruptcy.

[3] Section 95(2) provides a presumption that where the payment has the effect of giving any creditor a preference over other creditors it shall be presumed in the absence of evidence to the contrary to have been made with a view to giving a preference. The subsection provides further that when the payment was made voluntarily or under pressure shall not be evidence admissible to support the transaction.

[4] Various issues or questions are raised including the following:

1) The defendant must be a creditor within the meaning of the legislation.

2) The payment must be within three months of bankruptcy.

3) The payer at the relevant time or times must have been insolvent.

4) The payment must create a preference in fact.

5) There is the issue of the intent of the payer being expressed as a intent to pay with a view to give that creditor a preference over other creditors.

6) There is the issue of the presumption in ss. 2.

7) There is the issue of rebuttal of the presumption.

[5] Medler-McKay Holdings Ltd. carried on business under the trade name Krazy Kellys involved with the retail sale of electronic consumer goods such as T.V.'s, VCR's, and audio equipment. Teac Canada Ltd. had been a supplier since 1989 of audio equipment. As at July 17, 1991 there was owing by Medler-McKay to the defendant $113,027.56. On that date Medler-McKay gave to the defendant a cheque postdated to July 31, 1991 in the amount of $108,589.80, the difference of $4,437.76 being a trade discount. The cheque was certified on July 31, 1991, the result being that the account was paid in full.

[6] Medlar-McKay [sic] filed a proposal September 23, 1991. The proposal was voted upon October 8, 1991 and defeated. In the result Medlar-McKay [sic] was deemed bankrupt as at September 23, 1991.

[7] It is agreed that the payment above referred to was a payment within three months of the bankruptcy and that the payment was in fact made July 31, 1991. ... My approach is that it is essential for the plaintiff to establish that the payer, Medler-McKay, was an insolvent person as at July 17 and July 31, 1991. On the fact situation before me the most material date for considera-

tion of the intent of the debtor is July 17, 1991.

[8] The legislation defines creditor as being a person having a claim provable under the Act. For the purposes of the matters before me I conclude the defendant to be such a creditor.

[The judge reviewed the statutory definition of insolvent persons, the factual evidence prepared on behalf of the plaintiff and concluded.]

...Medler-McKay was an insolvent person at the material times of July 17 and July 31, 1991.

[13] The next issue to be addressed is was there a preference in fact or did the payment of July 31 have the effect of giving Teac Canada Ltd. a preference over other creditors. ... It is sufficient for there to be a finding of preference in fact that there be a preference over one or more of the other creditors. The payment herein reduced the balance due to the defendant to zero. During the three-month period preceding bankruptcy there is evidence of payment to other creditors and there was evidence dealing with the number of cheques written during that time period. I am satisfied, however, that there was little business in the normal sense of supply of inventory and/or payment upon a timely basis. Indeed, payment upon a timely trade term basis was not possible. There is no evidence before me of any other substantial creditor whose account was satisfied substantially, let alone in full. I am satisfied that the creditors giving evidence before me had accounts outstanding well outside of credit or usual trade terms and that they were outstanding at the date of bankruptcy and outstanding as of the relevant dates July 17 and July 31. I find the payment made July 31, 1991 to have been a preference in fact.

[14] The general scheme of the Bankruptcy Act is that ordinary creditors should rank equally. Balancing that policy is the equally valid policy that a creditor being paid in the ordinary course of their business or diligently pursuing collection efforts with success should not be penalized simply because

there is a preference in fact. However, the preference in fact once found results in the presumption (in the absence of evidence to the contrary) that the payment was made with a view to giving the creditor a preference over other creditors. The issue of "with a view to giving that creditor a preference over the other creditors" must be looked at in the context not only of the presumption but it must be looked at in the context of the motive and/or intention of the payer.

[The judge reviewed the dealings between Teac and the debtor including an angry meeting in which the cheque was given to Teac.]

... In the result I find on the evidence without reliance upon the presumption that the dominant purpose of the debtor was to make a payment by the old company to obtain credit and/or the supply of inventory for [a] ... new company and that in the result the dominant purpose for the payment was "with a view to giving that creditor a preference over the other creditors." I base my conclusion upon the facts without reliance upon the statutory presumption but if reliance was placed upon the statutory presumption I would find that the evidence of the defendant would not rebut the presumption. In the result I find on the evidence without reliance upon the presumption that there was a plan or scheme as contemplated by s. 95 to prefer this particular creditor over other creditors and that the payment is deemed fraudulent and void as against the Trustee in the bankruptcy.

[21] There shall be judgment declaring the payment made to Teac Canada Ltd. by Medler-McKay Holdings Ltd. in the amount of $108,589.80 July 31, 1991 fraudulent and void as against the Trustee, being a preference pursuant to the provisions of s. 95 of the *Bankruptcy and Insolvency Act*. There shall be judgment against Teac Canada Ltd. in the amount of $108,589.80.

Judgment for the plaintiff

Note: This decision was upheld by the Ontario Court of Appeal [1997] OJ. No. 2680 File No. C18236 and 35-039605

5. Fraudulent Conveyances Act/Fraudulent Preference Act

Questions

How can the family home be protected from creditors?
How angry can the court be when assets are moved to defraud creditors?

The matrimonial home, valued near $500,000, was registered in the name of Cheryl Hennessey. Three days before she was served with a claim against her arising from fraudulent stock manipulation on the Vancouver Stock Exchange she conveyed the home to her husband Ian. The plaintiff, United Services Fund, which had lost $20 million in the stock fraud, obtained judgment against her for $3.25 million. While that case was under appeal the United Services Fund commenced an action alleging that she had fraudulently conveyed the matrimonial home with the intent to thwart its enforcement of the judgment against her.

The court found that the conveyance of the home was a fraudulent conveyance made with fraudulent intent on the part of both Cheryl and her husband Ian. As the plaintiff had the right to trace the proceeds of the sale, the court reviewed the disposition of the funds and found that they had, through the complex and "deceitful" efforts of Ian, been exhausted. The court granted a monetary judgment in substitution for an order setting aside the fraudulent conveyance. "The result was judgment for the plaintiffs for the amount of the Lyndhurst property net proceeds in the amount of $475,038.77 plus pre-judgment interest at 13 percent from May 19, 1988."

The court also allowed the amendment of the Statement of Claim to include a claim for punitive damages. The judge, who had referred to the testimony of the defendants as "complete fabrication" and "a pack of lies," concluded "I find that the conduct of the defendants in their participation in the fraudulent conveyance and their subsequent deceitful activities to deny the plaintiffs access to any assets to satisfy even a small portion of the judgment against Cheryl is conduct which merits punishment by an award of punitive damages in order to demonstrate to the defendants that the law will not tolerate conduct which willfully disregards the rights of others. ... There will be judgment against the plaintiffs for punitive damages in the amount of $100,000.

The plaintiffs are not the only victims of the fraudulent activities of the defendants. By their fraudulent defence to this action they have perpetrated a fraud on counsel of the plaintiffs, on this court and on the public generally who have had to provide court facilities and court staff at the tax payers expense for a seven-day trial. There was no defence to the plaintiffs' action. The seven days of trial time could have been used for parties who have a legitimate court action. Cheryl and Ian came to court to defend a fraudulent conveyance action knowing the conveyance was fraudulent, failing to disclose relevant documents, and lying under oath. ... 'Oh, what a tangled web we weave, when first we practise to deceive.'

United Services Funds v. Hennessey
Ontario Court (General Division)[30]

In the Matter of: Babbitt and Paladin Inc., Gary Husbands and Excalibur Technologies Inc.

ONTARIO COURT (GENERAL DIVISION) IN BANKRUPTCY
TORONTO FILE NO: B274/92
NOVEMBER 26, 1992

The background facts are as follows: The plaintiff, Babbitt, had successfully sued Paladin Inc. and Gary Husbands, its majority shareholder. At the examination in aid of execution it was learned that the defendant Husbands had shut down Paladin and transferred all its assets to a newly created company, Excalibur Technologies Inc. The plaintiff then applied to have the transfer of assets set aside under the *Fraudulent Conveyances Act*. As a creditor of a corporation, the plaintiff used the oppression remedy under s. 248 of the *Ontario Business Corporations Act*.[31]

Carruthers, J. (given orally) This matter comes before the Court by way of a motion within an action which was terminated by a Judgment in favour of the plaintiff against the defendants, Paladin Inc. and Gary Husbands. It was with a view to satisfying this Judgment that this motion has been made pursuant to the provisions of the *Business Corporations Act*.

The basic issue concerns the fact that all the business and assets of Paladin, of which the defendant Husbands at all relevant times had the majority interest and was its sole operating mind, have ended up with a company known as Excalibur Technologies Inc. This company was the creation of Husbands and at all relevant times was also under his sole control and direction.

Essentially what happened was that Husbands shut down Paladin and started Excalibur, and in the process of doing so took all of the assets of Paladin, including 45 service contracts, all of the employees required to service those contracts and its goodwill and gave or transferred them, without cost, to Excalibur. As a result Paladin was left as an empty shell, thereby rendering the claims of outstanding creditors, and in particular the plaintiff, Cynthia Babbitt, unenforceable.

There appears to be no disagreement between counsel that all of the circumstances surrounding these dealings between Paladin and Excalibur, all of which are not disputed, give rise to a presumption in favour of the plaintiff against the validity of the transaction between Paladin and Excalibur. ...

In the course of testifying the defendant Husbands said without any reservation or qualification that a factor, if not the factor, in changing his business operations from Paladin to Excalibur was his inability to overcome what he described as being "a mountain of debt" that had been generated on behalf of Paladin. He testified that he could see "no way out of the situation" but to start a new business in the manner in which he did.

It is said on behalf of the defendants that there was no intention to defeat creditors of Paladin because Husbands only intended to start a new business because the situation with Paladin rendered a desired new business relationship ... impossible. ... As I said to counsel during argument, what Mr. Husbands had to say comes about as close to an admission that he intended to defeat or defraud Paladin's creditors as one could expect in a case of this kind.

Frankly I am surprised and concerned that any business man in this Province would not understand that what was done here is wrong. Surely Husbands had to know that one cannot by simply organizing a succession of new companies, utilizing new labels and transferring assets, without any consideration avoid the indebtedness of those left behind. That surely is a simply straightforward common sense basic principle. To permit what Husbands did would create havoc in the business and commercial world.

In my opinion the defendants have not succeeded at all in rebutting the presumption which the circumstances of this case give rise to. ...

[H]ad there been a claim for punitive damages, I would have most probably assessed punitive damages against the defendants. This is just absolutely a case in which we have someone who is virtually thumbing his nose at the Law and the rights of others, and abusing the processes of this Court in the process. It is very difficult for me to understand how anyone of his apparent intelligence can think that he is entitled to do what he has done and then come to this Court and say, it is right. And, I might add at this point, bring with him a strong attitude, as well, that it is wrong to criticize him for what he did.

While lots of people might do these things, it is rare that they would then try and justify them in a Court of Law. The whole thing is just an absolute waste of everyone's time, except of course for the defendants. I am sure they thought time was in their favour. ...

I have endorsed the record for oral reasons given, Judgment for the plaintiff against Paladin Inc., Gary Husbands and Excalibur Technologies Inc., for $31,339.85, and costs on a solicitor and client basis at $16,330. The liability of each of the parties, Paladin Inc., Gary Husbands and Excalibur Technologies Inc., is on a joint and several basis.

Judgment for the plaintiff

D. Negotiable Instruments

Question

---

*When can the drawer of the cheque say to the holder of the cheque
"I don't want to pay you" and succeed in law?*

- ***A*** British mail order firm received a cheque for £100 with an order for toys. Although the cheque was not completely filled out, the firm sent the order. The cheque had been forged—by the owner's seven-year-old son.[32]

Confederation Leasing Ltd. v. *Cana-Drain Services Inc. et al.*

[1994] O.J. No. 1660 (Q.L.)
DRS 95-05235
Action No. 92-CQ-20320-CM
Ontario Court of Justice—General Division
July 26, 1994

Background facts: The plaintiff received a promissory note when it purchased assets of a bank which included the assignment of the bank's accounts receivable. The makers of the note who dealt with the bank resist paying on the basis of a misrepresentation made to them by the bank.

Wilson J.:—...

DEFENCE OF MISREPRESENTATION

[5] Confederation Leasing is a holder in due course under s. 55(1) of the *Bills of Exchange Act*, R.S.C. 1985, c.B-4 which states:

55(1) A holder in due course is a holder who has taken a bill, complete and regular on the face of it, under the following conditions, namely:

(a) that he became the holder of it before it was overdue and without notice that it had been previously dishonoured, if such was the fact;

(b) that he took the bill in good faith and for value, and that at the time the bill was negotiated to him he had no notice of any defect in the title of the person who negotiated it.

(2) In particular the title of a person who negotiates a bill is defective within the meaning of this Act when he obtained the bill, or the acceptance thereof, by fraud, duress or force and fear, or other unlawful means, or for an illegal consideration, or when he negotiates it in breach of faith, or under such circumstances as amount to a fraud.

[6] As endorsers of the promissory note, the defendants Persichilli and Cornacchia (P & C) [the makers of the note] are liable for the amount of the promissory note to a holder in due course, subject only to what are known as real or absolute defences. Section 132 of the Act states:

132. The endorser of a bill by endorsing it, subject to the effect of any express stipulation authorized by this Act,

(a) engages that on due presentment it shall be accepted and paid according to its tenor, and that if it is dishonoured he will compensate the holder or a subsequent endorser who is compelled to pay it, if the requisite proceedings on dishonour are duly taken;

(b) is precluded from denying to a holder in due course the genuineness and regularity in all respects of the drawer's signature and all previous endorsements; and

(c) is precluded from denying to his immediate or a subsequent endorsee that the bill was, at the time of his endorsement, a valid and subsisting bill, and that he had then a good title thereto.

[7] Defences on a bill of exchange, cheque or note fall into three categories: real or absolute defences, defects of title and personal defences. Real or absolute defences, available against even a holder in due course, include, for example, the inca-

pacity to incur contractual liability or forgery of a party's signature. No defence of this type has been raised here.

[8] A defect of title defence affects the title of a person owning or assigned the bill. Crawford and Falconbridge ... *Banking and Bills of Exchange* (8th ed.) (Toronto: Canada Law Book, 1986), vol. 2, p. 1524] gives some examples. If a person obtains an instrument by fraud or undue influence, or for illegal consideration, his or her title to the instrument is defective: *Pacific Finance Acceptance Co. Ltd. v. Turgeon et al.* (1978), 93 D.L.R. (3d) 301 (B.C. Co. Ct.). The title defect may prevent a transferee or a signee from obtaining a good title.

[9] By way of contrast, a personal defence is a defence raising equities between the parties. They do not affect title to the instrument. These include contractual defences such as misrepresentation, or a right of set-off arising out of another transaction between the maker of the instrument and the payee of a note. According to Crawford and Falconbridge at p. 1524:

> The [personal] defence may be good as between the two parties between whom it arises, that is, between immediate parties, but it is not available as against a remote party taking in good faith.

[10] In *Banque de la Societe, Generale de Belgique v. McKissock*, [1961] O.W.N. 121 (H.C.J.), the Court affirmed this principle. ...

[11] If a transferee takes as holder in due course, the assignment is not affected by personal defences. Section 73 of the Bills of Exchange Act provides as follows:

73 The rights and powers of the holder of a bill are as follows:

(a) he may sue on the bill in his own name;

(b) where he is a holder in due course, he holds the bill free from any defect of title of prior parties, as well as from mere personal defences available to prior parties among themselves, and may enforce payment against all parties liable on the bill;

(c) where his title is defective, if he negotiates the bill to a holder in due course, that holder obtains a good and complete title to the bill; and

(d) where his title is defective, if he obtains payment of the bill the person who pays him in due course gets a valid discharge for the bill.

[12] As misrepresentation is a personal defence between the Bank and the defendants, the enforceability of the promissory note by Confederation as holder in due course is not affected. . .

[14] I therefore conclude that Confederation Leasing is a holder in due course and therefore is entitled to rely on the promissory note as endorsed. The defendants may well have a remedy against the Bank, but that is a matter for another day. ...

Boma Manufacturing Ltd. v. Canadian Imperial Bank of Commerce

FILE NO.: 24520

http://www.droit.umontreal.ca/

SUPREME COURT OF CANADA

NOVEMBER 21, 1996

[1] Iacobucci, J. — In the main, this appeal raises issues concerning the tort of conversion with respect to cheques, the meaning of fictitious or non-existing persons in s. 20(5) of the Bills of Exchange Act, R.S.C., 1985, c. B-4 (the "Act"), and the defence of a holder in due course under s. 165(3) of the Act.

I. BACKGROUND

[2] The appellants Boma Manufacturing Ltd. and Panabo Sales Ltd. are associated companies in the business of manufacturing and marketing small souvenir items. The only shareholders and officers of the companies are Boris Mange and Ursula Mange. [3] The appellants' bookkeeper Donna Alm committed fraud against the companies by way of issuing a long series of fraudulent cheques. These cheques were honoured by her bank, the respondent Canadian Imperial Bank of Commerce ("CIBC") over the course of five years. The appellants [the companies] brought an action in negligence, and in the alternative, conversion, against their bank, [the drawee bank] the Royal Bank of Canada, and against the respondent.

[4] Donna Alm … was never an officer, director or shareholder of the companies. She was, however, a duly authorized signing officer on the bank accounts maintained by the companies, along with Boris and Ursula Mange. Cheques drawn on these accounts required only one authorized signature. It was understood that Alm was to sign cheques only when the others were unavailable to do so, and only with respect to legitimate obligations of the companies.

…

[7] Between December 8, 1982 and May 6, 1987, Alm used the appellants' pre-printed cheque forms to create some 155 cheques totalling $91,289.54, payable to a number of persons connected with the appellants, including Boris Mange, Ursula Mange, several employees, and one of the subcontractors, Van Sang Lam. The cheques payable to Lam were, with one exception, made to "J. Lam" or "J. R. Lam," the initials and the last name mimicking the name of Donna Alm's first husband. Alm signed 146 of the cheques on behalf of the appellants, and fraudulently obtained Boris Mange's signature on the other nine. Alm deposited all the cheques into one of her accounts at the CIBC.

…

V. ANALYSIS

[29] I have found it helpful to consider this appeal in terms of three broad issues, as follows: the doctrine of conversion with respect to cheques; s. 20(5) as a defence to an action in conversion; and s. 165(3) as a defence to an action in conversion.

A. Conversion in relation to cheques

[30] It is a commonly accepted proposition that a bill of exchange is a chattel that can be negotiated from party to party. An individual obtains title to a bill through negotiation. Once an individual has obtained title, that individual has the right to present the bill to the drawee for payment, as well as a right of recovery against the drawer if the bill is dishonoured by the drawee. [31] The tort of conversion involves a wrongful interference with the goods of another, such as taking, using or destroying these goods in a manner inconsistent with the owner's right of possession. The tort is one of strict liability, and accordingly, it is no defence that the wrongful act was committed in all innocence. … If the customer is not entitled to the cheque which he delivers to his banker for collection, the banker, however innocent and careful he might have been, would at common law be liable to the true owner of the cheque for the amount of which he receives payment, either as damages for conversion or under the cognate cause of action … for money had and received. [32] The fact that liability for the tort of conversion is strict suggests that the respondent's submission that the appellants were contributorily negligent must fail.

[35] As I see it, the strict liability feature of conversion is well engrained in the jurisprudence concerning bills of exchange. … [41] The money on deposit in the appellants' Royal Bank accounts was owed to the lawful holder of those accounts, the appellants. Through the CIBC's actions, money owed to the appellants was paid to Alm, who was not entitled to the money. She was not a payee, and none of the cheques was endorsed by any of the named payees. The forged endorsements were "wholly inoperative" pursuant to s. 48 of the Act. The CIBC presented fraudulent cheques for payment to the Royal Bank, and collected the proceeds therefrom. The CIBC then accounted for the proceeds to Ms. Alm, one not "rightfully entitled" to the funds. Thus, the CIBC is prima facie liable in conversion to the appellants. However, it remains to be seen whether the CIBC can avail itself of a defence.

B. Unauthorized signatures and the fictitious payee defence

[42] As noted above, Alm created some 155 cheques payable to a number of persons connected with the appellants. One hundred and seven of the cheques were payable to "J. Lam" or "J. R. Lam", and were accepted for deposit without endorsement. The remaining Lam cheques, and all of the cheques payable to other third parties, bore the forged endorsement of the payee, the forgeries having been perpetrated by Donna Alm. … [45] … [S.] 20(5) of the Act, the fictitious payee provision, … provides that, where the payee is a fictitious or non-existing person, the bill may be treated as payable to bearer. The significance of a cheque that is payable to bearer, rather than to order, is that it can be negotiated by simple "delivery" to the bank; endorsement is not required. The presence or absence of a legitimate or forged endorsement is irrelevant to a bearer cheque. A bank becomes the lawful holder of a bearer cheque simply through delivery. By contrast, in order for a bank to

become the lawful holder of a cheque that is payable to order, not only must the cheque be delivered to effect negotiation, but the cheque must also be endorsed.

[Ed. note: If the payees are "fictitious" under s. 20(5) the bank, CIBC, is a holder in due course and is entitled to payment from the Royal Bank (the drawee bank) and the companies must suffer the loss.]

[53] …The key issue [under s. 20(5)] is whether the drawer intended the payees to receive payment, which itself raises the question of who the drawer is. Can Donna Alm's intention be imputed to the appellants? …

[55] With respect, it seems to me that the Court of Appeal erred in focusing on Alm's intention. It is the intention of the drawer that is significant for the purpose of s. 20(5), not the intention of the signatory of the cheque. While a "drawer" is often defined to mean "[t]he person who signs or makes a bill of exchange" (cf. *The Dictionary of Canadian Law* (2nd ed. 1995)), in my view, it is important in the circumstances of this case to distinguish between the signatory and the drawer. The drawer, in this case, is the entity out of whose bank account the cheques were drawn, that is, the appellant companies. Alm was not the drawer, but was simply the signatory. Thus, it is the intention of the appellant companies, as the drawer, that must be determined.

[60] … Mange knew that one of the subcontractors retained by the companies was a "Mr. Lam." He did not specifically recall Lam's first name, which, incidentally, was Van Sang. However, when Mange approved the cheques to "J. Lam" and "J. R. Lam," he honestly believed that the cheques were being made out for an existing obligation to a real person known to the companies. The trial judge's comments in this regard were tantamount to a finding of fact, and were not disturbed on appeal; as these are concurrent findings of fact, this Court should not intervene.

[61] Accordingly, the cheques made out to "J. Lam" and "J. R. Lam" … were payable to order, and in order to be negotiable to the bank, delivery alone was not sufficient. Valid, non-forged endorsements were required.

[67] … [I]t is my conclusion that the cheques in question certainly were "delivered" by Alm to the CIBC within the meaning of s. 2 of the Act. However, the cheques were not bearer cheques, but were payable to order. Accordingly, for negotiation to be effected, endorsement by the payee was required in order for the CIBC to acquire valid title to the cheques.

[68] It remains to be seen, however, whether s. 165(3) of the Act is of application in this situation so as to give the CIBC the rights of a holder in due course, including immunity against a claim in conversion.

C. Section 165(3) [defence]

[69] It should be noted at the outset that the CIBC in this case cannot be an actual holder in due course under the Act, because it is not a valid "holder" of the cheques in question. A bill must be negotiated to an individual in order for him or her to be a holder. As set out above, the cheques in this case were not validly negotiated, since they were payable to order, and bore no endorsement, or bore forged endorsements which amounted to a nullity under s. 48 of the Act.

[70] However, it is argued that the CIBC acquired the rights of a holder in due course pursuant to s. 165(3), which provides that:

> Where a cheque is delivered to a bank for deposit to the credit of a person and the bank credits him with the amount of the cheque, the bank acquires all the rights and powers of a holder in due course of the cheque.

. . .

[74] The respondent [CIBC] submits that, within the plain meaning of s. 165(3), it has acquired the rights of a holder in due course, since the cheques in question were indeed "delivered to a bank for deposit to the credit of a person", and since the CIBC credited the person "with the amount of the cheque. At first blush, this interpretation seems to be attractive. However, the consequence of this approach would be far-reaching and overly broad.

[75] If the respondent's interpretation were adopted, a bank would never need to require an endorsement, and the distinction between cheques payable to order and payable to bearer would be insignificant. A bank would always be immune from the consequences of having accepted unendorsed cheques into third party accounts. This result cannot be supported.

[76] In my view, the "person" in s. 165(3) must mean a person who is entitled to the cheque. This means that only the payee or the legitimate endorsee of the payee would qualify as a "person" for the purposes of s. 165(3). …

[78] Section 165(3) represents a policy decision with respect to the allocation of risk. When a collecting bank is presented with a cheque for deposit to the credit of the payee, the bank is entitled, essentially, to assume that it was truly the intention of the drawer that the payee receive the proceeds of the cheque. It is more difficult for a fraudulent employee to manage to have cheques wrongfully made out in their own name; the likelihood with respect to cheques presented by the payee is that they are genuine. Accordingly, a policy decision has been made to overlook the lack of endorsement with respect to these cheques, to prevent the bank from being exposed to personal defences and defects in title should the cheque be dishonoured. The collecting bank is permitted to overlook endorsement with respect to these cheques, because it is very likely that they are indeed genuine.

[79] However, the likelihood of fraud is dramatically higher when a person presents a third party cheque, particularly when it bears no endorsement. A collecting bank is not permitted to assume that the transaction is genuine in the face of circumstances that are so clearly prone to fraud. This is why the collecting bank is required, in the case of third party cheques, to ensure that they have been endorsed. It should be remembered that it was the respondent's own internal policy that third party cheques were not to be accepted without endorsement.

[80] To some, the allocation of risk in the bills of exchange system may seem arbitrary, but in my view a necessary and coherent rationale sustains this allocation. With respect to forged endorsements, for example, no party in particular is in any better position to detect the fraud than any other. It is a risk that all parties must bear, including collecting banks. It is a price that must be paid if one wishes to enjoy the significant benefits of the bills of exchange scheme, not the least of which is, from the bank's perspective, the facilitation of huge numbers of financial dealings conducted rapidly, and without overwhelming transaction costs. While the banks are accorded the important advantage of holder in due course status in many situations, it would not be appropriate, as the respondent would have it, to exempt any party, including collecting banks, from all exposure to the risk and consequence of fraud.

[81] In my view, s. 165(3) does not apply to the facts of this case. Alm was not the payee or a legitimate endorsee of the cheques in question. Accordingly, she was not a "person"

within the meaning of s. 165(3). Absent valid endorsements, the cheques were not validly negotiated to the bank. As a result, CIBC took the cheques subject to the equities of the situation. Alm was not entitled to the cheques, but CIBC credited her with the amount of those cheques. This constitutes conversion, for which CIBC is strictly liable.

VI. Conclusions and Disposition
[87] Accordingly, I would … set aside the judgment of the Court of Appeal, and restore the trial judgment against the CIBC for the full amount of the cheques in question, that is $91,289.54 plus interest.

Appeal allowed [CIBC liable]

Majority: Lamer, L'Heureux-Dubé, Sopinka, Gonthier, Cory, Iacobucci and Major; La Forest and McLachlin dissenting arguing on policy grounds that between the two innocent parties, the companies and CIBC, it is the drawer of the cheques at the companies which has the greater opportunity to avoid the fraud. Regarding the defence offered in s. 20(5), they found all 114 cheques payable to "D. Lam," "J. Lam" or "J.R. Lam" as cheques payable to non-existent persons. Thus the bank would have received them as payable to bearer and therefore the bank would be a holder in due course with a complete defence.

ENDNOTES

1. For a more detailed summary of *Deonanan v. Wingate* see *The Lawyers Weekly*, October 7, 1994, p. 37.

2. A more detailed account is given in the *Vancouver Sun*, November, 1979.

3. For a more detailed account see the *Vancouver Sun*, September 6, 1994, p. A6.

4. For a more detailed account see *The Maui News*, February 24, 1995, p. A2.

5. For a more detailed account see the *Vancouver Sun* , February 1992.

6. Summarized from *The Lawyers Weekly*, February 27, 1987, pp. 11, 13.

7. Adapted from *The Globe and Mail*, October 16, 1990, p. A18.

8. For a more detailed account see *Newsweek*, October 1, 1990.

9. A more detailed account is given in *Newsweek*, April 22, 1991, p. 48.

10. For a summary of *Royal LePage Real Estate Services Ltd.* see *The Lawyers Weekly*, November 19, 1993, p. 21.

11. Summarized from an AP release, November 11, 1997, EduPage.

12. A more detailed account is given in the *Vancouver Sun*, January 1990.

13. A more detailed account is given in the *Vancouver Sun*.

14. Summarized from *The Lawyers Weekly*, January 22, 1988, p. 12.

15. A more detailed account is given in the *Vancouver Sun*, November 21, 1990.

16. A more detailed account is given in *Newsweek*, January 6, 1992, p. 43.

17. A more detailed account is given in the *Vancouver Sun*, November 20, 1990.

18. A more detailed account is given in the *Vancouver Sun*, October 23, 1992.

19. A more detailed account is given in the *Vancouver Sun*, November 6, 1990.

20. *Fittingly Yours*, Aug/Sept/Oct, 1992, p. 47.

21. Summarized from *The Globe and Mail*, January 11, 1991.

22. For a more detailed account see *Newsweek*, November 13, 1995, p. 60.

23. Summarized from *The Lawyers Weekly*, August 25, 1989, p. 20.

24. For more detailed accounts see *Maclean's*, December 19, 1994, p. 30 and *The New York Times*, June 28, 1995, p. A7.

25. *The Globe and Mail*, November 16, 1992.

26. For a more detailed account see the *Vancouver Sun*, April 6, 1996, p. F8.

27. Summarized from *The Globe and Mail*, November 11, 1993, p. A13.

28. A more detailed account is given in *The Miami Herald*, December 29, 1993, p. 2A.

29. Summarized from a review in *The Lawyers Weekly*, August 19, 1994, p. 34.

30. Summarized from an extract of the case printed in *The Lawyers Weekly*, September 2, 1994, p. 11. For a discussion of the case see *The Lawyers Weekly*, July 22, 1994, p. 1.

31. Summarized from *The Lawyers Weekly*, February 26, 1993, p. 21.

32. Summarized from *The Globe and Mail*, October 28, 1992, p. A28.

V

THE LAW OF EMPLOYMENT AND AGENCY

A. Employment

1. The Distinction Between an Employee and an Independent Contractor

Formosa Mutual Insurance Co. v. Tanner

[1997] O.J. No. 2605 (Q.L.)
File No. 54/1997
Ontario Court of Justice (General Division)
June 11, 1997

O'Connor J.:— When Susan Tanner's occasional babysitter walked off with some of her antique porcelain doll collection, she claimed the loss under her homeowners' insurance policy. The Formosa Mutual Insurance Company turned her down, saying theft by an employee is not covered. Ms. Tanner argues her babysitter was not an employee. She was an independent contractor and the theft by her is not excluded by the contract, she says.

I agree with Ms. Tanner. The babysitter was an independent contractor. Since the exclusion clauses in the contract do not mention independent contractors, Formosa must pay the claim.

BACKGROUND

Ms. Tanner lives in Walkerton with her children. Her job as an airline flight attendant often takes her away from home for a few days at a time. So she went to her local Canada Employment Centre to see about a babysitter for the children during her trips. They gave her some names and told her she should do her own background checks. She interviewed Brenda Peterson and got some references from her. They appeared satisfactory. Ms. Peterson had other clients. She was hired. Ms. Peterson cared for the children several times before Ms. Tanner was surprised to learn from a friend one of her antique porcelain dolls was sold at a local auction. She did an inventory around the house and discovered the doll and other contents were missing, including a credit card and cash, all totalling several thousand dollars. The babysitter was the prime suspect. The police did an investigation and charged Ms. Peterson with

theft. Some of the stuff was recovered. But she had spent the money and sold most of the more valuable items. About $5,800 was lost. Ms. Tanner then made her insurance claim.

Formosa denied coverage. The contract does not cover theft by the insured's employees and a babysitter is an employee, it says.

The contract contains clauses excluding coverage for loss by theft by employees of the insured "... or other persons to whom the property insured may be loaned, rented or entrusted (carriers for hire excepted)." It also defines a "Residence Employee" as "... a person employed by the Insured to perform duties in connection with the maintenance or use of the insured premises. This includes persons who perform household or domestic services or duties of a similar nature for the Insured. This does not include persons while performing duties in connection with the Insured's business." (emphasis added). Curiously, although defined, residence employee is not referred to anywhere else in the policy.

APPLICANT'S POSITION

Formosa says "employee" should be given its plain and ordinary meaning. It relies on the definition of the master/servant relationship, now generally referred to as the employer/employee relationship, found in *Black's Law Dictionary*, 5th ed. (St. Paul Minn.: West Publishing Co., 1979). The relationship is found where one person, for pay, enters into the service of another and devotes to him personal labour for an agreed upon period and where the employer has the right select the employee, the power to remove and discharge him, and the right to direct both what work shall be done and the manner in which it will be done. A babysitter fits these criteria. Further, she is caught under the definition of "Residence Employee." Formosa argues a residence employee is a subset of employee and is indicative of the intentions of the parties to include a person who does domestic chores in the residence of the insured. If a babysitter satisfies the residence employee definition, then she is also included under the broader definition of an employee. Because employees are specifically excluded from theft coverage, Formosa should not be ordered to pay the claim.

RESPONDENT'S POSITION

Ms. Tanner says her thieving babysitter was not an employee, but an independent contractor, a significantly different category of servant with responsibilities and rights different from those of an employee. Independent contractors are not mentioned in the exclusionary clauses of the contract. The contract is clear and unambiguous. The intention of the parties must be determined from the ordinary meaning of the wording used. If they intended to exclude coverage for theft by independent contractors of the insured they would have said so.

ANALYSIS

"Employee" is not defined in the contract. The definition of "Residence Employee," is not helpful. The use of the undefined term "employee" with a modifier simply begs the question of the meaning of "employee." It is still not defined. Formosa appears content to live with the general definition in *Black's*, (supra).

An independent contractor is one who operates her own business enterprise. To distinguish between an employee and an independent contractor one test is whether or not the employer retains the power, not only of directing what work is to be done, but also controlling the manner of doing the work. If the person doing the work is free to carry it out as she thinks proper and is able to make decisions about exigencies as they arise, solve problems without direction or decide how to perform the contractual obligations as she sees fit, she is an independent con-

tractor. *Dallantonio v. McCormick* (1913), 29 O.L.R. 319 (C.A.). Later cases place emphasis on the question of whether the person is in a general sense in business for herself. If so she is an independent contractor. See *Bodnarchuk et. al. v Stevenson and Co. et. al.* (1994), 98 Manitoba Reports (2d) 161. This approach has been called the business organization test. One asks the question: "Whose business is it?" A typical employee works for only one employer, whereas a typical independent contractor is available to anyone who will pay for her services. See P. Atiyah, *Vicarious Liability in the Law of Torts* (London: Butterworths, 1967), p. 63. The fact one sells her services in the market generally rather than to a single employer suggests she is an entrepreneur, running her own business.

Here the babysitter made her livelihood by caring for the children of several people. She was not available exclusively to Ms. Tanner. when performing her duties she was not under the continuous supervision of Ms. Tanner, whose own job made her unavailable, often for days at a time, to provide hands-on direction or supervision. The babysitter would be required to make decisions about the carrying out of her responsibilities, e.g. when and what to feed the children, how to entertain them, how to manage medical emergencies.

Ms. Tanner paid her a set contract price, based on the time spent. The babysitter was responsible for her own source deductions and remittances to Revenue Canada. She was in a real sense in business for herself, offering her services to several people.

CONCLUSION

The babysitter more closely meets the definition of an independent contractor than of an employee. Her thefts are not excluded from coverage. Formosa must pay the claim of $5,802, less the $500 deductible, plus pre and post judgment interest until payment, in accordance with the *Courts of Justice Act*.

Unless counsel make submissions as to a different costs disposition before July 10, 1997, costs are to the Respondent on a party/party basis after assessment.

---

2. TERMS OF THE EMPLOYMENT CONTRACT

Questions

When you say "yes" to a job offer, what are you promising your employer?
What is the employer promising you?

- *T*he head office introduced a non-smoking policy, but it was not implemented at Ms. Scholem's centre in a suburb of Sydney, Australia. Ms. Scholem, in her action against her employer for failure to provide a smoke-free working environment, stated that her centre was a "tobacco-laden environment" and she was obliged to take part in consulting sessions with heavy smokers in a room with closed windows and doors. She alleged that the passive smoke, which she had to endure for her 12 working years, aggravated her asthma, led to bronchial spasms, shortness of breath and caused her to be on constant medication. The court held in her favour and awarded her about $80,000 (Can.) in damages. Ms. Scholem, a psychologist, worked with the New South Wales health department.[1]

- **D**rexel Burnham Lambert Inc. sued its former employee Michael Milken "junk bond pioneer" for more than one billion dollars, the compensation he received from the company over a four-year period. Milken received a ten-year prison sentence after pleading guilty to federal securities law violations. The prison term was reduced by a U.S. Federal Court in August of 1992. The lawsuit against Milken and other former employees was part of an agreement that would free the company from bankruptcy proceedings.[2]

    Details of a proposed $1.3 billion settlement indicate that Milken would retain about $125 million.[3]

3. JUST CAUSE/WRONGFUL DISMISSAL

Question

In a non-union job, if your contract is silent on the matter, what are the implied terms about dismissal?

- **J**ohn Pulitzer, the U.S. publisher, in whose name the Pulitzer prize for journalism is awarded, fired several employees because of the way they ate soup.[4]

Durand was a long-time employee of the defendant of the Quaker Oats Company of Canada Ltd. One of the company's customers made it possible for employees of the company to take a "trade trip." Durand's superior, the regional manager, cancelled the trade trip, but Durand surreptitiously arranged for his wife and her friend to go. After the company learned what he had done and questioned him about it, it terminated his employment. He received the following letter:

April 18, 1986

H.L. Durand
[Address]

Dear Sir:

This is to confirm that your employment with Quaker has been terminated for cause.

We have discussed with you in detail our concern, and have listened carefully to your comments on the matter.

It is clear that you have broken the bond of trust required between us.

You have breached specific provisions of our Conflict of Interest Rules. Further, you have committed an act of direct insubordination in order to derive personal gain.

Your conduct with regard to this matter leaves us no choice.

Yours truly,
"Bruce E. Barbour"
Bruce E. Barbour
Zone Manager
Western Canada

The following are excerpts from the reasons for the judgment of the Court of Appeal which held Durand had been dismissed for just cause and thereby reversed the decision of the lower court judge:

Locke, J.A. concludes:

"The evidence establishes clearly that there was secrecy, that there was insubordination, that there was a conflict of interest and that there had been an acquisition of a "perk" by Durand for his own or his family's personal advantage.

It was because, I think, of the trial judge's original error in characterizing the breach of the conflict of interest rules as "technical" that led him, in my view, to the decision he enunciated. In my opinion, on the facts and on the law there were substantial reasons for the executives of the Quaker Oats Company determining that the taking of the unauthorized trip had placed the company in a sense in hostage to a potential contractor for advertising and that the confidence that they would feel in Durand in handling advertising matters in the future could not be justified any longer.

I think that the express and implied terms of the contract of employment were breached and that the discharge was justified. I would correspondingly allow the appeal and dismiss the action.

Seaton J.A.: I agree.

Southin J.A.: Mr. Justice Locke has stated the facts and I agree with him that the appeal must be allowed. I would like to put my legal foundation for that opinion in my own words.

The appeal is from a judgment granting judgment for what is called wrongful dismissal. What such an action is usually, and is in this case, is an action for damages for breach of the implied term of a contract of employment which lacks an express term on the point that it can only be terminated by either side on reasonable notice, and that in itself leads to the action being founded on the proposition that the employer's act in not giving reasonable notice was itself a repudiation. But here the employer says that the employee repudiated and thus its notice of dismissal was in law an acceptance of that repudiation.

As my learned brother has referred to the implied term of the contract of employment, however one puts it, it is a promise by the employee that he will faithfully, honestly and diligently serve his employer. If he commits a fundamental breach of that term the employer is entitled to say "I have no further obligations to perform and that includes the obligation of giving you reasonable notice."

I approach the matter this way because, despite much of the language in the cases, contracts of service are not governed by any different legal principles from those governing all other contracts. (See on that point, *Laws V. London Chronicle* [*(Indicator Newspapers) Ltd.*, [1959] 1 W.L.R. 698, [1959] 2 All E.R. 285 (C.A.)]). What constitutes a fundamental breach of the implied term is not always easy to determine, but it must be determined objectively. It is not a question of the intention, necessarily or at all, of the employee—that is, did it ever occur to him that he was about to be in breach of an implied term is not material. It may well be in this case that the respondent never thought for a moment that anything that he was doing was in breach of the implied term of his contract of employment.

The learned judge below called what the respondent did deceptive, dishonest and bordering on insubordinate. Those terms are descriptive. They do not come, in my opinion, to grips with the issue. The gravamen of the appellant's case is that the respondent obtained for his wife and a friend from a supplier to the company, two tickets for a trip to Las Vegas worth about $800 each, without the knowledge of his superiors, and that is the kind of conduct that an employer can look upon as a fundamental breach because it exposes the employee to the importunings, possibly of the supplier, in connection with his duties.

Thus, in my view, that sort of thing, even if it did not occur to Mr. Durand (as I hope that it did not) that it was dishonest, is in fact a fundamental breach. Where, in my opinion, the learned judge erred was first, in not asking himself whether to do this thing was a fundamental breach and secondly, in considering that the company was under any legal obligation to choose a different way of dealing with this fundamental breach than the course it did choose. The company was under no obligation to choose any other course once there was a fundamental breach and for that, of course, I need only refer to *Port Arthur Shipbldg. Co. v. Arthurs*, [1969] S.C.R. 85, 70 D.L.R. (2d) 693 [Ont.]. I would therefore allow the appeal.

Seaton J.A.: The appeal is allowed. The action dismissed."

Appeal allowed.

Durand v. The Quaker Oats Company of Canada Ltd.
45 B.C.L.R. (2d) 354
British Columbia Court of Appeal
February 21, 1990

Q u e s t i o n s

Who has the burden of proving there was just cause for dismissal?
What types of behaviour give the employer "just cause" for dismissing the employee
without notice or even pay in lieu of notice?

An e-mail message based on a vulgar monologue by Andrew Dice Clay was altered to refer to a co-worker and sent by the plaintiffs to other co-workers. When asked by their superior in several meetings about the distribution of the message, both lied about the extent of the distribution of the "joke" (which eventually did come to the attention of the worker ridiculed).

After reviewing the character of the message. the facts of its distribution, and the subsequent meetings with the plaintiffs, Justice Drost states:

"… In an action for wrongful dismissal, the onus is on the defendant employer to satisfy the Court, on a balance of probabilities, that just cause existed for the summary dismissal of the employee. …

[23] Here, the onus is on the defendant to establish misconduct on the part of the dismissed employees which is serious enough to amount to a fundamental breach of their contracts of employment.

[24] MDA advances two grounds which it says establish cause. First, that the plaintiffs engaged in hurtful and malicious conduct toward a co-worker which so seriously affected the work environment that their termination was necessary to rehabilitate it. Second, that the plaintiffs were so dishonest in all their dealings with management during the investigation of the incident that they can no longer be trusted. …

[26] The argument advanced by the defendant is that, by engaging in a "prank" which was intentionally hurtful and vicious, the plaintiffs have revealed character flaws that are so serious as to justify their dismissal. It is not only their conduct, but also the fact that they were capable of such conduct, which concerns the defendant.

[27] In order to determine whether the sending of the e-mail is, in itself, serious enough to amount to a fundamental breach of their employment contracts, some analysis of the law is required. …

[Although the judge concluded that the prank ridiculed, demeaned and humiliated the worker, he concluded on this point:]

[34] Nonetheless, I am not persuaded that the conduct of the plaintiffs, so far as their involvement in the distribution of the e-mail message is concerned, is alone sufficient grounds for their summary dismissal. I am of the view that, standing alone, that conduct warranted a severe reprimand, but nothing more.

[35] However, such conduct, when combined with the plaintiffs' subsequent dishonesty during the investigation, does, in my opinion, clearly amounts to just cause for dismissal.

[36] As I mentioned above, the plaintiffs must have recognized the seriousness of their conduct. Nonetheless, they continued to be evasive and dishonest through three meetings with their supervisor. The leading statement concerning dishonesty as a just cause can be found in the judgment of Hollinrake J.A. in *McPhillips v. British Columbia Ferry Corp.* (1994), 94 B.C.L.R. (2d) l C.A., at p. 6:

Dishonesty is always cause for dismissal because it is a breach of the condition of faithful service. It is the employer's choice whether to dismiss or forgive.

[37] The case of *Marshal v. Pacific Coast Savings Credit Union* concerned the termination of the employment of a credit union bank manager who lied during an investigation into his use of credit. Drake J. found that the conduct which was under investigation was not in itself objectionable, but he dismissed the plaintiff's action for wrongful dismissal because he had lied to his employer during the course of the investigation.

[38] In my view, the same principle applies in the circumstances of this case.

[39] While, as Braidwood J. noted in the Wright, an employee's failure to disclose his own wrongdoing does not amount to cause, once the employee's conduct comes under investigation, he or she must be honest or risk dismissal for cause. ...

[41] I find that neither of the plaintiffs lived up to their implied duties of honesty or faithfulness.

[42] [The plaintiff] ... concedes that he lied to his employer and that fact, when taken together with his participation in the distribution of the offensive material, amounts to a breach of his implied duty of honesty and faithfulness and thus constitutes just cause for his dismissal.

[43] [The second plaintiff] ... is in an even worse position. He lied to his supervisor on at least three occasions. ... His dishonesty, when taken in conjunction with his earlier conduct, also gives rise to just cause for his dismissal.

[44] For those reasons, the plaintiffs' action is dismissed. Counsel are at liberty to make submissions regarding costs if they are unable to resolve that matter.

Di Vito v. Macdonald Dettwiler & Assoc. Ltd.
Vancouver Registry No. C944l98
The Supreme Court of British Columbia
June 27, 1996

Stanley Scott Werle *v.* SaskEnergy Incorporated

SASK. QUEEN'S BENCH
FILE NO. 1215-003
JUNE 3, 1992

Kyle J.: The defendant, SaskEnergy Incorporated ("SaskEnergy"), conducted a search for a Vice-President of its Sales and Marketing Department in September of 1990. The plaintiff, Mr. Stanley Scott Werle, was the successful applicant. Fifty-one people had applied. SaskEnergy is a public utility which sells natural gas to residents of Saskatchewan. It had recently been separated from SaskPower, the provincial electrical utility, and though it was a Crown corporation, it had plans to become privately held, plans which had excited some political controversy. When Mr. Werle sought the position of Vice-President of Sales and Marketing Department, it was a new position and the advertisement described aspects both of sales and of marketing as being part of the job.

Mr. Werle sent an application letter with a resume attached. In the resume he detailed his background as a salesperson with Xerox. He had been most successful in that role, and he was hoping that the new job, if he got it, would entitle him to a salary at or near the $100,000 level which he had attained at Xerox. In his resume he outlined his level of education which was stated to be a Bachelor of Commerce (Marketing) from the University of Saskatchewan. In fact, Mr. Werle had tried for four years to get his Bachelor of Commerce, but he had never passed even one year and he had certainly never been granted a degree. Mr. Werle has advanced no explanation for this misrepresentation which he says was an error resulting from a failure to carry forward some qualifying words which appeared in an earlier version of the resume.

Mr. Werle was hired after a number of interviews and a newsletter announcing his hiring was sent to the 500 or so employees of the company. It mentioned a Bachelor of Commerce and he noticed it, but did nothing. After a month or two, the personnel department asked him for a record of his university training, either a statement of marks or a copy of the diploma. After some delay, he indicated that he could not find his diploma. The personnel officer said: "Didn't you have it framed?" and he answered: "I am not a plaque collector."

When the personnel officer's suspicions were aroused, she called the University and discovered the truth and advised her superiors.

Mr. Bill Baker, President of the company, testified that he

had hired Mr. Werle because of his sales experience and background of education in marketing at the University of Saskatchewan. He says he would not have hired Mr. Werle had he known that he did not have a degree. When he found out that indeed he did not have the education, his concerns were twofold. First he felt that Mr. Werle could not do the marketing work he was, in part, hired to do. Secondly, he was concerned that they had hired someone who had lied about his credentials. He was disappointed by this turn of events. He liked Mr. Werle, although some doubts as to his ability in the planning area had started to surface. He says that to have someone in the company who would do such a thing was simply unacceptable. It was something that everyone would know about and it would be a terrible precedent or signal. Mr. Baker was most sympathetic with Mr. Werle. He respected the effort which Mr. Werle had made to get where he was, he respected the success he had achieved, and he liked his motivated style. He would have liked to have been a forgiving boss in these circumstances, and he toyed with the idea. He was, however, fully aware that his duty to the company was on a higher level and he felt that dismissal was required.

Mr. Werle's testimony was not convincing, not only could he not explain how the inaccuracy occurred, but when the newsletter announced that he had a degree, he did nothing and when personnel asked for his diploma he prevaricated. One can only conclude that he was living a lie, if not from the beginning when he filed the false resume, at least from the time of the newsletter. It is not surprising that the company would find this to be evidence of a lack of the integrity requisite in a vice-president. The fact that he allowed the error, as he called it, to continue is quite clearly consistent with the view that the original misrepresentation of his educational status was intentional, a conclusion which the company reached. I find that the company was fully entitled to conclude, as it did, that it had a dishonest employee. Its reluctance to fire him is understandable—his wife was expecting, he was remorseful, and he was a valuable employee, notwithstanding his shortfall in the marketing area. The transfer to a lower position as opposed to termination would, of course, have constituted constructive dismissal so his consent would be essential if that were to be done. Mr. Labas, President of a subsidiary of SaskEnergy, was really in charge of resolving the problem which had arisen. Against Mr. Baker's better judgment, he made an offer of a much reduced status for Mr. Werle, one which would have allowed him to regain the company's confidence. He did not accept the terms proposed and accordingly his employment was terminated for the cause referred to above.

That the company would dismiss a vice-president for what can only be described as fraud, is not surprising. Indeed, the willingness of the company to give Mr. Werle a second chance is surprising; it can only be related to a humane and forgiving nature on the part of the officers of the company. It was in no sense a condonation of Mr. Werle's misdeeds. It would have involved a reduction in salary of some $35,000 and a significant loss of status. In Mr. Werle's action for wrongful dismissal, he claims that the misstatement in the resume was inadvertent, that in ignoring the newsletter, he simply fell prey to the pressure of other matters, and that in his evasion of the personnel department's requests, he was unaware that his resume contained the aforementioned error.

There are no cases where an employee whose dishonesty was so clearly established has been found to have been wrongfully dismissed. The cases cited by Mr. Werle which raise the level of proof to a higher level than that of balance of probabilities, are not relevant here as I am in no doubt as to the dishonesty of Mr. Werle in respect of his credentials. His efforts to rationalize his behavior as presented at trial were not credible and they simply reinforce the impression of dishonesty which the events themselves had justified. His decision to bring this action was simply another example of his bad judgment. Accordingly, the action is dismissed and SaskEnergy is entitled to its costs.

[The plaintiff's action for wrongful dismissal is dismissed.]

Note: In the following cases the employee challenged the employer's allegation of just cause for dismissal. They lost.

- *K*ennedy had a co-worker punch his time card for him each morning. His employer told them to stop and warned that continuation of the practice could lead to Kennedy's dismissal. His continuation of the practice came to light on the day he called the company to say he wouldn't be in because of a car accident. Unfortunately his time card had already been punched by his faithful but uninformed co-worker.[5]

- *A* discreet surveillance by an outside security specialist documented that the cashier allowed her friends to take away items that were not paid for or were entered under an improper code.[6]

- *A* company chauffeur claiming neck and back injuries after an accident on the job was receiving disability payments equivalent to a full salary. The company obtained evidence that its disabled worker was able to play golf, do renovation work, load wood and drive for hours at a time.[7]

- *A* computer programmer, the only employee who "knew the answers, or the keys, or the passwords" was *suspended* because of his refusal to document his work and because of his responding to their requests "with derision, insubordination and laughter." The employee asked for a letter of termination, but he never was terminated in hopes that he would be cooperative. After he left voluntarily, the company had to hire additional programmers "to find out what were the keys to the kingdom." In his rather impassioned judgment the judge remarked "This is one of the simplest cases I have ever had to decide in eleven years as a judge. I can't believe this is before me.'[8]

Note: In the following cases the employee's action for wrongful dismissal was successful.

• *W*hen Mr. Mackenzie told a co-worker about the Seinfeld episode in which Seinfeld doesn't know a girl's name but knows it rhymes with a female body part, the co-worker alleged sexual harassment which cost Mackenzie his job with the Miller Brewing Company. He sued for wrongful dismissal, *inter alia*, and won. The brewery intends to appeal.[9]

• *M*r. Ditchburn was one of the best salesmen of an Ontario company for which he had worked for almost thirty years. Unfortunately, after dining and drinking with one of the company's most important customers, Ditchburn and the customer got into an argument which escalated into a physical fight. Ditchburn was fired and offered two months' salary. He sued for wrongful dismissal and won. The court found the fight was an isolated incident of bad judgment and not cause for dismissal.[10]

• *T*he former top manager of Triton Biosciences Inc., a subsidiary of Shell Oil Co. was dismissed after his secretary discovered a private memo outlining rules for a gay "safe sex" party. The judge of the California Alameda County Superior Court found the firing a "totally inappropriate over-reaction" to the memo.[11]

4. DAMAGES FOR WRONGFUL DISMISSAL

Q u e s t i o n

What factors does the court consider in determining what constitutes reasonable notice?

Bardal *v.* **The Globe & Mail Ltd.**

[1960] 24 D.L.R. (2D) 140
ONTARIO HIGH COURT
APRIL 21, 1960

Background facts: The plaintiff was hired as an advertising manager for an indefinite term. After sixteen years of service he was dismissed without cause and without notice. After reviewing the particulars of the plaintiff's work, remuneration, and the termination of his employment, McRuer, C.J.H.C. continues:

It remains only for me to consider what damages the plaintiff is entitled to recover.

In every case of wrongful dismissal the measure of damages must be considered in the light of the terms of employment and the character of the services to be rendered. In this case there was no stipulated term during which the employment was to last. Both parties undoubtedly considered that the employment was to be of a permanent character. All the evidence goes to show that the office of advertising manager is one of the most important offices in the service of the defendant. In fact, it is by means of the revenue derived under the supervision of the advertising manager that the publication of a newspaper becomes a profitable enterprise. The fact that the plaintiff was appointed to the Board of Directors of the defendant goes to demonstrate the permanent character or his employment and the importance of the office.

It is not argued that there was a definite agreement that the plaintiff was employed for life but the case is put on the basis of an indefinite hiring of a permanent character which could be terminated by reasonable notice.

In *Carter v. Bell & Sons,* [1936], 2 D.L.R. 438 at p. 439, O.R. 290 at p. 297, Mr. Justice Middleton concisely and with great clarity stated the law applicable to this case in this way: "In the case of master and servant there is implied in the contract of hiring an obligation to give reasonable notice of an intention to terminate the arrangement."

On this branch of the case, the only remaining matter to be considered is what should be implied as reasonable notice in the circumstances of the contract in question. In *Carter v. Bell* Middleton J.A. went on at p. 439 D.L.R., p. 297 O.R. to say: "This notice in a case of an indefinite hiring is generally 6 months, but the length of notice is always a matter for inquiry and determination, and in special circumstances may be less."

The contractual obligation is to give reasonable notice and to continue the servant in his employment. If the servant is dismissed without reasonable notice he is entitled to the damages that flow from the failure to observe this contractual obligation, which damages the servant is bound in law to mitigate to the best of his ability. ...

... I think I must determine what would be reasonable notice in all the circumstances and proper compensation for the loss the plaintiff has suffered by reason of the breach of the implied term in the contract to give him reasonable notice of its termination.

There can be no catalogue laid down as to what is reasonable notice in particular classes of cases. The reasonableness of the notice must be decided with reference to each particular case, having regard to the character of the employment, the length of service of the servant, the age of the servant and the availability of similar employment, having regard to the experience, training and qualifications of the servant.

Applying this principle to this case, we have a servant who, through a lifetime of training, was qualified to manage the advertising department of a large metropolitan newspaper. With the exception of a short period of employment as manager of a street car advertising agency, his whole training has been in the advertising department of two large daily newspapers. There are few comparable offices available in Canada and the plaintiff has in mitigation of his damages taken employment with an advertising agency, in which employment he will no doubt find useful his advertising experience, but the employment must necessarily be of a different character.

I have come to the conclusion, as the jury did in the *Sun Printing & Publishing Assn.* case and as the Court of Appeal agreed, that one year's notice would have been reasonable, having regard to all the circumstances of this case.

That being true, the next question to decide is what damages have flowed from the failure of the defendant to give a year's notice and how far have those damages been mitigated by the receipt by the plaintiff of a salary from another employer. ...

Judgment for plaintiff.

Note: In a Supreme Court of Canada decision (6-3), an employee wrongfully dismissed was awarded additional damages by way of an extended notice period because of the employer's lack of fair-dealing; it alleged, for two years, that it had just cause to dismiss him but admitted at trial time that it did not.[12]

Ansari et al. *v.* British Columbia Hydro and Power Authority

(1986) 2 B.C.L.R. (2D) 33
SUPREME COURT OF BRITISH COLUMBIA
APRIL 3, 1986

McEachern C.J.S.C.:—The separate actions of these four plaintiffs against the defendant for damages for wrongful dismissal were tried summarily together under R. 18A.

I. GENERAL

In 1984 a great many graduate engineers employed by B.C. Hydro were deemed surplus to its requirements and they were terminated without cause and without reasonable notice. They were given a severance allowance based upon years of employment with B.C. Hydro plus a percentage allowance of 25 per cent or 30 per cent for benefits. I understand that about 660 employees not covered by collective agreements were terminated in this way and some of them have brought actions for damages for wrongful dismissal. ...

The present four cases have been chosen not as test cases, for no other plaintiffs are bound by the result except, of course, by the possible application of *stare decisis* (the doctrine of precedence in which courts consider themselves bound by some previous decisions), but rather to explore the question of notice and to obtain a judgment on the questions of pensions and other benefits that were not specifically decided in the other four cases. ...

The principles relating to the assessment of damages for wrongful dismissal, which has been too much before the courts during the recent economic unpleasantness, are well established. These are stated and restated in case after case. In fact, in *Nicholls v. Richmond,* 60 B.C.L.R. 320, [1985] 3 W.W.R. 543, 50 C.P.C. 171 (S.C.), Mr. R.H. Guile, Q.C., furnished a 100-page summary of nearly 500 recent Canadian reported wrongful dismissal cases. It is not my function to rationalize the law but it is obvious that the profession is urgently in need of guidance.

The underlining principle which arises out of the law of master and servant (as they were called at common law) is that, absent contractual provisions, the master who terminates the employment of a servant must give reasonable notice and, upon doing so, he is not required to compensate the servant in any way. If the master does not give reasonable notice, then the law requires him to compensate the servant by an award of damages that is intended to put the servant in the position he would be in if he had received proper notice. In the assessment of these damages, the recovery of lost income is not limited to salary, but includes other benefits incidental to the employment being terminated: *Lawson v. Dom. Securities Corp.*, [1977] 2 A.C.W.S. 259 (Ont. C.A.).

It is not the function of damages for wrongful dismissal to penalize the employer for the manner of dismissal nor to compensate the employee over and above the damages flowing from the breach of the contract of employment for his loyal or useful service to the employer. This had been settled law since at least 1883 when the Supreme Court of Canada held that vindictive damages cannot be awarded for breach of contract: *Guilford v. Anglo-French SS. Co.* (1883), 9 S.C.R. 303 [N.S.].

The House of Lords reached a similar conclusion. …

In short, damages for wrongful dismissal are founded in contract and the focus of the inquiry is what damages, assessed in accordance with the principles I shall discuss, flow from the breach.

II. THE PERIOD OF REASONABLE NOTICE

In what is often regarded as a leading case, *Bardal v. Globe and Mail Ltd.*, [1960] O.W.N. 253, 24 D.L.R. (2d) 140 (H.C.), McRuer C.J.H.C. said at p. 145:

There can be no catalogue laid down as to what is reasonable notice in particular classes of cases. The reasonableness of the notice must be decided with reference to each particular case, having regard to the character of the employment, the length of service of the servant, the age of the servant and the availability of similar employment, having regard to the experience, training and qualifications of the servant.

In *Gillespie v. Bulkley Valley Forest Indust. Ltd.*, [1975] 1 W.W.R. 607, 50 D.L.R. (3d) 316 (B.C.C.A.), it was said that the factors enumerated by McRuer C.J.H.C. should not be regarded as exhaustive but, with great respect, they are indeed the most important factors, and other matters which have crept into the assessment of this kind of damages are not of great significance.

[After reviewing the other matters which he does not consider useful, Judge McEachern concludes:]

At the end of the day the question really comes down to what is objectively reasonable in the variable circumstances of each case, but I repeat that the most important factors are the responsibility of the employment function, age, length of service and the availability of equivalent alternative employment, but not necessarily in that order.

In restating this general rule, I am not overlooking the importance of the experience, training and qualifications of the employee but I think these qualities are significant mainly in considering the importance of the employment function and in the context of alternative employment.

What all this means, in my view, is that the general statement of factors quoted above from *Bardal* are the governing factors, and it would be better if other individual or subjective factors had not crept into the determination of reasonable notice. In my view such other matters are of little importance in most cases.

I turn to a consideration of the individual cases…

Note: This case was affirmed by the B.C. Court of Appeal on November 19, 1986; Doc. CA 005827.

Q u e s t i o n

How can a judge challenge the assumptions upon which accepted precedents are based?

Cronk **v.** *Canadian General Insurance Co.*

128 D.L.R. (4TH) 147
ONTARIO COURT OF APPEAL
SEPTEMBER 21, 1995

Summary of the facts: Edna Cronk had worked for Canadian General Insurance in a clerical position for 28 years when she was terminated without cause at the age of 55. She refused the money offered to her by the company as pay in lieu of notice and sued for wrongful dismissal claiming she was entitled to reasonable notice or a payment in lieu of reasonable notice. On her motion for summary judgment, the judge hearing the matter concluded she was entitled to 20 months notice, a period significantly longer than those usually awarded for a person in a clerical position.

Lacourciere J.A.:—This is an appeal from the summary judgment of the Honourable Mr. Justice MacPherson, dated July 14, 1994 … awarding damages of 20 months' salary in an action for wrongful dismissal against the appellant. Among other issues, this appeal raises the central question of the weight to be given to the character of an employee's occupation in setting the period of compensation to which the employee is entitled when he or she is dismissed without cause. …

… In granting judgment in her favour, MacPherson J. noted that "the factors to be considered in determining reasonable notice have remained more or less constant for over 30 years," having been enunciated by McRuer C.J.H.C. in *Bardal v. Globe and Mail Ltd.* (1960), 24 D.L.R. (2d) 140 at p. 145, [19601 O.W.N. 253 (H.C.J.):

> There can be no catalogue laid down as to what is reasonable notice in particular classes of cases. The reasonableness of the notice must be decided with reference to each particular case, having regard to the character of the employment, the length of service of the servant, the age of the servant and the availability of similar employment, having regard to the experience, training and qualifications of the servant.

It was the opinion of MacPherson J. that some of the factors enumerated in *Bardal* militated in favour of a generous notice period for the respondent. In this regard, he felt that her age made her particularly vulnerable, as she was probably too old to embark on a lengthy or strenuous retraining program, yet may well have been too young to contemplate retirement. As well, her limited training rendered her qualified only for clerical jobs within the insurance industry; her lack of mobility meant that even those jobs, were they to be found, would have to be in the Hamilton area. Finally, the learned motions judge took account of the fact that the respondent had devoted virtually her entire career to the appellant company, pointing out that the case law throughout Canada attaches great significance to what he termed the "long and loyal service factor". …

Addressing the role played by the character of employment in determining the requisite notice period, MacPherson J. observed the length of notice requested by the respondent had traditionally been reserved for persons with positions more senior to hers. Having said that, he could find no principled reason why this should be so. He rejected the proposition that senior employees are more stigmatized by the loss of employment than are their underlings. Likewise, he could find no support for the notion, frequently articulated in the case law, that senior, specialized employees have greater difficulty in securing new employment. …MacPherson J. [also] found another basis on which to dismiss the proposition (at p. 25):

> Third, the reality is—as we are all told by our parents at a young age that education and training are directly related to employment. The senior manager and the professional person are better, not worse, positioned to obtain employment, both initially and after in a post-dismissal context. Higher education and specialized training correlate directly with *increased* access to employment.

In support of this assertion, the learned motions court judge cited two studies published by the Council of Ontario Universities, as well as a May 21, 1994 article in the *Economist* magazine. He discovered these materials through his own research. For those reasons, he refused to accept the defendant's argument based on a managerial-clerical distinction. …

VII. THE DISTINCTION BETWEEN CLERICAL AND MANAGERIAL EMPLOYEES IN CHARACTERIZING THE EMPLOYMENT

… [The judge reviews the company's written arguments in support of the contention that clerical workers should receive less notice than managers and cites the multitude of cases that have adopted the "principle." He continues:]

In my opinion, the learned motions court judge's reasons do not justify departing from the widely accepted principle. He erred in doing so on the basis of his own sociological research without providing counsel an opportunity to challenge or respond to the results of the two studies relied upon. …

Before taking new matters into account based on statistics which have not been considered in the judgment under appeal, the adversarial process requires that the court ensure that the parties are given an opportunity to deal with the new information by making further submissions, oral or written, and allowing, if requested, fresh material in response.

The result arrived at has the potential of disrupting the practices of the commercial and industrial world, wherein employers have to predict with reasonable certainty the cost of downsizing or increasing their operations, particularly in difficult economic times. As well, legal practitioners specializing in employment law and the legal profession generally have to give advice to employers and employees in respect of termination of employment with reasonable certainty. Adherence to the doctrine of *stare decisis* plays an important role in that respect: *Cassell & Co. v. Broome*, [1972] 1 All E.R. 801 (H.L.) at p. 809.

VIII. CONCLUSION AND DISPOSITION

In my opinion, the character of the employment of the respondent does not entitle her to a lengthy period of notice. …

In calculating the period of notice for this respondent it is necessary to balance the traditional factors enumerated in *Bardal*, supra, which the motions court judgment appears to have improperly collapsed into the re-employability factor. While the character of the respondent's employment will restrict her to the level of a clerical, non-managerial employee, the respondent's age and lengthy faithful service for the appellant properly qualify her for the maximum notice in her category.

For these reasons, I would vary the judgment of MacPherson J. so that the respondent will recover damages based on a salary calculation covering 12 months . …

[Appeal allowed.]

Weiler J.:—[Justice Weiler agreed with Lacourciere that the appeal must be allowed. However, in a lengthy judgment he reviewed the motion court judge's attack on the assumptions underlying the precedent set in the *Bardal v. Globe and Mail* and asserted that the judge had a right to question the assumptions, but should have the arguments thoroughly canvassed in a full trial]

A trial is a search for the truth. When a trial judge reviews jurisprudence and finds it rests on a factual assumption, that may no longer be true or which may not apply in all cases, the judge is not obliged to continue to accept this assumption as a fact. Naturally, the judge wishes to avoid the expense and delay of requiring counsel to reattend for further argument concerning the material he has discovered and upon which he seeks to rely. However, where a judicial approach rests on a factual proposition with which the judge disagrees, and counsel are unaware that the judge is considering a break with the past, I can see no alternative but for the judge to allow counsel an opportunity to call evidence and to make submissions. The reason for this is twofold. The general studies or material that the judge sees as rebutting the factual proposition may, as a result of expert evidence, be susceptible to other interpretation. In addition, the parties have a right to expect that if a judge disagrees with a factual assumption, which has found its way into the jurisprudence and which has gone unchallenged, the judge will give the parties an opportunity to make submissions concerning the studies he sees as rebutting this assumption. MacPherson J. erred in not doing so. The parties should have been recalled.

Alternatively, it was open to MacPherson J. to dismiss the motion for summary judgment with respect to the issue of reasonable notice and to indicate that, in his opinion, there was a genuine issue for trial as to the weight to be given to character of employment. He could tell counsel about the studies that he felt were relevant. He could suggest that at a trial, if counsel desired, these and other studies could be introduced into evidence through experts who could be cross-examined as to their ramifications respecting Ms. Cronk. Inasmuch as the purpose of reasonable notice is to give the employee time to find other employment, the court's prediction as to the amount of reasonable notice required should if possible be based on correct assumptions.

… I would allow the appeal, set aside the judgment of MacPherson J. respecting reasonable notice, and in its place substitute an order … directing the trial of an issue as to the amount that Ms. Cronk is entitled to be paid in lieu of notice.

Appeal allowed.

MITIGATION

Question

How can an employee wrongfully dismissed mitigate his losses?

Mifsud *v.* MacMillan Bathurst Inc.

63 D.L.R. (4TH) 714; 70 O.R. (2D) 701
ONTARIO COURT OF APPEAL
NOVEMBER 21, 1989

Summary of the facts and of the judgment of the trial court given in the law report, reprinted with permission of Canada Law Book Inc., 240 Edward Street, Aurora, Ontario, L4G 3S9.

The plaintiff had been employed by the defendant for 18 years, and had been promoted first to the position of foreman, and later to that of supervisor. After some dissatisfaction with the plaintiff's work, the defendant reassigned him to the position of foreman. There was no reduction of salary, but the new position involved shift work and had reduced prospects of promotion and reduced responsibilities. The plaintiff started work in the new position, but left after a few days. An action for wrongful dismissal succeeded at trial on the basis of constructive dismissal. The defendant appealed to the Ontario Court of Appeal.

McKinlay J.A.:—The defendant, MacMillan Bathurst Inc., appeals a judgment in favour of the plaintiff, Frank George Michael Mifsud, awarding him the sum of $38,332.13 plus costs as a result of a finding that he was constructively dismissed from his position as a shift superintendent at the appellant's Etobicoke plant on September 4, 1984. This sum represents a notice period of 10 months. …

Counsel for the appellant argues that where there is a constructive dismissal, but where the new assignments involve no subjection to degrading work or humiliating relationships, the employee is obliged to mitigate his loss by accepting the position that was offered to him, and to work out his period of reasonable notice in that position. …

The doctrine of mitigation was concisely stated by Chief Justice Laskin in *Red Deer College v. Michaels* (1975), 57 D.L.R. (3d) 386 at p. 390, [1976] 2 S.C.R. 324, [1975] 5 W.W.R. 575 (S.C.C.):

The primary rule in breach of contract cases, that a wronged plaintiff is entitled to be put in as good a position as he would have been in if there had been proper performance by the defendant, is subject to the qualification that the defendant cannot be called upon to pay for avoidable losses which would result in an increase in the quantum of damages payable to the plaintiff. The reference in the case law to a "duty" to mitigate should be understood in this sense.

In short, a wronged plaintiff is entitled to recover damages for the losses he has suffered but the extent of those losses may depend upon *whether he has taken reasonable steps to avoid their unreasonable accumulation.*
(Emphasis added.)

There is no doubt that the duty of the plaintiff to take steps to mitigate his damages applies in all wrongful dismissal cases. The question is simply whether or not the steps taken by the plaintiff were reasonable.

When an employer wishes to dismiss an employee (other than for cause) the employer may choose either to give the employee reasonable notice of his termination date and require that he work out the notice period, or he may require the employee to leave immediately, thus rendering the employer liable for damages equal to the employee's remuneration and benefits for the reasonable notice period. If the employee leaves immediately, he is required to take reasonable steps to mitigate his loss and, barring any agreement to the contrary between the parties, any moneys earned in mitigation must be credited against his damages.

Is the situation substantially different when an employer does not wish to dismiss an employee but, being unsatisfied with his performance, or for some other valid reason, wishes to place him in a different position at the same salary? Why should it not be considered reasonable for the employee to mitigate his damages by working at the other position for the period of reasonable notice, or at least until he has found alternative employment which he accepts in mitigation?

The fact that the transfer to a new position may constitute in law a constructive dismissal does not eliminate the obligation of the employee to look at the new position offered and evaluate it as a means of mitigating damages. In all cases, comparison should be made to the contractual entitlement of the employer to give reasonable notice and leave the employee in his current position while a search is made for alternative employment. Where the salary offered is the same, where the working conditions are not substantially different or the work demeaning, and where the personal relationships involved are not acrimonious (as in this case) it is reasonable to expect the employee to accept the position offered in mitigation of damages during a reasonable notice period, or until he finds acceptable employment elsewhere.

It must be kept in mind, of course, that there are many situations where the facts would substantiate a constructive dismissal but where it would be patently unreasonable to expect an employee to accept continuing employment with the same employer in mitigation of his damages.

In this case, Mr. Mifsud improperly rejected the opportunity to mitigate his damages by maintaining an employed status from which to seek a preferable position elsewhere.

I would allow the appeal, replace the judgment of the trial judge with a judgment dismissing the plaintiff's claim, and allow the appellant its costs here and below.

Appeal allowed.

---

5. WRONGFUL RESIGNATION

Question

If you are not a member of a union and your employment contract is silent on the point, how much notice must you give your employer if you want to quit your job?

Systems Engineering and Automation Ltd. *v.* Power et al.

78 NFLD. & P.E.I.R. 65
NEWFOUNDLAND SUPREME COURT
OCTOBER 12, 1989

Wells, J.: The parties, I will refer to as SEA, Power, Guy and Avalon, respectively. SEA is a Newfoundland company, incorporated in 1983 and is a "high tech" supplier of services and hardware to other companies which require design, installation, and repair services for computer and control systems. Messrs. Power and Guy are technicians who were employed by SEA until May 7, 1987. Avalon was incorporated in May of 1987, and is owned by Messrs. Power and Guy.

SEA says that Messrs. Power and Guy, acting in concert, resigned from their employment on May 7, 1987 without notice and that in so doing they seriously prejudiced the work of SEA and caused it severe financial losses in the amount of $171,974.00.

SEA says that Messrs. Power and Guy secretly and improperly formulated a plan to incorporate Avalon to compete with it, and to take its customers, and that they asked fellow workers to leave SEA and work for the new company. It also says that Messrs. Power and Guy removed documents and records from the offices of SEA when they left.

Messrs. Power and Guy admit that they resigned without notice, however they say that SEA's demands upon them were such that their personal and family lives were being destroyed, and that they were justified in resigning without notice.

Avalon denies all allegations against it, and says that it did not commence business until more than two months after its incorporation which was at the time of the resignations of Messrs. Power and Guy.

The main issues are:

(a) were Messrs. Power and Guy justified in leaving the employ of SEA without notice?
(b) did Avalon do anything improper, and is it liable to SEA as a result of its entry into a similar business?
(c) If the defendants are liable, what is the measure of damages?
(d) who should bear the costs of this action?

In order to clarify the allegations, it is necessary to review the history of SEA, and the work histories of the individuals concerned.

[The judge reviewed the struggle of the company and the work and contributions of the defendants.]

A variety of reasons caused SEA to demand such working hours of Mr. Guy, but in my opinion the main reason was that the company could not afford to hire and train the number of technicians that it needed. Consequently it placed an increasingly heavy burden on the technicians which it already had, of whom Mr. Guy was the most senior and experienced. ...

Although Messrs. Power and Guy did not work together, their work histories at SEA somewhat paralleled each other and the company's records show that Mr. Power also worked as much as fifty, sixty, seventy and even eighty hours per week, mostly away from home and living in hotels. ...

By the spring of 1987, Messrs. Power and Guy found themselves vis-a-vis their employment and their family lives, in roughly comparable situation, which were far from satisfactory. [They talked about their frustrations and eventually they incorporated a company and resigned from SEA]. ...

The evidence indicated that the resignation enraged the management of SEA. ...

The first issue is whether or not Messrs. Power and Guy were justified in leaving their employment without notice.

I have no doubt that their working conditions which included long hours and the frustrations of working away from home, were difficult. Neither of them could have been expected to continue indefinitely to work these hours under these conditions. Nevertheless they were well aware that their particular jobs were important to their employer, and despite the frustrations which they felt, they must have known that to leave their employment without notice, would cause some difficulties and expense for SEA. Furthermore, nothing new or startling had taken place, for they had been working under similar conditions for months prior to May 7th.

[Their solicitor advised] that in the circumstances, they would have been justified in giving the minimum notice required by law.

It is agreed that there were no written contracts between the parties nor was their employment governed by a collective agreement. For these reasons it was argued that the *Labour Standards Act* applies, and I accept that argument as it applies to the minimum requirements.

Section 48 says:

Subject to sections 49 and 50, no employer or employee shall terminate a contract of service unless written notice of termination is given by or on behalf of the employer or employee, as the case may be, within the period set out in paragraph (a) or (b) of Section 51.

Section 51 says in its relevant parts:

The period of notice required to be given by the employer and employee under section 48 is

(a) one week, if the employee has been continuously employed by the employer for a period of one month or more but less than two years; and
(b) two weeks, if the employee has been continuously employed by the employer for a period of two years or more, ...

Accordingly I find as provided for in the Act, that Mr. Power should have given at least one week's notice and Mr. Guy, two.

[The Judge reviewed various projects on which the defendants were working at the time of their resignations to determine the extent of damages suffered by the plaintiffs because of their resigning without notice].

In summary therefore, I am prepared to allow under the various headings of damage:

(a) $2,000.00 for lost profits from Marystown Shipyard Limited,
(b) $3,000.00 for additional expenses in completing projects on which Mr. Power might have been able to assist,
(c) $5,000.00 for additional expenses in completing projects on which Mr. Guy might have been able to assist.

Total $10,000.00 ...

The evidence of Messrs. Power and Guy was to the effect that considerably more than $1,000.00 was owed to each of them, but they did not have records from which the amounts owing could be calculated. On a balance of probabilities, I am satisfied that they are owed at least $1,000.00 each, so that the sum of $2,000.00 should be deducted from the sum of $10,000.00 to which I have found the Plaintiff is entitled.

Judgment will therefore be entered for the plaintiff against the defendants jointly and severally in the amount of $8,000.00 together with prejudgment interest calculated from May 7, 1987. ...

Order accordingly.

6. LEGISLATION TO PROTECT EMPLOYEES

- *T*wenty-six men died by methane fire, carbon-monoxide poisoning and coal-dust explosion caused by concentrations of methane gas and coal dust in the Westray mines. Two managers of the mines face charges of criminal negligence and manslaughter, but the fault of the explosion was also attributed to the inspectors of the Department of Labour who failed to force the company to keep the mine safe.[13]

- *A* worker was crushed to death in a die-casting machine. The supervisor was unable to use a protection switch because the workers hung a spray gun on a wire that held the switch in an off position. The company which knew its workers frequently blocked safety switches was fined $200,000 under the Ontario *Occupational Health and Safety Act.*[14]

A woman began her employment as a cleaner at the airport for $5 an hour. When her supervisor learned she was pregnant he was very concerned about the effect of the cleaning chemicals on the fetus. He requested that she discuss the situation with her doctor. The employee reported back that the doctor advised that she could continue working. The supervisor himself wrote to the doctor who again responded that the chemicals would not adversely affect the unborn child. A few days later, the supervisor gave the employee a lay-off notice on the grounds that they were cutting staff. The employee complained under *The Saskatchewan Human Rights Code*, alleging that she was discriminated against on the grounds of her sex and pregnancy.

Her complaint was upheld. It was found that she was laid off because of her pregnancy and, although the supervisor's concern was praiseworthy, the firing was discriminatory. She was awarded damages for lost wages, hurt feelings and loss of self-esteem.

Nguyen v. Pacific Building Maintenance Ltd.
Summarized from The Lawyers Weekly
October 25, 1991, p. 29

- *T*he plaintiff, a nanny from Indonesia, gave testimony of serious exploitation by her employers. Her claim, aided by the *Employment Standards Act* (R.S.B.C.), the legislation creating the Canada Pension Plan and Employment Insurance as well as the law of contract and the principles of equity, was successful. The Court of Appeal dismissed the appeal by her employers.[15]

7. WORKERS' COMPENSATION

- *O*n the national day for honoring workers killed or injured on the job, government buildings fly flags at half staff. In British Columbia in 1995 152 workers died from workplace accidents and disease (although as many as 200,000 workers sought treatment).[16]

See p. 236 for Pasiechnyk v. Saskatchewan (Workers' Compensation Board)*, a Supreme Court of Canada decision in which the history and purpose of the Workers Compensation legislation are reviewed and in which the issue of judicial review is addressed.*

The *Workers' Compensation Act* of Newfoundland provided that:

> 43(2) The commission shall pay compensation to a worker who is seriously and permanently disabled as a result of an injury arising out of and in the course of employment notwithstanding that the injury is attributable solely to the serious and wilful misconduct of the worker.

A worker who was seriously and permanently disabled in a car accident when returning on a business trip was denied compensation by the Workers' Compensation Commission when it learned that the blood alcohol test taken some hours after the accident revealed that the reading was approximately four times that permitted by the *Criminal Code*. The worker's appeal to the Workers' Compensation Appeal Tribunal was dismissed. His appeal to the Newfoundland Supreme Court was dismissed. All found that the presumption that the injury arose out of employment had been rebutted.

Justice Cameron of the Newfoundland Court of Appeal wrote:

"The words 'in course of employment' refer to the time, place and circumstances under which the accident takes place. The words 'arising out of employment' refer to the origin of the cause of the injury. There must be some causal connection between the condition under which the employee worked and the injury which he received (*Blacks Law Dictionary*). In *MacKenzie v. G.T.P.R. Co.*, [1926] 1 D.L.R. 1 S.C.R. 178, Mignault J. cited with approval the statement of Lord Atkinson in *St. Helens Colliey Co. v. Hewitson*, [1924] A.C. 59 (H.L.), that the words 'arising out of' suggest the idea of cause and effect, the injury by accident being the effect and the employment, i.e., the discharge of the duties of the workman's service, the cause of that effect." Today, doing something incidental to his or her employment would be sufficient, the discharge of a duty having been rejected as too narrow a view. ...

"The Appeal Tribunal stated that to hold the accident arose out of the employment 'it must be satisfied that the degree of intoxication was incidental to the occurrence of the accident'. This test results, in my view, in a misapplication of s. 43, and amounts to an error in law. In light of the finding that the injury occurred in the course of employment and the application of the presumption contained in s. 61, the question which should have been asked is whether it had been proven that the employment was not a significant causative factor in the injury. As noted above, a finding that the applicant was the sole cause of the injury does not preclude a finding that the injury arose out of the employment. An example of an occasion where a worker might be said to be in the course of employment but the injury does not arise out of employment is an injury resulting from an act of violence against an employee at his place of employment but which was not motivated by nor connected with the employment. ...

"I have no difficulty with the conclusion of fact by the Appeal Tribunal that the accident probably would not have happened except for the appellant's intoxication. However, it was not the intoxication per se that injured him (as if, for example, he had been blinded by alcohol poisoning) but the combination of the intoxication with the driving of the car, the latter being a hazard of the appellant's employment. The injury was contributed to in a material degree by the appellant's employment; that is, it arose out of the employment....

"For these reasons the appeal is allowed and the decision of the Appeal Tribunal is set aside ..."

Appeal allowed.

Gellately v. Workers' Compensation Appeal Tribunal
126 D.L.R. (4th) 530
Newfoundland Court of Appeal
July 28, 1995

- *M*r. Ethier, angry with two co-workers, "saw red" and punched a metal filing cabinet with his fist. Off work for two months because of a fractured bone, he claimed workers' compensation but it was denied by the commission on the grounds that the injury was the result of a voluntary act or the result of gross negligence. The revisory board hearing the appeal rejected his claim; the appeals commission rejected his claim. Still arguing that the act could not be reasonably qualified as voluntary or the result of gross negligence, the worker has now appealed to the Quebec Superior Court.[17]

8. Collective Bargaining

A. Jurisdiction Disputes

- *I*n Quebec, The Quebec Federation of Labor and the Teamsters fought over which union would represent the workers of Molson-O'Keefe and Purolator. In these two instances the Teamsters won. In November of 1993 these two unions, "arch-rival," joined forces.[18]

B. Interests Dispute

Bargaining in Bad Faith

- *T*he Canada Labour Relations Board ruled that the owner of the Giant gold mine in Yellowknife had bargained in bad faith leading up to a May, 1992 strike action. The board ordered the company and union to negotiate a settlement within 30 days or face binding arbitration. The workers subsequently accepted an offer from the owner, Royal Oak Mines. The offer left some contentious issues to be negotiated by representatives from both sides or by a mediator if the two sides could not agree.[19] Labour peace came too late for some miners. Four months after the strike began, nine miners died in an explosion. A union member charged with murder was found guilty of nine counts of second-degree murder.

Strikes and Lockouts

- *I*n November of 1996, the baseball owners, in a 26-4 vote, ratified a new collective agreement. The approval of the contract by the owners and players ended a four-year fight during which the players went out on strike. The strike which began on August 12, 1994 lasted for 232 days and knocked out the World Series for the first time in 90 years The strike was ended by a court order.[20]

- *I*n the fall of 1994, the National Hockey League, failing to negotiate a new collective agreement with the NHL Players Association, commenced a lockout which threatened the 1994-95 season. The lockout continued for over 100 days; it wasn't until January of 1995 that the players ratified a new collective agreement. The concluded agreement allowed 26 teams to compete in a shortened 48-game season.[21]

- *I*n September of 1995, in a 226-134 vote, the National Basketball Association players voted to keep their union and for a six-year collective bargaining agreement. The agreement was subsequently ratified by the players' representatives of the N.B.A.'s 27 teams. After the owners voted on the contract the lockout which had begun on July 1, 1995 ended.[22]

- *M*r.Devries of Victoria, B.C. had tickets for a Canucks–L.A. Kings game in Vancouver. When the ferries quit running because of an illegal strike called by the B.C. Ferry and Marine Workers Union he missed the game. He sued. He won.[23]

The Supreme Court of Canada upheld two criminal contempt convictions which had imposed a $400,000 fine on the United Nurses Alberta. The nurses had continued to strike despite directives from the Alberta Labour Relations Board forbidding them to do so. Justice McLachlin, for the majority, held that civil contempt for the breach of a court order (the directives were filed and enforced as court orders) became criminal contempt when the nurses defied the court with intent, knowledge or recklessness as to the fact that the disobedience would lower respect for the court's authority.

> **United Nurses Alberta v. Alberta Attorney General**
> *Summarized from* The Lawyers Weekly
> *May 15, 1992 p. 15*

LABOUR RELATIONS BOARDS

- *I*n the summer of 1997, 96% of the 1,600 members of the Union of B.C. Performers voted in favour of a strike against the producers of *Police Academy: The Series* in response to the inability of the two sides to agree on the terms of an agreement. The performers were especially upset by the producers offering to buck tradition and pay them 30% less for "buy-out residuals" than is customary in the trade. Usually producers pay 105% of an actor's day rate to buy out the actor's right to future royalties. The Labour Relations Board mediator invoked a "rarely used" section of the Labour Code and ruled against UBCP's right to strike. The union appealed the ruling;[24] The appeal was denied.

B. AGENCY

Questions

If you are acting as an agent, what are your obligations to your principal?

What are your duties as a fiduciary?

Ocean City Realty Ltd. *v.* A & M Holdings Ltd. et al.

36 D.L.R. (4TH) 94
BRITISH COLUMBIA COURT OF APPEAL
MARCH 5, 1987

I

Wallace J.A.:—The appellant appeals from a decision wherein the trial judge awarded the plaintiff a real estate commission earned in connection with the sale of real property in the City of Victoria.

II

Facts

The plaintiff, Ocean City Realty Ltd. (Ocean City), is a licensed real estate agency. The defendant, A & M Holdings Ltd. (A & M), was the owner of a commercial building in Victoria, British Columbia known as the Weiler Building.

At all material times Mrs. Patricia Forbes was a licensed real estate sales person employed by Ocean City.

In January of 1983, Mr. Holm Halbauer contacted Mrs. Forbes for assistance in locating a commercial building in downtown Victoria which he might be interested in purchasing.

Mrs. Forbes contacted the principals of A & M to inquire as to whether the Weiler Building might be for sale. She also inquired as to the sales commission A & M would be willing to pay.

Following a series of negotiations an interim agreement for the sale of the Weiler Building was concluded between A & M

and Mr. Halbauer. It included a commission agreement between A & M and Ocean City whereby Ocean City was to receive 1.75% of the sale price of $5.2 million.

The trial judge found that at some point during the negotiations Mr. Halbauer advised Mrs. Forbes of his intention to proceed no further with the transaction unless Mrs. Forbes agreed to pay him, on completion of the sale, the sum of $46,000, representing approximately one-half of the total prospective commission.

Mrs. Forbes apparently indicated she was prepared to share her commission but declared that she could not agree to such an arrangement without first obtaining the approval of Mr. Fife, nominee of Ocean City.

Mrs. Forbes brought the proposal to Mr. Fife hoping that he would quash it, but he did not. Moreover, because Mr. Halbauer was not satisfied with her written confirmation of the arrangement and required a confirming letter from Ocean City, Mr. Fife advised her it could be provided if she actually owed money to Mr. Halbauer and if it was paid from her portion of the commission and not from Ocean City's. She told Mr. Fife that she did not in fact owe any money to Mr. Halbauer apart from the tentative arrangement she had made with him to share her commission. Mr. Fife none the less gave Mr. Halbauer a letter stating:

I understand that Mrs. Pat Forbes owes you the sum of $46,000.00. I hereby authorize you to deduct this amount from the commission monies you will be forwarding to us on behalf of A & M Holdings Ltd. on the sale of 921 Government Street.

The transaction contemplated by the interim agreement was not completed. Mr. Halbauer brought an action for specific performance against A & M, which was resolved by a compromise settlement, which resulted in the sale of the Weiler Building to Halbauer on different terms for the price of $5.6 million.

After the compromise settlement it was discovered by the solicitors for A & M that, prior to the conclusion of the agreement, Mrs. Forbes had made an arrangement with Halbauer whereby she agreed to rebate to him the sum of $46,000 from her portion of the commission to be paid to Ocean City. Up to that time A & M were unaware of that agreement.

A & M refused to pay the commission claimed by Ocean City with respect to the transaction. Ocean City brought this action against A & M for the commission.

At the trial Ocean City discontinued its claim against the personal defendant, Mr. Ellis, and abandoned its claim for compensation on a *quantum meruit* basis.

III
Issues

The issues raised by this appeal are of narrow compass:
(1) Is the real estate agent obliged to disclose to its principal the fact that it has agreed to rebate to the purchaser a portion of its real estate commission from the sale?
(2) If it is under such an obligation what effect does such nondisclosure have upon its claim to the real estate commission?

IV

The trial judge in addressing these issues made the following remarks:

The relationship between a real estate agent and a person retaining him to sell property is a fiduciary and confidential one and the real estate agent's duty to his principal is to be construed strictly. The agent has a duty to obtain the highest price possible for his client and he has a duty to disclose all material facts which might affect the value of the property (*Re Crackle et al. and Deputy Superintendent of Insurance & Real Estate* (1983), 150 D.L.R. (3d) 371, 47 B.C.L.R. 256, 29 R.P.R. 276, *sub nom. Re Crackle and/or Greyfriars Realty Ltd.* (B.C.C.A.)).

In *Canada Permanent Trust Co. v. Christie* (1979), 16 B.C.L.R. 183, Mr. Justice Esson, in the Supreme Court of British Columbia, considered whether an agent had a right to recover a real estate commission from the principal Christie and quoted with approval the following test [at pp. 185-6]:

"The onus is upon the agent to prove that the transaction was entered into after full and fair disclosure of all material circumstances and of everything known to him respecting the subject matter of the contract which could be likely to influence the conduct of his principal. The burden of proof that the transaction was a righteous one

rests upon the agent, who is bound to produce clear affirmative proof that the parties were at arm's length, that the principal had the fullest information upon all material facts and that having this information he agreed to adopt what was done."

The trial judge further stated:

The defendant says that Mrs. Forbes had made an unusual arrangement with the purchaser, Holm Halbauer, to pay over to the purchaser $46,000 of the proceeds of her commission on the sale. The defendant says that this arrangement was a material circumstance and should have been disclosed to the defendant as a matter likely to influence his conduct and that the failure to disclose this arrangement constitutes a breach of fiduciary duty, disentitling the broker to commission.

And further:

The authorities relied on by the defendant concern situations where the broker gained an advantage in the transaction and failed to disclose all material elements of the arrangement to his principal. In the case at bar the plaintiff says that no advantage was being sought by the broker and, indeed, Mrs. Forbes agreed to suffer a very considerable reduction in the anticipated commission in order, on her testimony, to secure the deal for the vendor and to permit the vendor to realize the full asking price for the property, that is, $5.6 million. ...

In the case at bar the legal duty of the agent, if she engaged herself in the subject of her arrangement with the defendant, was to find a buyer for the Weiler Building ready willing and able to pay the sum that the defendant had declared to be the price which the defendant required to be paid, that is $5.6 million. The agent also had an obligation to avoid any conflict of interest with the defendant. In my view, the agreement to pay over to the purchaser a portion of the agent's commission on completion of the sale did not put the plaintiff into conflict with the defendant, as both the defendant and the plaintiff had the same interest to advance, that is to say, to complete the sale at the plaintiff's asking price. Obviously, the defendant had more to gain than did the plaintiff by the completion of the sale on the terms negotiated by the plaintiff.

In my opinion, the trial judge's interpretation of the obligation owed to a principal by its agent is too restrictive. The duty of disclosure is not confined to those instances where the agent has gained an advantage in the transaction or where the information might affect the value of the property, or where a conflict of interest exists. The agent certainly has a duty of full disclosure in such circumstances; they are commonly occurring circumstances which require full disclosure by the agent. However, they are not exhaustive.

The obligation of the agent to make full disclosure extends beyond these three categories and includes "everything known to him respecting the subject-matter of the contract which would be likely to influence the conduct of his principal" (*Canada Permanent Trust Co. v. Christie, supra*) or, as expressed in 1 Hals., 3rd ed., p.191, para. 443, everything which "...would be likely to operate upon the principal's judgment."

In such cases the agent's failure to inform the principal would be material nondisclosure. ...

The test is an objective one to be determined by what a reasonable man in the position of the agent would consider, in the circumstances, would be likely to influence the conduct of his principal.

I would emphasize that the agent cannot arbitrarily decide what would likely influence the conduct of his principal and thus avoid the consequences of non-disclosure. If the information pertains to the transaction with respect to which the agent is engaged, any concern or doubt that the agent may have can be readily resolved by disclosure of all the facts to his principal. In the instant case the very withholding from the principal of the information concerning the payments to the purchaser of a portion of the commission could be evidence from which one might properly infer that the agent was aware that such circumstances would be a matter of concern to the principal.

One can readily appreciate that a vendor may wish not to enter into a complex sale arrangement which is subject to a variety of terms, such as vendor financing; a mortgage agreement; or a management agreement with a related company, unless that vendor was confident the purchaser was a person of integrity. ...

In the instant case the trial judge found that the agent justified her non-disclosure of the arrangement to pay the purchaser a percentage of the commission on the ground that she sought no advantage from the arrangement and indeed suffered a considerable reduction in her anticipated commission in order to secure the deal for the vendor and to permit the vendor to realize the full asking price for the property.

One may excuse a somewhat skeptical reaction to this altruistic rationale for non-disclosure of information by Mrs. Forbes. It ignores the fact that, if one accepts the premise that the arrangement was solely for the benefit of the principal, the agent would anticipate that the principal would approve of the agent's beneficience and proceed with the transaction. Accordingly, there would be no reason to withhold the information. ...

In the circumstances of this case, I find that the agent's nondisclosure was motivated by her desire to earn at least a portion of her commission and constituted a breach of her fiduciary duty to her principal and as a consequence she is not entitled to the commission claimed. ...

I would allow the appeal with costs here and below.

Taggart J. A.:—I agree.
Macfarlane J.A.:—I agree.
Taggart J.A.:—The appeal is allowed.

Question

What is the result if you sign on behalf of a company not in existence?

The president of a land development company purported to sign a contract on behalf of his company for the delivery and installation of steel. Unknown to him, at the time he signed, the company had been dissolved pursuant to the *Ontario Business Corporations Act* for failure to pay its taxes. The supplier, not paid in full, sued the president himself for breach of contract, and, in the alternative, for breach of warranty of authority.

The court held that the president of the company was liable, not for breach of contract because he was not a party to the contract, but for breach of warranty of authority. By purporting to sign for the company he was warranting that he had the authority to sign on behalf of an existing company.

Unfortunately for the plaintiff, the court concluded that, with regard to the quantum of damages to be awarded, the plaintiff was entitled to receive what it would have received from the company, i.e. what the plaintiff would have received if the defendant's representation were true, that he signed for the company. As the company had no assets, the plaintiff would have gotten nothing from the company and, therefore, could get nothing from the president of the company.

Falvo Steel Co. Ltd. v. Roccari
For a more detailed account see The Lawyers Weekly
May 29, 1987.

Question

What remedy is available if an agent breaches a fiduciary duty?

Soulos *v.* Korkontzilas

FILE NO.: 24949
http://www.droit.umontreal.ca/
SUPREME COURT OF CANADA
MAY 22, 1997

McLachlin, J

I

[1] This appeal requires this Court to determine whether a real estate agent who buys for himself property for which he has been negotiating on behalf of a client may be required to return the property to his client despite the fact that the client can show no loss. This raises the legal issue of whether a constructive trust over property may be imposed in the absence of enrichment of the defendant and corresponding deprivation of the plaintiff. In my view, this question should be answered in the affirmative.

II

[2] The appellant Mr. Korkontzilas is a real estate broker. The respondent, Mr. Soulos, was his client. In 1984, Mr. Korkontzilas found a commercial building which he thought might interest Mr. Soulos. Mr. Soulos was interested in purchasing the building. Mr. Korkontzilas entered into negotiations on behalf of Mr. Soulos. He offered $250,000. The vendor, Dominion Life, rejected the offer and tendered a counter-offer of $275,000. Mr. Soulos rejected the counter-offer but "signed it back" at $260,000 or $265,000. Dominion Life advised Mr. Korkontzilas that it would accept $265,000. Instead of conveying this information to Mr. Soulos as he should have, Mr. Korkontzilas arranged for his wife, Panagiota Goutsoulas, to purchase the property using the name Panagiot Goutsoulas. Panagiot Goutsoulas then transferred the property to Panagiota and Fotios Korkontzilas as joint tenants. Mr. Soulos asked what had happened to the property. Mr. Korkontzilas told him to "forget about it;" the vendor no longer wanted to sell it and he would find him a better property. Mr. Soulos asked Mr. Korkontzilas whether he had had anything to do with the vendor's change of heart. Mr. Korkontzilas said he had not.

[3] In 1987 Mr. Soulos learned that Mr. Korkontzilas had purchased the property for himself. He brought an action against Mr. Korkontzilas to have the property conveyed to him, alleging breach of fiduciary duty giving rise to a constructive trust. He asserted that the property held special value to him because its tenant was his banker, and being one's banker's landlord was a source of prestige in the Greek community of which he was a member. However, Mr. Soulos abandoned his claim for damages because the market value of the property had, in fact, decreased from the time of the Korkontzilas purchase.

[4] The trial judge found that Mr. Korkontzilas had breached a duty of loyalty to Mr. Soulos, but held that a constructive trust was not an appropriate remedy because Mr. Korkontzilas had purchased the property at market value and hence had not been "enriched": (1991), 4 O.R. (3d) 51, 19 R.P.R. (2d) 205 (hereinafter cited to O.R.). The decision was reversed on appeal, Labrosse J.A. dissenting: (1995), 25 O.R. (3d) 257. ...

[5] For the reasons that follow, I would dismiss the appeal. In my view, the doctrine of constructive trust applies and requires that Mr. Korkontzilas convey the property he wrongly acquired to Mr. Soulos. ...

IV

[9] This brings us to the main issue on this appeal: what remedy, if any, does the law afford Mr. Soulos for Mr. Korkontzilas' breach of the duty of loyalty [as a fiduciary, by] acquiring the property in question for himself rather than passing the vendor's statement of the price it would accept on to his principal, Mr. Soulos? ...

[13] The difference between the trial judge and the majority in the Court of Appeal may be summarized as follows. The trial judge took the view that in the absence of established loss, Mr. Soulos had no action. To grant the remedy of constructive trust in the absence of loss would be "simply disproportionate and inappropriate," in his view. The majority in the Court of Appeal, by contrast, took a broader view of when a constructive trust could apply. It held that a constructive trust requiring reconveyance of the property could arise in the absence of an established loss in order to condemn the agent's improper act and maintain the bond of trust underlying the real estate industry and hence the "integrity of the laws" which a court of equity supervises. ...

[15] It is my view that the second, broader approach to constructive trust should prevail. This approach best accords with the history of the doctrine of constructive trust, the theory underlying the constructive trust, and the purposes which the constructive trust serves in our legal system.

V

...

[17] The history of the law of constructive trust ... suggests that the constructive trust is an ancient and eclectic institution imposed by law not only to remedy unjust enrichment, but to hold persons in different situations to high standards of trust and probity and prevent them from retaining property which in "good conscience" they should not be permitted to retain. This served the end, not only of doing justice in the case before the court, but of protecting relationships of trust and the institutions that depend on these relationships. These goals were accomplished by treating the person holding the property as a trustee of it for the wronged person's benefit, even though there was no true trust created by intention. In England, the trust thus created was thought of as a real or "institutional" trust. In the United States and recently in Canada, jurisprudence speaks of the availability of the constructive trust as a remedy; hence the remedial constructive trust. ...

[The judge reviews English and Canadian jurisprudence and several scholarly articles.]

VI

[26] Various principles have been proposed to unify the situations in which the English law found constructive trust.. ..

[27] McClean, [McClean, A. J. "Constructive and Resulting Trusts—Unjust Enrichment in a Common Law Relationship—*Pettkus v. Becker* (1982), 16 U.B.C. L. Rev. 155] among others, regards the most satisfactory underpinning for unjust enrichment to be the concept of "good conscience" which lies at "the very foundation of equitable jurisdiction" (p. 169). ...

[28] Other scholars agree with McClean that good conscience may provide a useful way of unifying the different forms of constructive trust. ...

[29] Good conscience as the unifying concept underlying constructive trust has attracted the support of many jurists. ...

[34] It thus emerges that a constructive trust may be imposed where good conscience so requires. The inquiry into good conscience is informed by the situations where constructive trusts have been recognized in the past. It is also informed by the dual reasons for which constructive trusts have traditionally been imposed: to do justice between the parties and to maintain the integrity of institutions dependent on trust-like relationships. Finally, it is informed by the absence of an indication that a constructive trust would have an unfair or unjust effect on the defendant or third parties, matters which equity has always taken into account. Equitable remedies are flexible; their award is based on what is just in all the circumstances of the case. ...

[43] I conclude that in Canada, under the broad umbrella of good conscience, constructive trusts are recognized both for wrongful acts like fraud and breach of duty of loyalty, as well as to remedy unjust enrichment and corresponding deprivation. While cases often involve both a wrongful act and unjust enrichment, constructive trusts may be imposed on either ground: where there is a wrongful act but no unjust enrichment and corresponding deprivation; or where there is an unconscionable unjust enrichment in the absence of a wrongful act, as in *Pettkus v. Becker*, supra. Within these two broad categories, there is room for the law of constructive trust to develop and for greater precision to be attained, as time and experience may dictate. ...

VII

[45] In *Pettkus v. Becker*, supra, this Court explored the prerequisites for a constructive trust based on unjust enrichment. This case requires us to explore the prerequisites for a constructive trust based on wrongful conduct. Extrapolating from the cases where courts of equity have imposed constructive trusts for wrongful conduct, and from a discussion of the criteria considered in an essay by Roy Goode, "Property and Unjust Enrichment," in Andrew Burrows, ed., *Essays on the Law of Restitution* (1991), I would identify four conditions which generally should be satisfied:

(1) The defendant must have been under an equitable obligation, that is, an obligation of the type that courts of equity have enforced, in relation to the activities giving rise to the assets in his hands;

(2) The assets in the hands of the defendant must be shown to have resulted from deemed or actual agency activities of the defendant in breach of his equitable obligation to the plaintiff;

(3) The plaintiff must show a legitimate reason for seeking a proprietary remedy, either personal or related to the need to ensure that others like the defendant remain faithful to their duties and;

(4) There must be no factors which would render imposition of a constructive trust unjust in all the circumstances of the case; e.g., the interests of intervening creditors must be protected.

VIII

[46] Applying this test to the case before us, I conclude that Mr. Korkontzilas' breach of his duty of loyalty sufficed to engage the conscience of the court and support a finding of constructive trust for the following reasons.

[47] First, Mr. Korkontzilas was under an equitable obligation in relation to the property at issue. His failure to pass on to his client the information he obtained on his client's behalf as to the price the vendor would accept on the property and his use of that information to purchase the property instead for himself constituted breach of his equitable duty of loyalty. He allowed his own interests to conflict with those of his client. He acquired the property wrongfully, in flagrant and inexcusable breach of his duty of loyalty to Mr. Soulos. This is the sort of situation which courts of equity, in Canada and elsewhere, have traditionally treated as involving an equitable duty, breach of which may give rise to a constructive trust, even in the absence of unjust enrichment.

[48] Second, the assets in the hands of Mr. Korkontzilas resulted from his agency activities in breach of his equitable obligation to the plaintiff. His acquisition of the property was a direct result of his breach of his duty of loyalty to his client, Mr. Soulos.

[49] Third, while Mr. Korkontzilas was not monetarily enriched by his wrongful acquisition of the property, ample reasons exist for equity to impose a constructive trust. Mr. Soulos argues that a constructive trust is required to remedy the deprivation he suffered because of his continuing desire, albeit for non-monetary reasons, to own the particular property in question. No less is required, he asserts, to return the parties to the position they would have been in had the breach not occurred. That alone, in my opinion, would be sufficient to persuade a court of equity that the proper remedy for Mr. Korkontzilas' wrongful acquisition of the property is an order that he is bound as a constructive trustee to convey the property to Mr. Soulos.

[50] But there is more. I agree with the Court of Appeal that a constructive trust is required in cases such as this to ensure that agents and others in positions of trust remain faithful to their duty of loyalty: see *Hodgkinson v. Simms,* supra, per La Forest J. If real estate agents are permitted to retain properties which they acquire for themselves in breach of a duty of loyalty to their clients provided they pay market value, the trust and confidence which underpin the institution of real estate brokerage will be undermined. The message will be clear: real estate agents may breach their duties to their clients and the courts will do nothing about it, unless the client can show that the real estate agent made a profit. This will not do. Courts of equity have always been concerned to keep the person who acts on behalf of others to his ethical mark; this Court should continue in the same path.

[51] I come finally to the question of whether there are factors which would make imposition of a constructive trust unjust in this

case. In my view, there are none. No third parties would suffer from an order requiring Mr. Korkontzilas to convey the property to Mr. Soulos. Nor would Mr. Korkontzilas be treated unfairly. Mr. Soulos is content to make all necessary financial adjustments, including indemnification for the loss Mr. Korkontzilas has sustained during the years he has held the property.

[52] I conclude that a constructive trust should be imposed. I would dismiss the appeal and confirm the order of the Court of Appeal that the appellants convey the property to the respondent, subject to appropriate adjustments. The respondent is entitled to costs throughout.

Appeal dismissed.

Majority: La Forest, Gonthier, Cory, McLachlin and Major; Sopinka and Iacobucci JJ. dissenting.

ENDNOTES

1. A more detailed account is given in the *Vancouver Sun*, May 28, 1992, p. A14.

2. Summarized from *The Globe and Mail*, September 12, 1991, p. B6. Milken's name keeps resurfacing. He served 22 months for securities fraud and had obligations in a halfway house for three years. The day he left he was diagnosed with prostate cancer. He subsequently established a prostate-cancer research foundation, CapCure. (*Newsweek*, June 17, 1996). It was later reported that he was to receive a $50-million fee for participating in the deal in which Time Warner bought Turner Broadcasting (owner of, among other things, CNN) (*Newsweek*, September 23, 1996, p. 85).

3. A more detailed account is given in *Newsweek*, March 9, 1992.

4. Adapted from *The Globe and Mail*, October 29, 1992, p. A20.

5. See *The Lawyers Weekly*, April 12, 1991, p. 16 for the summary of *Kennedy v. MTD Products Ltd.* of the Ontario Court (General Division).

6. See the unreported case *Murphy v. Canadian Tire Corp.*, Ontario Court of Justice (General Division Registry O. 25752, November 25, 1991).

7. For a more detailed account see *The Lawyers Weekly*, January 25, 1991 for a summary of *Caruso v. Northern Telecom Ltd.*

8. *Kim v. Wray Energy Controls Ltd.*, Ontario Court (General Division) Toronto Region, June, 1992.

9. For a more detailed account of this U.S. case see *The Lawyers Weekly*, August 8, 1997, p. 24.

10. For a more detailed account see the summary of *Ditchburn v. Landis & Gyr Powers, Ltd.* in *The Lawyers Weekly*, October 27, 1995, p. 1; November 3, 1995, pp. 15, 16.

11. *The Lawyers Weekly*, August 30, 1991, p. 8.

12. For a discussion of *Wallace v. United Grain Growers Ltd.* see *The Lawyers Weekly*, November 14, 1997, p. 1 or see the case at http://www.droit.umontreal.ca/.

13. For a more detailed account of the released report "The Westray Story: A Predictable Path to Disaster" see *The Globe and Mail*, December 2, 1997, p. 1.

14. For a more detailed account see *The Lawyers Weekly*, January 20, 1995, p. 16.

15. See *Mustaji v. Tjin*, Vancouver Registry CA019954 for the Court of Appeal decision, June 21, 1996.

16. For a more detailed account see the *Vancouver Sun*, April 28, 1996, p. B8.

17. For a more detailed account see *The Lawyers Weekly*, February 11, 1994, p. 16.

18. *Maclean's*, November 22, 1993, p. 37.

19. For detailed accounts see *Maclean's*, January 30, 1995, p. 23; February 6, 1995, p. 11.

20. For the history of the negotiations and strike see *Maclean's*, August 8, 1994; October 24, 1994, p. 35; January 9, 1995, p. 28; February 6, 1995, p. 37; February 20, 1995; for news of the ratification, the *Vancouver Sun*, November 27, 1996, D1.

21. *Maclean's*, October 3, 1994, p. 17; January 9, 1995, p. 29; January 23, 1995, p. 42.

22. For a more detailed account see *The New York Times*, September 13, 1995, p. B9 and September 14, 1995, p. B5.

23. Summarized from *The Lawyers Weekly*, October 29, 1993, p. 12.

24. *Playback*, July 28, 1997 and *The Hollywood Reporter British Columbia Special Issue*, September 30, 1997, p. s-10.

VI
BUSINESS ORGANIZATIONS

A. PARTNERSHIP

Questions

What is the consequence to you of your partner being incompetent, negligent or dishonest?
What are the terms of the partnership agreement?
What is the consequence of a partner breaching the express or implied terms of that contract?

1. LIABILITY OF PARTNERS TO THIRD PARTIES

Victoria and Grey Trust Company *v.* Crawford et al.

(1986) 57 O.R. (2D) 484
HIGH COURT OF JUSTICE
NOVEMBER 12, 1986

Summary of the facts: A partner in a law firm was acting on behalf of an estate which maintained a savings account at Victoria and Grey Trust Company, the plaintiff. The lawyer was given a cheque for $60,025.61 signed by the executrix of the estate and instructed to transfer the funds from the plaintiff Trust Company to a bank in California. Instead, without the knowledge of his partners, the lawyer destroyed that cheque and created another one on which he made himself the payee and forged the signature of the executrix. He negotiated the cheque at his bank, the Toronto-Dominion Bank in Orillia. The plaintiff trust company, having been told by the estate accountant that the account was being cleared out and knowing that the lawyer was a partner of the defendant firm, honoured the cheque. Later, when the fraud was discovered, the plaintiff trust company (pursuant to the *Bills of Exchange Act*) indemnified (paid back) the Estate because it had paid out on a forged cheque. In this case the trust company is suing the partnership to recover its loss.

Holland J. (orally): — This case involves a claim against partners carrying on the practice of law for the fraud of one of the partners. ...

The plaintiff relies on two sections of the *Partnerships Act*, R.S.O. 1980, c. 370. The defence is that, on the facts of this case, the sections do not apply and that a partnership is not liable for the independent fraud of one of its partners.

Section 11 of the Act reads as follows:

11. Where by any wrongful act or omission of a partner acting in the ordinary course of the business of the firm, or with the authority of his co-partners, loss or injury is caused to a person not being a partner of the firm, or any penalty is incurred, the firm is liable therefor to the same extent as the partner so acting or omitting to act.

Section 12 of the Act reads as follows:

12. In the following cases, namely,

    (a) where one partner, acting within the scope of his apparent authority, receives the money or property of a third person and misapplies it…the firm is liable to make good the loss.

Dealing with s. 11, it is admitted that there was a wrongful act by a partner, that in acting for the estate and in receiving estate funds or property, Mr. Farr was acting in the ordinary course of the business of the firm, and that loss occurred. It is also agreed that the word "person" in the section includes a corporation. It is submitted, however, that the section does not apply because the "person" who sustained the loss — Victoria & Grey Trust Company — was not dealing with the firm.

Sections 11 and 12 of the Act fall under a heading which reads: "Relation of Partners to Persons Dealing with Them". This raises the point to what extent, in considering the meaning of a section, may or should I have reference to this heading.

Section 9 of the *Interpretation Act*, R.S.O. 1980, c 219, reads as follows:

The marginal notes and headings in the body of an Act and references to former enactments form no part of the Act but shall be deemed to be inserted for convenience of reference only.

The 12th edition of *Maxwell on the Interpretation of Statutes* (1989), at p. 11, has this to say:

Headings.

The headings prefixed to sections or sets of sections in some modern statues are regarded as preambles to those sections. They cannot control the plain words of the statute, but they may explain ambiguous words, a rule which, whatever the assistance which it may render in construction, cannot stand logically with the exclusion of marginal notes, for headings like marginal notes are — as Avory J. pointed out in *R. v. Hare* —"not voted on or passed by Parliament but are inserted after the Bill has become law."

I can see no ambiguity in the section. There is no indication in the section that the Legislature intended to limit liability of persons who suffer loss to persons dealing with the partnership, and in my opinion there is liability by virtue of s. 11 alone.

I turn now to s. 12(a) of the Act. It is submitted on behalf of the defence that what occurred here was really two transactions. In the first, Mr. Farr received the client's cheque, which was the property of the client. He improperly destroyed this cheque, and it is argued that there was no loss as a result of this act. Mr. Farr then had another cheque prepared and forged the client's signature. It is suggested that this was a separate act and distinct transaction in which he acted on his own, not within the scope of his apparent authority, and that therefore this section does not apply. Reliance is replaced [sic] on the decision of *Hughes v. Twisden* (1886), 55 L.J. Ch. 481, in which a member of a firm of solicitors was negligent in connection with the mortgage in 1875. The court held that the claim arising out of the 1869 transaction was statute-barred, and that the action itself failed because the fraud was not committed in the ordinary course of business. I point out that these two claims dealt with matters that involved separate transactions that were six years apart. One was based on negligence and the other on fraud.

In the present case we are dealing with what I consider to be one transaction — that is, the deposit of the cheque with a firm of solicitors, with the funds to be placed in the partnership account, and it would be improper to break the transaction down into isolated parts; see *Lloyd v. Grace, Smith & Co.*, [1912] A.C. 716, and particularly at p. 739.

For the above reasons there will be judgment for the plaintiff against all defendants for $60,025.61 together with interest at 11% from April 1, 1982, the date upon which the money was replaced in the estate account, together with costs to be assessed.

I have endorsed the record as follows: "Oral Reasons. Judgment for $60,025.61 with interest at 11% from April 1, 1982, together with costs to be assessed."

Thank you, gentlemen.

Judgment for plaintiff.

2. OBLIGATIONS OF PARTNERS TO EACH OTHER

Norman Olson v. *Antonio Gullo and Gullo Enterprises Limited*

ONTARIO COURT OF JUSTICE NO. 32867/88
JULY 9, 1992

Boland J.: This action arises out of the purchase and sale of ninety acres of land situate in the Township of Georgina and involves claims for damages for breach of contract, breach of fiduciary duty and payment for unjust enrichment. The counterclaim was not pursued at trial. …

It is the plaintiff's position that during the month of February, 1988, he and Gullo entered into an oral partnership agreement for the purpose of acquiring, developing and eventually disposing of the 1,000 acres situate on the west side of Woodbine Avenue. Gullo was to contribute his expertise as a real estate speculator and developer, and Olson was to provide his skills in marketing, promotion, public relations and financing. Olson further contends that it was also agreed that he and Gullo would contribute equal amounts of capital as required to purchase the various farms and they would share equally in the profits.

The defendants, on the other hand, flatly deny that there ever was any partnership agreement. They contend that at no time was there any relationship of trust, confidence and dependence created between the parties. It is their position that Gullo was interested in developing an industrial park and devoted a great deal of time attempting to purchase lands within the 1,000 acre tract. His offers were turned down by the farmers and he abandoned the project because of the high price of agricultural land. He decided to purchase the Walshe farm as a long-term investment. Assuming the land assembly went ahead, Olson's sole function was to find investors interested in developing the project and for this service he would receive a finder's fee or commission.

According to the evidence, in March, 1988, Gullo retained real estate agents at Family Trust Corporation. Over the next few months, these agents submitted agreements of purchase and sale in the name of Gullo Enterprises Limited in Trust to a number of farmers owning land within the 1,000 acre parcel. During this period Olson arranged for funds to purchase his share of the various parcels and discussed the project with prospective investors.

The evidence also establishes that during this period the price of farmland in the area increased dramatically and, consequently Gullo led Olson to believe that the project was no longer feasible as it would be virtually impossible to purchase any farms in the 1,000 acre tract because of rising prices. Nevertheless, unknown to Olson, in May of 1988, Gullo Enterprises Limited in Trust, entered into an agreement to purchase a ninety-acre farm, known as the Walshe Property, for approximately $20,000 an acre and, prior to closing, assigned the purchase agreement to Wesrow Estates Inc. at a profit of approximately $2,500,000. The Walshe farm was part of the 1,000 acres located on the west side of Woodbine Avenue in the Township of Georgina and is shown as parcel 7 on the preliminary study, dated March 1988. In September, 1988, Olson discovered that Gullo had secretly entered into agreements to purchase and sell the Walshe property at a considerable profit. He expressed his disappointment and anger to Gullo and his employment with [Gullo's company] Glacier Clear Marketing Inc. terminated the end of that month. This action was commenced November 4, 1988.

The evidence is overwhelming that in February, 1988, Norman Olson and Antonio Gullo orally agreed that they would be equal partners in purchases of parcels of land in a defined 1,000 acres located on the west side of Woodbine Avenue in the Township of Georgina. It was agreed that the parties would each provide half the moneys required to purchase the various farms and the land would be registered in both their names in due course. It was also agreed that Gullo would negotiate the purchases because of his experience in land assembly and that Olson would find interested investors and prepare promotional material related to the property and the project. Their respective roles were in keeping with their background and expertise.

[The judge reviewed the evidence]. ...

There was a mountain of evidence to support a finding that in February, 1988, Gullo and Olson orally agreed to become equal partners in the purchase of farms within the 1,000 acre tract of land and they anticipated making a great deal of profit. Furthermore, all this evidence supports a finding that the Walshe property was to be purchased and held as partnership lands.

It follows that Gullo and Olson, as partners, were in a fiduciary relationship and each had a duty of the utmost good faith and loyalty to the other and to the partnership. Once the partnership was established, it was not possible for either partner to utilize a partnership opportunity or divert a maturing business opportunity for his exclusive personal gain. Gullo owed a fiduciary duty to disclose all material facts to Olson. The evidence establishes that at no time did Gullo advise Olson of the purchase and sale of the Walshe farm and he never asked Olson to pay his share of the purchase money. He surreptitiously planned to pocket the entire profit of approximately $2,500,000. By secretly purchasing the Walshe property for himself and not for the partnership, Gullo failed to meet the minimum standards the law imposes on a partner and I find this was a serious breach of the fiduciary duty he owed to Olson.

Having found that there was partnership agreement and that Gullo breached that agreement, as well as the fiduciary duty he owed to Olson, one is faced with the difficult issue in this trial which is the appropriate measure of damage to be awarded in these circumstances. Unquestionably Gullo was unjustly enriched as a result of the breach of his fiduciary duty to Olson. At the time the partnership was established, Gullo and Olson had agreed to divide the partnership profits equally. Certainly, Olson is entitled to at least fifty per cent of the profits from the sale of the ninety-acre parcel comprising the Walshe farm. The contentious issue is whether the court should prevent Gullo from retaining any of the proceeds of the sale, including those profits which he was entitled to under the partnership agreement.

Counsel for the defendants argue that should the court find that there was a partnership agreement, Olson is only entitled to his share of the profits in accordance with the terms of that agreement. Counsel for the plaintiff seeks judgment for the entire profit. ...

I cannot agree with the defendants' position. I have given a great deal of consideration to the evidence heard during the trial and in my view this is not an appropriate disposition of the profit made on the sale of the Walshe property as there would be no penal aspect to the result. Gullo would receive precisely what he would have received if he had acted honestly and shared the proceeds equally with his partner, Olson. The result provides no disincentive. If this were the rule of law, a fiduciary could breach his trust hoping to hide the breach and after a lengthy trial retain his share of the secret profit. In my view, this is the same type of truly repugnant behaviour found in *Lavigne v. Robern* [which held that a fiduciary who has made a secret profit must not be allowed to profit from his wrongdoing] and I am bound by that case.

Gullo compounded his wrongful conduct by attempting to avoid this litigation by obstructing justice and contracting to kill Olson. He pleaded guilty to two charges of attempt [sic] murder and was sentenced to three years in the penitentiary on each charge to be served concurrently. He was punished for this conduct. However, he also threatened witnesses and police officers were required in the courtroom throughout the trial. The court must demonstrate that it will not tolerate this type of behaviour. ...

In this case, the appropriate measure of damages is for Gullo to hand over to Olson the entire secret profit. The court is merely removing the millions of dollars secretly pocketed by Gullo and placing them in the pocket of the plaintiff. In my view this is preferable to encouraging fraudulent conduct and weakening our structures of trust.

For the above reasons there will be a declaration that Norman Olson and Antonio Gullo were partners with each entitled to one-half of the profits. The defendants hold fifty per cent of the profits on the purchase and sale of the Walshe farm in trust for the plaintiff. ...

[Judgment for the plaintiff]

Note: On the issue of the proper way to distribute the profit the decision of the trial judge was overturned on appeal

Olson *v.* Gullo

ONTARIO COURT OF APPEAL
113 D.L.R. (4TH) 42
MARCH 1994

Morden A.C.J.O.:—Antonia Gullo Jr., as administrator of the estate of Antonio Gullo Sr., deceased, and Gullo Enterprises Limited appeal from a judgment against them in favour of the plaintiff, Norman Olson, in the amount of $2,486,940. Mr. Olson cross-appeals, with leave, from the costs order in the judgment, seeking to have his costs awarded on a solicitor-and-client basis in place of the party-and-party basis awarded in the judgment. (Antonio Gullo Sr. died after the evidence at the trial was given. His son, Antonio Gullo Jr., was appointed administrator of his estate and an order to continue this proceeding has been granted.) [The judge reviews the basic facts as found by the trial judge and the court's decision.] For the reasons which I shall give, I have concluded, however, that it was contrary to principle and authority in the present case to deprive the defendants of their one-half share in the transaction in question.

The relevant fiduciary principle with which to begin the analysis is expressed in s. 29(1) of the *Partnerships Act*, R.S.O. 1990, c. P5, which reads:

> 29(1) Every partner *must account to the firm* for any benefit derived by the partner without the consent of the other partners from any transaction concerning the partnership or from any use by the partner of the partnership property, name or business connection. (Emphasis added.)

> The same principle is expressed in s. 30 of the Act which reads:

> 30. If a partner, without the consent of the other partners, carries on a business of the same nature as and competing with that of the firm, the partner *must account for and pay over to the firm* all profits made by the partner in that business. (Emphasis added.)…

We must … begin our consideration with the basic premise that the profit in question is the property of the partnership, not of all the partners except the defaulting partner. To exclude the wrongdoer would be to effect a forfeiture of his or her interest in this partnership property. The point may be understood by considering a starker form of wrongdoing—a case where a partner misappropriates partnership funds for his own benefit. In such a case I am not aware of any principle or decision to the effect that not only must the partner account to the partnership for the money but must also suffer a forfeiture of his or her interest in it. In fact, the case law of which I am aware is to the contrary. …

[He then reviews a Supreme Court of Canada decision in *Sutton v. Forst* (1924) and a Massachusetts case *Shulkin v. Shulkin* (1938) which supported that position.]

I have not found any United States decision to the contrary. On the other hand, the following (all Massachusetts decisions) all cite *Shulkin* with approval on point. …

[The judge quotes extensively from a discussion on the matter by M.V. Ellis in *Fiduciary Duties in Canada* (Toronto: Carswell, 1993) including the following:

Simply put, it is arguable that the exclusion of the defaulting party from its lawful participation in the relationship sought to be enforced is untenable even where supported by the simple maxim that the fiduciary cannot benefit through its wrongdoing. That maxim is easily used to remove from a trustee or agent gain *not envisaged* by the pre-breach relationship but is more problematic in the context of a relationship whereunder gain *was envisaged* despite the fiduciary relationship.

I have no doubt that stripping the wrongdoing partner of the whole of the profit, including his or her own share in it, is a strong disincentive to conduct which breaches the fiduciary obligation. Further, as a host of equity decisions have shown for at least two centuries, the fact that this would result in a windfall gain to the plaintiff cannot, in itself, be a valid objection to it.

I do not however, think that it can accurately be said that the defaulting partner does profit from his wrong when he receives his pre-ordained share of the profit. With respect to this share, the partner's conduct in the impugned transaction does not involve any breach of duty. Under the terms of the relationship, with respect to this share, it was expected that the partner would act in his own interest. To the extent that there is a dilemma, I resolve the issue, in accordance with what I consider to be the more appropriate principles and authorities, against the forfeiture of the wrongdoing partner's interest in the profit.

I mention, for the sake of completeness, that in awarding the penal remedy the trial judge appears to have taken into account very serious criminal conduct of Mr. Gullo related to this litigation. This conduct took place after the events giving rise to Mr. Olson's claim and Mr. Gullo was convicted and sentenced for it. In my view it is not relevant to the remedy and it is not submitted on Mr. Olson's behalf that it is.

I turn now to the cross-appeal respecting the basis on which the plaintiff's costs should be assessed … [I]n light of the variation of the judgment which I propose, I think that this is now an entirely proper case for the award of solicitor-and-client costs of the action. The plaintiff as been the victim of the breach of a fiduciary obligation and it is appropriate for the court to express its disapproval of the defendants' conduct: see *Maximillian v. M. Rash & Co.* (1987), 62. O.R. (2d) 206 … The criminal conduct referred to in the proceeding paragraph, which involved counselling to have Mr. Olson killed, is also relevant to this issue.

For the foregoing reasons I would allow the appeal, with costs, and vary the trial judgment to provide that the plaintiff recover one-half of the profit in question. …

I would allow the cross-appeal, without costs, and vary the costs order to provide that the plaintiff be awarded the costs of the action on a solicitor-and-client basis.

Appeal allowed; cross-appeal allowed.

> Mr. Schmidt told his partners that he was taking an early retirement to help his sons on their farms. The partners gave him a very golden handshake. It was learned that while he was negotiating his early retirement he had intended to join a competing firm in the same city and was, in fact, soliciting colleagues to join him. He took sixty-five of the partnership's clients when he did leave. The partnership refused to pay out as per the retirement agreement. Schmidt sued. The B.C. Supreme Court held that the contract was voidable for misrepresentation and that Schmidt had breached his duty as a partner both at common law and under s. 22 of the B.C. *Partnership Act.*

> *Schmidt v. Peat Marwick Thorne*
> *Summarized from* The Lawyers Weekly
> *September 11, 1992 p. 2;*
> *September 25, 1992 p. 34*

- *A*dvocates of legal reform in the U.S. have promoted legislation regarding "domestic partnership" which would apply to gays and unmarried straight couples to eliminate injustices and difficulties that arise partly because of the law's failure to recognize gay marriages.[1]

B. The Corporation

1. The Company is a Separate Legal Entity.

Rich *v.* Enns

[1995] M.J. No. 198 (Q.L.)
DRS 95-16147
Suit No. AI 93-30-01374
Manitoba Court of Appeal
May 25, 1995

[l] Twaddle, J.A.:—The interesting question raised by this appeal is whether the sole shareholder and alter ego of a corporation can enforce a contract purportedly made by it [the company] after it has been dissolved.

THE FACTS

[2] The contract in question was one for the sale of land. It was prepared by the solicitors for the vendor, Sargent Properties Ltd. (hereinafter "Sargent"), as an offer to be made by the defendant [purchaser] and returned to them "for the acceptance of Sargent Properties Ltd." The defendant, however, treated the offer as one made to him by Sargent. He accepted it, but subject to conditions. The document was then returned to Sargent's solicitors. Sargent did not sign the document, either as offeror or offeree, but its solicitors certainly acted as though it constituted a contract between Sargent and the defendant. ...
[4l] ... What the solicitors overlooked was that ... Sargent, had been dissolved for a failure to file annual returns. ...
(6) For reasons which need not be detailed here, the defendant repudiated the contract before completion. Sargent, if it had not been dissolved, would certainly have had a cause of action for damages. It was, however, the plaintiff [the sole shareholder] who commenced the proceedings. The defen-

dant responded by saying, amongst other things, that he had not agreed to purchase the property from the plaintiff. ...

THE RELEVANT LAW

[13] It is unnecessary to cite authority for the proposition that a corporation is a distinct legal person. Its rights and obligations are its own, not those of its members, and that is so even where it is a corporation owned and controlled by a single shareholder. The corporation and the shareholder are not interchangeable. The shareholder has no right to enforce the corporation's contract.
[14] The inability of a sole shareholder to enforce his corporation's contracts is of little moment when the company is alive and well. The corporation can enforce them and, in the event that an action is commenced inadvertently in the shareholder's name, can be substituted as the proper plaintiff. The difficulties arise where the corporation has not yet been incorporated or has been dissolved.
[15] The two leading cases in this area are from other parts of the Commonwealth, one from England and the other from Australia.
[16] In *Newborne v. Sensolid (Great Britain) Ltd.,* [1953] 1 All E.R. 708 (C.A.), the plaintiff, Leopold Newborne, was the pro-

moter and prospective director of a limited company, Leopold Newborne (London) Ltd., which at the material time had not been registered. A contract for the supply of goods to the defendants was signed: "Leopold Newborne (London) Ltd." The plaintiff's name was written underneath. The market for the goods went down and the defendants refused delivery. While the litigation was in progress, the solicitors for the plaintiff company realized that it had not been registered at the time of the contract and took steps to substitute Mr. Leopold Newborne for the company.

[17] In agreeing with the defendants that substitution was not possible, Lord Goddart, … [said]:

> The company contracts and its contract is authenticated by the signature of one or more of the directors. This contract purports to be made by the company, not by Mr. Newborne. He purports to be selling, not his goods, but the company's goods. The only person who has any contract here is the company

[18] Later, Lord Goddart said:

> [As] the company was not in existence when the contract was signed, there never was a contract, and the plaintiff cannot come forward and say: "It was my contract."

[19] Morris L.J. (as he then was) endorsed the opinion of the chambers judge who had stated:

> The company was not in existence and that signature on that document, and indeed, the document itself, was an utter nullity.

[20] The Australian case is *Black v. Smallwood*, [1965] 117 C.L.R. 52 (H.C.). That case involved a contract for the sale of land between the plaintiffs as vendors and Western Suburbs Holdings Pty. Limited as purchaser. At the place for the purchaser's signature appeared the words "Western Suburbs Holdings Pty. Limited" beneath which were the signatures of the defendants as directors. At the date of execution of the contract the company had not been incorporated, although each of the defendants then believed that it had.

[21] The plaintiffs' suit against the individual defendants for specific performance was dismissed, the Court following the decision in *Newborne v. Sensolid (Great Britain) Ltd.*. …

[23] These Commonwealth cases have been cited with approval and followed in a number of Canadian cases:. …

[24] Turning to contracts with dissolved companies, I refer to *Falvo Steel v. Roccari* (unreported, released May 14, 1987, Ont. H.C.). in that case, the plaintiff had agreed to sell steel to San Rocco Imports Ltd. Unbeknownst to the plaintiff, the purchasing company had been dissolved. The plaintiff sought to recover from the company's principal who had signed a proposal for the delivery of the steel on behalf of the company. Watt J. dismissed the claim applying essentially the same principles as those applied where the company, instead of being dissolved, had not yet been incorporated. …

APPLICATION

[26] On the strength of the foregoing authorities, I think it can be said that, for the plaintiff to succeed, he must show that he at least intended himself to be a party to the contract. This he cannot do as his solicitors throughout were at pains to refer to Sargent as the contracting party. Moreover, Sargent alone had the right to transfer the property it was acquiring from M.D.R. to another. … The plaintiff must therefore have intended Sargent to be the contracting party.

[27] The trial judge did not consider the plaintiff's intention. Instead, he decided the case on the basis of the defendant knowing "Rich … to be the company." That is plainly wrong. The sole shareholder of a company is not the company. Each has a distinct legal personality. Indeed, it is to create a separate person that a sole shareholder incorporates a company. …

[31] The contract having been made by Sargent, a dissolved corporation, it is a nullity. No one can sue upon it: not even the plaintiff.

[Action dismissed.]

Q u e s t i o n s

When will the law not allow a person to rely on the priniciple that a company is a separate legal entity?

If a person chooses to use the corporate structure for carrying on business, can he or she avoid personal liability?

---

2. LIFTING THE CORPORATE VEIL / LIABILITY OF DIRECTORS

Lockharts Ltd. **v.** *Excalibur Holdings Ltd. et al.*

210 A.P.R. 181
NOVA SCOTIA SUPREME COURT
DECEMBER 14, 1987

Summary of the facts: Mr. Harrison and his wife were the sole shareholders of two companies, Baron Developments Ltd. (Baron), a construction company, and Excalibur Holdings Ltd., (Excalibur), an investment company. Baron bought a piece of property under an Agreement for Sale from Clayton Developments Limited (Clayton) and began construction of a house. The plaintiff Lockharts Ltd. contracted with Baron to supply building materials. When Baron failed to pay its account, Lockharts Ltd. sued Baron and a default judgment was entered in favour of Lockharts Ltd. for $19,513.80 on March 14, 1986. Both Baron and Excalibur had notice of the judgment.

On June 24, 1986 Excalibur bought the land from Clayton and took an assignment from Baron of all Baron's interest in the land under the Agreement for Sale with the result that Excalibur had both legal and equitable interest in the property and Baron, the judgment debtor, no longer owned any property.

Davison, J.: ...

ISSUES: ...

[T]he plaintiff's submissions to me were:

(1) That the events which took place in June, 1986, constituted a fraudulent scheme designed to defeat the rights of the plaintiff under the judgment. Therefore, it is submitted I should ignore the separate corporate entity of Excalibur and grant an order declaring the judgment "binding upon... the assets and land of the defendant, Excalibur."

(2) That an order should issue declaring the judgment against Baron an encumbrance against the land known as lot 9-44 Grenadier Drive by reason of s. 18 of the *Registry Act*, R.S.N.S. 19967, c. 265, and the equitable interest of Baron in the land pursuant to the agreement of purchase and sale. ...

LIFING THE CORPORATE VEIL

Since *Salomon v. Salomon & Co. Ltd.*, [1897] A.C. 22, it has been a clear principle of law that a company is an independent legal entity distinct from its shareholders. In this case the plaintiff asks me to "lift the corporate veil" on the grounds of fraud. The plaintiff says Mr. Harrison used Excalibur to strip the assets of Baron to avoid payment to the plaintiff of the amount of the judgment.

In England there have been signs that the firm principle of *Salomon* has been the subject of some erosion and the most often quoted comments are those of Lord Denning in *Littlewoods Mail Order Stores Ltd. v. McGregor*, [1969] 3 All E.R. 855, at 860:

> ... I decline to treat the Fork Company as a separate and independent entity. The doctrine laid down in *Salomon v. Salomon & Co. Ltd.* has to be watched very carefully. It has often been supposed to cast a veil over the personality of a limited company through which the courts cannot see. But that is not true. The courts can and often do draw aside the veil. They can, and often do, pull off the mask. They look to see what really lies behind. ... I think that we should look at the Fork Company and see it as it really is — the wholly-owned subsidiary of the taxpayers. It is the creature, the puppet, of the taxpayers in point of *fact*: and it should be so regarded in point of *law*.

The facts in *Jones v. Lipman* [1962] 1 W.L.R. 832, are sim-

ilar to the facts before me. The defendant, Lipman, entered an agreement with the plaintiff to sell a parcel of land but before completion under the agreement Lipman transferred the land to a company the sole shareholders of which were Lipman and a clerk at the office of Lipman's solicitor. The court granted an order requiring both defendants to perform the agreement with the plaintiff. Mr. Justice Russell found that the company was a sham or "a mask which he (Lipman) holds before his face in an attempt to avoid recognition by the eye of equity."

In *Merchandise Transport Ltd. v. British Transport Commission*, [1962] 2 Q.B. 173, a transport company which owned vehicles applied for licences in the name of a subsidiary company because it feared it would be unsuccessful if the application was in its own name. The court refused to treat parent and subsidiary companies as independent bodies and decided the issue as if they were one commercial unit. ...

In Canada, the principle enunciated in *Salomon* is alive and well, but it is also clear that courts will disregard the corporate entity in certain circumstances including situations involving "fraud or improper conduct." Authors of texts on company law are fond of saying that the only consistent principle which has evolved is that in the *Salomon* case (see Gower, *The Principles of Modern Company Law* (3rd Ed.) p. 189). In my respectful opinion the courts have been equally consistent in clearly enunciating an exception to the basic principle by refusing to permit a corporate entity to be used for fraudulent or improper purposes. It is true that there has been inconsistency in the application of this exception but the existence of the exception has been recognized by all levels of Canadian Courts.

In his dissenting judgment in *Jodrey's Estate v. Province of Nova Scotia* (1980), 41 N.S.R. (2d) 181; 76 A.P.R. 181; 32 N.R. 275, Chief Justice Dickson was clearly of the view that the principle of *Salomon* has been rigidly applied in the Canadian Courts but also recognized the exception with these words at page 228 N.W.R., A.P.R.:

> Generally speaking in the *absence of fraud or improper conduct* the courts cannot disregard the separate existence of a corporate entity: (emphasis added).

...

The Saskatchewan Court of Appeal in *Nedco v. Clark et al.* (1973) 43 D.L.R. (3d) 714, referred to *Toronto v. Famous Players Canadian Corp.*, [1936] 2 D.L.R. 129, as an illustration of how the Supreme Court of Canada has recognized "the right to pierce the corporate veil for a specific purpose." After reviewing a number of authorities, Chief Justice Culliton concluded at p. 721:

…while the principle laid down in *Salomon v. Salomon & Co. Ltd.*, supra, is and continues to be a fundamental feature of Canadian law, there are instances in which the court can and should lift the corporate veil, but whether it does so depends upon the facts in each particular case. Moreover, the fact that the court does lift the corporate veil for a specific purpose in no way destroys the recognition of the corporation as a independent and autonomous entity for all other purposes.

The recognition of the right by the Supreme Court of Canada is even more apparent since the dicta of Madame Justice Wilson in *Kosmopoulos v. Constitution Insurance Co. of Canada* (1987), 74 N.R. 360: 21 O.A.C. 4; 34 D.L.R. (4th) 208, at 213-214. …

What can be drawn from the foregoing authorities? In my assessment, the fundamental principle enunciated in the *Salomon* case remains good law in Canada and "one man corporations" should be considered as separate entities from their major shareholder save for certain exceptional cases. A judge should not "lift the veil" simply because he believes it would be in the interest of "fairness" or of "justice." If that was the test the veil in Salomon case would have been lifted. On the other hand the courts have the power indeed the duty, to look behind the corporate structure and to ignore it if it is being used for fraudulent or improper purposes or as a "puppet" to the detriment of a third party.

One of the fundamental purposes of establishing a corporate existence is to limit the liability of the shareholders. In doing so, growth of commerce is encouraged by providing a vehicle by which monies can be invested with the knowledge that losses would be restricted to an amount usually equivalent to the extent of the investment.

The purpose of the corporate entity was not to defraud or mislead others including creditors and shareholders and in my opinion where a company is being used for this purpose the "veil" should be lifted and a remedy made available to the victims of such conduct.

In the case before me the plaintiff supplied materials to Baron when Baron had an equitable interest in the lands on which the building, for which the material was to be used, was to be constructed. After Baron defaulted in payment, the plaintiff secured a judgment which, if the agreement for purchase and sale had been completed, would have attached to Baron's legal interest in the land and dwelling. After the judgment was obtained no effort was made to complete under the purchase and sale agreement and the property was conveyed to Excalibur which, like Baron, is solely owned by the principal, Harrison.

The sequence and nature of the documents and events raised a strong *prima facie* inference that the conveyance from Clayton Developments Limited to Excalibur was intended to defeat the rights of the plaintiff. It was incumbent upon the defendants to adduce evidence to rebut that inference. In my opinion, the defendants failed to meet that burden. The plaintiff has convinced me, on the balance of probabilities, having regard to the gravity of the finding (see *Hanes v. Wawanesa Mutual Ins. Co.*, [1963] S.C.R. 154, at 162) that Mr. Harrison made use of Excalibur for a fraudulent and improper purpose.

Mr. Harrison would have the court believe that the reason for having the conveyance in the name of Excalibur was because Excalibur could complete the construction; whereas Baron did not have financial resources to do so. I do not accept this evidence and it is not supported by any other evidence. …

I was not convinced by the evidence that Baron could not have completed under the agreement of sale. There was no evidence of any attempts by Mr. Harrison to secure funds other than the two conversation he had with Mr. Lisson [the lender]. Even if Baron did not have the ability to secure funds by itself why couldn't Excalibur have guaranteed to loan Baron? This would have achieved the same result and would have permitted the agreement to have been completed as originally contemplated.

If the situation had been such that the agreement of purchase and sale had been completed before the judgment was entered and legal title conveyed from Baron to Excalibur after the entry of the judgment, that conveyance could have been set aside pursuant to the terms of the *Assignments and Preferences Act*, R.S.N.S. 1967, c.16. In effect, that is precisely what occurred in this case, except that title was retained in Clayton Developments Limited until the appropriate time.

In my opinion, the evidence clearly establishes that the corporate entities owned by Mr. Harrison were used as "puppets" to the detriment of the plaintiff and in that respect were used for fraudulent and improper purposes.

My conclusion is that the plaintiff is entitled to declaratory relief and that an order, declaring that the plaintiff's judgment against Baron is binding upon and forms a charge upon the interest of Excalibur on the lands referred to in the deed of conveyance from Clayton Developments Limited to Excalibur dated the 24th day of June 1986 should issue. …

The plaintiff shall recover from the defendants its costs.

Judgment for plaintiff.

Property owned by Riverside Fisheries Ltd. of Windsor, Ontario was destroyed by fire. When the insurance company refused to compensate the company for its loss on the grounds that the fire was deliberately set, Riverside Fisheries Ltd. sued the insurance company.

The following are the concluding words of Judge Walsh of the Ontario Supreme Court. "There is no doubt whatsoever but that the fire was deliberately set, most probably the work of a professional arsonist. After a most careful and anxious scrutiny of all the facts and circumstances I find that the defendants have satisfied the onus imposed on them.

"Mr. Shulgan [counsel for the plaintiff], in a most novel argument, submitted that even if I should find, as I have, that the plaintiff Irving Goldhar was responsible for the fire, it should not prevent recovery by the corporate plaintiff, Riverside Fisheries Limited on the ground that it is a separate legal entity and its recovery should not be barred by the guilt or wrongdoing of Irving Goldhar, even though he is its president and principal shareholder.

"This submission is based by analogy to the recent decision of the Ontario Court of Appeal in *Higgins v. Orion Insurance Co.*, 50 O.R. (2d) 352, 10 C.C.L.I. 139, [1985] I.L.R. 1-1886, 17 D.L.R. (4th) 90, 8 O.A.C. 259, which held that arson on the part of one partner did not deprive a co-insured innocent partner from recovering from the insurer the loss actually sustained by him.

"A close perusal of the reasons of Robins J.A. in the Higgins case makes it abundantly clear that given the interwoven family business relationships here existent public policy considerations would never qualify Riverside as 'an innocent partner' as that term was used in that judgment.

"The plaintiffs' action is therefore dismissed. ..."

Riverside Fisheries Ltd. et al. v. Economical Mutual Insurance Co. et al.
(1986) 19 C.C.L.I. 130
Ontario Supreme Court

3. Duties of a Director

Questions

What are your duties as a director and to whom are they owed?
What is the consequence of being in breach of those duties?

China Software Corp. v. *Leimbigler et al.*

(1989) 27 C.P.R. (3D) 215
Supreme Court of British Columbia
June 15, 1989

Callaghan J.: — The plaintiff claims damages from the defendants, two of its former directors and shareholders, for breach of fiduciary duty in intentionally misleading the plaintiff as to the state and cost of completion of the TM (Tianma) Chinese Text Generator and Word Processor System in order to induce the plaintiff to sell the system to Malaspina College.

The Chinese text generation and word processing system is a system for generating and handling Chinese character text (Hanzi text). The system automatically converts text from the standard romanized form of Chinese (Pinyin) into Hanzi text . ...and permits the user to look up the English equivalent of a Chinese word, as well as the Chinese synonyms of a Chinese word, a useful feature for individuals who work with the Chinese language.

[By 1985 a group consisting of Dr. Leimbigler, a linguist, Mr. Slade, who had expertise in the computer field, Mr. Green a lawyer who could assist in raising venture capital and Kambeitz, who had computer equipment and the willingness to work on the project, formed a company, China Software Corporation, the plaintiff in this case. The development of the software system proceeded on schedule. Regular project review meetings were held. At one such meeting it was agreed that Leimbigler and Kambeitz should go to China and Japan to demonstrate the soft-

ware system. On their return from the trip, Leimbigler reported to Green that neither Sony or NCR was interested in the system and that it would take another eight to ten months to complete the prototype at a cost of approximately $200,000 to $300,000. The information with regard to timing and cost was contrary to what he had led his partners to believe before the trip.

Later that month, in August of 1985, the company rejected an offer to purchase the system for $100,000 from International Geosystems Corporation. Within a few days Leimbigler advised that Malaspina College was prepared to offer $100,000 cash and urged acceptance. At the meetings in which the offer was discussed, Leimbigler again said the prototype could not be completed for another eight to ten months and would cost an additional $200,000 to $300,000 and that similar systems were being developed. Furthermore, Leimbigler and Kambeitz indicated they would abandon their work on the system if the sale was not completed. Green and Slade reluctantly concluded the company should accept the Malaspina offer.

Unknown to the company, Leimbigler and Kambeitz had surreptitiously negotiated an agreement with Malaspina College under which they would form a limited partnership which would benefit Leimbigler and Kambeitz. When Green learned of the agreement, he demanded the disclosure of its contents to the company. Despite initial statements to mislead the company about the nature of the agreement and reluctance to disclose its contents, meetings were held at which the details of the agreement were disclosed and the parties negotiated an arrangement to resolve the matter. Malaspina rejected the arrangement.

The company later agreed to proceed with the sale without a satisfactory arrangement because it was clear that Leimbigler and Kambeitz would not complete the project. The College insisted that with the sale of the system the company execute a general release of Leimbigler, Kambeitz and Malaspina. The company agreed. Leimbigler and Kambeitz transferred their shares in the company back to the company and gave up their share of the $100,000 of the sale proceeds.

The system was soon sold to three men who sold it to International Geosystems Corporation. Malaspina received $150,000 cash and a promissory note for $150,000. Leimbigler and Kambeitz received $100,000 and 250,000 shares of International Geosystems Corporation valued at $2.00 a share.] ...

Clearly there was a fiduciary relationship. The defendants breached that relationship in order to obtain a more abundant award through the agreement entered into with Malaspina College.

Counsel for the defendants candidly acknowledges that the defendants likely have no defence on the merits since there are no extenuating circumstances sufficient to justify the defendants' positioning themselves as they did to take a corporate opportunity that belonged to China Software Corporation. The defence proceeded on the assumption that the two defendants were guilty of misrepresentation and non-disclosure in order to induce the sale by China Software to Malaspina College, as pleaded. Counsel submits, however, that the plaintiff gave these two defendants a full release and discharge in connection with a claim of breach of trust which was not induced by any fraud or misrepresentation and consequently cannot be set aside. As counsel said, the defendants acknowledged by their actions in giving up their shares in the plaintiff corporation as well as their 48% interest in the $100,000 sale price, that they were in breach of their fiduciary obligations. He argues that just because the fraud was much greater than the plaintiff suspected or was disclosed in the negotiations leading up to the giving of the release, does not justify setting it aside. Counsel for the defendants went on to say that the giving of a general release must release and discharge the releasee from any and all actions up to that time, even though the releasor is unaware of the true extent of any wrongdoing on the part of the party to whom the release is given.

While the argument in many respects at first blush is inviting, it is clear that the plaintiff would not have consummated an agreement with Malaspina College if it had been aware of the ongoing interest of International Geosystems Corporation and Sony, all of which was kept from it by the secretive conduct of the defendants. Malaspina had no interest in keeping to itself the technology acquired but was desirous of marketing the system in order to recoup its $100,000 investment. The defendants' failure to divulge information of the interest of other parties, the representation (which was false) that it would take eight to ten months and $200,000 to $300,000 to complete the prototype, and the refusal of the defendants to work further on the project were the effectual causes of the sale to Malaspina. The plaintiff, because of the intractable position of Malaspina (it refused to purchase unless it and the two defendants Leimbigler and Kambeitz were provided with a final

release and discharge), as well as the misrepresentation of the defendants, was left, because of the disparity in their positions, with little choice. To accede to the defendant's' argument would be tantamount to condoning the fraudulent misrepresentations perpetrated by the two defendants. The plaintiff was induced to grant the release as a result of non-disclosure of material information and because of the fraudulent misrepresentations already alluded to.

In dealing with the submission of the defendants that the final release was effective to bar the claim of the plaintiff because the release was not obtained by a fraud or misrepresentation on the part of the defendants, I need only point out that the release and sale were inextricably bound. If the defendants had divulged to the plaintiff that International Geosystems Corporation and Sony had shown great interest in the China Software System and if they had represented the true state of affairs as to the system's cost and completion time, the release would not have been executed, nor would the sale to Malaspina have been proceeded with.

There need not be misrepresentation with respect to the document itself. The releasor may be fully cognizant as to what he is signing but if the defendants, who are in a fiduciary position, have misrepresented the true state of affairs to which the release is directed, breaching their fiduciary duty and thereby inducing the plaintiff to execute the release, the release will be set aside: *Francis v. Dingman* (1983) 2. (4th) 244, 43 O.R. (2d) 641, 23 B.L.R. 234 (C.A.)

The release was obtained as a result of deliberate non-disclosure and fraudulent misrepresentations and, accordingly, is vitiated.

Considering the admissions or concessions made by counsel for the defendants, it hardly seems necessary for me to proceed to discuss the doctrine that company directors stand in a fiduciary relationship to the company they represent, in that they must:

(a) act honestly and in good faith and in the best interests of the company;
(b) disclose the nature and extent of any personal interest they have in a proposed contract, and
(c) disclose any and all conflicts.

These basic principles have been enshrined in ss. 142, 144 and 147 of the Company Act, R.S.B.C. 1979, c. 59.

It is of course a fundamental rule of equity that a person in a fiduciary capacity must not place himself in a position where his duty and personal interest conflict. The rule is clearly enunciated by Lord Herschell in *Bray v. Ford*, [1896] A.C. 44 (H.L.), at p. 51:

> It is an inflexible rule of a Court of Equity that a person in a fiduciary position, such as the respondent's, is not, unless otherwise expressly provided, entitled to make a profit; he is not allowed to put himself in a position where his interest and duty conflict. It does not appear to me that this rule is, as has been said, founded upon principles of morality. I regard it rather as based on the consideration that, human nature being what it is, there is danger, in such circumstances, of the person holding a fiduciary position being swayed by interest rather than by duty, and thus prejudicing those whom he was bound to protect. It has, therefore, been deemed expedient to lay down this positive rule.

The leading Canadian case on fiduciary obligations is *Canadian*

Aero Service Ltd. v. O'Malley (1973), 11 C.P.R. (2d) 206, 40 D.L.R. (3d) 371, [1974] S.C.R. 592. At p. 219, Laskin J. (as he then was), in discussing the fiduciary duties of directors, said:

> An examination of the case law in this Court and in the Courts of other like jurisdiction on the fiduciary duties of directors and senior officers shows the pervasiveness of a strict ethic in this area of the law. In my opinion, this ethic disqualifies a director or senior officer from usurping for himself or diverting to another person or company with whom or with which he is associated a maturing business opportunity which his company is actively pursuing; he is also precluded from so acting even after his resignation where the resignation may fairly be said to have been prompted or influenced by a wish to acquire for himself the opportunity sought by the company, or where it was his position with the company rather than a fresh initiative that led him to the opportunity which he later acquired.

After quoting from the judgment of Viscount Sankey and Lord Russell of Killowen in *Regal (Hastings), Ltd. v. Gulliver*, [1942] 1 All E.R. 378 (H.L), at pp. 381 and 389, he went on to say, at p. 220: "The reaping of a profit by a person at a company's expense while a director thereof is, of course, an adequate ground upon which to hold the director accountable." Further, at p. 221:

What these decisions indicate is an updating of the equitable principle whose roots lie in the general standards that I have already mentioned, namely, loyalty, good faith and avoidance of a conflict of duty and self interest. Strict application against directors and senior management officials is simply recognition of the degree of control which their positions give them in corporate operations, a control which rises above day accountability to owning shareholders and which comes under some scrutiny only at annual general or at special meetings. It is a necessary supplement, in the public interest, of statutory regulation and accountability which themselves are, at one and the same time, an acknowledgment of the importance of the corporation in the life of the community and of the need to compel obedience by it and by its promoters, directors and managers to norms of exemplary behaviour.

The conduct of the two defendants falls far short of the conduct that one would expect of a director and employee and, in effect, was a stratagem concocted and developed in order to appropriate unto themselves a business opportunity which in fairness belonged to the plaintiff.

As a result of this breach there must be a disgorgement of profits. ...

Judgment accordingly.

- *T*hree directors of Levy-Russell Ltd. [Levy] a company in need of new financing, gave secret financial information to Shieldings Inc., a venture capital company and potential purchaser of Levy, in return for equity in a new company to be formed. Shieldings used the information against Levy in its negotiations and succeeded in buying Levy for less than its fair value.

  Justice Lane of the Ontario Court found that the directors had breached their common law and statutory duty to their company and found them personally liable for $5.26 million, the difference in the price paid and the fair price.[2]

4. RIGHTS OF THE SHAREHOLDERS / RELIEF FROM OPPRESSION

Question

Do the statutes that provide for business corporations afford any protection to the shareholders?

Lenstra *v.* Lenstra, et al.

COURT FILE NO. A3340/95
ONTARIO COURT (GENERAL DIVISION
JUNE 30, 1995

Walters, J.: This is an application by Natalie Olga Lenstra for relief under the oppression remedy provisions of the *Ontario Business Corporations Act*. The applicant is the widow of the deceased William Lenstra, the brother of the respondent Hendrik Lenstra. William Lenstra died on January 11, 1994. William

Lenstra and Hendrik Lenstra are the sole registered shareholders, directors and officer[s] of the respondent corporations. William Lenstra and Hendrik Lenstra each owned 50% of all of the shares in each corporation. William Lenstra and Hendrik Lenstra were involved in a partnership which spanned some

35 years. Each was equally involved in the operation of their companies, which primarily dealt in real estate. Prior to his death, William Lenstra and Hendrik Lenstra would each receive profits of between $5–$7,000.00 each month, plus additional amounts in each year. In 1993, they each received between $100–$150,000.00. No profits from the corporations were paid or distributed to the estate of William Lenstra since his death. William Lenstra's will provided that the applicant was to receive 25% of his estate. Under the subsequent codicil, the applicant is to receive a life interest in his estate. The applicant and the respondent Hendrik Lenstra are the named co-executors and trustees in both the will and codicil.

It is the applicant's contention that since the death of her husband, the respondent is acting in a manner designed to ensure that the corporations do not generate any income to the detriment of the estate. Further, the applicant contends that Hendrik Lenstra is abusing the assets of the corporation and allowing his sons to profit or benefit from the said corporations.

The respondent denies these allegations and instead insists that the reduction in profitability of the companies is due to decline in real estate market conditions.

Section 248 of the *Ontario Business Corporations Act,* R. S. 0. 1990, chap. B 16, provides:

(1) A complainant, the Director and, in the case of an offering corporation, the Commission may apply to the court for an order under this section;

(2) Where, upon an application under subsection (1), the court is satisfied that in respect of a corporation or any of its affiliates,

(a) any act or omission of the corporation or any of its affiliates effects or threatens to effect a result;

(b) the business or affairs of the corporation or any of its affiliates are, have been or are threatened to be carried on or conducted in a manner; or

(c) the powers of the directors of the corporation or any of its affiliates are, have been or are threatened to be exercised in a manner, that is oppressive or unfairly prejudicial to or that unfairly disregards the interest of any security holder, creditor, director or officer of the corporation, the court may make an order to rectify the matters complained of.

Section 245 of the *Ontario Business Corporations Act* defines "complainant" as follows:
"complainant" means,

(a) a registered holder or beneficial owner, and a former registered holder or beneficial owner, of a security of a corporation or any of its affiliates,

(b) a director or an officer or a former director or officer of a corporation or of any of its affiliates,

(c) any other person who, in the discretion of the court, is a proper person to make an application under this Part.

The respondent argues that the applicant has no status to bring this application as she does not come within any of the classes of individuals whose interests are dealt with under this section, and further, that she is not acting in good faith or in the interests of the corporation, but rather is acting on a personal vendetta against Hendrik Lenstra.

The applicant contends that in fact she is the only proper person to bring such an application before the court. She is one of the co-executors of the estate. Clearly, the other co-executor, Mr. Hendrik Lenstra, is one of the named respondents and one of the individuals the applicant is alleging is acting in an oppressive fashion. William Lenstra's shares have passed to his estate and the estate is now the beneficial owner of a security of a corporation. Counsel for the applicant has provided me with several reported decisions showing the discretion of the court in determining who a proper person to make an application is. I refer specifically to the cases of *Csak v. Aunwn* (1990), 69 D.L.R. (4th) 567 (Ont. H.C.); *Moriarity v. Slater* (1989), 67 O.R. (2d) 758 (H.C.J.); and *First Edmonton Place Ltd. v. 315888 Alberta Ltd.* (1988), 40 B.L.R. 28 (Alta. Q.B.) at page 63.

These cases make it clear that the oppression remedy provisions are remedial in nature and should be given a broad and liberal interpretation. On the facts of this case, I am satisfied that the applicant is a proper person to make this application under Part 17 of the *Business Corporations Act.*

Having determined that the applicant has status to bring this application, I must decide if in fact the conduct complained of by the applicant is oppressive or unfair. Obviously what is oppressive or unfair in one case may not necessarily be so in another.

Again, counsel for the applicant has provided me with a comprehensive list of authorities.

In *Re National Trust Company and Grace Holding, Inc. et al.* [indexed as *Henderson (Estate) v. Grace Holding, Inc.*] 63 D.L.R. (4th) 415 (Ont. Div. Crt.). The court found that the corporation and its officers had not operated in an appropriate manner.

> However, as Mr. Justice Campbell found in that regard, the corporation is doing nothing to which Henderson did not agree. Henderson was one of the active participants in the initial stages of the creation of the corporation, the purchase of the property, etc. and it cannot be said to be oppressive to his estate to have continued the policies which he was part of creating. However, since his death the estate has not received notice of meetings, been treated as a shareholder or been recognized as being entitled to whatever rights flowed with regard to the largest penthouse. The estate has not been a party to the continuing of the operation which appears to be contrary to a number of Ontario statutes.

This is precisely the conduct the respondent here has exhibited towards his deceased brother's estate.

Further, the respondents refusal or unwillingness to provide updated financial statements for the corporations along with the questionable, non-arms-length transactions with his sons give rise to a concern that he has taken advantage of his position to secure personal benefits for himself at the expense of the corporations. This is a breach of his fiduciary duty and where there has been a breach of fiduciary duty, the test for oppression has been met. ...

On the facts of this case, I find that the actions of the respondent Hendrik Lenstra have been oppressive.

Section 248 of the *Ontario Business Corporations Act* sets out a wide list of remedies available to the court on an interim or final basis. Counsel for the applicant has urged me to remove the respondent Hendrik Lenstra as a Director of the respondent corporations and in his place appoint the applicant as a Director of the respondent corporations. Further, the applicant asks that a receiver/manager be appointed for the purpose of managing the affairs of the corporations. I am reluctant to make such drastic orders at this juncture. I am mindful of the fact that the respondent is a 50% owner of these companies, and with his deceased brother has always operated these businesses. The appointment of a receiver/manager might affect the public's perception of these businesses and that would not be in anyone's economic best interests.

However, I do feel it is appropriate for the applicant to have a say in the running of these corporations and therefore, an order will go appointing her as a Director of the respondent corporations. The registers and other records of these corporations shall be amended to include Natalie Olga Lenstra as a Director.

This application will be adjourned in order that both parties may provide me with further submissions as to any further interim or final orders they feel are appropriate in the circumstances. I am hopeful that the parties will be able to agree on the orderly management of these corporations. However, if that is not possible, then I am prepared to entertain and consider the other relief requested by the applicant.

Counsel may speak to me regarding costs of this application.

As a shareholder of Harold E. Ballard Ltd., W. Ballard, son of Harold E. Ballard whose company, by 1972, owned approximately a 70% interest in Maple Leaf Gardens Ltd., sought a remedy under the relief from oppression sections of the *Ontario Business Corporations Act* on the grounds that Harold E. Ballard Ltd. had been conducted by Harold and two directors appointed by him in a manner that was oppressive or unfairly prejudicial or which unfairly disregarded his interests and the interests of his company. He alleged that the company was conducted as if its assets were the property of Harold E. Ballard personally. His applications were granted by Judge Farley in his 172-page decision.

820099 Ontario Inc. v. Harold E. Ballard Ltd.
Summarized from The Lawyers Weekly
March 29, 1991 p. 24

Derivative Action

Question

What if the company has been wronged but the company through its directors won't sue?

Hercules Managements Ltd. *v.* Ernst & Young

Background facts of this Supreme Court of Canada case are given on p. 53 above. In short, investors allege that their investment loss was caused by the company auditors who prepared the annual financial statements. The Court dismissed their claims on policy grounds. It held that the statements were prepared for the shareholders as a collective body, not for the shareholders to make investment decisions and that to hold otherwise would subject auditors to indeterminate liability. The following is the decision of Justice La Forest on the issue of whether or not the shareholders' action against the auditors hired by the company should properly be a derivative action.

La Forest, J.:—
… Does the rule in *Foss v. Harbottle* affect the appellants' action? …

ISSUE 2: THE EFFECT OF THE RULE IN FOSS V. HARBOTTLE

[58] All the participants in this appeal—the appellants, the respondents, and the intervener—raised the issue of whether the appellants' claims in respect of the losses they suffered in their existing shareholdings through their alleged inability to oversee management of the corporations ought to have been brought as a derivative action in conformity with the rule in *Foss v. Harbottle* rather than as a series of individual actions. The issue was also raised and discussed in the courts below. In my opinion, a derivative action—commenced, as required, by an application under s. 232 of *the Manitoba Corporations Act*—

would have been the proper method of proceeding with respect to this claim. Indeed, I would regard this simply as a corollary of the idea that the audited reports are provided to the shareholders as a group in order to allow them to take collective (as opposed to individual) decisions. Let me explain.

[59] The rule in *Foss v. Harbottle* provides that individual shareholders have no cause of action in law for any wrongs done to the corporation and that if an action is to be brought in respect of such losses, it must be brought either by the corporation itself (through management) or by way of a derivative action. The legal rationale behind the rule was eloquently set out by the English Court of Appeal in *Prudential Assurance Co. v. Newman Industries Ltd.* (No. 2), [1982] 1 All E.R. 354, at p. 367, as follows:

> The rule [in *Foss v. Harbottle*] is the consequence of the fact that a corporation is a separate legal entity. Other consequences are limited liability and limited rights. The company is liable for its contracts and torts; the shareholder has no such liability. The company acquires causes of action for breaches of contract and for torts which damage the company. No cause of action vests in the shareholder. When the shareholder acquires a share he accepts the fact that the value of his investment follows the fortunes of the company and that he can only exercise his influence over the fortunes of the company by the exercise of his voting rights in general meeting. The law confers on him the right to ensure that the company observes the limitations of its memorandum of association and the right to ensure that other shareholders observe the rule, imposed on them by the articles of association. If it is right that the law has conferred or should in certain restricted circumstances confer further rights on a shareholder the scope and consequences of such further rights require careful consideration.

To these lucid comments, I would respectfully add that the rule is also sound from a policy perspective, inasmuch as it avoids the procedural hassle of a multiplicity of actions.

[60] The manner in which the rule in *Foss v. Harbottle*, supra, operates with respect to the appellants' claims can thus be demonstrated. As I have already explained, the appellants allege that they were prevented from properly overseeing the management of the audited corporations because the respondents' audit reports painted a misleading picture of their financial state. They allege further that had they known the true situation, they would have intervened to avoid the eventuality of the corporations' going into receivership and the consequent loss of their equity. The difficulty with this submission, I have suggested, is that it fails to recognize that in supervising management, the shareholders must be seen to be acting as a body in respect of the corporation's interests rather than as individuals in respect of their own ends. In a manner of speaking, the shareholders assume what may be seen to be a "managerial role" when, as a collectivity, they oversee the activities of the directors and officers through resolutions adopted at shareholder meetings. In this capacity, they cannot properly be understood to be acting simply as individual holders of equity. Rather, their collective decisions are made in respect of the corporation itself. Any duty owed by auditors in respect of this aspect of the shareholders' functions, then, would be owed not to shareholders qua individuals, but rather to all shareholders as a group, acting in the interests of the corporation. And if the decisions taken by the collectivity of shareholders are in respect of the corporation's affairs, then the shareholders' reliance on negligently prepared audit reports in taking such decisions will result in a wrong to the corporation for which the shareholders cannot, as individuals, recover.

[61] This line of reasoning finds support in Lord Bridge's comments in *Caparo*, supra, at p. 580:

> The shareholders of a company have a collective interest in the company's proper management and in so far as a negligent failure of the auditor to report accurately on the state of the company's finances deprives the shareholders of the opportunity to exercise their powers in general meeting to call the directors to book and to ensure that errors in management are corrected, the shareholders ought to be entitled to a remedy. But in practice no problem arises in this regard since the interest of the shareholders in the proper management of the company's affairs is indistinguishable from the interest of the company itself and any loss suffered by the shareholders ... will be recouped by a claim against the auditor in the name of the company, not by individual shareholders. [Emphasis added.]

...

[62] One final point should be made here. Referring to the case of *Goldex Mines Ltd. v. Revill* (1974), 7 O.R. (2d) 216 (C.A.), the appellants submit that where a shareholder has been directly and individually harmed, that shareholder may have a personal cause of action even though the corporation may also have a separate and distinct cause of action. Nothing in the foregoing paragraphs should be understood to detract from this principle. In finding that claims in respect of losses stemming from an alleged inability to oversee or supervise management are really derivative and not personal in nature, I have found only that shareholders cannot raise individual claims in respect of a wrong done to the corporation. Indeed, this is the limit of the rule in *Foss v. Harbottle*. Where, however, a separate and distinct claim (say, in tort) can be raised with respect to a wrong done to a shareholder qua individual, a personal action may well lie, assuming that all the requisite elements of a cause of action can be made out.

[63] The facts of *Haig*, supra, provide the basis for an example of where such a claim might arise. Had the investors in that case been shareholders of the corporation, and had a similarly negligent report knowingly been provided to them by the auditors for a specified purpose, a duty of care separate and distinct from any duty owed to the audited corporation would have arisen in their favour, just as one arose in favour of Mr. Haig. While the corporation would have been entitled to claim damages in respect of any losses it might have suffered through reliance on the report (assuming, of course, that the report was also provided for the corporation's use), the shareholders in question would also have been able to seek personal compensation for the losses they suffered qua individuals through their personal reliance and investment. On the facts of this case, however, no claims of this sort can be established.

CONCLUSION

[64]. ...With respect to the claim regarding the appellants' inability to oversee management properly, I would agree with the courts below that it ought to have been brought as a derivative action. ...

[65] I would dismiss the appeal with costs.

RIGHTS REGARDING THE AGM

Yves Michaud, a shareholder of both the Royal Bank and the National Bank of Canada wanted some shareholders' proposals to be included in the annual information circular and put to a vote at the annual general meeting. Among the proposals was one to limit the salaries of bank executives to twenty times the salary of the average employee; a move that would cause some top salaries to plummet. The banks resisted. The issue, pressed to the Quebec Court of Appeal, was decided in favour of Michaud, in favour of certain "inalienable" rights of the shareholders. In his review of this case, Mr. Seeman said this was the first time "that a publicly traded Canadian company has been compelled to vote on shareholder proposals relating to corporate governance at their annual meeting."

Michaud v. National Bank of Canada
Summarized from The Lawyers Weekly
January 31, 1997, p. 32.

The proposals were defeated.[3]

ENDNOTES

1. A more detailed account is given in *Newsweek*, September 14, 1992.

2. For a full review of this 403-page decision in *Levy-Russell Ltd. v. Tecmotiv Inc.* see *The Lawyers Weekly*, April 29, 1994, p. 1.

3. *The Lawyers Weekly*, October 31, 1997, p. 2.

VII
PROPERTY

A. PERSONAL PROPERTY

Who gets the ring?
"Resolution of this question, I think, involves a choice between conflicting authorities. The plaintiff [he] relies upon *Cohen v. Sellar*, [1926] 1 K.B. 536. At p. 548, McCardie J. defined the law on this topic, in the following words:

> If the engagement to marry be dissolved by mutual consent, then in the absence of agreement to the contrary, the engagement ring and like gifts must, I think, be returned by each party to the other.

The defendant [she] relies upon *Vezina v. Blais*, [1953] C.S. 48 (P.Q.S.C.). Mr. Wilson contends that the law on this topic is described by Collins J. at p. 49, in the following words:

> … [An engagement ring is] an outright gift by the [donor] to the [recipient]. … It [becomes] the absolute property of the [recipient] upon … acceptance of it.

I apply the principle of law stated in Cohen. I think Cohen contains an accurate statement of the current law in this province. That principle was not referred to in *Vezina*. And in any event, in my opinion, the principle expressed in Cohen is more in harmony with contemporary notions of matrimonial property dispute resolution. I am persuaded that an analysis founded upon principles of commercial and contract law are more sound, than an analysis founded upon principles of gift.

Hitchcox v. Harper
Victoria Registry No. 96/3296
Supreme Court of British Columbia
August 21, 1996

B. INTELLECTUAL PROPERTY

1. COPYRIGHT

Question

Who owns copyright?

| *Cselko Associates Inc. and Ernie Cselko* | *v.* | *Zellers Inc. and Display Industries of Canada (Eastern) Ltd.* |

ONTARIO COURT OF JUSTICE
COURT FILE NO. 33515/88Q
JULY 10, 1992

Hawkins, J:—This is a motion by the defendant Zellers to dismiss the plaintiffs' action. The plaintiff Cselko is a commercial illustrator who carries on his business through the vehicle of the corporate plaintiff of which he is sole proprietor.

Zellers is a retail merchant and the defendant Display Industries of Canada (Eastern) Limited (Display Ltd.) is a commercial art broker.

Zellers developed an advertising and merchandising gimmick which they named "Zeddy Bear." They had some commercial illustrations done of Zeddy with which they were not entirely satisfied. They retained Display Ltd. to find them an illustrator to do some drawings of Zeddy in various activity poses. Display Ltd. engaged Cselko on behalf of Zellers, to do drawings. Zellers had no direct contact with Cselko. Zellers' end of the transaction was handled entirely through Display Ltd. and in particular by the late Mr. James Renwick, Sr.

It was made known to Cselko that the illustration he was commissioned to do were going to be used by Zellers for advertising purposes. No limitation on the use to which Zellers could put the illustrations was ever discussed. The plaintiff billed Display Ltd. by means of invoices which contained no limitations or copyright warnings. He was paid approximately $16,000.00 for his work.

Zellers used the illustrations in connection with usual advertising, packaging and promotional material (e.g. a colouring book) and has even reproduced some of the drawings to be sold in frames.

The plaintiff, after he discovered the extent to which his drawings were being put, registered his copyright in them. He now sues for substantial damages for breach of copyright and injunctive relief.

There is only one issue in this law suit—what limitations on use, if any, are to be implied in the circumstances of this case.

There was, as I have already noted, no limitation discussed. The plaintiff asserts that "advertising" and "packaging" are different and that art sold for use in advertising does not encompass packaging. It is clear from his cross-examination that he did not make this view known to Mr. Renwick.

In his affidavit the plaintiff alleges as follows in paragraph 2(b):

I negotiate fees for my artwork based on the complexity of the artwork, the extent of the use required by the client and the duration of the use. Payment may be negotiated in the form of a royalty arrangement or straight fees or both. The use of artwork on packaging for products requires a special contractual relationship and special remuneration to the artist, as packaging normally has a long shelf life of many years.

The plaintiff admitted on his cross-examination that in twenty-three years as an artist he has never received royalties on his work.

The plaintiff, in response to this motion has filed an affidavit of David Yaxley who is Art Director of Sears Canada. Mr. Yaxley's affidavit is laudatory, and no doubt rightly so, of the plaintiff's skill and reputation. The thrust of Mr. Yaxley's affidavit is that Sears' practice is to negotiate specific separate fees for each of the various uses to which the artist's work is to be put. He states, in paragraph 4 of his affidavit, that such is "the custom in the advertising industry as far as I am aware." It is clear from his cross-examination that he has no experience whatever in situations where commercial artwork is purchased with no express restrictions placed on its use.

Chris Yaneff has sworn an affidavit filed in support of this motion. It is his evidence that it is the custom of the trade that a commercial artist assigns all rights in the work to his customer and that the custom is so widely known that a written assignment is rarely executed. In other words, it is up to the artist to specifically limit the uses if there are to be limits. Mr. Yaneff's evidence was not shaken on cross-examination.

Danielle Jones a commercial illustrator since 1980, swore an affidavit filed on behalf of the defendant. She testifies that it is standard practice in the industry that all rights are assigned to the client unless the artist expressly limits other use. She was not cross-examined.

Carol Green Long has sworn an affidavit filed by the defendant in support of this motion. She has been involved in marketing commercial artwork since 1983. It is her view that the client is entitled to use the purchased artwork without restriction. She was not cross-examined.

The plaintiff, in his affidavit in opposition to the motion says, in paragraph 8 "the custom of the trade of commercial advertising is to negotiate with the artist the rights for advertising purposes separately from any other rights such as the right to use the work on products ... *I intend to present many expert witnesses at the trial of this action attesting to the aforesaid custom.*" (emphasis mine)

As Bolan J. said in *Vaughan v. Warner Communication Inc.* (1986) 56 O.R. (2d) 242 at p. 247

... Rule 20 should not be eviscerated by the practice of deferring actions for trial *at the mere suggestion that future evidence may be made available.* (emphasis mine)

I am satisfied that the plaintiffs' claims do not survive a good hard look on the material presented on this motion.

THE COPYRIGHT ACT PROBLEM

Section 13(4) of the *Copyright Act* R.S.C. Ch. C-42 provides "the owner of the copyright in any work may assign the right

... and may grant any interest in the work by licence but no assignment or grant is valid unless it is in writing ...."

It has been held that a licence to use may be implied by the conduct of the parties and need not be in writing. *Howard Drabble Ltd. v. Hycolith Manufacturing Company* (1928), 44

T.L.R. 264 (Ch.Div.). See also Fox *Copyright* (2nd edition) 298 ff.

Judgment may issue dismissing the plaintiff's claim against both defendants. ...

[Plaintiff's claim dismissed]

- *A*round Christmas one movie seems to dominate the TV selections —*It's a Wonderful Life* with Donna Reed and Jimmy Stewart. The theme is appropriate to the season, but the more important factor affecting its availability is the price — the stations are paying no royalties to the creators because the copyright lapsed.[1]

Question

What can be copyrighted?

- *I*n a U.S. action, the NBA sued Motorola Corp. and STATS Inc. for misappropriating its property and infringing copyright by broadcasting professional basketball scores and statistics to sport afficionados through electronic pagers. The appeal court—overturning the trial court—held that they were only reporting facts and facts are not copyrightable.[2]

- *F*reelance writers and photographers who contracted with Thomson newspapers have launched a class-action suit against Thomson Corp. et al. for infringing copyright by selling their stories or pictures to electronic databases accessible through the Internet. They claim $50 million in compensatory damages and as much again as punitive damages.[3]

THE *"LOOK AND FEEL"* CASES

- *R*eferred to as the "look and feel" case, Lotus sued to stop the sale of a program, VP Planner, developed by a Vancouver company, Stephenson Software Inc., because the program looks and feels like the popular spreadsheet program, Lotus 1-2-3. Lotus sought an injunction to bar Paperback Software International of Berkeley, California from selling the program, compensatory damages of $14 million and punitive damages of $10 million. Lotus based its case not only on copyright infringement, but also on unfair trade practices.[4]

  Judge Keeton of the U.S. District Court which first heard the case concluded that the menu command structure of 1-2-3 is an original and nonobvious way of expressing a command structure and is a creative expression deserving copyright protection. It had been settled that a creator could protect underlying source and object code but the court was being faced with questions of the protection of noncode characteristics of software.[5]

  Lotus Development Corp. v. Paperback Software and International and Mosaic Software Inc.

  Note: *This suit prompted the League for Programming Freedom to picket the Lotus headquarters urging Lotus to 'innovate not litigate.' The group's founder says such law suits stifle innovation, since new programs have borrowed ideas from previous innovations and that users want compatible software. A more detailed account is given in* Newsweek *August 27, 1990.*

- *A*pple Computer, in a case which "stunned" the computer industry, sued Microsoft Corp. and Hewlett-Packard Co. for $5.5 billion for illegally copying computer screen symbols used by the company's Macintosh computer. The defendants argued that the symbols were generic and thus not suitable for copyright protection and that the symbols were derived form those used earlier by other companies including Xerox Corp. In April of 1992 a U.S. District Judge ruled that most of the symbols used by Apple were not protected by copyright.[6]

On April 24, a few days after Walker's ruling, Apple asked the judge to reconsider his decision; the motion was granted.[7]

On August 7, 1992 Walker reaffirmed his ruling that most of the symbols are not protected by copyright or that they were allowed by a 1985 agreement between Apple and Microsoft.

* *I*n *Lotus Development Corporation v. Borland International Inc.* a U.S. Court of Appeal held that Borland had not infringed copyright; the Lotus 1-2-3 "command menu hierarchy constituted part of the method of operation of the program and copyright law does not protect methods of operation. Lotus appealed to the United States Supreme Court.[8] The U.S. Supreme Court split 4-4 thus allowing Borland's previous appeal victory to stand.[9]

Q u e s t i o n s

What are the consequences of infringing copyright?
In an action for damages, how much should the infringer have to pay to the copyright owner?

Society of Composers, Authors and Music Publishers of Canada *v.* *348803 Alberta Ltd. et al.*

REPORT OF REFERENCE: AS TO THE AMOUNT OF DAMAGES, INTEREST AND COSTS OWING BY THE DEFENDANT TO THE PLAINTIFF FOR THE PERIOD 01 JANUARY 1994 TO 09 JANUARY 1997.
http://www.fja-cmf.gc.ca/en/cf/1997/recents/html/
FEDERAL COURT OF CANADA
JULY 3, 1997

John A. Hargrave, Prothonotary, :
This Reference, pursuant to the designation of the Administrator of the Court, 12 March 1997, to determine the profits, damages, interest and costs owing by 348803 Alberta Ltd. and Damir Zoranic to the Society of Composers, Authors and Music Publishers of Canada (the "Society of Composers") arises out of the Plaintiff's action claiming an accounting and various other relief for the use of copyright music, including royalties payable in accordance with the applicable tariffs set out from time to time in the Supplement to the *Canada Gazette*. The claim for relief is based on a Judgment obtained by the Society of Composers, in default of defence, on 20 February 1997.

The Reference took place at Vancouver, BC, on the afternoon of 24 June, 1997. The Defendants, who are now in the position of judgment debtors, with profits, damages, interest and costs payable to the Plaintiff to be determined by this reference, all as set out in Federal Court rules 500 through 507, have had ample notice from time to time of these proceedings, including the present reference. No one attended to represent the Defendants.

APPLICABLE TARIFFS

The Society of Composers is the only performing rights society authorized by the Copyright Board of Canada to issue licences and to collect licence fees from parties wishing to perform copyright musical works in public in Canada. The tariffs and fees are authorized by Section 67 through Section 67.2 of the *Copyright Act*, R.S.C. 1985, Chapter C-42. The Copyright Board publishes, each year, in the *Canada Gazette*, a statement of the royalties which the Society of Composers may collect. These are in the form of tariffs. The relevant tariff, in this instance, is Tariff 18, applicable to recorded music for dancing. In the present instance the applicable tariffs are those of 13 August 1994, for the 1994 year, 11 March 1995 for 1995, and 21 September 1996 for 1996. the Plaintiff's evidence establishes the Defendants' establishment is still in operation, but not that it presently plays recorded music. Thus there is no claim for 1997.

APPROACH TO ASSESSMENT

The relief sought in this case involves the determination of a royalty or licence fee as damages, the portion of net profits to go to the Society of Composers and exemplary damages.

Damages
Where it is customary to licence the use of a work, music in this instance, damages may be measured on the basis of the usual royalty or licence fee. The licence fees for music are calcu-

lated using given figures and rates from the Copyright Board Tariffs and various statistics as to the operation of the licensee. Where a licence fee alone is inadequate recompense, general damages at large may be in order: *Hay v. Sloan* (1957) 27 C.P.R. 132 at 140 (Ont. H.C.).

Profits

Recompense does not necessarily end with damages, but may also, in a copyright infringement matter, at a court's discretion, include an accounting of profit. This is touched on indirectly in section 34 (1.01) of the *Copyright Act*, in the context of an accounting, and is specifically provided for in section 35 (1) of the Act. I have treated damages and profits not as alternative, but as cumulative relief.

[He reviews arguments that it should be damages or profits in the alternative, but concludes that the *Canadian Copyright* Act clearly allows both.]

An award of profits is, in a sense, an equitable approach, although one that by recognition in the Copyright Act has become a legal remedy to be applied equitably. It is a determination of the Defendants' gain by reason of wrongful use of the Plaintiff's property, an amount which is awarded to the Plaintiff. ... One must, however, in the present instance, keep in mind. that the award of profit is based on a default judgment specifying profit as a remedy: the outcome might well have been different had the Defendants appeared.

Estimating Licence Fees and Profits

By reason of the absence of representation on behalf of the Defendants, and the fact that there has been no access to the Defendants' records, an accurate calculation of the licence fees owing and of profits is not possible. Therefore I must calculate the licence fees and profits as best I can: see for example *Performing Rights of Canada Ltd. v. 497227 Ontario Ltd.* [and others].

In summary, it is not improper to calculate damages and profit in a rough and ready manner, particularly if the necessity to do so is the result of omissions on the part of defendants to attend and to protect their interests by providing appropriate information and documents.

Material Tendered by the Plaintiff

[After reviewing the material supplied by plaintiff he moves to the calculations.]

CALCULATION OF LICENCE FEES

... To summarize, I have calculated the licence fee for the full years 1994 through 1996 as though the lounge operated between four and seven days a week at the basic licence fee, together with a premium of 160% for the 150 patron capacity over the basic 100 patrons.

The calculations are as follows:

1994 $334.93 × 260% =	$	868.40
1995 $347.34 × 260% =		903.08
1996 $359.72 × 260% =		935.27
Total		$2,706.75
GST @ 7%		193.72
TOTAL		$2,900.47

CALCULATION OF AWARD OF PROFITS

As I noted earlier, an award in the nature of profits derived from infringement is an equitable approach, made into a legal remedy by section 35(1) of the *Copyright Act*. It is the confiscation of and transfer to the Plaintiff of the portion of profits made by the Defendants through their unauthorized use of the Plaintiff's works. I have decided to recommend this transfer of profit, in addition to damages, for an award merely of the usual licence fee and of the court's tariff based costs for legal expenses does not adequately reimburse the Plaintiff for the time and trouble it has taken to enforce its rights. It is thus proper to transfer a portion of the profit. The more difficult conclusion to reach is the value of the Plaintiff's music to the Defendants.

Mr. Justice Holmes of the Supreme Court of the United States recognized the inherent value of music in a restaurant setting in a 1917 case, *Victor Herbert v. Shanley Company*, reported (1917) 61 Law. Ed. 511. The case involved infringement of Mr. Herbert's "Sweethearts" by a live performance in a Broadway restaurant. The Defendant argued that there was no infringement because diners paid nothing at the door, but only for their food and drink. A portion of the final paragraph of the reasons is worth reading:

> The defendants' performances are not eleemosynary. They are part of a total for which the public pays, and the fact that the price of the whole is attributed to a particular item which those present are [595] expected to order is not important. It is true that the music is not the sole object, but neither is the food, which probably could be got cheaper elsewhere. The object is a repast in surroundings that to people, having limited powers of conversation, or disliking the rival noise, give a luxurious pleasure not to be had from eating a silent meal. If music did not pay, it would be given up. If it pays, it pays out of the public's pocket. Whether it pays or not, the purpose of employing it is profit, and that is enough. (page 514).

It matters not that the Defendants had no specific charge, for example a cover charge at the door, for the music at their establishment. Music adds an ambiance to such establishments. The music added a value to the Defendants' operation, otherwise they would have given up playing music. Just what the value of the music might be I must now arrive at in a rough and ready manner.

Earlier in this report I referred to ratios of profit to statutory licence fees derived from four references in which the plaintiffs were either The Performing Rights Organization of Canada Ltd. or, as in the present instance, The Society of Composers, Authors and Music Publishers of Canada. I also noted the circumstances in each of those four cases were analogous to those in the present instance, with obvious differences in the facts cancelling out each other.

To simplify the calculation I have revised the average ratio from 18.38 to 18. Thus the portion of the net profit which I have attributed to music and which I recommend as an award of profit to the Plaintiff is 18 times the licence fee in each year:

1994 - 18 × $868.40 =	$15,631.20
1995 - 18 × $903.08 =	$16,255.44
1996 - 18 × $935.27 =	$16,834.86
Total	$48,721.50

PRE-JUDGMENT INTEREST

[Pre-judgment interest on the license fees: $355.16; on the profits $3,239.84.]

EXEMPLARY DAMAGES

In its Statement of Claim the Society of Composers asks for exemplary damages. Exemplary damages, also referred to as punitive damages, are not compensatory, but rather are to punish and must be sufficient to act as a deterrent.

In *Vorvis v. ICBC* [1989] 1 S.C.R. 1085, the Supreme Court of Canada dealt with exemplary damages at pages 1107 and 1108. There, Mr. Justice McIntyre, who gave the reasons for the majority, wrote as follows:

> Moreover, punitive damages may only be awarded in respect of conduct which is of such nature as to be deserving of punishment because of its harsh, vindictive, reprehensible, and malicious nature. I do not suggest that I have exhausted the adjectives which could describe the conduct capable of characterizing a punitive award, but in any case where such an award is made the conduct must be extreme in its nature and such that by any reasonable standard it is deserving of full condemnation and punishment.

This idea of punishment was coupled with the idea of deterrence, by the Supreme Court of Canada, in *Hill v. Church of Scientology* [1995] 2 S.C.R. 1130 at 1208 and 1209. The test applied by the Supreme Court of Canada was whether the conduct of the defendant was so outrageous that punitive damages were rationally required to act as a deterrent: see pages 1209 and 1210.

Very recently the Federal Court of Appeal awarded punitive damages in *Profekta International Inc. v. Theresa Lee*, an unreported decision of 30 April 1997 in action A-23-96. The facts involved a continued violation of a copyright, which had included a criminal conviction and warnings issued by the plaintiff. ...

In the present instance, I am of the view that there ought to be punitive damages for a number of reasons. First, the material shows that the Plaintiff visited the premises of the Defendants five times, over a period of 4 years, to ask them to voluntarily pay the required licence fee. Second, the Society of Composers provided the licence fee forms to the Defendants on a number of occasions. Third, the Society of Composers and subsequently their lawyers, sent some dozen letters to the Defendants, ranging from form letters enclosing the licence forms, through follow up letters, letters explaining what steps they would take if the licence fees were not paid, and finally, a letter from their lawyers not long before the present action was commenced, all of which appear to have been ignored. Fourth, at one point the affidavit of material indicates that the Defendant, Damir Zoranic, had thrown the licence application material in the garbage and subsequently said that he had no intention of paying the licence fees. Finally, the Defendants had ample notice of the present proceedings and yet chose to ignore them, thus putting the Plaintiff to additional expense. I would also observe that while many establishments using music for which the Society of Composers collects a royalty, pay the required fee, a number of others do not and thus an award of exemplary damages in this instance might act as a deterrent to those who use others' music without payment.

In view of the substantial recommended award of profit to the Plaintiff, I have tempered what would otherwise be a larger exemplary award. However exemplary damages are in order as a caution to those who would capitalize by using another's property and then not only ignore requests for properly payable licence fees, but also ignore a copyright holder's rights in a willful and flagrant manner, or to those whose conduct is uncooperative and disdainful. I therefore recommend exemplary damages in the amount of $5,000.

TAXATION OF BILL OF COSTS

... . A copy of the bill of costs is attached as Schedule A. I recommend that it be allowed as presented at $ 2,808.80.

CONCLUSION

I recommend to the Court that the Plaintiff be awarded:

1. Licence fees, including GST	$2,900.47
2. Interest on licence fees	355.16
3. Net profit attributable to use of Plaintiff's music	48,721.50
4. Interest on net profits	3,239.84
5. Exemplary damages	5,000.00
6. Costs and disbursements	2,808.80
Total	$63,025.77

This amount should be payable jointly and severally by the Defendants.

I thank Counsel for the Plaintiff for good material and a complete presentation.

Question

Can infringement of copyright lead to a criminal conviction?

R. *v.* J.P.M.

C.A.C. No. 121549
NOVA SCOTIA COURT OF APPEAL
MARCH 29, 1996

Roscoe, J.A.:—This is an appeal by a young offender from convictions entered by Judge Atton on three counts of distributing infringing copies of computer software contrary to s. 42(l)(c) of the *Copyright Act*, R.S. 1985, c.C-42, which is as follows:

42. (1) Every person who knowingly

(c) distributes infringing copies of any work in which copyright subsists either for the purpose of trade or to such an extent as to affect prejudicially the owner of the copyright, is guilty of an offence and liable

(d) on conviction on indictment, to a fine not exceeding one million dollars or to imprisonment for a term not exceeding five years or to both.

Other provisions of the *Copyright Act* relevant to this matter are:

2. In this Act,

"literary" work includes tables, compilations, translations and computer programs; "telecommunication" means any transmission of signs, signals, writing, images or sounds or intelligence of any nature by wire, radio, visual, optical or other electromagnetic system …

Judge Atton's critical findings of fact respecting the [appellant's bulletin board] and the appellant's role as operator of it are as follows:

… As operator of the system Mr. M. was the person who organized the files and determined the areas in which each would be stored. He also monitored and reviewed the operation of the system and granted access to various areas of the bulletin board to callers. As he became more familiar with callers he would upgrade their access allowing them further entry to different areas. It appears that the most restricted area was area 20 or Hacker's Delight. This also appears to be the only area which contained commercial copyrighted protected programs. Access to this area was restricted to persons to whom Mr. M. had granted priority known as special. This allowed those persons access to commercial programs and the ability to download or copy them even though they were copyright protected. There were 16 such accesses granted, according to the evidence, by Mr. M. There was evidence that on at least three occasions that this downloading was done during a time period in question, and in documents filed there's also evidence that this was done on other occasions by other persons other than the ones that were witnesses. What Mr. M. had done was through his bulletin board made available for distribution and assisted in the distribution of the copyright programs without license from commercial producers and copyright owners of those materials. He also, on occasion personally downloaded or distributed the programs to computers belonging to third parties at a separate location. These activities were clearly in contravention of the licensing agreement, and I'm satisfied, the copyrights of the producers of the materials in which were made known to purchasers of the legal copies when purchased. This action was clearly prejudicial to the owners of the copyright in that they were deprived of control over their product which they required to ensure quality and also interferes with a legitimate commercial distribution and sale of the product for profit …

Since computer programs are expressly protected by the *Act* as literary works, and the owners of the copyrights have the sole right to communicate the work to the public by telecommunication, there can be no doubt that the appellant created infringing copies of the software by placing them on the bulletin board in such a way that they were available to be used and copied by the 16 "special" users.

It is also clear that when he accessed his computer by modem from his friends' homes and downloaded the programs onto their computers, he was "distributing" the infringing copies.

Furthermore, by controlling the means and manner by which the users of the bulletin board accessed area 20, and providing the software to assist in the downloading by modem by those users, the appellant was also distributing, that is giving out, or sharing the infringing copies. Although it is suggested that the programs were "scrambled" so that they could not be copied or downloaded by the callers, the evidence accepted by the trial judge was that they were "packaged" or "compressed" for efficient [transmission]. …

Appeal dismissed.

- *T*wo operators of bulletin boards were charged under the *Copyright Act* for distributing unlicensed software. Michael Solomon of BBS "90 North" in Montreal and Sergio Arana, of the Toronto "Legion of Death" BBS, both pleaded guilty. Solomon was fined $20,000: Arana, $2,500.[10] The Litigation Report of the Canadian Alliance Against Software Theft (CAAST) gives the specifics of numerous actions before and since. It also states the consequences which include the forfeiture of the seized equipment. For a copy call the CAAST hotline 1-800-263-9700.[11]

Piracy Cases in the Entertainment Field Include:

• *S*teven Spielberg was sued before his film *Amistad* was even released. Barbara Chase-Riboud claimed that the film, about the mutiny of Africans on a slave ship, was stolen from her novel.
His lawyers maintained that the film is based on history and another book on the topic.[12]

• *R*occo Mastrangelo, operating a business for Radio City Film Exchange Ltd. under the name of Master Video Productions, pleaded guilty to two charges of copyright infringement; the company pleaded guilty to one. The RCMP had "seized 125 copies of unauthorized Italian-language versions of [three Disney films:] *The Aristocats, Beauty and the Beast*, and *The Rescuers Down Under.*" Judge Bruno Cavion of the Ontario Court fined the defendants $9,000 and sentenced Mastrangelo to three years' probation.[13]

• *A* class action suit filed in 1993 against CompuServe and involving 384 music publishers who alleged 941 songs had been infringed was settled out of court. CompuServe agreed to pay $568,000 and agreed to create a licensing agreement for online forum managers to upload and download recordings of copyrighted songs.[14]

• *A* "Web robot" will surf the web to find sites using music. "Musicot" was developed by BMI, a music licensing agency that represents 180,000 songwriters.[15]

• *H*umorist Art Buchwald successfully sued Paramount Pictures for pirating his story for its production of the film *Coming to America* and was awarded 19% of the profit. Although the film had grossed $300 million, Paramount alleged there was no profit.[16] Paramount appealed, but before the appeal was heard Paramount and Buchwald settled their seven-year legal battle. Paramount paid Buchwald and Alain Bernheim, also a plaintiff, more than $1 million.[17]

• *T*he Chiffons (composers of "He's So Fine") sued George Harrison for "My Sweet Lord." Harrison lost the case even though the infringement was found to be done unconsciously.[18]

• *A* U.S. court stopped the sale of rapper Biz Markie's album "I Need a Haircut" because of Markie's unauthorized "sampling" of music from Gilbert O'Sullivan's song "Alone Again (Naturally)." Sampling, using pieces of old songs to create new music, had not been tested in the court; hereafter, the record companies may insist that every sample used be authorized.[19]

• *A* U.S. Superior Court Judge in Los Angeles ruled that Ms. Cynthia Plaster Caster was entitled to the return of her plaster mouldings of the genitalia of famous male rock stars.[20]

INTERNAL COPYING

• *I*n 1984 Lotus Development Corporation, without warning, sued Rixon, a company that manufactures modems and other computer products, for $10 million for software piracy. Lotus alleged that Rixon had violated the licensing agreement and copyright laws by making thirteen copies of Lotus 1-2-3 for use in their branch offices. The action was seen as a test case because it was not an action against a company who had made copies to sell for a profit, but against a company who merely made copies for internal use.[21] This matter was settled out-of-court for an undisclosed amount of cash plus Rixon's agreement to a permanent injunction. As is the custom in out of court settlements, Rixon did not admit to any wrongdoing.[22]

INFRINGEMENT OF MORAL RIGHTS

Q u e s t i o n

What rights remain with a creator, even if he has assigned or sold his copyright?

• *T*hree days after the death of Peter Sellers, who had starred in films as the blundering Inspector Clouseau, the owners of the copyright of his films approached his wife with their plan to make a movie from the clips of his previous films. She did not want pieces of film to be used "in a film meant to be a tribute to Peter. Peter would have hated it, and we can't let a film like that come out."

• *T*he artist, Walt Spitzmiller, was commissioned by L.L.Bean, Inc. to illustrate the cover of its mail-order catalogue with a hunting scene. He painted a rough hunter with his Labrador retriever. The released cover showed a clean-shaven hunter with a "preppified pooch."

   Spitzmiller sued the company, *inter alia*, with copyright infringement and breach of contract. He asked for the destruction of the altered copies and damages equal to the total fall catalogue earnings. Spitzmiller's lawyer is quoted as saying "It's a good thing the dog can't sue."[23]

• *B*ryan Adams took court action against David Duke, a right-wing political figure in the U.S., for using "Everything I Do I Do for You" in his political campaigns.

PARODY

Q u e s t i o n

Is parody saved by the "fair dealing" clause of the Copyright Act?

Compagnie Generale des Establissements Michelin- Michelin & Cie.	*v.*	*National Automobile, Aerospace, Transportation and General Workers Union of Canada (CAW-Canada)*

[1997] 2 F.C. 306
FEDERAL COURT

Teitelbaum J.:

...

   As I stated briefly above, the defendant CAW conducted an organizing campaign at Michelin Canada's plants in Nova Scotia in February and March 1994. The defendant CAW distributed 2,500 leaflets to Michelin workers outside the factory gates at the three Nova Scotia Michelin Canada plants. ... The top right hand corner of the leaflet displays the CAW logo, a mark with the letters "CAW' and "TCA" separated by a stratified maple leaf and the word "Canada" underneath a thinly drawn line. The contentious portion of the leaflet depicts a broadly smiling "Bibendum," arms crossed, with his foot raised, seemingly ready to crush underfoot an unsuspecting Michelin worker. In the same leaflet, another worker safely out of the reach of "Bibendum's" looming foot has raised a finger of warning and informs his blithe colleague, "Bob, you better move before he squashes you!" Bob, the worker in imminent danger of "Bibendum's" boot has apparently resisted the blandishments of the union since a caption coming from his mouth reads, "Naw, I'm going to wait and see what happens". Below the roughly drawn figures of the workers is the following plea in bold letters, "Don't wait until it's too late! Because the job you save may be your own. Sign today for a better tomorrow." The leaflet also gives the phone number for the CAW office in Granton. Defendant Wark, the defendant CAW's organizer for Nova Scotia, admitted that he had photocopied and prepared the leaflet with the offending "Bibendum" figure in the CAW office.

The leaflet was also reproduced as a poster and displayed on the windows of CAW offices in Granton, Waterville and Bridgewater. ...

As I have ruled that the defendants have reproduced a substantial part of the plaintiff's work and thus infringed the copyright, the burden now shifts to the defendants to prove that they fall under an exception to copyright infringement. Like the plaintiff in regards to the *Trade-marks Act,* the defendants have offered a novel argument and radical interpretation of the law. In this case, the defendants argue that parody is a form of "criticism" under paragraph 27(2)(a. 1), the relevant exception to copyright infringement.

Paragraph 27(2)(a.1) reads:

27.—

(2) The following acts do not constitute an infringement of copyright:

  (a.1) any fair dealing with any work for the purposes of criticism, review or newspaper summary, if

    (i) the source, and

    (ii) the author's name, if given in the source, are mentioned.

Parody is not explicitly discussed in the *Copyright Act.* ... [The judge reviews the case law cited.] I am not satisfied that these cases are applicable to the current matter. ... Under the *Copyright Act,* "criticism" is not synonymous with parody. Criticism requires analysis and judgment of a work that sheds on the original. Parody is defined in the *Collins Dictionary of the English Language* (2nd ed., London: Collins, 1986) as "a musical, literary or other composition that mimics the style of another composer, author, etc. in a humorous or satirical way." In *Zamacois, Miguel v. Douville, Raymond et al.* 1944] Ex. C.R. 208; (1943), 3 Fox P.C. 44, Justice Angers, at page 71 of Fox P.C. held that the court will consider the wider context, both the quantity and quality of quotations from the original, in its evaluation of a work as "criticism": "The right of literary criticism includes the right of citation of passages from the work criticized and the number or importance of the citations does not modify the character of the publication if they serve only to contribute to the demonstration of the criticism undertaken." In the Canadian and Commonwealth courts, parody has never been held to figure as criticism although the term criticism is not confined to "literary criticism."

The defendants have added a twist to this usual reasoning by urging the Court to consider in line with the recent decision of the American Supreme Court in *Luther R. Campbell a.k.a. Luke Skywalker v. Acuff-Rose Music, Inc.,* 114 S. Ct. 1164 (1994), (hereinafter *Acuff-Rose)* that parody is a form of "criticism", under paragraph 27(2)(a.1). The defendants submitted that even though their "Bibendum" constituted a reproduction of a substantial part of the plaintiff's copyright, this was a type of parody that by the very definition of the term parody required substantial reproduction of the original to make its point. The addition of the men under "Bibendum's" upraised leg, the dialogue and the alteration in "Bibendum's" expression created a new, integrated "Bibendum" design that was meant to ridicule and mock "Bibendum's" usual corporate image as a benign, smiling and safe father figure. The defendants further argued that they had no need to cite the source, a requirement

under paragraph 27(2)(a.1) since in a parody, the source is implicitly known to the onlooker.

As with the plaintiff's creative and novel interpretations of the *Trade-marks Act,* I have rejected the defendants' submissions. The defendants fall short because American case law permitting parody as criticism under the American doctrine of "fair use" is not applicable nor terribly persuasive in the Canadian context of a different legal regime and a longstanding trend to deny parody as an exception. As well, exceptions to copyright infringement should be strictly interpreted. I am not prepared to read in parody as a form of criticism and thus create a new exception under paragraph 27(2)(a.1).

...

The defendants pointed to the recent unanimous decision of the American Supreme Court in *Acuff-Rose, supra,* as sole authority for reading in parody as a component of criticism or the exception to infringement. In effect, the defendants are admitting, "Yes, we did infringe the plaintiff's copyright by copying a substantial part of the original but as a defence, we can plead that we were parodying the original, a form of fair dealing for the purpose of criticism under paragraph 27(2)(a.1)." The defendants admitted that they were urging the Court to accept a new interpretation of paragraph 27(2)(a.1) in the light of the American decision. In *Acuff-Rose,* the defendant [2 Live Crew] had used the characteristic bass riff and opening line from Roy Orbison's classic rock song, *Pretty Woman* in its own rap song with new lewd and crude lyrics and distinctive rap background motifs. Justice Souter writing for the Court held at page 1173 that the Court of Appeals had erred in overstating the parodist's commercial motive to deny the fairness of the use… : " The rap version of *Pretty Woman* could still qualify as a parody or critique of the romantic fantasy embodied in the original song and could be considered an exception to copyright infringement as fair use for the purpose of criticism under section 107 of the American statute. The United States Supreme Court remanded the case to the trial level to reconsider the rap version of *Pretty Woman* against all of the factors for "fair use" in section 107.

While the American case is most fascinating from both a cultural and legal perspective, I have not found it to be persuasive authority in the context of Canada's particular copyright regime. Chief Justice Laskin in *Morgentaler v. The Queen,* [1976] 1 .C.R. 616, held at page 629 that a court should be prudent in applying American precedents to the Canadian context and should take into consideration the particular rules of each system of law: "they do not carry any authority beyond persuasiveness according to their relevance in the light of context, with due regard to the obvious differences that exist." American decisions are only persuasive to the extent that the laws in both jurisdictions are similar: ... [The judge examines the differences between the American and Canadian copyright provisions.] I cannot accept that I should give the word "criticism" such a large meaning that it includes parody. In doing so, I would be creating a new exception to the copyright infringement, a step that only Parliament would have the jurisdiction to do.

...

Thus, I hold, in line with the prevailing Canadian authorities, that parody does not exist as criticism, an exception to acts of copyright infringement. And even if I were to follow the American authority in *Acuff-Rose* and state that parody exists as a fair dealing exception to infringement, the defendants would have failed under the two secondary elements of paragraph 27(2)(a. 1). First, the defendants did not mention the source and author's name of the original on their "Bibendum" leaflets and poster. This is condition of the fair dealing exception. ...

In addition, the defendants did not treat the original work in a fair manner, a further requirement of the "fair dealing" exception. The defendants argued that as a parody, their work could not be held to treat the copyright in a kid glove fashion. Parody has to bite and in some way batter the reputation of the original, However, once again, the defendants have sought to dilute the usual rules of the fair dealing exception and defeat the wording of paragraph 27(2)(a. 1) simply by labelling the "Bibendum" posters and leaflets a parody. It is not enough that because it is a parody, there is no need to mention the source. Now the defendants would have the Court rule that by the mere fact of the parody label, the defendants are per-

mitted to forego treating the plaintiffs copyright in a fair manner, a requirement for all the existing exceptions like criticism, review and summary. To accept the defendants' submissions on parody would be akin to making the parody label the last refuge of the scoundrel since the Court would have to do away with two of the usual strictures of paragraph 27(2)(a.1): mentioning the source and fair treatment.

(V) CONCLUSIONS ON COPYRIGHT

I am not prepared to take the two leaps of faith urged by the defendants. The first is that parody is synonymous with criticism. The second is that the defendants can dispense with the need to mention the source and fair treatment because of the peculiar nature of parody with its implicit acknowledgment of the source. My role is not to create legislation but to apply the existing rules crafted by Parliament. ...

Note: This decision was appealed, but the Federal Court advised that the parties filed Notices of Discontinuance.[24]

LICENSING

- *I*n 1989 Bill Gates, the chairman of Microsoft, incorporated Interactive Home Systems to acquire the electronic rights to photos and works of art. The company, now Corbis Corp. [Corbis = woven basket, Lat.] turns photographic negatives into electronic images. CEO Doug Rowan stated the objective of the company was to "capture the entire human experience throughout history." The licensing agreements are nonexclusive. The company operates from Bellevue, Washington, and employs photographers, photo editors, art historians, and copyright lawyers.[25]

2. BREACH OF CONFIDENCE / TRADE SECRET

Question

What does the plaintiff have to prove in order to win an action against a defendant on the grounds that the defendant breached a confidence?

International Corona Resources Ltd. was drilling exploratory holes on land on which it owned mining rights when it was approached by LAC Minerals Ltd. Discussions followed with a view to a possible partnership or joint venture. Corona revealed the results of its drilling and its interest in purchasing mineral rights of an adjacent property, the Williams property, which looked promising. At one meeting Corona discussed its efforts to secure the property. Three days later, LAC's vice-president for exploration spoke to Mrs. Williams and soon submitted a bid which led to LAC's acquisition of the property to Corona's exclusion. LAC developed a gold mine on the property.

Per La Forest of the Supreme Court of Canada on the issue of breach of confidence [p. 20]:
Breach of confidence

I can deal quite briefly with the breach of confidence issue. I have already indicated that LAC breached a duty of confidence owed to Corona. The test for whether there has been a breach of confidence is not seriously disputed by the parties. It consists in establishing three elements: that the information conveyed was confidential, that it was communicated in confidence, and that it was misused by the party to whom it was communicated. In *Coco v. A.N. Clark (Engineers) Ltd.*, [1989] R.P.C. 41 (CH.), Megarry J. (as he then was) put it as follows (p. 47):

> In my judgment, three elements are normally required if, apart from contract, a case of breach of confidence is to succeed. First, the information itself, in the words of Lord Greene, M.R. in the *Saltman* case on page 215, must "have the necessary quality of confidence about it." Secondly, that information must have been imparted in circumstances importing an obligation of confidence. Thirdly, there must be an unauthorized use of that information to the detriment of the party communicating it.

This is the test applied by both the trial judge and the Court of Appeal. Neither party contends that it is the wrong test. LAC, however, forcefully argued that the courts below erred in their application of the test. LAC submitted that "the real issue is whether Corona proved that LAC received confidential information from it and [whether] it should have known such information was confidential."

Sopinka J. has set out the findings of the trial judge on these issues, and I do not propose to repeat them. They are all supported by the evidence and adopted by the Court of Appeal. I would not interfere with them. Essentially, the trial judge found that the three elements set forth above were met: (1) Corona had communicated information that was private and had not been published. (2) While there was no mention of confidence with respect to the site visit, there was a mutual understanding between the parties that they were working towards a joint venture and that valuable information was communicated to LAC under circumstances giving rise to an obligation of confidence. (3) LAC made use of the information in obtaining the Williams property and was not authorized by Corona to bid on that property. I agree with my colleague that the information provided by Corona was the springboard that led to the acquisition of the Williams property. ... [and] that LAC committed a breach of confidence. ...

LAC Minerals Ltd. v. International Corona Resources Ltd.
61 D.L.R. (4th) 14
S.C.C.
August 11, 1989

William Black, president of the plaintiff company Wil-Can Electronics, developed a suppressor which protects electrical equipment from damage from a sudden surge of electricity. After three years of testing, the suppressor received approval of the Canadian Standards Association (CSA).

In 1984, the Ontario Provincial Police (OPP) bought a dozen of these surge suppressors for use in its telecommunications network. In 1987 the OPP called for tenders for construction of buildings the specifications for which included the Wil-Can surge suppressors "or approved equivalent."

One bidder, Mechron Energy Ltd. claimed it would provide its own model of surge suppressors with the cost of each $700 less than the Wil-Can model. To evaluate Mechron's bid, an engineer with OPP asked Black of Wil-Can to explain how Wil-Can's model worked which he did in some detail. The judge found as a fact that the information was given in confidence, but that it was passed on to Mechron which used it to duplicate the superior model of Wil-Can.

Wil-Can sued successfully for breach of confidentiality and was awarded damages equivalent to the gross profit of $1,200 per unit for 131 units, which the company most probably would have made but for the misuse of the trade secret, and $10,000 punitive damages.

Wil-Can Electronics Can Ltd. v. Ontario Ministry of the Solicitor General
Summarized from The Lawyers Weekly *January 29, 1993, p. 18. See also the editions of February 19, 1993 p. 13 for a summary of the case and March 5, 1993, p. 3 for Jeffrey Miller's comment.*

- *A* company that was licensed to manufacture and market Clamato Juice for the Canadian market and which used the recipe to develop and market Caesar cocktail after the license agreement expired was sued and found liable for the misuse of confidential information. The trial took six weeks.[26]

- *P*ierre Marion, former head of the French spy agency, admitted that the French spied on their allies' industries for years. He maintained the spying was essential to keep France abreast of technological advances. Among other projects, the agency schemed to infiltrate IBM and Texas Instruments to recruit employees as agents to pass on trade secrets useful to French companies.[27]

Question

What can I take when I leave the company?
When is it know-how and not a trade secret?

In the high-stakes business of drug manufacturing, time, secrecy and ownership are of essence. By agreement the employee promises not to disclose confidential information and agrees that inventions are the property of the employer. When Jagroop Dahiya, the biochemist who invented a process for the manufacture of an anti-cholesterol drug left Apotex Fermention Inc. for Novopharm Ltd. he took information. Was the information confidential information belonging to the company or general knowledge? Justice Monnin, in a 148-page decision, found it was a confidential trade secret and awarded the plaintiff $3.7 million.

Apotex Fermentation Inc. v. Novopharm Ltd.[28]

---

3. Passing Off

Questions

Why is the tort of passing-off significant in protecting a person's intellectual property?
What is its relationship to the law of trade marks?

Institute National des Appellations d'Origine des Vins & Eaux-de-Vie v. *Andres Wines Ltd.*

40 D.L.R.(4TH) 239
ONTARIO SUPREME COURT
JULY 2, 1987

Dupont J.:

INTRODUCTION

The plaintiffs seek injunctive relief restraining the defendants from using the appellation "Champagne" in the manufacture and sale of their products; they also seek damages for loss of sales, diminution of their market, and depreciation of goodwill allegedly resulting from the defendants' use of the appellation "Champagne." ...[T]hey base their claim for injunctive relief upon the common law action of passing off.

The plaintiff, L'Institut National des Appellations d'Origine des Vins et Eaux-de-Vie (I.N.A.O.), is a national organization established by French law; its primary duty is to regulate the areas and conditions of production and sale of wines and spirits bearing controlled appellations of origin. Its co-plaintiffs are companies incorporated under the laws of the Republic of France and carry on business as producers of wine in geographically designated areas located in that part of France described as the Champagne District.

The defendants are companies duly incorporated in Canada who for many years have been producing, advertising and selling sparkling and still wines under various names, some of which incorporate the word "champagne"; in particular, "Canadian Champagne."

The plaintiffs claim the right to sue together on their own behalf as producers of wine in the Champagne District who are engaged in the sale of champagne in Ontario. The common interest they assert is in the goodwill associated with the word "champagne"; they argue that their goodwill has been detrimentally affected by the defendants' alleged improper use of the term.

The defendants strongly take issue with such joint or collective action, submitting that this procedure is without precedent in Canadian jurisprudence and should be rejected.

They also challenge I.N.A.O.'s status as a plaintiff. Although it is not a wine producer, the I.N.A.O. is vested with legal personality and is entitled to be a party to legal proceedings. In fact, one of its functions is to institute legal proceedings for the purpose of protecting the rights of French producers of wines and spirits and of preventing the misuse of appellations of origin nationally and internationally. …

CANADIAN CASE-LAW

The Ontario Court of Appeal had occasion to deal with the law of passing off, in *Orkin Exterminating Co. Inc. v. Pestco Co. of Canada Ltd. et al.* (1985), 5 C.P.R. (3d) 433, 50 O.R. (2s) 726, 19 D.L.R. (4th) 90. … [in which it] did consider the general nature of the tort of passing off and clearly stated that, in its view, misrepresentation leading to confusion was a requisite element of the action. Quoting from *Spalding v. Gamage*, Morden J.A. wrote (p. 442 C.P.R., P. 735 O.R., p. 99 D.L.R.: "A fundamental principle upon which the tort of passing off is based is that 'nobody has any right to represent his goods…as the goods… of somebody else'." Later on, he explained (p. 450 C.P.R., p. 744 O.R., p. 108 D.L.R.): "In this kind of case I think that the main consideration should be the likelihood of confusion with consequential injury to the plaintiff."

The Supreme Court of Canada has also approved of the principle that misrepresentation is the underlying basis for an action in passing off. In *Consumers Distributing Co. Ltd. v. Seiko Time Canada Ltd.* (1984), 1 C.P.R. (3d) 1, 10 D.L.R. (4th) 161, 3 C.I.P.R. 223, the respondent, the authorized dealer of Seiko watches for Canada, sued the appellant for passing off on the ground that the appellant, who purchased genuine Seiko watches from an authorized dealer, sold the watches without warranty, point of sale service or instruction booklet. The respondent argued that without these additional features, the watches could not be sold as "Seiko" watches. It had been established by evidence that once the appellant posted a notice declaring that it was not an authorized dealer, that the watches were not purchased from the appellant and were not internationally guaranteed, no instance of public confusion had ever occurred.

The absence of confusion was considered critical by the Supreme Court because of its conception of the basis of the tort (pp. 15-6 C.P.R., p. 175 D.L.R.):

…the passing-off rule is founded upon the tort of deceit, and while the original requirement of an intent to deceive died out in the mid-1800's there remains the requirement, at the very least, that confusion in the minds of the public be a likely consequence by reason of the sale…by the defendant of a product not that of the plaintiff's making, under the guise or implication that it was the plaintiff's product or the equivalent.

In its judgment the Supreme Court of Canada quoted and approved of the following passage which defines the nature of passing off (pp. 13-4 C.P.R., p. 173 D.L.R.):

It consists of the making of some false representation to the public…likely to induce them to believe that the goods…of another are those of the plaintiff…The test laid down in such cases has been whether… the defendant's conduct results in a false representation, which is likely to cause confusion or deception, even though he has no such intention. (Prosser, *The Law of Torts*, 4th ed.)

This test is found, in various formulations, throughout reported cases. There seems no doubt that for both the House of Lords in England and the Supreme Court in Canada, a necessary, constitutive element of the tort of passing of, the very thing which causes damage to the plaintiff's goodwill, is the defendant's misrepresentation of its product which is likely to cause confusion in the public's mind between the defendant's goods and those of the plaintiff. Although the misrepresentation may take a variety of different forms, as indeed it does in each particular case, it must nevertheless exist and be established through admissible evidence by the plaintiff in order for the plaintiff to succeed in an action for passing off. In a sense "passing off" is a synonym for "misrepresentation" or "false description."

CONCLUSION

A detailed consideration of the evidence brought before the court has led me to conclude that Canadian champagne is a distinct Canadian product not likely to be confused or even compared with French champagne. This conclusion is based on the following evidence: the many years during which the defendant wine producers marketed Canadian champagne in Ontario; the manner in which the defendants' products are labelled, with the word "Canadian" displayed as prominently as the word "champagne," in compliance with government directives, so as to clearly identify the products as Canadian; the way the Canadian product has, for many years, been physically separated from French champagnes in L.C.B.O. stores and listed separately by them as well as by restaurants on their wine lists; the vast body of evidence confirming that Canadian champagne has attained a reputation of its own in Ontario.

The evidence further establishes that the Ontario public concerned with or interested in wines, as purchasers or otherwise, have not been misled and do not confuse the French and the Canadian products. The purchaser who is completely ignorant about wine and wishes to purchase a bottle of champagne for a special occasion will very likely realize the difference between the two products either by the clear labelling of both, or the difference in listing and physical location at the L.C.B.O. stores, or, finally, by the vast price differential between the products.

The evidence indicates quite clearly that the high regard and reputation of French champagne has not been affected by Ontario sales of Canadian champagne and remains well established in this province. This is supported by evidence illustrating the constantly growing sales of French champagne notwithstanding its dramatic price increases, while the price of Canadian champagne, by comparison, has remained basically stable.

I cannot agree with the plaintiffs' submission that the defendants have and continue to engage in conduct designed or likely to deceive the public; they do not misrepresent their Canadian product as one originating from the Champagne District of France or produced by any French champagne houses, nor one which is in any way connected or associated with French champagne. The marketing, advertising, labelling and general reputation of Canadian champagne, and the evidence as a whole in this regard, has satisfied the court that deception and confusion are not likely to occur in Ontario.

The evidence in support of the parties' submissions, as well as the exhibits illustrating and clarifying them, has been copious. While I have not dealt with each in this judgment, I have considered them all in order to draw justifiable inferences of fact to permit the court to arrive at a decision.

This court has concluded, for the reasons detailed throughout this judgment, that the plaintiffs have not established the defendants' misrepresentation and have therefore failed to prove all the elements which constitute the tort of passing off.

The Plaintiff's claim is dismissed.

Note: The appeal from this decision was dismissed by the Ontario Court of Appeal on January 18, 1990. The reasons for judgment began: "Mr. Justice Dupont delivered very full and careful reasons for judgment. … He dealt with all of the issues arising at trial and anticipated all of those arising in this appeal. We are in complete agreement with his conclusions" 30 C.P.R. (3d) 279. Leave to appeal to the Supreme Court of Canada was denied.[29]

- *W*alt Disney Productions successfully enjoined the West Edmonton Mall from using the name "Fantasyland" for its indoor amusement park.[30], but did not succeed in obtaining an injunction and damages against Fantasyland Hotel for passing off its hotel as "being licensed by, associated with or having the approval of Walt Disney."[31]

The patent protection period expired for the well-known drug Prozac. Manufactures of generic drugs began manufacturing a look-alike pill. The manufacturers of Prozac alleged that because the pills had the size, shape and colour of the original, the generic manufacturer was liable for, among other things, the tort of passing-off, but their action failed in the Federal Court of Appeal.

Eli Lilly and Co. v. Novopharm Ltd.
http//www.fja-cmf.gc.ca
Federal Court Trial Division
April 25, 1997

---

4. TRADE MARK

Q u e s t i o n

What constitutes infringement of one's trade mark?

697234 Ontario Inc. carrying on business as The Loose Moose Tap & Grill *v.* **The Spruce Goose Brewing Co.**

(1991) C.P.R. (3D) 449
FEDERAL COURT, TRIAL DIVISION
NOVEMBER 7, 1991

Jerome A.C.J.—This application for an interlocutory injunction came on for hearing at Toronto, Ontario, on October 7, 1991. The plaintiff owns the trade mark THE LOOSE MOOSE TAP & GRILL and seeks to restrain the defendant, pending trial, from commencing operations of a restaurant also in Toronto under the name The Spruce Goose. At the conclusion of argument, for reasons given orally from the bench, I dismissed the application and indicated that these brief written reasons would follow.

The plaintiff has operated continuously since March of 1989, a restaurant in downtown Toronto known as The Loose Moose. I accepted submissions that through the expenditure of effort and money it has had a successful operation and has established substantial goodwill. In late August of this year, the plaintiff became aware that the defendant intended to operate a restaurant called The Spruce Goose Brewing Co. Ltd. at 130 Eglinton Avenue East. It is the plaintiff's concern that the public will inevitably refer to the defendant's restaurant simply as the Spruce Goose and through an advertising campaign in the publication *Now Magazine*, it will propose to offer the same service and atmosphere to the same clientele, causing confusion with the plaintiff's registered trade mark and resulting damage.

My reasons for the dismissal of the application are that I find all relevant issues, the facts, the law and the discretionary considerations involved in injunctive relief to be uncertain at best.

FACTS

The plaintiff argues that the defendant's use of the words "spruce goose" is the focal point of this dispute and that I should find them to be so similar to the trade mark or trade name Loose Moose as to enjoin them. It is the plaintiff's contention that any connection between the defendant's intended trade name and the well-known aircraft built by Howard Hughes is incidental, the purpose and in any event the effect being to create confusion with the plaintiff's trade name and trade mark.

The defendant's documentary evidence contains photographs of the signage on the restaurant's exterior and interior decor. The exterior sign has a depiction of the Howard Hughes aircraft. The theme is carried through to the interior decor which includes murals depicting Howard Hughes, the Spruce Goose aircraft and the head and neck of the Canadian goose. Clearly, therefore, the principal factual allegations are vigorously disputed.

THE LAW

I have in mind my earlier decision in *Horn Abbot Ltd. v. Thurston Hayes Development Ltd.* (1985), 4 C.P.R. (3d) 376 (F.C.T.D.), and that of former Chief Justice Thurlow in *Mr. Submarine Ltd. v. Amandista Investments Ltd.* (1987), 19 C.P.R. (3d) 3, [1988] 3 F.C. 91, 16 C.I.P.R. 282 (C.A.). These are cases where the duplication of a substantial part of the trade mark led to interlocutory injunctions to restrain copying of high profile and highly successful trade marks. In the present case, the plaintiff asks me to do the same with respect to words that may sound the same, but are in fact different. Not only are they different, but they have a distinctive connotation in the connection with Howard Hughes and the famous aircraft. As a matter of law, therefore, the plaintiff's right to the relief sought is far from clear.

DISCRETION

The plaintiff's business has enjoyed success for over two years. The defendant's business at the time of this hearing was yet to open. If I am wrong in my conclusion and confusion is established at trial, it seems unlikely that in the interim the defendant's restaurant would inflict severe damage on the plaintiff. I also expect that what harm will occur will be capable of calculations and monetary compensation. The defendant, on the other hand, has completed all negotiations with advertisers, staff and landlord to open soon. If I were to wrongly enjoin them from opening, I would consider the injury to them to be more severe and more difficult to redress with monetary compensation. The difference is not great, but what difference there is favours the defendant.

For these reasons, on October 7, 1991, I declined the application and directed counsel to prepare the appropriate order which I signed and filed on October 17, 1991.

Application dismissed.

- *I*n Newark, New Jersey, the proprietor called his business "Dom Knows Pizza." Domino's Pizza Corporation was not amused and sued for trade mark infringement.[32]

- *I*n 1990, the proprietor of a tavern decorated with velvet paintings named his bar "Velvet Elvis" and registered the trademark. He argues the bar celebrates the phenomenon of velvet oil paintings, not Elvis. He argues that and more because Elvis Presley Enterprises Inc. has gone to court to force him to change the name.[33]

- *H*ormel Foods Corporation, the makers of Spam, a pressed meat product, has demanded that the e-mail distributor Cyber Promotions Inc. not use a picture of a can of Spam at its web site. Hormel Foods would be pleased that people not use the term "spamming" for wholesale distribution of junk e-mail.[34]

- *W*atch for the lawsuits against those who register domain names such as "the-spice-girls.com." In 1996 a court in the U.K. ruled that the person who had registered "harrods.com" had to relinquish it to the famous Harrods department store.[35]

- *I*n 1981 the Beatles' company Apple Corps Limited gave the California Computer company, Apple Computer Inc. the right to use the Apple name and logo similar to its own as long as it did not sell machines "intended for synthesizing music." By 1989 Apple computers were used to compose and play music. Apple Corps Limited asked the court to order them to call the musical computers something else or pay a substantial licensing fee.[36]

Miss Universe Inc. had its appeal dismissed by the Federal Court Trial Division. The company appealed the decision of the Registrar of trade-marks who allowed the registration of the trade mark "Miss Nude Universe." Among his reasons for dismissing the appeal, Judge Strayer said "while the two trade-marks have two words in common, my first impression when looking at the two is that the word "Nude" in the middle of the Applicant's trade-mark is of an arresting significance which would convey to all but the most indifferent reader a profound difference between the two contests. Therefore the Applicant's trade-mark is distinctive."

Miss Universe, Inc. v. Dale Bohna
Court No. T-976-91
Federal Court of Canada, Trial Division
July 3, 1992

The Federal Court of Appeal allowed the appeal and refused registration of the applicant's mark Miss Nude Universe. It found that the 30-year use of the mark Miss Universe in promotion of beauty pageants and goods resulted in its being a very distinctive and famous mark that should be given a "wide scope" of protection. It noted as one of the errors of the trial court was its focusing on the word "nude" where the resemblance of the two marks was evident.[37]

- *H*ogg Wyld Ltd. and Oink, Inc. of New Mexico, manufacturers of jeans to fit large women, were unsuccessfully sued by Jordache Enterprises for using a mark that included the name "Lardashe."[38]

- *M*attel Inc. the manufacturers of Barbie and Ken dolls successfully sued Michael and Saundra Cherwenka for trademark infringement. The Cherwenkas performed as nude dancers under the names of Malibu Barbie and Malibu Ken. In a consent decree the couple agreed to quit using references to the Ken and Barbie dolls and Ms. Cherwenda also agreed to stop wearing the type of chiffon dresses associated with the Barbie doll.[39]

Q u e s t i o n s

Can you use your competitor's trademark in comparison advertising?
What does the court consider before it will grant an interlocutory injunction prohibiting the use of the trademark?

Future Shop Ltd. *v.* *A. & B. Sound Ltd.*

[1994] 8 W.W.R. 376
BRITISH COLUMBIA SUPREME COURT
APRIL 14, 1994

MacKenzie J.:—The plaintiffs (hereinafter referred to as "Future Shop") apply for an interlocutory injunction to restrain the defendants (hereinafter referred to as "A. & B. Sound") from referring to Future Shop trademarks in comparative advertising. The parties are each engaged in the retail sale of commercial electronic products. Future Shop operates nationwide in Canada with a few outlets in the United States. A. & B. Sound's outlets are confined to British Columbia and Alberta. Future Shop's sales overall are substantially greater than sales of A. & B. Sound but both have annual sales in excess of $100,000,000.

"The Future Shop" is a registered trademark of Future Shop; the plaintiffs have also applied for registration of "Future Shop" and "Future Shop Ltd." For the purposes of this application, A. & B. Sound concedes that all three names are trademarked and they are treated as interchangeable hereafter.

The complaint before me relates to the use by A. & B. Sound of the Future Shop trademark in comparative advertisements of A. & B. Sound. For the purposes of this application, the ads are otherwise accepted as fair and accurate. Both sides are competitors in a highly price-sensitive mass market and both use advertising techniques that could be described as aggressive. Each side accuses the other of publishing advertisements that are false and misleading. However, the issues of falsity and deceptiveness of some of the advertisements have been left to other motions to be heard on another day and it is agreed that only the reference to the Future Shop trademark in A. & B. Sound ads is put in issue on this motion.

Future Shop claims that A. & B. Sound's use of its trademark name is in violation of its trademark rights pursuant to s. 19 and s. 22(1) of the *Trade Marks Act*, R.S.C. 1985, c.T-13. Future Shop also relies on the definition of "use" in s. 2 of the statute and the "deemed use" provision of s.4.

For ease of reference, s. 19 and s. 22(I) are as follows:

Rights conferred by registration

19. Subject to sections 21 and 32, the registration of a trade-mark in respect of any wares or services, unless shown to be invalid, gives to the owner of the trade-mark the exclusive right to the use throughout Canada of the trade-mark in respect of those wares or services.

Depreciation of goodwill

22.(1) No person shall use a trade-mark registered by another person in a manner that is likely to have the effect of depreciating the value of the goodwill attaching thereto.

The authorities establish a two-part test for interlocutory injunctive relief which may be conveniently summarized as, first, a threshold question whether there is "a fair issue to be tried" and, if the applicant satisfies the threshold test, secondly whether the balance of convenience favours granting the relief. ...

"FAIR QUESTION TO BE TRIED"

The proposition pressed most strenuously by Mr. Dyer on behalf of Future Shop was that the use of the Future Shop name in a comparative ad was "likely to depreciate the value of the goodwill attaching" to the Trademark in breach of s. 22(l). This section was first interpreted by Thurlow J. in *Clairol International Corp. v. Thomas Supply & Equipment Co.*, [1968] 2 Ex. C.R. 552. ...

There is no provision similar to s. 22 in any other jurisdiction and it is capable of a sweeping ambit. Thurlow J. notes that it could be interpreted to extend to comparative price lists identified by trademarks displayed in a poster by a shopkeeper on his counter. He concludes that s. 22 was not intended "to forbid legitimate comparisons or criticisms of that kind." There is no difference in principle between a counter display of comparative prices and a newspaper, radio or T.V. advertisement containing the same information. ...

Thurlow J. was persuaded that the injunction should be granted, as I read his reasons because Revlon tried to attach to its products the favourable image which the Clairol colour chart had in the market. Clairol was the colour leader and Revlon did not seek to distance its colours from Clairol's. Rather, Revlon's use of the Clairol colour chart was intended to convey the message in effect, "Our colours are so close to Clairol's as to be just as good. "Revlon thereby sought to capitalize on the similarities of its products to those of Clairol and appropriate a part of the Clairol goodwill in so doing. A comparative ad which by obvious and reasonable implication stresses the differences between the advertiser's product and that of the competition does not attach itself to the competitor's goodwill in the same manner. Rather, it seeks to distance itself from that goodwill by stressing the differences. This would explain the contrast between the result which Thurlow J. reached with respect to the Revlon package, which he enjoined, and his illustration of the comparative pricing poster, which he concluded would not offend s. 22(l).

The question, depending on the evidence in any particular case, is whether the use of the competitor's trademark is for a purpose which stresses the similarities or the differences with the trademarked competition. If the purpose is to stress the similarities, the value of the goodwill associated with the trademark is appropriated in a manner contrary to the intent of s. 22. If use stresses the differences with the trademark, then the use is for the purpose of distancing the trademarked ware or service and 22 is not offended. ...

... In my view, the *Clairol* decision supports the position of A. & B. Sound that their fair and accurate comparative price ads do not offend s. 22(l) of the *Trade Marks Act*. ...

Returning to *Clairol*, as Thurlow J. noted, s. 22 is a unique provision capable of substantially divergent interpretation. Insofar as I am aware, it has not been definitively interpreted by an appellate court in Canada. The broad construction pressed by Future Shop would preclude comparative pricing, at least of services, and prohibit comparative price ads of a type that are commonplace in contemporary retail advertising of price-sensitive products, among grocery stores for example. For that reason, I share the reservations of the merits of a broad interpretation of s. 22 expressed by Thurlow and Reed JJ. I doubt that an expansive interpretation will ultimately prevail. But at the present stage of the evolution of the jurisprudence, I cannot say that the position advanced by Future Shop is untenable. Accordingly, I conclude that Future Shop's position raises a "fair issue to be tried" and Future Shop has met the threshold test.

I do not think that s. 19 adds anything to the strength of Future Shop's argument. I do not think that a reference to a trademark for the purpose of distinguishing the trademarked ware or service offends the exclusive right to use the trademark confirmed by s. 19.

BALANCE OF CONVENIENCE

In *Canadian Broadcasting Corp. v. CKPG Television Ltd.* (1992), 64 B.C.L.R. (2d) 96 [[1992] 3 W.W.R. 279] (C.A.), Lambert J.A. summarized the second prong, of the *Wale* test in these terms (at p. 102)-

> I would also adopt and follow the approach of Madam Justice McLachlin to the second prong of the test, namely, the assessment of balance of convenience. I would summarize that approach in this way: in assessing the balance of convenience. a judge should consider these points: the adequacy of damages as a remedy for the applicant if the injunction is not granted, and for the respondent if an injunction is granted; the likelihood that if damages are finally awarded they will be paid; the preservation of contested property; other factors affecting whether harm from the granting or refusal of the injunction would be irreparable; which of the parties has acted to alter the balance of their relationship and so affect the status quo; the strength of the applicant's case; any factors affecting the public interest; and any other factors affecting the balance of justice and convenience.
>
> It should be noted that the strength of the applicant's case is a separate factor, which should be considered under the second prong of the test, quite apart from the question under the first prong of the test of whether the applicant has established a fair question to be tried. But the assessment of the relative strength of the parties' cases must recognize the degree to which those cases have not yet been revealed because of the nature of the evidence and the way it has been presented on the injunction application, which may be markedly different from the way it would be presented at trial.

This case does not raise a question of preservation of contested property or the ability of either party to pay an award of damages made at trial. The other factors referred to are in issue. The approach to be taken to these factors, according to Lambert J.A. is as follows (at p. 103):

> ... the process of applying the second prong of the test is not a process of considering each possible factor separately, and then doing a tally, nor is it a process that can be

regarded as effectively discharged by the mechanical application of a formula or checklist of points. Rather, it is a process of assessing all of the relevant factors at one time and in one unified context and reaching a single overall conclusion about where the balance of convenience rests.

Future Shop contends that it will suffer harm that cannot be compensated for in damages if the injunction is not granted. It submits that the potential damage to its reputation is unquantifiable and cannot be adequately repaired by an award of damages.

The parties are large retailers of consumer items where price competition is intense. A. & B. Sound pursues a strategy of seeking to attract customers by highlighting its low prices in comparison with those of its competitors by ads which, for the purposes of this application, are assumed to be otherwise fair and accurate. An injunction would deprive A. & B. Sound of that option, at least with respect to Future Shop, and likely work to its disadvantage in the battle for market share. Consumers face a bewildering array of products and prices; comparative information helps them to make better choices. The public has an interest in comparative advertising, providing it is fair and accurate. I think that the impact upon the market share of the parties from either granting or refusing an injunction is difficult to measure but equally imponderable either way. ...

As discussed above, Future Shop's case is arguable but weak. The dispute involves two large and, I think, essentially responsible retailers engaged in a hotly contested struggle for market share. To the extent there is a status quo, refusal of the injunction will best maintain the status quo until all the issues between the parties can be thoroughly canvassed at trial. I conclude that the balance of convenience favours refusing this injunction.

This application has been argued against a background of advertisements by each side which have been challenged by the other as false and deceptive. Each has responded to this criticism by modifying its advertising. Some of those modifications have been confirmed by solicitors' unndertakings. Irritants still remain and criticism continues, but the parties seem to have made considerable progress in resolving their differences. Future Shop fears a repetition, at a sensitive time in the marketing year, of an ad similar to the so-called "Pinocchio" ad of A. & B. Sound which portrayed Future Shop with a long liar's nose. A. & B. Sound has agreed not to repeat the Pinocchio ad but has not ruled out ads of a similar nature in the future. The Pinocchio ad was offensive and Future Shop's indignation and desire to avoid any repetition is understandable. In a struggle for customers, emotions can run high even for large, sophisticated retailers. It appears to me that the Pinocchio ad was probably an over-reaction to any provocation present in Future Shop ads. The parties ought not to let emotion overcome good judgment. There are limits to legitimate advertising and the courts of necessity will determine those limits if the issues are pressed. But limits set by the courts are unlikely to be as satisfactory to either side as limits which they devise themselves as experienced retailers and agree to respect. The progress which the parties have made to date suggests that they ought to be able to complete the process.

The application for an interlocutory injunction on the terms argued before me is denied.

Application dismissed.

- *T*he ad showed two pies. One had a bottom crust inverted over the bottom crust. It looked silly. It was labelled "Maple Leaf" with the words "their idea of a top crust." Robin Hood's pie had a proper "lattice-work" top. Maple Leaf applied for an injunction. It argued that the ads were false and misleading. The court found that the balance of convenience favoured Maple Leaf and granted the injunction.[40]

Q u e s t i o n

Could I make an agreement with my competitor about the use of my trademark in comparative advertising?

Eveready Canada v. *Duracell Canada Inc.*

64 C.P.R. (3D) 348
ONTARIO COURT (GENERAL DIVISION)
NOVEMBER 9, 1995

Lane J. (orally)—This motion involves a dispute over whether the defendant is in breach of obligations under the *Trade-marks Act,* R.S.C. 1985, c. T-13, and under an agreement between the parties, in broadcasting a T.V. commercial in which it makes a claim that its batteries are superior to the batteries of the plaintiff.

Strictly speaking, I am faced with an application brought on very short notice and a request by the defendant for an adjournment. However, bearing in mind the evidence that the next several weeks are the heaviest selling season for the products in question, I have elected to treat this matter as if it was an application for the injunction itself realizing that if I place the defendant upon terms that it withdraw the advertisement pending the completion of preparation for the formal motion, the effect is the same as enjoining it for an important part of the selling season. ...

The advertisement in question is called "Staying Alive." It is a colour TV commercial of 30 seconds in length. There is a brief showing of a superscript which reads "The Copper Top Tops Them All" which is agreed to be a claim for superiority of the defendant's product over all other batteries and therefore, clearly over the batteries of the plaintiff.

The theme of superiority is also carried through the imagery of the commercial. The commercial shows a party going on. The partygoers are in costume. A unicorn, which has the defendant's battery strapped to his back and is therefore powered by it, outdances all other dancers until at the last, he dances with a masked dancer in a blue dress. He dances vigorously, she dances more languorously. She collapsed in a heap, her mask falls away revealing a pink bunny whose eyes close as she expires. The unicorn then dances up the stairs.

There was some debate over whether or not the pink bunny was actually dead or not, but I regard this as a somewhat esoteric debate. The implication is very, clear that the battery of the defendant powering the unicorn is far superior to the battery of the plaintiff powering the pink bunny.

These parties both have pink bunnies as trade marks. It is conceded by Mr. Skea [Vice-President of Marketing for the defendant] in giving his evidence this afternoon that the pink bunny in the commercial is intended to represent the plaintiff's trade mark pink bunny. The bunny is, however, not dressed in the fashion that is characteristic of the plaintiff's bunny in that it is not

beating a drum and it is not wearing sun-glasses. This, however, does not seem to be a distinction with a lot of difference for the present since, as I say, it is conceded that the pink bunny is intended to represent the plaintiffs trade mark. Having seen the commercial myself in court, I would not have any doubt that it would be so recognized by at least a good many consumers.

Now the fact that these parties both have pink bunnies, albeit differently got up, has apparently led to some confusion in the past and in order to minimize that confusion the parties have entered into an agreement, one clause of which is of some importance in this litigation. That is an agreement of January 10, 1992, which recites the background of the use of pink bunnies by each of them, defines the plaintiff's pink bunny as one that wears sun-glasses, carries a drum bearing an Eveready trade mark and shoes known as flip-flops and the defendant's bunny as a pink bunny with and without a drum. There are also drawings of these bunnies attached.

The agreement requires the parties to exercise good faith efforts to avoid confusion between the two bunnies and then in para. 5 provides as follows:

> The parties agree that neither party will use the other's bunny, or a bunny confusingly similar thereto, in comparative advertising unless the advertising party makes an unambiguous and truthful claim that the advertiser's brand possesses service-life superiority.

Also of importance in the litigation is s. 52(l) of the *Competition Act,* R.S.C. 1985, c. C-34, which reads as follows:

52(l)   No person shall, for the purpose of promoting, directly or indirectly, the supply or use of a product or for the purpose of promoting, directly or indirectly, any business interest, by any means whatever,

   (b) make a representation to the public in the form of a statement, warranty or guarantee of the performance, efficacy or length of life of a product that is not based on an adequate and proper test thereof, the proof of which lies on the person making the representation;

The plaintiff submits that there is a serious issue to be tried here as to the right of the defendant to broadcast this commercial. In the first place, it says that claim for superiority is contrary to s. 52 just read because, the defendant does not have in its possession any testing of the plaintiff's product that can support the claim of superiority.

The facts appear to be these: in 1994 the defendant made an adjustment in its product to make its batteries somewhat more long-lived than the batteries of the plaintiff. The defendant has in its possession tests, a summary of which was put in as ex. "1," showing that its batteries had an average superiority of about 13% over the batteries of the plaintiff in testing done of batteries manufactured by the plaintiff in March, April, May and June of this year.

The plaintiff contends, however, that as of the broadcasting of this advertisement beginning I am told some 15 days ago and therefore in the last week of October, the tests of the defendant are no longer accurate because commencing in July, 1995, the plaintiff began to manufacture a different battery which is more powerful and which, on the defendant's own evidence, has never been tested by the defendant against the plaintiff's battery. This battery was manufactured starting in July and no batteries of the older kind have been manufactured since then. By October the new battery was beginning to appear on retail shelves.

Mr. Skea testified for the defendant that upon being advised by the president of the plaintiff on November 1, 1995, that it was the president's opinion that the advertisement could no longer be supported because of this change in manufacture, he, that is Mr. Skea, personally went out and examined retail stock in three stores in the western part of Metropolitan Toronto and sent a colleague to examine stock in an unidentified number of stores and neither he nor his colleague could find any batteries that had been manufactured by the plaintiff with the new formula. He also said that the reports from field representatives of the defendant across Canada had so far not revealed any batteries of the plaintiff bearing any kind of special insignia or advertising material to indicate that they were new or improved or anything like that. However, his evidence fell short of saying that there were no such batteries on the market.

Now there are in evidence certain tests of the plaintiff which the defendant argues show that its batteries have a continuing small, but in its submission important, superiority over the plaintiff's batteries. The plaintiff counters that its evidence shows parity in one important category of battery and statistically insignificant differences in another category of battery. The two categories together account for about 80% of the market, so that for most consumers, these two sizes are the batteries they will assume are being compared. They are the commercially important batteries for our purposes.

Can the defendant on this evidence meet the test of s. 52 of the *Competition Act* or the truthfulness requirement in the agreement? ... I take "truthful" in the agreement to have been used in a commercially reasonable sense. The parties could not have meant to rely upon statistically and commercially insignificant differences in their products and so I approach the matter from the viewpoint that in order for the commercial's claim for superiority to be regarded as truthful, it must be based upon some kind of significant differences between the products.

I think from a technical point of view the defendant would have trouble meeting the test of s. 52 because it has done no testing of its own on the latest batteries and I think it is stretching the section somewhat to suggest that the defendant can justify its advertisement by seizing, after the event, on the plaintiff's testing. The intent of the section is clearly that no one shall put a commercial of this sort out into the stream of commerce without doing testing himself in advance to ensure that the claim that is being made is true.

I am also of the view that the differences that are demonstrated by the plaintiffs evidence of testing may well, as the plaintiff's witness suggests in his affidavit, fall into the category of differences that are not statistically or commercially significant.

I conclude that there is a serious issue to be tried as to whether in the last 15 days while this commercial has been aired, the necessary proof of superiority existed and whether the claim is indeed a truthful one within the meaning of the agreement between the parties. Having concluded there is a serious issue to be tried, I turn to the balance of convenience and the question of irreparable harm.

The harm to both parties that is most obvious is in the area of lost sales. If I permit the commercial to continue, the plaintiff will likely lose sales. If I direct that it be withdrawn, the defendant, will likely lose sales. Neither party could readily measure the sales which it has lost. If the advertisement is continued, the plaintiff cannot be sure to what extent any reduction in its sales can be attributed to the advertisement as opposed to other factors. Likewise, if the advertisement is withdrawn, the defendant cannot readily measure the sales impact of the loss of the advertising because it cannot know what it would have sold if it had continued the advertising. So both such losses are irreparable in the sense in which the cases use that term.

If the advertisement is withdrawn, the defendant will also lose the cost of making the commercial. However, that is not irreparable harm; that is a known figure and compensation can be given for that.

The plaintiff argues that the commercial directly attacks its trade mark bunny and denigrates it. Although, as I have noted, the dying bunny is not wearing sun-glasses nor is she beating a drum, it is admitted that it is intended to depict the plaintiffs bunny trade mark and, as I have said, it so appears to me.

The defendant responds that the agreement allows the use of the plaintiff's trade mark by the defendant in a comparative advertisement making an unambiguous and truthful claim and accordingly, the use of the trade mark cannot form the basis for a lawsuit. I have already mentioned that I think there is a serious issue about whether or not the claim is a truthful one. But there is a further point and that is, that having considered the nature of this agreement, I cannot accept that these two enormous business enterprises with the huge investments that each has, on the evidence, in their respective trade marks, intended to subject their trade marks to visual humiliation at the hands of the other party in comparative advertising. It makes no commercial sense to think that these parties had the intention of putting their trade marks at that kind of risk. And it is not essential in giving full meaning to the language of the clause, to take it that far. It makes commercial sense to read the clause as allowing the fair depiction of the other side's trade mark so as to make clear who is the target of the superiority claim. But it seems to me that a very serious issue exists as to the fairness of the treatment of the plaintiff's trade mark by the defendant within the context of the activity permitted under the agreement cl. 5.

For these reasons, I have concluded that the potential damage to the plaintiff is in a different realm than the potential damage to the defendant. The loss of sales is one thing. Damage which may be long lasting or even permanent to a valuable

trade mark is another thing altogether. For these reasons, I find that the balance of convenience favours the plaintiff.

Accordingly, the motion for an injunction will be adjourned but upon terms that the advertisement is withdrawn during the term of the adjournment.

Motion adjourned.

Question

What kind of evidence can be introduced to defend against a claim of passing-off or trade mark infringement?

Tony the Tiger v. Esso Tiger: The plaintiffs alleged passing-off and trademark infringement by the Esso Tiger. The defendant pleaded that TONY THE TIGER has coexisted with the ESSO TIGER for 30 years in 17 countries. When the plaintiffs refused to produce evidence relating to the co-existence claim, the Senior Master ordered them to do so. This action is an appeal to the court to determine whether evidence of co-existence without confusion in other countries may be relevant to the passing-off and trade-mark infringement claims asserted by the plaintiff. The following is an excerpt from the decision of Justice Kiteley.

"… Based on this review, a number of conclusions can be drawn.

"Firstly, the discretion of the Registrar in applications for registration is circumscribed by the fact that the *Trade-marks Act* applies in Canada. The territorial jurisdiction for which the trade-mark is granted is Canada. Consequently, on appeals from decisions of the Registrar, the court is similarly circumscribed.

"Secondly, even in that context, the authorities seem to be evolving in the direction that there may be circumstances in which co-existence in other countries without confusion may be relevant.

"Thirdly, when civil proceedings are involved in which the plaintiff claims damages or injunctive relief, the pleadings have a significant impact. If the pleadings raise confusion in other countries, the evidence is relevant. It follows that if the evidence is relevant, oral and documentary discovery is also relevant.

"Earlier, I referred to two paragraphs of the pleadings. A more detailed review of the pleadings is required. The plaintiff Kellogg Company is a U.S. corporation. The plaintiff Kellogg Canada Inc. is a Canadian corporation and a wholly owned subsidiary of the U.S company. The defendant is a Canadian company. The plaintiffs allege that TONY THE TIGER was introduced in Canada in 1952, and that it has become strongly identified in the Canadian public with the plaintiffs' [cereal] products. The plaintiffs also allege that the defendant did not use the ESSO TIGER in Canada until 1992 when the whimsical tiger was introduced which is "strikingly similar" to TONY THE TIGER. The plaintiffs allege that the defendant's activities have given rise "to a likelihood of confusion … amongst the Canadian public, that the plaintiffs or either of them and Imperial Oil are associated in some way."—The plaintiffs' claims pursuant to sections 7(b), 19 and 20 of the *Trade-marks Act* are related to use and confusion in Canada. The claims for depreciation of goodwill pursuant to section 22, for misappropriation of reputation, goodwill and personality, and for infringement of copyright are not geographically limited.

"The defendant alleges that the ESSO TIGER was created in 1964 and used in television advertising in Canada from 1965 to 1969. Since then the ESSO TIGER has been used in print advertising and product brochures, for local and regional programs and special events, and as a corporate identifier. The defendant alleges that the ESSO TIGER is recognized as one of the most famous international corporate identifiers in the world. In that context, it alleges the co-existence without confusion has occurred for almost 30 years in 17 countries other than Canada. The defendant denies the similarity and asserts that, in any event, there are different fields of use. The defendant denies that there is any passing-off or trademark infringement. In reply, the plaintiffs allege that if the defendant did use the ESSO TIGER in Canada in 1964, it had long since abandoned use.

"It is apparent from this summary that the focus of the plaintiffs' claims is damages for activities of the defendant within Canada. But that does not mean that the defendant is compelled to answer only with respect to Canada; the defendant had the option to put into issue a history of co-existence without confusion in other countries.

"For the foregoing reasons, I answer the first question of law in the affirmative. Co-existence without confusion outside Canada is relevant. ...

"... On the basis of the above review, I cannot find that it is plain and obvious that co-existence without confusion in other countries over a prolonged period of time does not disclose a defence to a claim based on passing-off and trade-mark infringement. I agree with the defendant's counsel that, at best the plaintiffs have shown that such evidence was, historically, viewed with some hesitation, but that such evidence is currently, more likely considered relevant, particularly if the issue is raised in the pleadings. The test is the likelihood of confusion. The burden of proof is on the plaintiff to prove that there is a likelihood. If, as alleged by the plaintiffs, there was a hiatus of many years in Canada, co-existence without confusion in other countries may be significant on the issue of likelihood of confusion in Canada. Where the issue is the tendency of similar marks to cause confusion, experience in similar market places, at least at this stage, is *prima facie* relevant."

Kellogg Co. et al. v. Imperial Oil Ltd.
136 D.L.R. (4th) 686
Ontario Court (General Division)
April 30, 1996

• *T*he trial judge held that the survey used by the plaintiff was inadmissible because it was improperly conducted. Without the admission of the survey results, the plaintiff's passing-off action failed. The court of appeal upheld the lower court's decision not only with regard to the passing-off action, but also with the trial judge's dismissal of the plaintiffs' claims of trademark infringement, unlawful interference with contractual relations, violations of the *Trade Practice Act*, the *Competition Act* and the *Criminal Code*. The successful defendant against this onslaught? Pepsi-Cola. The defeated plaintiffs? Twenty-one hockey teams, their unincorporated organization—The National Hockey League—and the National Hockey League Services Inc. The cause of the excitement? Pepsi's contest called the "Diet-Pepsi $4,000,000 Pro-Hockey Play-offs Pool" advertised during the 1990 Stanley Cup Play-offs.[41]

5. PATENT

Question

What is patentable?

- *T*he Fellows of Harvard College are appealing to the Federal Court of Appeal for a reversal of the decision of the Commissioner of Patents who rejected its petition for a patent on its mouse on the grounds that the mouse is primarily created by nature, not man. The mouse has been genetically altered to be more susceptible to cancer.[42]

- *M*r. Moore suffered from leukemia which resulted in an enlarged spleen. The spleen was removed and without his knowledge his doctor at the University of California Los Angeles Medical Centre used some of the tissue to create a laboratory cell line which he patented. The cells could be used to make drugs capable of controlling the count of white blood cells, which would be useful for the treatment of leukemia and AIDS. Mr. Moore sued for battery, fraud, unjust enrichment and conversion.

  The California Supreme Court held that he should have been informed of the doctor's research interests but he did not have a property right in the cell line. The Court of Appeal, in a 2-1 decision, held that Moore did have a property right to his spleen. The issue as to whether or not human tissue is considered tangible personal property was appealed to the U.S. Supreme Court.[43]

INFRINGEMENT

- *D*igital Equipment Corporation has sued Intel Corporation, which Digital alleges stole its patented chip designs and used them to develop the Pentium chip.[44]

- *T*he allegations of patent infringement by the brand-name drug companies against the manufacturers of generic drugs will continue to occupy front page news until the Parliamentarians settle Canada's position on the issue of generic drugs. Since the passage of C-91 which increased patent protection for the drug companies the increase in the cost of drugs has threatened our health care system.[45]

- *I*n 1985 Polaroid won its case (begun in 1976) against Eastman Kodak Co. for infringing on its patent on instant photography. In 1990 the court assessed the damages at $909.4 million.[46]

6. INDUSTRIAL DESIGN

- *M*irabai Art Glass of Ontario asked the court for an interlocutory injunction against Paradise Designs of Vancouver to stop it from selling designer toilet plungers, a popular Christmas present. The request was refused.[47]

7. REMEDIES

ANTON PILLER ORDER

Profekta International Inc. *v.* *Mai*

T-1995-95
http//www.fja-cmf.gc.ca
FEDERAL COURT TRIAL DIVISION
AUGUST 29, 1996.

McKeown J.: The plaintiff seeks an Anton Piller order on an *ex parte* and *in camera* basis, for the detention, custody and preservation of copies of video-cassette taped programs allegedly in the control of the defendant and allegedly infringing the plaintiff's rights as the exclusive Canadian licensee for those programs.

THE FACTS

The plaintiff filed a statement of claim on September 22, 1995. The plaintiff's statement of claim alleges that: 1) the defendant has knowingly infringed copyright in video-cassette taped programs owned by Television Broadcasts Limited of Hong Kong; 2) it is the exclusive Canadian licensee for the programs and as such possesses an interest protected pursuant to the provisions of the *Copyright Act*, R.S.C., 1985, c. C-42 (the Act) and the plaintiff licenses retail video stores to rent the programs to the public, and; 3) the defendant, who operates a retail store, rents out the programs on video-cassette tapes without the plaintiff's permission in violation of the Act.

[Although the plaintiff requested an affidavit of documents— and video-cassette tapes are "documents" within the meaning of the Federal Court Rules [C.R.C., c. 663]—the defendant has twice failed to give an accurate listing. The plaintiff knows they are inaccurate because the plaintiff's investigator has rented offending videos from the defendant's store.]

The plaintiff has brought this motion for an Anton Piller order in part on the basis that the defendant's failure to provide an accurate and complete affidavit of documents, despite having been expressly asked. ...

ANALYSIS

An Anton Piller order is a remedy which should be granted in only the rarest of circumstances as it confers on the moving party a search and seizure power which runs contrary to the principles of private property and trespass. Accordingly, an Anton Piller order must only be granted where the moving party has satisfied a burdensome test. As was enunciated in the original case dealing with such an order, *Anton Piller K.G. v. Manufacturing Processes Ltd.*, [1976] R.P.C. 719 (C.A.), the moving party must first demonstrate that it has an extremely strong *prima facie* case; secondly, that the potential for damage is very serious, and; thirdly, there must be clear evidence that the other party has in its possession incriminating documents or things, and that there is a real possibility that the other party may destroy such material before any application *inter partes* can be made. Furthermore, in my view, after an action has been commenced, I must be satisfied that it is appropriate to proceed in the absence of the other party.

I will indicate at the outset of these reasons that I am satisfied that the plaintiff has demonstrated that there is an extremely strong *prima facie* case. The plaintiff provided documentary evidence of its interest in the copyright which subsists in these programs through an exclusive licensing agreement with the owners of the copyright. There is no evidence that the defendant has any authority to rent video-cassette tapes of the programs to the public. Thus, there is a serious issue to be tried. Furthermore, the potential for damage is very serious and there is clear evidence that the defendant has in her possession video-cassette tapes which she rents out without the plaintiff's permission in violation of the Act and I am satisfied that there is a real possibility that the defendant may destroy the tapes before any application *inter partes* can be made.

Practically speaking, so that these orders have their intended effect, Anton Piller orders are most often sought on an *ex parte* basis. This is to ensure the element of surprise in the sense that, as the defending party is not given notice of the order, there is no opportunity for the offending documents or things to be destroyed or removed. In addition, Anton Piller orders are, generally speaking, sought either before or at the onset of court proceedings as it is at this point that the plaintiff becomes aware that such an order is necessary. This particular motion is unusual in the sense of its timing. The plaintiff brings this motion midway through the proceedings, after the usual discovery process has begun. Because the matter is so far advanced, both parties are represented by counsel. It is because this motion is brought *ex parte* and because of its timing that it poses difficulties which in my view had to be addressed by counsel for the plaintiff.

[The judge reviews the case law including *Yousif v. Salama* in which an Anton Piller order was granted. He quotes Lord Denning for the majority and Justice Donaldson for a very strong dissent.] ...

In my view, as was the case in *EMI Ltd.* and in *Yousif*, there is compelling evidence that if the defendant were provided with notice of this motion, the plaintiff's litigation will be "unfairly and improperly frustrated." The plaintiff has, through the affidavit of its private investigator, provided this Court with compelling evidence that there is a probability, and more than a possibility, that were the defendant to be given notice of this motion, the evidence being sought would disappear. I must state, however, that I come to this conclusion reluctantly as I am loathe to proceed in any matter where there is legal counsel, without providing counsel with the opportunity to be heard.

The second issue which counsel for the plaintiff addressed was whether seeking an Anton Piller order is appropriate at this stage of the proceedings, where the parties have already begun the ordinary discovery process. The Federal Court Rules provide for discovery between parties through the exchange of affidavits of documents and in the case at bar, the parties have, at least in form, complied with this requirement. The plaintiff is not satisfied with the affidavit of documents provided by the defendant, and has tendered to the Court, evidence that the affidavit of documents is deficient. In these circumstances, I am faced with two applicable Federal Court Rules. First, there is Rule 453. ... Under ordinary circumstances, where a party is dissatisfied with an affidavit of documents, Rule 453 provides the appropriate course of action. Upon motion for an order under that Rule, the opposing parties would be afforded the opportunity to satisfy the Court as to whether or not the affidavit of documents at issue is accurate.

However, in the present circumstances, there is also Rule 470, under which Rule the plaintiff in the case at bar moves, which contemplates that this Court may make, *inter alia*, an order such as an Anton Piller order, for the detention, custody and preservation of property. In this case, the plaintiff is relying on the allegedly inaccurate affidavit of documents as the evidence that an Anton Piller order is required. Rather than seek to obtain an order requiring an accurate affidavit of documents, the plaintiff has chosen the more extreme route of being granted the power to enter onto the defendant's premises and seize those documents which it alleges are present there and which are not listed on the affidavit of documents. To proceed in this manner is to circumvent the ordinary discovery process in a major way. Counsel for the plaintiff has cited authority for the proposition that Anton Piller orders may be granted long after the proceedings between the parties have commenced and advanced. ...

... Thus, the plaintiff in this case had the choice of which Rule under which to proceed and it chose Rule 470; the only limitation on proceeding in that manner is, of course, that the plaintiff must meet the stringent test that is applicable to the granting of Anton Piller orders. ... To use Mr. Justice Sharpe's words, quoted above, the plaintiff must demonstrate that this is a case where there is "compelling evidence that the defendant is bent on flouting the process of the court by refusing to abide by the ordinary procedure of discovery." In my view, the affidavit evidence of the plaintiff's private investigator provides this compelling evidence. The defendant has twice remitted an affidavit of documents to the plaintiff, each of which, on the evidence presented to this Court, is inaccurate; the private investigator's evidence is that he has rented seven programs which properly should have been disclosed, but have not been. The defendant has been given two opportunities to comply with this Court's Rules, and I am satisfied on the evidence that she has failed to do so. … [I]n my view, this is one of the rare cases where the evidence demonstrates that the ordinary discovery process will not have its intended effect and an Anton Piller order is appro-

priate. It should be noted that the courts are careful to ensure that Anton Piller orders are not used as tools for fishing expeditions. I am satisfied, in light of the private investigator's evidence with respect to his having rented seven allegedly infringing videos, that the plaintiff is not seeking this motion as part of a fishing expedition. On the evidence, I draw the inference that there are additional allegedly infringing video-cassette tapes at the defendant's retail premises.

In my view, the plaintiff has met the three parts of the test for an Anton Piller order. In addition, the plaintiff has satisfied me that this motion should be done on an *ex parte* basis and that it is a remedy which is available at this point in the proceedings.

For these reasons, an Anton Piller order is granted.

- *L*awyers representing the Software Publishers Association (SPA), Lotus Development Corp., Microsoft, Activision, Ashton-Tate, Broderbund, Infocom and Lifetree, obtained a court order which allowed them to seize evidence from the offices of a Vancouver firm, Software Information Services, a software rental agency. The plaintiffs claimed that the firm, which rented popular software to potential purchasers, was renting illegal copies of copyrighted software. The executive director of SPA reported that during the raid materials were thrown from an office window to a person below waiting on a motorcycle; all were recovered. The Copyright Infringement Fund of the SPA paid the legal bill.[48]

CONTEMPT OF COURT

- *I*n its Statement of Claim, Apple Computer alleged that the defendants were importing, assembling and selling computers that contained programs for which Apple owned the copyright. It also alleged that the defendants used a computer case and symbols that would confuse the public. Apple was awarded an interlocutory injunction. The defendants continued to import and assemble the Apple clones. Apple then returned to court for a contempt of court ruling.

  The court found the defendants were in contempt of court, and fined Minitronics of Canada, O.S. Micro Systems and Comtex Micro System $1000, $10,000 and $20,000 respectively. The court further fined Lam of Minitronics $1,000, Lam, Lieu and Wu of Micro Systems and Comtex, $5,000 each and ruled that they would be sent to jail unless they paid the fines, apologized to the court, conducted themselves properly for a year and posted a $100,000 performance bond. Lam of Minitronics had to pay Apple's legal costs up to the morning on which he entered a guilty plea; the other defendants had to pay costs of $60,000.[49]

C. INSURANCE

Moscarelli v. *Aetna Life Insurance Co. of Canada*

24 O.R. (3D) 383 (Q.L.)
[1995] O.J. No. 1709
COURT FILE NO. 12250/91U
ONTARIO COURT (GENERAL DIVISION)
JUNE 14, 1995

Pitt J..: —This application comes before the court in the form of a legal issue to be determined. The issue is framed by the parties as follows:

Can an accident and sickness insurer, when properly voiding a policy of accident and sickness insurance being of fraudulent misrepresentation made by the insured in his application, retain the insurance premiums paid by the insured or must they return the premiums to the former insured?

We must first turn to the relevant sections of the *Insurance Act*, R.S.O. 1980, c. 218 ("the Act") [which includes] ... s. 261 which provides as follows:

> 261(1) An applicant for insurance on his own behalf and on behalf of each person to be insured, and each person to be insured, shall disclose to the insurer in any application, on a medical examination, if any, and in any written statements or answers furnished as evidence of insurability, every fact within his knowledge that is material to the insurance and is not so disclosed by the other.
>
> (2) Subject to sections 262 and 265, a failure to disclose or a misrepresentation of such a fact renders a contract voidable by the insurer.
>
> (3) In the case of a contract of group insurance, a failure to disclose or a misrepresentation of such a fact with respect to a group person insured or a person insured under the contract does not render the contract voidable, but if evidence of insurability is specifically requested by the insurer, the insurance in respect of such a person is, subject to section 262, voidable by the insurer. ...

By notifying the insured in writing that it intended to void the policy and retain all premiums, the insurer, in fact, exercised its option under s. 261. That section does not provide for disposition of premiums and, accordingly, it is necessary to import common law rules for the resolution of the problem.

[The judge reviews the arguments of the plaintiff and the defendant and the cases cited.]

He [counsel for the insurer] also argues that: A return of premiums constitutes restitution *in integrum,* an equitable remedy. The maxim "he who has committed inequity, cannot claim equity," applies to the return of insurance premiums on a voided life insurance policy.

ANALYSIS

Although *Brophy v. North American Life Assurance Co.* (1902), 32 S.C.R. 261, is cited for that proposition, that case is no beacon of clarity as what it decided was that where a policy is cancelled on the ground that it was a wagering contract,

the company should not be required to return the premiums. But there is little doubt that the consensus among the judges was that the "clean hand doctrine" was sound public policy and applies in insurance law. There is, however, the distinct impression left in that case that the result could depend in some cases of fraud on whether the insured or the insurer is the plaintiff.

Brody v. Dominion Life Assurance Co., [1928] S.C.R. 582, [1928] 4 D.L.R. 529, is another case out of the Supreme Court which does not help to elucidate the issue. ...

There does not seem to be one case decided in Canada where an insured, having made a fraudulent representation in an insurance application, has been able to successfully sue for the return of premiums.

Brophy and *Brody,* supra, both suggest that where an insurer brings an action it would be prudent to offer to return the premiums. Nevertheless, in *Brophy* perhaps the strongest language against the return of the premiums in any case is found at p. 271 where Taschereau J. said:

> An interference, in the name of equity, to alleviate the offender's punishment by ordering the return of the premiums into his guilty hands would seem to me an inconsistency. The insured is not in a position to ask the assistance of the court, nor to invoke rules of equity the sole effect of which would be then to benefit the sole culprit. He has received no consideration from the company for the moneys he has paid, it is true, but he owes his loss to his own turpitude, and the court should have no pity upon him and no mercy for him, under any circumstances. I would apply to him the rule that he who has committed iniquity cannot claim equity.

Yet Sedgewick J.'s statement on p. 275, namely:

> Why the company began hostilities, instead of waiting for Father Brophy to make the first attack, has not been explained. Had the latter begun, making his counterclaim his statement of claim his action would have been dismissed and no return of premiums would have been decreed.

indicates that there is some advantage in being a defendant in these circumstances. ...

While the matter is not free from doubt, I believe that the authorities support the position of the insurer, and I also believe that it is the more principled and rational position.

Judgment for the defendant, insurer.

Andryechen **v.** *Transit Insurance Co.*

[1992] I.L.R. 1-2830 AT 1820 (Q.L.)
[1992] O.J. No. 145
DRS 93-08614 No. 542/89
ONTARIO COURT OF JUSTICE—GENERAL DIVISION
JANUARY 22, 1992

VALIN J.:—In 1988, Edward Andryechen owned and operated a Mack diesel truck which was used for long distance haulage of trailers loaded with freight. He was engaged in hauling freight for C.A. Farmer Cartage Ltd. as an independent broker. His truck was insured by the Transit Insurance Company. The vehicle was stolen some time during the early morning hours of April 5, 1988. It was found about 24 hours later. When the truck was recovered, there was substantial damage to the engine, front bumper and windshield. As well, a CB radio had been removed. The cost to repair the damage and replace the radio was appraised at $19,464.33.

The Transit Insurance Company refused to pay for the cost of repairing Mr. Andryechen's truck on the grounds that the theft of, and subsequent damage to, the truck was fraudulent. The insurer alleged that its investigation revealed that Mr. Andryechen either caused or assisted in the damage to the truck. … [D]espite repeated requests by the plaintiff, the defendant refused to pay for the repairs. The plaintiff was forced to pay the repair account himself in order to get his truck back on the road. He did this on May 17, 1988 with the assistance of loans which he obtained from two of his brothers. …

As a result of the defendant's continued refusal to pay, the plaintiff felt compelled to sell his [rental] home on Pasmore Ave. in order to repay the loans which had been advanced to him by his brothers; this was done some six or seven months later. I accept the plaintiff's testimony that he would not have sold the home but for the refusal of the defendant to pay.

ISSUE OF FRAUD

The defendant's refusal to pay resulted in the plaintiff consulting a lawyer and the commencement of this action. The defendant has maintained throughout that its investigation suggested that there was fraud on the part of the plaintiff in that he either caused or assisted in the damage to the truck. As previously stated, one of the issues in this case is whether the defendant is excused from the requirement to pay under the policy as a result of the alleged fraud on the part of the plaintiff.

STANDARD OF PROOF

In a civil action, the plaintiff is required to establish his case on a balance of probabilities. I find that Mr. Andryechen has discharged the onus on him of proving that there was in place a valid automobile insurance policy, that there had been a theft of his truck which resulted in damage to the vehicle which was covered by that policy, and that he filed a proof of loss as required.

It is up to the defendant insurance company to show that the plaintiff was fraudulent in that he either caused or assisted in the damage to the truck. In effect, the defendant is alleging criminal conduct on the part of the plaintiff, even though this is a civil action. The question arises as to what is the standard of proof required in order for the defendant to be successful in establishing its defence. … In *Hanes v. Wawanesa Mutual Insurance Company*, [1963] S.C.R. 154, Ritchie, J. delivering the judgment of the court, referred with approval to what was said by Denning, L.J. in *Bater v. Bater*, [1950] 2 All E.R. 458 at 459 which reads in part as follows:

In criminal cases the charge must be proved beyond a reasonable doubt, but there may be degrees of proof within that standard. Many great judges have said that, in proportion as the crime is enormous so ought the proof to be clear. So also in civil cases. The case may be proved by a preponderance of probability, but there may be degrees of probability within that standard. The degree depends on the subject-matter. A civil court, when considering a charge of fraud will naturally require a higher degree of probability than that which it would require if considering whether negligence were established. It does not adopt so high a degree as a criminal court, even when considering the charge of a criminal nature, but still it does require a degree of probability which is commensurate with the occasion.

In the case of *Tsalamatas v. Wawanesa Mutual Insurance Co.* (1983), 141 D.L.R. (3d) 322, Lacourciere J.A., speaking for the Ontario Court of Appeal stated at p. 324:

Accordingly, in those cases involving criminal or quasicriminal conduct, the trier of fact must examine the totality of the circumstances, including the gravity of the allegations with "special scrutiny" and be satisfied only with a clear preponderance of proof.

I take these to be accurate statements of principle as to the burden of proof which must be met by the defendant in this action. In order for the defendant to be successful in establishing its defence, it must prove on a balance of probabilities that the only reasonable conclusion to be drawn from the facts which have been found in this case is that the truck was taken and damaged by the plaintiff or by someone at his request. Since this defence depends on proof that the plaintiff has committed a criminal offence, even though this is a civil action, the degree of probability must be commensurate with the gravity of the offence of fraud. I must examine closely the elements of motive and opportunity. Indeed, I must give the matter special scrutiny in all respects. [The judge then reviews all the allegations of the insurance company and all the testimony relating to those allegations.] …

Having closely scrutinized all of the evidence, I am unable to conclude that Mr. Andryechen had a better motive or opportunity for being involved in the theft of or damage to his truck than anyone else. There simply is not a preponderance of proof of the theories advanced by the defendant that the plaintiff had both the motive and opportunity to participate in the alleged fraud. I therefore conclude that the defence to this action must fail.

DAMAGES

(a) *Under the Policy*

Counsel for the parties agree that the plaintiff is entitled to be paid the following damages under the policy:

(i) repairs as per appraisal	$19,464.33
(ii) loss of income during repairs	$ 5,690.90
	$25,155.23

(b) *Punitive Damages*

In addition to damages payable under the policy, the plaintiff seeks punitive damages. He advances this claim on the proposition that punitive damages are payable where an insurance company refuses to pay a claim by reason of an alleged criminal act on the part of the insured, or where the insurer acts unreasonably or arbitrarily. While there is no doubt that a court may award punitive damages in a case where there has been a breach of contract, the circumstances under which such an award is made are rare. A helpful statement of the legal principle which governs the circumstances which must exist before such an award will be made is found in the case of *Vorvis v. Insurance Corp. of British Columbia*, [1989] 1 S.C.R. 1085 where McIntyre J. stated at p. 1108:

> Moreover, punitive damages may only be awarded in respect of conduct which is of such nature as to be deserving of punishment because of its harsh, vindictive, reprehensible and malicious nature. I do not suggest that I have exhausted the adjectives which could describe the conduct capable of characterizing a punitive award, but in any case where such an award is made the conduct must be extreme in its nature and such that by any reasonable standard it is deserving of full condemnation and punishment.

The investigation conducted by the defendant insurance company caused it to believe that the plaintiff had participated in a fraud under the policy. The defendant chose to defend the action on that basis. In doing so, counsel for the plaintiff argued that the defendant acted unreasonably and without any evidence to support the defence. He argued forcefully that the theories of the defence were based on suspicion or speculation and not on facts proven at trial.

In my view, although the defence failed, it was not unreasonable for the defendant to defend this action. Although the effect of defending the action no doubt placed the plaintiff in harsh circumstances which ultimately caused him to sell his house in order to pay off the loans he obtained to pay the repair account, there is nothing in the evidence which would support a finding that the defence of the action was in any way malicious, vindictive or reprehensible. The fact that the defence failed does not convince me that the decision to defend was unreasonable or totally without merit. I am therefore unable to find that the decision to defend is deserving of full condemnation and punishment in the form of punitive damages. Although no loss was proven by the plaintiff with respect to the sale of his house, any such loss or inconvenience can be addressed by way of pre-judgment interest.

RESULT

The plaintiff is entitled to judgment against the defendant in the amount of $25,155.23. In addition the plaintiff has claimed, and is entitled to recover, prejudgment interest on that amount at the rate of 11% from May 9, 1988, the date on which the proof of claim was filed, to the date of judgment. He is also entitled to post-judgment interest at the rate applicable as of the date of judgment.

Judgment for the plaintiff

- *I*nsurance premiums for young male drivers were attacked under *the Alberta Individual's Rights Protection Act* (IRPA) as discriminatory because those rates were about twice as high as those for young females. The Alberta Court of Appeal agreed young men were treated differently but that treatment was not unfair given that, among other things, young males accounted for approximately 40% of all road accidents resulting in injury or death. The court concluded that there was no fair alternative.[50]

D. REAL PROPERTY

1. LEGAL INTERESTS IN LAND

Question

When a person buys property, what is included, what is one getting?

The Minister of Finance of Manitoba, pursuant to the Manitoba *Retail Sales Tax*, submitted a tax bill of $1,375,387 to Air Canada in respect of aircraft, aircraft engines and parts consumed and services, meals and liquor consumed in and over the Province of Manitoba. One of the arguments by Air Canada in its appeal from the assessment of the Minister of Finance was that the Province of Manitoba did not have the power to tax aircraft in the airspace over the Province. Justice Morse considering this issue wrote:

The respondent in the present case relied on the hoary maxim: *Cujus est solum ejus est usque ad coelum and ad inferos* ("Whoever owns the soil owns all that lies above it to the sky and to the centre of the earth"). However, in my view, there has never been in England or Canada any interpretation of this maxim requiring me to hold that the owner of the land does, in fact, own or have the right to possession of the airspace above his land to the sky. I adopt the following statement made by Mr. Richardson in the article to which I have referred (at p. 134):

1. It has not been necessary for an English court to give literal effect to the maxim *cujus est solum, ejus est usque ad coelum*, and no court has done so…

In my view, the effect of the maxim goes no further than to protect the owner or occupier of land in his enjoyment of the land and to prevent anyone else from acquiring any title or exclusive right to the space above the land which would limit the landowner or occupier in making whatever proper use he can on his land. And in Fleming, *The Law of Torts*, 4th ed. (1971), the following is stated (at pp. 43-4):

The extent of ownership and possession of superincumbent air-space has become a topic of considerable controversy since the advent of air navigation. Much play has been made of the maxim *cujus est solum ejus est usque ad coelum*, but the 'fanciful phrase' of dubious ancestry has never been accepted in its literal meaning of conferring unlimited rights into the infinity of space over land. The cases in which it has been invoked establish no wider proposition than that the air above the surface is subject to dominion in so far as the use of space is necessary for the proper enjoyment of the surface.

The appeal was allowed.

Re Air Canada and the Queen in Right of Manitoba
77 D.L.R. (3d) 68
Manitoba Queen's Bench
February 18, 1977

The further appeal by the Province of Manitoba to the Manitoba Court of Appeal was allowed in part, but on the issue of ownership of the airspace the Court of Appeal agreed with the Queen's Bench. About the maxim, argued even in the Court of Appeal, Justice Monnin said:

The Latin phrase, much more picturesque than the English, speaks of 'up to heaven and down to hell'. … The maxim cannot go further than direct the owner or occupier of land in his enjoyment of the land and also to prevent anyone else from acquiring any title or exclusive right to the space above such land so as to limit a person to whatever proper use he can make of his land. Further than that it cannot go. Academic writers and modern jurisprudence reject its literal application. So must I in this age of jet aircrafts, satellites, supersonic Concordes, orbital travel and visits to the moon. The sooner the maxim is laid to rest, the better it will be.

Re the Queen in Right of Manitoba and Air Canada
86 D.L.R. (3d) 631
Manitoba Court of Appeal
January 19 and February 16, 1978

Question

In Canada, can one obtain title to land without a formal transfer or bequest in a will?

Teis *v.* Ancaster (Town)

[1997] O.J. No. 3512 (Q.L.)
Docket: C17900
Ontario Court of Appeal
September 3, 1997

[1] Laskin J.A.:—John and Elsie Teis claimed possessory title to two strips of land—the "ploughed strip" and the "laneway"—located on the western edge of Jerseyville Park, a public park owned by the Town of Ancaster and used mainly to play baseball. For more than 10 years, both the Teis and the Town mistakenly believed that the Teis owned these two strips of land. In a judgment dated January 18, 1994, Lazier J. declared that the Teis were owners by adverse possession of the ploughed strip and the laneway but that the public was entitled to travel over part of the laneway by car and all of the laneway by foot. The Town appeals and asks that the Teis' action be dismissed. The Teis cross-appeal and ask to delete that part of the judgment granting the public a right-of-way over the laneway. ...

[2] The main issue on the appeal is whether a person claiming possessory title must show "inconsistent use" when both the claimant and the paper title holder mistakenly believe that the claimant owns the land in dispute. Inconsistent use means that a claimant's use of the land is inconsistent with the true owner's intended use of the land. The other issue on the appeal is whether the trial judge made a "palpable and overriding error" in holding that the Teis had "actual possession" of the disputed strips for the ten-year period prescribed by the *Limitations Act*, R.S.O. 1980, c. L.15.

[3] In my opinion, the test of inconsistent use does not apply to a case of mutual mistake and the trial judge did not err in finding actual possession. Accordingly, I would dismiss the appeal. I would also dismiss the cross-appeal because of the findings of fact made by the trial judge. ...

THE APPEAL

[8] Under ss. 4 and 15 of the *Limitations Act* the interest of the true owner of land may be extinguished by a person who has been in adverse possession of that land for ten years. ...

At the end of the ten-year period these provisions bar the remedy and extinguish the title of the true owner.

[9] The requirements a claimant must satisfy to establish possessory title were set out by Wells J. in *Pflug and Pflug v. Collins*, [1952] O.R. 519, a case relied on by Lazier J. and referred to with approval by Wilson J.A. in the following passage of her majority judgment in *Keefer v. Arillotta* (1976), 13 O.R. (2d) 680 at 692 (C.A.):

> In *Pflug and Pflug v. Collins*, ... Mr. Justice Wells (as he then was) made it clear that a person claiming a possessory title must establish (1) actual possession for the statutory period by themselves and those through whom they claim; (2) that such possession was with the intention of excluding from possession the owner or persons entitled to possession; and (3) discontinuance of possession for the statutory period by the owner and all others, if any, entitled to possession. If he fails in any one of these respects, his claim fails.

...

(a) *Actual Possession*

[13] The first requirement is actual possession for the ten-year period. To succeed, the acts of possession must be open, notorious, peaceful, adverse, exclusive, actual and continuous. If any one of these elements is missing at any time during the statutory period, the claim for possessory title will fail. The trial judge found that all of these elements had been met for more than ten years. This finding is a finding of fact, which cannot be set aside on appeal unless the trial judge made a "palpable and overriding error." In my view, the Town has failed to demonstrate such an error. ...

(b) *Inconsistent Use...*

[25] ... Inconsistent use means that the claimant's use of the land is inconsistent with the true owner's intended use. If the true owner mistakenly believes that the claimant owns the disputed land, then the owner can have no intended use for the land and, correspondingly, the claimant's use cannot be inconsistent with the owner's intended use. ... Therefore, if a claimant were required to show inconsistent use when both parties were honestly mistaken about the true boundary line, the claimant could never make out a case of adverse possession. Such a result would offend established jurisprudence, logic and sound policy. ...

[27] It makes no sense to apply the test of inconsistent use when both the paper title holder and the claimant are mistaken about their respective rights. The application of the test would defeat adverse possession claims in cases of mutual mistake, yet permit such claims to succeed in cases of knowing trespass. Thus applied, the test would reward the deliberate squatter and punish the innocent trespasser. Policy considerations support a contrary conclusion. ...

[28] ... I therefore conclude ... that the test does not apply to cases of mutual mistake about ownership. ...

[30] ... [Also] in cases of mutual mistake the court may reasonably infer, as indeed I infer in this case, that the claimants, the Teis, intended to exclude all others, including the paper title holder, the Town.

THE CROSS-APPEAL

[34] The Teis submit that the trial judge erred in declaring that the public had a right-of-way over the laneway. A possessory title may be subject to a right-of-way. See *Ziff*, supra, at p. 119. The trial judge granted a right-of-way because he found that

> This particular lane has not been in the exclusive domain of the plaintiffs. Members of the public have traversed these lands on foot and at times when the lands to the east were being used for recreation, including Little League Baseball, vehicles were parked on part of the [laneway] from time to time.

This finding was supported by the evidence of Town residents and Mr. Teis. I would not interfere with it. Accordingly, in my view the cross-appeal must fail.

ADVERSE POSSESSION OF MUNICIPAL PARK LAND

[35] Most adverse possession claims involve disputes between private property owners. In this case, the Teis claim adverse possession of municipally owned land. I have some discomfort in upholding a possessory title to land that the Town would otherwise use to extend its public park for the benefit of its residents. Still, the Town did not suggest that municipally owned park land cannot be extinguished by adverse possession or even that different, more stringent requirements must be met when the land in dispute is owned by a municipality and would be used for a public park. This case was argued before the trial judge and in this court on the footing that the ordinary principles of adverse possession law applied. The application of those principles to the evidence and the trial judge's findings of fact justify extinguishing the Town's title to the ploughed strip and the laneway.

[36] Several American states have legislation that prevents a limitation period from running against "municipal property devoted to public use." See 3 Am. Jur. (2d) section 271. Even at common law, some American courts have decided that municipally owned land used for a public purpose, such as a park, cannot be acquired by adverse possession. ...

[37] In Canada, Alberta is the only province with legislation protecting all municipally owned land against claims of adverse possession. *Municipal Government Act*, S.A. 1994, c. M.26.1, s. 609. In Ontario, streets, highways, and road allowances have been protected from adverse possession or encroachment claims. ...

[38] Whether, short of statutory reform, the protection against adverse possession afforded to municipal streets and highways should be extended to municipal land used for public parks, I leave to a case where the parties squarely raise the issue.

CONCLUSION

[39] I would dismiss both the appeal and the cross-appeal with costs.

Note: This law may not be applicable in your jurisdiction because of the operation of the Torrens system of land registration. Gaining title by adverse possession may be expressly prohibited by statute.

VARIATIONS OF WILLS

Pattie *v.* Standal Estate

DOCKET: 16908 REGISTRY: VERNON
http://www.courts.gov.bc.ca
THE SUPREME COURT OF BRITISH COLUMBIA
SEPTEMBER 12, 1997

[1] Smith, J.:—Arthur Gordon Standal ("Mr. Standal") died on December 15, 1985 [sic 1995?], at age 50. His will, made on April 21, 1995, left his $133,000 estate to Mary Jane Breau, his common-law wife of two years. It made no mention of, or provision for, his only child, an adopted son, Robert Gordon Pattie ("Robert") born February 9, l964. Letters probate were granted on April 22, l996. Robert applies to this Court to vary the terms of his father's will. ...

[3] Mr. Standal and Robert's mother married in l960. They lived in Alberta. In May 1965, they adopted Robert. Two years later, when Robert was only 3, they separated; on February 4, l970, they were divorced. The Decree Nisi order awarded Mrs. Standal custody of Robert and gave her the right to apply for maintenance. She never did so and after their separation Mr. Standal never contributed to Robert's maintenance.

[4] When Robert was 7 he moved with his mother from Alberta to B.C. Thereafter, he had no further contact with his father. On May 11, 1984, Robert legally changed his surname from Standal to Pattie. ...

[10] Prior to executing his will, Mr. Standal was advised by his lawyer of the provisions of s. 2(1) of the *Wills Variation Act*, R.S.B.C. 1979, Ch. 435 ("the Act"):

2(1) Notwithstanding any law or statute to the contrary, if a testator dies leaving a will which does not, in the court's opinion, make adequate provision for the proper maintenance and support of the testator's wife, husband or children, the court may, in its discretion, in an action by or on behalf of the wife, husband or children, order that the provision that it thinks adequate, just and equitable in the circumstances be made out of the estate of the testator for the wife, husband or children.

[11] Mr. Standal excluded his son from his will in spite of any legal advice he received. He provided no reasons for so doing and no evidence of his reasons was tendered.

[12] Robert brings an application for summary judgment pursuant to s. 2(1) of the Act, seeking a share of his father's estate. He submits that his father had a moral obligation to provide for him under his will. Ms. Breau opposes Robert's claim. ...

[The testator is subject to legal obligations and to moral obligations.]

[14] Problems arise where there are competing claims between legal and moral obligations. If the estate is large enough, all claims can be, and should be met. Where it is not, legal obligations will take priority over moral claims.

[15] Further conflicts may occur between a testator's duty to provide what is adequate, just and equitable, and the freedom to dispose of his or her estate as the testator sees fit. While Courts will not lightly interfere with a testator's wishes, under s. 2(1) of the Act, testamentary autonomy is limited by the Act's primary requirement, namely, that a testator provide what is adequate, just and equitable.

[16] Whether a testator has fulfilled his or her legal and moral obligations to provide what is adequate, just and equitable for an adult child, while at the same time being free to exercise his testamentary autonomy, may require a balancing of these competing claims. ... However, as stated by McLachlin J. in *Tataryn*, supra, at 157:

> In many cases, there will be a number of ways of dividing the assets which are adequate, just and equitable. In other words, there will be a wide range of options, any of which might be considered appropriate in the circumstances. Provided that the testator has chosen an option within this range, the will should not be disturbed. Only where the testator has chosen an option which falls below his or her obligations as defined by reference to legal and moral norms, should the court make an order which achieves the justice the testator failed to achieve. ...

[19] The moral claim of an adult child can still be defeated, provided the testator gives reasons for disinheriting or inadequately providing for the child. The reasons need not be justifiable; it is sufficient if they are valid, i.e., based on fact, and rational, i.e., having a connection between the reasons and the act of disinheritance: *Kelly v. Baker*, (1996), 82 B.C.A.C. 150 (C.A.); *Bell v. Roy Estate*, supra.

[20] Only where there is evidence as to the testator's reasons, can the Court properly assess if he or she has acted as a judicious parent in discharging their duty to family members. ...

THE CIRCUMSTANCES OF THIS CASE

[22] There is no question Mr. Standal had a legal obligation to Ms. Breau to provide for her support and maintenance after his death. ...

[24] However, Mr. Standal's legal obligation to Ms. Breau, while taking priority over his moral obligation to his adult independent son, does not preclude him having an additional moral duty to make adequate, just and equitable provisions in his will for Robert, in the absence of circumstances which might negate the existence of such an obligation.

[25] There is no evidence before the Court, either from Mr. Standal in a written expression of his reasons, or from any other witness or documentary evidence, to allow the Court to assess Mr. Standal's reasons for disinheriting Robert. In the absence of such evidence, the Court must fall back upon the wealth of judicial authority that has accepted the premise of a parent's moral obligation to provide for his or her child unless that duty is displaced by special circumstances. No such special circumstances exist here.

[26] The legal obligation for a parent to support his or her child, during the parent's lifetime, if unfulfilled, may create circumstances for an adult child to advance a moral claim against the parent's estate if the support is inadequate or if no provision is made for the child from the estate. In this case, I find Mr. Standal had a legal obligation during his lifetime to contribute to Robert's maintenance. He failed to do so. This failure, in the absence of any evidence of special circumstances, creates a basis upon which Robert may advance a moral claim to a share of his father's estate.

[27] Mr. Standal has provided for Ms. Breau's maintenance after his death, by her receipt of two pensions totalling $1,600 per month which she will continue to receive for the rest of her life, and by her receipt of the proceeds of a life insurance policy for $57,000. Her contribution of domestic services, without compensation, and his moral obligation to her as his spouse, in my opinion, is more than adequately met by Ms. Breau receiving one-half of his estate.

[28] By failing to make any provision for Robert in his will, I find that Mr. Standal did not meet his moral obligation to his son. In exercising the broad discretion given to this Court pursuant to s. 2(1) of the Act, I conclude that an adequate, just and equitable provision for Robert, in these circumstances, is for him to receive the remaining one-half of his father's estate.

[29] There will be an order accordingly to vary Mr. Standal's will.

[30] Costs are payable from the estate.

TENANCY IN COMMON AND JOINT TENANCY

Questions

If a person decides to co-own property with another, should he or she buy as a joint tenant or as a tenant in common?

What is the significance of the difference?

Caluori v. *Caluori*

ONTARIO COURT OF JUSTICE
COURT FILE NO. 59859/92
JULY 16, 1992

Rutherford, J.: The applicant [Mrs.], a dependant within the meaning of s. 57 of the *Succession Law Reform Act* R.S.O. 1990, Chapter S. 26, seeks relief by way of proper support from the estate of her late husband, pursuant to s. 58 of the Act.

It is clear from the evidence that this 72 year old widow is not destitute. Her monthly income from all sources will be between $1,200 and $1,700 a month depending on how this application is determined. The real issue concerns the house in which she and her husband lived since 1964. It was their matrimonial home for all those years and the house in which the applicant insisted on maintaining and caring for her late husband during his declining years. He was not well in his last 6 years and required close care and attention in his final year or two. The applicant expresses a strong, emotional attachment to the home saying she wants to die there, as did her husband.

The marriage was the second for each of them. It lasted almost 20 years and the Caluoris were close. They shared the burdens and benefits of life equally. Their financial contribution to their overall situation was roughly equal.

When the Caluoris purchased the house in question at 1284 Lambeth Walk in the City of Nepean, they took title to it as joint tenants, having discussed the mutual objective they had at that time of having the house left to the survivor of the two. Sometime later, without disclosing it to his wife, the late Mr. Caluori obviously changed his mind about that mutual objective and conveyed his interest in the home to himself in a deed to uses, thus creating a tenancy in common. Then, in a will created at about the same time, he left his entire estate to the children of his first marriage, making no provision for the applicant. The respondent as executor of the will, seeks an order by way of counter application to sell the house and divide the proceeds between the estate and the applicant. The house is worth about $130,000 and if sold, the applicant would receive approximately $60,000 for her own use. This would be her sole asset, apart from savings of about $15,000 and pension and old age security income of about $1,200 per month.

In assessing the applicant's claim that she has not been adequately provided for, I have evaluated the evidence against the criteria set out in s.62 of the *Succession Law Reform Act*. In particular, I have considered the 19 year, close, caring relationship between the applicant and her late husband; the length of time they lived in the house in question; the applicant's expectation which was reciprocal as far as she knew, that the house was jointly owned and she and her late husband each intended the survivor to have it; the relatively equal sharing and contributing the applicant and her late husband had and made to their financial circumstances; and of course, the contextual circumstances including the applicant's assets, means and other legal recourse for support together with the estate of the

applicant's late husband and his testamentary wishes.

I am guided by the views expressed in such cases as *Re Davies v. Davies* (1980) 27 O.R. 98 and *Re Dentinger* [1981] 128 D.L.R. (3d) 613, holding that "proper support" as contemplated by s. 58 of the *Succession Law Reform Act* includes more than necessities of life and may extend to non-essentials and even luxuries. The difference between "adequate support" and "adequate proper support" involves consideration of the life-style of the parties. such that the support is fitting or appropriate to the circumstances.

In *Re Mannion* (1984) 45 O.R. (3d) 339, Dubin J.A. (now Chief Justice of Ontario) said at page 342 concerning s. 58:

> The new statute being remedial, it should be given a broad and liberal interpretation...

When I balance the evidence as applied to the criteria in s.62 and apply the s. 58 formula of "adequate provision for the proper support of the applicant," I am driven to the conclusion that her proper support must include being able to live in the house at 1284 Lambeth Walk for as long as she wishes. It is the matrimonial home, her home for the last 18 years and one, in a neighborhood, to which she attaches a strong emotional tie. The applicant shuns apartment life as "living in a tomb" and in my view, is entitled, by the legislation, to stay where she is.

I appreciate that the half-interest in the house is the only asset in the estate, apart from a few items of personal property of relatively small economic value, but the beneficiaries under the will are the next generation and all good things come to those who wait, especially each in their proper turn.

Accordingly, under the authority of subsection 58(1) of the *Succession Law Reform Act*, it is the order of the Court that the respondent as executor and trustee of the Will of Eugene Caluori hold the interest of the estate in the house at 1284 Lambeth Walk, more particularly described in the Deed of Land registered as instrument no. 671288 in the Registry Office for the Registry Division of Ottawa on May 30, 1975, in trust for the benefit of the applicant and for her use as long as she wishes to live in that house. Upon her death or upon her no longer residing in the house, the estate's interest therein shall be disposed of as directed in the will. While the applicant resides in the house, she will be responsible for maintaining it and will bear all the expenses necessary therefor.

Because there are no other liquid assets in the estate, I make no order as to costs in this application. The counter-application for sale of the estate's interest in the house is dismissed and no costs are awarded in relation to it either.

Dated at Ottawa, this 16th day of July, 1992.

2. TRANSFER OF LAND

Note: For a story underlining "buyer beware" see Tony's Broadloom & Floor Covering Ltd (in trust) *v. NMC Canada Inc.* p. 230.

> The vendor didn't know but her real estate agent and lawyer knew, that her property was to be designated a heritage site and that would thwart the express purpose of the buyer to raze the old farmhouse, barn and blacksmith's shop to replace them with new commercial establishments. The failure to disclose was considered a misrepresentation entitling the buyer to an award of damages.[51]
>
> *Goldstein v. Davison*

3. REMEDIES FOR BREACH OF CONTRACT

SPECIFIC PERFORMANCE AND DAMAGES IN LIEU THEREOF

Semelhago *v.* Paramadevan

FILE NO.:24325
http://www.droit.umontreal.ca/
SUPREME COURT OF CANADA
JUNE 20, 1996

...

[2] The judgment of Sopinka, Gonthier, Cory, McLachlin, Iacobucci and Major JJ. was delivered by Sopinka, J.:—This appeal concerns the principles that apply in awarding damages in lieu of specific performance. The appellant vendor refused to close a transaction for the sale of residential property to the respondent purchaser. The latter sued for specific performance and, in the alternative, damages in lieu thereof. At the commencement of the trial, the respondent elected the latter. Subsequent to the date fixed for closing, property values rose. If the closing date is the date on which damages are assessed, the respondent would not recover the increase in the value of the property he agreed to purchase. If, however, damages are assessed as of the date of trial, the question is whether the respondent is entitled to recover not only this increase but also to retain the increase in value of the residence which the respondent owned at the time of the agreement of purchase and sale and which was not sold as a result of the aborted transaction.

I. FACTS

[3] In August 1986, the respondent purchaser agreed to buy a house under construction in the Toronto area from the appellant vendor Sinnadurai Paramadevan for $205,000, with a closing date of October 31, 1986. To finance the purchase, the respondent was going to pay $75,000 cash, plus $130,000 which he was going to raise by mortgaging his current house. The respondent negotiated a six-month open mortgage, so that he could close the deal on the new house and then sell his old one at an appropriate time in the six months following closing. Before the closing date, the appellant vendor reneged and in December 1986, title to the house was taken by the appellant Blossom Paramadevan. The respondent stayed in his old house, which was worth $190,000 in the fall of 1986, and $300,000 at the time of the trial.

[4] The respondent sued the appellants for specific performance or damages in lieu thereof and put a caution on the title. At the time of trial, the market value of the property was $325,000. The respondent elected to take damages rather than specific performance and on December 5, 1990, Corbett J. of the Ontario Court of Justice (General Division) awarded him $120,000, that being the difference between the purchase price he had agreed to pay and the value of the property at the time of trial. The appellants appealed to the Court of Appeal for Ontario on the ground that the assessment was a "windfall" because the respondent was benefiting not only from the increase in the value of the new house, but also from the gain in the value of the old house. The respondent cross-appealed against the disallowance of legal and appraisal fees. On June 17, 1994, the Court of Appeal allowed the appeal and the cross-appeal: (1994), 19 O.R. (3d) 479, 39 R.P.R. (2d) 215, 73 O.A.C. 295 [and awarded $81,733.96]. ...

III. ISSUE

[9] What principles apply to the assessment of damages in lieu of specific performance and, further, how do those principles apply to the facts of this case?

IV. ANALYSIS

[10] The trial judge expressed reservations about the propriety of an award of specific performance in this case. While I share those reservations and will return to the question as to the circumstances under which specific performance is an

appropriate remedy, this appeal should be disposed of on the basis that specific performance was appropriate. The case was dealt with by the parties in both courts below and in this Court on the assumption that specific performance was an appropriate remedy.

[11] A party who is entitled to specific performance is entitled to elect damages in lieu thereof. …

[Judge Sopinka continues to reason that if the plaintiff seeks specific performance the acceptance of the breach is delayed. If the plaintiff subsequently elects damages in lieu of specific performance the amount awarded needs to be the amount necessary for the plaintiff to purchase the asset.]

[18] I therefore conclude that, in the circumstances of this case, the appropriate date for the assessment of damages is the date of trial as found by the trial judge. Technically speaking, the date of assessment should be the date of judgment. That is the date upon which specific performance is ordered. For practical purposes, however, the evidence that is adduced which is relevant to enable damages to be assessed will be as of the date of trial. It is not usually possible to predict the date of judgment when the evidence is given.

[19] The difference between the contract price and the value "given close to trial" as found by the trial judge is $120,000. I would not deduct from this amount the increase in value of the respondent's residence which he retained when the deal did not close. If the respondent had received a decree of specific performance, he would have had the property contracted for and retained the amount of the rise in value of his own property. Damages are to be substituted for the decree of specific performance. I see no basis for deductions that are not related to the value of the property which was the subject of the contract. To make such deductions would depart from the principle that damages are to be a true equivalent of specific performance.

[20] This approach may appear to be overly generous to the respondent in this case and other like cases and may be seen as a windfall. In my opinion, this criticism is valid if the property agreed to be purchased is not unique. While at one time the common law regarded every piece of real estate to be unique, with the progress of modern real estate development this is no longer the case. Residential, business and industrial properties are all mass produced much in the same way as other consumer products. If a deal falls through for one property, another is frequently, though not always, readily available.

[21] It is no longer appropriate, therefore, to maintain a distinction in the approach to specific performance as between realty and personalty. It cannot be assumed that damages for breach of contract for the purchase and sale of real estate will be an inadequate remedy in all cases. The common law recognized that the distinction might not be valid when the land had no peculiar or special value. In *Adderley v. Dixon* (1824), 1 Sim. & St. 607, 57 E.R. 239, Sir John Leach, V.C., stated (at p. 240):

> Courts of Equity decree the specific performance of contracts, not upon any distinction between realty and personalty, but because damages at law may not, in the particular case, afford a complete remedy. Thus a Court of Equity decrees performance of a contract for land, not because of the real nature of the land, but because damages at law, which must be calculated upon the general money value of land, may not be a complete remedy to the purchaser, to whom the land may have a peculiar and special value.

[22] Courts have tended, however, to simply treat all real estate as being unique and to decree specific performance unless there was some other reason for refusing equitable relief. See *Roberto v. Bumb.* … Some courts, however, have begun to question the assumption that damages will afford an inadequate remedy for breach of contract for the purchase of land. In *Chaulk v. Fairview Construction Ltd.* (1977), 14 Nfld. & P.E.I.R. 13, the Newfoundland Court of Appeal (per Gushue J.A.), after quoting the above passage from *Adderley v. Dixon*, stated, at p. 21:

> The question here is whether damages would have afforded Chaulk an adequate remedy, and I have no doubt that they could, and would, have. There was nothing whatever unique or irreplaceable about the houses and lots bargained for. They were merely subdivision lots with houses, all of the same general design, built on them, which the respondent was purchasing for investment or re-sale purposes only. He had sold the first two almost immediately at a profit, and intended to do the same with the remainder. It would be quite different if we were dealing with a house or houses which were of a particular architectural design, or were situated in a particularly desirable location, but this was certainly not the case.

Specific performance should, therefore, not be granted as a matter of course absent evidence that the property is unique to the extent that its substitute would not be readily available. The guideline proposed by Estey J. in *Asamera Oil Corp. v. Seal Oil & General Corp.*, [1979] 1 S.C.R. 633, with respect to contracts involving chattels is equally applicable to real property. At p. 668, Estey J. stated:

> Before a plaintiff can rely on a claim to specific performance so as to insulate himself from the consequences of failing to procure alternate property in mitigation of his losses, some fair, real and substantial justification for his claim to performance must be found.

A similar position has been taken by the British Columbia Supreme Court in *McNabb v. Smith* (1981), 124 D.L.R. (3d) 547, at p. 551.

[23] The trial judge was of the view in this case that the property was not unique. She stated that, "It was a building lot under construction which would be interchangeable in all likelihood with any number of others." Notwithstanding this observation, she felt constrained by authority to find that specific performance was an appropriate remedy. While I would be inclined to agree with the trial judge as to the inappropriateness of an order for specific performance, both parties were content to present the case on the basis that the respondent was entitled to specific performance. The case was dealt with on this basis by the Court of Appeal. In the circumstances, this Court should abide by the manner in which the case has been presented by the parties and decided in the courts below. In future cases, under similar circumstances, a trial judge will not be constrained to find that specific performance is an appropriate remedy.

[24] This takes me to the deductions made by the Court of Appeal. While I have some reservations about the propriety of these deductions, there was no cross-appeal by the respondent with respect to the award of damages. No argument was presented with respect to these deductions. ...

DISPOSITION

[27] In the result, the appeal is dismissed with costs.

Appeal dismissed with costs.

Note: Judge La Forest agreed with the disposition of the case but did not want to join the majority in its consideration of a person's right to specific performance or damages in lieu of that remedy.

---

4. THE LANDLORD/TENANT RELATIONSHIP

Minto Developments Inc. ***v.*** *Nuttall, et al.*

IN THE MATTER OF THE *LANDLORD AND TENANT ACT*, R.S.O. 1990 C.L.7, AS AMENDED
[1993] O.J. NO. 2543 (Q.L.)
ACTION NO. 75616/93
ONTARIO COURT OF JUSTICE—GENERAL DIVISION
AMENDED REASONS FOR JUDGMENT JANUARY 24, 1994

[1] Binks J.:—The applicant is a landlord and the respondent Sue Nuttall (Carter) is the tenant of Unit 18 of an 18 unit townhouse at 83 Woodridge Crescent, in the City of Nepean. On June 21st, 1993 the respondent Legault's reticulated python which is between 13 and 20 feet long and 4 to 6 inches wide appeared at the window of Unit 18 where children were sitting below, creating alarm in the area. The police were summoned, along with City by-law officials at which time various constrictor snakes, tarantulas and lizards were found in Unit 18. The applicant commenced this application and obtained an interim injunction removing the pythons, boa constrictors and similar animals by an order of McWilliam J. dated July 2nd, 1993.

[2] In her application for a lease, the respondent Nuttall (Carter) stated that only she and her sister Mary Carter would be occupying the premises. Minto entered into a lease with Nuttall (Carter) dated March 21st, 1992 which stipulated in part that only two adults might occupy the subject premises being the respondents Sue Nuttall and Mary Carter and this was set out in the application for lease.

[3] The lease was dated March 21st, 1992 and was extended on a month to month basis by the parties and stipulated *inter alia*:

(i) the subject premises will be used and occupied by the respondent Nuttall and one adult in her immediate family;

(ii) the subject premises will only be used for the purposes of a private dwelling and residence;

(iii) the tenant will not do or permit to be done any act on the subject premises that will be deemed by the landlord to be a nuisance or that will cause disturbance or inconvenience to any other tenant of the building;

(iv) the tenant shall not alter or caused to be altered the lock on any entry door or affix a night latch upon any entry door to the subject premises without the landlord's written consent;

(v) the tenant cannot assign or sublet the subject premises without the landlord's consent, which consent shall not be arbitrarily withheld;

(vi) no tenant shall do, or permit anything to be done in said premises or bring or keep anything therein which will in any way ... obstruct or interfere with the rights of other tenants, or in any way injure or annoy them, or conflict with ... any statute or municipal by-law;

(vii) tenants, their families, guests, visitors and servants shall not make or permit ... do anything that will annoy or disturb or interfere in any way with other tenants or those having business with them.

(vii) "NO DOGS OR PETS ALLOWED" clause—at the end of the lease in bold letters.

[4] In December, 1992 the respondent Nuttall allowed a third adult the respondent Todd Legault to occupy the premises without the applicant's knowledge or consent, contrary to paragraphs 6 and 11 of the lease.

[5] When she signed the lease Sue Nuttall indicated her intention was to house only cats in the premises. The intention of the respondent Legault was substantially different. His intention was set out in his employment resume when he stated "in the future I hope to have one of the largest and healthiest collection of reptiles in the country."

...

[7] As a result of his intention the respondent Legault brought the following animals into the subject premises:

one (1) reticulate python

one (1) Burmese python

two (2) royal pythons

one (1) carpet python

two (2) rainbow boa constrictors

one (1) Mexican boa constrictor

one (1) Columbia boa constrictor

one (1) Kenyan sand boa constrictor

one (1) corn snake

one (1) Californian king snake

one (1) yellow anaconda

one (1) African house snake

one (1) rose hair tarantula

one (1) Mexican brow tarantula

one (1) nile monitor lizard

one (1) savannah monitor lizard

one (1) tokay gecko lizard

one (1) gold tegu lizard

...

[9] Legault looks after the snakes and because they are tropical, the bedroom where they are kept is quite warm, warm enough that Legault finds it necessary from time to time to open the window when he is in the bedroom tending to the reptiles. On June 21st, 1993 Legault left the bedroom window part way open (1 inch) and a reticulate python between 13 and 20 feet long and 4 to 6 inches wide called "Taipan" crawled onto a terrarium (which is really an aquarium with sand in it and a lid on top) housing other snakes and opened the window while no one occupied the premises.

[10] There are conflicting versions of what happened that evening. ...

[15] The first notice the applicant had that there were snakes, lizards and tarantulas in Unit 18 was on the night of June 21st, 1993 when the 13 1/2 to 20 foot long python appeared at the window of Unit 18 and the police and Nepean by-law officials were called in to investigate. A spotlight was beamed on the snake and a multitude of people gathered around the unit to witness the events as they transpired. Police officials on the scene indicated at the time they were prepared to "deal with dogs and cats but there was no way there were going to deal with snakes."

...

[18] The respondents' boas and pythons are referred to in paragraph 11, of schedule "B" of the City of Nepean By-law regarding keeping of animals in a residence. ... The respondents are in breach of paragraph 30 (d) of that by-law by failing to keep their large pythons in an escape-proof enclosure, when one of the animals was next to a window screen trying to get out of a window and another of the pythons was being kept in a child's swimming pool in one of the bedrooms in the subject premises. A breach of any by-law also constitutes a breach of the lease (paragraph 25K) and therefore constitutes grounds for termination under the *Landlord and Tenant Act*, R.S.O. 1990, c.L.7 s. 107 (1) (c) as an "illegal act." The respondents do not deny this breach, they simply allege that no escape of the pythons has ever taken place. In my opinion they were not in an escape-proof container simply by being in the room. The room itself is not an "enclosure." ...

[20] The respondent Legault has already tried to persuade the neighbourhood to adopt his view regarding the subject of constrictor snakes, tarantulas and lizards by an open invitation to discuss the issue, but only a twelve year old took him up on his invitation because the neighbours are just "set in

their ways" according to Legault. The respondent Legault also tried to allay the neighbourhood's fears by approaching the *Ottawa Sun* and co-operating in an article appearing therein on June 24th, 1993 in that paper. Unfortunately, the article did nothing to stop the alarm in the neighbourhood. ...

[21] As a result of the respondent Legault using the subject premises as a zoo for exotic animals the respondents have breached paragraphs 6, 25K and 25M of the lease by not using them solely as a private dwelling and residence and have thereby caused a disturbance, annoyance, interference and inconvenience to their neighbouring tenants who fear for their safety and that of their children. ...

[24] A residential lease may be terminated on the following grounds:

"107.—(1) [where]

(b) a tenant at any time during the term of the tenancy exercises or carries on, or permits to be exercised or carried on, in or upon the residential premises or any part thereof, any illegal act ...;

(c) the conduct of the tenant or a person permitted in the residential premises by the tenant is such that it substantially interferes with the reasonable enjoyment of the premises for all usual purposes by the landlord or the other tenants;

(d) the safety or other lawful right, privilege or interest of any other tenant in the residential premises is or has been seriously impaired by an act or omission of the tenant or a person permitted in the residential premises by the tenant where such act or omission occurs in the residential premises or its environs;

[25] Pursuant to a recent amendment to the Act, Section 107 (6) and 108 of the *Landlord and Tenant Act* permits eviction of a tenant or removal of a pet only when the presence of the pet constitutes a breach of s. 107 (1).

[26] Subsection (6) of Section 107 of the *Landlord and Tenant Act* recites as follows:

Where the notice of termination is served under clause (1) (c) or (d) and is based on the presence, control or behaviour of an animal in or about the rented premises, a judge hearing an application under section 113 brought by the landlord under subsection (3) or (4) shall not direct the issue of a writ of possession unless the judge is satisfied that the tenant is keeping an animal and that,

(a) the past behaviour of an animal of that species has substantially interfered with the reasonable enjoyment of the premises for all usual purposes by the landlord or the other tenants;...

(c) the presence of an animal of that species or breed is inherently dangerous to the safety of the landlord or the other tenants. ...

[28] The court has already ruled that the fear of an animal is sufficient to constitute a substantial interference with the neighbours' enjoyment of their premises. ...;

[30] The evidence shows that the Legault animals belonged to dangerous species. There is no evidence regarding the individual specimens' temperament involved in this case but there need not be. The *Landlord and Tenant Act* refers to inherently

dangerous species that interfere with a reasonable enjoyment of property, both without regard to the nature of the individual specimen. This follows the common law which holds that the nature of the species is to see if it is inherently dangerous, and disregards the fact whether the particular specimen was not tame.

> If a person wakes up in the middle of the night and finds an escaping tiger on top of his bed and suffers a heart attack, it would be nothing to the point that the intentions of the tiger were quite amiable. ... It is not, in my judgment, practicable to introduce conceptions of *mens rea* and malevolence in the case of animals. *Behrens v. Bertram Mills Circus Ltd.* [1957] 2 Q.B. 1 at 17-18 cited in *Lewis v. Oeming* (1983) 24 C.C. L.T. 81, at 95 (Alta T.D.).

[31] In Fleming, *The Law of Torts* 345 (5th ed, 1977) it is stated that classification of a particular species is dangerous is a matter of law for the court and it does not depend on the nature of the particular specimen. ...

[33] It should be noted that the respondent Legault does not have a legal right he can assert against the landlord to reside in the subject premises, and the lease itself prohibits him from residing in Unit 18.

[34] I am satisfied that the keeping of the animals by Legault and the tenant in Unit 18 at 83 Woodridge Crescent, in the City of Nepean, has substantially interfered with the reasonable enjoyment of the premises by the landlord and by the other tenants and the presence of animals is inherently dangerous to the safety of the landlord and the other tenants.

[35] On the basis of all of the evidence, it is appropriate therefore to issue an order:

(a) terminating the tenancy agreement between the applicant and the respondent Sue Nuttall dated March 21st, 1992 as extended on a month-to-month basis;

(b) a writ of possession in favour of the applicant with respect to the subject premises to issue;

(c) an order requiring the respondents to remove the boa constrictors, pythons, tarantulas and monitor lizards from the subject premises within 15 days of the date of this order.

[36] There shall also be a declaration that Todd Legault is not entitled to occupy Unit 18, of 83 Woodridge Crescent, in the City of Nepean, and an order prohibiting him from residing there.

...

RELATIONSHIP BETWEEN THE WORDING OF THE LEASE AND THE RELEVANT STATUTE

Pinheiro *v.* *Bowes*

[1994] O.J. No. 115 (Q.L.)
DRS 94-11881
ACTION NO. 11539/93
ONTARIO COURT OF JUSTICE—GENERAL DIVISION
JANUARY 7, 1994

[1] Killeen J.:— This application by the landlord under s. 113 of the *Landlord and Tenant Act*, R.S.O. 1990, c.L.7 has been narrowed down, by agreement, to one issue, namely, whether a contractual provision as to notice of termination may override s. 80(1) of the Act.

THE AGREED FACTS

[2] The parties entered a lease which contained ... [a provision that] a monthly tenancy may be terminated by giving written notice to terminate on or before the last day of one month of the tenancy to be effective on the last day of the following month of the tenancy.

[3] It is acknowledged that ... the tenant stayed in the premises for some time and, on October 27, 1993, served a written notice purporting to terminate the tenancy as of November 30, 1993. In doing so, the tenant thought that she was lawfully complying with the one-month notice proviso set out in paragraph 19(d) of the lease.

[4] If the tenant was entitled to rely on paragraph 19(d), then, of course, she owes nothing further to the landlord. If, however, that clause cannot be relied upon, then the tenant owes the landlord one additional month's rent by virtue of s. 99 of the Act.

THE RESOLUTION OF THE NOTICE ISSUE

[5] The parties acknowledge that two provisions of the Act must be considered in deciding the central issue of this case. These sections are as follows:

> 80.-(1) This Part applies to tenancies of residential premises and tenancy agreements despite any other Act or Parts I, II, or III of this Act and despite any agreement or waiver to the contrary except as specifically provided in this Part.

> 99.-(1) A notice to terminate a monthly tenancy shall be given not less than sixty days before the date the termination is specified to be effective and shall be specified to be effective on the last day of a month of the tenancy.

[6] Mr. Schlemmer, for the tenant, argues that s. 99 ... does not bind the tenant in this case because of the express provision in the lease which permits termination on notice for the lesser period of 30 days.

[7] Mr. Schnurr, on the other hand, argues that s. 80(1), in clear and unambiguous language, invalidates the shorter one-

month notice period in the lease for all purposes and, in combination with s. 99(1), effectively requires the tenant, or landlord, to give 60 days notice. ...

[9] ... [S]. 80(1) ... seems to be crystal clear in its intent. Section 80 (1) says, in explicit terms, that every provision of Part IV applies to all residential tenancy agreements and that this is so "despite any agreement or waiver to the contrary except as specifically provided in this Part." (Emphasis added.)

[10] I can identify no ambiguity in s. 80(1) and the parties acknowledge that there is nothing in Part IV which permits any agreement or waiver to the contrary.

[11] I must express some discomfiture at permitting a landlord to rely on the statutorily-created invalidation of that landlord's own lease proviso but it is not for a judge to run roughshod over a statute in an effort to protect a tenant. ...

[13] Judges must accept statutes as they find them if they are clear and unambiguous and catch the factual situation under consideration.

[14] In my view, while s. 99 was largely created to protect tenants, it cannot be said to be contrary to public policy to enforce it in favour of a landlord. Section 99 provides a broadly-gauged protective rule for landlord-tenant relationships and must be enforced as it plainly reads and provides. On its face, it invalidates the lease proviso in issue and makes the tenant liable for one month's additional rent.

...

INTERPRETATION

80,100 Canada Corp. *v.* Reid

[1992] O.J. No. 2511 (Q.L.)
ACTION NO. 5232/92
ONTARIO COURT OF JUSTICE—GENERAL DIVISION
SEPTEMBER 30, 1992

Byers J.:—This is an application to interpret a lease. The applicant/landlord is a holding company owned by a law firm. The respondents are Karen Reid and her father, Carmen Reid. Karen Reid is 34 years of age with a grade 12 education. She signed the lease and became the tenant. Carmen Reid signed as guarantor.

The lease was for five (5) years. It was prepared by the law firm. The respondents did not have independent legal advice.

Karen Reid operated a gift shop on the premises. That business failed after two years, and she became insolvent.

She abandoned the premises. She tendered three months' additional rent pursuant to Clause "h" in the lease. She says that is the end of her obligation. The applicant/landlord declined to accept the tender. It takes the view that the lease is still in effect and the obligations under that lease continue, even today.

I am now required to determine the meaning of Clause "h."

For the purposes of this argument all parties agree that the respondents read Clause "h" before signing the lease, and that they relied on its plain meaning.

The applicant's position is that Clause "h" does not really mean what it seems to say. The applicant says that the law is that Clause "h" really means that in the event of insolvency the lease is voidable at the option of the landlord.

Clause "h", in its material portions, says:

"That ... if the Lessee ... shall become ... insolvent ... the said term shall immediately become forfeited and void, and an amount equivalent to the next ensuing three months' rent shall be at once due and payable.

Clause "h" uses the word "void:" it does not use the word "voidable". Clause "h" does not have in it the words, "at the option of the landlord."

Strange as it may seem, the cases cited by the applicant in its case book do support its position and the courts have, in effect, added the words, "at the option of the landlord" into clauses, on many occasions.

But must they always be added in every case? ...

In my view Clause "h," in this particular lease, [means her insolvency ends the lease and she must pay three months rent].

I say that because:

1. the plain meaning of the words say that;
2. it was open to the applicant to add the words "at the option of the landlord" if it so desired. After all, It was made up of lawyers. It was their lease.
3. In the context of the whole lease, it makes sense to assume that the applicant intended those words ("at the option of the landlord") not to be there. I note that those words are there, in black and white, in the clause dealing with voidance of the lease for vacancy or improper use. Here are two clauses in the same document dealing with much of the same things: one clause has "at the option of the landlord", the other clause, (Clause "h") does not. I conclude it does not, because the landlord/applicant intended that it not be there. And I am not prepared to put it there, now, despite that intention.

In my view, therefore, this lease is void and the damages are fixed by Clause "h" at three months' rent. The parties themselves can do the exact calculations. Judgment accordingly. Costs to the respondent fixed at $750.

THE APPLICATION OF THE DOCTRINE OF FRUSTRATION

Binder **v.** *Key Property Management Corp.*

[1992] O.J. No. 1732 (Q.L.)
DRS 93-02594
ACTION No. 5270/92
ONTARIO COURT OF JUSTICE—GENERAL DIVISION
JULY 21, 1992

Jenkins J. :
...

CONCLUSIONS

I find that Ms. Binder suffers from chronic fatigue syndrome and is allergic to latex paint and other chemical substances found in the Key Properties apartment. As a result her symptoms were exacerbated when she moved into the freshly painted apartment and she was forced to move out.

S. 86 of the *Landlord and Tenant Act* R.S.O. 1990 ch.L.4 provides as follows:

The doctrine of frustration of contract applies to tenancy agreements and the Frustrated Contracts Act applies thereto. ...

Fridman in *The Law of Contract in Canada* deals with physical incapacity as it relates to the doctrine of frustration starting at p. 600. In determining whether a contract is frustrated by physical incapacity the most important factor is the nature of the contract and whether it is a contract of personal service. At p. 601 he says:

Whether illness of a party will operate to terminate a contract will depend upon the nature of the contract and the type of illness. If it is of the kind which renders the contract incapable of performance as agreed, for example, to play at a concert on a particular night, it would seem that frustration takes place. If it does not disrupt the ultimate fulfilment of the contract a different result will occur.

Ms. Binder's lease with Key Properties is obviously not a contract of personal service. Her obligation is to pay rent for the use of the premises which she has done to date. In addition, her son has continued to live in the apartment and to attend school in London.

The apartment is in habitable condition and it is Ms. Binder's allergies that have forced her to move out. If Ms. Binder had been hospitalized due to an illness unrelated to the chemical substances in the apartment, the lease would still be enforceable even though its purpose was partially frustrated by her hospitalization.

While I have great sympathy for Ms. Binder I find that her special needs resulting from her allergies are not sufficient to terminate the tenancy. As a result I find that the lease is enforceable and the application is dismissed with costs if demanded.

---

5. MORTGAGES

Question

What is the relationship between the mortgagee and the mortgagor?

Bayshore Trust Company **v.** *Assam*

ONTARIO COURT OF JUSTICE
No. 75510/90
APRIL 9, 1992

MacDonald, J: At the opening of trial in this matter, I was advised by counsel for the parties that there was consent to judgment on the claims advanced by Bayshore Trust Company against the defendant Philip Assam. Accordingly, I have endorsed the record for judgment to go in the form provided to me on the consent of counsel. There remains to be determined the issues arising from the counterclaim advanced by the defendant, Mr. Assam.

The relevant background is the following:

Philip Assam is the owner of a residential property municipally known as 2117 Lawrence Avenue West. Mr. Assam obtained from Bayshore Trust Company, a first mortgage which was registered on title on April 7th, 1989 for a period of one year in the principal amount of $210,000. Monthly payments were $2,540.00. Interest was at the rate of 14% per annum. By agreement between the plaintiff and the defendant, this mortgage was renewed on April 25th, 1990 for one year with an interest rate of 14.5%. Default occurred in or about February, 1991 and continued at the time of proceedings before me.

In April, 1991, the defendant Bayshore advised Mr. Assam in writing that they would not consider further renewal of the mortgage due to poor prepayment history.

Mr. Assam has consented to judgment in the amount of $241,667.06. He has also agreed to deliver possession of the land and premises in question to the plaintiff.

The amended counterclaim is against Bayshore Trust Company and one Robert Christopher, jointly and severally. Robert Christopher was then the Chief Executive Officer of Bayshore Trust Company, although at the time of trial, he was no longer associated with the company. Mr. Assam's claim is for $50,000 in general damages together with special damages in an undefined amount. Mr. Assam alleges that the plaintiffs caused him to suffer economic loss by reason of granting him the mortgage. Mr. Assam states that the monthly obligations for service of the mortgage were so high as to make it impossible for him to meet these obligations. Mr. Assam was employed at the time of the application for mortgage in a position that had income of $28,000 a year on a gross basis. He indicated to Bayshore Trust Company that he would have additional income by reason of certain undefined tenancies which he proposed to have on the premises in question. His intentions were to rent out rooms in the premises, but there was never a precise estimate given of the rental income which he anticipated. The monthly mortgage obligation was in fact significantly more than Mr. Assam's monthly income on a net basis, and he alleges that Bayshore, with this information in hand, ought not to have granted him the mortgage in question. It was also known to Bayshore Trust that a second and third mortgage were being postponed by the placement of the first mortgage with Bayshore on the property in question. The second and third mortgages were privately held. Mr. Assam also suggested that he was induced into the transaction by Bayshore and its agents. ...

Mr. Assam alleges that the activities of Bayshore induced him into a situation of financial disaster and it is on this basis that his counterclaim is based. Mr. Christopher gave evidence. He was very familiar with all aspects of the transaction as it related to Mr. Assam. Mr. Christopher struck me as a straightforward witness who tried to accommodate Mr. Assam as much as possible. Mr. Christopher advised me that Bayshore Trust is what is known as an "equity lender;" that is to say that Bayshore Trust assesses a prospective borrower on the basis of the equity of the property in question. Bayshore loans up to 70% of the value of the property, and in Mr. Assam's case, the loans extended to Mr. Assam by Bayshore never exceeded 70% of the value of the property in question. Mr. Christopher indicated to me that the application form does make enquiries about the level of one's income, but the only consideration in respect of the decision to extend funds is based on the equity in the property. ...

The issue is whether or not Bayshore Trust, an equity lender, owes a fiduciary duty of care to the borrower, Mr. Assam? If Bayshore Trust is found to have a fiduciary duty of care, then the court would have to address the question of damages that may arise from any breach of this duty.

It is well settled that as a general rule, a mortgagee is not in a fiduciary relationship with the mortgagor. In the absence of evidence of special circumstances upon which to base a fiduciary duty, the relationship between the parties is purely one of a lender and a borrower or debtor and creditor.

The Supreme Court of Canada considered the test to be applied to determine whether a fiduciary relationship had arisen in *Lac Minerals Ltd. v. International Corona Resources Ltd.*, [1989] 2 S.C.R. 574. Mr. Justice Sopinka was of the opinion a fiduciary obligation is one that arises out of a fiduciary relationship. He concluded that there was no precise test, but that certain characteristics were so frequently found in relationships which had been found to be fiduciary, that they served as a guide. He quoted with approval the enumeration of those characteristics by Madam Justice Wilson in *Frame v. Smith*, [1978] 2 S.C.R. 99 at pp. 135 and 136. They are as follows:

1) The fiduciary has scope for the exercise of some discretion or power.

2) The fiduciary can unilaterally exercise that power or discretion so as to affect the beneficiary's legal or practical interests.

3) The beneficiary is peculiarly vulnerable to or at the mercy of the fiduciary holding the discretion or power.

Mr. Justice Sopinka pointed out that a fiduciary relationship could exist even though not all of the above characteristics were present. However, he stated that the third, that of dependency or vulnerability, was indispensable.

In *Northland Bank v. 230720 Alberta Ltd.* [1990] A.J. No. 838, the defendant debtors sought to establish a fiduciary relationship between themselves and the plaintiff creditor. ... The Alberta Court of Queen's Bench held that it was a straightforward case of a lender-borrower with no "special circumstances" to create a fiduciary relationship of any kind. The court stated as follows:

It is not a defense for a borrower to say that the lender knew or should have known that he did not have the ability to repay the loan so the lender should not have made it.

The wisdom of a lender in giving a loan is not a defense to why the loan should not be repaid. Poor business decisions belong in a court of business, not a court of law.

Houlden J.A. in *Hayward v. Bank of Nova Scotia et al.* (1985), 51 O.R. (2d) 193 (C.A.) reviewed the law with respect to when a fiduciary relationship comes into existence in a relationship between a bank and its customer, and considered *Lloyds Bank Ltd. v. Bundy*, [1974] 3 All E.R. 757 and the more recent case of the House of Lord's of *National Westminster v. Morgan*, [1985] 1 All E.R. 821. *Litwin Construction (1973) Ltd. v. Pan, Nicholson and Nicholson* (1988), 29 B.C.L.R. (2d) 88 C.A.) discusses the "exceptional cases" where the law imposes a fiduciary obligation in a commercial relationship.

The facts in this case do not fit into this line of authorities. The three characteristics to establish a fiduciary relationship are not disclosed in the evidence before me. I do not find that Mr. Assam was vulnerable or dependent upon Bayshore Trust. He was an educated person who understood the extent of the obligation he was undertaking. He had legal counsel. The relationship between him and Bayshore was that of a lender and a borrower. There was a lot of contact between Mr. Assam and Bayshore Trust and its agents, particularly over his inability to make monthly payments, but I cannot find that Bayshore had any duty of a fiduciary nature to Mr. Assam. It is not appropriate to transform the relationship of a lender and a borrower into a fiduciary relationship. I cannot find that Bayshore exercised a dominating influence over Mr. Assam and there is nothing in the evidence that would bring me to the conclusion that Bayshore went beyond a normal business relationship so as to place itself in the position of a fiduciary. The counterclaim against both defendants is, therefore, dismissed.

In the judgment on the main action which I referred to earlier, costs were reserved both in the main action and the counterclaim. If arrangements cannot be made between the parties with respect to costs, I may be spoken to.

TERMS

To complete a real estate transaction, a borrower, through a series of transactions, ended up obligated to pay a total of $2,113,660 plus monthly interest on a mortgage debt of $1,556,8300. The borrower defaulted on the loan. The lender began foreclosure proceedings. The borrower argued that the rate of interest was contrary to s. 347(2) of the *Criminal Code* which prohibits a rate of interest that exceeds 60%. The judge, in a chambers hearing, held for the borrower.

The B.C. Court of Appeal dismissed the appeal by the lender and concluded that in this case the effective rate of interest was 148.2 9%.

Kebet Holdings Ltd. v. 351173 B.C. Ltd
Summarized from The Lawyers Weekly
January 29, 1993 p. 27

The borrower claimed the bank calculated the interest rate improperly and contrary to s. 4 of the *Federal Interest Act* which provides that the lender must contain an express statement of the yearly rate of interest when interest is payable at any rate or percentage for any period less than a year. The contract did stipulate an annual interest rate of 24% but also stated that the rate would be calculated and paid monthly which meant the actual interest paid was close to 27%. Furthermore, because the interest was paid monthly the bank had use of the borrower's money which it could reinvest for the remainder of the year and thus gained while the borrower lost the opportunity.

The outcome of the case would affect the payment of millions of dollars to lenders. The Alberta Court of Queen's Bench agreed that the borrower, Dunphy Leasing had overpaid by $85,000 but this decision was overturned on appeal which held that on the wording of the contract the parties had agreed that the lender could calculate the interest each month and because it was paid each month it did not trigger s. 4 of the *Interest Act* given the wording of that provision.

The Supreme Court of Canada in a six-sentence comment dismissed the appeal by the borrower. In the words of Chief Justice Lamer speaking for a unanimous court of seven judges:

> Mr. Willis, you gave the very difficult case you had the best possible day in Court a barrister can. Unfortunately we cannot accede to your arguments. Essentially this case rests upon the interpretation of a contract and the statutory interpretation of s. 4 of the *Interest Act*, R.S.C. 1985, c.I-15. Both matters were carefully considered by the Court of Appeal and we feel that we cannot usefully add to the reasons below, with which we are in substantial agreement.
>
> The appeal is accordingly dismissed with costs in this Court only.
>
> Judgment accordingly.

The Bank of Nova Scotia, et al. v. Dunphy Leasing Enterprises Ltd., et al.[52]

ENDNOTES

1. Summarized from *The Globe and Mail*, July 1, 1993, p. A9.

2. Internet from the *Wall Street Journal*, August 29, 1996, p. B3 and *The Lawyers Weekly*, February 21, 1997, p. 12.

3. For a full account of this action see *The Lawyers Weekly*, February 21, 1997, p. 8.

4. Summarized from *The Province*, January 16, 1987.

5. Summarized from *BYTE*, September 1990, p. 19.

6. A more detailed account is given in the *Vancouver Sun*, April 16, 1992, p. D11.

7. A more detailed account is given in the *Vancouver Sun*, August 8, 1992, p. B11.

8. *The Lawyers Weekly*, June 30, 1995, p. 10.

9. For a more detailed account see the summary in *PATSCANnews*, Winter 1996, p. 1 in an article by David Wedge, an intellectual property lawyer in Vancouver, who concluded that the "look and feel concept [is] dead."

10. For a more detailed account see *The Lawyers Weekly*, October 28, 1994, p. 25.

11. *CAAST Litigation Report*, October 15, 1997.

12. For a more detailed account see *The Province*, November 25, 1997.

13. For a more detailed account see *The Lawyers Weekly*, February 16, 1996, p. 5. In 1994 the Canadian Motion Picture Distributors Association, through its Film/Video Security Office, and the local police conducted 20 raids in Ontario and with RCMP and Canada Customs were involved with eight seizures of illegal videos. In B.C., Ravinderjit Kandola was fined $36,000 under the *Copyright Act* following the seizure of 1,200 pirated video cassettes by RCMP Commercial Crime Section at two outlets owned by Kandola. For a more detailed account see *The Lawyers Weekly*, June 30, 1995, p. 17.

14. For a more detailed account see *The Lawyers Weekly*, February 16, 1996, p. 11.

15. For a more detailed account see AP, October 15, 1997, on the Internet.

16. For a more detailed account see *Newsweek*, January 22, 1990.

17. For a more detailed account see *The New York Times*, September 12, 1995, p. C2.

18. *The Lawyers Weekly*, July 28, 1989.

19. A more detailed account is given in *Newsweek*, January 6, 1992, p. 55.

20. Summarized from *The Globe and Mail*, April 28, 1993, p. A7.

21. A more detailed account is given in *Infoworld*, March 5, 1984, p. 6.

22. A more detailed account is given in *Datamation*, May 1, 1984.

23. A more detailed account is given in *Newsweek*, March 16, 1987, p. 53.

24. This case was followed for years in *The Lawyers Weekly*. The U.S. case involving 2 live Crew's use of Roy Orbison's 1964 song, "Oh, Pretty Woman," was also covered by *Time magazine*, December 13, 1993, p. 93.

25. For a more detailed account see *Newsweek*, June 24, 1996, p. 89.

26. See *Cadbury Schweppes Inc. v. FBI Foods Ltd.*, The British Columbia Court of Appeal, Vancouver Registry CAO 18889, http://www.courts.gov.bc.ca/.

27. A more detailed account is given in *Newsweek*, September 23, 1991, p. 40.

28. For a summary of this trial decision of the Manitoba Queen's Bench see *The Lawyers Weekly*, September 22, 1995, p. 20 and October 6, 1995, p. 13.

29. See *The Lawyers Weekly*, October 7, 1994, p. 9.

30. For a summary of *Walt Disney Productions v. Triple Five Corp.*, see *The Lawyers Weekly*, July 24, 1992, p. 3.

31. See *The Lawyers Weekly*, October 14, 1994, p. 33 regarding the dismissal of the appeal, June 7, 1996, p. 12.

32. For a more detailed account see *The Lawyers Weekly*, June 25, 1993, p. 23.

33. For a more detailed account see *The Hollywood Reporter*, November 26, 1996.

34. Received by e-mail from Edupage, *USA Today*, June 3, 1997.

35. See *Net Insider*, October 15, 1997, by internet.

36. A more detailed account is given in *Newsweek*, March 6, 1989.

37. For a summary of the Federal Court of Appeal's decision see *The Lawyers Weekly*, February 24, 1995, p. 32.

38. *The Lawyers Weekly*, Jeffrey Miller, December 16, 1988.

39. *The Lawyers Weekly*, July 13, 1990.

40. For a summary of *Maple Leaf Foods Inc. v. Robin Hood Multifoods Inc.* see *The Lawyers Weekly*, November 4, 1994, p. 28.

41. For a full examination of these wrongs and acceptable evidence see *National Hockey League v. Pepsi-Cola Canada Ltd.* (1995) 2 B.C.L.R. (3d) 13 for the decision of the trial judge and [1995] 5 W.W.R. 404 for the decision of the B.C. Court of Appeal.

42. For a full report on this case see *The Lawyers Weekly*, June 28, 1996, p. 11.

43. Summarized from *The Globe and Mail*, November 10, 1992.

44. Received by e-mail from Edupage, *New York Times*, May 14, 1997.

45. For a more detailed account of this issue see *The Globe and Mail*, November 19, 1997, p. 1.

46. Summarized from *The Globe and Mail*, October 13, 1990, p. B5.

47. For a more detailed account see *The Ottawa Citizen*.

48. A more detailed account is given in *Datamation*.

49. A more detailed account is given in the *Vancouver Sun*, March 19, 1988, pp. 1, D12.

50. For a more complete summary of *Co-operators General Insurance Co. v. Alberta Human Rights Commission* see *The Lawyers Weekly*, January 21, 1994, p. 18.

51. For a more detailed account see the reviews in *The Lawyers Weekly*, July 8, 1994, pp. 5, 42.

52. The decision of the Court of Appeal was summarized from the review of the case in *The Lawyers Weekly*, April 8, 1994, p. 3; April 22, 1994, p. 16 and the Supreme Court of Canada decision was taken from http://www.droit.umontreal.ca/.

VIII

THE REGULATION OF BUSINESS

A. GOVERNMENTAL REGULATION

Question

In what ways can government affect your business plans and practices?

Tony's Broadloom & Floor Covering Ltd. v. NMC Canada Inc.

31 O.R. (3D) 481 (Q.L.)
[1996] O.J. No. 4372
No. C21028
COURT OF APPEAL FOR ONTARIO
DECEMBER 12, 1996

Doherty, J.A.:—The appellants purchased certain property in Etobicoke in September 1988. In November 1988, they were told of the presence of Varsol and oil contaminant in the soil and the groundwater on the property. Some four-and-a-half years later, in February 1993, the appellants commenced this action claiming rescission of the agreement of purchase and sale and damages on the basis that the contaminants rendered the property of no value. The appellants and respondents brought motions for summary judgment in December 1994. White J. dismissed the appellants' motion. ...

The property ... was zoned for industrial use. It had a long history of industrial use and the respondents had operated a factory on the property under the name Venco Metals ("Venco"), since 1974. Venco manufactured metal stamps and used Varsol to clean the machinery used in that process. Between 1979 and 1985, the dirty Varsol was dumped on the ground behind the factory. In 1985, the owner of the adjoining property complained about the presence of oil and Varsol in its sump pump pit. Representatives from the Ministry of the Environment and the City of Etobicoke investigated and determined that the dirty Varsol was likely migrating from the respondents' property to the neighbour's property through the groundwater. The respondents retained Monenco Consultants Ltd. ("Monenco") to investigate the problem and to advise as to what steps should be taken. ... A short time later, in November 1985, Varsol and other solvents were classified as registerable hazardous waste material by O. Reg. 322/85 passed pursuant to the *Environmental Protection Act*, R.S.O. 1980, c. 141. Monenco reported that the soil and groundwater were contaminated with Varsol and oil and recommended that certain wells be installed on the property to capture the contaminant and control its spread. The respondents installed the recommended system in 1985 and retained Monenco to monitor the condition of the soil and groundwater.

Mr. Tony Tolomei, who controlled both corporate appellants, became interested in purchasing the property late in 1987. His carpet business was located about 100 metres from the property, and he had previously purchased and developed two other smaller properties in the area. Mr. Tolomei knew that Venco operated a manufacturing plant on the property, but he did not know the specific nature of that business.

Mr. Tolomei negotiated the purchase of the property with George Arndt, the Director of Finance for one of the respondent companies. On January 8, 1988, the parties entered into an agreement of purchase and sale calling for the sale of the property for a price of $1,250,000. ... Although Mr. Arndt was well aware of the contaminant in the groundwater and soil, he made no mention of it to Mr. Tolomei either before entering into the agreement in January or prior to closing in September. The appellants [buyers] were unaware of the existence of the contaminant in the soil and groundwater before the closing of the transaction.

Mr. Tolomei wanted to build a multi-storey residential condominium on the property. ... [However,] he did not tell Mr. Arndt or anyone connected with the respondents about his intended use of the property. ...

When he agreed to buy the property, Mr. Tolomei knew that the property was zoned for industrial use, and he knew that a factory had been operated on the site for many years. Mr. Tolomei also knew that the property would have to be re-zoned before he could proceed with his condominium development. Despite these facts, Mr. Tolomei chose not to investigate the property prior to agreeing to purchase it, or to make the agreement conditional upon appropriate re-zoning. ...

Although the respondents gave the appellants full access to the property between January and September 1988, the appellants did nothing to determine the suitability of the property for the proposed use. Nor, as provided for in the agreement of purchase and sale, did the appellants obtain the respondents' consent to an inspection of the property by any governmental authority. According to Mr. Tolomei he did not even bother to visually inspect the property before the closing date.

In August 1988, the appellants did ask the respondents for permission to conduct certain soil tests on the property. The respondents gave that permission. For reasons which had nothing to do with the respondents, the tests were not done until after closing and the appellants did not receive a report from their consultant until December 1988. Although the tests were done to determine the feasibility of erecting a multi-storey building on the property, they clearly revealed the contaminant in the soil and groundwater. ...

The appellants were told of the contaminant problem in November 1988 by officials from the Ministry of the Environment. They continued to attempt to develop the property. ... The appellants' efforts to develop the property were finally abandoned in 1991 when, according to Mr. Tolomei, the economy precluded any further attempt to develop the property. ...

In oral argument, counsel for the appellants submitted that the classification of the contaminant as "hazardous industrial waste" in a regulation passed pursuant to the *Environmental Protection Act* established that any use of the property posed a danger. He also argued that the contaminant rendered the property "valueless." The evidence does not support the first submission and flatly contradicts the second. ... The appellants' own evidence established that the property had value in its existing state. The most that can be said on this record is that the presence of the contaminant could significantly increase the costs of developing the property for use as a residential condominium.

Much of the argument on the motion turned on whether the presence of the contaminant should be classified as a latent or patent defect in the property. I agree with the respondents' primary submission that it was neither. ...

In this case, the respondents agreed to sell, and the appellants agreed to buy industrial property. ... [T]he respondents were not told of the appellants' intention to use the property for a very different purpose. The respondents had no reason to believe that the appellants would use the property for any purpose other than an industrial one. The question of whether the contaminant constituted a defect in the property must be considered in this context. This record offers no support for the contention that the contaminant impaired the continued use of the property for industrial purposes. The appellants got exactly what they bargained for—industrial land. Their undisclosed intention to use the property for residential purposes does not alter the bargain the appellants made, or create a latent defect in the industrial property which the appellants agreed to purchase.

If I am wrong and the presence of the contaminant was a defect, I agree with the conclusion of White J. [the trial judge] ... that the defect was a patent one. It would have been readily discoverable by the appellants had they exercised reasonable vigilance in the circumstances. In deciding whether the appellants exercised reasonable vigilance, it must be remembered that the appellants were buying industrial land on which they proposed to build a residential condominium. A reasonable inspection of the property, reasonable inquiries of the respondents, and reasonable inquiries of the local and provincial authorities would have put the appellants on notice of the existence of the contaminant. Indeed, had the appellants pursued the taking of soil samples with reasonable diligence after the respondents had permitted them to take those samples, they would have learned of the existence of the contaminant before closing. Instead, the appellants chose not to disclose their intended use of the property and to take no steps to satisfy themselves that the property could be used for that purpose. ...

The appellants also submit that apart from the characterization of any defect as latent or patent, the vendors had a duty to bargain in good faith and breached that duty when they failed to advise the appellants of the information provided by Monenco in the spring and summer of 1988. The existence of a duty to bargain in good faith in an arms-length commercial transaction involving the sale of real property is debatable: see annotation of J. Lem to Justice White's decision at 44 R.P.R. (2d) 29 at pp. 30–31. In any event, I can see no evidence on this record of any basis for a finding of bad faith against the respondents. They made no misrepresentations. They gave the appellants ready access to information concerning the property and full physical access to the property, even to the extent of permitting investigations which were not required by the agreement of purchase and sale. Furthermore, they had no knowledge that the appellants intended to radically change the use of the property. I cannot agree that the failure to disclose information which did not affect the continued use of the property for industrial purposes, and which could have been obtained by the appellants through their own reasonable efforts, constitutes bad faith.

I would dismiss the appeal with costs.

Appeal dismissed.

Campbell et al. *v.* Federal Express Canada Ltd.

[1997] O.J. No. 3510 (Q.L.)
COURT FILE NO. 512/97
ONTARIO COURT OF JUSTICE (GENERAL DIVISION)
AUGUST 27, 1997

[1] Bolan, J.:—The Applicants Campbell reside at 871 Main Street West and the Applicants Bryer reside at 863 Main Street West, all in the City of North Bay. Directly behind their property at 881 Jet Avenue, the Respondent carries on a courier business which involves the loading and unloading of trucks on week days sometime between 3:00 a.m. and 4:00 a.m. The Applicants allege the Respondent's nocturnal operations affect their sleep, health and mental state in that they are awakened on a regular basis in the middle of the night during these operations. They seek an injunction prohibiting the Respondent from emitting sounds from 7:00 p.m. to 7:00 a.m. This relief is sought on three grounds:

> First: The Respondent's activities are in contravention of the City Planning By-Law 28-80 as amended;
>
> Second: The Respondent is contravening the City Noise By-Law 142-76, as amended;
>
> Third: The actions of the Respondent constitute a nuisance of [sic] common law.

[The judge reviews the facts regarding the *"modus operandi"* of the Respondent, the consequent woes of the Applicants "such as moving their beds into the living room, keeping their windows closed in summer in spite of the heat, wearing ear plugs and even moving into the basement," the experience of other neighbours, and the complaints received by the North Bay City Council.]

[12] I am satisfied that the noise as described by the Applicants and others to whom I have referred does in fact seriously affect the sleep habits of the Applicants and others in the neighbourhood. Furthermore, the noise causes material discomfort and annoyance. The issue to determine is what remedy, if any, is available to the Applicants.

[He reviews the wording of the Noise By-Law and its Schedule 2.]

[17] I am satisfied that the noise emanating from the Respondent's courier operation between the hours of 7:00 p.m. to 7:00 a.m. constitutes a breach of the Noise By-Law. The Respondent's operation comes under the heading of loading and unloading and occurs during the prohibited period. In my view, the Respondent is in breach of the Noise By-Law unless it is an essential service. The decision of Dickson C.J.C. in *Re Public Service Employee Relation Act* [1987] 1 S.C.R. 313 describes essential service as "one the interruption of which would threaten serious harm to the general public or to a part of the population." Surely, this kind of operation is not an essential service which can only be carried out at this location. Courier services flourish in this city—the Respondent is not the only courier in this area. There is no evidence which prevents the Respondent for relocating somewhere else in the city.

[18] There is no evidence of serious harm being inflicted on anyone should the service be discontinued at this location.

[19] There will accordingly be an Order prohibiting the Respondent from conducting their loading and unloading operation at 881 Jet Avenue in the City of North Bay between the hours of 7:00 p.m. and 7:00 a.m.

[20] The operation of this Prohibition Order is stayed until November 1, 1997 to allow the Respondent to relocate or to take such steps as are required to discontinue the noise.

[21] Having granted the relief sought on the second ground, I need not deal with the first and third grounds.

[22] I invite written submissions on costs.

- *I*n *R. v. Bata Industries,* two former directors of the company involved with the day-to-day operations were convicted under environmental protection legislation for *not* taking steps to prevent the release of pollutants by the company. Furthermore, the court order against the convicted company prohibited the company from indemnifying the convicted directors.[1]

  On appeal the court upheld the order that prohibited the company from indemnifying the directors.[2]

B. CHALLENGES TO A BY-LAW OR A DECISION OF AN ADMINISTRATIVE TRIBUNAL

Q u e s t i o n

How can you challenge a by-law that interferes with your business?
What are your defences if you must face a hearing before an administrative tribunal?

The facts were stated by Judge Grange of the Court of Appeal for Ontario as follows:

"An exotic dancer at Jilly's Tavern in the east end of Toronto performed her act with the assistance of a declawed Siberian tiger. The tiger, when not required for the act, was sometimes kept on a leash behind the tavern. There were no incidents of harm, either to persons or the tiger, but a city councilor for the area, spurred on by animal rights groups, brought the matter before City Council."

A city by-law was passed and later amended to regulate the keeping of animals. The inclusive language of the by-law prohibited circuses and similar shows from using exotic animals unless the performance related to certain films or education. The circus companies challenged the by-law.

One issue before the Court of Appeal was whether or not the city by-law was within the power of the city as granted by the *Municipal Act* of Ontario. After a careful review of the exact wording of the by-laws, the relevant section of the *Municipal Act*, sections of the *Ontario Society for the Prevention of Cruelty to Animals Act*, and Supreme Court of Canada cases concerning municipal power, Judge Grange concluded:

"We no longer concern ourselves with the reasonableness of municipal by-laws. But that does not mean that the municipality is free to exceed the powers given to it by statute. As Lacourciere J. said in *Re Regional Municipality of Ottawa-Carleton and Township of Marlborough*, [1974] 2 O.R. (2d) 297 at 305:

> A by-law must be passed for the purpose allowed by the statute, and council must not see, in enacting a by-law, to accomplish indirectly that which cannot be directly accomplished in the manner provided by legislature.

… In my view the Legislature in enacting s. 210(1) [of the Municipal Act] did not intend the City to use it to control the conduct of circuses. What was intended instead was that the by-laws passed under the section would control the keeping of exotic animals such as, perhaps, the tiger associated with the dancer at Jilly's Tavern and would restrain the activities of persons who fancied boa constrictors or barracudas as domestic pets.

For these reasons, I am of the opinion that council of the city exceeded its powers in attempting to prohibit the use of exotic animals in circuses visiting the city. The aims of city council may well be commendable but those aims must be legislated or fulfilled by the appropriate authorities.

I would allow the appeal, set aside the order of the Divisional Court and grant judgment ordering a declaration that the prohibition against the keeping of animals used in live public entertainment in the city of Toronto under City of Toronto By-law No. 212-86 as amended is *ultra vires* the legislative authority of the city of Toronto and is therefore of no force or effect. The appellants are entitled to their costs here and below. There will be no costs to or against the Attorney General.

Stadium Corporation of Ontario Ltd. v. City of Toronto
Registry No. C13313
Court of Appeal for Ontario Court
April 1993

DID THE TRIBUNAL ILLEGALLY RESTRAIN TRADE?
DID THE TRIBUNAL FAIL TO ADHERE TO THE RULES OF NATURAL JUSTICE?

Johnson **v.** *Athletics Canada and International Amateur Athletics Federation*

[1997] O.J. No. 3201 (Q.L.)
COURT FILE NO. A4947/97
ONTARIO COURT OF JUSTICE (GENERAL DIVISION)
JULY 25, 1997

[1] Caswell J.:— The applicant Benjamin Johnson has applied to the court for the following relief:

1. a declaration that the life-time ban issued by the respondents, Athletics Canada (A.C.) and the International Amateur Athletics Federation (I.A.A.F.), preventing him from participating in amateur athletic events governed by the respondents is contrary to the common law doctrine of restraint of trade;

2. an order reinstating Mr. Johnson's eligibility to participate in all activities governed by the respondents; and

3. costs on a solicitor and client basis.

FACTS

...

[11] At the Seoul Olympics in 1988, Mr. Johnson tested positive for the use of stanozolol, a prohibited substance. He was stripped of his gold medal and ultimately was banned from competition for two years. In 1990 he was re-instated as a member of A.C. He competed thereafter at various events and at the 1992 Olympics in Barcelona as a member of the Canadian team. Subsequent to his re-instatement Mr. Johnson was tested after every event in which he participated. ...

[13] On January 17, 1993 Mr. Johnson participated in an I.A.A.F. competition held in Montreal. At the conclusion of the race he provided a urine sample for testing. The sample was collected and sent to INRS-Sant, for analysis in accordance with the approved scientific protocols as set out in I.A.A.F. Procedural Guidelines 4.8–4.11. The urine sample was divided between two containers and they were labelled "A" and "B". ...

[14] Sample "A" was tested between January 19 and January 25 and the results revealed a testosterone to epitestosterone ratio of 10.3:1 [where 6:1 constitutes an offence]. ...

[15] ... The testing and analysis of sample "B" occurred on February 15 and 16, 1993. Mr. Johnson's lawyer, Terrence O'Sullivan, and his expert, Dr. David Black, President and Laboratory Director of Aegis Analytical Laboratories in Nashville, Tennessee were present on both days. Mr. Johnson's representatives examined the integrity of the "B" sample and agreed that there was no evidence of tampering, improper sealing of the "B" sample or any difficulties as to the coding of the sample bottles. The results of the testing [of] ... sample "B" had a ratio of testosterone to epitestosterone identical to sample "A", namely 10.3:1. ...

[17] ... Mr. Johnson [was informed] ... that the I.A.A.F. Doping Commission had ruled that the positive test contravened I.A.A.F. Rules 55 and 60 and constituted a doping offence. Since this was a second doping offence under I.A.A.F. Rule 60 2(a)(ii), pursuant to Rule 59.1 and 59.2, he was suspended from competition. The letter further stated ... [that he had the right to appeal the ruling, but Johnson did not appeal].

[22] On April 21, 1993 A.C. again wrote to Mr. Johnson to advise that the period had expired within which he could launch his appeal from the finding of the I.A.A.F. Doping Commission. The letter stated that since the deadline for return of the notice of application for a hearing expired as of midnight April 1, 1993, Mr. Johnson was declared ineligible for competition for life.

THE LAW

Restraint of Trade

[23] Competition among world class "amateur" athletes provides the successful athlete with considerable financial rewards including support from his national body as a carded athlete and payments from companies whose products he endorses. In order to preserve the athlete's amateur status, the monies that the athlete earns are deposited in an athlete reserve trust fund. In the 1980's and even after the Seoul Olympics, Mr. Johnson continued to be considered a world class athlete with lucrative endorsement contracts.

[24] It is the position of the applicant that the court should find that the life-time ban from competition is in restraint of Mr. Johnson's common law rights to carry on the trade or business from which he earns his livelihood: running. ...

[25] There is no "bright line" test with respect to the categories to which the doctrine of restraint of trade applies. ...

[26] In the English case of *Gasser v. Stinson et al.*, unreported, June 15, 1988 (Ch. Div.), Scott J., ... on the issue of restraint of trade, found as follows:

The policy underlying restraint of trade law is that people should be free to exploit for their financial gain the talents and abilities that they may have. I would accept that restraint of trade law would not be applicable to activities that were undertaken for no financial reward at all (for example, school sport). ... But, in a sport which allows competitors to exploit their ability in the sport for financial gain and which allows that gain to be a direct consequence of participation in competition, a ban on competition is, in my judgment, a restraint of trade.

[27] I adopt Scott J.'s reasoning and I find that the life-time ban imposed on Mr. Johnson is in restraint of trade.

Justification for the Restraint

[28] In *Nordenfelt v. Maxim Nordenfelt Guns & Ammunition Co. Ltd.*, [1894] A.C. 535 (H.L.) Lord Macnaghten stated at p. 565:

> The public have an interest in every person's carrying on his trade freely: so has the individual. All interference with individual liberty of action in trading, and all restraints of trade of themselves, if there is nothing more, are contrary to public policy, and therefore void. That is the general rule. But here are exceptions: restraints of trade and interference with individual liberty of action may be justified by the special circumstances of a particular case. It is a sufficient justification, and indeed it is the only justification, if the restriction is reasonable—reasonable, that is, in reference to the interests of the parties concerned and reasonable in reference to the interests of the public, so framed and so guarded as to afford adequate protection to the party in whose favour it is imposed, while at the same time it is in no way injurious to the public. That, I think, is the fair result of all the authorities.

[29] I am persuaded that this statement represents the present state of the law in Canada: *Connors v. Connors Brothers Limited et al.*, [1939] S.C.R. 162. A.C. and the I.A.A.F. have argued that the life-time ban after a second doping offence is reasonable for many reasons. I agree that the ban is reasonable and is not an illegal restraint of trade. It is necessary to protect Mr. Johnson for the sake of his own health from the effects of consistently using prohibited substances. It is necessary to protect the right of the athlete, including Mr. Johnson, to fair competition, to know that the race involves only his own skill, his own strength, his own spirit and not his own pharmacologist.

[30] The public has an interest in the protection of the integrity of the sport. Governments around the world subsidize their elite athletes through carding systems. The public pays to attend the events. The elite athlete is viewed as a hero and his influence over the young athlete cannot be underestimated. Mr. Johnson became both rich and famous during his athletic career as a result of his athletic performances. In at least some of the races he has admitted that he was cheating. Most major sports impose a life-time ban after an athlete has been caught for a second time using banned substances. …

[32] This court is required to extend a measure of deference to the justifications advanced by the I.A.A.F. as the world governing body for amateur athletes when considering the reasonableness of the ban. It is not this court's function to serve as a court of appeal on the merits of decisions reached by tribunals exercising jurisdiction over specialized fields. The I.A.A.F. has special expertise not only in regulating amateur athletics but also in regulating, detecting and preventing drug abuse. …

Denial of Natural Justice

[34] The position of Mr. Johnson is that the actions and proceedings of the I.A.A.F. and A.C. in 1993 were inherently unfair and as a result he was denied natural justice. The requirements of natural justice are set out by the Supreme Court of Canada in many cases including *Lakeside Colony of Hutterian Brethren v. Hoffer*, [1992] 3 S.C.R. 165 Gonthier J. at p. 195:

> The content of the principles of natural justice is flexible and depends on the circumstances in which the question arises. However, the most basic requirements are that of notice, opportunity to make representations, and an unbiased tribunal.

[35] … Mr. Johnson now raises the issue of apprehension of bias as the reason for his failure to initiate appeal proceedings during the 28-day period following March 5, 1993. Mr. Johnson claims that this bias was revealed in certain statements reported in the press that were made by Dr. Ljungqvist [Chairman of the Doping Control Commission] and by Mr. Dupr [President of A.C.].The statements suggested the futility of any appeal by Mr. Johnson in view of the findings of the Doping Commission. When Mr. Johnson announced his resignation on March 7, 1993, however, he stated that he did not wish to appeal the ban for three reasons; his age, the potential cost of an appeal, and the obligations that he felt to spare his family any further trauma. He did not at that time mention any apprehension of bias by A.C.'s and/or I.A.A.F.'s appellate panels.

[36] Both A.C. and I.A.A.F. referred to the procedures open to Mr. Johnson, after the Doping Commission confirmed his suspension, as being appeal procedures. … These procedures were really in the nature of hearings "de novo," that is new hearings. Mr. Johnson was entitled notice of the hearing(s) to be represented by counsel, to be present personally and to present further evidence including witnesses. The panels were required to consider existing and additional evidence and to hear submissions from counsel. It is important to note that Mr. Johnson was represented at the time by Terrence O'Sullivan, a very experienced and capable counsel. The pleadings in this application contain voluminous correspondence between Mr. O'Sullivan and A.C. and the I.A.A.F.

[37] There is insufficient evidence before me that any appeal panel would have been biased against Mr. Johnson, in order to justify Mr. Johnson's failure to enforce his rights at the time. While I consider the remarks of Mr. Ljungqvist and Mr. Dupr, to be most improper given their positions, I have no evidence that either person would have affected the decision of an appeal panel.

[38] Even if I were to find that on March 5, 1993, the Doping Commission should have heard from Mr. Johnson's counsel and should have considered any additional evidence, I am faced with the fact that Mr. Johnson did not avail himself of any of the several opportunities that were available to him for further hearings on the merits. Such hearings were capable of curing any perceived lack of fairness at the Doping Commission hearing and it must be assumed that they would do so: *Grey v. Canadian Track and Field and Association* (1986), 39 A.C.W.S. (2d) 483 (Ont. H.C.) … [and others].

[39] Mr. Johnson failed to exhaust the remedies that were available to him without sufficient justification. The procedures in place in 1993 complied with the requirements of natural justice and were procedurally fair. In my view there was no violation of the rules of natural justice.

DISPOSITION

[40] The application is therefore dismissed.

- *I*n a criminal action, the judge charged the accused with "complete nincompoopery." This comment with others was sufficient to raise an apprehension of bias. The accused was successful in obtaining a prohibition and his case was assigned to a different judge.[3]

Was the behaviour the result of official misinformation

In a case involving a criminal action against the owner and operator of an adult video store, the accused argued that he did not "knowingly" sell obscene material because the films were approved by the Ontario Film Review Board. The majority of the court did not consider the excuse of "officially induced error of law" because it was not raised, but Justice Lamer said the following:

> In my view, the circumstances of this case permit the accused to be excused from conviction on the basis of an officially induced error of law by virtue of the OFRB's approval of the films in question. While I do not believe film board approval negatives *mens rea* or justifies the accused's criminal actions, I believe that reasonable reliance on this type of official advice is sufficient basis for a judicial stay of proceedings to be entered. Requiring that a stay be entered only in the clearest of officially induced error of law cases does not offend the maxim that ignorance of the law does not excuse. Rather, it provides an exception from this provision, in line with the existing exceptions, which ensures that the morally blameless are not made criminally responsible for their actions.

R. v. Jorgenson
File No.: 23787
http://www.droit.umontreal.ca/
Supreme Court of Canada
November 16, 1995

Privative Clauses

Question

Does a privative clause in the legislation creating the tribunal prevent a judicial review of a tribunal's decision?

Pasiechnyk et al. v. *Saskatchewan (Workers' Compensation Board)*

File No.: 24913
http://www.droit.umontreal.ca/
Supreme Court of Canada
August 28, 1997

Sopinka, J.:

[1] This case raises the issue of the correct standard of review of a determination of the Saskatchewan Workers' Compensation Board (the Board) that an action was barred by *The Workers' Compensation Act*, 1979, S.S. 1979, c. W-17.1 (the "Act"). It also raises the issue of whether the government, when it acts as a regulator, is an "employer" within the meaning of the Act. I find that the determination made by the Board was protected by a full privative clause, and that it was within the jurisdiction of the Board. The Board's decision that the government was an "employer" and thus entitled to benefit from the statutory bar was not patently unreasonable.

FACTS

[2] On May 25, 1990 a crane owned by Procrane fell over onto a trailer in which employees at a Saskatchewan Power Corporation construction site were taking their morning coffee break. Two workers died and six others suffered serious and debilitating injuries. The injured workers and the dependents of the deceased workers qualified for and received Workers' Compensation Benefits.

[3] In January 1991, the respondents launched an action against SaskPower, Procrane, and the Saskatchewan Government. The claim against the government alleged that it failed to meet its duties under *The Occupational Health and Safety Act*, R.S.S. 1978, c. O-1, by failing adequately to inspect the crane. ...

[4] The Board held that the government, Procrane and SaskPower were "employers" within the meaning of the Act, and accordingly the actions were barred by the Act. The Saskatchewan Court of Queen's Bench dismissed the respondents' application for judicial review. The Saskatchewan Court of Appeal allowed the respondents' appeal with respect to the action against the government but not with respect to the actions against Procrane and SaskPower. This appeal involves only the action against the Government of Saskatchewan.

RELEVANT STATUTORY PROVISIONS

[5] *The Workers' Compensation Act*, 1979, S.S. 1979, c. W-17.1 ...

22.—(1) The board shall have exclusive jurisdiction to examine, hear and determine all matters and questions arising under this Act and any other matter in respect of which a power, authority or discretion is conferred upon the board and, without limiting the generality of the foregoing, the board shall have exclusive jurisdiction to determine: ...

(h) whether any industry or any part, branch or department of any industry is within the scope of this Act and the class to which it is assigned;

(2) The decision and finding of the board under this Act upon all questions of fact and law are final and conclusive and no proceedings by or before the board shall be restrained by injunction, prohibition or other proceeding or removable by certiorari or otherwise in any court. ...

44. No employer and no worker or any dependent of a worker has a right of action against an employer or a worker with respect to an injury sustained by a worker in the course of his employment. ...

167. The right to compensation provided by this Act is in lieu of all rights of action, statutory or otherwise, to which a worker or his dependants are or may be entitled against the employer of the worker for or by reason of any injury sustained by him while in the employment of the employer. ...

180. Except as otherwise provided in this Act, all rights of action against the employers for injuries to workers, either at common law or under The Workmen's Compensation Act, are abolished. ...

ISSUES

[14] There are three issues in this appeal:

1. the standard of review;
2. if the standard of review is patent unreasonableness was the decision of the Board [to find the government an employer and thus barred from an action] patently unreasonable; and
3. if the standard of review is correctness, was the Board correct in determining that the action against the government was statute barred?

[15] I have decided that the standard of review is patent unreasonableness and therefore the third issues does not arise.

ANALYSIS

Standard of Review

[16] To determine the standard of review, I must first decide whether the subject matter of the decision of the administrative tribunal was subject to a privative clause having full privative effect. If the conclusion is that a full privative clause applies, then the decision of the tribunal is only reviewable if it is patently unreasonable or the tribunal has made an error in the interpretation of a legislative provision limiting the tribunal's powers. In either circumstance the tribunal will have exceeded its jurisdiction. These principles are summarized in *U.E.S., Local 298 v. Bibeault*, [1988] 2 S.C.R. 1048. ...

[17] A "full" or "true" privative clause is one that declares that decisions of the tribunal are final and conclusive from which no appeal lies and all forms of judicial review are excluded. ... Where the legislation employs words that purport to limit review but fall short of the traditional wording of a full privative clause, it is necessary to determine whether the words were intended to have full privative effect or a lesser standard of deference. ...

[18] ... Factors such as the purpose of the statute creating the tribunal, the reason for its existence, the area of expertise and the nature of the problem are all relevant in arriving at the intent of the legislature. ... See *Bibeault* ...

HISTORY AND PURPOSE OF WORKERS' COMPENSATION

[23] The history and purpose of workers' compensation supports the proposition that the Board in this case had exclusive jurisdiction to decide the question of whether the statutory bar applies, because this question is intimately related to one side of the historic trade-off embodied in the system.

[24] Workers' compensation is a system of compulsory no-fault mutual insurance administered by the state. [The judge summarizes the history of our legislation and the "historic trade off]... by which workers lost their cause of action against their employers but gained compensation that depends neither on the fault of the employer nor its ability to pay. Similarly, employers were forced to contribute to a mandatory insurance scheme, but gained freedom from potentially crippling liability. ...

[26] The importance of the historic trade off has been recognized by the courts. ...

[28] The cases also support the conclusion that the legislature intended to commit exclusively to the Board the question of whether the statutory bar applied. ...

[There follows a thorough review of the purpose, role and expertise of the Board.]

[38] The composition, tenure, and powers of the Board demonstrate that it has very considerable expertise in dealing with all aspects of the workers' compensation system. Not only does the Board have day-to-day expertise in handling claims for compensation, in setting assessment rates and promoting workplace safety; but it also has expertise in ensuring that the purposes of the Act are not defeated. …

The Problem before the Board

[39] The Act contains three provisions that bar actions. Section 44 takes away the right of action of an employer or a worker against an employer or a worker for an injury sustained by a worker in the course of his employment. Section 167 simply provides that the right to compensation in the Act is in lieu of all rights of action that a worker may have against his or her employer by reason of an injury sustained in the course of employment. Section 180 abolishes all rights of action against employers for injuries to workers. …

[41] Essentially, then, the question before the Board on an application under s. 168 is whether the plaintiff is eligible for compensation, and whether the defendant is immune from suit by virtue of being a contributor to the workers' compensation system. In both cases, the Board is passing on a matter that relates intimately to the purposes and structure of the workers' compensation system. …

[42] There can be no question that the question of eligibility for compensation is one that is within the Board's exclusive jurisdiction. It is also clear upon examination that the issue of whether an action is barred is equally within the Board's ex-clusive jurisdiction. It would undermine the purposes of the scheme for the courts to assume jurisdiction over that question. It could lead to one of the problems that workers' compensation was created to solve, namely, the problem of employers becoming insolvent as a result of high damage awards. The system of collective liability was created to prevent that, and thus to ensure security of compensation to the workers. Individual immunity is the necessary corollary to collective liability. The interposition of the courts could also lead to uncertainty about recovery. …

[43] In view of the above, the issue as to whether the proposed action is barred is one that is committed to the Board for final decision and is not reviewable unless it is patently unreasonable.

IS THE DECISION PATENTLY UNREASONABLE?

[After reviewing the procedure by which the Board held the government to be an "employer" and after considering the argument of the Court of Appeal, the judge concluded:]

Applying the standard which I have determined is appropriate, I conclude that clearly the decision of the Board is not patently unreasonable.

CONCLUSION

[52] I would allow the appeal, set aside the judgment of the Court of Appeal and restore the judgment of Scheibel J. The appellants are entitled to costs both here and in the Court of Appeal.

Appeal allowed

C. REMEDIES

PREROGATIVE WRITS

A community association, to block a development on land zoned multiple dwelling, requested the city to rezone the area. The city complied and passed a resolution to have the city solicitor prepare the necessary by-law. The next day, the Cheungs, the owners of the property, were told by the city that under s. 981(2) that they had seven days to apply for the building permit or they would be caught by the new zoning bylaw. The Cheungs filed their application for a building permit within six days. The city purported to freeze all building permit applications under s. 981(1).

The Cheungs sought an order of *mandamus* to force the city to issue the building permit. It was granted. In the reasons for decision of the appeal case the relevant statutory provision was given:

981. (1) Where a local government passes a resolution identifying what it considers to be a conflict between a development proposed in an application for a building permit and

(a) an official community plan,

(b) a rural land use bylaw, or

(c) a bylaw under sections 963 or 969

that is under preparation, the local government may direct that the permit be withheld for a period of 30 days, commencing on the day the application for the permit was made.

(2) Subsection (1) does not apply unless a local government has, by resolution at least 7 days prior to the application for a building permit, commenced the preparation of a plan or bylaw that is in conflict with the application.

Justice Cumming continued:

"The new s. 981 made two important changes:

(a) First, it set out with some precision the circumstances that must exist, and the procedures which must be followed, for a building permit, which would otherwise be issued as of right, to be withheld.

(b) Second, it provided that a building permit could not be withheld unless the rezoning process had been commenced at least 7 days prior to the building permit application. This second change is one of principle. The effect of this change is the issue on this appeal.

The purpose of subs. (2) of s. 981 was explained by Esson C.J.S.C. in *Taina Developments (Blackford) Ltd. v. New Westminster (City) (28* February 1990), Vancouver Registry A900370 (B.C.S.C.), as follows ... : (At pp 8-9

> The broad purpose of s. 981 is to provide machinery to block developments, which comply with existing zoning but will be in conflict with proposed zoning, from being pressed ahead during the time required to enact the bylaw that is "under preparation". The purpose of s. 981(2), in my view, is not to give an opportunity to developers who hear of the intention to amend the law to crystallize their position under existing law by advising the city's officials of a concept which meets the requirements of that law. *Rather it is, as Mr. de Villiers suggests, to provide relief to those who at the time preparation commences are ready to build and who take the step of applying for a building permit within 7 days.* For a building of any substantial size and complexity, the application could be ready within 7 days of the resolution only if it was in an advanced state of readiness at the date of the resolution. (Emphasis added.)

[Sections 981(1) and 981(2)] are necessarily linked and must work together. To hold otherwise would allow a municipality to both approbate and reprobate s. 981. ...

Section 981(1) is not applicable here as the application for a building permit, complete in all its essentials, was made within 7 clear days from the City Council's December 9, 1993 resolution to instruct the City solicitor to prepare the down-zoning by-law. ...

... The Cheungs were rightly entitled to the order made in their favour.

Appeal dismissed; mandamus granted."

Cheung v. Victoria (City)
100 B.C.L.R. (2d) 235
British Columbia Court of Appeal
December 22, 1994

Judge Stone of the Federal Court Appeal Division dismissed an application under the regulations made pursuant to the *Narcotic Control Act* "for an order of mandamus compelling the Minister of National Health and Welfare to issue a licence forthwith so that the appellant may legally cultivate, gather or produce hemp (*Cannabis stiva L.*) for scientific purposes." The application had been rejected by the Minister on the grounds that the applicant did not have the necessary academic qualifications to support scientific research nor the details of a project to show that scientific research would be conducted. The Motions Judge who reviewed the Minister's decision held that the applicant had not shown that the Minister's discretionary power had been used "for some improper purpose, in bad faith or ... on irrelevant considerations." Judge Stone agreed and also rejected the applicant's attack on the relevant legislation as being against his Charter rights.

Klevering v. Her Majesty the Queen
Docket: A-1026-96
http://www.fja-cmf.gc.ca/
Federal Court Appeal Division
November 7, 1997

Declarations

Sue Rodriguez was afflicted with Amyotrophic Lateral Sclerosis (known as Lou Gehrig's Disease) which causes a person to lose control of muscle functions. Death is ultimately caused by the inability to swallow and breathe because of the failure of the requisite muscles. The disease, however, does not affect the mind.

Unwilling to endure such a death, Ms. Rodriguez wanted to end her life when it became unbearable, but was physically unable to do it without assistance. Because s. 241 of the *Criminal Code* makes it a crime to assist anyone in committing suicide, she commenced a court action in which she asked for a declaration that s. 241 of the *Criminal Code* violates her rights under s. 7 of the *Charter* which reads:

> Everyone has the right to life, liberty and security of the person and the right not to be deprived thereof except in accordance with the principles of fundamental justice.

Her application was dismissed by the B.C. Supreme Court.

She appealed to the B.C. Court of Appeal. The three justices who heard the appeal agreed that s. 241 of the *Criminal Code* did violate her rights under s. 7 of the *Charter*; nevertheless, the appeal was dismissed. Justice Hollinrake held that the violation was not contrary to the principles of fundamental justice; Justice Proudfoot held that the declaration sought would establish a bad precedent in that it would exempt unnamed persons from future criminal liability. Justice McEachern, dissenting, interpreted s. 7 of the *Charter* as ensuring individual control and held that s. 241 of the *Criminal Code* denied her rights, and those rights were not deprived in accordance with the principles of fundamental justice. He would not have struck down s. 241, but instead would have allowed a doctor-assisted suicide, for Ms. Rodriguez only, if she would follow certain prescribed rules.[4]

Ms. Rodriguez appealed to the Supreme Court of Canada which heard argument on May 20, 1993 in a nationally televised session.[5]

The reserved judgment, released in October, held against her. By a 5-to-4 vote, the court rejected her argument that the ban on assisted suicide should be struck down. The majority felt, *inter alia*, that society had not reached a consensus on the issue of assisted suicides and that allowing assisted suicides could lead to abuse affecting the more vulnerable members of society.[6]

On February 12, 1994, Sue Rodriguez died. It was determined that it was an assisted suicide. The response has ranged from cries to prosecute, to the full extent of the law, the person who assisted her to calls for a bill to be presented to Parliament to legalize assisted suicide.

Rodriguez v. British Columbia (Attorney General)

Question

If the court orders a person or company to stop polluting a water system or stop blocking the roads, what can be done if they don't obey the court order?

D. CONTEMPT OF COURT

Regina *v.* Jetco Manufacturing Ltd. et al.

C.E.L.R. (N.S.) 243
ONTARIO SUPREME COURT
MAY 21, 1986

Montgomery J. (orally):—The Municipality of Metropolitan Toronto brought contempt proceedings against Jetco Manufacturing Limited ("Jetco"), and its president, Keith Alexander, for alleged contempt of an order of a Justice of the Peace pursuant to s. 326 of the *Municipal Act*, R.S.O. 1980, c. 302, dated April 30, 1985.

Jetco operates an electroplating plant in Weston, Ontario, and has operated it since August 8, 1974. Jetco has been convicted of 69 violations of the anti-water pollution by-laws of the Municipality of Metropolitan Toronto, specifically By-law 148-83 and its predecessor, By-law 2520, with respect to discharging waste water containing chemical substances in excess of permissible limits. Jetco has been fined $97,950.

On April 30, 1985, Justice of the Peace White made an order referring to Jetco convictions on January 18, 1985, for discharge of waste water containing excess amounts of nickel and chromium into sanitary sewers prohibiting Jetco pursuant to s. 326 of the *Municipal Act* from continuation or repetition of the offences. Since that order, there have been five separate incidents of breaches of the by-law between May 27 and October 28, 1985, resulting in 14 separate convictions of Jetco and fines imposed of $28,000.

Tests conducted on March 11, 1986, indicate that Jetco waste water continued to violate By-law 148-83.

Jetco has failed to install pollution control abatement equipment which successfully ensures that plant operation will comply with the court order and By-law 148-83.

According to expert evidence, the conduct of Jetco discharging excess nickel, cadmium and cyanide into the water system has the tendency and effect to:

(i)   interfere with, impair, upset or completely retard sewage treatment plants and processes;

(ii) enhance the toxicity of other chemicals in the system;

(iii) interfere with and poison biological systems in Lake Ontario;

(iv) cause contamination of surface and ground water in the area of landfill sites where sludge containing cyanide is applied;

(v)   cause air pollution when sludge containing cyanide is incinerated;

(vi) corrode sewers requiring their costly replacement.

The issue raised by the respondents is whether the respondents had notice of the order of the Justice of the Peace.

Jetco saw fit to absent itself from Court when facing summonses. It was not, therefore, made immediately aware of the prohibition order of the Justice of the Peace, but that was because it saw fit to absent itself from the criminal trials. I am satisfied, however, beyond a reasonable doubt that Jetco and Alexander had knowledge of the prohibition order of April 30, 1985. The attitude of Alexander is exemplified in his cross-examination when he said: "I treated the fines as licencing fees for doing business."

The bald statement in his affidavit that he was not aware of the order is not credible in light of the evasive nature of his answers under cross-examination. ...

The criminal standard of proof is applicable to these proceedings. I have considered the totality of the evidence before me and I have applied the strict criminal test. I have no difficulty on the evidence in finding that Alexander acted knowingly and in contravention of the order of the Court, as did Jetco. I find the conduct of Jetco and of Alexander to be a contempt of the order of the Justice of the Peace, and as such, they are both guilty of criminal contempt.

It was never suggested that the Court lacked the jurisdiction to impose a finding of contempt. That power is inherent in a superior Court. Mr. Justice O'Leary commented in *Can. Metal Co. v. CBC* (No. 2) (1974), 4 O.R. (2d) 585, 19 C.C.C. (2d) 218, 48 D.L.R. (3d) 641 (Ont. H.C.), affirmed (1975), 11 O.R. (2d) 167, 29 C.C.C. (2d) 325, 65 D.L.R. (3d) 231 (Ont. C.A.), on matters of contempt and stated in clear language [at 4 O.R. 613] that: "To allow Court orders to be disobeyed would be to tread the road toward anarchy."

That is clearly what has happened here. The remaining question for my determination is, therefore, the question of sentence. The sole consideration in determining sentence is one of deterrence. ...

If Courts fail to enforce their orders and allow the continuation of the attitude displayed by Mr. Alexander of treating fines for pollution as a cost of doing business, there can be no deterrence to the evils of pollution. One hundred thousand dollars in fines have had no effect so far. I therefore assess a fine for contempt against Jetco in the sum of $200,000.

I now turn to the conduct of the president, the directing mind of the corporation, Mr. Alexander. I consider the conduct of anyone who permits excessive amounts of contaminants, including arsenic, to enter our water supply, to be grossly offensive. Such conduct must be deterred, specifically and generally. I therefore sentence Keith Alexander to 1 year in jail. On May 12, the respondent's solicitor wrote to the Municipality of Metropolitan Toronto and said:

It is obvious that Jetco will not undertake a major works program while contemplating the simultaneous closure of the factory. As a result, any works project will be adjourned by the company until litigation has been adjudicated or otherwise disposed of.

That means that pollution will continue until the respondents decide to amend their operation. It flies in the face of any attempt to purge contempt. I therefore sentence Keith Alexander to a further 1 month in jail for every single day that he delays his decision to undertake a major works program to comply with the by-law and the order of this Court up to a maximum of a further 15 months. That, of course, would result in a penitentiary sentence.

The message is clear to these and all other polluters—clean up or close up. In the absence of the accused Alexander, I direct the sheriff of the County of York to apprehend Mr. Alexander on his return and take him into custody so that he may commence serving his sentence.

Costs to the applicants on a solicitor-and-client basis forthwith after assessment.

Application granted.

COURT OF APPEAL 57 O.R. (2D) 776 AT P. 780

…In my respectful view the trial judge erred in convicting the appellants. I think he erred in law in finding that the appellants or either of them had notice of the prohibition order on the basis of the affidavit evidence and hearsay evidence before him. …

From the moment of the filing of the appellant Alexander's affidavit, the matter was no longer one in which, as the applicant alleged, none of the facts were in dispute. When there are controverted facts relating to matters essential to a decision as to whether a party is in contempt of court, those facts cannot be found by an assessment of the credibility of deponents who have not been seen or heard by the trier of fact, as was done in this case. The judge here quite simply was in no position to make the factual determination upon which his contempt order was predicated. On the disputed state of the evidence before him he could not properly conclude that the municipality had established beyond a reasonable doubt that the appellants were aware of the prohibition order of the justice of the peace. In the circumstances of this case, a trial of the issue raised by the application ought to have been ordered.

It follows that the order finding the appellants guilty of contempt of court cannot stand and their convictions and sentences must be set aside.

In the result, I would allow the appeal and set aside the order appealed from. The municipality should be at liberty to take such further or other proceedings in this matter as it may be advised. I would make no order as to costs.

Appeal allowed.

Background Facts:

When the government of British Columbia made a decision to allow some logging in Clayoquot Sound on Vancouver Island, protesters began a blockade. Those who ignored a court order against disrupting the logging were arrested in the "largest mass arrest in B.C. history" for contempt of court.[9]

By November 11, 1993 more than 800 protesters had been arrested.[10]

The following are excerpts from Justice Bouck's decision reprinted by the *Times-Colonist* of Victoria, B.C.

Before fixing the actual sentences, something must be said about the legal concept of contempt of court. …[D]emocracy allows a society to govern itself by the rule of law and not by the rule of the individual…Some Canadians take democracy for granted. It is easy to forget that democracies have failed. It can happen to us unless we as a people co-exist by the rule of law. If we do not, Canada could collapse into a form of tyrannical rule. Our country will ultimately deteriorate if people feel they are entitled to abuse the rights of others when they are unable to convince the majority of the rightness of their cause. …[T]he right to peacefully protest brings with it the responsibility of avoiding interfering with the rights of others. …

Preserving the dignity of the court is only a minor part of contempt proceedings. The fundamental issue is much deeper. Underneath it all, contempt proceedings are taken primarily to preserve the rule of law. Without the rule of law democracy will collapse. Individuals will then decide which laws they will obey and which ones they won't. Government by the rule of law will disappear. People will then be controlled by the rule of the individual. The strongest mob will rule over the weak. Anarchy will prevail.

Most of you have indicated that you prefer to follow the law of God. No doubt encouraged by submissions of your counsel, who ought to have known better, some of you have invited me to apply the law of God. This court does not apply the law of God, irrespective of whose interpretation of that law is offered for consideration. This court applies the law as it is determined to be by the legislators of this country and by the decisions of this court, which have accumulated now for 700 years. …

The rule of law exists in this society only because the overwhelming majority of citizens, irrespective of their different views on religion, morality, or science, agree to be bound by the law. That agreement, which cannot be found recorded in a conventional sense, has survived the deepest and most profound conflicts of religion, morality and science. In that sense it might be thought that its strength is overwhelming and its future secure. But that is not the case at all, for the continued existence of that agreement is threatened by its own inherent fragility. That fragility was described by former Chief Justice Farris of this court in the celebrated case of *Canadian Transport Co. Ltd. v. Alsbury* (1952), 6 W.W.R. (N.S.) 473 (B.C.S.C.), to which counsel have referred, I quote from p. 478:

> Once our laws are flouted and orders of our courts treated with contempt the whole fabric of our freedom is destroyed. We can then only revert to conditions of the dark ages when the only law recognized was that of might. One law broken and the breach thereof ignored, is but an invitation to ignore further laws and this, if continued, can only result in the breakdown of the freedom under the law which we so greatly prize. …

[In response to the contention that the actions of the protesters followed the path of Ghandi, Martin Luther King and the suffragettes, Judge Bouck said:] But here, the elected representative of the people of this province made the law allowing MacMillan Bloedel Ltd. to log the timber in Clayoquot Sound. It was not decreed. … Except for the out-of-province defendants, the others have the right to vote. They were simply unable to persuade the elected representatives of the people to adopt their point of view. Unlike Mr. Gandhi, Mr. King and the suffragettes, they could attempt to change the law through their vote and the votes of others whom they could persuade. Unlike Mr. Gandhi, Mr. King and the suffragettes, they infringed a legal right: the right of MacMillan Bloedel Ltd. to cut timber in Clayoquot Sound. Their behavior in no way follows the noble ideals of Mr. Gandhi, Mr. King or the suffragette movement. …

I turn now to fix the sentence for each of the defendants found guilt of contempt of the court orders made 20 July 1992 and 16 July 1993. It is not a pleasant duty. I take no joy in the task. …

Despite repeated comments by various judges concerning the necessity of working within the democratic system, and despite relatively modest sentences, disobedience of court orders continues. Many people do not seem to get the message. …

The only way the law can deal with continuous breaches of court orders is to increase the penalty in the hope it will dissuade others from committing the same kinds of acts.

The sentences I am about to impose should reflect a degree of penalty for their unlawful behaviour. Mostly, it should serve as a deterrent to others who contemplate undermining the rule of law.

[The sentences imposed ranged from fines of $1,000 to $3,000 and jail terms from 45 to 60 days.]

MacMillan Bloedel Limited v. Simpson
Times-Colonist
October 15, 1993 p. A5

ENDNOTES

1. *The Lawyers Weekly*, May 1, 1992, p. 1, 13.

2. See *The Lawyers Weekly*, August 20, 1993, p. 9

3. For a more detailed account see the summary of *R. v. Gerlach* in *The Lawyers Weekly*, July 15, 1994.

4. *The Lawyers Weekly*, March 26, 1993, pp. 1, 22; April 9, 1993, p. 16.

5. Summarized from *The Globe and Mail*, May 21, 1993, p. A1.

6. For a more detailed account see *Maclean's*, October 11, 1993, p. 27.

7. Summarized from *Maclean's*, August 23, 1993, p. 13 and October 25, 1993, p. 11.

8. *The Globe and Mail*, November 11, 1993, p. A6.